Cracking the

CSET®

California Subject Examinations for Teachers

2nd Edition

The Staff of The Princeton Review

PrincetonReview.com

Penguin
Random
House

The Princeton Review, Inc.
110 East 42nd St, 7th Floor
New York, NY 10017
E-mail: editorialsupport@review.com

Published in the United States by Penguin Random House LLC, New York, and in Canada by Random House of Canada, a division of Penguin Random House Ltd., Toronto.

ISBN: 978-0-525-56762-2
eBook ISBN: 978-0-525-56774-5
ISSN: 2156-4892

Editor: Meave Shelton
Production Editors: Liz Dacey and Kathy G. Carter
Production Coordinator: Deborah A. Weber
Content Contributors: Jean Hsu, Christine Lindwall, Anne Bader, Parisun Shoga, Ali Landreau, and Kevin Baldwin

Printed in the United States of America on partially recycled paper.

10 9 8 7 6 5 4 3 2 1

2nd Edition

Editorial
Rob Franek, Editor-in-Chief
Mary Beth Garrick, Executive Director of Production
Craig Patches, Production Design Manager
Selena Coppock, Managing Editor
Meave Shelton, Senior Editor
Colleen Day, Editor
Sarah Litt, Editor
Aaron Riccio, Editor
Orion McBean, Associate Editor

Penguin Random House Publishing Team
Tom Russell, VP, Publisher
Alison Stoltzfus, Publishing Director
Amanda Yee, Associate Managing Editor
Ellen L. Reed, Production Manager
Suzanne Lee, Designer

Acknowledgments

The Princeton Review would like to extend special thanks to Kate Smith and Riley Dacosta for authoring the first edition of this book, and to the following contributors to the second edition update: Jean Hsu, Christine Lindwall, Anne Bader, Parisun Shoga, Ali Landreau, and Kevin Baldwin.

We are also very grateful to the time and attention given to each page by Deborah Weber, Liz Dacey, and Kathy Carter.

Contents

Get More (Free) Content

1 Go to **PrincetonReview.com/cracking.**

2 Enter the following ISBN for your book: 9780525567622

3 Answer a few simple questions to set up an exclusive Princeton Review account. (If you already have one, you can just log in.)

4 Click the "Account Home" button, also found under "My Account" from the top toolbar. You're all set to access your bonus content!

Need to report a potential **content** issue?

Contact **EditorialSupport@review.com.**

Include:

- full title of the book
- ISBN number
- page number

Need to report a **technical** issue?

Contact **TPRStudentTech@review.com** and provide:

- your full name
- email address used to register the book
- full book title and ISBN
- computer OS (Mac/PC) and browser (Firefox, Safari, etc.)

The **Princeton Review**®

Once you've registered, you can...

- Download and print 3 full-length CSET: Multiple Subjects practice tests, with complete explanations

- Download and print 3 full-length CSET: Writing Skills practice tests, with sample responses and scoring information

- Access a Writing Skills strategy tutorial

- Check to see if there have been any corrections or updates to this edition

- Get our take on any recent or pending updates to the CSET

Look For These Icons Throughout The Book

 PRACTICE TESTS

 PROVEN TECHNIQUES

 APPLIED STRATEGIES

 OTHER REFERENCES

Chapter 1
Getting Started

WHAT IS THE CSET?

CSET stands for **California Subject Examinations for Teachers.** These tests fulfill the basic skills requirements for prospective K–12 teachers. CSET: Multiple Subjects combined with CSET: Writing Skills is one option for fulfilling the basic requirement. Other options include the MSAT, Praxis, SSAT, and CBEST.

A passing score on all three subtests that comprise CSET: Multiple Subjects (MS), and on CSET: Writing Skills, is a requirement for prospective elementary school teachers as part of the teacher credentialing process. Although most elementary schools in California end at fifth grade, the Multiple Subjects teaching credential is designated for grades K–6.

Taking CSET: Single Subjects (SS) is one way to verify subject matter competence in a single content area, such as Physical Education or Social Science. Generally, Single Subject credentials are required to teach individual subjects in grades 7–12, often referred to as the secondary-level grades.

The CSET may also be required for some teachers who received their teacher training in other states, and it can be taken by current educators adding authorizations.

Who Writes the CSET?

The CSET was developed by the California Commission on Teacher Credentialing (CTC) and is administered by National Evaluation Systems, Inc. (NES). Test materials are aligned with current California K–12 Student Academic Content Standards, textbooks, Common Core curriculum, and CTC standards.

Official information about the CSET, including test dates and locations, registration deadlines and requirements, and a practice test, can be found online at www.cset.nesinc.com. Here's additional contact information for the CSET Program:

Address: CSET Program
    Evaluation Systems Group of Pearson
    P.O. Box 340880
    Sacramento, CA 95834-0880

Phone: 1-800-205-3334 or 1-916-928-4003
    Monday–Friday 9:00 A.M.–5:00 P.M. PST
    (except for U.S. holidays)
    Saturday paper-test days only 6:30 A.M.–10:00 A.M. PST
    (Automated Information System available 24 hours daily)

What's on the CSET: Multiple Subjects Test?

CSET: Multiple Subjects consists of three subtests, and you must receive a passing score on all three to meet the basic requirements.

*   Subtest I (101)
    Reading, Language, and Literature
    History and Social Science

*   Subtest II (214)
    Science
    Math

*   Subtest III (103)
    Physical Education
    Human Development
    Visual and Performing Arts

Don't Forget Your Practice Tests!
Included for free, with your purchase of this book, are three full-length Multiple Subjects practice tests and three full-length Writing Skills practice tests. To download them, register your book at PrincetonReview.com, following the steps outlined on pages vi–vii.

How Is the CSET: Multiple Subjects Test Structured?

*   If you choose to take Subtest I or Subtest II individually, you will have three hours to complete the subtest.
*   If you choose to take Subtest III individually, you will have two hours and fifteen minutes to complete the subtest.
*   If you choose to take all three subtests together, you will have five hours to complete the testing session. You will be presented with one subtest at a time, but you may work on the subtests in any order. The subtests will not be individually timed.
*   Any breaks you take during the session will be considered part of your available testing time.

One thing you should take comfort in is that, compared to most of the standardized tests out there, the CSET is a test taker's dream (if test takers actually dream about such things). First of all, regardless of how many subtests you're taking in one test session, you can choose how to allocate your testing time. At the beginning of the test session, you will be given access to the first subtest. You can move freely within the this test, and when finished, you will be given access to the next test. The five hours are entirely yours, but be aware that once you complete a test you cannot go back into that test.

Also, each subtest is divided equally by content area, so you know exactly how many questions there will be on each subject, and in what order. The breakdown of the test is shown in the following table.

CSET: MULTIPLE SUBJECTS			
Subtest	Domains	Number of Multiple-Choice Questions	Number of Constructed-Response Questions (short [focused] responses)
I	Reading, Language, and Literature	26	2
	History and Social Science	26	2
	Subtest Total	52	4
II	Science	26	2
	Mathematics	26	2
	Subtest Total	52	4
III	Physical Education	13	1
	Human Development	13	1
	Visual and Performing Arts	13	1
	Subtest Total	39	3

This is exactly how the test is structured, with no variations. When you take Subtest III, for example, you know that questions 1–13 will be multiple-choice questions on Physical Education, questions 14–26 will be multiple-choice questions on Human Development, and questions 27–39 will be multiple-choice questions on Visual and Performing Arts. These questions will be followed by one constructed-response question related to Physical Education, then one constructed-response question related to Human Development, and finally one constructed-response question related to Visual and Performing Arts.

How Is the CSET: Multiple Subjects Test Scored?

Each subtest is scored independently, which means that your score on any one subtest does not affect your scores on the others. This also means—more good news—that once you pass a subtest, you don't have to retake that one, even if you haven't yet passed one or both of the others.

Your score on each subtest is based on your overall performance on that test. The proportions of the questions are the same on all three subtests.

- multiple-choice questions: 70%
- constructed-response questions: 30%

Each of the multiple-choice questions has four answer choices, and they are machine scored as correct or incorrect. Your multiple-choice score is based strictly on the number of questions you answer correctly. There is no penalty for guessing and no point deduction for wrong answers. We'll discuss good specific test-taking strategies later in the book.

Constructed-response questions are open-ended questions requiring written answers. Your responses to these questions will be scored by two or more California educators, who base the scores on several performance characteristics.

- Purpose: How well do you answer the question?
- Subject matter knowledge: How well do you apply your knowledge of the content area?
- Support: How well do you back up your answer?
- Depth and breadth of understanding: How well do you know your stuff?

Then, of course, you have raw scores that are weighted and converted to a scaled score between 100 and 300, but unless you're absolutely fascinated with that process, all you have to do is focus on the magic number 220. That's the minimum passing score on each subtest.

How Many Subtests Should I Take in One Session?

This is entirely up to you, but here are some factors to consider as you make your decision:

- your reading/writing speed
- your ability to switch gears
- the time it takes you to study and prepare for a test
- the content area knowledge you already possess
- how soon you need to complete your teaching credential requirements

How Is the CSET: Multiple Subjects Test Formatted?

Computer Based Testing

Each of the three subtests is offered only as a Computer Based Test (CBT). While you will be provided a notepad and pencil for note taking or outline writing, all responses need to be recorded electronically in the computer-response format to be scored. Be careful to leave time to transfer any notes or answers from your notepad.

> CBT Testing: What to Know
>
> CBT testing can take some practice. We recommend that you review the official tutorial provided by the CSET test creators: https://www.testing.nesinc.com/cbttutorial/tutorial/tutorial_page_1.html.
>
> You should also be aware that certain items, such as packages, cell phones, electronic devices, and calculators, will not be permitted in the testing room. These items will be checked into a locker prior to the test and remain inaccessible till the end of the test. Yes, this means even during voluntary breaks, so be prepared.
>
> Test takers needing specific accommodations can request alternative testing conditions. An application for alternative testing conditions and all supporting documents must be submitted and approved prior to registering for a test date. More information is available at http://www.ctcexams.nesinc.com.

Calculators

While personal calculators are not allowed in the testing room, you will be provided an on-screen, four-function calculator during the test. This will be available only for Subtest II. It might be helpful to review the on-screen calculator tutorial on the CSET website: http://www.ctcexams.nesinc.com/content/docs/calculator_tutorial.pdf.

Hand-Written Responses and Scanning

Some questions require a handwritten response. You will be given a booklet and will need to use the scanner at your testing station to scan in your response. You may want to familiarize yourself with the scanner and handwritten responses on the Pearson testing website: http://www.esvideos.nesinc.com/HandDrawTutorialVideo.asp?detectflash=false.

What Is the CSET: Writing Skills Test?

The CSET: Writing Skills test (142) consists of two constructed-response questions, which are also scored by California educators using standardized procedures. It is a separate test, and it can be used only in conjunction with CSET: Multiple Subjects to satisfy the basic skills requirement. For more information, be sure to register your book online for free access to our Writing Skills strategy tutorial, as well as three full-length Writing Skills practice tests.

To download your free Writing Skills tutorial and practice tests, register your book online following the steps outlined on pages vi–vii.

Chapter 2
Cracking the System

HOW TO USE THIS BOOK

Well, for starters, don't skip this chapter. Our goal is to give you the test-taking techniques you need to boost your score on the CSET. You'll have a better idea of what you're doing when you have read and worked through this book and then taken the practice tests found online.

After you've taken the practice tests, make sure to read all of the explanations, even the explanations to the questions you answered correctly. You'll often find that your understanding of a question and the best way to have gone about answering it will be much clearer after you've read the explanation. You'll also catch some instances in which you got the question right, but for all the wrong reasons. Most important, many of the explanations contain content information you won't find elsewhere in the book.

What Is The Princeton Review?

The Princeton Review is an international test-prep company whose mission is to provide personalized, innovative, best-in-class private tutoring, test prep, and admission products and services to help students knock down barriers and achieve their academic goals.

For over 35 years, we have had phenomenal success in improving students' scores on standardized tests. This success is due to a simple, innovative, and radically effective philosophy: study the test, not just what the test claims to test. This approach has lead to the development of strategies based on the principles the test writers themselves use to write the tests.

Obviously you need to be well versed in many subjects to do well on the CSET, but a good score is also a measure of your ability to think like the test writers. This book will help you to do both.

For more about our products and services, visit our website at PrincetonReview.com.

This book is organized to provide as much—or as little—support as you need, so use it in whatever way will be helpful to improve your confidence with the CSET: Multiple Subjects test. This chapter will review some useful test-taking strategies to help you work efficiently through the multiple-choice section to achieve your highest score. However, the CSET: Multiple Subjects test is heavily content-based as well, so the following chapters will help to give you an essential review of all the subjects tested on all three subtests. The review found in this book will be most helpful if you've already taken coursework in the main subject areas and focus on the most important details that are likely to appear on this test. Just brushing up on basic facts and concepts will speed you up. If, for example, you haven't so much as glanced at the periodic table since your 8:00 A.M. freshman chemistry class, ten minutes spent looking it over will do you a world of good.

BASIC PRINCIPLES OF CRACKING THE SYSTEM

We'll now walk you through our best strategies for cracking both multiple-choice and constructed-response questions.

Proven Technique: Pacing

Did you know that slowing down can actually earn you points? Read on to find out how!

Pace Yourself

A big part of scoring well on an exam is working at a consistent pace. The worst mistake made by inexperienced or unsavvy test takers is that they come to a question that stumps them, and rather than just skip it, they panic and stall. Time stands still when you're working on a question you cannot answer, and it's possible for test takers to waste five minutes on a single question because they are too stubborn to cut their losses.

Don't make that mistake. Tests are like marathons; you do best when you work through them at a steady pace. You can always come back to a question you don't know. When you do, very often you will find that your previous mental block is gone, and you will wonder why the question perplexed you the first time around. Even if you still don't know the answer, you will not have wasted valuable time you could have spent on easier questions.

Keeping a consistent pace also means that you won't work too quickly and make careless mistakes. Let's say you do all 52 questions in Subtest I, but get only half of them right. This gives you a raw score of 26.

Now, let's say you slow down and focus on the first 35 questions that you know you can get right, and then guess on the remaining 17 questions. Using this method, you could earn 35 raw points—and you might even get a few more from guessing, which we will discuss later in this chapter.

In this case, slowing down can get you more points. Unless you are confident that you can complete these tests with high accuracy and with time to spare, you should slow down and focus on the points you know you can get.

> Slow down, score more. You're not scored on how many questions you do. You're scored on how many questions you answer correctly. Doing fewer questions can mean more correct answers and points overall!

Pacing is especially important on the CSET, because you have the option of taking one or more subtests in one test session. It's essential that you map out your time in advance.

If you take all three subtests in one session, then you will have a total of five hours to complete all three tests. Therefore, you can divide up the full five hours equally among the three subtests, or you may want to allot more time to the first two tests (remember that Subtest III taken individually is given less time because it is a shorter test with fewer questions).

For example, your testing time might look like this:

- Subtest I: 110 minutes
- Subtest II: 110 minutes
- Subtest III: 80 minutes

Your personal strengths and weaknesses should definitely factor into your planning. If, for example, you know that you'll need a little extra time for Subtest II because you work slowly on math problems, then plan accordingly! The point is to know your own needs, make a *strategic* decision about time limits for each portion of the test, and then monitor your time carefully during the exam.

When thinking about your pacing and timing strategies, keep in mind that the multiple-choice questions account for 70% of your score, while the two constructed-response questions account for only 30% of your score on each subtest. It would be a very poor strategy to start with the constructed-response questions and then spend so much time on them that you couldn't properly tackle the multiple-choice questions. The CSET official guide suggests that each constructed-response question should take about 10–15 minutes, so, once again, plan accordingly.

MULTIPLE-CHOICE QUESTIONS

There Is No Guessing Penalty on the CSET!

It's essential that you remember this fact, which is why it appears here first. On the CSET: Multiple Subjects test, you don't lose points or portions of points for an incorrect multiple-choice answer, and therefore, you *must* answer every single question, even if you are at the point at which you have to guess randomly. You can only help yourself by guessing, and you can only hurt yourself by leaving a question unanswered.

Sometimes you won't be able to eliminate any answers; other times you won't have time to even look at some questions. For cases like these, we have a simple solution. Pick a **letter of the day (LOTD)** from A to D, and use that letter to answer all the questions for which you aren't able to eliminate any choices.

This is a quick, easy way to make sure that you answer every question. It also has some potential statistical advantages. If each of the four letters has a one-in-four chance of being correct, and you pick the same letter every time you need to guess, you're likely to get a couple of freebies.

LOTD is your if-all-else-fails strategy that should be used *only* for those questions for which you are unable to eliminate any choices. LOTD is a perfect solution for second-pass guesses that we will talk about next.

The Two-Pass System

Proven Technique: The Two-Pass System
Here's another way to conserve your energy and make the best use of your time.

The **Two-Pass System** is The Princeton Review's term for judicious skipping. It means working through the test once (the first pass) to gather up all the quick, easy points, and then going back (the second pass) to work on the time-consuming, difficult questions you skipped initially.

In the first pass, follow your instincts. There is no magic number of questions to answer on your first pass. You might answer five questions on your first pass or you might answer 30. The main point of the Two-Pass System is to gather up the easy points quickly and efficiently first. Deciding whether a question is first pass or not is a snap decision. Five seconds is the absolute longest you should think about whether a question is first pass or not. Use the five-second rule:

If it takes more than five seconds to decide if it's a first or second pass question, it automatically becomes a second pass question. Skip it.

After finishing your first pass, you should be left with the medium and tough questions, the questions you didn't like at first glance. On the first pass, you undoubtedly answered some questions you wish you'd left for later. That's no cause for alarm. Since the CSET: Multiple Subjects test is a computer-based test, you'll see a navigation screen after your first pass that will show you all of the questions you skipped. You can click on any question to go back for your second pass. On the second pass, you'll find some questions that turn out to be easier than you'd expected. If you've done the first pass well, what you're left with are mostly the tougher questions.

And if you are staying mindful of your time, you can still skip to your heart's content. There's no law that says you can't do a third or even a fourth pass. Skip questions that look like they'll eat up your time without giving you anything back. At a certain point, you'll know it's time to just make your best guess and move on.

The CBT format of the test also allows you to "flag" questions for later review. If you guess on a tougher question but want to review it later, you can click on **flag for review** in the upper-right-hand corner of your screen. Your navigation screen will also show the questions that you flagged. Remember, flagging questions will not affect your final score—so flag away!

Process of Elimination (POE)

You are probably already acquainted with **Process of Elimination (POE)** in its simplest form: eliminate answers you know are wrong. The Cracking the System approach to POE isn't really different, just more intense.

You'll find that on a number of questions, the right answer will jump out at you. It will be based on a book you've read and remember well, or a math concept you're particularly good at. When that happens, you'll pounce on the right answer and move on.

Proven Technique: POE
What do you do when the answer isn't obvious?

Other times, however, the question topic will be unfamiliar and the answer choices may only ring vague bells. That's when POE should be a reflex. Through POE, you can take advantage of what partial knowledge you have. You may not know the information that leads you directly to the answer, but you could know information that tells you what the answer definitely is *not*. Let's look at an example.

The first important cash crop in the American colonies was:

A. cotton.

B. corn.

C. tobacco.

D. fresh fruit.

Apply the Strategy
...and may the odds be ever in your favor!

Here's How to Crack It

Let's look at the answer choices one at a time. You may think you don't know the answer, but it's what you know about the answer choices judged against the question that counts. It's what you know about the answer choices that allows you to use POE.

A.   cotton.

The cotton gin was not invented until the late eighteenth century. Eliminate this.

D.   fresh fruit.

Ridiculous! You know that fruit would hardly have remained fresh during the long sea journey from the colonies back to England. Eliminate this one too.

By using POE, you've narrowed down your choice to two possibilities. At this point, if you're still stumped, or pressed for time, you can make a guess. But now, instead of having a 25% chance of getting the right answer, you're up to 50%. That's a huge difference. The answer, by the way, is (C), tobacco.

———————○———————

It's always helpful to physically cross out wrong answers, because when answers are crossed out, you are less likely to mistakenly choose them. (Even the most attentive brain can wander during a test session that can take up to five hours.)

Since this is a computer-based test, we recommend that you use the notepad and pencil you are given to cross out answers and thus keep track of your POE. Just remember to transfer your answers!

Types of Questions

The directions for the multiple-choice section simply ask you to select the "best" answer choice for each question. That's code for "More than one of the answer choices might fit in some way or another, but we're looking for the one that makes the most sense." The test uses a variety of question types, though, and if you recognize the different types, you'll save yourself time and the possibility of choosing the wrong answer even when you know the right one.

Standard Questions

The majority of multiple-choice questions are pretty straightforward, like this one:

The first president of the United States was:

A.   George Washington.

B.   Abraham Lincoln.

C.   Franklin D. Roosevelt.

D.   Mickey Mouse.

In some cases (like this one), you can use common sense to choose the right answer. If you don't know the answer, then use POE to get yourself closer.

Component Questions

Here and there, you'll run into a question that has more than one component. In this case, look for the answer choice that fits all parts of the question, not just one. Remember this phrase: *part* wrong is *all* wrong. If there's *anything* that is somewhat wrong in the answer choice, even if there is other information that is correct, that answer choice cannot be right. Here's an example.

George Washington, Abraham Lincoln, and Franklin
D. Roosevelt were all:

A.   mice.

B.   born in the nineteenth century.

C.   Democrats.

D.   United States presidents.

Here's How to Crack It

The answer choice you need is one that relates correctly to all parts of the question, which, in this case, is three names. Sometimes, you'll know the correct answer, but other times, you'll have to work at it. If you need to use POE for this type of question, go through the answer choices one by one, like a checklist.

Let's just pretend that you don't know the answer to this one. Quickly check each answer against the components of the question. Choice (A) does not relate to any of the question components, so cross that out. Choice (B) relates to Abraham Lincoln and Franklin D. Roosevelt, but not George Washington, so cross that out. Choice (C) relates only to Franklin D. Roosevelt, so cross that one out as well. Even if you didn't know the answer, based on POE, you've successfully ruled out everything but (D).

CONSTRUCTED-RESPONSE QUESTIONS

You may be wondering why the CSET labels these as **constructed-response questions** and not simply essay questions. Actually, it's a good thing they don't, because that might throw you off track. The constructed-response questions are not supposed to be five-paragraph essays. The test guide tells you that each constructed-response question should take 10–15 minutes. How many people do you think can plan and write a full five-paragraph essay in under 15 minutes?

Here's what they *do* expect of you.

The Prompt

For one thing, they expect you to answer the question. If you write a great response that does not address the prompt, you'll get a poor score. Most prompts on the constructed-response questions have more than one component. Your first priority is to take apart the prompt and make sure you know exactly what's being asked of you. Let's look at an example of a typical constructed-response prompt:

The American colonies declared their independence from England in 1776.

Using your knowledge of this time period in U.S. history, prepare a response in which you

1. identify two factors that led to this decision;
2. select one of the factors you have identified; and
3. explain how that factor contributed to the event.

After you've read the prompt, take a minute to reword it into questions. Make a list:

1. What are two reasons the colonies wanted independence from England?
2. Which reason am I going to write about?
3. How did that reason contribute to the colonies' decision to declare independence from England?

As a general rule, you can answer the first two questions together in one paragraph. They're really just historical or subject-matter facts; you'll just want to make sure that you write them in complete, well-constructed sentences. The third question is the one you should spend most of your time on, as you should write one or two paragraphs to fully answer it. This is the place where you can synthesize ideas and explore the prompt. We have a few tips and tricks to help you.

Brainstorm

Take about one or two minutes to write down as many things as you can think of that relate to the question. Depending on the content area, you should try to come up with information and ideas about the following items:

- names
- dates
- places
- concepts
- vocabulary

Then sort out the results of your brainstorm. Some of what you write down will become your main point(s), some will be facts that can be used as evidence to support your conclusions, and some will be garbage.

As you will see in the practice tests, the CSET constructed-response questions are very specific. Many questions require you to use terms that are specific to the content area. The educators who score your responses are looking for these terms, and they want to know that you know what the terms mean. When you use them, define or explain them. Take particular care to define any such terms that appear in the question. The introductory paragraph is a good place to include any definitions.

Use the Multiple-Choice Section to Your Advantage

Remember, there's nothing to stop you from going back and skimming the multiple-choice questions. Sometimes, you'll run into questions that might relate to the material covered in the constructed-response questions. You might find key terms, names, and dates. It's worth a shot if you're having trouble getting started or if you want more facts to back up your ideas.

The Format

Remember the following as you write your response:

- Start strong.
- Make it clear.

Start Strong

It's up to you to write a brilliant beginning that will set the tone and sustain the reader's positive attitude. Put a lot of care into writing the first few sentences, and don't make any mistakes. Try to have a variety of sentence structures and be sure to double-check spelling and punctuation. If you're unsure about the spelling of a word, don't use it!

Don't worry so much about the rest of the response; the readers expect a few mistakes. If you try to write the whole response perfectly, you may write too slowly and waste time, or worry too much and write dull, overwrought, and perhaps recondite paragraphs (see how it comes across when you use vocabulary that's too obscure?). All it takes is three or four well-crafted, strong sentences at the start of your essay to convince the reader that you can write a good sentence when you have time to do so. As long as the rest of your response is clear and well organized, the glow of a good beginning can carry over the entire response.

Make It Clear

High-scoring responses are *clear*. They aren't perfect. They aren't moving and profound. They're simply clear. Clarity is your goal.

Keep your sentences as simple as possible. Long sentences become convoluted very quickly and will give your scorers a headache, putting them in a bad mood. Do not antagonize your reader! Remember that good writing does not have to be complicated; some great ideas can be stated simply.

Do not ever use a word if you are unsure of its definition or proper usage. A malapropism might give your scorers a good laugh, but it will not earn you any points, and it will probably cost you.

Do not use contractions or shorthand symbols such as "&" or "w/" or "tho." Get into the habit of using a relatively high level of discourse when you write. You will not impress anyone if your response reads like an email or a text message.

KEY TERMS

pacing
Two-Pass System
CBT flag for review
Process of Elimination (POE)
constructed-response questions
letter of the day (LOTD)

Summary

o   Plan your time management strategy in advance.

o   Answer every question. Answer every question. Answer every question.

o   In the multiple-choice section, use the Two-Pass System to collect easy points first.

o   Use Process of Elimination to help you narrow down the choices in multiple-choice questions when you're not sure of the answer.

o   In constructed-response questions, make sure you address each part of the prompt.

o   Start your written responses strong and error-free.

o   Use sentence constructions that are simple and clear.

Subtest I: Reading, Language, and Literature; History and Social Science

Reading, Language, and Literature

History and Social Science

Chapter 3
Language Structure, Linguistics, and Literacy

FIRST, A REFRESHER…

A NOUN's the name of any thing;
As, *school* or *garden, hoop* or *swing*.

ADJECTIVES tell the *kind* of noun;
As, *great, small, pretty, white*, or *brown*.
Three of these words we often see
Called ARTICLES—*a, an*, and *the*.

Instead of nouns the PRONOUNS stand;
John's head, *his* face, *my* arm, *your* hand.

VERBS tell of something *being done*;
As, *read, write, spell, sing, jump*, or *run*.

How things are done the ADVERBS tell;
As, *slowly, quickly, ill*, or *well*.
They also tell us *where* and *when*;
As, *here*, and *there*, and *now*, and *then*.

A PREPOSITION stands *before*
A noun; as, *in*, or *through*, a door.

CONJUNCTIONS sentences unite;
As, kittens scratch *and* puppies bite.

The INTERJECTION shows surprise;
As, *O*, how pretty! *Ah*, how wise!

From *First lessons in language, or, Elements of English grammar,* by David B. Tower and Benjamin F. Tweed, 1853.

NOW, THE BASICS

The poem above illustrates an important point: English grammar hasn't changed much since the 19th century. If you remember anything you learned in your elementary school English classes, you're off to a good start!

So let's begin by brushing up on the two main components of language structure, syntax and semantics, and soldier on from there.

SYNTAX

Syntax is the structure of language: how phrases, sentences, and paragraphs are put together. It's a perfect example of one of those things you know how to *do*, but not how to *explain*. You can probably drive a car without thinking actively about what you're doing, but if someone asked you to explain how the engine worked, could you easily launch into an explanation of alternators, fuel injection, and combustion chambers? By the same token, you may be able to write gorgeous, well-constructed sentences, but could you immediately identify the use of a non-defining relative clause?

The odds of the test asking something that specific, thankfully, are slim to none. Most likely, all you'll need to review are some general terms and concepts.

Parts of a Sentence

Sentence

A **sentence** consists of one or more clauses that express a complete thought.

- In 1865, Abraham Lincoln was assassinated.
- Leave the dishes there; I'll clean up later.

Clause

A **clause** is part of a sentence and must include at least a subject and a predicate.

- They left.
- Aunt Elaine bought Katie a Tonka truck.

Independent Clause

An **independent clause,** or main clause, can stand on its own.

- We'll see you later.
- The painting will be moved to a different museum.

Subordinate Clause

A **subordinate clause,** also known as a relative clause or a dependent clause, cannot stand on its own.

- which proved the defendant's guilt
- because she never showed up

Phrase

A **phrase** is a group of words that form a concept, but cannot stand alone as a sentence.

- out of nowhere
- her blue dress

Subject

A **subject** is a word or group of words defining who or what performs an action or is in a particular state of being.

- *The boy* jumped from the tree.
- *Winning the lottery* did not change their lifestyle.
- *I* am a man of constant sorrow.

Grammar Review
Check out The Princeton Review's *Grammar Smart* for additional grammar review.

Predicate

A **predicate** is a verb or verb phrase expressing an action performed or a state of being.

- The cat *meowed*.
- That *was* the last time anyone saw him alive.

Categories of Sentences

Declarative

A **declarative sentence** is the most common type of sentence, and it's named aptly. A declarative sentence states something, generally a fact, an opinion, or an arrangement of some kind. It ends with a period (.).

- I prefer vanilla over chocolate.
- The Boston Americans won the first World Series in 1903.
- The dog needs to go out.

Imperative

An **imperative sentence** is a command or request that ends with a period (.) or an exclamation point (!). This is the hardest type for students to deal with when they learn how to identify the subjects of sentences, because there is actually no subject in an imperative sentence. The subject is actually *you*, but it's not written or spoken; it's implied. *(You) Forget it!*

- Answer the phone.
- Please have the report done by Friday.
- Get in here now!

Interrogative

An **interrogative sentence** asks a question. The auxiliary, or helping, verb or verb phrase comes first, then the subject, followed by the main verb or verb phrase. Naturally, the interrogative form ends with a question mark (?).

- When does his flight arrive?
- How did you like the show?
- Will the author sign copies of her book after the reading?

Exclamatory

An **exclamatory sentence** emphasizes a declarative or imperative statement by using an exclamation point (!).

- I won the contest!
- Look out for that car!
- You're fired!

Types of Sentences

Simple

A **simple sentence** consists of one independent clause. Don't be deceived, though, into thinking that "simple" means that the sentence must be short. An independent clause can have a compound subject or verb, and it can include adjectives and adverbs. The only requirement is that it have no dependent clauses, or other independent clauses joined with a conjunction.

- I went to bed early.
- Heath Ledger, Christian Bale, and Michael Caine all starred in *The Dark Knight*.
- Ron's younger sister and her new boyfriend did their best to be on time for Ron's joint birthday and retirement party.

Compound

A **compound sentence** consists of two or more independent clauses. Just think of taking two or more complete sentences and attaching them together. One way to do that is by using a semicolon (;). The other option is to use a **coordinating conjunction.** The list of coordinating conjunctions has come to be known as the **fanboys:**

for, and, nor, but, or, yet, so.

- The sun is out, yet it's cold.
- Shelbie's boss was away on business Monday, so she spent the day playing solitaire on the computer.
- I don't understand why he's so angry; all I said was that his story was simplistic and trite.

Complex

A **complex sentence** contains one independent, or main, clause, and one or more dependent clauses. To link the dependent clauses to the main clause, use a **subordinating conjunction.** There is a long list of subordinating conjunctions. Some of the more common are *after, until, because, although, since,* and *while.*

- We won't know how Dad is doing until the doctor comes out.
- Even though she cheated on the exam, Sara was not expelled from school.
- I didn't think it was necessary to ask your permission because I knew you'd say yes.

Compound-Complex

Finally, a **compound-complex sentence** consists of at least two independent clauses and at least one dependent clause. To break it down, just start with the compound sentence rule. Take two independent clauses (or two simple sentences) and connect them. Then add a dependent clause to one of the independent clauses, and you've created a compound-complex sentence.

- Since my sister returned from her trip, I've been trying to plan a night out with her, but she's always too busy to return my calls.
- Gary's car emits horrible smoky exhaust; we had to fall far behind to avoid it while we were following him to the restaurant.

Other Conventions

The rest of the "mechanics" of language include **spelling, capitalization,** and **punctuation.** Because questions about these will probably be few, there's no need to go into too much detail, so we'll just review a few basic rules. (By the way, that was a compound-complex sentence.)

Spelling

There's an old saying: "German is a language of rules; English is a language of exceptions." Anyone who's suffered through elementary school spelling lessons can attest to that. Luckily, only a tiny percentage of all the words in the English language are used on the exam, and it's unlikely that you'll be asked a standard spelling question. Even if that does happen, as long as you read regularly—novels, newspapers—you should be able to handle any words you encounter.

Capitalization

Keep in mind the basic rules of capitalization. This is obviously not a complete list, but the questions on the test won't be obscure.

- the first word of a sentence
- names and initials of people
- titles preceding names, such as *Mr., Dr., Rev.*
- days of the week, months of the year, holidays

- continents, countries, states, cities, provinces
- the pronoun *I*
- names of languages, nationalities

As a general rule, remember that *proper nouns* (nouns that represent a specific person, place, or thing) are typically capitalized.

- What state do you live in?
  I live in New York State.

- Do you know the boy next door?
  Yes, we both joined the Boy Scouts.

- Is the governor in his office?
  No, Governor Jones is still at the meeting.

Punctuation

Once again, there's no reason to go into minute detail—we're not going to bother with the uses of the period and question mark, for instance—but certain concepts and rules bear revisiting.

There are a number of different uses for **commas.**

- to separate a list of items
- to separate phrases and clauses
- to separate independent clauses that are connected by one of the fanboys
- to introduce a direct quote
- to end a direct quote within a framing sentence

Semicolons are often used incorrectly. There are really only two proper uses (other than a couple of obscure optional ones).

- to separate two equally weighted independent clauses, in place of a period *or* a comma and one of the fanboys
- to separate groups of words that are internally separated by commas

There are also two uses for **colons.**

- to set off a list of words or phrases, used for additional explanation, generally after an independent clause
- to introduce a direct quote, although commas are more commonly used

Dashes are used occasionally in place of commas, usually when more emphasis is desired.

Parentheses are used to add information that is related to the sentence but is nonessential to understanding.

Apostrophes can be used in two ways.

- in a contraction, such as *I'm,* to indicate that one or more letters have been omitted from a word
- to show possession, generally before the "s" for singular nouns and after the "s" for plural nouns

So how might the CSET test you on your knowledge of syntax? Let's look at an example.

――――――――○――――――――

Identify the subject in the following sentence:

Much to the fans' delight, the band's new drummer turned out to be far better than the previous one.

A.   the fans' delight

B.   the band's new drummer

C.   far better

D.   the previous one

Here's How to Crack It

Rule number one: Don't fall into the "noun trap." Elementary school students begin learning about subjects by identifying nouns, but by now, you should know that nouns can appear anywhere in sentences: in dependent clauses, in prepositional phrases, even in verb phrases. By the same token, you know not to assume that the subject always comes at the beginning of the sentence. Step back, look at the sentence as a whole, and ask yourself, "What is it about?" It's really about the new drummer, so the answer is (B).

――――――――○――――――――

SEMANTICS

Semantics is commonly used in everyday English to refer to an issue based on words rather than issues. "Your Honor, I didn't *steal* the car; I *borrowed* it. Really, we're just arguing semantics here." Syntax is structure; semantics is meaning. Hold on—don't bother breaking out those vocabulary flashcards. The CSET won't test you on your memorization skills, but on your understanding of how meaning is constructed, and how words relate to each other.

Etymology

Etymology is the study of word origin. If you've ever watched a spelling bee, you know that one of the questions students are allowed to ask is "What is the language of origin?" There's a reason for that, and it's not just to stall for time. Often, English words (or words that have been adopted into the English language) that originate from the same foreign or ancient language have similar construction.

For example, the words *mezzanine*, *pizza* and *paparazzi* all come from the Italian language. One similarity is obvious—the use of the double "z"—but say the words aloud slowly and listen to the vowel sounds. Each "a" sounds like the others, as does each "i." Knowing that the word *mezzanine* is of Italian origin would help a student spell it correctly, as opposed to something like "mezaneen."

However, we also need to look at it the opposite way. Sometimes, the spelling of a word may help determine its origin, and that in turn can lead to an understanding of its meaning. Words that end in "-eur," such as *masseur* and *chauffeur*, are often derivations from the French describing a person with a particular job. When we see a word such as *restaurateur*, the connection of the word ending gives us a clue to its meaning. We recognize the first part of the word, and the suffix "-eur" helps us put it together: a *restaurateur* is a person who owns a restaurant.

Denotation and Connotation

Denotation refers to the literal definition of a word, while **connotation** refers to an implicit meaning. In other words, the denotative meaning of a word is found in the dictionary. The connotative meaning of a word is a "shade of meaning," used to elicit some kind of emotional response.

- They found a *shady* corner of the park for their picnic.

Here, the word *shady*, in its most literal definition, describes an area that is blocked from direct sunlight. But consider another example.

- No one really liked Bud; there was something *shady* about him.

Does no one like him because he blocks sunlight? Probably not. In this case, it is a connotative meaning of the word *shady*. There is a feeling associated with the word: one of concealment, of dishonesty.

Let's take it one step further. Understanding connotation doesn't just mean determining how a word is used in a sentence. It also means choosing words deliberately in order to evoke a particular emotion. Think about how the sentence changes when we exchange *shady* for similar words.

- No one really liked Bud; there was something *disgraceful* about him.
- No one really liked Bud; there was something *untrustworthy* about him.
- No one really liked Bud; there was something *ignominious* about him.

All three of those words are synonyms for *shady*, yet each one slightly changes the implicit meaning of the sentence.

Here's an example of a CSET question about denotation and connotation.

Which of the following sentences uses a denotative meaning of the underlined word?

A. "Don't give me any of your <u>lip</u>," my mother warned.

B. His teacher secretly felt that he was a little <u>thick</u>.

C. The <u>plot</u> of the story had some major holes in it.

D. After much deliberation, the committee decided to <u>shelve</u> the idea.

Here's How to Crack It

This is a tough type of question because there are so many dictionary-listed meanings for words. However, just because it's in the dictionary doesn't mean it's a literal meaning. The dictionary lists figurative meanings as well. What you want to do here is think as literally as possible, and use POE to eliminate incorrect answers. Picture what's going on. For instance, in (A), you know that the mother does not think the child is actually going to hand her a lip, right? In (B), it's unlikely that the teacher is making a judgment about the student's physical girth. Choice (D) may be tricky because "shelving" is a term widely used in this manner, but again, picture it. An *idea* is an abstract concept: Can it actually be placed on a shelf? The best answer here is (C), because it is a literal meaning of the word "plot."

Context

Looking at words in context is another way to determine a word's meaning. Initially, context is helpful when you're faced with a word that has more than one definition. Children are taught to look at the whole sentence in order to figure out which meaning of the word is used.

- We saw a black *bear* near our campsite. (animal)
- I can't *bear* to see you unhappy. (suffer)
- The tree will *bear* sweet apples once it's grown. (produce)
- *Bear* left at the intersection. (turn)

By upper elementary school, students are also taught to use **context clues** when they run into unfamiliar vocabulary words in their reading. It's an alternative to flipping back and forth between a book and a dictionary. And it makes sense. Imagine a student reading a short story for homework and coming to a word she doesn't recognize. She stops, sets aside the story, opens the dictionary, looks up the word, tries to understand the definition, which often includes more difficult words than the original word and necessitates looking up those words. By the time the poor girl gets back to the reading, she has completely forgotten what the story is about.

Using context clues, on the other hand, keeps the student actively involved in the reading. When she comes to an unfamiliar word, she examines the surrounding text to see if she can determine its meaning based on how it is used in the sentence or paragraph.

Let's look at an example:

- Due to his *opprobrious* conduct at the homecoming game, Rob was benched for the remainder of the season.

Before you balk at the word, think about it for a moment. What clues can you use to determine what it means? Well, there's *conduct*, which (let's assume) you know means *behavior*. That's a start. Next, there is a negative consequence to his behavior. Not only that, but it's a severe consequence—being benched for a game or two is one thing, but missing the rest of the season is extreme. Finally, pretend there's a blank space in place of *opprobrious*, and based on what you've inferred, insert your own word or phrase.

- Due to his *really bad* conduct at the homecoming game, Rob was benched for the remainder of the season.

Then just assume you're right, and move on. Unless you continue reading and realize that your understanding of the word was completely erroneous ("And so, Rob was awarded the school's highest honor for his brave conduct in breaking up that huge brawl—and both legs in the process"), attaching your own meaning to the word made the reading more accessible to you in the moment, and that's what matters. Later, you can look up *opprobrious* and see that it means "outrageously disgraceful or shameful." In other words, "really bad."

You might see a CSET question like this.

---○---

Read the sentence below; then choose the best possible definition of the underlined nonsense word.

Some of Jackie's friends decided to major in <u>schumpology</u>, but due to her phobia, she chose instead to major in a field that wouldn't require her to handle glass.

A. the study of jeans

B. the study of tire tread

C. the study of carpet

D. the study of picture frames

Here's How to Crack It

The test will sometimes use nonsense words in order to make you think about *how* to determine the correct answer, as opposed to just *knowing* the correct answer. This is a context question: they're asking you to look at the sentence as a whole in order to figure out what the nonsense word might mean. There are several context clues here. We see the word *but*, which indicates that she did *not* choose this major. Always keep your eyes peeled for words like "but," which indicate a change in direction. So we find out that Jackie has a phobia, or fear, of glass, which is *why* she does not want to study this subject. Based on these clues, we look at the answers and see that the study of picture frames is the one that would most likely require the handling of glass, so the answer is (D).

Diction Errors

Errors in **diction**, or word choice, are quite common and are often tested on the CSET. You can choose the wrong word for a variety of reasons—for example, somewhere along the line you may simply have got the idea in your head that a word means something other than what it means. (This, by the way, is why you should never use a word you're only vaguely familiar with on the constructed-response questions!) Often we think we know what a word means from hearing it in context many times, but we're actually wrong. For example, you've probably heard the phrase "ulterior motive" many times, but what precisely does "ulterior" mean? You'd be forgiven for thinking that it means "wicked" or "self-centered," but it actually means "hidden." However, a word can also be wrong because it's simply inappropriate in that context (like using the word "ain't" in a formal piece of writing). Some common types of diction errors are discussed below.

Frequently Confused Words

Using an incorrect word because it sounds or looks very similar to another word is a widespread diction error. Words that sound the same but have different meanings are called **homophones**: e.g., the first *principle* (rule) of school administration is that the *principal* (head of a school) is in charge. Here are some commonly confused homophones:

Their (possessive pronoun)
There (in or at that place)
They're (contraction of "they" and "are")
- If *they're* going to stay the night, tell them to put *their* suitcases over *there* in the corner.

Your (possessive pronoun)
You're (contraction of "you" and "are")
- *You're* not going to get very far without *your* car keys.

Its (possessive pronoun)
It's (contraction of "it" and "is")
- *It's* an imposing sight to see an elephant stand on *its* hind legs.

To (preposition)
Two (the number after one)
Too (also)

- Are the *two* of you coming with us *to* the party, or are you staying home *too*?

Whether (conjunction)
Weather (atmospheric conditions)

- Do you know *whether* we will have nice *weather* on Saturday?

Which (interrogative pronoun)
Witch (mythical person with wicked magical powers)

- *Which witch* won the prize for best Halloween costume?

Bear (to endure/a large carnivorous mammal)
Bare (unclothed or uncovered)

- I could hardly *bear* the pain of the *bear* chewing on my *bare* foot!

There are other words that don't sound exactly alike, but alike enough to cause confusion:

Except/Accept

- I invited everyone *except* Bill, whom I forgot; I hope he will *accept* my apology.

Than/Then

- If you can't even run faster *than* your little sister, *then* don't try out for the track team!

Affect/Effect

- The noise *affected* my concentration during the exam, which had a terrible *effect* on my grade.

> Remember that *affect* is always a verb and *effect* is always a noun when used in this context! However, there is a different word ("effect") that means "to cause" or "to bring about." When used in that sense, *effect* is a verb.

Then there are some words that really don't sound alike at all, but are still often confused:

Imply/Infer

- Did you mean to *imply* that I can't dance, because that is what I *inferred*.

> Remember that the speaker *implies* and the listener *infers!*

Conventional Usages

Some constructions are correct simply as a matter of convention, not any particular grammatical rule. In other words, we say it this way because our ancestors, for whatever reason, thought it was a good idea. Here are some examples:

Different from (not different than)

- Correct: Americans are different *from* Europeans in that the latter are soccer fanatics.

Either/or
- Correct: You can *either* stay *or* go, but make up your mind quickly!

Neither/nor
- Correct: My cat can *neither* sing *nor* dance, so I'm not a millionaire.

But/also
- Correct: The store *not only* sold me a defective toaster *but also* billed me for it twice.

BEYOND THE BASICS

The CSET is also going to test you on other fundamental components of linguistics. These are concepts you may be less familiar with.

Pragmatics

Pragmatics is the study of social language: how people communicate with each other. When a four-year-old child pipes up in a supermarket, "Daddy, that lady is so *old* " and over the father's stammering apologies, the woman smiles and says, "It's all right; he doesn't know any better," she's right. It's because the child's pragmatic skills aren't developed Pragmatics covers all aspects of social communication, including these concepts.

- Appropriate use of language for a given situation. This is usually the first aspect to develop—knowing when and how to greet someone, to ask a question, to provide information.
- Varying use of language depending on the situation or the listener. When a child is sitting in his living room watching TV with his parents, and needs to use the bathroom, for him to say, "Be back in a minute," would be fine. But if he's in class and needs to go, he wouldn't say that to the teacher; he'd ask permission.
- Understanding and using verbal and nonverbal signals, such as body language, facial expressions, volume, and tone.

Phonology

Phonology is the study of sounds and speech patterns: the distinctions between consonant and vowel sounds, and how they are combined to form words. **Phonological development** is the gradual process in which children develop adult speech patterns. In a child's early speech, the way a word sounds in his brain isn't usually what comes out of his mouth. That's why you'll hear small children say *tar* for *car*, *hagger* for *hamburger*, or *babing suit* for *bathing suit*. These deviations from adult speech are called phonological processes. When the patterns of pronunciation in a given language change over time, we call this **phonological change.** For example, if you were to hear somebody speaking English as it was pronounced in the middle ages, you would surely have a difficult time understanding what was said.

Phonemes

Phonemes are the smallest units of sound that convey meaning. When you divide words into individual phonemes, use slashes to identify them. Many of them are single letters.

- man   /m/ /a/ /n/
- zip   /z/ /i/ /p/
- get   /g/ /e/ /t/

Some phonemes are letter combinations.

- lash   /l/ /a/ /sh/
- thin   /th/ /i/ /n/
- chop   /ch/ /o/ /p/

You can figure out how to determine whether a pair of letters should be separated into two phonemes or kept as one by sounding the word out by each letter.

- jump   /j/ /u/ /m/ /p/
- play   /p/ /l/ /a/ /y/
- this   /th/ /i/ /s/
- ring   /r/ /i/ /ng/
- lick   /l/ /i/ /ck/

In the first two words, the letter sounds don't change when you say them separately. But read *this* aloud one letter at a time—/t/ /h/ /i/ /s/—and it changes the sound of the word. The same for *ring*. If you separate the last two letters, it might sound more like the "ng" in the word *engine*. And in the last word, the letters "ck" create one sound, "k," which is how the phoneme is identified.

Phonemic Awareness

Phonemic awareness is the understanding that words can be divided into phonemes, and conversely, that phonemes can be blended together to form words. Phonemic awareness is widely considered to be crucial in early reading development. Kindergarten and first-grade teachers use activities like rhyming, clapping out syllables, and filling in missing letters in their instruction.

Morphology

Morphology is the study of units of meaning in language.

Morphemes are the smallest units of meaning in words. It's probably easiest to remember what you learned in school about word construction: root words, prefixes, suffixes, plurals, and verb tense. Dividing a word into morphemes means dividing it up into its most basic parts.

One-morpheme words can have one or more syllables, but cannot be broken down into any smaller units of meaning.

- shirt
- love
- giraffe

Other words can be broken down into two or more morphemes.

- hats: hat + s (2)
- unbreakable: un + break + able (3)
- systematically: system + atic + al + ly (4)

The Alphabetic Principle

The **alphabetic principle,** finally, goes back to the very beginning. It refers to the basic understanding of letter-sound awareness, which is the first step in learning to read. Most of it can be figured out with common sense, but you may run into a few particular terms.

- **Alphabetic understanding** is the understanding that in printed words, the letters, representing phonemes, are read left to right.
- A **grapheme** is the term for each of the individual letters and letter combinations that represent the same phoneme. For example, the phoneme /f/ can be represented by more than just the letter "f," as in *fly*; it can also be represented by "ph" as in *phone* and "gh" as in *cough.*
- **Orthography** is the system of using symbols to represent sounds—in English, it is an alphabetic spelling system.

SECOND LANGUAGE ACQUISITION

Most of what we've already covered applies to learners of English both as a first and second language, but there are theories and concepts specifically related to English Language Learners (now referred to in education as ELL, not ESL) that you need to know. This should be basic review for anyone who's been through a teacher credentialing program in California.

Stages of Second Language Acquisition

There are five generally accepted stages of **second language acquisition.**

Preproduction

The **preproduction** stage is also known as the silent period. During this stage, students observe, listen, absorb, and develop an understanding of up to 500 words, but may not speak for several months, or may communicate only with gestures and a few basic words.

Early Production

Early production occurs when students understand and can use approximately 1,000 words. They speak in one- to two-word phrases and can demonstrate understanding by answering simple (yes/no, either/or) questions. This stage can last up to six months after preproduction.

Speech Emergence

The **speech emergence** stage can last up to another year; by now, students have usually developed about 3,000 words and are beginning to speak in short sentences, ask simple questions, and engage in basic conversation.

Intermediate Language Proficiency

Intermediate language proficiency is also known as intermediate fluency. At this stage, students have a vocabulary of about 6,000 words. They understand more complex concepts and use longer and more detailed sentences when speaking and writing, though their English is punctuated by frequent grammatical errors. This stage may take up to a year.

Advanced Language Proficiency

Advanced language proficiency is also known as advanced fluency. It takes several years for students to reach this stage, but by this point, their English is comparable to their grade-level native English-speaking peers.

Krashen's Hypotheses

Researcher and linguist **Dr. Stephen Krashen** is known for his second language acquisition theory, which is broken down into five hypotheses.

If you are interested in working with English language learners, check out our book *Cracking the TOEFL.*

The Acquisition-Learning Distinction

In Krashen's **acquisition-learning distinction,** he differentiates the acquisition of language from the learning of language: acquisition occurs naturally and subconsciously, while learning is conscious and formal. According to Krashen, acquisition is more important than learning.

The Natural Order Hypothesis

Krashen's **natural order hypothesis** is his belief that the acquisition of grammatical structures in a given language tends to follow a particular order. He does not, though, believe that this should be a basis for teaching grammar in that particular order.

The Monitor Hypothesis

Aptly named, a **monitor** is a learner's internal editor—when a learner has enough time to edit, is focused on form, and knows the rule, the monitor edits the output. Krashen makes three distinctions:

- **Monitor over-users** try to always use their monitors, and end up so worried about correctness that they prevent fluency.
- **Monitor under-users** either have not consciously learned or choose not to use their conscious knowledge of the language.
- **Optimal monitor users** employ the monitor when it is appropriate and does not interfere with communication.

The Input Hypothesis

The **input hypothesis** is the idea that a language acquirer develops competency over time by gradually receiving input one level higher than the learner's current level of competence. If a learner is said to be at level "i," acquisition occurs when he or she receives second language input at "i + 1."

The Affective Filter Hypothesis

Finally, Krashen believes that there are outside affective variables that play a role in second language acquisition, such as motivation and self-esteem (which should be high) and anxiety (which should be low). The **affective filter** can be likened to a brick wall: the higher the filter, the less acquisition will take place.

BICS and CALP

One last theory we'll mention is **Dr. Jim Cummins's** distinction between two types of language.

BICS

BICS stands for **Basic Interpersonal Communications Skills.** This generally refers to social or "playground" language, or low-risk academic language (simple yes/no questions, for example). Learners are socially surrounded and immersed in the second language, which makes it soak in faster—like holding a sponge under water—and they develop conversational fluency long before they develop academic fluency.

CALP

CALP stands for **Cognitive Academic Language Proficiency,** or academic fluency. If BICS is a small "social" sponge immersed in water, CALP is a giant "academic" sponge held under a trickling faucet. It takes several years for learners to acquire the technical and academic language needed to achieve academic proficiency.

KEY TERMS

syntax
sentence
clause
independent clause
subordinate clause (relative clause or
  dependent clause)
phrase
subject
predicate
declarative sentence
imperative sentence
interrogative sentence
exclamatory sentence
simple sentence
compound sentence
coordinating conjunction
fanboys
complex sentence
subordinating conjunction
compound-complex sentence
spelling
capitalization
punctuation
commas
semicolons
colons
dashes
parentheses
apostrophes
semantics
etymology
denotation
connotation
context clues
diction
homophone

conventional usage
pragmatics
phonology
phonological development
phonological change
phonemes
phonemic awareness
morphology
morphemes
alphabetic principle
alphabetic understanding
grapheme
orthography
second language acquisition
preproduction
early production
speech emergence
intermediate language proficiency
  (intermediate fluency)
advanced language proficiency
  (advanced fluency)
Dr. Stephen Krashen
acquisition-learning distinction
natural order hypothesis
monitor
monitor over-users
monitor under-users
optimal monitor users
input hypothesis
affective filter
Dr. Jim Cummins
Basic Interpersonal Communication Skills
  (BICS)
Cognitive Academic Language Proficiency
  (CALP)

Chapter 3 Drill

Answers and explanations can be found in the final section of this book, beginning on page 617.

1. What is generally considered a major flaw of the alphabetic principle?

    A. Children whose native language is not English have difficulty understanding it.

    B. Some children learn the alphabet earlier than others.

    C. Many letters and letter combinations have multiple sounds.

    D. It doesn't take into account the meanings of words.

2. Which of the following words contains exactly two morphemes?

    A. plant

    B. ankle

    C. speakers

    D. loaded

3. In which word can you separate the consonant blend into two phonemes?

    A. lau<u>gh</u>

    B. <u>fl</u>ow

    C. <u>ph</u>one

    D. fea<u>th</u>er

4. In which of the following sentences is the underlined word used correctly?

    A. He left her at the <u>alter</u>.

    B. Make sure you don't <u>altar</u> the meaning of the sentence.

    C. Traffic was diverted around the <u>site</u> of the accident

    D. The building <u>cite</u> was purchased by Donald Trump.

5. Which of the following is a complex sentence?

    A. Jill played the game of her life, but the team still lost the championship.

    B. You can go out tonight as long as you're home by ten.

    C. Why is Alaska not part of Canada?

    D. I'd hate to lose my scholarship; I'll do anything to raise my grade so that I can stay in school.

Summary

o   Syntax is the study of structure and form, while semantics is the study of meaning.

o   Pragmatics is the study of social language.

o   Phonology is the study of sound and speech patterns: how letter sounds are combined to form words.

o   Morphology is the study of units of meaning: how words are constructed.

o   There are five stages of second language acquisition.

o   Theories by researchers such as Dr. Stephen Krashen and Dr. Jim Cummins help us to understand how second language development occurs.

Chapter 4
Written and
Non-written
Communication

HIGH STANDARDS

Below is an excerpt from the content standards for English Language Arts, adopted by the California State Board of Education.

1.0 Writing Strategies

Students write clear and coherent sentences and paragraphs that develop a central idea. Their writing shows they consider the audience and purpose. Students progress through the stages of the writing process (e.g., prewriting, drafting, revising, editing successive versions).

Organization and Focus

    1.1   Select a focus when writing.

    1.2   Use descriptive words when writing.

2.0 Writing Applications
(Genres and Their Characteristics)

Students write compositions that describe and explain familiar objects, events, and experiences. Student writing demonstrates a command of standard American English and the drafting, research, and organizational strategies outlined in Writing Standard 1.0.

Using the writing strategies of grade one outlined in Writing Standard 1.0, students:

    2.1   Write brief narratives (e.g., fictional, autobiographical) describing an experience.

    2.2   Write brief expository descriptions of a real object, person, place, or event, using sensory details.

THE TIP OF THE ICEBERG

Do you think trying to teach students how to write good sentences is going to be hard? Multiply that by 25, or 50, or 100, and welcome to the world of essays, oral presentations, and research reports! The CSET will test you on your preparedness to teach students how to communicate effectively on and off the page.

Oh, and lest you think that you'll escape the need for such depth of instruction if you plan to teach younger students, take a closer look at the guidelines above: they are excerpted from the content standards for *first grade*.

THE WRITING PROCESS

The **writing process** is not as simple as assigning an essay and collecting it on the due date. Students need to be taught how to write, and that's your job.

You'll use a five-step process to help them learn: pre-writing, drafting, revising, editing, and publishing.

A sixth step, *evaluating*, is sometimes added.

Pre-writing

Pre-writing is what we used to call brainstorming. In addition to the old standard strategies of note-taking and outlining, teachers now employ a wide variety of techniques to guide students in gathering and developing ideas. **Graphic organizers,** or visual representations of ideas, are very effective. The type of graphic organizer depends on the purpose of the writing. Some examples of pre-writing activities are listed below.

- **KWL** refers to these questions: *What do we know? What do we want to know? What have we learned?* It is represented by a table with three columns. The first two sections of the chart—answering the first two questions—are filled in as a pre-writing activity, while the last section is completed later.
- A **Venn diagram** is a construction of overlapping circles, used in comparing and contrasting. For students in the lower grades, a two-circle (two-item) diagram is usually used, and it is sometimes extended to a three-circle diagram in the upper grades.
- **Webbing** is very popular in pre-writing. There are many different configurations that teachers and students may use, but the general purpose is to connect and categorize ideas.
- **SQ3R** is a systematic strategy for reading. The acronym stands for the five steps in the process: Survey (or Skim), Question, Read, Recall (or Recite), and Review.

Here's a web that a student might use to collect information about a character.

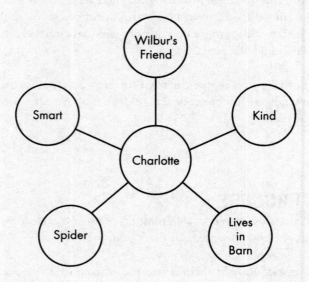

Drafting

Drafting is the step in which students write first drafts. At this point, they just need to focus on getting their ideas down, without worrying about proper essay format or mechanical details.

Revising

Don't get **revising** confused with editing, which we'll talk about next. Revising is all about concepts and ideas. Students sometimes have to do two or three revisions, and often at least one of these revisions is done in **peer groups** or **workshops.** These are the types of things to look for in revising:

- thesis strength
- organization/flow
- topic sentences
- supporting sentences/evidence
- transitions between paragraphs
- introduction/conclusion

Editing

Once a student has a well-revised draft, it's time to fix the errors, or start **editing.** As with revising, editing is sometimes done with classmates' help. The following items should be checked and fixed:

- spelling
- capitalization
- punctuation
- sentence structure
- grammar
- word choice

Publishing

How **publishing** is handled is really up to the teacher. Some simply have students hand in their papers. Others have students make books out of their papers, with covers and illustrations. Some may "publish" student work on a teacher web page. The point of this step is to give the students a sense of completion and pride in their work.

CSET questions about the writing process often come in the form of a paragraph, with one or more questions about the way it is written. That can mean anything from identifying mechanical errors to reorganizing the paragraph to make it flow better. Here's an example.

Read the following draft of an introduction by a fifth grader; then answer the two questions that follow.

[1]I've loved hockey for as long as I can remember. [2]However, I'm not sure exactly how I turned out to be a hockey fan. [3]My father was always a big football fan, my mom loves baseball. [4]And my brothers and sisters don't like hockey, either.

1. Which sentence has a punctuation error?

   A.   Sentence 1

   B.   Sentence 2

   C.   Sentence 3

   D.   Sentence 4

2. Based on what this student has written so far, which of the following sentences would be the best thesis statement?

    A.   My favorite team is the Detroit Red Wings.

    B.   For many reasons, I think hockey is the best sport there is.

    C.   A lot of my friends love hockey as much as I do.

    D.   I hope to become a professional hockey player someday.

Here's How to Crack It

The first question is a simple editing question, and it's asking you strictly for punctuation, so focus on that instead of any other issues you see with the sentences. As is, the only sentence with a punctuation error is (C), sentence 3, which has a **comma splice**—a comma separating two independent clauses without one of the fanboys. The second question seems more subjective, but remember that a correct answer is somewhere in there—it's not just about your opinion. Look at it with a "teacher's eye." A thesis statement lays out the purpose of the paper, and therefore, needs to leave the door open for some substantial material. All of these sentences are logical and grammatically correct, but (B) would be the best thesis because it allows the student to present several solid ideas.

NON-WRITTEN COMMUNICATION

Non-written communication is an important concept. It would make for a pretty boring school year—for students and teachers alike—if every assignment were a written one, not to mention the fact that we wouldn't be doing a very good job of preparing students for real life. Students need the experience of presenting information orally, and teachers can find ways to do that in every grade level. (Remember Show and Tell?)

Oral Presentations

There are many types of **oral presentations** that teachers assign their students, although some are more common than others.

Recitation

Recitation is memorizing a piece of writing and repeating it out loud in front of the teacher and, generally, the class, although some teachers allow students to make recitations privately, for various reasons. Often, a recital is comprised of multiple poem recitations.

Narrative Presentation

A **narrative presentation** is basically an oral presentation of a story. Criteria may include the following:

- sequence of events
- sensory details
- story elements (plot, setting, characters, and so on)

Persuasive Speech

Yes, we start them young! **Persuasive speech** is taught even in the early grades, when students learn to give short persuasive presentations. The prompts are generally simple at first: "Should we be allowed to bring pets to school?" Later, the prompts become more sophisticated: "How can we protect our environment?" No matter what the level, persuasive pieces should include the following basics:

- a clear statement of the speaker's position
- supporting evidence: data, statistics, quotes
- prior knowledge

Response to Literature

A **response to literature** is a very subjective term: it can be just about anything that the teacher or student comes up with as a way to interpret, analyze, or connect to the reading. Responses can include the following:

- monologue/soliloquy
- character analysis
- historical context
- letter
- poem
- song
- summary

Research Report

There's a lot more to a **research report** than just the culminating oral presentations, and we'll get to them in more detail later in this chapter.

Presentation Components

Presentation components include a number of different variables. Obviously, there's more to analyzing and evaluating an oral presentation than grading the information given; if that were the case, you may as well have the students just hand in the written portion. You need to consider other factors, such as the following:

- volume
- pace
- tone
- eye contact
- posture
- gestures
- facial expression
- pronunciation fluency

Make sure that you take into account any factors that may deviate from standard oral English: students who are English language learners, students with differing dialects, students who have hearing or speech problems, and the like.

This is how the CSET might pose a question in that vein.

———————————○———————————

Mrs. Hasner is evaluating oral presentations in her third-grade class. One of the students, E. J., gave an excellent speech in many respects, but stared at the floor throughout his presentation. What is one possible explanation that, if true, should negate Mrs. Hasner's inclination to mark E. J. down for this component of his speech?

A. E. J. is from a culture in which looking someone in the eye is considered rude.

B. E. J. was nervous in front of the class.

C. E. J. did not have time to rehearse his presentation.

D. E. J. forgot that eye contact was a component that would be graded.

Here's How to Crack It

This is first and foremost a cultural sensitivity question. Watch closely for these! Once you recognize it, the answer, (A), is obvious. The other three answers may all be true, but they are things that E. J. can be held accountable for within the parameters of the assignment.

———————————○———————————

RESEARCH STRATEGIES

Let's come back to **research strategies** and look at these in more detail. There are a lot of special considerations when it comes to guiding students in research, so it's important for teachers to be thorough and clear.

Preparation

Preparation is an important tool the students learn gradually, with help from you. Whether the research is for a written or an oral report, students need to be given detailed instructions. It's helpful to provide a series of steps, which can be adjusted by grade level or topic.

Determine the Topic

For the lower grades, a teacher may want to assign a very narrow topic, such as a particular historical figure, animal, or invention. As students get older, the topics become broader and they have more freedom to choose their own directions.

Outline the Main Points

Not unlike a standard essay, a research report should have a clear focus. Again, in the lower grades, a teacher may give the students a few ideas to choose from, while in the upper grades, students are encouraged to determine their own main points.

Identify Resources

Helping the students identify and utilize good resources is the hardest, and most important, step in preparation for the assignment. Except perhaps for the earliest grades, students will be required to draw information from multiple sources. You should provide access to a variety of print materials in the classroom and the school library, and/or guide the students on how to find print resources outside of school. You should provide detailed and carefully constructed instruction on conducting Internet research. This may include limiting the research to Internet sites of your choosing or suggestion, or allowing the students to conduct Internet research only in the classroom or school computer lab.

Interpreting Research

Students need to learn how to interpret their research—that is, determine the validity of the information they collect. *You* know that just because some guy named Geo in Illinois writes a blog about movies, it doesn't necessarily mean he's presenting objective and accurate facts, but your students may not.

To help them evaluate how reliable the research is, teach them about primary and secondary sources.

Primary Sources

A **primary source** is original, firsthand information. Think "straight from the horse's mouth." The following items are examples of primary sources:

- letters
- speeches
- eyewitness accounts
- government records
- autobiographies
- photographs
- contemporaneous film

Secondary Sources

Secondary sources analyze and interpret primary sources. They are one or more steps removed from the primary source. The following are some examples of secondary sources:

- textbooks
- encyclopedias
- magazine articles
- biographies
- documentaries

Citing Sources

Admit it, you just groaned, didn't you? **Citing sources** isn't fun for anyone, but it is necessary, and you'll appreciate it far more as a teacher than you ever did as a student. While formal bibliographies are generally not required until the upper elementary grades at the earliest, even the youngest students should understand the reasoning behind giving credit when using other people's ideas to support their arguments.

At some point in your career, there comes a time when you have to bite the bullet and have "the talk" with your students. It may be difficult and uncomfortable for you and for them, but it's for their own good, and who better to teach them than you? Yes, we're talking about **plagiarism.** Drill, drill, drill into them that plagiarism is the equivalent of stealing, with a healthy dose of cheating sprinkled on top. And be vigilant about checking their sources. *That's* why it's important for you to teach them proper citation methods, so that you can keep them honest.

In the upper elementary and middle school grades, students will begin to learn about two major formats for citations: **APA (American Psychological Association)** and **MLA (Modern Language Association).** APA is generally used in psychology, education, and other social sciences. MLA is used in literature, arts, and humanities. A citation in either format will contain the same basic information, but they differ slightly in the representation, as illustrated below in some of the more common sources your students may use.

Book by One Author

MLA: Author's Last Name, First Name. *Book Title.* Publisher, Year of Publication.

APA: Author's Last Name, First Initial. (Year of Publication). *Book title.* Location of Publication: Publisher.

Short Work from a Website

MLA: Author's Last Name, First Name. "Title of Article." *Title of Website.* Publisher/Sponsor of Website, update date (Day Month Year), URL of page or home page. Date of access (Day Month Year) (if no update date).

APA: Author's Last Name, First Initial. Date (Year, Month). *Title of article.* Retrieved from (URL—no hyperlink)

Journal Article in Print

MLA: Author's Last Name, First Name. "Title of Article." *Title of Journal,* Volume number (vol. x,), Issue Number (no. x), Date (Month, Year), Pages (pp. x–x).

APA: Author's Last Name, First Initial. (Year published). Article title. *Journal Name, Volume*(Issue), Pages (x–x).

Let's take a practice question.

MLA and APA handbooks would most likely agree with which of the following statements regarding proper citations?

A. Information found on the Internet does not need to be cited.

B. Direct quotations and paraphrases are the only types of information that should be cited.

C. Parenthetical acknowledgements are not necessary if there is a complete list of works cited at the end of a research paper.

D. It is not necessary to use *Anonymous* or *Anon* when a book has no author's name.

Here's How to Crack It

While you may not know each specific rule, you should be able to eliminate some of the answer choices by following the basic principles of citing sources. As a general rule, proper citations require you to account for all information that is borrowed—whether it is direct quotations or simply information and ideas. Though common knowledge statements are not necessary to cite, any specific information that furthers your ideas must be acknowledged. The first three answer choices all violate this premise. Choice (A) would be the most obvious; just ask Geo from Illinois when he finds out you quoted his *Superman* review without giving him credit. You may not be sure about (B), but based on standard test-taking sense, you know that any answer with an absolute (here, "the <u>only</u> types") is usually a wrong answer. And if you think about (C) for a moment, you'll realize the major flaw: Yes, there may be a list of works cited, but if you use a quote without a parenthetical reference, how will the reader know which of the works on your list the quote comes from? Once you've eliminated those answers, you know the correct answer is (D). To cement your confidence in the choice, ask yourself this: How often have you actually seen *Anonymous* or *Anon* in a book citation?

KEY TERMS

writing process

pre-writing

graphic organizers

KWL

Venn diagram

webbing

SQ3R

drafting

revising

editing

peer groups

workshops

editing

publishing

comma splice

non-written communication

oral presentations

recitation

narrative presentation

persuasive speech

response to literature

research report

presentation components

research strategies

preparation

primary source

secondary source

citing sources (citation)

plagiarism

APA (American Psychological Association)

MLA (Modern Language Association)

Chapter 4 Drill

Answers and explanations can be found in the final section of this book, beginning on page 617.

1. For which of the following essay prompts would a Venn diagram be most useful in pre-writing?

   A. Discuss the importance of setting in *The Cay.*

   B. Analyze the theme of social class in *The True Confessions of Charlotte Doyle.*

   C. Analyze the characters of Jesse and Leslie in *Bridge to Terabithia.*

   D. Discuss the theme of survival in *Island of the Blue Dolphins.*

2. Which would be the most appropriate persuasive speech topic for a second grader?

   A. "Why Bike Safety Is Important"

   B. "Our School Cafeteria"

   C. "How to Take Care of a Dog"

   D. "The Best Way to Study for a Test"

3. Which is a pair of primary sources?

   A. a photocopy of an original newspaper article within a textbook chapter

   B. the biography of a woman and her authentic birth certificate

   C. a video of a speech along with a review of the speech

   D. a letter with a photo enclosed

4. Renee is editing her essay and comes to the following sentence:

   In *Number the Stars,* either Uncle Henrik or Peter have to help Ellen and her family escape.

   What is the type of error in the sentence?

   A. subject-verb agreement

   B. punctuation

   C. capitalization

   D. There is no error.

5. In Richard's essay, he quotes material from a book about legendary punk rockers, written by Todd Oliver and Kristin Pfeifer. It was published in 2002, in New York, by Random House. How would he cite the book in his bibliography using MLA style?

   A. Oliver, Todd & Pfeifer, Kristin (2002). *Punk Paragons.* New York: Random House.

   B. Oliver, T. & Pfeifer, K. (2002). Punk Paragons. New York: Random House.

   C. Oliver, Todd, and Kristin Pfeifer. *Punk Paragons.* Random House, 2002.

   D. Oliver, Todd, and Pfeifer, Kristin. "Punk Paragons," 2002. New York: Random House.

Summary

o   There are five stages of the writing process: pre-writing, drafting, revising, editing, and publishing.

o   Students are asked to produce a number of different types of oral presentations, including recitations and persuasive speeches.

o   Teachers must guide student research carefully.

o   Knowing how to cite sources properly is vital, in order to properly give credit and to avoid plagiarism.

Chapter 5
Texts

ONCE UPON A TIME

> A young female, smaller than all of her peers, is nonetheless hardworking and trustworthy. One day, an emergency situation arises, and everyone who is bigger and stronger is asked for help. For various reasons—self-absorption, fear, apathy—they refuse, one by one. Finally, she is asked, and though reluctant and unsure of her abilities, she agrees to step up. To everyone's surprise, including her own, her courage and determination (along with an uplifting mantra) carry her through, and she succeeds in saving the day.

Does this story seem vaguely familiar? Or perhaps not so vague—it's the storyline of "The Little Engine That Could."

If you didn't know before that the little engine was female, you do now. You should also know that teachers can, and do, develop entire curriculum units around what seems to be the simplest of stories. The CSET will test you less on your general knowledge of children's literature than on your ability to look at the works you might use in your classroom from many different angles, from character analysis to themes to cultural implications. It's a lot to absorb, so as you study, just remember to stay positive: *I think I can, I think I can, I think I can.*

THE WORKS

No, you don't have to read every book, story, and poem ever written in order to get through the reading, language, and literature section of the CSET. You do, however, need to have some background knowledge of the concepts and conventions of children's literature.

Fiction Genres

The many options within the category of **fiction genres** are the most common types of novels and stories that children read.

Realistic Fiction

Realistic fiction is a broad designation referring to any story that *could* happen in real life. The characters are fictional, but the events in the story are based in the real world.

- *The Secret Garden*, Frances Hodgson Burnett
- *Ramona the Pest*, Beverly Cleary

Science Fiction and Fantasy

The terms *science fiction* and *fantasy* are sometimes used synonymously, but they aren't one and the same. **Science fiction** deals with current or futuristic science and technology, other life forms such as aliens, other planets or universes, and time travel; it refers to fiction that has more of a scientific basis, even if it's far-fetched. **Fantasy,** at the risk of being redundant, is more fantastical. It features witches, wizards, kings, queens, dragons, fairies, mermaids, talking animals, and the like.

- *A Wrinkle in Time*, Madeleine L'Engle (science fiction)
- *The Wizard of Oz*, L. Frank Baum (fantasy)

Fable

Fables are very short stories that teach a **moral** or **lesson.** The characters are usually animals, or sometimes plants or forces of nature, that are **anthropomorphized** (given human qualities).

- "The Tortoise and the Hare"
- "The Wolf in Sheep's Clothing"

Myth and Legend

Myths revolve around heroic, immortal, or extra-human characters. They take place either in other worlds or in other parts of the world, in the distant past, or both. **Legends** overlap with myths in some instances, but legends can also be based on historical figures or events.

- *Odysseus in the Serpent Maze*, Jane Yolen and Robert J. Harris (myth)
- *John Henry: An American Legend*, Ezra Jack Keats (legend)

Folktale

Folktales originated in the early stages of civilization and were passed along orally, which left room for a great deal of shifting and modification by the tellers. This is actually another broad designation, as there are many different categories within the genre. Some folktales are humorous; some have morals; they can be religious, romantic, or magical. The name itself is the explanation of the genre's origins: folktales are stories that spring from folks' imaginations.

- "The People with Five Fingers: A Native Californian Creation Tale," John Bierhorst
- "Anansi the Spider: A Tale from the Ashanti," Gerald McDermott

Mystery

Mystery stories entail solving a puzzle. They usually involve some kind of crime, or **whodunit,** and a detective or sleuth, professional or amateur, who tries to solve it. There is often a cast of colorful characters who may or may not be suspects in the crime.

- *The Westing Game,* Ellen Raskin
- *From the Mixed-Up Files of Mrs. Basil E. Frankweiler,* E. L. Konigsburg

Historical Fiction

Most teachers take advantage of **historical fiction** as a valuable teaching tool. Historical events can be too distant or removed for children to really understand, and reading stories about people and children living through those events makes history more accessible to them.

- *Number the Stars,* Lois Lowry (the Holocaust)
- *Johnny Tremain,* Esther Forbes (the American Revolution)

STORY ELEMENTS

Students are taught to write and to analyze stories based on four major **story elements.**

- **Plot**—the main events or basic storyline
- **Character**—the people (or animals, animated objects, etc.) represented in the story
- **Setting**—the time and place in which the story unfolds
- **Theme**—the underlying ideas and motifs that dominate or pervade the story

Freytag's Pyramid

When children are just beginning to grasp the concept of a story, they learn that all stories have a beginning, a middle, and an end. Later, they're able to dissect plots with more sophistication. One widely adopted system of analysis is **Freytag's Pyramid,** which divides a plot into five parts.

- **exposition:** setting the stage
- **rising action:** building the plot
- **climax:** the turning point
- **falling action:** the aftermath
- **resolution:** the conclusion

Theme

The **theme** is the main idea of a work, sometimes called the author's purpose or the moral. Teachers often plan theme units, in which students study several different works with similar themes.

Themes are generally broad, but their treatment can run the gamut from simple to complex. For instance, in a kindergarten-level story, the theme *be yourself* might come in the form of a young girl who likes to wear clothes that are different from the clothes of all the other girls. In a sixth-grade novel, *be yourself* could be presented as the story of a boy who doesn't feel comfortable with his family's religion.

Religion and culture are often inherent in themes. In each of the *be yourself* stories, the theme would change significantly if one of those elements changed: if the protagonists were Caucasian or African American, Jewish or Buddhist.

Perspective

In later studies of literature, **perspective,** or point of view, can become much more complex, but for grade school students, a few suffice.

First Person

A **first-person narrative** is easily identified by the use of *I* and *me* in the narration. (Be sure to make the distinction between the narration and the dialogue: when people speak, they speak in first person.) The **narrator** is a person, animal, creature, or even an object, who tells the story through his or her own eyes and ears. The reader is limited, then, to knowing only what the narrator knows.

Third-Person Limited

In a **third-person limited narrative,** the story still follows one main character, but it is told more from the perspective of a close observer, as if the narrator were shadowing the main character. Instead of first-person pronouns, the narrator uses the character's name and the third-person pronouns *he* or *she, him* or *her* and the corresponding plurals. Again, though, because the narration is centered on one character, the reader still primarily sees and hears only what happens in that character's presence.

Third-Person Omniscient

If the third-person limited narrator is a shadow, the **third-person omniscient narrator** is a ghost, able to move from person to person, room to room, city to city. All of the characters are referred to by name and by third-person pronouns, but while there still may be one or a few main characters, the narrator can see them all—and show them to the reader—at any time.

Poetry

As with prose, the use of **poetry** in the classroom varies significantly based on age. In elementary and middle school, some types of poems are used more frequently than others.

- **Lyric poems** describe a speaker's thoughts or feelings.
- **Narrative poems** are long poems that tell stories.
- **Haiku** have a specific structure and capture a fleeting moment in nature.
- **Odes** celebrate or praise.
- **Elegies** mourn.
- **Ballads** are song-like narrative poems, often of folk origin.
- **Concrete poems** use words to form a shape representative of the poem's subject.

Here's an example of a concrete poem:

A flock
    of geese
        elegantly
           soars through
                the clouds
                    as we tilt
                      our faces
                        toward the
                            skies.
                      and sunny
                  warmth
                them to
              drawing
            harmony,
        timed
      perfectly
    beat in
Their wings

Let's try a question.

Read the following passage from *Heidi,* by Johanna Spyri, and answer the question that follows.

"Oho!" thought Sebastian, laughing to himself, "the little miss has evidently been up to more mischief." Then, drawing the boy inside he said aloud, "I understand now, come with me and wait outside the door till I tell you to go in. Be sure you begin playing your organ the instant you get inside the room; the lady is very fond of music."

Sebastian knocked at the study door, and a voice said, "Come in."

"There is a boy outside who says he must speak to Miss Clara herself," Sebastian announced.

Clara was delighted at such an extraordinary and unexpected message.

"Let him come in at once," replied Clara; "he must come in, must he not," she added, turning to her tutor, "if he wishes so particularly to see me?"

Whose perspective is this story told from?

A.   first person: Clara

B.   first person: Sebastian

C.   third-person limited

D.   third-person omniscient

Here's How to Crack It

In the passage, the characters are all referred to by name or by third-person pronouns, which means that you can quickly use POE (review that on page 11 if you need a refresher) to rule out (A) and (B). Now, though, you have to pay attention to what else is going on in the passage. Initially, you might assume that the narration closely follows Sebastian, because you hear his thoughts in the first paragraph. But suddenly, in the fourth paragraph, the proverbial ghost passes through the wall. One minute, you're in the hallway with Sebastian, and in the next sentence you're in the room with Clara. And not only do you hear her speak, you are provided access to her thoughts as well (she is "delighted"). With close reading, you can determine that the answer is actually (D), third-person omniscient.

LITERARY DEVICES

If all you remember about creative elements in literature and poetry is how to spell onomato-poeia, there are a few other things you should probably revisit. Basic elements like **rhyme** and **repetition** really bear no examples, but here are some others.

Simile

A **simile** is the comparison of two dissimilar things using *like* or *as*.

- David is as sharp as a tack.
- The calm water looks like glass.

Metaphor

A **metaphor** is also a comparison of two dissimilar things, though without the use of *like* or *as*.

- In a crisis, Taria is a rock.
- A blanket of snow covered the earth.

There are more complex forms, including **extended metaphor,** which uses a symbol to represent something else throughout a long passage or entire work. "O Captain! My Captain!" by Walt Whitman is a classic example: on the surface, the poem is about a captain who has successfully navigated his ship through a storm, but dies just before reaching port. However, the poem is actually an extended metaphor: the captain represents Abraham Lincoln, the ship is America, the storm is the Civil War, and his sudden death is…well, his sudden death.

Personification

Personification is the assigning of human qualities to non-humans: animals, plants, inanimate objects, and the like.

- The wind whispered in the night.
- Every time Sam dove into the pile, the leaves leaped and danced in the air.

Alliteration

Alliteration is the repetition of initial consonant sounds.

- Little Lucy loves lavender and lilacs.
- Zach zigged and zagged around the zoo.

Hyperbole

Hyperbole is exaggeration. Hyperboles can sometimes be confused with similes, because they often use *like* or *as*.

- I'm so tired, I could sleep for a month!
- To Charlie, his father seemed as tall as a skyscraper.

Imagery

The tendency may be to assume that **imagery** is limited to the use of visual images, but in actuality, imagery is language that appeals to all of the senses.

- I stroked the papery skin of her hands.
- As she sang, Hillary's high, clear voice wafted through the hall.

Tone

Tone may also be referred to as mood. It's the overall attitude of a piece of writing. Look for words or phrases that evoke emotions.

- Chris trudged out into the bleak, gray dawn.
- The puppy bounded eagerly into Lindsey's arms.

Onomatopoeia

And of course, **onomatopoeia** is the term for words that represent sounds. Pretty much every animal sound is included in this group, as well as words such as *slap, crack, swish, click,* and *murmur.*

Now that we have reviewed literary devices, let's tackle a practice question.

Read this poem by Emily Dickinson and answer the question that follows.

A door just opened on a street—
    I, lost, was passing by—
An instant's width of warmth disclosed
    And wealth, and company.

The door as sudden shut, and I,
    I, lost, was passing by,—
Lost doubly, but by contrast most,
    Enlightening misery.

The speaker in the poem can best be characterized as:

A.   peaceful.

B.   lonely.

C.   nervous.

D.   delighted.

Here's How to Crack It

By scanning the answers, you can determine that this is a *tone,* or *mood,* question. First, isolate any "feeling" words in the poem: *lost, warmth, enlightening, misery.* At first glance, that list proves troublesome. The words seem to contradict each other. The only answer you can really eliminate using POE at this point is (C), *nervous.* When you look back at the poem, you discover a few things. One, the word *lost* is used three times, which gives it more weight. Two, the word *warmth* is part of a section depicting a scene from which the speaker is excluded. Three, the word *enlightening* is used here in conjunction with the word *misery,* as a way to prove that the speaker is now more acutely aware of his or her unhappiness. This eliminates (A) and (D). To be sure, you can go back to the repetition of the word *lost* to verify that your instinct is correct. The answer is (B), *lonely.*

Non-Literary Texts

Analyzing Arguments

In addition to having you decipher literary works, the CSET also tests your ability to analyze informational text as well. You will need to evaluate the soundness of a particular line of reasoning, as well as the sufficiency of the evidence presented in support of a given claim. While there are literally dozens of specific logical **fallacies**, or types of bad reasoning, you really just need to keep your wits about you for these questions. For example, does the speaker misstate the other person's position and then refute a "weaker" version of that argument? Does the speaker assume that something is true without any real proof or evidence? Does the speaker state that something is the case simply because nobody has proven otherwise? Take a look at the following question.

For more on logical fallacies, visit the Purdue University Online Writing Lab (OWL) at owl.english. purdue.edu/owl/ resource/659/03/.

Josie: If the faculty awards committee makes a fair decision, then Ms. Crabapple is a shoo-in to win the Best Teacher Award at the awards ceremony on Sunday! How could she not? Pretty much all of us students agree that she is the best-loved teacher in the entire school.

While on the surface Josie's argument might appear reasonable, closer analysis reveals that it is pretty unsound. Her position is, basically, that a fair decision by the faculty committee would require that the "Best Teacher" award be given to Ms. Crabapple. What's her evidence for this? She bases her argument that Ms. Crabapple is the best teacher on the fact that, according to the student consensus, she is the "best-loved" teacher in the school. But "best teacher" and "best-loved teacher" are not the same concept. Maybe Ms. Crabapple is so beloved by her students because she makes them do little or no work. Maybe Ms. Crabapple is on the verge of being fired because she allows her students to eat pizza and listen to rock music every day while the other ninth-graders are struggling through algebra problems. While we don't know the specific criteria that the faculty will use to determine who the best teacher is, we really don't have to have that information. "Best-loved teacher" is pretty far removed from the concept of "best teacher," so Josie's argument is flawed.

Assessing the Credibility of Sources

When the facts are basically agreed upon and someone is making an *argument* based on those facts, as in a formal logic problem, it's a fallacy to attack the speaker on a personal level instead of attacking the argument itself. However, in the real world we don't always agree about what's a fact and what isn't, so we need to assess the credibility of various sources and the information they present. In the age of the Internet, when virtually everybody has a blog or website on which they hold themselves out as some kind of authority, you have to take their assertions with a pretty large grain of salt. Your common sense will help you tremendously here. Is the individual who's making claims about a new miracle treatment a qualified medical doctor, a well-reputed scientist, just some guy on the Internet, or the owner of the company that manufactures that product? Be wary of any statements that seem extreme or implausible, especially when the supporting evidence sounds vague. Remember that numbers and statistics can easily be manipulated when someone's agenda involves convincing you of something. In short, people who have relevant expertise and no apparent motive to distort the facts tend to be credible, especially when they appear cautious and responsible in their statements.

KEY TERMS

fiction genres

realistic fiction

science fiction

fantasy

fables

moral (lesson)

anthropomorphized

myths

legends

folktales

mystery

whodunit

historical fiction

story elements

plot

character

setting

theme

Freytag's Pyramid

exposition

rising action

climax

falling action

resolution

perspective

first-person narrative

narrator

third-person limited narrative

third-person omniscient narrative

poetry

lyric poems

narrative poems

haiku

odes

elegies

ballads

concrete poems

rhyme

repetition

simile

metaphor

extended metaphor

personification

alliteration

hyperbole

imagery

tone

onomatopoeia

fallacy

credibility of sources

Chapter 5 Drill

Answers and explanations can be found in the final section of this book, beginning on page 617.

Read the following fable; then answer the two questions that follow.

The Wind and the Sun were arguing over which of them was stronger. Soon they saw a traveler coming down the road, and the Sun said: "Aha! Here is a way to decide our dispute. Whichever of us can make that traveler take off his cloak shall be regarded as the stronger." The Sun hid behind a cloud, and the Wind began to blow as hard as it could onto the traveler. But the harder he blew, the tighter the traveler wrapped his cloak around him, until at last the Wind had to give up in despair. Then the Sun came out and shone in all his glory upon the traveler, who soon grew warm and took off his cloak.

1. What is the moral of the fable?

   A. Be careful what you wish for.

   B. Kindness gets better results than cruelty.

   C. Birds of a feather flock together.

   D. Do not judge a book by its cover.

2. Which of the following elements most clearly reflects the style of traditional fables?

   A. the extended metaphor

   B. the argument between two characters

   C. the use of personification

   D. the one-sided dialogue

3. **Read the following sentence; then answer the question that follows.**

   The icy rain sliced Lynn's cheeks like razor blades.

   Which two literary devices does this sentence employ?

   A. simile and onomatopoeia

   B. simile and alliteration

   C. metaphor and personification

   D. metaphor and imagery

4. Which of the following is a narrative poem?

   A. "The Road Not Taken" by Robert Frost

   B. "The Tyger" by William Blake

   C. "Paul Revere's Ride" by Henry Wadsworth Longfellow

   D. "Boa Constrictor" by Shel Silverstein

5. Which is an example of hyperbole?

   A. Claire's laugh echoed throughout the school campus.

   B. In the dark room, the shadows looked like menacing monsters.

   C. Everyone always said that Jules was as sweet as pie.

   D. Our cat hacked up a hairball the size of Cleveland.

Summary

o   Students read a wide variety of fiction genres.

o   There are four story elements: plot, character, setting, and theme.

o   Freytag's Pyramid divides a plot into five parts.

o   The three most common perspectives are first person, third-person limited and third-person omniscient.

o   Students learn to classify and write poems of different types.

o   Writers employ literary devices to make their work more meaningful and interesting.

Chapter 6
History and Social Science Strategy

CRACKING THE HISTORY AND SOCIAL SCIENCE TEST

Use the map below to answer the two questions that follow.

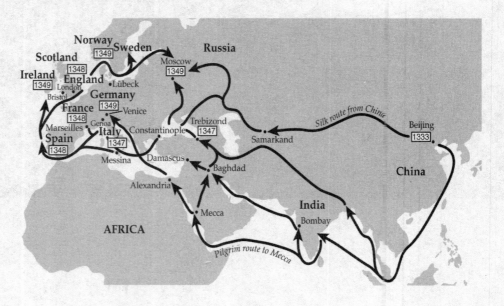

1333–1349 CE

1. The map above shows:

   A. the expansion of the Roman Empire.

   B. major routes of the Crusades.

   C. the spread of the Bubonic Plague.

   D. explorations by Ferdinand Magellan.

2. If you have absolutely no idea what this map represents, you should:

   A. eliminate as many wrong answers as possible.

   B. try to get the answer from someone else's test.

   C. select an answer choice and move on.

   D. cry.

PICK YOUR BATTLES

The History and Social Science subtest covers thousands of years, from ancient civilizations to modern California history. In the next chapter, we'll provide an overview of the essential content areas to help you focus your studies. In addition to reviewing history, we recommend honing the skills needed to answer the various types of questions you'll face.

PROCESS OF ELIMINATION

Obviously, applying POE is a skill you should be utilizing throughout the test, but it will prove especially valuable in the area of history, so it bears repeating. The trick is not to get hung up on what you *don't* know. Focus instead on what you *do* know. Eliminate answer choices you know aren't true based on your knowledge of history. You can also eliminate answer choices that don't represent the correct era—a question about the American Revolution can't be answered by a fact about the Civil War! Finally, use your common sense to eliminate bad answer choices; if an answer choice just doesn't make sense, eliminate it. If you can eliminate even one or two answers, you're in much better shape than you were before.

Give it a try on this quote question.

"An accountable peasantry subject to other men; much use of the service tenement (i.e., the fief) rather than salary, which was inconceivable; the dominance of a military class; agreements concerning obedience and protection which bound man to man and, in the military class, assumed the distinctive form called vassalage, the breakdown of central authority."

The quote above most likely describes conditions in:

A.   imperial Rome.

B.   thirteenth-century France.

C.   nineteenth-century Britain.

D.   sixteenth-century Japan.

Apply the Strategy
POE is particularly helpful on history questions.

Here's How to Crack It

What came to mind as you read the quote? Clues like "peasantry" and "fief" may have made you think of feudalism, which should also make you think of Europe (and maybe Japan). Feudalism arose after the fall of the Roman Empire, so eliminate (A). While (C) may be tempting, make sure to read carefully! Britain certainly wasn't feudal in the nineteenth century. While Japan had its own feudal system, the tracts of land weren't referred to as fiefs, so you can eliminate (D) and you're left with the correct answer, (B).

MAPS

Map questions require you to look at a map and answer one or more questions. Watch out because map questions can be a bit tricky, though. These types of questions require some basic outside knowledge of history and geography.

Let's take the map at the beginning of this chapter as an example. Look at the clues you have available to you. One major clue is the map's **date range:** 1333–1349 CE (Common Era, formerly known as AD; BCE is Before the Common Era). Based on that range, what can you rule out? Well, hopefully you know a bit about the Roman Empire, which developed in the first centuries of the Common Era. That is much too early for this map. Also, the Crusades lasted for several centuries, while this map spans only 16 years. At this point, you're down to two choices, and you can make an educated guess. Ferdinand Magellan sailed around the tip of South America in the early 1500s, so the answer is (C).

Let's look at another map question.

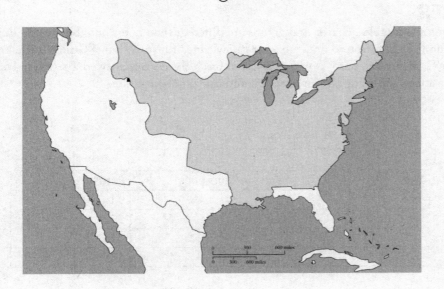

The shaded region on the map above shows the land held by the United States immediately following the:

A.   American Revolution.

B.   passage of the Northwest Ordinance.

C.   Louisiana Purchase.

D.   Mexican War.

Here's How to Crack It

Use any or all of what you know to eliminate incorrect answers. The American Revolution occurred when the Thirteen Colonies overthrew the governance of the British Empire. Picture the original colonies and the land they occupied: basically, a somewhat vertical strip along the East Coast. This map indicates far too much land for (A) to be the correct answer. Similarly, the Northwest Ordinance of 1787 allowed only for the creation of up to five states in the area between the Ohio River and the Great Lakes, east of the Mississippi. The shaded region on the map extends too far west, and covers a lot more than five states' worth of land, so (B) cannot be right. The Mexican War resulted in the United States' acquisition of land that would later become Texas, California, and most of the states in between, which rules out (D). The correct answer is (C), the Louisiana Purchase.

TABLES

Questions about tables, charts, and graphs are different than questions about maps in that they usually don't require you to draw on your knowledge of history. Some basic outside knowledge could be helpful, sure, but it is not required to reach the correct answer. These types of answers are more about analyzing the information and drawing conclusions.

Look at this example.

Year	Total in Thousands	Rate*
1881–1890	5,247	9.1
1891–1900	2,688	5.3
1901–1910	8,795	10.4
1911–1920	5,736	5.7

Immigration 1881–1920

*Annual rate per 1,000 U.S. population. Rates computed by dividing the sum of annual immigration totals by the sum of annual United States population totals for the same number of years.

Which of the following can be inferred from the above table?

A. More immigrants arrived in the United States between 1911 and 1920 than during any other period from 1881 to 1920.

B. The period between 1891 and 1900 marked the lowest rate of immigration between 1881 and 1920.

C. Political persecution in Europe led to a rise in immigration to the United States between 1881 and 1920.

D. World economic factors led to a rise in immigration from East to West.

Here's How to Crack It

You only need to apply the information from the chart to answer this question—the rate of 5.3 from 1891–1900 is the lowest (B). Choices (C) and (D) reflect political circumstances that may have influenced immigration but cannot be inferred from the chart.

Table questions in the CSET often ask you to select a line that correctly matches two categories. Here's an example.

————————◯————————

Which line below correctly matches an American colony with the primary reason it was founded?

Line	Colony	Reason for founding
1	Maryland	Economic gain
2	Virginia	A gift from the King
3	Massachusetts	Religious freedom
4	Connecticut	Economic gain

A. Line 1

B. Line 2

C. Line 3

D. Line 4

Here's How to Crack It

Just as in the previous questions, use what you know to eliminate answers. When you think colonial Virginia, think agriculture—it was founded for economic gain, so you can eliminate (B). Maryland was a haven for Catholics, so you can eliminate (A). Between (C) and (D), it's a pretty safe bet to go with religious freedom as the reason for a colony's founding, so if you're not sure, you can make an educated guess with (C), which is the correct answer (Connecticut was also founded for religious freedom).

————————◯————————

Let's try another one.

Which line in the table below best matches a California industry and the area in which it is concentrated?

Line	Industry	Area
1	Aerospace	Southern California
2	Electronics	Central Valley
3	Entertainment	San Francisco Bay Area
4	Mining	Central Coast

A. Line 1

B. Line 2

C. Line 3

D. Line 4

Here's How to Crack It

Use common sense to eliminate answer choices—the electronics industry is concentrated in Silicon Valley near San Francisco and the entertainment industry is concentrated in Southern California, so eliminate (B) and (C). Mining is concentrated in more inland communities and in the northern part of the state (think Gold Rush), so eliminate (D) and you're left with the correct answer, (A).

CHARTS

The key with chart questions is not to overanalyze. The questions are very direct: they just want to know that you can interpret a chart. As with tables, outside knowledge that you may have is helpful but not necessary. The correct answer will be indisputably supported by the information provided. They don't want you to think outside the box—literally!

Here's one type of chart you might see.

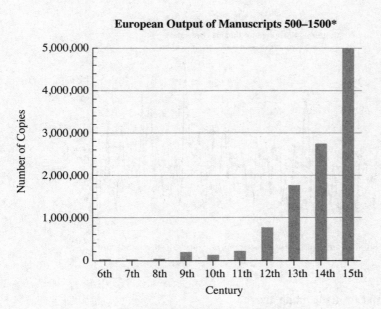

European Output of Manuscripts 500–1500*

*without Southeast Europe (Byzantine realm) and Russia

Based on the information in the graph above, which of the following conclusions is accurate?

A.   The production of manuscripts reached its peak in the 15th century and subsequently declined.

B.   Manuscript production almost doubled after the invention of the printing press.

C.   The number of manuscripts produced remained relatively constant as Europe entered The Renaissance.

D.   A stronger European economy in the 14th and 15th century led to greater purchasing power among citizens and the production of more manuscripts.

Here's How to Crack It

First, see which answer choices you can eliminate based on the information in the chart. As Europe entered the Renaissance, the production of manuscripts greatly increased, so eliminate (C). Simply because this chart ends at the year 1500 doesn't mean that production stopped at that point, so eliminate (A). While (D) may seem logical, this table provides no information about the economy in Europe, so eliminate it. The printing press was invented in the mid-15th century, and the numbers from the 14th to the 15th century almost double on the graph, so (B) is the conclusion best supported by this table.

You'll also need to be prepared to interpret graphs.

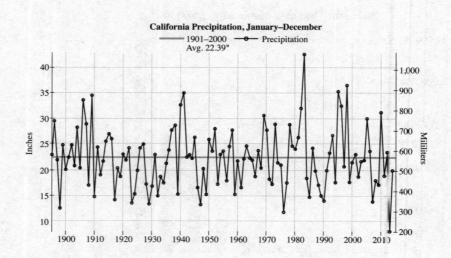

California Precipitation, January–December

What can you infer from the graph above?

A. California wildfires were likely at their worst in years that had precipitation amounts well below average.

B. California never sees more than 50 inches of precipitation.

C. Precipitation amounts vary from year to year, with most years within a few inches of the average.

D. California's water supply is difficult to predict in any given year.

Here's How to Crack It

Look for answers that are incorrect based on the graph (remember: don't infer anything!). There is a fair amount of variation, but most of the points on the graph are near the line down the center that represents the average. We have no information here about wildfires or the prediction of water supply, so eliminate (A) and (D). While California hasn't seen more than 50 inches of precipitation in the time period on this graph, we don't have evidence that this has never happened, so eliminate (B). You're left with (C), which matches the data in the graph.

Summary

- Process of Elimination (POE) is especially helpful in the history/social sciences portion of the test.

- With map questions, use all of the information you know about history and geography to analyze the map and question.

- With table, chart, and graph questions, remember that the answers are there in the figure. You just need to interpret information.

Chapter 7
World, United States, and California History Review

If you read through the CSET: Multiple Subjects Subtest I description, you'll see that this portion covers not just United States and world history but California history as well. Clearly, that's a *lot* of history—far more than can be comprehensively addressed in one book, let alone one chapter. Therefore, the following overviews are intended to focus on the essentials: the core of what you need to know. For a more in-depth review, check out some of our other titles:

California: A History and *The Elusive Eden* are comprehensive California history resources.

- *Cracking the SAT Subject Test in U.S. History* and *Cracking the SAT Subject Test in World History:* Comprehensive, textbook-style content review; each also includes drills and practice tests for their respective SAT Subject Tests.
- *ASAP U.S. History* and *ASAP World History:* "Class notes" study guides; each covers key concepts, people, events dates, and ideas for their respective AP Exams, and includes helpful visuals like tables, charts, and graphs.

Let's begin!

WORLD HISTORY REVIEW

Ancient Civilizations

Most of the world's early great civilizations were located in river valleys. Rivers provided a regular supply of water, which is, of course, necessary for survival. Also important is that the lowlands around rivers tend to be covered with soil that is loaded with nutrients, which are deposited, nourishing the soil when the river recedes after floods. The river itself may be home to animals and plants that could also provide food for people. Rivers were also a vital means of transportation.

Mesopotamia

Mesopotamia literally means "between the rivers"; the rivers were the Tigris and the Euphrates. A series of ancient civilizations thrived along their banks. Mesopotamia is part of a larger area of relatively arable land known as the **Fertile Crescent**, which extends westward from Mesopotamia toward the Mediterranean.

Sumerian civilization rose in the southern part of Mesopotamia. In addition to successful agriculture and river management, the Sumerians developed a form of writing known as **cuneiform**. Scribes used this form of writing to set down laws, treaties, and important social and religious customs; soon the use of cuneiform spread over the trade routes to many other parts of the region. Trade was also enhanced by the introduction of the wheel, a major development that greatly reduced the time it took to transport both goods and people between two points. Sumerians also developed a 12-month calendar and a mathematical system based on units of 60 (as in 60 seconds and 360 degrees). They also used geometry to survey the land and to develop architectural enhancements such as arches and columns.

Sumerians were **polytheistic**; they built temples, called **ziggurats**, which were terraced pyramids, to appease their gods. They believed that when disaster struck—such as a particularly devastating flood—it was because the gods were angry.

Egypt

The ancient Egyptian civilization developed along the Nile River, where the soil was rich and the agricultural opportunities were plentiful. The Nile cuts through an otherwise arid landscape, so the people clustered along the riverbanks, where, in addition to farms, they constructed towns and cities. Unlike the Tigris and Euphrates Rivers, the Nile floods at a predictable time of the year and in relatively predictable stages. This made it possible for the ancient Egyptians to follow a very stable agricultural cycle and compile substantial food surpluses.

Rulers, known as **pharaohs**, directed the construction of obelisks and the pyramids, enormous tombs for their afterlife. In addition, the Egyptians used a writing system to communicate. Known as **hieroglyphics**, this system consisted of a series of pictures (hieroglyphs) that represented letters and words. The Egyptians were also very interested in astronomy, which led to their creation of a fairly reliable calendar.

Over time, the civilization became dependent on trade because its people needed a constant supply of timber and stone for their many ambitious building projects and because Egyptian culture valued luxuries such as gold and spices.

Like most Mesopotamian societies, the Egyptians were polytheistic. The most significant aspect of their religious beliefs was the focus on life after death—the afterlife.

China

Shang China rose in the Hwang Ho River Valley (also known as the Yellow River Valley), and, like other river-basin communities, used its stable agricultural surplus to build a trade-centered civilization. At its height, the **Shang dynasty** controlled large parts of northern China and were militarily quite powerful.

Not only were they accomplished bronze workers, but they also used horse-drawn chariots, developed the spoked wheel, and became experts in the production of pottery and silk. What's more, they devised a decimal system and a highly accurate calendar.

The extended family was an important institution in many ancient civilizations across the globe, but nowhere was it more important than in Shang China. There, multiple generations of the same family lived in the same household in a **patriarchal** structure (led by the eldest male). Shang religion held that gods controlled all aspects of people's lives; people also believed that they could call on the spirits of their dead ancestors to act as their advocates with the gods. This gave the extended family even greater significance.

India

Around 321 BCE, the **Mauryan Empire** arose in India, which would come to be the largest in that country to date. A major reason that the Mauryan Empire became so powerful and wealthy was trade. Indian merchants traded silk, cotton, and elephants (among hundreds of other items) to Mesopotamia and the eastern Roman Empire.

Emperor Ashoka is known for his Rock and Pillar Edicts, which were carved on—you guessed it—rocks and pillars throughout the empire. These edicts reminded Mauryans to live generous and righteous lives. Following Ashoka's conversion and commitment to Buddhism, the religion spread beyond India into many parts of Southeast Asia.

After Ashoka's death in 232 BCE, the Mauryan Empire began to decline rapidly. However, between 375 and 415 CE, it experienced a revival under Chandra Gupta II. The **Gupta Empire** was more decentralized and smaller than its predecessor, but it is often referred to as a golden age because it enjoyed relative peace and saw significant advances in the arts and sciences. For example, Gupta mathematicians developed the concepts of pi and of zero. They also devised a decimal system that used the numerals 1 through 9.

The Hebrew People

Israel stretches inland from the eastern shore of the Mediterranean; it lies at a crossroads linking Egypt, Mesopotamia, and Arabia. Areas rich in resources, such as the coastal plain, were often controlled by others. The Hebrews were a **nomadic** people who occupied areas near settlements (sometimes raiding their farms and villages) and eventually developed an agricultural way of life. Their geographical location allowed them to integrate into the trading networks of the Middle East and Africa.

The Hebrews are significant because of their religious beliefs called **Judaism**. In contrast to previous civilizations in the Fertile Crescent and beyond, the Hebrews were **monotheistic**, meaning that they believed in one god. By around 1000 BCE, the Hebrews had established Israel in Palestine on the eastern shores of the Mediterranean Sea. Although they were frequently invaded by neighboring empires, they managed to maintain their identity, in large part because they believed they were God's chosen people. Under the Persians, the Hebrews were freed from captivity and continued to develop a distinct culture that would later lead to the development of major world religions.

The Classical Civilizations: The Mediterranean

From approximately 2000 BCE to around 500 CE, two Mediterranean civilizations, Greece and Rome, dominated the region. Simply put, Western civilization as we know it essentially began with these two empires. Perhaps their most important contribution is the concept of **representative government**, but the Greeks, Romans, and Persians also made lasting contributions to art, architecture, literature, science, and philosophy.

Greece

Ancient Greece was located on a peninsula between the waters of the Aegean and Mediterranean Seas. Because the land in Greece is mostly mountainous, there wasn't much possibility for agricultural development on the scale of the ancient river valley civilizations. But Greece did have natural harbors and mild weather, and its coastal position aided trade and cultural diffusion by boat, which is precisely how the Greeks conducted most of their commercial activity.

The Greeks were polytheistic. The myths surrounding their gods, like those of Zeus and Aphrodite, are richly detailed and still hold our interest to this day. Greek polytheism was unique in one major respect: the Greek gods were believed to possess human failings—they got angry, got drunk, took sides, and had petty arguments.

The **Golden Age of Pericles** (480–404 BCE) saw Athens become a cultural powerhouse under the leadership of Pericles. Pericles established **democracy** for all adult males. Philosophy and the arts flourished, and continued to do so for the next two centuries. During the Golden Age, Greek drama was dominated by the comedies and tragedies of Aeschylus and Euripides, the sculptures of Phidias adorned the streets, and Greek architecture earned its place in history with its distinctive Doric, Ionic, and Corinthian columns. Math and science thrived under the capable instruction of Archimedes, Hippocrates, Euclid, and Pythagoras.

Rome

Geographically, Rome was relatively well situated. The Alps to the north provided protection from an invasion by land. The sea surrounding the Italian peninsula limited the possibility of a naval attack unless a large armada floated across the sea. Yet, although it was somewhat isolated, Rome was also at a crossroads. It had easy access to northern Africa, Palestine, Greece, and the Iberian Peninsula (modern-day Spain and Portugal), which meant easy access to the rest of the world.

Early on, Rome developed civil laws to protect individual rights (in some ways similar to our Bill of Rights). The laws of Rome were codified and became known as the **Twelve Tables of Rome** (the concept of "innocent until proven guilty" originated here). Later, these laws were extended to an international code that Rome applied to its conquered territories.

Under imperial power, the Roman Empire expanded to its largest geographical proportions through additional military conquests. But more important in the history of the Roman Empire was the growth of the arts and sciences during this time. For centuries, Greece had been the arts center of the Western world. With the *pax romana* (Roman peace), however, the arts in Rome flourished, especially literature (notably, Ovid's *Metamorphoses* and Virgil's *Aeneid*) and architecture (marked by the building of the Pantheon, Colosseum, and Forum). Science also reached new heights. Ptolemy looked to the heavens and greatly influenced achievements in astronomy, while Roman engineers went to work on roads and aqueducts.

The Fall of Rome   In short, it can be said that it was internal decay, in combination with external pressure (Attila's Huns, among others groups), that brought about the fall of the Roman Empire. The sheer size of the empire and the huge expense of maintaining it, coupled by a succession of weak—or just plain bad—leaders and a series of epidemics, are all factors that caused the empire to collapse.

Emperor **Diocletian** attempted to deal with the increasing problems by dividing the empire into two regions run by co-emperors. He also brought the armies back under imperial control, and attempted to deal with the economic problems by strengthening the imperial currency, forcing a budget on the government, and capping prices to deal with inflation. Despite Diocletian's innovations and administrative talents, civil war erupted upon his retirement in 305 CE.

After rising to power in 306 CE as a co-emperor, **Constantine** defeated his rivals and assumed sole control over the empire in 322 CE. He ordered the building of Constantinople at the site of the Greek city of Byzantium, and in 340 CE this city became the capital of a united empire. Constantine, too, was an able emperor, but the problems of shrinking income and increased external pressures proved insurmountable. After Constantine's death the empire was again divided into two pieces, east and west. The eastern half thrived from its center at Constantinople; the western half, centered in Rome, continued its spiral downward.

Rome faced external pressure from invaders on all of its frontiers, especially from the middle of the third century on. One such invader was the powerful and well-organized **Sassanid Persian Empire**, which took over in Iran in 224 CE.

In addition to the Persians, Germanic tribes, such as the Visigoths, happened to attack the Roman empire at the same time that the Romans were embroiled in costly civil wars or wars against the Persians. The Visigoths sacked Rome in 410 CE, and by 476 CE, the Roman emperor had been deposed. The fall of the western half of the Roman Empire was complete. The eastern half survived, but not as the Roman Empire. It was later renamed the Byzantine Empire.

Medieval and Early Modern Times

Feudalism in Europe and Japan

The fall of Rome left a fragmented society in Europe. As various tribes and territorial lords battled for supremacy, trade declined and self-sufficiency became increasingly necessary. The estates of wealthy landowners became centers of agricultural production and provided a degree of protection the government could not.

Feudalism, the name of the European social, economic, and political system of the Middle Ages, had a strict hierarchy. **Nobles,** in exchange for military service and loyalty to the king, were granted power over sections of the kingdom. The nobles, in turn, divided their lands into smaller sections under the control of lesser lords called **vassals**. The estates that were granted to the vassals were called **fiefs**, and these later became known as **manors.** The lord and the peasants lived on the manor. The peasants worked the land on behalf of the lord, and in exchange the lord gave the peasants protection and a place to live.

The interesting thing about feudalism in Japan is that it developed at around the same time as feudalism in western Europe. Feudalism took root in Japan for many of the same reasons, such as weak central leadership, but it developed independently.

In 1192, **Yoritomo Minamoto** was given the title of chief general, or **shogun**, by the emperor. Below the shogun in the pecking order were the **daimyo**, owners of large tracts of land (the counterparts of the lords of medieval Europe). The daimyo were powerful **samurai**, who were like knights: part warrior, part nobility. They, in turn, divided up their lands to lesser samurai (vassals), who in turn split their land up again. Peasants and artisans worked the fields and shops to support the samurai class. Just as in European feudalism, the hierarchy was bound together in a land-for-loyalty exchange.

Compare and Contrast Them: European and Japanese Feudalism
They were similar in terms of political structure, social structure, and honor code. They were different in terms of treatment of women and legal arrangement. In Europe, the feudal contract was just that, a contract. It was an arrangement of obligations enforced in law. In Japan, on the other hand, the feudal arrangement was based solely on group identity and loyalty. In both cases, the feudal arrangement was based on culture, and so the feudal system stayed around for a very long time.

Christianity

In the early days, Christianity was spread by the disciples of **Jesus** and by **Paul of Tarsus**. With its emphasis on compassion, grace through faith, and the promise of eternal life regardless of personal circumstances, Christianity appealed widely to the lower classes and women. By the 3rd century C.E., Christianity had become the most influential religion in the Mediterranean basin. Following a period of sporadic and localized persecution, it became legal within, and then the official religion of, the Roman Empire; it continued to branch northward and westward into regions beyond the boundaries of the Roman Empire. In the ensuing centuries, this marriage of Christianity and empire would profoundly affect developments in a large segment of the world.

By 600 C.E., interaction through trade, warfare, and migration had spread Christianity, Hinduism, and Buddhism far beyond their areas of origin. Christianity became the dominant force in what was left of the Roman Empire, while the **Silk Road** and Indian Ocean trade routes brought Buddhism and Hinduism into East and Southeast Asia.

The Rise of Islam

Growing up in the city of **Mecca** in the Arabian desert (present-day Saudi Arabia), **Muhammad** was exposed to many different beliefs, in part because Mecca lay on the trade routes between the Mediterranean and the Indian Ocean. He was exposed to both Judaism and Christianity as a child, as well as the many polytheistic faiths that had traditionally influenced the region. Once he began preaching the monotheistic religion of Islam, which shares a foundation with Judaism and Christianity, he came into conflict with the leaders of Mecca, who had both a religious and economic interest in maintaining the status quo. Persecuted and threatened with death, Muhammad and his followers fled to Medina in 622 CE.

Muhammad's flight to Medina is known as the **hijra,** which marks year 1 on the Muslim calendar.

From Mecca, Islam spread rapidly and widely, stretching from the Indus River in the east to the northwest coast of Africa. The tenets of Islam came to be officially practiced in Arab culture, similar to the way the tenets of Christianity were practiced in the Roman and Byzantine Empires. Lands where Islam was practiced were known as **Dar al Islam**, or House of Islam.

The Renaissance

The **Renaissance** literally means "rebirth," and this was nowhere more apparent than in the arts. In Italy, where powerful families in city-states such as Florence, Venice, and Milan became rich on trade, art was financed on a scale not seen since the classical civilizations of Greece and Rome. The **Medici** family in Florence, for example, not only ruled the great city and beyond, but turned it into a showcase of architecture and beauty by acting as patron for some of the greatest artists of the time, including Michelangelo and Brunelleschi.

With the invention of the **printing press**, books became easy to produce and thus were far more affordable. The growing middle class fueled demand for books on a variety of subjects that were written in their own vernacular, such as German or French. The book industry flourished, as did related industries such as papermaking, a craft that was learned from the Arabs, who learned it from the Chinese. More books led to more literate and educated people. The newly literate people desired more books, which continued to make them more educated, which again increased their desire for books, and so on. The most commonly circulated books and pamphlets were religious in nature. New translations of the Bible into vernacular languages encouraged public debate and personal interpretation of the Bible and helped usher in the Reformation.

> The **Protestant Reformation** was a religious movement that sought to curb the excesses of the Church and correct Church doctrine.

The Scientific Revolution

Prior to the **Scientific Revolution,** Europe and most of the world believed, as Aristotle asserted, that Earth was the center of the universe and that the Sun, stars, and planets revolved around the Earth. As Europe changed dramatically due to the Renaissance and the Protestant Reformation, and as the growth of universities gave structure to burgeoning questions about the world, educated Europeans began to examine the world around them with new vigor. The results were revolutionary.

Nicolaus Copernicus developed a mathematical theory that asserted that the Earth and the other celestial bodies revolved around the Sun and that the Earth also rotated on its axis daily. In 1632, **Galileo Galilei** showed how the rotation of the Earth on its axis produced the apparent rotation of the heavens, as well as how the stars' great distance from the Earth prevented humans from being able to see their changed position as the Earth moved around the Sun.

Together, these men and others developed a widely used system of observation, reason, experiment, and mathematical proof that could be applied to every conceivable scientific inquiry. With precise scientific instruments, such as the microscope and the telescope, a scientist could retest what another scientist had originally tested. Many scientific inquires were conducted with practical goals in mind, such as the creation of labor-saving machines or the development of power sources from water and wind.

The Commercial Revolution: The New Economy

The trading, empire building, and conquest of the **Age of Exploration** was made possible by new financing schemes that now form the basis of our modern economies. Though many elements had to come together at once for the new economy to work, timing was on the side of the Europeans, and everything fell into place.

First, the church gave in to state interests by revising its strict ban on what are now standard business practices, like lending money and charging interest on loans. Once banking became respectable, a new business structure emerged: the **joint-stock company**, an organization created to pool the resources of many merchants, thereby distributing the costs and risks of colonization and reducing the danger for individual investors. Investors brought shares, or stock, in the company. If the company made money, each investor would receive a profit proportional to his or her initial investment. Because huge new ships were able to carry unprecedented cargoes, and because the goods were often outright stolen from their native countries, successful voyages reaped huge profits. A substantial middle class of merchants continued to develop, which in turn attracted more investors, and the modern-day concept of a stock market was well under way.

This concludes our overview of the most important CSET World History content. For more information on these topics, check out *ASAP World History* and *Cracking the SAT Subject Test in World History*.

Now, let's turn our attention to U.S. History.

UNITED STATES HISTORY

Early Exploration, Colonial Era, and the War for Independence

The Early Colonial Era: Spain Colonizes the New World

Christopher Columbus arrived in the New World in 1492. He was not the first European to reach North America, but his arrival marked the beginning of the **Contact Period**, during which Europe sustained contact with the Americas and introduced a widespread exchange of plants, animals, foods, communicable diseases, and ideas in the **Columbian Exchange**. When Columbus returned to Spain and reported the existence of a rich new world with easy-to-subjugate natives, he opened the door to a long period of European expansion and colonialism.

Once Spain had colonized much of modern-day South America and the southern tier of North America, other European nations were inspired to try their hands at New World exploration. They were motivated by a variety of factors: the desire for wealth and resources, clerical fervor to make new Christian converts, and the race to play a dominant role in geopolitics. The vast expanses of largely undeveloped North America and the fertile soils in many regions of this new land, opened up virtually endless potential for agricultural profits and mineral extraction.

Concurrently, improvements in navigation made sailing across the Atlantic Ocean safer and more efficient.

The English Arrive

Unlike other European colonizers, the English sent large numbers of men and women to the agriculturally fertile areas of the East. Despite our vision of the perfect Thanksgiving table, relationships with local Indians were strained, at best.

The four main colonizing powers in North America interacted with the native inhabitants very differently:

- **Spain** tended to conquer and enslave the native inhabitants of the regions it colonized. The Spanish also made great efforts to convert Native Americans to Catholicism. Spanish colonists were overwhelmingly male, and many had children with native women, leading to settlements populated largely by **mestizos,** people of mixed Spanish and Native American ancestry.
- **France** had significantly friendlier relations with indigenous tribes, tending to ally with them and adopt native practices. The French had little choice in this: French settlements were so sparsely populated that taking on the natives head-on would have been very risky.
- **The Netherlands** attempted to build a great trading empire, and while it achieved great success elsewhere in the world, its settlements on the North American continent, which were essentially glorified trading posts, soon fell to the English. This doesn't mean they were unimportant. One of the Dutch settlements was New Amsterdam, later renamed New York City.
- **England** differed significantly from the three other powers in that the other three all depended on Native Americans in different ways: as slave labor, as allies, or as trading partners. English colonies, by contrast, attempted to exclude Native Americans as much as possible. The English flooded to the New World in great numbers, with entire families (rather than just young men) arriving in many of the colonies, and intermixing between settlers and natives was rare. Instead, when English colonies grew to the point that conflict with nearby tribes became inevitable, the English launched wars of extermination. For instance, the Powhatan Confederacy was destroyed by English "Indian fighters" in the 1640s.

The Early Colonies

The colonies were established for a few primary reasons. Many were founded for religious reasons—freedom or reform—such as Plymouth Colony. Others were proprietorships, or gifts from the King, and ruled by their owners. Finally, some were founded for economic reasons, such as Virginia, where investors hoped to reap profits from cash crops.

Slavery in the Early Colonies

The extensive use of African slaves in the American colonies began when colonists from the Caribbean settled the Carolinas. Until then, indentured servants and, in some situations, enslaved Native Americans had mostly satisfied labor requirements in the colonies. As tobacco-growing and, in South Carolina, rice-growing operations expanded, more laborers were needed than **indenture** could provide. Slavery flourished in the South. Because of the nature of the land and the short growing season, the Chesapeake and the Carolinas farmed labor-intensive crops such as tobacco, rice, and indigo, and **plantation** owners there bought slaves for this arduous work. Slaves' treatment at the hands of their owners was often vicious and at times sadistic. While slavery never really took hold in the North the same way it did in the South, slaves were used on farms in New York, New Jersey, and Pennsylvania, in shipping operations in Massachusetts and Rhode Island, and as domestic servants in urban households, particularly in New York City. While slave owners benefited greatly, the slave trade created significant challenges in Africa such as loss of population and divisions among African peoples.

Reasons for the Founding of Selected Colonies
- Virginia (1607): Economic gain
- Plymouth (1620): Religious freedom (Separatist Pilgrims)
- Massachusetts (1629): Religious freedom (Non-separatist Puritans); later merged with Plymouth
- Maryland (1633): Religious freedom (Catholics)
- Connecticut (1636): Religious differences with Puritans in Massachusetts
- Rhode Island (1636): Religious freedom from Puritans in Massachusetts
- New York (1664): Seized from Dutch
- New Jersey (1664): Seized from Dutch
- Delaware (1664): Seized from Dutch, who took it from Swedes
- Pennsylvania (1682): Religious freedom (Quakers)
- Georgia (1732): Buffer colony and alternative to debtors' prison

The Age of Salutary Neglect

British treatment of the colonies during the period preceding the **French and Indian War** (also called the Seven Years' War) is often described as **salutary neglect** or **benign neglect.** Although England regulated trade and government in its colonies, it interfered in colonial affairs as little as possible. Because of the distance, England set up absentee customs officials and the colonies were left to self-govern, for the most part. England occasionally turned its back to the colonies' violations of trade restrictions. Thus, the colonies developed a large degree of autonomy, which helped fuel revolutionary sentiments when the monarchy later attempted to gain greater control of the New World.

During this century, the colonies "grew up," developing fledgling economies. The beginnings of an American culture—as opposed to a transplanted English culture—took root. One result of the Seven Years' War was that in financing the war the British government had run up a huge debt. The new king, George III, and his prime minister, George Grenville, felt that the colonists should help pay that debt. After all, they reasoned, the colonies had been beneficiaries of the war; furthermore, their tax burden was relatively light compared to that of taxpayers in England, even on the same goods. Meanwhile, the colonists felt that they had provided so many soldiers that they had fulfilled their obligation. Accordingly, Parliament imposed new regulations and taxes on the colonists. Over the next 11 years, the British government imposed a series of laws that were protested by the colonists, eventually resulting in the colonists convening the **First Continental Congress** in 1774.

The War for Independence

The British underestimated the strength of the growing pro-revolutionary movement. Government officials mistakenly believed that if they arrested the ringleaders and confiscated their arsenals, violence could be averted. However, in the spring of 1775, British forces met resistance from the colonial militia, and the first battles of the war were fought at Lexington and Concord. The **Second Continental Congress** convened just weeks after the battles of Lexington and Concord. Throughout the summer, Congress prepared for war by establishing a Continental Army, printing money, and creating government offices to supervise policy. The following year, Congress was looking for a rousing statement of its ideals, and it commissioned **Thomas Jefferson** to write the **Declaration of Independence**. He did not let them down. The Declaration not only enumerated the colonies' grievances against the Crown, but it also articulated the principle of individual liberty and the government's fundamental responsibility to serve the people. With the document's signing on July 4, 1776, the Revolutionary War became a war for independence. After several years of fighting, the British surrendered at Yorktown in October of 1781.

The Development of the Constitution and the Early Republic

The Articles of Confederation

In 1777, the Continental Congress sent the **Articles of Confederation,** the first national constitution, to the colonies for ratification. The colonists intentionally created little to no central government since they were afraid of ridding themselves of Britain's imperial rule only to create their own tyrannical government. The articles contained several major limitations, as the country would soon learn. For one, the Articles gave the federal government no power to raise an army. Some of the Articles' other major limitations on the federal government included the following:

- It could not enforce state or individual taxation, or a military draft.
- It could not regulate trade among the states or international trade.
- It had no executive or judicial branch.
- The legislative branch gave each state one vote, regardless of the state's population.
- In order to pass a law, 9/13 of the states had to agree.
- In order to amend or change the Articles, unanimous approval was needed.

A New Constitution

By 1787, it was clear that the federal government lacked sufficient authority under the Articles of Confederation and a Constitutional Convention was convened. The Constitution established the three branches of government: the **executive**, the **legislative**, and the **judicial**. The branches were set up with a system of **checks and balances** (or separation of powers) so that none of the three branches could attain too much power.

> **Federalism**
> A system of shared powers in which authority is distributed between the central government and the states.

The Origins of a Two-Party System

Following the ratification of the Constitution, those favoring a strong federal government came to be known as **Federalists** (not to be confused with the Federalists who supported ratification of the Constitution, even though they were often the same people). Those who favored stronger state governments called themselves the **Republicans** (not to be confused with the Republican Party created in the 1850s).

Our First Party System		
	Federalists	**Democratic-Republicans**
Leaders	Hamilton, Washington, Adams, Jay, Marshall	Jefferson, Madison
Vision	Economy based on commerce	Economy based on agriculture
Governmental Power	Strong federal government	Stronger state governments
Supporters	Wealthy, Northeast	Yeoman farmers, Southerners
Constitution	Loose construction	Strict construction
National Bank	Believed it was "necessary"	Believed it was merely "desirable"
Foreign Affairs	More sympathetic toward Great Britain	More sympathetic toward France

Westward Expansion

The **Louisiana Purchase** removed one major obstacle to U.S. western settlement, and the resolution of the **War of 1812** removed another by depriving Native Americans of a powerful ally in Great Britain. By 1820, the United States had settled the region east of the Mississippi River and was quickly expanding west. Americans began to believe that they had a God-given right to the Western territories, an idea that came to be known as America's **Manifest Destiny**.

Some took the idea of Manifest Destiny to its logical conclusion and argued that Canada, Mexico, and even all of the land in the Americas eventually would be annexed by the United States. Western settlement was dangerous. The terrain and climate could be cold and unforgiving, and these settlers from the East were moving into areas that rightfully belonged to Native Americans and Mexicans, none of whom were about to cede their homes without a fight.

Beginnings of a Market Economy

From the time they first arrived until the Revolutionary War era, most settlers in the United States raised crops for subsistence, rather than for sale at market. Most people made their own clothing and built their own furniture and homes, and they got by without many other conveniences. Cash transactions were relatively rare. Instead, people used ledgers to keep track of who owed what to whom and typically settled accounts when someone moved away or died. Developments in manufacturing and transportation changed all that, however. By making it possible to mass produce goods and transport them across the country cheaply, a market economy began to develop. Advances in machine technology, coupled with a U.S. embargo on British goods prior to and during the War of 1812, spurred the development of textile mills in New England.

Transportation: Canals, Railroads, Highways, and Steamships

Prior to the 1820s, travel and shipping along east-west routes was difficult, and most trade centered on the north-south routes along the Ohio and Mississippi Rivers. The construction of the National Road from Maryland to West Virginia (and ultimately to central Ohio) made east-west travel easier, but the big change came with the completion of the **Erie Canal** in 1825. Similarly, **railroads** redefined land travel. America's first railroads were built during the 1830s, the first typically connecting only two cities.

Farming

Although American manufacturing grew at a rapid pace, agriculture remained by far the most common source of livelihood throughout the first half of the 19th century. The Midwest became America's chief source of grains, such as wheat and corn. Midwestern farms—much larger than New England farms—were also much more adaptable to the new technology that allowed farmers to nearly double production.

Social History, 1800–1860

Middle-class families worked to reach the plateau at which the women could devote themselves to homemaking instead of wage earning. (Many middle-class women in their teens and early twenties worked—as salesclerks, teachers, and such—before settling down to marriage.) As wage-earning labor was more often performed away from the home, in factories and offices, the notion developed that men should work while women kept house and raised children. In working-class families, men often worked in factories or at low-paying crafts; women often worked at home, taking in sewing. Others worked as domestic servants, and most worked throughout their lives. Those in poverty were most often recent **immigrants**. Their numbers swelled in the 1840s and 1850s when the great immigration waves from Ireland (to the cities in the North) and then Germany (to the West) reached the United States. These immigration waves met with hostility, especially from the working classes, who feared competition for low-paying jobs.

The South was home to more than 250,000 free blacks, the descendants of slaves freed by their owners or freed for having fought in the Revolutionary War. Some owned land or worked at a trade, but most worked as tenant farmers or day laborers.

Frontier life was rugged, to say the least. To survive, settlers constantly struggled against the climate, elements, and Native Americans who were not anxious for the whites to settle, having heard about their treatment of Eastern tribes. Still, the frontier offered **pioneers** opportunities for wealth, freedom, and social advancement—opportunities that were less common in the heavily populated, competitive East and the aristocratic South. Those women who could handle the difficulties of frontier life found their services in great demand, and many made a good living at domestic work and, later, running boardinghouses and hotels. Because of the possibilities for advancement and for "getting a new start in life," the West came to symbolize freedom and equality to many Americans.

Toward the Civil War and Reconstruction

The Abolition Movement

Before the 1830s, few whites fought aggressively for the liberation of the slaves. The Quakers believed slavery to be morally wrong and argued for its end. Most other antislavery whites, though, sought gradual abolition, coupled with colonization, a movement to return blacks to Africa. As in other reform movements, women played a prominent role. Abolition associations formed in every large black community to assist fugitive slaves and publicize the struggle against slavery.

When congressional debate over slavery became too heated, Congress adopted a **gag rule** that automatically suppressed discussion of the issue. It also prevented Congress from enacting any new legislation pertaining to slavery. The rule, which lasted from 1836 to 1844, along with Southern restrictions on free speech, outraged many Northerners and convinced them to join the abolition movement.

Abolitionists' determination and the South's inflexibility pushed the issue of slavery into the political spotlight. Westward expansion, and the question of whether slavery would be allowed in the new territories, forced the issue further. Together, they set in motion the events that led up to the Civil War.

Sectional Strife: The Path to Civil War

Increasing sectional disagreements among the North, South, and West were in large part because of the differences in these regions' economies and cultures. The North was rapidly becoming an industrialized economy. The South, on the other hand, maintained its original economic orientation; the plantation system had remained largely unchanged since the colonial days. Meanwhile, the West had its own ideology, but its territories were often used as bargaining chips in the powerful play between Northern and Southern interests, increasing the tension between free and slave states in the populace and in Congress.

In the election of 1860, the issue of slavery came to the forefront. The Democratic Party was overwhelmingly pro-South and pro-slavery; the new Republican Party opposed slavery in the new territories; and a third party, the Constitutional-Unionists, sought further compromise on the slave question. In December 1860, three months before Lincoln's inauguration, South Carolina seceded from the Union. Within months, six other states had joined South Carolina to form the **Confederate States of America**; the states chose Jefferson Davis to lead the Confederacy. Cautiously, Lincoln decided to maintain control of federal forts in the South while waiting for the Confederacy to make a move. On April 12, 1861, it did, attacking and capturing Fort Sumter.

The Civil War and Reconstruction

For many people of the era, the Civil War was not solely (or even explicitly) about slavery. Except for active abolitionists, most Northerners believed they were fighting to preserve the **Union**. Most Southerners described their cause as fighting for their **states' rights** to govern themselves. But slavery was the issue that had caused the argument over states' rights to escalate to war.

The Civil War was fought at enormous cost. More than 3 million men fought in the war, and of them, more than 500,000 died. At least as many were seriously wounded. Both governments ran up huge debts during the war, and much of the South was ravaged by Union soldiers. From a political perspective, the war permanently expanded the role of government. On both sides, government grew rapidly to manage the economy and the war.

Reconstruction may be seen as both a time period and a process. As a time period, Reconstruction usually refers to the years between 1865 and 1877, that is, from the end of the Civil War until the end of military reconstruction when the Union army withdrew from the South. The *process* of reconstruction, however, was complicated and complex, and some argue it continues to this day. Reconstruction involved readmitting the Southern states that had seceded from the Union; physically reconstructing and rebuilding Southern towns, cities, and property that had been destroyed during the war; and finally, integrating newly freed blacks into American society. It is this last process that has proven to be most difficult.

The legal end of slavery did not mean an end to racial prejudice. Landowners were often unwilling to sell land to or hire former slaves for anything but low-paying jobs, and poll taxes and literacy tests were used to curtail voting rights granted by the 15th Amendment. Legal and illegal methods were used by those who wanted to maintain a pre-Civil War social and political order.

The Rise of Industrial America

In 1876, **Thomas A. Edison** built his workshop in Menlo Park, New Jersey, and proceeded to produce some of the most important inventions of the century. His advances allowed for the extension of the workday, which previously ended at sundown, and the wider availability of electricity. With that wider availability, Edison and other inventors began to create new uses for electricity, both for industry and the home. The last quarter of the 19th century is often called the **Age of Invention** because so many technological advances like Edison's were made. These advances, in turn, generated greater opportunities for **mass production**, which then caused the economy to grow at a tremendous rate.

Manufacturers cut costs and maximized profits in every way they could imagine. They reduced labor costs by hiring women and children. In cities, where most factories were located, manufacturers hired the many newly arrived immigrants who were anxious for work. Because manufacturers paid as little as possible, the cities in which their employees lived suffered many of the problems associated with poverty, such as crime, disease, and the lack of livable housing for a rapidly expanding population.

Factories were dangerous, and many families had at least one member who had been disabled at work. Insurance and workmen's compensation did not exist then, either. The poverty level in cities also rose because those who could afford it moved away from the city center. As factories sprang up, cities became dirtier and generally less healthy environments. Advances in **mass transportation**, such as the expansion of railroad lines, streetcars, and the construction of subways, allowed the middle class to live in nicer neighborhoods, including bedroom communities in the suburbs, and commute to work. (The growing middle class was made up of managers, secretaries, bureaucrats, merchants, and the like.) As a result, immigrants and migrants made up the majority of city populations. Starting around 1880, the majority of immigrants arrived from Southern and Eastern Europe. (Prior to 1880, most immigrants to America came from northern and western Europe.) Prejudice against the new arrivals was widespread, and many immigrants settled in ethnic neighborhoods, usually in tenements. Worse off still were black and Latino migrants. Many employers refused them any but the worst jobs.

To learn more about this and other topics in U.S. history, refer to *ASAP U.S. History* and/or *Cracking the SAT Subject Test in U.S. History*.

Now we'll home in on the state that puts the "C" in CSET!

CALIFORNIA HISTORY

Your students go to school in California; therefore, they learn about California history. You will be teaching them California history; therefore, you will be tested on your knowledge of it. The CSET divides this section into two time periods:

1. the pre-Columbian period through the Gold Rush
2. post-1850

FROM PANGAEA TO GOLD
(Pre-Columbian Period through the Gold Rush)

Geography

In many ways, California's history is defined by its distinctive physical geography.

Mountains

Notice a theme? Water, and how Californians get water, plays an important role alongside geography in California history.

The **Sierra Nevada** mountain range, which runs over 400 miles along the east side of the state, served to isolate much of California from the rest of the country until the mid-19th century. In part because the Sierra Nevada is one of the snowiest regions in the United States, the runoff in streams and rivers provided ample water for life in surrounding areas.

Desert

Most of southeast California is comprised of desert. The largest portion is what we now know as the **Mojave Desert,** which includes the hottest place in the Americas, **Death Valley.** The desert region also helped isolate California from the east and south.

Central Valley

The **Central Valley** is exactly that: a large valley spanning the entire middle section of the state. Due to its Mediterranean climate, fertile soil, and diverse land resources, early tribes in the area developed an agriculture-based culture.

Coast

California's extensive coastline provided protection from foreign conquest in the centuries predating ocean exploration. It also provided an abundance of sea life as a food source for coastal tribes.

American Indians

Several hundred thousand **American Indians,** or Native Americans, comprised of dozens of tribes and hundreds of languages, were indigenous to California before the 19th century.

Kinship

California Indian tribes were centered on familial associations. **Kinship networks** formed the basis for leadership, social organization, and economic activity.

Religion

The religious leaders can be classified generally as priests, shamans, and ritualists. California Indian religious communities were divided into two major systems: the **Kuksu** in the north and the **Toloache** in the south. The belief in magic, or supernatural power, was almost universal in California Indian society, and was believed to be both the cause and the effect for everything from health to behavior to natural phenomena.

Economics

California Indians were hunters, trappers, and gatherers. Sources of live game included animals such as deer, elk, rabbits, squirrels, and quail, as well as fish and other sea life in the coastal regions. Other food staples were acorns and other nuts, squash, and corn.

Trade within and among tribes promoted communication and expansion. Basketry was common, and became a widespread skill. California Indians also used redwood trees to make boats, planks, stools, cooking implements, and housing structures. From animal skins, they manufactured clothing and blankets.

Spanish Exploration and Colonization

Spanish explorers and sailors had visited California sporadically since the mid-16th century, when **Hernando Cortes** oversaw the fall of the **Aztec Empire** and established **New Spain,** also known as **Baja California,** which included territory that would later become Mexico and southern California. In 1769, **King Carlos of Spain,** in an attempt to claim **Alta California** before Russian settlers did, ordered the Spanish to send expeditions north and establish missions.

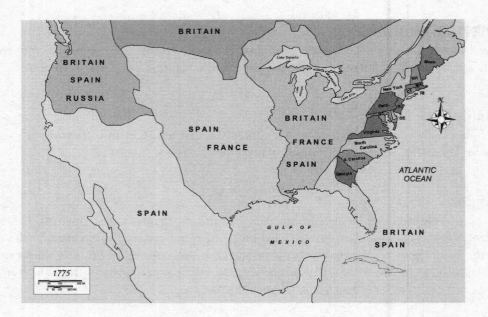

Junipero Serra

Father **Junipero Serra** was a **Franciscan** priest who accompanied one of the first Spanish expeditions. Serra wanted very much to Christianize the California Indians. He established the mission system, building the first nine missions before his death.

The Missions

In all, the Spanish built 21 **missions** between San Diego and San Francisco. No, you probably don't need to memorize all of their names, but there are a few things you should know.

The missions were all constructed similarly; they were almost like small feudal manors, in that they were self-contained communities, gated and surrounded on all sides by the outer perimeter of the buildings. The church was the main building, and there were also living quarters, kitchens, workshops, storerooms, and a large central patio with a fountain.

The California missions were first and foremost in the world in terms of prosperity and functionality. This is due in large part to California's mild climate and bountiful natural resources, but also because Father Serra was persistent in attracting the California Indians to the missions. Many Indians were converted to Christianity and worked in the missions voluntarily; many more were forced to convert. The missionaries taught the natives skills in farming and crafting, and educated them in the Christian religion. Eventually, many of the mission operations depended on Indian labor.

Agriculture

The missionaries and other Spanish settlers introduced a great number of plants and animals to California, including oranges, lemons, apples, figs, wheat, corn, almonds, walnuts, cattle, horses, sheep, and grapes (which ultimately led, of course, to wine vineyards!).

Mexican Rule

In 1821, Mexico won independence from Spain, and four years later, California was officially proclaimed a territory of the **Republic of Mexico.**

Effect on the Missions

In a series of decrees and acts, the Mexican government gradually dismantled the mission system, freeing the Indians and confiscating and plundering the missions, forcing the Franciscans out completely by 1836.

The Rancho Period

To bring more settlers to California, the Mexican government gave out large land grants. **Ranchos,** which were large ranches, dominated the landscape for a period of time in the late 1830s to mid-1840s. Rancheros lived pleasant lives, raised cattle and sheep, rode horses, and employed Indians to work the land and tend the animals. Cattle hides and cattle fat, or **tallow,** which was used to make candles and soap, were major exports.

The Mexican War

Most of the events leading up to the **Mexican War,** which lasted from 1846 to 1848, revolved around Texas, but its repercussions affected California enormously.

The Bear Flag Revolt

The one major prewar incident that did take place in California was the **Bear Flag Revolt.** As tensions mounted between the United States and Mexico, a group of men, inspired by **John C. Fremont,** an Army major who encouraged rebellion against Mexican rule in California, devised a new flag with a bear and star on it. They declared themselves members of a new **Republic of California,** and captured General Mariano Vallejo. After a few brief skirmishes, word came that the United States had declared war on Mexico, and the **Bear Flaggers** joined the U.S. efforts. The bear flag, though, became the official flag of California.

The Treaty of Guadalupe Hidalgo

In February 1848, the United States, under President Polk, and Mexico signed the **Treaty of Guadalupe Hidalgo,** which granted the United States Texas, New Mexico, and California for the sum of $15 million.

California's Admission to the Union

California was not immediately granted statehood; it hung in a kind of limbo between Mexican and U.S. rule for over two years, during which California was governed by the U.S. military. In September and October of 1849, forty-eight representatives from cities all over California convened at Colton Hall in Monterey to draw up California's first constitution.

On October 13, 1849, the delegates signed the constitution—in which they had redrawn the state boundaries—knowing that the land California currently occupied was far too vast for Congress to agree to confirm it as a free state. They presented the constitution to then-governor Brigadier General Bennett Riley. In the months following, the people of California ratified the constitution and elected state officials and representatives.

> ### The Modern California Constitution
> The California Constitution has grown significantly and is now one of the longest constitutions in the world. Its protections of individual rights are, in many instances, broader than the protections set in the U.S. Constitution and Bill of Rights. Additionally, the California Constitution grants three important powers to voters: **initiative** (the ability of citizens to place a measure on the ballot), **referendum** (the ability of citizens to use a ballot measure to repeal an act of the legislature), and **recall** (the ability of citizens to remove an elected official from office by vote).

The two senators traveled to Washington, D.C., to petition Congress to accept California as a free state, and on September 9, 1850, California became the 31st state of the United States. San Jose was the first capital of California, but by 1854, state officials decided on Sacramento as the capital city.

The Gold Rush

Here's a quick rundown of the facts, the figures, and the folks involved in the **Gold Rush.**

In the Beginning

On January 24, 1848, James Marshall discovered small gold nuggets at (John) Sutter's Fort— also known as **Sutter's Mill,** when digging a small canal. In the days that followed, Sutter's workers began to dig for gold in their time off, eventually abandoning their work altogether to search full-time.

In mid-spring, Sam Brannan, a merchant at Sutter's Fort, traveled to San Francisco and ran through the streets shouting that gold had been discovered on the American River. Men in San Francisco, Sacramento, and neighboring areas left their work and flocked to the area to search for gold.

Word Spreads

Within weeks, the news traveled throughout California and into the nearby states, and more men abandoned their jobs to mine for gold. By the fall, word had reached all the way across the country.

In November, a delegate from the California government took a sample to Washington, D.C., and on December 5, 1848, President Polk confirmed the discovery in an address to Congress.

The Forty-Niners

Gold miners came in droves and were nicknamed **forty-niners.** Most people traveled by boat at first, though later more land passages were developed. No matter what the method, it was often a difficult journey.

Almost overnight, San Francisco turned into a booming metropolis. Ships poured into the harbors. Tents and shacks were set up as interim resting places for those newly arrived before they headed up to gold country; later, as settlers stayed longer in one place, more permanent housing was erected, and businesses developed by the hundreds. Similar expansions gradually hit Sacramento and other large cities like Stockton, which were close to the **Mother Lode**—the hundred or so miles along the foothills of the Sierra Nevada, which were packed with mining camps.

The Effect on California

The population of the state grew exponentially in a matter of just a few years, and at first, the influx of people proved extremely hazardous. Mining was hard work, subject to accidents and disease, the most common of which was cholera. Also, gold mining was, at first, essentially a free-for-all, which led to theft, fights, murders, and lynchings. The California Indian population was nearly decimated. Mining also took a terrible toll on the environment: the mountains and foothills were ravaged, and the rivers and creeks were filled with silt and debris.

There were some positive effects, though: the timing coincided with California's admission to the Union, and the overflow of settlement camps grew into cities. With immigrants from other states and countries came commerce, trade, and better transportation, including steamships and railroads. By the mid-1860s, San Francisco was the 10th largest city in the United States, and California had become the most ethnically diverse area in the world.

...AND ALL THE REST (Post-1850)

Railroads
California had a few short-distance railroads, such as one connecting San Jose and San Francisco, but between the excitement of the gold rush and the impending Civil War, plans for a **transcontinental railroad** began to take shape.

The **Central Pacific Railroad** was an integral part of the country—it was the west half of the railroad that eventually linked the two coasts—and of California. The railroad was the brainchild of engineer **Theodore Judah,** who had built the first short-distance railroads. His associates, who took over after Judah's death in 1863, were known as the **Big Four:** Collis Huntington, Mark Hopkins, Leland Stanford (yes, he's the guy who founded Stanford University), and Charles Crocker.

Crocker took advantage of the thousands of Chinese immigrants who were having difficulty finding work due to racial inequality, and it was these Chinese workers who were largely responsible for constructing the western segment of the transcontinental railroad.

Water
It became apparent soon after the population explosion of the 1850s that water was not going to come easily to California cities and farms. Rainfall was sufficient in the northern part of the state, but almost nonexistent in large areas of central and southern California. Engineer William Hammond Hall's research and studies were instrumental in developing California's irrigation systems.

Oil
In the 1890s and early 1900s, oil wells were dug in southern California and on platforms in the Pacific. Oil is considered to be the foundation of the industrial infrastructure of Los Angeles and much of southern California.

Agriculture
After the gold rush, wheat became a huge industry in California. Vast wheat ranches sprawled across much of the Central and Sacramento Valleys. By the late 1870s, California was exporting wheat all over the world.

With the creation of irrigation ditches came more ranches and fields, with crops of every kind, from grains to fruits to vegetables to cotton. California had solidified its status as an agricultural state.

Labor

Here are some key dates and facts concerning labor in California:

- 1850s: The first California unions developed.
- 1870s and 1890s: Depressions hit the state's workers hard.
- 1880s–1890s: Migrant workers became commonplace.
- 1927: The **Confederation of Mexican Workers** was formed.
- 1933: Cotton pickers in the San Joaquin Valley staged the largest agricultural strike in U.S. history.
- 1975: Due to the efforts of **Cesar Chavez,** the **United Farm Workers Union** won the right to unionize agricultural laborers.

Ethnic/Racial Tensions

Though California has virtually always been a diverse state, there have been periods of particular significance in terms of racial inequality.

Skilled and hardworking Chinese laborers were a great threat to Anglo men in the decades following the gold rush. This situation led to discrimination and even lynchings.

Mexican immigrants were targeted during the Great Depression.

Japanese immigrants and Japanese-born citizens were treated equally unfairly, even before World War II, though after the bombing of Pearl Harbor, over one hundred thousand Californians of Japanese descent were sent to **internment camps.**

During and after World War II, thousands of African Americans came to California seeking work, but encountered discrimination in housing and unions. In 1965, racial tension erupted in riots in the Watts section of Los Angeles.

The **Immigration and Nationality Act of 1965** resulted in a substantial increase in the Asian population of California.

Most recently, the 1992 Los Angeles riots, sparked by the acquittal of four police officers accused in the videotaped beating of African American motorist Rodney King, showed that racial tensions still persist.

KEY TERMS

World History

Fertile Crescent
Sumerian civilization
cuneiform
polytheism
ziggurats
pharaohs
hieroglyphics
Shang dynasty
Patriarchal
Mauryan Empire
Gupta Empire
Nomadic
Judaism
monotheism
representative government
Golden Age of Pericles
democracy
Twelve Tables of Rome
pax romana
Diocletian
Constantine
Sassanid Persian Empire
feudalism
nobles
vassals
fiefs (manors)
Yoritomo Minamoto
shogun
daimyo
samurai
Jesus
Paul of Tarsus
Silk Road
Mecca
Muhammad
hijra
Dar al Islam
Renaissance
Medici family
printing press
Protestant Reformation
Scientific Revolution
Nicolaus Copernicus
Galileo Galilei
Age of Exploration
joint-stock company

U.S. History

Christopher Columbus
Contact Period
Columbian Exchange
Spain
mestizos
France
The Netherlands
England
indenture
plantation
French and Indian War
salutary neglect (benign
  neglect)
First Continental Congress
Second Continental
  Congress
Thomas Jefferson
Declaration of Independence
Articles of Confederation
executive branch
legislative branch
judicial branch
checks and balances
federalism
Federalists
Republicans
Louisiana Purchase
War of 1812
Manifest Destiny
Erie Canal
railroads
immigrants
pioneers
gag rule
Confederate States of
  America
Union
states' rights
Reconstruction
Thomas A. Edison
Age of Invention
mass production
factories
mass transportation

California History

Sierra Nevada
Mojave Desert
Death Valley
Central Valley
American Indians
  (Native Americans)
kinship networks
Kuksu
Toloache
Spanish explorers
Hernando Cortes
Aztec Empire
New Spain (Baja California)
King Carlos of Spain
Alta California
Junipero Serra
Franciscan
missions
Republic of Mexico
ranchos
tallow
Mexican War
Bear Flag Revolt
John C. Fremont
Republic of California
Bear Flaggers
Treaty of Guadalupe
  Hidalgo
initiative
referendum
recall
Gold Rush
Sutter's Mill
forty-niners
Mother Lode
transcontinental railroad
Central Pacific Railroad
Theodore Judah
Big Four
Confederation of Mexican
  Workers
Cesar Chavez
United Farm Workers Union
internment camps
Immigration and
  Nationality Act of 1965

Chapter 7 Drill

Answers and explanations can be found in the final section of this book, beginning on page 617.

1. Which religion had the greatest impact on West African culture?

   A.   Buddhism

   B.   Islam

   C.   Zoroastrianism

   D.   Christianity

2. Which of the following most likely accounts for the growth in human population between 3000 B.C.E. and 200 C.E.?

   A.   the development of plant and animal domestication

   B.   the use of more efficient methods of warfare

   C.   the decline of species that competed with humans for food

   D.   the invention of spoken language

3. **Use the map to answer the question that follows.**

   The shaded region of the map above indicates lands that, in 1510, were under the control of which empire?

   A.   the Inca Empire

   B.   the Spanish Empire

   C.   the Olmec Empire

   D.   the Aztec Empire

4. Which of the following contributed LEAST to the decline of the Roman Empire?

   A.   civil wars between rivals for the throne

   B.   incursions of barbarian peoples into the empire

   C.   the persistence of the senate as a body of government in the empire

   D.   demographic weakness on account of diseases and epidemics

5. Johannes Gutenberg's invention has been described as revolutionary because:

   A. with easier access to books, more people learned to read and more books were printed.

   B. with oil paints, Renaissance artists could paint much more detail than they could with watercolors.

   C. coupled with a large pool of unemployed workers, it led to early industrialization in parts of Central Europe.

   D. until guilds were created, craftspeople were unable to control the goods they produced.

6. In the sixteenth century, Spain was the dominant colonial force in the New World because:

   A. no other European nations knew of the existence of the Americas.

   B. Spanish settlers adopted the indigenous religions and cultures of the New World.

   C. Spain had negotiated with other countries for the exclusive rights to settle the New World.

   D. the Spanish Armada controlled the Atlantic Ocean.

7. The system under which national and state governments share constitutional power is called:

   A. federalism.

   B. nationalism.

   C. autocracy.

   D. socialism.

8. Following the Civil War, most freed slaves:

   A. stayed in the South and worked as sharecroppers.

   B. joined the pioneering movement as it headed West.

   C. moved to the North to work in factories.

   D. took work building the nation's growing railroad system.

9. All of the following contributed to the growth of manufacturing during the middle of the nineteenth century EXCEPT:

   A. the development of labor-saving machines.

   B. the perfection of the assembly line.

   C. increased production made possible by the economies of scale available to large companies.

   D. the completion of the transcontinental railroad.

10. The Louisiana Purchase was an important factor in the development of U.S. trade because it:

    A. opened new markets among the western Indian nations.

    B. gave the country complete control of the Mississippi River.

    C. added numerous French factories in the Louisiana Territory to the U.S. economy.

    D. facilitated the immediate completion of the transcontinental railroad.

11. Which of the following was considered to be a negative repercussion of the transcontinental railroad on California?

    A. the discrimination against Chinese laborers

    B. the loss of isolation

    C. the destructive effects of the railroad tracks on farmland

    D. the dramatic reduction of ocean travel

12. In 2003, a special election was held and California Governor Gray Davis was replaced by Arnold Schwarzenegger. This is an example of:

    A. initiative.

    B. representative democracy.

    C. recall.

    D. impeachment.

13. A primary goal of the mission system in California was:

    A. to generate wealth for Spain.

    B. to house explorers as they traveled north.

    C. to develop the agricultural industry.

    D. to convert Native Americans to Christianity.

14. *The Grapes of Wrath* by John Steinbeck is written about a family traveling from Oakland to California during what period in history?

    A. the Great Depression

    B. the gold rush

    C. World War II

    D. the Mission Period

15. The geography and climate of California's Central Valley resulted in:

    A. a sparse population in this area of the state.

    B. an agriculture based economy in the region.

    C. the movement of the state capital from San Jose to Sacramento.

    D. regional conflict over the availability of resources.

Summary

World History

o   Physical geography is a key factor in the development of society, from the earliest civilizations establishing themselves near water sources in Europe, Africa, and Asia to regional identities in the United States and the location of cities and industries in California.

o   Early civilizations such as Mesopotamia, Egypt, and China live on through their timeless cultural and intellectual contributions.

o   Religion affects history: societies change in fundamental ways with the rise of the great religions, and religious beliefs shape politics, economics, and social structures.

U.S. History

o   Colonies in the United States were founded for a few main reasons, chief among them religious freedom and economic gain.

o   The American Revolution coincided with a change in the way people viewed their government: a belief in egalitarianism and democracy replaced trust in monarchy and aristocracy. This is reflected in principals of government such as separation of powers.

o   The new United States struggled to define its ideals as boundaries changed and regional opinions clashed. New developments in technology, agriculture, and commerce built wealth and infrastructure.

o   Regional tensions over slavery and states' rights led to the Civil War, an event that radically changed American society and the role of the federal government in state affairs. It took many years for the South to fully recover from the economic and social upheaval of the Civil War.

California History

o   For centuries, Native Americans were California's only residents.

o   Spanish missionaries built a series of missions along California's coastline.

o   California's admission to the Union coincided with the gold rush, which in turn contributed to a huge population boom.

Subtest II: Science and Math

Science

Math

Chapter 8
Structure and
Properties of Matter

INTRODUCTION TO MATTER

Matter Defined

Although organisms exist in many diverse forms, they all have one thing in common. They are all made up of **matter.** Objects that take up space and have mass are known as matter. Matter is made up of **elements,** which by definition are substances that cannot be broken down into simpler substances by chemical means. Everything in the physical world is made up of microscopic matter comprised of **atoms** or **molecules.**

Subatomic Particles

If you break down an element into smaller pieces, you'll eventually come to the atom—the smallest unit of an element that retains its characteristic properties. Atoms are the building blocks of the physical world.

Within atoms are even smaller subatomic particles called **protons, neutrons,** and **electrons.**

Let's take a look at a typical atom:

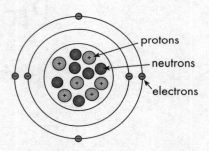

Protons and neutrons are particles that are packed together in the core of an atom called the **nucleus.** You'll notice that protons are positively charged (+) particles whereas neutrons are uncharged particles.

Electrons, on the other hand, are negatively charged (–) particles that spin around the nucleus. Electrons are quite small compared to protons and neutrons. In fact, for our purposes, electrons are considered massless. Most atoms have the same number of protons and electrons, making them electrically neutral. Some atoms have the same number of protons but differ in the number of neutrons in the nucleus. These atoms are called **isotopes.**

PHYSICAL PROPERTIES OF MATTER

All matter is categorized as being in the **solid** phase, the **liquid** phase, or the **gas** phase.

The solid phase is characterized by the inability of the material to conform to the shape of the container that holds it and an inability of the material to expand to fill the available volume.

The liquid phase is characterized by the ability of the material to conform to the shape of the container that holds it, but an inability of the material to expand to fill the available volume.

The gas phase is characterized by the ability of the material to take the shape of the container that holds it and the ability of the material to expand to fill the available volume.

Matter can undergo **physical changes** and **chemical changes.** The CSET requires that you be familiar with both of these concepts. Physical changes are changes in state, such as the evaporation of water. During evaporation, water goes from being a liquid (for example, water in your cat's water bowl) to a gas (water vapor, and kitty is thirsty again). Chemical changes occur when bonds are broken and new bonds are formed between different atoms. Examples of chemical changes include rusting of metal, ripening of fruit, mixing of ingredients in cake batter to become a new type of matter, photosynthesis, and many more.

Matter has physical, thermal, electrical, and chemical properties. These specific properties can include **color** (the human eye response to light as reflected by matter), **density** (the amount of mass contained in a given substances), **hardness** (the resistance to penetration by a given substance, and **conductivity** (the ability to transmit heat [thermal] or current [electrical]).

Thermal Properties of Matter

When heated or cooled, matter undergoes phase changes. That is, matter can actually change states. Generally, the most common progression of phase changes is observed when a substance is heated. The progression is solid to liquid to gas. The reverse progression occurs when cooling is in progress—gas to liquid to solid. In a phase change, the initial properties of the matter substance remain constant and unchanged.

Electrical Properties of Matter

Matter is classified as a **conductor** or **non-conductor.** Conductors have a high number of free electrons, while non-conductors do not.

Chemical Properties of Matter

Matter can react with other types of matter when chemically combined. These products can be either liberated (**exothermic**) or absorbed (**endothermic**).

The Periodic Table

The **periodic table** is a method of classifying chemical elements. The location of a substance on the periodic table determines how it will react to another substance.

Each element is represented by its one- or two-letter chemical symbol. Above each chemical symbol is the **atomic number** (number of protons) for that element. Below each chemical symbol is that element's **atomic weight.** There's no need for you to memorize the periodic table for the CSET. However, it may serve you well to be familiar with the location of the more popular elements: H, O, and Fe.

Elements in the periodic table can be classified as part of a period (row) or a group (column). Elements are listed in order of increasing atomic number (the number of protons in the atomic nucleus). Rows, or periods, are arranged so that elements with similar properties fall into the same columns (groups or families). There are 18 columns in the periodic table (numbered 1 through 18) and many different categories within the table. These columns and categories are a useful shorthand for knowing a bit of information about an element based on its location.

Periodic Table of the Elements

1 H 1.0																	2 He 4.0
3 Li 6.9	4 Be 9.0											5 B 10.8	6 C 12.0	7 N 14.0	8 O 16.0	9 F 19.0	10 Ne 20.2
11 Na 23.0	12 Mg 24.3											13 Al 27.0	14 Si 28.1	15 P 31.0	16 S 32.1	17 Cl 35.5	18 Ar 39.9
19 K 39.1	20 Ca 40.1	21 Sc 45.0	22 Ti 47.9	23 V 50.9	24 Cr 52.0	25 Mn 54.9	26 Fe 55.8	27 Co 58.9	28 Ni 58.7	29 Cu 63.5	30 Zn 65.4	31 Ga 69.7	32 Ge 72.6	33 As 74.9	34 Se 79.0	35 Br 79.9	36 Kr 83.8
37 Rb 85.5	38 Sr 87.6	39 Y 88.9	40 Zr 91.2	41 Nb 92.9	42 Mo 95.95	43 Tc (98)	44 Ru 101.1	45 Rh 102.9	46 Pd 106.4	47 Ag 107.9	48 Cd 112.4	49 In 114.8	50 Sn 117.7	51 Sb 121.8	52 Te 127.6	53 I 126.9	54 Xe 131.3
55 Cs 132.9	56 Ba 137.3	57 *La 138.9	72 Hf 178.5	73 Ta 180.9	74 W 183.9	75 Re 186.2	76 Os 190.2	77 Ir 192.2	78 Pt 195.1	79 Au 197.0	80 Hg 200.6	81 Tl 204.4	82 Pb 207.2	83 Bi 209.0	84 Po (109)	85 At (210)	86 Rn (222)
87 Fr (223)	88 Ra 226.0	89 †Ac 227.0	104 Rf (261)	105 Db (268)	106 Sg (269)	107 Bh (267)	108 Hs (277)	109 Mt (278)	110 DS (281)	111 Rg (282)	112 Cn (285)	113 Nh (286)	114 Fl (289)	115 Mc (290)	116 Lv (293)	117 Ts (294)	118 Og (294)

*Lanthanide Series:	58 Ce 140.1	59 Pr 140.9	60 Nd 144.2	61 Pm (145)	62 Sm 150.4	63 Eu 152.0	64 Gd 157.3	65 Tb 158.9	66 Dy 162.5	67 Ho 164.9	68 Er 167.3	69 Tm 168.9	70 Yb 173.0	71 Lu 175.0
†Actinide Series:	90 Th 232.0	91 Pa (231)	92 U 238.0	93 Np (237)	94 Pu (244)	95 Am (243)	96 Cm (247)	97 Bk (247)	98 Cr (251)	99 Es (252)	100 Fm (257)	101 Md (258)	102 No (259)	103 Lr (260)

Each horizontal row in the periodic table is called a **period.** The outermost electrons of every atom in a period have the same principal **quantum number,** or **shell number.** Each vertical column in the periodic table is a **group.** Every member of a group has the same number of valence electrons and may be expected to have similar chemical properties to other members of the group.

In general, elements from the same group will not react, while elements from different groups may. Remember that the more separated or distinguished the groups are, the greater potential for reaction.

Compounds

When two or more different types of atoms are combined, they form a chemical **compound.** You'll sometimes find that a compound has different properties from those of its elements. For instance, hydrogen and oxygen exist in nature as gases. Yet, when they combine to make water, they often pass into a liquid state. When hydrogen atoms get together with oxygen atoms to form water, a **chemical reaction** occurs.

$$2H_2 \ (g) + O_2 \ (g) \ \rightarrow \ 2H_2O \ (l)$$

The atoms of a compound are held together by **chemical bonds,** which may be ionic bonds, covalent bonds, or hydrogen bonds.

An **ionic bond** is formed between two atoms when one or more electrons are transferred from one atom to the other. In this reaction, one atom loses electrons and becomes a positively charged ion (cation) and the other atom gains electrons and becomes a negatively charged ion (anion). Ions are the charged forms of atoms. For example, when Na reacts with Cl, charged ions, Na^+ and Cl^-, are formed.

A **covalent bond** is formed when electrons are shared between atoms. If the electrons are shared equally between the atoms, the bond is called **nonpolar covalent.** If the electrons are shared unequally, the bond is called **polar covalent.** When two pairs of electrons are shared, the result is a double covalent bond. When three pairs of electrons are shared, the result is a triple covalent bond.

A **hydrogen bond** is a weak chemical bond that forms between a hydrogen atom that is covalently bonded to an electronegative atom and another electronegative atom. The most common electronegative atoms you will come across in regards to a hydrogen bond are carbon, nitrogen, oxygen, and fluorine.

Evaporation is an example of:

A.   photosynthesis.

B.   matter undergoing a chemical change.

C.   a covalent bond.

D.   matter undergoing a physical change.

Here's How to Crack It

Hopefully the correct answer jumps out at you on this one. You know that photosynthesis is the process by which plants turn water and sunlight into energy, so (A) must be incorrect. Choice (C) is completely nonsensical in this context, so cross that one out. Choices (B) and (D) are left, but you remember that chemical changes occur when bonds are broken and new bonds are formed between different atoms, while a physical change is a change in state (liquid to gas, for example). So (D) must be the correct answer.

WATER, ACIDS, AND BASES

Water

One of the most important substances in nature is water. Did you know that 70 percent of your body weight consists of water? Water is considered a unique molecule because it plays an important role in chemical reactions.

Let's take a look at one of the properties of water. Water has two hydrogen atoms joined to an oxygen atom.

In water molecules, the hydrogen atoms have a partial positive charge and the oxygen atom has a partial negative charge. Molecules that have an unequal distribution of both partially positive and partially negative charges are said to be polar. Water is therefore a polar molecule. The positively charged ends of the water molecules strongly attract the negatively charged ends of other polar compounds. Likewise, the negatively charged ends strongly attract the positively charged ends of neighboring compounds. These forces are most readily apparent in the tendency of water molecules to stick together as in the formation of water beads or raindrops.

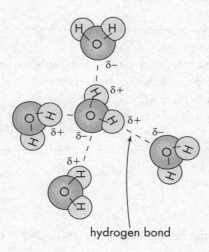

hydrogen bond

Water molecules are held together by hydrogen bonds. Although hydrogen bonds are individually weak, they are collectively strong when present in large numbers. Because it can react with other polar substances, water makes a great solvent; it can dissolve many kinds of substances. The hydrogen bonds that hold water molecules together contribute to a number of special properties.

As previously mentioned, water molecules have a strong tendency to stick together. That is, water exhibits cohesive forces. These forces are extremely important to life. For instance, when water molecules evaporate from leaves, they "pull" neighboring water molecules. These, in turn, draw up the molecules immediately behind them, and so on all the way down the plant vessels. The resulting chain of water molecules enables water to move up a stem.

Water molecules also like to stick to other substances—that is, they are adhesive. Have you ever tried to separate two glass slides stuck together by a film of water? They're difficult to separate because of the water sticking to the glass surfaces. These two forces taken together —**cohesion** and **adhesion**—account for the ability of water to rise up the roots, trunks, and branches of trees. Water has a high surface tension because of the cohesiveness of its molecules. This phenomenon is called **capillary action** since it occurs in thin vessels.

Another remarkable property of water is its **heat capacity.** Heat capacity refers to the ability of a substance to store heat. For example, when you heat an iron kettle, it gets hot pretty quickly. Why? Because it has a low specific heat. It doesn't take much heat to increase the temperature of the kettle. Water, on the other hand, has a high heat capacity. You have to add a lot of heat to get an increase in temperature. Water's ability to resist temperature changes is one of the things that helps keep the temperature in our oceans fairly stable. It's also why organisms that are composed mainly of water, like human beings, are able to keep a constant body temperature.

Let's review the unique properties of water:

- Water is polar and can dissolve other polar substances.
- Water has cohesive and adhesive properties.
- Water has a high heat capacity.
- Water has a high surface tension.

Acids and Bases

Reactions are influenced by whether the solution in which they occur is **acidic, basic,** or **neutral.**

A solution is acidic if it contains a lot of hydrogen ions (H^+). That is, if you dissolve an acid in water, it will release a lot of hydrogen ions. When you think about acids, you usually think of substances with a sour taste, like lemons. For example, if you squeeze a little lemon juice into a class of water, the solution will become acidic.

Bases, on the other hand, release a lot of hydroxide ions (OH^-) when added to water. These solutions are said to be **alkaline.** Bases usually have a slippery consistency. Common soap, for example, is composed largely of bases.

The acidity or alkalinity of a solution can be measured on a **pH scale.** The pH scale is numbered from 1 to 14. The midpoint, 7, is considered neutral pH. The concentration of hydrogen ions in a solution indicates whether it is acidic, basic, or neutral. Here's the trend:

An increase in H^+ ions causes a decrease in the pH.

Notice from the scale below that stronger acids have lower pHs. If a solution has a low concentration of hydrogen ions, it will have a high pH.

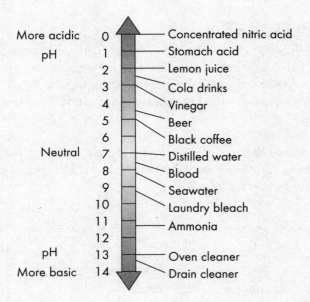

More acidic — pH — 0 — Concentrated nitric acid
1 — Stomach acid
2 — Lemon juice
3 — Cola drinks
4 — Vinegar
5 — Beer
6 — Black coffee
Neutral — 7 — Distilled water
8 — Blood
9 — Seawater
10 — Laundry bleach
11 — Ammonia
12
pH — 13 — Oven cleaner
More basic — 14 — Drain cleaner

The pH scale is not a linear scale—it's logarithmic. That is, a change of one pH number actually represents a tenfold change in hydrogen ion concentration. For example, a pH of 3 is actually ten times more acidic than a pH of 4. This is also true in the reverse direction: a pH of 4 represents a tenfold decrease in acidity compared to a pH of 3.

Your doctor says that your diet is too acidic and it's causing stomach distress. What should you drink with lunch that day?

A. distilled water

B. coffee

C. beer

D. lemonade

Here's How to Crack It
Choice (D), lemonade, probably sounds like a terrible idea if you're looking to eliminate acid from your diet, right? So cross out that one. From the scale that you saw before, you remember that coffee has a pH of 5 and beer has a pH of about 4.5, while neutral is 7. So (A) is correct, distilled water with a pH of 7, neutral.

ORGANIC MOLECULES

Now that we have discussed chemical compounds generally, let's turn to a special group of compounds. Most of the chemical compounds in living organisms contain a selection of carbon atoms. These molecules are known as **organic compounds.** By contrast, molecules that do not contain carbon atoms are called **inorganic compounds.** For example, salt (NaCl) is an inorganic compound.

Carbon is important for life because it is a versatile atom, meaning that it has the ability to bind with other carbons as well as a number of other atoms. The resulting molecules are key in carrying out the activities necessary for life.

To review:

- Organic compounds contain carbon atoms.
- Inorganic compounds do not contain carbon atoms (except carbon dioxide).

Next, let's take a look at four classes of organic compounds central to life on Earth:

- carbohydrates
- proteins
- lipids
- nucleic acids

Carbohydrates

Organic compounds that contain carbon, hydrogen, and oxygen are called **carbohydrates.** They usually contain these three elements in a ratio of 1:2:1, respectively.

Most carbohydrates are categorized as either **monosaccharides, disaccharides,** or **polysaccharides.** The term *saccharides* is a fancy word for sugar. The prefixes *mono-, di-,* and *poly-* refer to the number of sugars in the molecule. Mono means "one," di- means "two," and poly means "many." A monosaccharide is therefore a carbohydrate made up of a single type of sugar molecule.

Monosaccharides: The Simplest Sugars

Monosaccharides, the simplest sugars, serve as an energy source for cells. While there are many different types of monosaccharides, the two most common sugars are glucose and fructose. Both of these monosaccharides are six-carbon sugars with the chemical formula $C_6H_{12}O_6$. **Glucose,** the most abundant monosaccharide, is the most popular sugar around. Plants produce it by capturing sunlight for energy, while cells break it down to release stored energy.

Glucose can come in two forms: α-glucose and β-glucose, which differ simply by a reversal of the −H and −OH on the first carbon. For example, if the −OH is above the ring, the molecule is β-glucose. **Fructose,** a common sugar in fruit, is the other monosaccharide you should be familiar with.

Glucose and fructose can be depicted as either straight chains or rings. Both of them are pretty easy to spot; just look for the six carbon molecules. These are the two different forms.

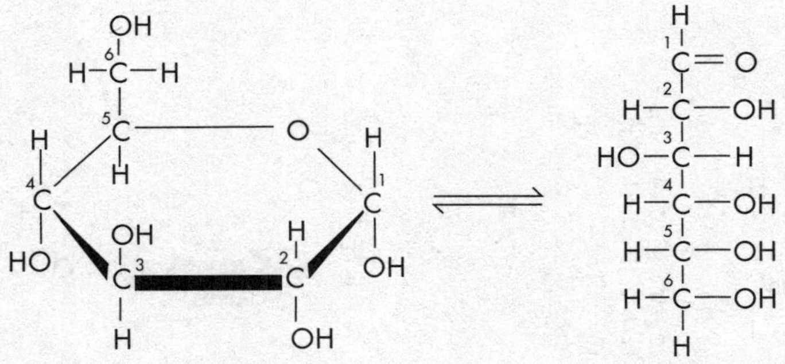

Ring form of glucose

Straight-chain form of glucose

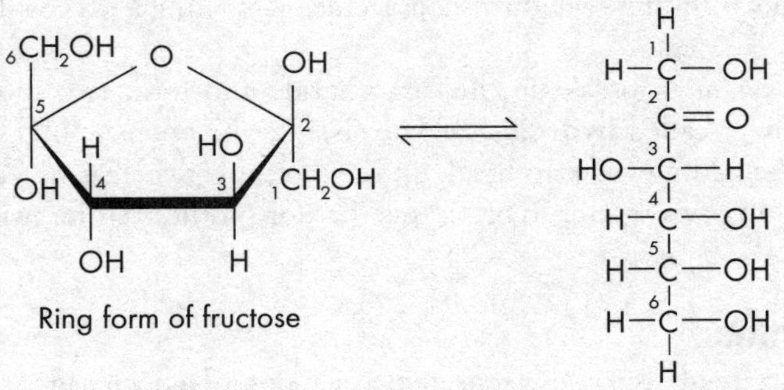

Ring form of fructose

Straight-chain form of fructose

Disaccharides

What happens when two monosaccharides are brought together? The hydrogen (−H) from one sugar molecule combines with the hydroxyl group (−OH) of another sugar molecule. What do H and OH add up to? Water (H_2O)! So a water molecule is removed from the two sugars. This process can be referred to as a **dehydration synthesis reaction, condensation reaction,** or **polymerization reaction.** During this process, a water molecule is lost and two molecules of monosaccharide are chemically linked and form a disaccharide.

Maltose is an example of a disaccharide:

Glucose   Glucose

Maltose

Maltose is formed by linking two glucose molecules—forming a **glycosidic bond.**

Now what if you want to break up the disaccharide and form two monosaccharides again? Just add water! That's called **hydrolysis.** Hydrolysis is the opposite of a dehydration reaction. In hydrolysis you're adding water to break up the molecule, whereas in a dehydration synthesis reaction you're taking away water to bring together (or synthesize) the two molecules.

Polysaccharides

Polysaccharides are made up many repeated units of monosaccharides. Therefore, a polysaccharide is a kind of **polymer,** a molecule with repeating subunits of the same general type. And any time we're bringing together monomers to create a polymer, a polymerization reaction will take place. Common polysaccharides you should be familiar with include **starch, cellulose,** and **glycogen.** Polysaccharides are often storage forms of sugar or structural components of cells. For instance, animals store glucose molecules in the form of glycogen in the liver and muscle cells while plants store α-glucose in the form of starch. On the other hand, cellulose, which is made up of β-glucose, is a major part of the cell wall in plants. Its function is to lend structural support. What to remember: starch is for plant storage, cellulose is for plant structure, and glycogen is for animal storage. Chitin, a polymer of β-glucose molecules, serves as a structural molecule in the walls of fungus and in the exoskeletons of arthropods.

Here's something to think about: why can't humans digest cellulose? The glycoside bond in polymers that have α-glucose can easily be broken down by humans but the glycoside bond in polymers containing β-glucose polymers, such as cellulose, cannot. This is because the bonds joining the glucose subunits in cellulose are different than those in starch. Starch is composed of α-glucose subunits held together by 1–4 glycoside linkages, while cellulose contains β-glucose subunits held together by 1–4 linkages.

Of the choices below, which is the simplest sugar, which serves as an energy source for cells?

A.   carbohydrate

B.   polysaccharide

C.   monosaccharide

D.   disaccharide

Here's How to Crack It

Carbohydrates are organic compounds that contain carbon, hydrogen, and oxygen, but they are not the simplest sugars, so eliminate (A). From your reading, you recall that "saccharide" is a fancy word for sugar and the prefixes *poly-*, *mono-*, and *di-* indicate the number of sugars in the molecule. From words like monotone and monologue, you know that mono means "one," and it stands to reason that the simplest sugar is the one that hasn't come together with any other molecules yet, so the correct answer is (C), monosaccharide.

Proteins

Amino acids are organic molecules that serve as the building blocks of proteins. They contain carbon, hydrogen, oxygen, and nitrogen atoms. There are 20 different amino acids commonly found in proteins. You should remember that every amino acid has four important parts: an **amino group** (–NH$_2$), a **carboxyl group** (–COOH), a **hydrogen atom,** and an **R group.**

Here is a typical amino acid:

Amino acids differ only in the R group, which is also called the **side chain**. The R group associated with an amino acid could be as simple as a hydrogen atom (as in the amino acid glycine) or as complex as a carbon skeleton (as in the amino acid arginine).

Glycine   Arginine

It is a good idea to be familiar with the chemical structure of different functional groups. Functional groups are distinct groups of atoms within molecules that have specific properties that are unique to them. When it comes to spotting an amino acid, simply keep an eye out for the amino group (NH_2), and then look for the carboxyl molecule (COOH). The most common functional groups of organic compounds are as follows:

CLASS	GENERAL FORMULA	EXAMPLE	COMMON NAME (SYSTEMATIC NAME)	COMMON SUFFIX/PREFIX (SYSTEMATIC)
Hydrocarbons				
Alkanes	RH	CH_3CH_3	ethane	-ane
Alkenes	$RR'C = CR''R'''$	$H_2C = CH_2$	ethylene (ethene)	-ene
Alkynes	$RC \equiv CR'$	$HC \equiv CH$	acetylene (ethyne)	(-yne)
Arenes	ArH^a		benzene	-ene
Halogen-Containing Compounds				
Alkyl halides	RX	CH_3CH_2Cl	ethyl chloride (chloroethane)	halide (halo-)
Aryl halides	ArX^a	—Cl	chlorobenzene	halo-
Oxygen-Containing Compounds				
Alcohols	ROH^a	CH_3CH_2OH	ethyl alcohol (ethanol)	-ol
Phenols	$ArOH^a$	—OH	phenol	-ol
Ethers	ROR'	$H_3CH_2COCH_2CH_3$	diethyl ether	ether
Aldehydes	RCHO	$CH_3\overset{O}{\overset{\|}{C}}H$	acetaldehyde (ethanal)	-aldehyde (-al)
Ketones	$RR'C = O$	$CH_3\overset{O}{\overset{\|}{C}}CH_3$	acetone (2-propanone)	-one
Carboxylic acids	RCO_2H	$CH_3\overset{O}{\overset{\|}{C}}OH$	acetic acid (ethanoic acid)	-ic acid (-oic acid)
Carboxylic Acid Derivatives				
Esters	RCO_2R'	$CH_3\overset{O}{\overset{\|}{C}}OCH_3$	methyl acetate (methyl ethanoate)	-ate (-oate)
Amides	$RCONHR'$	$CH_3\overset{O}{\overset{\|}{C}}NHCH_3$	N-methylacetamide	-amide
Nitrogen-Containing Compounds				
Amines	RNH_2, $RNHR'$, $RNR'R''$	$CH_3CH_2NH_2$	ethylamine	-amne
Nitriles	$RC \equiv N$	$H_3CC \equiv N$	acetonitrile	-nitrile
Nitro compounds	$ArNO_2{}^a$	—NO$_2$	nitrobenzene	nitro-

^{a}R indicates an alkyl group ^{b}Ar indicates an *aryl* group.

Polypeptides

When two amino acids join, they form a **dipeptide.** The carboxyl group of one amino acid combines with the amino group of another amino acid. Here's an example:

Here's the
peptide bond

This is the same process we saw earlier: dehydration synthesis (also known as a condensation reaction or polymerization reaction). Why? Because a water molecule is removed to form a bond. The bond between two amino acids has a special name—a **peptide bond.** If a group of amino acids is joined together in a "string," the resulting organic compound is called a **polypeptide.** Once a polypeptide string twists and folds on itself, it forms a three-dimensional structure called a **protein.**

Lipids

Like carbohydrates, **lipids** consist of carbon, hydrogen, and oxygen atoms, but not in the 1:2:1 ratio typical of carbohydrates. The most common examples of lipids are fats, oils, phospholipids, and **steroids.** A typical fat consists of three fatty acid molecules and one molecule of **glycerol.** The fancy name for this kind of molecule is a *triglyceride.* Your body prefers this type of fat molecule because it is efficiently stored and used for energy. The main reason for this is because there is no need to modify the triglyceride molecule in order for the body to use it—it is stored and used as is.

To make a triglyceride, each of the carboxyl groups (–COOH) of the three fatty acids must react with one of the three hydroxyl groups (–OH) of the glycerol molecule. This happens by the removal of a water molecule. So, the creation of a fat requires the removal of three molecules of water. Once again, what have we got? You probably already guessed it—dehydration synthesis! The linkage now formed between the glycerol molecule and the fatty acids is called **ester linkage.**

A fatty acid can be **saturated,** which means it has a single covalent bond between each pair of carbon atoms or it can be **unsaturated,** which means adjacent carbons are joined by double bonds instead of single bonds. A **polyunsaturated** fatty acid has many double bonds within the fatty acid.

Butyric Acid — Saturated Fatty Acid

Oleic Acid—Monounsaturated Fatty Acid

Linoleic Acid — Polyunsaturated Fatty Acid

Lipids are important because they function as structural components of cell membranes, sources of insulation, and a means of energy storage.

Phospholipids

Phospholipids are a special class of lipids that contain two fatty acid "tails" and one negatively charged phosphate "head." Take a look at a typical phospholipid.

Typical Phospholipid

```
        H           O
        |           ||
  H  —  C  — O — P — O — R  } phosphate
        |           |
                    O


                    H   H   H   H   H   H   H   H   H   H
                    |   |   |   |   |   |   |   |   |   |
  H  —  C — O — C — C — C — C — C — C — C — C — C — C —  ... etc.
        |       |   |   |   |   |   |   |   |   |   |
                H   H   H   H   H   H   H   H   H   H


                    H   H   H   H   H   H   H   H   H   H
                    |   |   |   |   |   |   |   |   |   |
  H  —  C — O — C — C — C — C — C — C — C — C — C — C —  ... etc.
        |       |   |   |   |   |   |   |   |   |   |
        H       H   H   H   H   H   H   H   H   H   H

      glycerol                    fatty acids
```

Phospholipids are extremely important, because of some of the unique properties they possess.

The two fatty acid tails are **hydrophobic** (water-hating). Fatty acid tails are nonpolar, and nonpolar substances don't mix well with polar ones, such as water.

On the other hand, the phosphate head of the lipid is **hydrophilic** (water-loving) meaning that it does mix well with water. Why? It carries a negative charge, and this charge draws it to the positively charged end of a water molecule. A molecule that has both a hydrophilic region and a hydrophobic region is **amphipathic.** A phospholipid is an example of an amphipathic molecule.

This arrangement of the fatty acid tail and the phosphate group head provides phospholipids with a unique shape. The two fatty acid chains orient themselves away from the water, while the phosphate portion orients itself toward the water. Phospholipids are a major component of our cell membranes. The cell membrane, also known as the plasma membrane, is composed of two layers of phospholipids. The phospholipid tails face toward the center of the membrane creating a nonpolar or hydrophobic environment in the center of the membrane. On the other hand, the phospholipid heads are on the outside of the membrane exposed to the cytoplasm and the outside of the cell, which are both polar or hydrophilic environments. Because the cell membrane is composed of two layers of phospholipids, it can also be referred to as the lipid (or phospholipid) bilayer.

Another class of lipids is known as steroids. All steroids have a basic structure of four linked carbon rings. This includes cholesterol, vitamin D, and a variety of hormones. Take a look at a typical steroid.

Nucleic Acids

The fourth class of organic compounds is the **nucleic acid.** Like proteins, nucleic acids contain carbon, hydrogen, oxygen, and nitrogen but nucleic acids also contain phosphorus. Nucleic acids are molecules made up of simple units called **nucleotides.**

Nucleotides

Nucleotides are the building blocks of nucleic acids. There are two kinds of nucleic acids you should be familiar with: **deoxyribonucleic acid (DNA)** and **ribonucleic acid (RNA).**

Ribose　　　　**Deoxyribose**

The three components that make up a nucleotide are the base, sugar, and phosphate group.

There are five nitrogenous bases to know: adenine, thymine, guanine, cytosine, and uracil. All of the bases can be used in DNA or RNA with the exception of thymine and uracil. Thymine is exclusively found only in DNA and uracil is exclusively found only in RNA. These bases can be categorized either as a pyrimidine or a purine. Adenine and guanine are purines. Cytosine, uracil, and thymine are pyrimidines. Base pairing occurs between adenine and thymine, guanine and cytosine (in DNA), and guanine and uracil (in RNA).

In DNA and RNA, the sugar is a ribose. By looking at the 2′ carbon on the ribose sugar, we can determine if the molecule is DNA or RNA. The presence of the −OH on the 2′ carbon results in the monomer for an RNA molecule, whereas the absence of the −OH on the 2′ carbon results in the monomer for a DNA molecule.

The phosphate group is attached to the 5′ carbon on the ribose sugar.

We will talk more about DNA in a few chapters!

KEY TERMS

matter
elements
atoms
molecules
protons
neutrons
electrons
nucleus
isotopes
solid, liquid, gas
physical change
chemical change
color
density
hardness
conductivity
conductor
non-conductor
exothermic
endothermic
periodic table
atomic number
atomic weight
period
quantum number (shell number)
group
compound
chemical reaction
chemical bonds
ionic bonds
covalent bonds
nonpolar covalent
polar covalent
hydrogen bonds
cohesion
adhesion
capillary action
heat capacity
acidic
basic
neutral
alkaline
pH scale

organic compounds
inorganic compounds
carbon
carbohydrates
monosaccharide
disaccharide
polysaccharide
glucose
fructose
dehydration synthesis reaction
    (condensation reaction or polymerization
    reaction)
glycosidic bond
hydrolysis
polymer
starch
cellulose
glycogen
amino acids
amino group
carboxyl group
hydrogen atom
R group (side chain)
dipeptide
peptide bond
polypeptide
protein
lipids
steroids
glycerol
ester linkage
saturated
unsaturated
polyunsaturated
phospholipids
hydrophobic
hydrophilic
amphipathic
nucleic acids
nucleotides
deoxyribonucleic acid (DNA)
ribonucleic acid (RNA)

Chapter 8 Drill

Answers and explanations can be found in the final section of this book, beginning on page 617.

1. Which of the following organic molecules is a major storage carbohydrate used to store energy in plants?

   A. cellulose

   B. maltose

   C. fructose

   D. glycogen

2. A solution with a pH of 10 is how many times more basic than a solution with a pH of 8?

   A. 2

   B. 4

   C. 10

   D. 100

3. The conversion of lactose to glucose and galactose involves the addition of which of the following molecules to the lactose molecule?

   A. O_2

   B. H_2

   C. ATP

   D. H_2O

4. A scientist is studying a type of matter called WC22. All that scientists know about WC22 is that it's unable to expand to fill the available volume, but it's able to conform to the shape of the container that holds it. What type of matter must WC22 be?

   A. liquid

   B. solid

   C. gas

   D. conductor

5. Which of the following is something that plants produce by capturing sunlight for energy and cells break it down to release stored energy?

   A. fructose

   B. glucose

   C. disaccharides

   D. photosynthesis

Summary

- Everything in the world is made up of matter comprised of atoms or molecules.

- Within atoms are protons, neutrons, and electrons.

- Matter can be a gas, a liquid, or a solid.

- Matter can undergo physical changes and chemical changes.

- The periodic table is a useful tool for organizing all elements.

- Solutions can be acidic, basic, or neutral and the acidity or alkalinity of a solution is measured with a pH scale.

- Most of the chemical compounds in living organisms contain a selection of carbon atoms, also known as organic compounds. Molecules without carbon atoms are inorganic compounds.

- Most carbohydrates are categorized as either monosaccharides, disaccharides, or polysaccharides.

- Amino acids are organic molecules that serve as the building blocks of proteins.

Chapter 9
Principles of
Motion and Energy

Subtest II will test your knowledge of the principles of motion and energy. Like the content in the last chapter, you need to know a variety of different topics, but not in extreme depth.

To successfully tackle this section, you should review the following:

Principles of Motion and Energy
- Description of object motion based on speed, velocity, and acceleration
- Forces such as gravity, magnetism, and friction
- Forms of energy, including solar, chemical, electrical, magnetic, nuclear, sound, light, and electromagnetic
- Heat, thermal energy, and temperature as well as measurement systems
- Transfer of heat by conduction, convection, and radiation
- Sources of light
- Optical properties of waves including light, sound, and reflection
- Conservation of energy resources for renewable and nonrenewable natural resources

MOTION BASICS

The basics of motion are seen in everyday life. **Motion** is any physical movement or change in position or place. Motion may be characterized by **position,** the location of an object; **displacement,** the distance an object has moved; **speed,** the time-rate of displacement or object movement; **velocity,** the direction of speed; and **acceleration,** the rate of velocity change.

POSITION, DISTANCE, AND DISPLACMENT

Position is an object's location on a coordinate axis system. **Distance** is a scalar quantity that represents the total amount traveled by an object. **Displacement** is an object's change in position. It's the vector that points from the object's initial position to its final position, regardless of the path actually taken. Since displacement means change in position, it's generically denoted Δs, where Δ denotes *change in* and s means spatial location. (The letter **p** is not used for position because it's reserved for another quantity: **momentum.**)

Let's try a problem.

In a track-and-field event, an athlete runs exactly
once around an oval track, a total distance of 500 m.
Find the runner's displacement for the race.

A.   0 m

B.   500 m

C.   1,000 m

D.   2,000 m

Here's How to Crack It
If the runner returns to the same position from which she left, then her displacement is zero.

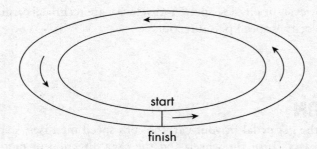

The *total* distance covered is 500 m, but the net distance—the displacement—is 0. Don't be tricked into picking 500 m, (B), because you didn't read the question carefully. The correct answer is (A).

SPEED AND VELOCITY
When we're in a moving car, the speedometer tells us how fast we're going; it gives us our speed. But what does it mean to have a speed of say, 10 m/s? It means that we're covering a distance of 10 meters every second. By definition, **average speed** is the ratio of the total distance traveled to the time required to cover that distance:

$$\text{average speed} = \frac{\text{total distance}}{\text{time}}$$

The car's speedometer doesn't care in what direction the car is moving (as long as the wheels are moving forward). You could be driving north, south, east, west, whatever; the speedometer would make no distinction. A speed of 55 miles per hour, north and 55 miles per hour, east register the same on the speedometer: 55 miles per hour.

However, we will also need to include direction in our descriptions of motion. We just learned about displacement, which takes both distance (net distance) and direction into account. The single concept that embodies both speed and direction is called **velocity**, and the definition of average velocity is

$$\text{average velocity} = \frac{\text{displacement}}{\text{time}}$$

$$\bar{v} = \frac{\Delta s}{\Delta t}$$

(The bar over the **v** means average.) Because Δ**s** is a vector, $\bar{v}$ is also a vector, and because Δt is a positive scalar, the direction of $\bar{v}$ is the same as the direction of Δ**s**. The magnitude of the velocity vector is called the object's speed, and it is expressed in units of meters per second (m/s).

Note the distinction between speed and velocity. In everyday language, they're often used interchangeably. However, in physics, speed and velocity are technical terms whose definitions are not the same. Velocity is speed plus direction.

ACCELERATION

When you step on the gas pedal in your car, the car's speed increases; step on the brake and the car's speed decreases. Turn the wheel, and the car's direction of motion changes. In all of these cases, the velocity changes. To describe this change in velocity we need a new term: **acceleration.** In the same way that velocity measures the rate-of-change of an object's position, acceleration measures the rate-of-change of an object's velocity. An object's average acceleration is defined as follows:

$$\text{average acceleration} = \frac{\text{change in velocity}}{\text{time}}$$

$$\bar{a} = \frac{\Delta v}{\Delta t}$$

The units of acceleration are meters per second, per second: $[a]$ = m/s². Because Δ**v** is a vector, $\bar{a}$ is also a vector; and because Δt is a positive scalar, the direction of $\bar{a}$ is the same as the direction of Δ**v**.

Furthermore, if we take an object's original direction of motion to be positive, then an increase in speed corresponds to a positive acceleration, while a decrease in speed corresponds to a negative acceleration (deceleration).

Note that an object can accelerate even if its speed doesn't change. (Again, it's a matter of not allowing the everyday usage of the word *accelerate* to interfere with its technical, physics usage.) This is because acceleration depends on $\Delta\mathbf{v}$, and the velocity vector $\mathbf{v}$ changes if (1) speed changes, (2) direction changes, or (3) both speed and direction change. For instance, a car traveling around a circular racetrack is constantly accelerating even if the car's speed is constant, because the direction of the car's velocity vector is constantly changing.

Let's tackle a sample problem.

A car is traveling in a straight line along a highway at a constant speed of 80 miles per hour for 10 seconds. What is its acceleration?

A.   0

B.   80

C.   600

D.   3,600

Here's How to Crack It

This is another example of a tricky question that requires careful reading. Since the car is traveling at a constant velocity, its acceleration is zero. If there's no change in velocity, then there's no acceleration. Choice (A) is correct.

GRAVITY AND FORCE

Gravity's value at Earth's surface, denoted g, is approximately expressed below as the standard average.

$$g = 9.81 \text{ m/s}^2 = 32.2 \text{ ft/s}^2$$

This means that, ignoring air resistance, an object falling freely near Earth's surface increases its velocity with 9.81 m/s (22 mph) for each second of its descent.

An interaction between two bodies—a push or a pull—is called a **force.** If you lift a book, you exert an **upward force** (created by your muscles) on it. If you pull on a rope that's attached to a crate you create a **tension** in the rope that pulls the crate. When a skydiver is falling through the air, the Earth is exerting a downward pull called **gravitational force,** and the air exerts and upward force called **air resistance.** When you stand on the floor, the floor provides an upward, supporting force called the **normal force.** If you slide a book across a table, the table exerts a **frictional force** against the book, so the book slows down and then stops. Static cling provides a directly observable example of the **electrostatic force.** Protons and neutrons are held together in the nuclei of atoms by the **strong nuclear force,** and radioactive nuclei decay through the action of the **weak nuclear force.**

NEWTON'S LAWS

Sir Isaac Newton began the modern study of principles associated with these concepts. Three of the laws that Newton stated in *Principia* are known as **Newton's Laws of Motion.** They form the basis for dynamics—that is, why things move the way they do.

The First Law

Newton's First Law says that an object will continue in its state of motion unless compelled to change by a force impressed upon it. That is, unless an unbalanced force acts on an object, the object's velocity will not change: If the object is at rest, then it will stay at rest; and if it is moving, then it will continue to move at a constant speed in a straight line.

Basically, no force means no change in velocity. This property of objects, their natural resistance to changes in their state of motion, is called **inertia.** In fact, the first law is often referred to as the **Law of Inertia.**

The Second Law

Newton's Second Law predicts what will happen when a force *does* act on an object: the object's velocity will change; the object will accelerate. More precisely, it says that its acceleration, **a**, will be directly proportional to the strength of the total—or *net*—force ($\mathbf{F}_{net}$) and inversely proportional to the object's mass, *m*:

$$\mathbf{F}_{net} = m\mathbf{a}$$

This is the most important equation in mechanics!

The **mass** of an object is the quantitative measure of its inertia; intuitively, it measures how much matter is contained in an object. Two identical boxes, one empty and one full, have different masses. The box that's full has the greater mass, because it contains more stuff; more stuff, more mass. Mass is measured in **kilograms,** abbreviated kg. (Note: An object whose mass is 1 kg weighs about 2.2 pounds.) It takes twice as much force to produce the same change in velocity of a 2 kg object than of a 1 kg object. Mass is a measure of an object's inertia, its resistance to acceleration.

The Third Law

The Third Law is commonly remembered as to every action, there is an equal, but opposite, reaction. More precisely, if Object 1 exerts a force on Object 2, then Object 2 exerts a force back on Object 1, equal in strength but opposite in direction. These two forces, $F_{1\text{-on-}2}$ and $F_{2\text{-on-}1}$, are called an **action/reaction pair.**

Let's try a problem.

Newton's Third Law of motion states that for every action, there is an equal and opposite reaction. Which of the following is the best example of the application of this law?

A. Less energy is used to roll a wheelbarrel over ice than to roll it over sand.

B. A paper airplane thrown across a classroom remains in motion until it bumps into the force of a student's head.

C. When swimming, your hands push the water behind you and the water pushes you in the forward direction.

D. More fuel is needed to drive a car 35 miles when the trunk is full of sandbags, than when the trunk is empty.

Here's How to Crack It

Choices (A) and (D) are obviously wrong—they have nothing to do with Newton's Third Law. Choice (B) might sound familiar, because it's an example of Newton's First Law. Don't fall for that trap. That leaves the only correct example of an action (pushing water behind you) and its reaction (being propelled forward), (C).

WEIGHT

Mass and **weight** are not the same thing—there is a clear distinction between them in physics—but they are often used interchangeably in everyday life. The weight of an object is the gravitational force exerted on it by Earth (or by whatever planet it happens to be on). Mass, by contrast, is an intrinsic property of an object that measures its inertia. An object's mass does not change with location. Put a baseball in a rocket and send it to the Moon. The baseball's weight on the Moon is less than its weight here on Earth (because the Moon's gravitational pull is weaker than Earth's due to its much smaller mass), but the baseball's mass would be the same.

FRICTION

When an object is in contact with a surface, the surface exerts a contact force on the object. The component of the contact force that's parallel to the surface is called the **friction force** on the object. Friction, like the normal force, arises from electrical interactions between atoms that comprise the object and those that comprise the surface.

We'll look at two main categories of friction: (1) **static friction** and (2) **kinetic (sliding) friction.** If you attempt to push a heavy crate across a floor, at first you meet with resistance, but then you push hard enough to get the crate moving. The force that acted on the crate to cancel out your initial pushes was static friction, and the force that acts on the crate as it slides across the floor is kinetic friction. Static friction occurs when there is no relative motion between the object and the surface (no sliding); kinetic friction occurs when there *is* relative motion (when there's sliding).

Let's try a problem.

On a chilly winter day, Selena rubs her hands together while waiting at the bus stop. As she rapidly rubs them against each other, her hands become warm. What is this an example of?

A.   Newton's First Law

B.   static friction

C.   Newton's Third Law

D.   friction between surfaces converting kinetic energy into thermal energy

Here's How to Crack It

You can eliminate (A) and (C) immediately—this question isn't about inertia or a force acting on an object outside itself. With (B), the word "friction" might catch your eye and entice you—don't fall for it! As we covered before, static friction occurs when there is no relative motion between the object and the surface, so (B) must be wrong. Choice (D) is the perfect explanation and the correct answer.

ENERGY

It wasn't until more than one hundred years after Newton's studies that the idea of energy became incorporated into physics. Today it permeates every branch of the subject.

It's difficult to give a precise definition of energy; there are different forms of energy because there are different kinds of forces. The CSET focuses on the following forms of energy:

- **Solar energy** is radiant light and heat from the Sun, and it is used along with secondary solar-powered resources such as wind, wave power, and hydroelectricity. One example of solar energy is the use of solar panels to harness energy that can be used even when it's nighttime.
- **Chemical energy** is the interrelation of work and heat with chemical reactions. Natural gas, coal, and petroleum are examples of stored chemical energy.
- **Electrical energy** is associated with conservative Coulomb forces (electrostatic interaction between electrically charged particles). Examples include batteries and lightning.
- **Magnetic energy** and electrical energy are related by Maxwell's equations (equations can be combined to show that light is an electromagnetic wave). Magnets align with magnetic fields. One example of magnetic energy in action includes the compass.
- **Nuclear energy** is released by the splitting (**fission**) or merging (**fusion**) of atoms. Examples include nuclear power plants and atomic and hydrogen bombs.
- **Sound energy** is the same thing as sound waves. Sound is a traveling wave that is an oscillation of pressure transmitted through a solid, liquid, or gas. One example is an opera singer hitting a high note and shattering a glass.
- **Energy of light** is also known as **luminous energy.** This is not the same as radiant energy. The human eye can see light only in the visible spectrum and has different sensitivities to light of different wavelengths within the spectrum. Examples include the way in which you process the physical world.
- **Electromagnetic energy** is a phenomenon that takes the form of self-propagating waves in a vacuum or matter. Examples include radio waves, micro waves, X-rays, gamma rays, and much more.

All energy can be put into one of two categories: potential and kinetic.

Potential energy is energy of position—gravitational energy. Examples include chemical, mechanical, nuclear, gravitational, and electrical energy.

Kinetic energy is energy of motion—of waves, objects, substances, and molecules. Examples include radiant, thermal, motion, and sound energy.

Energy can come into a system or leave it via various interactions that produce changes. One of the best definitions we know reads as follows:

> **Force** is the agent of change, **energy** is the measure of change, and **work** is the way of transferring energy from one system to another.

And one of the most important laws in physics (the **Law of Conservation of Energy,** also known as the **First Law of Thermodynamics**) says that if you account for all its various forms, the total amount of energy in a given process will stay constant; that is, it will be conserved. For example, electrical energy can be converted into light and heat (this is how a light bulb works), but the amount of electrical energy coming into the light bulb equals the total amount of light and heat given off. Energy cannot be created or destroyed; it can only be transferred (from one system to another) or transformed (from one form to another).

WORK

When you lift a book from the floor, you exert a force on it, over a distance; when you push a crate across a floor, you also exert a force on it, over a distance. The application of force over a distance, and the resulting change in energy of the system that the force acted on, gives rise to the concept of work. When you hold a book in your hand, you exert a force on the book (normal force), but since the book is at rest, the force does not act through a distance, so you do no work on the book. Although you did work on the book as you lifted it from the floor, once it's at rest in your hand, you are no longer doing work on it.

> If a force **F** acts over a distance d, and **F** is parallel to **d**, then the work done by **F** is the product of force and distance: $W = Fd$.

Notice that, although work depends on two vectors (**F** and **d**), work itself is not a vector. Work is a scalar quantity.

Let's try a problem.

A man pushes against a rock for 15 minutes to move it out of his driveway, but the rock never budges.

Work is defined as the force it takes to actually move an object. Using this definition, how much work did the man do?

A.   none

B.   more than was necessary

C.   15 minutes' worth

D.   enough to tire him out

Here's How to Crack It
Choices (B), (C), and (D) might seem appealing, but they are wrong. Focus on the definition of work to solve this problem. The man actually did no work, even though he is completely exhausted from the effort.

POWER
Simply put, **power** is the rate at which work gets done (or energy gets transferred, which is the same thing). Suppose you and I each do 1000 J of work, but I do the work in 2 minutes while you do it in 1 minute. We both did the same amount of work, but you did it more quickly; you were more powerful. Here's the definition of power:

$$\text{Power} = \frac{\text{Work}}{\text{time}} \qquad \text{(in symbols)} \ \rightarrow \ P = \frac{W}{t}$$

The unit of power is the joule per second (J/s), which is renamed the **watt**, and symbolized W (not to be confused with the symbol for work, W). One watt is 1 joule per second: 1 W = 1 J/s.

FORMS OF ENERGY

Heat

Energy can present in the form of **heat.** But **temperature** is best characterized as a measure of the aggregate atomic or molecular activity pertaining to a particular object. Measurements of temperature may be calculated using such devices as thermometers, thermocouples, and optical methods.

When heated to a certain temperature, a mercury or alcohol **thermometer** will use principles of expansion properties. Fluids, when heated, will expand or contract to an exact amount which can then be read by the identifiers on the thermometer.

TRANSFER OF HEAT

Conduction, radiation, and **convection** are different ways in which the transfer of heat may occur. Conduction refers to instances in which heat flows from a hotter object to a cooler one. Radiation refers to heat transfer in a vacuum where there is no possibility of conduction. The heat radiates or emits from the heated object into a space area. Convection involves the heating and circulation of a substance that changes density when it is heated.

Light Sources

The CSET requires that you know about light sources including the Sun, light bulbs, and excited atoms. The light given off by the Sun enables photosynthesis (more below). We can also produce light, as in light bulbs. The basic idea behind light bulbs is simple. Electricity runs through the filament. Because the filament is so thin, it offers some resistance to the electricity, and this resistance converts electrical energy into heat. The heat is enough to make the filament white hot, and the "white" part is light. That is how an **incandescent light bulb** works. A **fluorescent light bulb** works differently. It has electrodes at both ends of a fluorescent tube, and a gas containing argon and mercury vapor inside the tube. A stream of electrons flows through the gas from one electrode to the other. These electrons bump into the mercury atoms and excite them. As the mercury atoms move from the excited state back to the unexcited state, they give off ultraviolet photons. These photons hit the phosphor, coating the inside of the fluorescent tube, and this phosphor creates visible light. Light sources emanate from wavelengths (meaning color). **Polychromatic** refers to a mixture of colors, or a white light source. Single-color sources are known as **monochromatic.**

Light and Matter Interaction

Vision, photosynthesis, and **photoemission** are modes of light and matter interaction. Vision (light in the visible spectrum) interacts with the human eye, producing electrical signals that the brain is able to read and decipher as color. We perceive color in an object because of the way the object reflects the light reaching it. For example, we see bananas as yellow because bananas absorb all the colors of the spectrum except yellow. Photosynthesis is the process by which organisms (plants and bacteria) use energy in the form of light and convert it to chemical form (oxygen and reduced carbon compounds). Photoemission refers to the interaction of light with certain types of materials. Electrons are emitted by the lighted material.

Let's try a problem.

---○---

Which of the following is an explanation for why we perceive a red apple as red?

A. The apple reflects all the colors of the spectrum except for red, which is absorbed.

B. The apple absorbs all the other colors of the spectrum, but reflects red.

C. The apple reflects green and blue, the other two primary colors, but absorbs red.

D. The apple absorbs green, blue, and red.

Here's How to Crack It

Primary colors have nothing to do with anything here, so scratch out (C) immediately. Choice (A) gets the information that we know about light and color backward. We see color because that color is reflected back to us, not absorbed. So you can eliminate (A). Choice (B) gets the information right exactly—this is the correct answer. Choices (C) and (D) maintain that we see colors that are absorbed by the object, rather than reflected by the object, so cross them off.

---○---

WAVES

Waves are designated as **transverse** or **longitudinal.** A transverse wave has a wave disturbance, or amplitude perpendicular or transverse to the direction of propagation. Examples of transverse waves include an ocean wave, light waves, and "the wave" (the one you do at a basketball or football game). However, in a longitudinal wave, wave disturbances are parallel to the direction of propagation. Sound waves are an example of a longitudinal wave. One way to think about a wave's energy is simply a disturbance traveling through a medium at speeds that depend on the medium.

Waves are reflected or refracted. **Reflection** occurs when all or part of a wave bounces off a surface and is redirected to another surface. **Refraction** refers to a wave's penetration of a surface.

Frequency is one way to measure sound waves. The frequency is the number of complete cycles of a sound wave within one second. One cycle per second is called 1 **hertz.** Human ears can detect sounds from about 20 hertz (the lowest sound) to about 20 000 hertz (the highest sound). Below 20 hertz, humans feel only the vibration of the sound. Above 20,000 hertz, they can't hear the sound at all (but dogs can!). All sound travels at the same speed, regardless of frequency.

The wave formula is a formula that will help you out when dealing with wave-related questions.

$$v = f\lambda$$

v is for wave speed
f is for frequency
λ is for wavelength

There are two main rules to remember when dealing with waves.

1. Wave speed depends only on the type of wave and the medium through which it travels. Wave speed does not depend on frequency or wavelength.
2. When a wave enters from one medium into another, its frequency stays the same, but the speed and wavelength change.

MAGNETS

A **magnet** is a material or object that produces a magnetic field. This magnetic field is a force that pulls or repels other magnets, depending on their magnetism. A magnet pulls unlike charges and repels like charges. In short, opposites attract. The magnetic force surrounding a magnet isn't uniform. Each end of a magnet has a great concentration of force, while the center of a magnet has a weak magnetic force. The two ends of a magnet are called the **poles,** much like the poles on Earth.

A **compass** works because its needle is a freely rotating magnet. The painted end, or **needle,** of a compass is drawn to the north (magnetic) pole of Earth to align itself in a northerly direction. It seems confusing, but the needle labeled "N" in a compass is actually a magnet of the opposite charge (S)—it is drawn to north because opposites attract. The area to which the needle points is called the **North Magnetic Pole,** which is close to the geographic North Pole (but not the exact same place).

Let's tackle a magnetism question of the type you may encounter on the CSET.

———————◯———————

Magnets are often made of polarized metal bars, especially bars made of iron. Magnets are attracted only to certain types of metal. Typically, metals that make good magnets are also attracted to magnets. Based on this information, which of the following is a magnet most likely attracted to?

A. copper penny

B. aluminum can

C. plastic wrap

D. iron fillings

Here's How to Crack It

Choice (C) is obviously wrong—plastic is not magnetic, even in the best of science fiction movies. The passage states that magnets are often made of iron and also that the materials used to make magnets are also attracted to magnets. Thus, it can be inferred that magnets and iron attract, so (D) is correct.

———————◯———————

KEY TERMS

motion
position
displacement
speed
velocity
acceleration
distance
momentum
average speed
force
upward force
tension
gravitational force
air resistance
normal force
frictional force
electrostatic force
strong nuclear force
weak nuclear force
Newton's Laws of Motion
inertia
Law of Inertia
mass
kilogram
action/reaction pair
mass
weight
friction force
static friction
kinetic (sliding) friction
force
energy (solar, chemical, electrical,
  magnetic, nuclear, sound, light,
  electromagnetic, potential, kinetic)

work
Law of Conservation of Energy
  (First Law of Thermodynamics)
power
watt
heat
temperature
thermometer
conduction
radiation
convection
incandescent light bulb
fluorescent light bulb
polychromatic
monochromatic
vision
photosynthesis
photoemission
waves
transverse waves
longitudinal waves
reflection
refraction
frequency
hertz
magnet
pole
compass
needle
North Magnetic Pole

Chapter 9 Drill

Answers and explanations can be found in the final section of this book, beginning on page 617.

1. Which of the following is/are true?

   I.   If an object's acceleration is constant,
        then it must move in a straight line.

   II. If an object's acceleration is zero,
        then its speed must remain constant.

   III. If an object's speed remains constant,
        then its acceleration must be zero.

   A. I and II only

   B. I and III only

   C. II only

   D. III only

2. A baseball is thrown straight upward.
   What is the ball's acceleration at its highest
   point?

   A. 0

   B. $\frac{1}{2}g$, downward

   C. g, downward

   D. $\frac{1}{2}g$, upward

3. A person standing on a horizontal floor
   feels two forces: the downward pull of
   gravity and the upward supporting force
   from the floor. These two forces:

   A. have equal magnitudes and form an
      action/reaction pair.

   B. have equal magnitudes but do not
      form an action/reaction pair.

   C. have unequal magnitudes and form
      an action/reaction pair.

   D. have unequal magnitudes and do not
      form an action/reaction pair.

4. Which of the following statements is true?

   A. A white shirt absorbs all colors of
      light.

   B. A blue shirt absorbs blue light.

   C. A black shirt reflects all colors of
      light.

   D. A red shirt reflects red light.

5. Below is a figure of a science experiment in which three donut-shaped magnets were stacked on a pole.

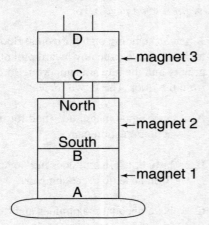

Based on the figure, which of the following represent(s) north poles?

A. A only

B. B only

C. B and C

D. A, B, and C

Summary

- The basics of motion are seen in everyday life.

- Average speed is the ratio of the total distance traveled by the time required to cover that distance.

- Velocity is a concept that embodies both speed and direction. Average velocity = displacement / time.

- Acceleration measures the rate of change of an object's velocity.

- Force is an interaction between two bodies.

- Gravity on Earth's surface is 9.81 m/s^2, which is denoted by the letter g.

- Newton's Laws of Motion are the basis of dynamics.

- The weight of an object is the gravitational force exerted on it by Earth.

- The mass is the intrinsic property of an object that measures its inertia.

- Friction force is the component of the contact force that is parallel to the surface.

- There are two main categories of friction: static and kinetic.

- All energy is either potential or kinetic.

- Energy is a measurement of change; work is the way of transferring energy from one system to another.

- Power is the rate at which work gets done.

- Temperature is a measure of the aggregate atomic or molecular activity pertaining to a particular object.

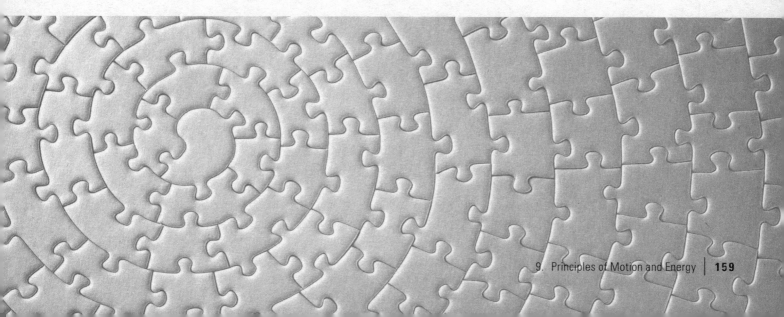

o   Conduction, radiation, and convection are different ways in which the transfer of heat may occur.

o   The Sun, incandescent light bulbs, and fluorescent bulbs are three different sources of light.

o   All waves are either transverse or longitudinal. They can be reflected or refracted.

o   In the world of magnets, as in romantic clichés, opposites attract.

Chapter 10
Structure and Function of Living Organisms

This chapter covers the structure of living organisms and their function. The CSET requires that you be familiar with the concepts listed below.

> Structure of Organisms and Their Function
> - Levels of organization and related functions in plants and animals including organ systems
> - Structures and related functions of plants and animals such as reproductive, respiratory, circulatory, and digestive functions
> - Principles of chemistry underlying the function of biological systems including carbon, water and salt, DNA, and photosynthesis

LIVING THINGS

All living things—plants and animals—are composed of **cells.** According to the cell theory, the cell is life's basic unit of structure and function. In other words, the cell is the smallest unit of living material that can carry out all the activities necessary for life. Cells are studied using different types of microscopes.

WHAT ARE THE DIFFERENT TYPES OF CELLS?

For centuries, scientists have known about cells. However, it wasn't until the development of the electron microscope that scientists were able to figure out what cells do. We now know that there are two distinct types of cells: **eukaryotic cells** and **prokaryotic cells.** A eukaryotic cell contains a membrane-bound structure called a **nucleus** and **cytoplasm,** filled with tiny structures called **organelles** (literally "little organs"). Examples of eukaryotic cells are fungi, plant cells, and animal cells.

A prokaryotic cell, which is a lot smaller than a eukaryotic cell, lacks both a nucleus and membrane-bound organelles. An example of a prokaryotic cell is bacteria. The genetic material in a prokaryote is one continuous, circular DNA molecule that lies free in the cell. In addition to a plasma membrane, most prokaryotes have a cell wall composed of peptidoglycan. Prokaryotes may also have ribosomes (although smaller than those found in eukaryotic cells) as well as a **flagellum.** Flagella can be found in both prokaryotic and eukaryotic cells. The structure and movement of the flagella is completely different between the two cell types, but the function of movement remains the same.

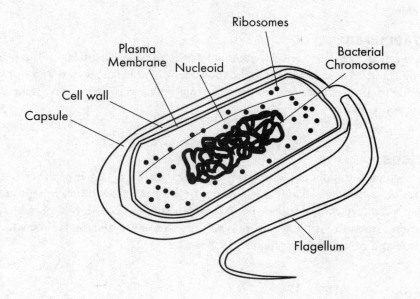

Organelles

A eukaryotic cell is like a microscopic factory. It's filled with organelles, each of which has its own special task. Let's take a tour of a eukaryotic cell and focus on the structure and function of each organelle. Here's a picture of a typical animal cell and its principal organelles:

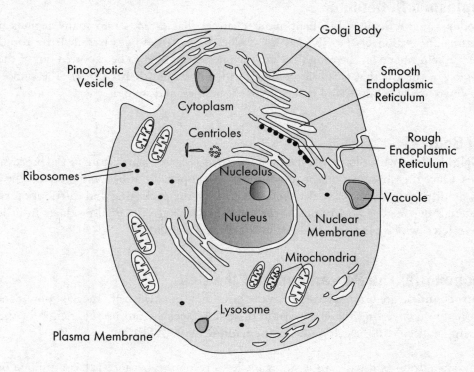

Plasma Membrane

A eukaryotic cell has an outer envelope known as the **plasma membrane.** The plasma membrane is important because it regulates the movement of substances into and out of the cell. The membrane itself is semipermeable, meaning that only certain substances, namely proteins, pass through it unaided.

The Nucleus

The nucleus, which is usually the largest organelle, is the control center of the cell. The nucleus directs what goes on in the cell and is also responsible for the cell's ability to reproduce. It's the home of the hereditary information—DNA—which is organized into large structures called **chromosomes.** The most visible structure within the nucleus is the **nucleolus,** which is where rRNA is made and ribosomes are assembled.

Ribosomes

Ribosomes are the sites of protein synthesis. Their job is to manufacture all the proteins required by the cell or secreted by the cell. Ribosomes are round structures composed of RNA and proteins. They can be either free floating in the cell or attached to another structure called the **endoplasmic reticulum (ER).**

Endoplasmic Reticulum

The endoplasmic reticulum is a continuous channel that extends into many regions of the cytoplasm. The region of the ER that is "studded" with ribosomes is called the **rough ER (RER).** Proteins made on the rough ER are the ones earmarked to be exported out of the cell. The region of the ER that lacks ribosomes is called the **smooth ER (SER).** The smooth ER breaks down toxic chemicals and makes lipids, hormones, and steroids

Golgi Bodies

The **Golgi bodies,** which look like stacks of flattened sacs, also participate in the processing of proteins. Once the ribosomes on the rough ER have completed synthesizing proteins, the Golgi bodies modify, process, and sort the products. They're the packaging and distribution centers for materials destined to be sent out of the cell. They package the final products in little sacs called **vesicles,** which carry the products to the plasma membrane.

Mitochondria: The Powerhouses of the Cell

The **mitochondria** are often referred to as the powerhouses of the cell. They are power stations responsible for converting the energy from organic molecules into useful energy for the cell. The energy molecule in the cell is **adenosine triphosphate (ATP).**

The mitochondrion is usually an easy organelle to recognize because it has a unique oblong shape and a characteristic double membrane consisting of an inner portion and an outer portion.

Since mitochondria are the cell's powerhouses, you're most likely to find more of them in cells that require a lot of energy. Muscle cells, for example, are rich in mitochondria.

Lysosomes

Throughout the cell are small, membrane-bound structures called **lysosomes.** These tiny sacs carry digestive enzymes, which they use to break down old, worn-out organelles, debris, and large ingested particles. The lysosomes make up the cell's cleanup crew, helping to keep the cytoplasm clear of unwanted flotsam.

Centrioles

The **centrioles** are small, paired, cylindrical structures that are found within **microtubule organizing centers (MTOCs).** Centrioles are most active during cellular division. When a cell is ready to divide, the centrioles produce microtubules, which pull the replicated chromosomes apart and move them to opposite ends of the cell. Although centrioles are common in animal cells, they are not found in plant cells.

Vacuoles

In Latin, the term *vacuole* means "empty cavity." But **vacuoles** are far from empty. They are fluid-filled sacs that store water, food, wastes, salts, and pigments.

Peroxisomes

Peroxisomes are organelles that detoxify various substances, producing hydrogen peroxide as a byproduct. They also contain enzymes that break down hydrogen peroxide (H_2O_2) into oxygen and water. In animals, they are common in the liver and kidney cells.

Cytoskeleton

Have you ever wondered what actually holds the cell together and enables it to keep its shape? The shape of a cell is determined by a network of fibers called the **cytoskeleton.** The most important fibers you'll need to know are **microtubules** and **microfilaments.**

Microtubules, which are made up of the protein **tubulin,** participate in cellular division and movement. These small fibers are an integral part of three structures: centrioles, cilia, and flagella. We've already mentioned that centrioles help chromosomes separate during cell division. Cilia and flagella, on the other hand, are threadlike structures best known for their locomotive properties in single-celled organisms. The beating motion of cilia and flagella structures propels these organisms through their watery environments.

Though we usually associate such structures with microscopic organisms, they aren't the only ones with cilia and flagella. As you probably know, these structures are also found in certain human cells. For example, the cells lining your respiratory tract possess cilia that sweep constantly back and forth (beating up to 20 times per second), helping to keep dust and unwanted debris from descending into your lungs. And every sperm cell has a flagellum, which enables it to swim through the female reproductive organs to fertilize the waiting ovum.

Microfilaments, like microtubules, are important for movement. These thin, rodlike structures are composed of the protein actin. They are involved in cell mobility, and play a central role in muscle contraction.

If you were inside a cell and giving directions to the location where water, food, wastes, salt, and pigments are stored, you would be talking about the:

A.   nucleus.

B.   ribosomes.

C.   vacuoles.

D.   centrioles.

Want More Practice?
Download your 3 free online practice tests. Details are on pages vi–vii.

Here's How To Crack It

After your careful review of the cell and its different sections, this one should be a breeze. Choice (A), the nucleus, can't be right because the nucleus is the brain center of the cell—that's not where waste and water is stored. Choice (B), the ribosomes, are the sites of protein synthesis, and (D), the centrioles, facilitate cell division, which is not what the question asks about. The correct answer must be (C), vacuoles. Go back and review this section if those concepts are confusing.

Plant Cells Versus Animal Cells

Plant cells contain most of the same organelles and structures seen in animal cells, with several key exceptions. Plant cells, unlike animal cells, have a protective outer covering called the **cell wall** (made of cellulose). A cell wall is a rigid layer just outside of the plasma membrane that provides support for the cell. It is found in plants, protists, fungi, and bacteria. In fungi, the cell wall is usually made of **chitin.** In addition, plant cells possess **chloroplasts** (organelles involved in photosynthesis). Chloroplasts contain chlorophyll, the light-capturing pigment that gives plants their characteristic green color. Another difference between plant and animal cells is that most of the cytoplasm within a plant cell is usually taken up by a large vacuole that crowds the other organelles. In mature plants, this vacuole contains the **cell sap.** Plant cells also differ from animal cells in that plant cells do not contain centrioles

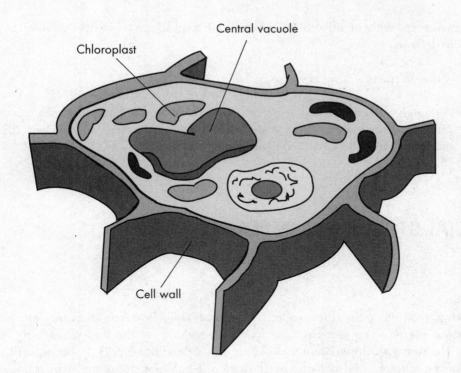

Chloroplast

Central vacuole

Cell wall

To help you remember the differences among prokaryotes, plant cells, and animal cells, we've put together this simple table.

STRUCTURAL CHARACTERISTICS OF DIFFERENT CELL TYPES			
Structure	**Prokaryote**	**Plant Cell**	**Animal Cell**
Cell Wall	Yes	Yes	No!
Plasma Membrane	Yes	Yes	Yes
Organelles	No!	Yes	Yes
Nucleus	No!	Yes	Yes
Centrioles	No!	No!	Yes
Ribosomes	Yes	Yes	Yes

Transport: The Traffic Across Membranes

We've talked about the structure of cell membranes. Now let's discuss how molecules and fluids pass through the plasma membrane. What are some of the patterns of membrane transport? The ability of molecules to move across the cell membrane depends on two things: (1) the semipermeability of the plasma membrane and (2) the size and charge of particles that want to get through.

First let's consider how cell membranes work. For a cell to maintain its internal environment, it has to be selective in the materials it allows to cross its membrane. Since the plasma membrane is composed primarily of phospholipids, lipid-soluble substances cross the membrane without any resistance. Why? Because "like dissolves like." Generally speaking, the lipid membrane has an open-door policy for substances that are made up of lipids. These substances can cross the plasma membrane without any problem. However, if a substance is not lipid-soluble, the bilipid layer won't let it in.

One exception to the rule is water:

> Although water molecules are polar (and therefore not lipid-soluble), they can rapidly cross a lipid bilayer because they are small enough to pass through gaps that occur as a fatty acid chain momentarily moves out of the way.

SPECIAL STRUCTURES IN PLANTS

Roots

A growing **root** includes three regions: the **root tip,** the **elongation region,** and the **maturation region.** The root tip and elongation regions are the sites of ongoing primary growth. The **root apical meristem** includes tiny, undifferentiated cells that continually divide and form the zone of cell division. As cell division in the root apical meristem continues, the new cells left behind grow rapidly in length and push the root tip along. As the cells absorb water, elongation occurs. Tiny **root hairs,** extensions of the epidermal cells, form and provide an increased surface area through which water and dissolved minerals can move into the plant.

All roots have an **epidermis** (an outer protective covering), a **cortex** (a middle region which stores starch and other minerals), and a **stele** (the inner cylinder, which contains xylems and phloems). How do water and minerals enter the root? They travel through the root cortex either by the **apoplast** (porous cell walls) or **symplast** (through plasmodesmata). Once water and minerals reach the inner layer of the cortex, called the **endodermis,** they must cross the **endodermal cells,** tightly packed cells that regulate the selective passage of water and minerals into the vascular tissue, in order to reach the root's interior.

Leaves

Leaves play an important role in photosynthesis. But did you know that leaves are sometimes modified for other purposes?

Here's a list of some of the other functions of leaves:

- Leaves can be modified to form **spines,** as in a cactus. This adaptation is great for protection.
- Leaves can be adapted for water storage. Fleshy leaves allow plants to survive particularly harsh environments where the water supply is intermittent or undependable.

- Leaves can also be modified to trap prey. Insectivorous plants have specialized leaves that digest insects. Because they grow in soils deficient of essential nutrients, especially nitrogen, these plants are forced to eat insects. There are basically two general forms of these adaptations:
  1. Some leaves have tiny hairs that act like bear traps. For example, an insect brushing against the hairs in a Venus flytrap triggers the leaves to snap shut.
  2. Other leaves are adapted to form a "slippery slope" that traps insects. In a pitcher plant, for example, once an insect gets inside, it can't get out. It slips down into the bell-shaped interior of the leaf, where it drowns in a mixture of water and enzymes. These enzymes then finish the job by digesting the insect.

Flowering Plants

Let's take a look at what you do need to know about flowering plants.

Flowering plants have several organs: the **stamen, pistil, sepals,** and **petals.**

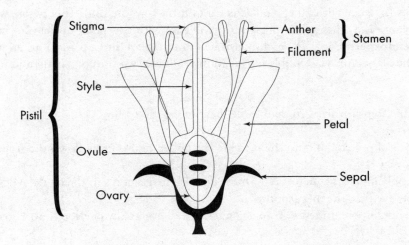

The male parts are collectively called the stamen, and the female parts are called the pistil. The sepals are the green, leaf-like structures that cover and protect the flower, while the brightly colored petals attract potential pollinators. Let's review each of these structures.

The Stamen

The stamen consists of the **anther** and the **filament.** The anther is the structure that produces pollen grains. These **pollen grains,** called **microspores,** are the plant's male gametophytes, or sperm cells. Pollen grains are produced and released into the air. The filament is the thin stalk that holds up the anther.

The Pistil

The pistil includes three structures: the **stigma, style,** and **ovary.** The stigma is the sticky portion of the pistil that captures the pollen grains. The style is a tubelike structure that connects the stigma with the ovary.

The ovary is the structure in which fertilization occurs. Within the ovary are the **ovules,** which contain the plant's equivalent of the female gametophytes. In a fertilized plant, the ovary develops into the fruit. Apples, pears, and oranges are all fertilized ovaries of flowering plants. The female gametes of plants are known as **megaspores.** They undergo meiosis to produce eight female nuclei, including one **egg nucleus** and two **polar nuclei.**

Double Fertilization

Now that we've seen both the male and the female organs in plants, let's take a look at how they actually reproduce. Flowering plants carry out a process called **double fertilization.** When a pollen grain lands on the stigma, it germinates and grows a thin pollen tube down the style, which meets up with the ovary. The pollen grain then divides into two **sperm nuclei.** One sperm nucleus (n) fuses with an egg nucleus (n) to form a zygote (2n). This zygote will eventually form a plant. The other sperm nucleus (n) will fuse with two polar nuclei (2n) in the ovary to form the **endosperm** (3n). The endosperm will not develop into a plant. Rather, it will serve as food for the plant embryo. Double fertilization produces two things: a plant and food for the plant.

Let's review the steps involved in double fertilization:

- Grains of pollen fall onto the stigma. The pollen grains grow down the style into the ovary.
- The pollen grains (microspores) meet up with megaspores in the ovule. Microspores fertilize the megaspores.
- One microspore unites with an egg nucleus and eventually develops into a complete plant.
- The other microspore unites with two polar nuclei and develops into food for the plant, often in the form of a fruit.

As the embryo germinates, different parts of the plant begin to develop. The **cotyledons** are the first embryo leaves to appear. They temporarily store all the nutrients for the plant. The **epicotyl** is the part at the tip of the plant. This portion becomes the stems and leaves. The **hypocotyl** is the stem below the cotyledons. This portion becomes the roots of the plant. In some embryos, root development begins early, and the well-defined embryonic root is referred to as a **radicle.**

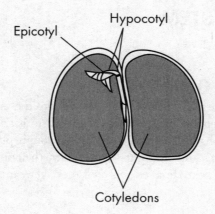

Epicotyl

Hypocotyl

Cotyledons

What triggers sexual reproduction in plants? Plants flower in response to changes in the amount of daylight and darkness. This is called **photoperiodism.** Plants fall into three main groups: **short-day plants, long-day plants,** and **day-neutral plants.** Although you'd think that plants bloom based on the amount of sunlight, they actually flower according to the amount of uninterrupted darkness.

Short-day plants require a long period of darkness, whereas long-day plants need short periods of darkness. Short-day plants usually bloom in late summer or fall when daylight is decreasing. Long-day plants, on the other hand, flower in late spring and summer when daylight is increasing. Day-neutral plants don't flower in response to daylight changes at all. They use other cues such as water or temperature.

The light receptor involved in photoperiodism is a pigment called **phytochrome.** In short-day plants, it inhibits flowering, whereas in long-day plants it induces flowering.

Vegetative Propagation

Flowering plants don't always reproduce via fertilization. In some cases, flowering plants can reproduce asexually. This process is known as **vegetative propagation.** That means parts of the parent plant—such as the roots, stems, or leaves—can produce another plant. Some examples of plant parts that can reproduce this way include **tubers, runners,** and **bulbs.** For instance, suppose you wanted to make white potatoes without fertilization. All you'd have to do is cut out the eyes of a potato, the tubers, and plant them. Each of the eyes will develop into a separate potato plant. **Grafting** is another way plants can be reproduced asexually.

Here's a list of the different types of vegetative propagation:

VEGETATIVE PROPAGATION		
Types	**Description**	**Examples**
Bulbs	Short stems underground	Onions
Runners	Horizontal stems above the ground	Strawberries
Tubers	Underground stems	Potatoes
Grafting	Cutting a stem and attaching it to a closely related plant	Seedless oranges

THE DIGESTIVE SYSTEM

The Purpose of the Digestive System

All organisms need nutrients to survive. But where do the nutrients—the raw building blocks—come from? That depends on whether the organism is an **autotroph** or **heterotroph.** As you may recall, autotrophs make their own food through photosynthesis, and all of the building blocks—CO_2, water, and sunlight—come from their immediate environment. Heterotrophs, on the other hand, can't make their own food; they must acquire their energy from outside sources.

When we talk about digestion, we're talking about the breakdown of large food molecules into simpler compounds. These molecules are then absorbed by the body to carry out cell activities. In fact, everything we'll discuss in this section revolves around three simple questions:

1.   What do organisms need from the outside world in order to survive?
2.   How do they get those things?
3.   What do they do with them once they get them?

Multicellular organisms have come up with a variety of ways of getting their nutrients. In simple animals, food is digested through **intracellular digestion**—that is, digestion occurs within food vacuoles. For example, a hydra encloses the food it captures in a food vacuole. Lysosomes containing digestive enzymes then fuse with the vacuole and break down the food. More complex animals have evolved a digestive tract and digest food through **extracellular digestion.** That is, the food is digested in a gastrovascular cavity. For example, in grasshoppers, food passes through specialized regions of the gut: the **mouth, esophagus, crop** (a storage organ), **stomach, intestine, rectum,** and **anus.**

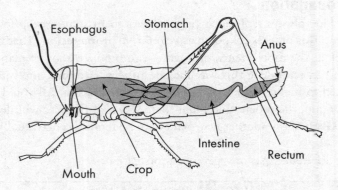

The Human Digestive System

The human digestive tract consists of the **alimentary canal** and accessory organs. The alimentary canal is the tube that leads from the mouth to the anus and includes the mouth, esophagus, stomach, **small intestine,** and **large intestine.** The **accessory organs** consist of the liver, pancreas, gall bladder, and salivary glands. Four groups of molecules must be broken down by the digestive tract: **starch, proteins, fats,** and **nucleic acids.**

The Mouth

The first stop in the digestive process is the mouth, or **oral cavity.**

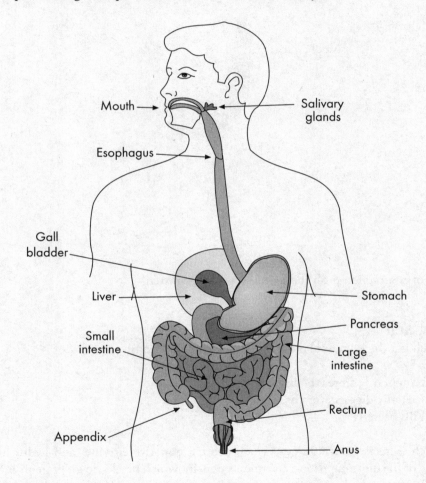

When food enters the mouth, mechanical and chemical digestion begins. The chewing, softening, and breaking up of food is called mechanical digestion. The mouth also has **saliva** in it. Saliva, which is secreted by the **salivary glands,** contains an important enzyme known as **salivary amylase.** Salivary amylase begins the chemical breakdown of starch into maltose.

Esophagus

Once chewed, the food, now shaped into a ball called a **bolus,** moves through the **pharynx** and into the esophagus. The job of the esophagus is to carry food to the stomach. The esophagus begins as skeletal muscle and ends as smooth muscle. Food moves through the esophagus in a wavelike motion known as **peristalsis.** At the end of the esophagus is a structure known as the cardiac sphincter. The only job of the cardiac sphincter is to separate the stomach from the esophagus. The stomach's acidic environment is dangerous to the esophageal cells so this sphincter separates the two environments. Please take note that the other sphincter, the pyloric sphincter, in this system plays a different role.

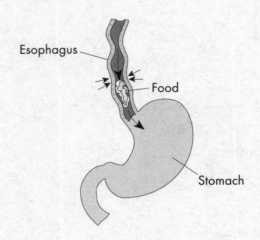

Peristalsis

The waves of contraction push the food toward the stomach.

The Stomach

The stomach is a thick, muscular sac that has several functions:

- It temporarily stores the ingested food.
- It partially digests proteins.
- It kills bacteria.

The stomach secretes **gastric juices,** which contain digestive enzymes and hydrochloric acid (HCl). One of the most important enzymes is **pepsin,** which breaks down proteins into smaller peptides. Pepsin works best in an acidic environment. When HCl is secreted, it lowers the pH of the stomach and activates pepsinogen into pepsin to digest proteins. The stomach also secretes mucus, which protects the stomach lining from the acidic juices. Finally, HCl kills most bacteria.

Food is also mechanically broken down by the churning action of the stomach. Once that's complete, this partially digested food, now called **chyme,** is ready to enter the small intestine.

The Small Intestine

The small intestine has three regions: the duodenum, the jejunum, and the ileum. The chyme moves into the first part of the small intestine, the duodenum, through the **pyloric sphincter.** The pyloric sphincter controls gastric motility by regulating entry of food into the small intestine. The small intestine is very long—about 23 feet in an average man. In the small intestine, all three food groups are completely digested and the body can now absorb all of the nutrients from the food. The walls of the small intestine secrete enzymes that break down proteins (peptidases) and carbohydrates (maltase, lactase, and sucrase).

The Pancreas

The **pancreas** secretes a number of enzymes into the small intestine: **trypsin, chymotrypsin, pancreatic lipase,** and **pancreatic amylase**. Trypsin and chymotrypsin break down proteins into dipeptides. Pancreatic lipase breaks down lipids into fatty acids and glycerol. Pancreatic amylase, on the other hand, breaks down starch into disaccharides. Ribonuclease and deoxyribonuclease break down nucleic acids into nucleotides.

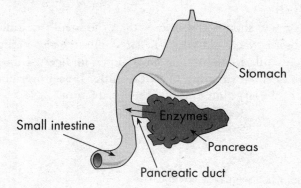

These enzymes are secreted into the small intestine via the **pancreatic duct.**

Another substance that works in the small intestine is called **bile.** Bile is not a digestive enzyme. It's an **emulsifier,** meaning that it mechanically breaks up fats into smaller fat droplets. This process makes the fat globules more accessible to pancreatic lipase. Bile enters the small intestine by the bile duct, which merges with the pancreatic duct.

Here's something you should memorize:

> Bile is made in the **liver** and stored in the **gall bladder.**

Once food is broken down, it is absorbed by tiny, fingerlike projections of the intestine called **villi** and **microvilli.** Villi and microvilli are folds that increase the surface area of the small intestine for food absorption. Within each of the villi is a capillary that absorbs the digested food and carries it into the bloodstream. Within each villus are also lymph vessels, called **lacteals,** which absorb fatty acids.

Don't forget that hormones are also involved in the digestive system: **gastrin** (which stimulates stomach cells to produce gastric juice), **secretin** (which stimulates the pancreas to produce bicarbonate and digestive enzymes), and **cholecystokinin** (which stimulates the secretion of pancreatic enzymes and the release of bile).

Here's a summary of the pancreatic enzymes:

THE PANCREATIC ENZYMES AND THE FOODS THEY DIGEST	
Pancreatic Enzymes	**Food Substance**
pancreatic amylase, pancreatic lipase, trypsin, chymotrypsin	starch fat protein
proteolytic enzymes, maltase, lactase	proteins carbohydrates

The Large Intestine

The **large intestine** is much shorter and thicker than the small intestine. The large intestine has an easy job: it reabsorbs water and salts. The large intestine also harbors harmless bacteria that are actually quite useful. These bacteria break down undigested food and in the process provide us with certain essential vitamins, like **vitamin K.** The leftover undigested food, called **feces**, then moves out of the large intestine and into the rectum.

———————⚬———————

In food digestion, what begins the chemical breakdown of starch into maltose?

A. salivary amylase

B. bolus

C. esophagus

D. oral cavity

Here's How To Crack It

Don't be misled by (D) (oral cavity) and think, "That's the first step in the digestive process! That must be the answer." Be sure to read each question on the CSET carefully so that you don't make a careless error. From your careful review of the digestive process, you know that the esophagus is the tube that leads food to the stomach and bolus is the name of food once it is chewed, so (B) and (C) must be wrong. That leaves only (A), salivary amylase. Even if you didn't come up with "salivary amylase" off the top of your head, POE can lead you to the correct answer.

———————⚬———————

THE RESPIRATORY SYSTEM

The Purpose of the Respiratory System

All cells need oxygen for aerobic respiration. For simple organisms, such as platyhelminthes, no special structures are needed because the gases can easily diffuse across every cell membrane. In other multicellular organisms, however, the cells are not in direct contact with the environment. These organisms must find other ways of getting oxygen into their systems. For some animals, such as segmented worms, gas exchange occurs directly through their skin. Others, such as insects, have special tubes called **tracheae.** Air enters these tubes through tiny openings called **spiracles.** Among vertebrates, the respiratory structures you should be familiar with are **gills** (used by many aquatic creatures) and **lungs.**

The Human Respiratory System

Air enters the human body through the nose or mouth.

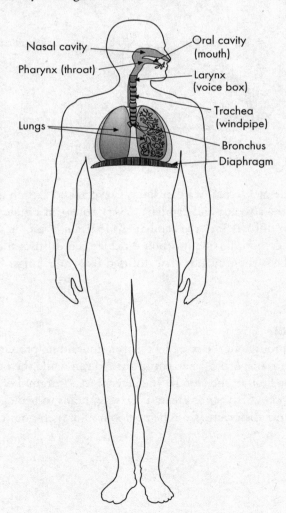

Nasal cavity

Oral cavity (mouth)

Pharynx (throat)

Larynx (voice box)

Trachea (windpipe)

Lungs

Bronchus

Diaphragm

The nose cleans, warms, and moistens the incoming air and passes it through the **pharynx** (throat) and **larynx** (voice box). Next, air enters the trachea. A special flap called the **epiglottis** covers the trachea when you swallow, preventing food from going down the wrong pipe. The trachea also has cartilage rings to help keep the air passage open as air rushes in.

The trachea then branches into two bronchi: the **left bronchus** and the **right bronchus.** These two tubes service the lungs. In the lungs, the passageways break down into smaller tubes known as **bronchioles.** Each bronchiole ends in a tiny air sac known as an **alveolus.** These sacs enable the lungs to have an enormous surface area: about 100 square meters. Let's take a look at one of these tiny air sacs:

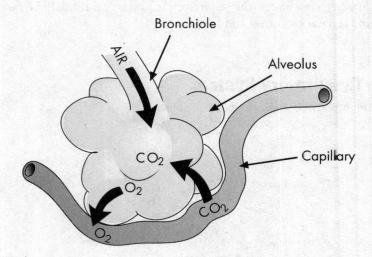

You'll notice that alongside the alveolus is a **capillary.** Oxygen and carbon dioxide diffuse across the membrane of both the alveolus and capillary. Every time you inhale, you send oxygen to the alveoli. Oxygen then diffuses into the capillaries. The capillaries, on the other hand, have a high concentration of carbon dioxide. Carbon dioxide then diffuses into the alveoli. When you exhale, you expel the carbon dioxide that diffused into your lungs. Gas exchange occurs via passive diffusion.

Transport of Oxygen

Oxygen is transported throughout the body by the iron-containing protein **hemoglobin** in red blood cells. Hemoglobin transports 97 percent of the oxygen while the other 3 percent is dissolved in the **plasma** (the fluid of the blood). The percent O_2 saturation of hemoglobin is highest where the concentration of oxygen is greatest. Oxygen binds to hemoglobin in oxygen-rich blood leaving the lungs and dissociates from hemoglobin in oxygen-poor tissues.

Transport of Carbon Dioxide

We've just mentioned that carbon dioxide can leave the capillaries and enter the lungs. However, carbon dioxide can travel in many forms. Most of the carbon dioxide enters red blood cells and combines with water to eventually form **bicarbonate ions** (HCO_3^-). Here's a summary of the reaction:

$$CO_2 \quad + \quad H_2O \quad \rightarrow \quad H_2CO_3 \quad \rightarrow \quad H^+ \quad HCO_3^-$$

Carbon dioxide   Water   Carbonic Acid   Hydrogen ion
Bicarbonate ion

Sometimes carbon dioxide combines with the amino group in hemoglobin and mixes with plasma, or is transported to the lungs.

Mechanics of Breathing

What happens to your body when you take a deep breath? Your diaphragm and intercostal muscles contract and your rib cage expands. This action increases the volume of the lungs, allowing air to rush in. This process of taking in oxygen is called **inspiration.** When you breathe out and let carbon dioxide out of your lungs, that's called **expiration.** Your respiratory rate is controlled by **chemoreceptors.** As your blood pH decreases, chemoreceptors send nerve impulses to the **diaphragm** and intercostal muscles to increase your respiratory rate.

Hemoglobin transports 97 percent of the oxygen that is transported throughout your body. What happens to the other 3 percent?

A.   It is dissolved in the lipids.

B.   It is dissolved in the plasma.

C.   It is lost.

D.   It forms bicarbonate ions.

Here's How To Crack It

You can cross off (A) immediately, as lipids aren't related to the respiratory system at all. Choice (C) is too vague; it must be wrong. Bicarbonate ions probably sound familiar, but don't be thrown off by that choice. The correct answer is (B); the other 3 percent of oxygen that is not transported by hemoglobin is dissolved in plasma (the fluid of the blood).

THE CIRCULATORY SYSTEM

The Purpose of the Circulatory System

Most organisms need to carry out two tasks: (1) supply their bodies with nutrients and oxygen and (2) get rid of wastes. Many simple aquatic organisms have no trouble moving materials across their membranes since their metabolic needs are met by diffusion. Larger organisms, on the other hand, particularly terrestrial organisms, can't depend on diffusion. They therefore need special circulatory systems to accomplish internal transport.

There are two types of circulatory systems: an **open circulatory system** and a **closed circulatory system.** In an open circulatory system, blood is carried by open-ended blood vessels that spill blood into the body cavity. In arthropods, for example, blood vessels from the heart open into internal cavities known as **sinuses.** Other organisms have closed circulatory systems. That is, blood flows continuously through a network of blood vessels. Earthworms and some mollusks have a closed circulatory system, as do vertebrates.

The Human Circulatory System

The heart is divided into four chambers, two on the left and two on the right. The four chambers of the heart are the **right atrium,** the **right ventricle,** the **left atrium,** and the **left ventricle.** Let's take a look at a picture of the heart:

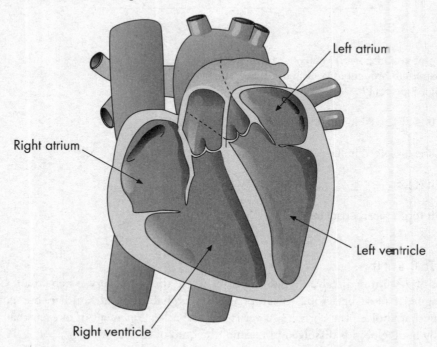

Left atrium

Right atrium

Left ventricle

Right ventricle

The heart pumps blood in a continuous circuit. Since blood makes a circuit in the body, it doesn't matter where we begin to trace the flow of blood. For our purposes, we'll begin at the point in the circulatory system where the blood leaves the heart and enters the body: the left ventricle. When blood leaves the left ventricle it will make a tour of the body. We call this **systemic circulation.**

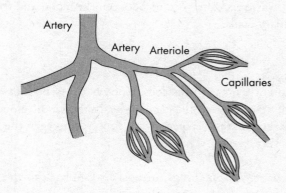

Systemic Circulation

Blood leaves the heart through the **aortic semilunar valve** and enters a large blood vessel called the **aorta.** The aorta is the largest artery in the body. The aorta then branches out into smaller vessels called **arteries.**

Arteries always carry blood away from the heart. Just remember "A" stands for "away" from the heart. They're able to carry the blood because arteries are thick-walled, elastic vessels. The arteries become even smaller vessels called **arterioles,** and then the smallest vessels called **capillaries.**

There are thousands of capillaries. In fact, some estimate that the capillary routes in your bloodstream are as long as 100 kilometers! These vessels are so tiny that red blood cells must squeeze through them in single file. Capillaries intermingle with the tissues and exchange nutrients, gases, and wastes. Oxygen and nutrients leave the capillaries and enter the tissues; carbon dioxide and wastes leave the tissues and enter the capillaries.

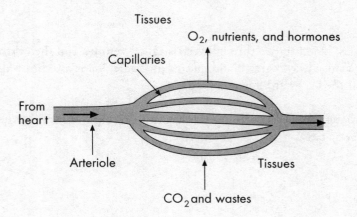

Before we take a look at the next stage of circulation, let's recap the pathway of blood through the body:

- Blood leaves the heart's left ventricle via the aorta.
- It travels through the arteries to the arterioles, and eventually to the capillaries.
- Gas and nutrient/waste exchange occurs between the blood and the tissues through the capillary walls.

Back to the Heart

After exchanging gases and nutrients with the cells, blood has very little oxygen left. Most of its oxygen was donated to the cells through the capillary walls. Since the blood is now depleted of oxygen, it is said to be **deoxygenated.** To get a fresh supply of oxygen the blood now needs to go to the lungs.

But the blood doesn't go *directly* to the lungs. It must first go back to the heart. As the blood returns to the heart, the vessels get bigger and bigger.

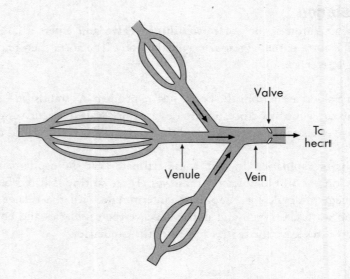

From the capillaries, blood travels through vessels called **venules** and then through larger vessels called **veins.** Veins always carry blood *toward* the heart. Veins are thin-walled vessels with valves that prevent the backward flow of blood.

Blood eventually enters the heart's right atrium via two veins known as the **superior vena cava** and the **inferior vena cava.**

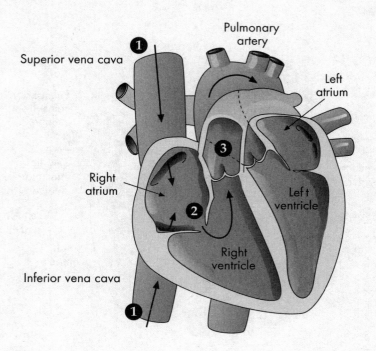

Blood now moves through the heart. Blood travels from the right atrium to the right ventricle through the **right atrioventricular (AV) valve** (or **tricuspid**). From the right ventricle, blood will go out again into the body, but this time toward the lungs. This process is called **pulmonary circulation.**

The Pulmonary System

Blood leaves the right ventricle through the pulmonary semilunar valve and enters a large artery known as the **pulmonary artery.** Remember what we said about arteries? Blood vessels that leave the heart are always called arteries.

There's one major feature you must remember about the blood in the pulmonary system. Whereas in systemic circulation the blood was rich with oxygen, the pulmonary artery is carrying deoxygenated blood. The pulmonary artery branches into the right and left pulmonary arteries which lead, respectively, to the right and left lungs. These arteries become smaller arterioles and then once again capillaries.

We just said that these vessels carry deoxygenated blood. In the lungs, the blood will pick up oxygen and dump carbon dioxide. Sounds familiar? It should. It's just like the gas exchange we discussed in the respiratory system. In the lungs, the blood fills with oxygen, or becomes **oxygenated.** The blood returns to the heart via the **pulmonary veins** and enters the left atrium.

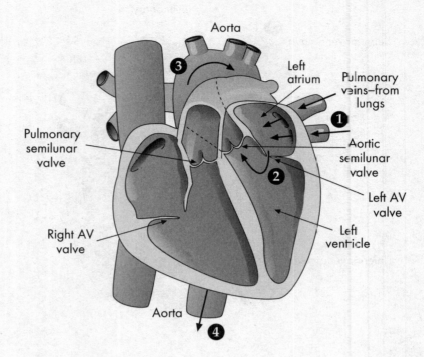

Blood then moves to the left ventricle through the **left atrioventricular (AV) valve** (or **bicuspid** or **mitral valve**). Now we've completed our tour of the heart. Let's recap the events in pulmonary circulation:

- Deoxygenated blood leaves the right ventricle via the pulmonary artery.
- The pulmonary artery branches into the right and left pulmonary arteries, carrying the blood to the lungs.
- Blood travels from the arteries to the arterioles, and eventually to the capillaries.
- Gas exchange occurs between the capillaries and alveoli in the lungs.
- Once the blood is oxygenated, it returns to the heart through the pulmonary veins.

The Contents of Blood

Now let's take a look at blood itself. Blood consists of two things:

- plasma
- cells and cell fragments suspended in the fluid

Blood carries three types of cells: **red blood cells** (also called **erythrocytes**), **white blood cells** (also called **leukocytes**), and **platelets.** Red blood cells are the oxygen-carrying cells in the body. They contain hemoglobin, the protein that actually carries the oxygen (and carbon dioxide) throughout the body. Mature red blood cells lack a nucleus. White blood cells fight infection by protecting the body against foreign organisms.

Platelets are cell fragments that are involved in blood clotting. When a blood vessel is damaged, platelets stick to the collagen fibers of the vessel wall. The damaged cells and platelets release substances that activate clotting factors, and a series of reactions occur. First, a prothrombin activator converts prothrombin (a plasma protein) to thrombin. Then thrombin converts fibrinogen to fibrin threads, which strengthen the clot.

Here's something you should remember for the test:

> All of the blood cells are made in the **bone marrow.** The bone marrow is located in the center of the bones.

Blood Types

There are four blood groups: **A, B, AB,** and **O.** Blood types are pretty important and are based on the type of antigen(s) found on red blood cells. If a patient is given the wrong type of blood in a transfusion, it could be fatal! Why? Because red blood cells in the blood will clump if they are exposed to the wrong blood type. For example, if you have blood type A (that is, your red cells carry the A antigen) and you receive a blood transfusion of blood type B, your blood will clump. That's because your blood contains **antibodies,** an immune substance that will bind and destroy the foreign blood.

What is important to remember about the different blood types is that type O blood is the universal donor and that type AB is the universal recipient.

Use the diagram below to answer the question that follows.

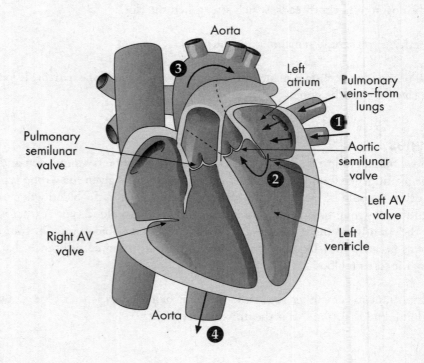

Which chamber of the heart labeled in the diagram above is primarily responsible for pumping blood to most of the organs and tissues of the body?

A.   left atrium

B.   left ventricle

C.   right atrium

D.   right ventricle

Here's How To Crack It

This is yet another question that requires simple memorization. You know that blood makes a tour of the body, called systemic circulation, but where does that tour begin? Like a band kicking off a tour in their hometown, blood starts its tour in the left ventricle, (B), and then takes the show on the road.

THE LYMPHATIC AND IMMUNE SYSTEM

The Lymphatic System

The **lymphatic system** is made up of a network of vessels that conduct **lymph,** a clear, watery fluid formed from interstitial fluid. Lymph vessels are found throughout the body along the routes of blood vessels. It plays an important role in fluid homeostasis.

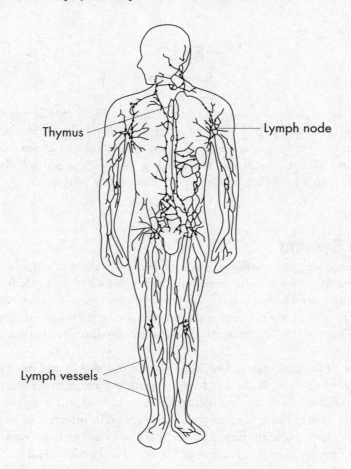

Thymus

Lymph node

Lymph vessels

The lymphatic system has three functions:

- It collects, filters, and returns fluid to the blood by the contraction of adjacent muscles.
- It fights infection using lymphocytes, cells found in lymph nodes.
- It removes excess fluid from body tissue.

Sometimes a lymph vessel will form a **lymph node,** a mass of tissue found along the course of a lymph vessel. A lymph node contains a large number of lymphocytes:

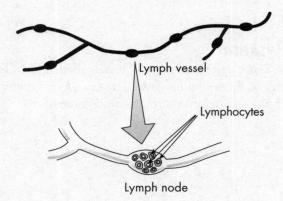

Lymph vessel

Lymphocytes

Lymph node

Lymphocytes are important in fighting infection. They multiply rapidly when they come in contact with an **antigen,** or foreign substance recognized by the immune system. (We'll talk about this in a second.) The lymph nodes swell when they're fighting an infection. That's why when you have a sore throat, one of the first things a doctor does is touch the sides of your throat to see if your lymph nodes are swollen, a probable sign of infection.

The Immune System

The **immune system,** generally speaking, is one of the body's defense systems. It is a carefully and closely coordinated system of specialized cells, each of which plays a specific role in the war against bodily invaders. As we mentioned above, foreign molecules—be they viral, bacterial, or simply chemical—that can trigger an immune response are called antigens. The appearance of antigens in the body stimulates a defense mechanism that produces antibodies.

The body's first line of defense against foreign substances is the skin and mucous lining of the respiratory and digestive tracts. If these defenses are not sufficient, other nonspecific defense mechanisms are activated. These include **phagocytes** (which engulf antigens), **complement proteins** (which lyse [disintegrate] the cell wall of the antigen), **interferons** (which inhibit viral replication and activate surrounding cells that have antiviral actions), and **inflammatory response** (a series of events in response to antigen invasion or physical injury).

Types of Immune Cells

The primary cells of the immune system are lymphocytes—T-cells and B-cells. The plasma membrane of cells has **major histocompatibility complex markers (MHC markers)** that distinguish between self and nonself cells. When **T-lymphocytes** encounter cells infected by pathogens, they recognize the foreign antigen-MHC markers on the cell surface. T-cells are activated, multiply, and give rise to clones. Some T-cells become **memory T-cells,** whereas others become **helper T-cells.** Helper T-cells activate **B-lymphocytes** and other T-cells in responding to the infected cells. Memory T-cells recognize bacteria or viruses that they have encountered before. Other T-cells, **cytotoxic T-cells,** recognize and kill infected cells. The activation of T-cells is referred to as a **cell-mediated response.** T-cells are made in the bone marrow, but mature in the thymus.

In antibody-mediated immunity (humoral immunity), when B-lymphocytes encounter antigen-presenting cells (like **macrophages**) with foreign MHC markers, they are activated and produce clones. Some B-cells become memory cells that can rapidly divide and can produce plasma cells after an infection has been overcome. These plasma cells produce antibodies that bind to the antigens that originally activated them. Helper T-cells are also involved and produce interleukins. Both memory T- and memory B-cells are responsible for long-term immunity.

AIDS

Acquired immunodeficiency syndrome (AIDS) is a devastating disease that interferes with the body's immune system. AIDS essentially wipes out the helper T-cells, preventing the body from defending itself. Those afflicted with AIDS do not die of AIDS itself but rather of infections that they can no longer fight off due to their compromised immune systems.

One thing to remember about the immune cells and blood cells: All blood cells, white and red, are produced in the bone marrow. To summarize:

- T-lymphocytes actually fight infection and help the B-lymphocytes proliferate.
- B-lymphocytes produce antibodies.

THE EXCRETORY SYSTEM

The Purpose of the Excretory System

As you already know, all organisms must get rid of wastes. We'll now focus primarily on how organisms get rid of **nitrogenous wastes** (products containing nitrogen) and regulate water. When cells break down proteins, one of the byproducts is **ammonia** (NH_3), a substance that is toxic to the body. Consequently, organisms had to develop ways of converting ammonia to a less poisonous substance. Some animals convert ammonia to **uric acid,** while others convert ammonia to **urea.** Some examples of excretory organs among invertebrates are **nephridia** (found in earthworms) and **Malpighian tubules** (found in arthropods).

The Human Excretory System

In humans, the major organ that regulates excretion is the **kidney.** Each kidney is made up of a million tiny structures called **nephrons.** Nephrons are the functional units of the kidney. A nephron consists of several regions: the **Bowman's capsule,** the **proximal convoluted tubule,** the **loop of Henle,** the **distal convoluted tubule,** and the **collecting duct.**

Here's an illustration of a nephron:

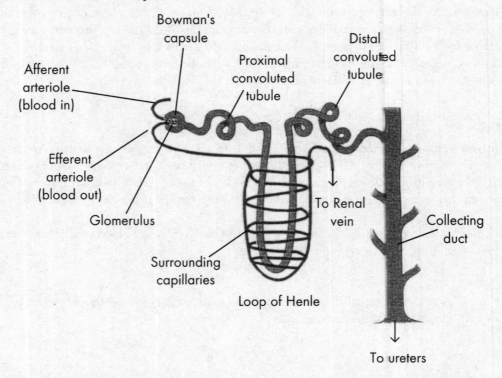

How does a nephron work? Let's trace the flow of blood in a nephron. Blood enters the nephron at the Bowman's capsule. A blood vessel called the **renal artery** leads to the kidney and branches into arterioles, then tiny capillaries. A ball of capillaries that "sits" within a Bowman's capsule is called a **glomerulus.** Blood is filtered as it passes through the glomerulus, and the plasma is forced out of the capillaries into the Bowman's capsule. This plasma is now called a **filtrate.**

The filtrate travels along the entire nephron. From the Bowman's capsule, the filtrate passes through the proximal convoluted tubule, then the loop of Henle, then the distal convoluted tubule, and finally the collecting duct. As it travels along the tube, the filtrate is modified to form urine.

What happens next? The concentrated **urine** moves from the collecting ducts into the **ureters,** then into the **bladder,** and finally out through the **urethra.**

THE NERVOUS SYSTEM

The Purpose of the Nervous System

All organisms must be able to react to changes in their environment. As a result, organisms have evolved systems that pick up and process information from the outside world. The task of coordinating this information falls to the nervous system. The simplest nervous system is found in the hydra. It has a **nerve net** made up of a network of nerve cells, the impulse of which travels in both directions. As animals became more complex, they developed clumps of nerve cells called **ganglia.** These cells are like primitive brains. More complex organisms have a brain with specialized cells called **neurons.**

Neurons

The functional unit in the nervous system is a neuron. That's because neurons receive and send the neural impulses that trigger organisms' responses to their environments. Let's talk about the parts of a neuron. A neuron consists of a **cell body, dendrites,** and an **axon.**

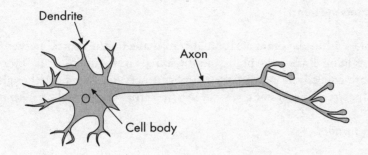

The cell body contains the nucleus and all the usual organelles found in the cytoplasm. Dendrites are short extensions of the cell body that receive stimuli. The axon is a long, slender extension that transmits an impulse from the cell body to another neuron or to an organ. A nerve impulse begins at the top of the dendrites, passes through the dendrites to the cell body, and moves down the axon.

Types of Neurons

Neurons can be classified into three groups: **sensory neurons, motor (effector) neurons,** and **interneurons.** Sensory neurons receive impulses from the environment and take them to the body. For example, sensory neurons in your hand are stimulated by touch. A motor neuron transmits the impulse to muscles or glands to produce a response. The muscle responds by contracting or the gland responds by secreting a substance (for example, a hormone). Interneurons are the links between sensory neurons and motor neurons. They're found in the brain and spinal cord.

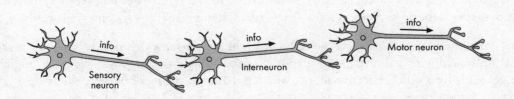

How Neurons Communicate

There are billions of neurons running throughout the body, firing all the time. More often than not, one or more neurons are somewhat "connected." This means that one neuron has its dendrites next to another neuron's axon. In this way, the dendrites of one cell can pick up the impulse sent from the axon of another cell. The second neuron can then send the impulse to its cell body and down its axon, passing it on to yet another cell.

Parts of the Nervous System

The nervous system can be divided into two parts: the **central nervous system** and the **peripheral nervous system.**

All of the neurons within the brain and spinal cord make up the central nervous system. All of the other neurons lying outside the brain and the spinal cord—in our skin, our organs, and our blood vessels—are collectively part of the peripheral nervous system. Although both of these systems are really part of one system, we still use the terms *central* and *peripheral*.

So keep them in mind:

- The central nervous system includes the neurons in the brain and spinal cord.
- The peripheral nervous system includes all the rest.

The peripheral nervous system is further broken down into the **somatic nervous system** and the **autonomic nervous system.**

- The somatic nervous system controls voluntary activities. For example, the movement of your eyes across the page as you read this line is under the control of your somatic nervous system.
- The autonomic nervous system controls involuntary activities. Your heartbeat and your digestive system, for example, are under the control of the autonomic nervous system.

The interesting thing about these two systems is that they sometimes overlap. For instance, you can control your breathing if you choose to. Yet most of the time you do not think about it: your somatic system hands control of your respiration over to the autonomic system.

The autonomic system is broken down even further to the **sympathetic nervous system** and the **parasympathetic nervous system.** These two systems actually work antagonistically.

The sympathetic system controls the **fight-or-flight response,** which occurs when an organism confronted with a threatening situation prepares to fight or flee (thus "fight" or "flight"). To get ready for a quick, effective action, whether that be brawling or bolting, the sympathetic nervous system raises your heart and respiration rates, causes your blood vessels to constrict, increases the levels of glucose in your blood, and produces goose bumps on the back of your neck. It even reroutes your blood sugar to your skeletal muscles in case you need to make a break for it. After the threat has passed, the parasympathetic nervous system brings the body back to **homeostasis**—that is, back to normal. It lowers your heart and respiratory rates and decreases glucose levels in the blood.

The flowchart below gives you a nice overview of the different parts of the nervous system:

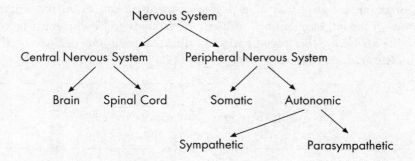

Parts of the Brain

The brain can also be divided into parts. Here's a summary of the major divisions within the brain.

DIVISIONS WITHIN THE BRAIN	
Parts of the Brain	**Function**
Cerebrum	Controls all voluntary activities; receives and interprets sensory information; largest part of the human brain
Cerebellum	Coordinates muscle activity and refinement of movement
Hypothalamus	Regulates homeostasis and secretes hormones; regulates the pituitary gland
Medulla	Controls involuntary actions such as breathing, swallowing, heartbeat, and respiration
Pons	Connects parts of the brain with one another and contains the respiratory center
Midbrain	Center for visual and auditory reflexes (pupil reflex and blinking)
Thalamus	Main sensory relay center for conducting information between the spinal cord and cerebrum

DNA: THE BLUEPRINT OF LIFE

All living things possess an astonishing degree of organization. From the simplest single-celled organism to the largest mammal, millions of reactions and events must be coordinated precisely for life to exist. This coordination is directed from the nucleus of the cell, by **deoxyribonucleic acid,** or **DNA.**

> DNA is the hereditary blueprint of the cell.

The DNA of a cell is contained in structures called chromosomes. The chromosomes consist of DNA wrapped around proteins called histones. When the genetic material is in a loose form in the nucleus, it is called **euchromatin,** and its genes are active, or available for transcription. When the genetic material is fully condensed into coils, it is called **heterochromatin,** and its genes are generally inactive. Situated in the nucleus, chromosomes direct and control all the processes necessary for life, including passing themselves, and their information, on to future generations.

Structure of DNA

The DNA molecule consists of two strands that wrap around each other to form a long, twisted ladder called a **double helix.** The structure of DNA was brilliantly deduced in 1956 by two scientists named James Watson and Francis Crick.

DNA is made up of repeated subunits of **nucleotides.** Each nucleotide has a **five-carbon sugar,** a **phosphate,** and a **nitrogenous base.** Take a look at the nucleotide below. This particular nucleotide contains a nitrogenous base called **adenine:**

The name of the pentagon-shaped sugar in DNA is **deoxyribose.** Hence, the name *deoxyribo-nucleic acid.*

The Importance of DNA

Enzymes are proteins that are essential for life. This is true not only because they help liberate energy stored in chemical bonds, but also because they direct the construction of the cell. This is where DNA comes into the picture.

DNA's main role is directing the manufacture of proteins. These proteins, in turn, regulate everything that occurs in the cell. But DNA does not *directly* manufacture proteins. Instead, DNA passes its information to an intermediate molecule known as **ribonucleic acid (RNA).** These RNA molecules carry out the instructions in DNA, producing the proteins that determine the course of life.

The flow of genetic information is therefore

$$DNA \rightarrow RNA \rightarrow proteins$$

This is the central doctrine of molecular biology.

DNA is the hereditary blueprint of the cell. By directing the manufacture of proteins, DNA serves as the cell's blueprint. But how is DNA inherited? For the information in DNA to be passed on, it must first be copied. This copying of DNA is known as **DNA replication.**

KEY TERMS

cells
eukaryotic cells
prokaryotic cells
nucleus
cytoplasm
organelles
nucleoid
flagellum
plasma membrane
chromosomes
nucleolus
ribosomes
endoplasmic reticulum (ER)
rough ER (RER)
smooth ER (SER)
Golgi bodies
vesicles
mitochondria
adenosine triphosphate (ATP)
lysosomes
centrioles
microtubule organizing centers (MTOCs)
vacuoles
peroxisomes
cytoskeleton
microtubules
microfilaments
tubulin
cell wall
chitin
chloroplasts
cell sap
roots
root tip
elongation region
maturation region
root apical meristem
root hairs
epidermis
cortex
stele
apoplast
symplast
endodermis
endodermal cells
spines
stamen

pistil
sepals
petals
anther
filament
pollen grains (microspores)
stigma
style
ovary
ovules
megaspores
egg nucleus
polar nuclei
double fertilization
sperm nuclei
endosperm
cotyledons
epicotyls
hypocotyls
radicle
photoperiodism
short-day plants
long-day plants
day-neutral plants
phytochrome
vegetative propagation
tubers
runners
bulbs
grafting
autotroph
heterotroph
intracellular digestion
extracellular digestion
mouth
esophagus
crop
stomach
intestine
rectum
anus
alimentary canal
small intestine
large intestine
accessory organs
starch
proteins

fats
nucleic acids
oral cavity
saliva
salivary glands
salivary amylase
bolus
pharynx
peristalsis
gastric juices
pepsin
chime
pyloric sphincter
pancreas
trypsin
chymotrypsin
pancreatic lipase
pancreatic amylase
pancreatic duct
bile
emulsifier
liver
gall bladder
villi
microvilli
lacteals
gastrin
secretin
cholecystokinin
large intestine
vitamin K
feces
tracheae
spiracles
gills
lungs
pharynx
larynx
epiglottis
left bronchus
right bronchus
bronchioles
alveolus
capillary
hemoglobin
plasma
bicarbonate ions

inspiration
expiration
chemoreceptors
diaphragm
open circulatory system
closed circulatory system
sinuses
right atrium
right ventricle
left atrium
left ventricle
systemic circulation
aortic semilunar valve
aorta
arteries
arterioles
capillaries
deoxygenated
venules
veins
superior vena cava
inferior vena cava
right atrioventricular valve (tricuspid)
pulmonary circulation
pulmonary artery
oxygenated blood
pulmonary veins
left atrioventricular valve (bicuspid,
   or mitral valve)
red blood cells (erythrocytes)
white blood cells (leukocytes)
platelets
bone marrow
blood types
antibodies
lymphatic system
lymph
lymph node
lymphocytes
antigen
immune system
phagocytes
complement proteins
interferons
inflammatory response
major histocompatibility complex
   markers (MHC markers)

T-lymphocytes
memory T-cells
helper T-cells
B-lymphocytes
cytotoxic T-cells
cell-mediated response
macrophages
acquired immunodeficiency
  syndrome (AIDS)
nitrogenous wastes
ammonia
uric acid
urea
nephridia
Malpighian tubules
kidney
nephrons
Bowman's capsule
proximal convoluted tubule
loop of Henle
distal convoluted tubule
collecting duct
renal artery
glomerulus
filtrate
urine
ureters
bladder
urethra
nerve net
ganglia
neurons
cell body

dendrites
axon
sensory neurons
motor (effector) neurons
interneurons
central nervous system
peripheral nervous system
somatic nervous system
autonomic nervous system
sympathetic nervous system
parasympathetic nervous system
fight-or-flight response
homeostasis
cerebrum
cerebellum
hypothalamus
medulla
pons
midbrain
thalamus
deoxyribonucleic acid (DNA)
euchromatin
heterochromatin
double helix
nucleotides
five-carbon sugar
phosphate
nitrogenous base
adenine
deoxyribose
ribonucleic acid (RNA)
DNA replication

Chapter 10 Drill

Answers and explanations can be found in the final section of this book, beginning on page 617.

1. A major difference between bacterial cells and animals cells is that bacterial cells have:

   A. a plasma membrane.

   B. ribosomes, which are involved in protein synthesis.

   C. a cell wall.

   D. a nuclear membrane.

2. The nucleolus is:

   A. the site at which rRNA is formed.

   B. a channel inside the cytoplasm that is the site of lipid synthesis.

   C. a polymer of the protein tubulin that is found in cilia, flagella, and spindle fibers.

   D. a semi-rigid structure that lends support to the cell.

3. Which of the following structures is NOT part of the pistil?

   A. ovule

   B. ovary

   C. style

   D. anther

4. The digestive enzyme that hydrolyzes molecules of fats into fatty acids is known as:

   A. bile.

   B. lipase.

   C. amylase.

   D. protease.

5. The blood type that is the universal recipient is:

   A. O.

   B. A.

   C. AB.

   D. B.

Summary

- All living things are composed of cells.

- Inside cells are many organelles that perform important, specific tasks. You should memorize these for the CSET.

- Plants have special structures including roots and leaves.

- Flowering plants contain both male and female parts and reproduce through a process called double fertilization.

- In human digestion, food travels from the oral cavity, is broken down by salivary amylase, travels through the pharynx and into the esophagus, then into the stomach, small intestine, large intestine, and is finally expelled as feces.

- Gills and lungs are respiratory structures among vertebrates.

- Taking in oxygen is called inspiration; breathing out is called expiration.

- The two types of circulatory systems are the open circulatory system and the closed circulatory system.

- In the human body, blood leaves the heart from the left ventricle and then makes a tour of the body that is called systemic circulation.

- The lymphatic system is important for fluid homeostasis in the body.

- The immune system is the body's defense system.

- The excretory system rids the body of nitrogenous wastes and regulates water.

- The nervous system is an elaborate system that picks up and processes information from the outside world.

Chapter 11
Living and Nonliving Components in Environments (Ecology)

LIVING AND NONLIVING COMPONENTS

Living and nonliving components coexist on Earth in a careful balance. Life is the condition that distinguishes active organisms from inorganic matter. Living organisms undergo metabolism, maintain homeostasis, possess a capacity to grow, respond to stimuli, reproduce, and adapt to their environment in successive generations. To maintain homeostasis, all living things require four basic things: food, water, air, and space.

CYCLES IN NATURE

Nutrients such as carbon, oxygen, nitrogen, phosphorus, sulfur, and water all move through the environment in complex cycles known as **biogeochemical cycles.**

As you can probably tell from the collective name of these natural cycles, living organisms, geologic formations, and chemical substances are all involved in these cycles. Keep in mind that when we describe the movement of these inorganic compounds, it's important to understand both the destinations of the compounds and how they move to their destinations. For example, for the CSET, it won't be enough for you to know that water moves from the atmosphere to Earth. You'll need to know the different ways it has of getting there. In other words, you'll need to know that water moves from the atmosphere to Earth's surface through precipitation, either in the form of snow or rainfall.

But, let's talk about a few things that all of these cycles have in common before we go into each one in detail. First of all, the term **reservoir** is used to describe a place where a large quantity of a nutrient sits for a long period of time (in the water cycle, the ocean is an example of a reservoir). The opposite of a reservoir is an **exchange pool,** which is a site where a nutrient sits for only a short period of time (in the water cycle, a cloud is an example of an exchange pool). The amount of time a nutrient spends in a reservoir or an exchange pool is referred to as its **residency time.** In the water cycle, water might exist in the form of a cloud for a few days, but it might exist as part of the ocean for a thousand years! Perhaps surprisingly, living organisms can also serve as exchange pools and reservoirs for certain nutrients; we'll delve into more about this later.

The energy that drives these biogeochemical cycles in the biosphere comes primarily from two sources: the Sun and the heat energy from the mantle and core of Earth. The movements of nutrients in all of these cycles may be via abiotic mechanisms, such as wind, or through biotic mechanisms, such as living organisms. Another important fact to note is that while the **Law of Conservation of Matter** states that matter can be neither created nor destroyed, nutrients can be rendered unavailable for cycling through certain processes—for example, in some cycles, nutrients may be transported to deep ocean sediments where they are locked away interminably.

Though we won't get into a discussion of trace elements here, you should also know that certain trace elements such as zinc, copper, and iron are necessary in small amounts for living organisms. Trace elements can cycle in conjunction with the major nutrients, but there's still much to be discovered about these elements and their biogeochemical cycles. For the CSET, just know that there are certain trace elements required by living things that cycle, along with the major elements, through the biosphere.

Let's start with perhaps the most famous biogeochemical cycle: the water cycle.

The Water Cycle

As you might imagine, the water that exists in the atmosphere is in a gaseous state, and when it condenses from the gaseous state to form a liquid or solid, it becomes dense enough to fall to Earth because of the pull of gravity. This process is formally known as **precipitation.** When precipitation falls onto Earth, it may travel below ground to become **groundwater,** or it may travel across the land's surface and enter a drainage system, such as a stream or river, that will eventually deposit it into a body of water such as a lake or an ocean. Lakes and oceans are reservoirs for water. In certain cold regions of Earth, water may also be trapped on Earth's surface as snow or ice; in these areas, the blocks of snow or ice are reservoirs.

Water is also cycled through living systems. For example, plants consume water (and carbon dioxide) in the process of photosynthesis, in which they produce carbohydrates. Because all living organisms are primarily made up of water, they act as exchange pools for water.

Water is returned to the atmosphere from both Earth's surface and from living organisms in a process called **evaporation.** Specifically, animals respire and release water vapor and additional gases to the atmosphere. In plants, the process of **transpiration** releases large amounts of water into the air. Finally, other major contributors to atmospheric water are the vast number of lakes and oceans on Earth's surface. Incredibly large amounts of water continually evaporate from their surfaces.

Take a look at the graphic below, which shows all of the forms that water takes in the biosphere and atmosphere.

The Water Cycle

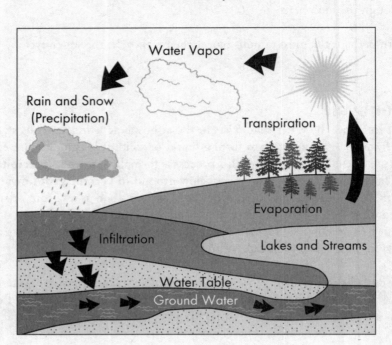

The Carbon Cycle

Now let's talk about carbon. The key events in the carbon cycle are **respiration,** in which animals breathe and give off carbon dioxide (CO_2); and **photosynthesis,** in which plants take in carbon dioxide, water, and energy from the Sun to produce carbohydrates. In other words, living things act as exchange pools for carbon.

When plants are eaten by animal consumers, the carbon locked in the plant carbohydrates passes to other organisms and continues through the food chain (more on this later in the chapter). In turn, when organisms—both plants and animals—die, their bodies are decomposed through the actions of bacteria and fungi in the soil; this releases CO_2 back into the atmosphere.

One aspect of the carbon cycle that you should definitely be familiar with for the exam is this: when the bodies of once-living organisms are buried and subjected to conditions of extreme heat and extreme pressure, eventually this organic matter becomes oil, coal, and gas. Oil, coal, and natural gas are collectively known as fossil fuels, and when **fossil fuels** are burned, or **combusted,** carbon is released into the atmosphere. Finally, carbon is also released into the atmosphere through volcanic action.

There are two major reservoirs of carbon. The first is the world's oceans, because CO_2 is very soluble in water. The second large reservoir of CO_2 is Earth's rocks. Many types of rocks—called carbonate rocks—contain carbon, in the form of calcium carbonate.

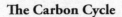

The Carbon Cycle

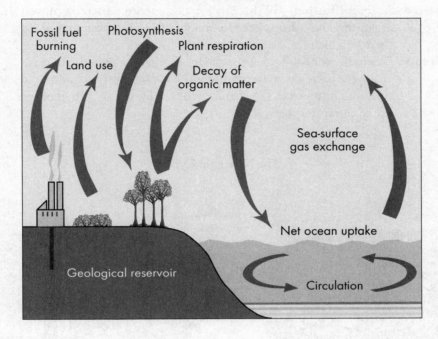

The Nitrogen Cycle

Earth's atmosphere is made up of approximately 78 percent nitrogen (N_2) and 21 percent oxygen (the other components of the atmosphere are trace elements), so as you can see, nitrogen is the most abundant element in the atmosphere. For this reason, it might not seem like living organisms would find it difficult to get the nitrogen they need in order to live. But it is! This is because atmospheric N_2 is not in a form that can be used directly by most organisms. In order to keep this rather complicated cycle straight, let's look at it in steps.

Step 1: **Nitrogen fixation**—In order to be used by most living organisms, nitrogen must be present in the form of ammonia (NH_3) or nitrates (NO_3^-). Atmospheric nitrogen can be converted into these forms, or "fixed," by atmospheric effects such as lightning storms, but most nitrogen fixation is the result of the actions of certain soil bacteria. One important soil bacteria that participates in nitrogen fixation is *Rhizobium*. These nitrogen-fixing bacteria are often associated with the roots of legumes such as beans and clover. In the future, we may be able to insert the genes for nitrogen fixation into crop plants, such as corn, and reduce the amount of fertilizer that is used.

Step 2: Nitrification—In this process, soil bacteria converts ammonium (NH_4^+) into one of the forms that can be used by plants—nitrate (NO_3).

Step 3: Assimilation—In assimilation, plants absorb ammonium (NH_3), ammonia ions (NH_4^+), and nitrate ions (NO_3^-) through their roots. Heterotrophs then obtain nitrogen when they consume plants' proteins and nucleic acids.

Step 4: Ammonification—In this process, decomposing bacteria convert dead organisms and other waste to ammonia (NH_3) or ammonium ions (NH_4^+), which can be reused by plants.

Step 5: Denitrification—In denitrification, specialized bacteria (mostly anaerobic bacteria) convert ammonia back into nitrites and nitrates and then into nitrogen gas (N_2) and nitrous oxide gas (N_2O). These gases then rise to the atmosphere.

The Nitrogen Cycle

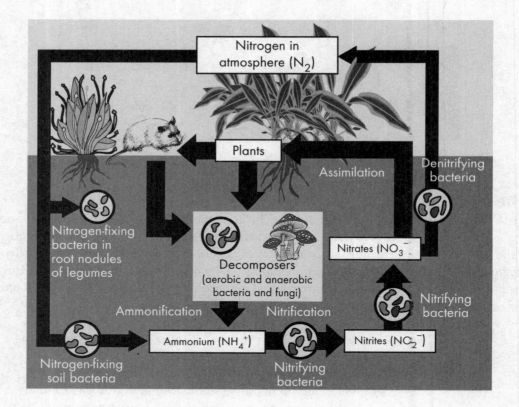

The Phosphorus Cycle

The last biogeochemical cycle we'll talk about is the phosphorus cycle. The **phosphorus cycle** is perhaps the simplest biogeochemical cycle, mostly because phosphorus does not exist in the atmosphere other than in dust particles. Phosphorus is necessary for living organisms because it's a major component of nucleic acids and other important biological molecules. One important idea for you to remember about the phosphorus cycle is that phosphorus cycles are more local than those of the other important biological compounds.

For the most part, phosphorus is found in soil, rock, and sediments; it's released from these rock forms through the process of chemical weathering. Phosphorus is usually released in the form of phosphate (PO_4^{3-}), which is very soluble and can be absorbed from the soil by plants. You should know that phosphorus is also often a limiting factor for plant growth, so plants that have little phosphorus are stunted.

Phosphates that enter the water table and travel to the oceans can eventually be incorporated into rocks in the ocean floor. Through geologic processes, ocean mixing, and upwelling, these rocks from the seafloor may rise up so that their components once again enter the **terrestrial cycle.** Take a look at the phosphorus cycle shown below.

Humans have affected the phosphorus cycle by mining phosphorus-rich rocks in order to produce fertilizers. The fertilizers placed on fields can easily leach into the groundwater and find their way into aquatic ecosystems where they can cause eutrophication and overgrowth of algae.

The Phosphorous Cycle

We are almost done with the chemistry. But we need to discuss one more element before we move on to discuss the biosphere, and that's sulfur.

Sulfur

Sulfur is one of the components that make up proteins and vitamins, so both plants and animals need sulfur in their diets. Plants absorb sulfur when it is dissolved in water, so they can take it up through their roots when it's dissolved in groundwater. Animals obtain sulfur by consuming plants.

Most of Earth's sulfur is tied up in rocks and salts or buried deep in the ocean in oceanic sediments, but some sulfur can be found in the atmosphere. The natural ways that sulfur enters the atmosphere are through volcanic eruptions, certain bacterial functions, and the decay of once-living organisms. When sulfur enters the atmosphere through human activity, it's mainly via industrial processes that produce sulfur dioxide (SO_2) and hydrogen sulfide (H_2S) gases.

All right! It's time to move on to our discussion of the biotic components of Earth. Let's start with a review of how energy moves through ecosystems. First, let's look at a sample question.

Nitrogen from the atmosphere must be incorporated into living organisms to make proteins. Which of the following plants is a vehicle for organisms that add nitrates to the soil?

A. rice

B. lima bean

C. rose

D. Venus flytrap

Here's How To Crack It

Remember that we discussed the nitrogen-fixing bacteria associated with legumes, back in our discussion of the nitrogen cycle? Keep that one in mind and it's obvious that (B) is the correct answer.

FOOD CHAINS AND FOOD WEBS

You might recall that the nonliving components of the environment are known as the **abiotic components.** These include the atmosphere, hydrosphere, and lithosphere. Well, it's time to begin our study of the living, **biotic components** of Earth. Together, all of the living things on Earth constitute the biosphere.

All living things can be classified by the manner in which they obtain food. You might recall that plants are capable of making their own food through photosynthesis, and that some animals (for example, mice) eat plants. Some animals (for example, humans) eat both plants and animals, and some animals (for example, wolves) eat only other animals. There are actually two fancy terms that are normally used to describe these broad categories of organisms: **autotrophs** are those organisms that can produce their own organic compounds from inorganic chemicals, while **heterotrophs** obtain food energy by consuming other organisms or products created by other organisms.

Finally, as unpleasant as it might be to think about, some animals feed only on the remains of other plants and animals! All of these different types of living things fall into specific categories.

Producers

Producers are organisms that are capable of converting radiant energy or chemical energy into carbohydrates. The group of producers includes plants and algae, both of which can carry out photosynthesis. The unbalanced overall reaction of photosynthesis is shown below.

$$H_2O + CO_2 + \text{solar energy} \rightarrow CH_2O + O_2$$

While most producers make food through photosynthesis, a few autotrophs make food from inorganic chemicals in anaerobic (without oxygen) environments, through the process of chemosynthesis. Chemosynthesis is carried out by only a few specialized bacteria, called **chemotrophs,** some of which are found in hydrothermal vents deep in the ocean. This unbalanced reaction is shown below.

$$O_2 + H_2S + O_2 + \text{energy} \rightarrow CH_2O + S + H_2O$$

At this point, let's discuss a few other environmental science terms that you may be required to know for the exam. The **net primary productivity (NPP)** is the amount of energy that plants pass on to the community of herbivores in an ecosystem. It is calculated by taking the **gross primary productivity (GPP),** which is the amount of sugar that the plants produce in photosynthesis, and subtracting from it the amount of energy the plants need for growth, maintenance, repair, and reproduction. NPP is measured in kilocalories per square meter per year ($kcal/m^2/y$). In other words, the gross primary productivity of an ecosystem is the rate at which the producers are converting solar energy to chemical energy (or, in a hydrothermal ecosystem, the rate of productivity of the chemotrophs). Perhaps not surprisingly, the net productivity of an ecosystem is a limiting factor for its number of consumers. Let's talk about them next.

Consumers

Consumers are organisms that must obtain food energy from secondary sources, for example, by eating plant or animal matter. There are a number of different types of consumers:

- **Primary consumers** include the herbivores, which consume only producers (plants and algae).
- **Secondary consumers** consume primary consumers.
- **Tertiary consumers** consume secondary consumers.
- **Detritivores** derive energy from consuming nonliving organic matter such as dead animals and fallen leaves.
- **Decomposers** are bacteria or fungi that absorb nutrients from nonliving organic matter such as plant material, the wastes of living organisms, and corpses. They convert these materials into inorganic forms. Generally, fungi and bacteria are decomposers. They serve as the "garbage collectors" in our environment.

Note that one organism may occupy multiple levels of a food chain. By eating a hamburger and bun, you are both a primary consumer because you are eating tomatoes and lettuce, and a secondary consumer by eating the beef.

Let's move on and talk about how energy flows through all of these different types of organisms in ecosystems.

Food Chains

As you probably recall, energy flows in one direction through ecosystems from the Sun to producers, to primary consumers, to secondary consumers, to tertiary consumers. In an ecosystem, each of these feeding levels is referred to as a **trophic level.** With each successive trophic level, the amount of energy that's available to the next level decreases. In fact, only about 10 percent of the energy from one trophic level is passed to the next; most is lost as heat, and some is used for metabolism and anabolism. Interestingly enough, this is why food chains rarely have more than four trophic levels.

Food chains are usually represented as a series of steps, in which the bottom step is the producer and the top step is a secondary or tertiary consumer. In food chains, the arrows depict the transfer of energy through the levels, and in fancier food chains, the relative **biomass** (the dry weight of the group of organisms) of each trophic level will often be represented. Here's a simple food chain.

Food Chain

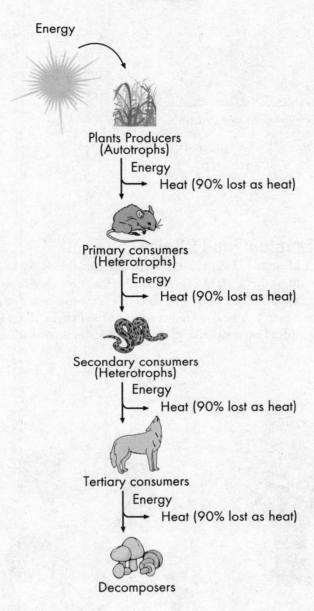

Energy

Plants Producers
(Autotrophs)

Energy
Heat (90% lost as heat)

Primary consumers
(Heterotrophs)

Energy
Heat (90% lost as heat)

Secondary consumers
(Heterotrophs)

Energy
Heat (90% lost as heat)

Tertiary consumers

Energy
Heat (90% lost as heat)

Decomposers

What we're showing here is a typical terrestrial food chain, but keep in mind that there are aquatic food chains as well, with algae and different types of fish.

One final note about food chains: at each successive level in a food chain, much energy is lost. The amount of energy (in kilocalories) available at each trophic level organized from greatest to least is an **energy pyramid.** In other words, the producers have the most energy in an ecosystem; the primary consumers have less energy than producers; the secondary consumers have less energy than the primary consumers; and the tertiary consumers will have the least energy of all.

Energy Pyramid

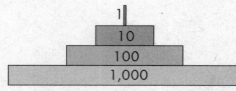

1	Tertiary consumers
10	Secondary consumers
100	Primary consumers
1,000	Producers

Hypothetical units of energy

Note: 90% of energy is lost
at each step

Food Webs—Tangled Food Chains

As you're probably already aware, food chains are an oversimplified way of demonstrating the myriad feeding relationships that exist in ecosystems. Because there are so many different types of species of plants and animals in ecosystems, their relationships in real-world ecosystems are much more complicated than can be depicted in a single food chain. Therefore, we use a **food web** in order to represent feeding relationships in ecosystems more realistically.

Food Web

Again, this is a typical terrestrial food web, but keep in mind that very complicated aquatic food webs exist as well! Let's take a step back for a minute and discuss the setting for food chains and food webs—ecosystems. But first, let's try a question.

———————○———————

Which of the following organisms serve as decomposers in the ecosystem?

A.   bacteria and viruses

B.   fungi and bacteria

C.   viruses and protists

D.   fungi and viruses

Here's How To Crack It

Both fungi and bacteria serve as decomposers, so (B) is correct. Fungi and bacteria break down organic matter. Viruses invade other organisms, but they're not decomposers. Protists are unicellular organisms, such as paramecium and euglena. They're not decomposers either.

———————○———————

THE WORLD'S ECOSYSTEMS

Because different geographic areas on Earth differ so much in their abiotic and biotic components, we can easily place them in broad categories. The two largest categories are broken down in this way: ecosystems that are based on land are called **biomes,** while those in aqueous environments are known as **aquatic life zones.** Aquatic ecosystems are categorized primarily by the salinity of their water—freshwater and saltwater ecosystems fall into separate categories. Land environments are separated into biomes based on their climate.

Although it might seem that each biome listed in the following table is very distinct, in reality, biomes blend into each other; they do not have distinct boundaries. The transitional area where two ecosystems meet actually has a name—these areas are called **ecotones.** Another important term that you should be familiar with for the exam is **ecozones:** ecozones (also called **ecoregions**) are smaller regions within ecosystems that share similar physical features.

Information about the Earth's Biomes

Biome	Annual Rainfall, Soil Type	Major Vegetation	World Location
Deciduous forest (temperate and tropical)	75–250 cm, rich soil with high organic content	Hardwood trees	North America, Europe, Australia, and Eastern Asia
Tropical rainforest	200–400 cm, poor quality soil	Tall trees with few lower limbs, vines, epiphytes, plants adapted to low light intensity	South America, West Africa, and Southeast Asia
Grasslands	10–60 cm, rich soil	Sod-forming grasses	North American plains and prairies; Russian steppes; South African velds; Argentinean pampas
Coniferous forest (Taiga)	20–60 cm (mostly in summer), acidic soil due to vegetation	Coniferous trees	Northern North America, northern Eurasia
Tundra	Less than 25 cm, permafrost soil	Herbaceous plants	The northern latitudes of North America, Europe, and Russia
Chaparral (scrub forest)	50–75 cm (mostly in winter), shallow and infertile soil	Small trees with large hard leaves, spiny shrubs	Western North America, the Mediterranean region
Deserts (cold and hot)	Less than 25 cm (sandy soil with a coarse texture)	Cactus, other low-water adapted plants	30 degrees north and south of the equator

Not surprisingly, each biome has specific characteristics that determine the types of organisms that are capable of living in it. Some of these characteristics are the type and availability of nutrients, the ecosystems' temperature, the availability of water, and the amount of sunlight the region receives. One important law to be familiar with for this test is the **Law of Tolerance**. The Law of Tolerance describes the degree to which living organisms are capable of tolerating changes in their environment. Living organisms exhibit a range of tolerance, and even individuals within a population tolerate changes to their environment differently: this concept is the basis for natural selection, which drives evolution. We'll cover that thoroughly in Chapter 12.

Another important law for you to know is the **Law of the Minimum,** which states that living organisms will continue to live, consuming available materials until the supply of these materials is exhausted.

Environmental **accommodation** and **adaptation** are important phenomena that you should be familiar with. Accommodation is the process by which mental structures and behaviors are modified to adapt to new experiences. For example, dogs were wild at one time and have been domesticated. They are capable of learning specific behaviors and generalizing that knowledge. A dog doesn't instinctively know not to urinate or defecate indoors, but can be taught not to do so. If you trained your dog not to urinate or defecate in your house, and then took him to a friend's home, his modified behavior would carry over to that environment, and he knows that he may not urinate or defecate there, either. He has made a generalization about his environment and can accommodate his surroundings.

An adaptation is a change that an organism must make for survival. It enables the organism (plant or animal) to adjust to different conditions within the environment. Structural adaptation happens over a long period of time, unlike accommodation. Examples of adaptation include behavior adaptation, hibernation, teeth, body covering, and many more. The polar bear is a perfect example of adaptation. Polar bears are closely related to the brown bear, but have adapted for cold temperatures; for moving across snow, ice, and open water; and for retaining heat.

Ecosystem Diversity

The term **biodiversity** is used to describe the number and variety of organisms found within a specified geographic region, or ecosystem. It also refers to the variability among living organisms, including the variability within and between species and within and between ecosystems.

Therefore, when we talk about the biodiversity of an area, we must specifically state the aspect of biodiversity that we're describing, or else the term is too vague to be comprehensible. In general, however, biodiversity in an ecosystem is a good thing. The more biodiversity in a certain species within an ecosystem, the larger and more diverse the species' gene pool is, and the greater its chance of adaptation, and thus survival.

SHARE AND SHARE ALIKE?

When people talk about managing common property resources such as air, water, and land, a paper published in *Science* magazine by Garret Hardin in 1958, called "The Tragedy of the Commons," often comes to mind. In this paper, Hardin referenced a parable from the 1880s in which a piece of open land, a commons, was to be used collectively by the townspeople for grazing their cattle. Each townsperson who used the land continued to add one cow or ox at a time until the commons was overgrazed. Hardin quite eloquently says, "Each man is locked into a system that compels him to increase his herd without limit—in a world that is limited.

Ruin is the destination toward which all men rush, each pursuing his own best interest in a society that believes in the freedom of the commons. Freedom in a commons brings ruin to all."

This parable serves as a foundation for modern conservation. **Conservation** is the management or regulation of a resource so that its use does not exceed the capacity of the resource to regenerate itself. This is different from **preservation,** which is the maintenance of a species or ecosystem in order to ensure its perpetuation, with no concern as to its potential monetary value.

Next, we'll show how human economics often influences how we interact with Earth's resources. Ecosystems (both biotic and abiotic) are often referred to as **natural resources.** When we describe something as a *resource*, we are essentially putting an economic value on it; therefore, natural resources are described in terms of their value as **ecosystem capital.**

Some Terms Used to Describe Resources

Let's start by discussing the two main types of resources:

- **Renewable resources** such as plants and animals, can be regenerated quickly.
- **Nonrenewable resources** such as minerals, fossil fuels, and soil, are typically formed by very slow geologic processes, so we consider them incapable of being regenerated within the realm of human existence.

There are a couple more terms you should know before we dive into our review of the major resources available to humans on Earth. The **consumption** of natural resources refers to the day-to-day use of environmental resources such as food, clothing, and housing. On the other hand, **production** refers to the use of environmental resources for profit. An example of this might be a fisherman who sells his fish in a market. Got those terms? Let's move on.

AGRICULTURE

How do resources relate to your dinner? Well, 77 percent of the world's food comes from croplands, 16 percent comes from grazing lands, and 7 percent of the world's food comes from ocean resources. Despite the importance of our crops, and although the population of the United States has increased significantly, fewer people than ever in the history of the United States now farm the land. Why is this? The short answer is that it has a lot to do with increasing urbanization and industrialization. Now that machines are readily available to work the land and harvest crops, farms have become more like factories—currently only 15 percent of the entire workforce of the United States produces the food to feed the entire country—and for exporting. Farms in the United States today are quite a bit larger than farms of the past; the average farm is 400 acres, while in the early 20th century the average farm size was about 100 acres.

The use of machinery in farming has allowed a farmer to work more land and do so more efficiently; however, one of the drawbacks of the machinery is the amount of fossil fuel needed to power it. As the cost of fuel rises, the cost of food will also rise.

This rise in agricultural productivity can be tied to the new pesticides and fertilizers, expanded irrigation, and the development of new high-yield seed types. However, it has also resulted in a significant decrease in the genetic variability of crop plants, and led to huge problems in erosion.

Traditional Agriculture and the Green Revolution

Throughout most of history, agriculture all over the world was such that each family grew crops for themselves, and families primarily relied on animal and human labor to plant and harvest crops. This process is called **traditional subsistence agriculture,** and it provides enough food for one family's survival. Traditional subsistence agriculture is still practiced in developing nations, and is currently practiced by about 42 percent of the world's population.

Another component of traditional agriculture that's still practiced in many developing countries today is a method called **slash and burn;** this practice actually dates back to early man. In slash and burn, an area of vegetation is cut down and burned before being planted with crops. Then because soils in these developing countries are generally poor, the farmer must leave the area after a relatively short time and find another location to clear. This practice severely reduces the amount of available forest; it is a significant contributor to deforestation.

The **Green Revolution** is generally thought of as the time after the Industrial Revolution when farming became mechanized and crop yields in industrialized nations boomed. Don't confuse the Green Revolution, which is about farming, with the Green Movement, which is about conservation.

Norman Borlaug is considered by many to be the founder of the Green Revolution. He was born in 1914 on a farm in Iowa, and throughout his career, Borlaug collaborated with scientists worldwide on problems of wheat improvement. He worked with India and Pakistan, attempting to find ways to adapt the newly created strains of wheat to these lands. His work has allowed developed and developing countries to produce higher yields of crops on less land, which is quite advantageous; the use of less land saves forests, grasslands, mountainsides, and wetlands from being degraded and also preserves their biodiversity. Borlaug received the Nobel Peace prize in 1970 for his work with high-yield crops.

Fertilizers and Pesticides

One factor that contributed to the Green Revolution was an increase in the use of fertilizers and pesticides. Interestingly, when the non-native settlers (the first white settlers) planted their first corn crops, certain tribes of Native Americans taught them to plant a fish along with the corn seed; the fish acted as a natural fertilizer for the crops. As you can see, manures and other organic materials have been used as fertilizers by farmers for many years. However, the development of inorganic (chemical) fertilizers brought about the huge increases in farm production seen during the Green Revolution. It's estimated that if chemical fertilizers were suddenly no longer used, then the total output of food in the world would drop about 40 percent!

Of course, there are downsides to the widespread use of chemical fertilizers, and these include the following: the reduction of organic matter and oxygen in soil; the fact that these fertilizers require large amounts of energy to produce, transport, and supply; and the fact that once they are washed into watersheds, they are dangerous pollutants.

Similarly, the increased use of pesticides in the Green Revolution has significantly reduced the number of crops lost to insects, fungi, and other pests, but these chemicals have also had an effect on ecosystems in and surrounding farms. It's estimated that the average insect pesticide will be useful for only 5–10 years before its target insect evolves to become immune to its effects; therefore, new pesticides must constantly be developed. However, even with this constant development, crop loss due to pests has not decreased since 1970, although the use of pesticides has tripled!

Because the use of pesticides is so prevalent in the United States, Congress passed the **Federal Insecticide, Fungicide, and Rodenticide Act (FIFRA)** in 1947 and amended it in 1972. This law requires the EPA to approve the use of all pesticides in the United States.

Irrigation

Another major contributor to the increased crop yields seen in the Green Revolution was advanced irrigation techniques, which allowed crops to be planted in areas that normally would not have enough precipitation to sustain them. However, repeated irrigation can cause serious problems, including a significant buildup of salts on the soil's surface that make the land unusable for crops. To combat this **salinization** of the land, farmers have begun flooding fields with massive amounts of water in order to move the salt deeper into the soil. The drawback to this, however, is that the large amounts of water can waterlog plant roots, which will kill the crops. This process also causes the water table of the region to rise.

Genetically Engineered Plants

The third and last significant contributor to the Green Revolution was the introduction of genetically engineered plants. When genetically engineered plants were first introduced to the public, they were met with hostility and fear. This is in part because many people feared the eventual creation of hybrid humans and other genetic abominations.

Arguably, one of the most important developments in the genetic modification of plants has been the creation of golden rice, which contains vitamin A and iron. The introduction of this rice addresses two of the serious health problems that are seen in developing nations: vitamin A deficiency, which can result in blindness and other serious health problems; and iron deficiency, which leads to anemia. This is just one example of the potentially multitudinous uses of genetic engineering in solving global hunger problems!

So far, the only empirical problem that has arisen as a result of the introduction of genetically engineered plants has been that pollen from these plants can spread, and hybrids between genetically engineered and non-genetically engineered plants can arise. This is a concern for some, since it may result in a loss of certain indigenous plant strains, such as the blue corn of Mexico.

Genetically engineered plants enable us to develop foods with higher nutritional value, and they also have the potential to enable us to decrease the amount of pesticides we use. For example, one particular strain of cotton has been genetically modified in such a way that it produces a pesticide in its leaves—but only at times when the insect population is a problem. Some other potential benefits of genetically engineered plants include producing their own nitrogen (which is often hard for plants to derive from the soil) or tolerating higher levels of salt in the soil. As you know, this latter development would allow plants to grow in areas where over-irrigation previously rendered the soil unusable.

Monotonous Monoculture

Believe it or not, three grains provide more than half of the total calories that are consumed worldwide! These three crops are rice, wheat, and corn, and the phenomenal increase in the yield of these crops was a result of genetic engineering. Genetic engineers discovered a way to cause plants to divert more of their photosynthetic products (called **photosynthate**) to becoming grain biomass rather than plant body biomass.

It's estimated that, of the roughly 30,000 plant species that could possibly be used for food, only 10,000 have been used historically, with any regularity. Today 90 percent of the caloric intake worldwide is supplied by just 14 plant species and 8 terrestrial animal species! In other words, today's agriculture represents a major reduction in agricultural biodiversity.

On a smaller scale, much of the farming that occurs today is characterized by **monoculture.** In monoculture, just one type of plant is planted in a large area. As we discussed earlier, this has proved to be an unwise practice for numerous reasons. **Plantation farming,** which is practiced mainly in tropical developing nations, is a type of industrialized agriculture in which a monoculture cash crop, such as bananas, coffee, or vegetables, is grown and then exported to developed nations.

Soil Degradation

Great Plains droughts in the 1930s were the major causative factors that created the Dust Bowl, but also, farming practices used at that time contributed to the destruction of the land.

In an effort to address the Dust Bowl and other agricultural problems, the United States Soil and Conservation Service (today it's called the National Resources Conservation Service) was established, and it passed the Soil Conservation Act in 1935. Conservation districts were set up by the Service and these franchises provided education to farmers.

Today, farmers can protect soil from degradation in numerous ways. The practice of **contour plowing,** in which rows of crops are plowed across the hillside, prevents the erosion that can occur when rows are cut up and down on a slope. **Terracing** also aids in preventing soil erosion on steep slopes. Terraces are flat platforms that are cut into the hillside to provide a level planting surface; this reduces the soil runoff from the slope. Additionally, **no-till methods** are quite beneficial; in no-till agriculture, farmers plant seeds without using a plow to turn the soil. Soil loses most of its carbon content during plowing, which releases carbon dioxide gas into the atmosphere.

Finally, **crop rotation** can provide soils with nutrients when legumes are part of the cycle of crops in an area. An alternate to crop rotation is **intercropping** (also called **strip cropping**), which is the practice of planting bands of different crops across a hillside. This type of planting can also prevent some erosion by creating an extensive network of roots. As you might be aware, plant roots hold the soil in place and reduce or prevent soil erosion.

The Livestock Business

Perhaps not surprisingly, the introduction of all these new agricultural techniques has significantly affected the livestock business. As long as the grazing area is sufficient for the number of animals, livestock grazing is a sustainable practice. If, however, grass is consumed by animals at a faster rate than it can re-grow, land is considered **overgrazed.** Overgrazing is harmful to the soil because it leads to erosion and soil compaction. One solution to the problem of overgrazing is similar to crop rotation—animals can be rotated from site to site. Another solution involves the overall control of herd numbers.

Various tracts of public lands are available for use as rangeland, and cooperation between government agents, environmentalists, and ranchers can help avoid problems of overgrazing on these lands.

Another problem that arises from the large number of grazing animals worldwide is the large amount of animal waste produced. Instead of this waste being used as a natural fertilizer, it has instead become the most widespread source of water pollution in the United States. Grazing animals also consume 70 percent of the total grain crop consumed in the United States, making them expensive food stuff.

The law that describes the degree to which living organisms are capable of tolerating changes in the environment is called the:

A.   Law of Adaptation.

B.   Law of Accommodation.

C.   Law of Tolerance.

D.   Law of Ecosystem.

Here's How To Crack It
This question is a great example of how, sometimes, the answer is right under your nose. Read the question carefully and you will see that (C), Law of Tolerance (the correct answer), is staring you in the face. Adaptation and accommodation are certainly important parts of the study of ecology, but they are not the correct answers here.

ECONOMICS AND RESOURCE UTILIZATION

The study of how people use limited resources to satisfy their wants and needs is called **economics.** As you can imagine, some of those needs are tangible (food and shelter are two examples) while others are intangible (the beauty of a forest and clean air are two examples). A resource can have both tangible and intangible properties.

A forest has value for supplying jobs and wood (tangible) as well as for its beauty and ability to remove CO_2 from the air (intangible). When private citizens, governments, and corporations make a decision on how to use a forest, they must weigh the benefits (more jobs and lumber) against the cost of cutting down the trees (less recreation space, the loss of biodiversity, and loss of CO_2 removal). This process is called **cost-benefit analysis.** It may be easy to assign a monetary value to the tangible properties (like the amount of lumber in the forest), but how do you assign a monetary value to the intangible properties (like the beauty of a forest)? While cost-benefit analysis helps make decisions on how to use resources, you can see that the process is very difficult, and it can lead to different estimates by different groups.

Economists also want to figure out the cost of each step in a process. From our forest example, what is the cost to the economy of adding one more acre to the forest; or what is the benefit to us if we add one more acre to the forest? The additional costs are termed **marginal costs,** and the added benefits are called **marginal benefits.** It is important to remember that resources are not free and unlimited. Some resources must be expended in order for us to use them. While we may benefit from more acres to hike in, the lumber company will suffer from not having as many trees to cut. In other words, marginal benefits and costs help us understand tradeoffs. By preserving a forest, we trade more hiking space with less profit for local economies.

KEY TERMS

biogeochemical cycles
reservoir
exchange pool
residency time
Law of Conservation of Matter
water cycle
precipitation
groundwater
evaporation
transpiration
carbon cycle
respiration
photosynthesis
fossil fuels
combusted
nitrogen fixation
nitrification
assimilation
ammonification
dentrification
phosphorus cycle
terrestrial cycle
sulfur
abiotic components
biotic components
autotrophs
heterotrophs
producers
chemotrophs
net primary productivity (NPP)
gross primary productivity (GPP)
consumers
primary consumers
secondary consumers
tertiary consumers
detritivores
decomposers
trophic level
food chains
biomass

energy pyramid
food web
biomes
aquatic life zones
ecotones
ecozones (ecoregions)
Law of Tolerance
Law of the Minimum
accommodation
adaptation
biodiversity
conservation
preservation
natural resources
ecosystem capital
renewable resources
nonrenewable resources
consumption
production
traditional subsistence agriculture
slash and burn
Green Revolution
Norman Borlaug
Federal Insecticide, Fungicide, and
    Rodenticide Act (FIFRA)
salinization
photosynthate
monoculture
plantation farming
contour plowing
terracing
no-till methods
crop rotation
intercropping (strip cropping)
overgrazed
economics
cost-benefit analysis
marginal costs
marginal benefits

Chapter 11 Drill

Answers and explanations can be found in the final section of this book, beginning on page 617.

1. Which organisms in the food chain are producers?

    A.   birds

    B.   insects

    C.   grass

    D.   mice

2. Which of the following species are considered autotrophs?

    I.   mice

    II.   fungi

    III. plants

    A.   I

    B.   I and III

    C.   II and III

    D.   III

3. Organisms use different resources in the same habitat, and in this way avoid competition. This is referred to as:

    A.   the Law of Tolerance.

    B.   hunting and gathering.

    C.   predator-prey relationship.

    D.   resource partitioning.

4. Humans, being living things, are classified as which of the following?

    A.   chemoautotrophs

    B.   photoautotrophs

    C.   chemoheterotrophs

    D.   photoheterotrophs

5. In a very polluted river, it costs $3 per kilogram to remove the first 80 percent of the pollution. It costs $25 per kilogram to remove the last 20 percent of the pollutant. This phenomenon is correctly referred to as:

    A.   cost-benefit analysis.

    B.   external costs.

    C.   marginal costs.

    D.   marginal benefit.

Summary

o   All living things require four basic things: food, water, air, and space.

o   Nutrients move through the environment in biogeochemical cycles including the water cycle, the carbon cycle, the nitrogen cycle, and the phosphorous cycle.

o   Energy flows in one direction through the ecosystem: from the Sun to producers to primary consumers to secondary consumers to tertiary consumers to decomposers, in a system called the food chain.

o   Ecosystems based on land are called biomes; those based in aqueous environments are aquatic life zones.

o   Biodiversity is the variety of organisms in a specified region or ecosystem.

o   Renewable resources and nonrenewable resources are the two main types of resources available.

o   Conservation is the regulation of a resource so that its use doesn't exceed the capacity to regenerate itself. Preservation is the regulation of a resource to ensure its perpetuation.

o   Norman Borlaug is considered by many to be the founder of the Green Revolution.

o   Economics is the study of how people use limited resources.

Chapter 12
Life Cycle, Reproduction, and Evolution

LIFE CYCLE

How does a tiny, single-celled egg develop into a complex, multicellular organism? By dividing, of course. The cell will change shape and organization many times by going through a succession of stages. This process is called **morphogenesis.** In order for the human sperm to fertilize an egg it must dissolve the **corona radiata,** a dense covering of follicle cells that surrounds the egg. Then the sperm must penetrate the **zona pellucida,** the zone below the corona radiata.

When an egg is fertilized by a sperm, it forms a **diploid cell** called a **zygote.**

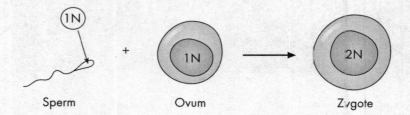

Sperm   +   Ovum   →   Zygote

Fertilization triggers the zygote to go through a series of rapid cell divisions called **cleavage.** What's interesting at this stage is that the embryo doesn't grow. The cells just keep dividing to form a solid ball called a **morula.**

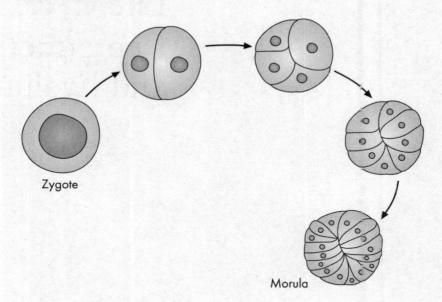

Zygote

Morula

One cell becomes two cells, two cells become four cells, and so on.

Blastula

The next stage is called **blastula.** As the cells continue to divide, they press against each other and produce a fluid-filled cavity called a **blastocoel.**

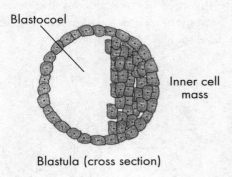

Blastula (cross section)

Gastrula

During **gastrulation,** the zygote begins to change its shape. Cells now migrate into the blastocoel and differentiate to form three germ layers: the **ectoderm, mesoderm,** and **endoderm.**

- The outer layer becomes the ectoderm.
- The middle layer becomes the mesoderm.
- The inner layer becomes the endoderm.

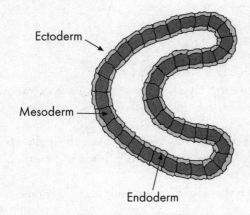

Gastrula (cross section)

Each germ layer gives rise to various organs and systems in the body. Here's a list of the organs that develop from each germ layer.

- The ectoderm produces the **epidermis** (the skin), the eyes, and the nervous system.
- The endoderm produces the inner linings of the digestive tract and respiratory tract, as well as accessory organs such as the pancreas, gall bladder, and liver. These are called "accessory" organs because they are offshoots of the digestive tract, as opposed to the channels of the tract itself.
- The mesoderm gives rise to everything else. This includes bones and muscles as well as the excretory, circulatory, and reproductive systems.

Neurulation and Organogenesis

The **neurula** stage begins with the formation of two structures: the **notochord,** a rod-shaped structure running beneath the nerve cord, and the **neural tube** cells, which develop into the central nervous system. During this time organogenesis is also taking place. Organogenesis, just as the name implies, is the formation of all of the organs and structures. By the end of this stage, we're well on our way to developing a nervous system.

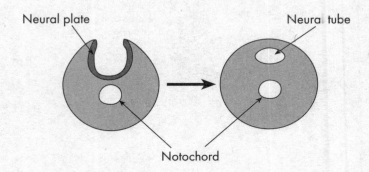

The *order* of the stages and the various events is extremely important. Think of it this way: when a couple are trying to have a baby and they find out they're pregnant, then it Must Be Good News (M = morula, B = blastula, G = gastrula, N = neurula). For our purposes, think of the order of embryological development in this way:

Zygote → Cleavage → Morula → Blastula → Gastrula → Neurula → Organogenesis

What About Chicken Embryos?

In addition to the primary germ layers, some animals have **extraembryonic membranes.** An average developing chicken, for example, possesses these membranes.

There are basically four extraembryonic membranes: the **yolk sac, amnion, chorion,** and **allantois.** These extra membranes are common in birds and reptiles.

You should be familiar with these membranes and their functions:

FUNCTIONS OF EXTRAEMBRYONIC MEMBRANES	
Extraembryonic membrane	**Function**
Yolk sac	Provides food for the embryo
Amnion	Forms a fluid-filled sac that protects the embryo
Allantois	Is involved in gas exchange; stores uric acid
Chorion	Surrounds all the other extraembryonic membranes

Fetal Embryo

The fetal embryo also has extraembryonic membranes during development: the amnion, chorion, allantois, and yolk sac. The **placenta** and the **umbilical cord** are outgrowths of these membranes. The placenta is the organ that provides the fetus with nutrients and oxygen and gets rid of the fetus's wastes. The placenta develops from both the chorion and the uterine tissue of the mother. The umbilical cord is the organ that connects the embryo to the placenta.

Development of an Embryo

During embryonic development, some tissues determine the fate of other tissues in a process called **induction.** Certain cells, called **organizers,** release a chemical substance (a **morphogen**) that moves from one tissue to the target tissue. It is now known that development involves many episodes of embryonic induction.

Homeotic genes control the development of the embryo. Some homeotic genes, called homeobox genes, consist of homeoboxes (short, nearly identical DNA sequences) that encode proteins that bind to DNA; these proteins tell cells in various segments of the developing embryo what type of structures to make. Interestingly, homeobox genes are shared by almost all eukaryotic species. Hox genes, which are a subset of homeobox genes, specify the position of body parts in the developing embryo. Mutations in Hox genes result in the conversion of one body part into another. For example, in *Drosophila,* a specific Hox mutation results in a leg developing where an antenna would normally be.

The cytoplasm can also have an influence on embryonic development. For example, chicken and frog embryos contain more yolk in one pole (the vegetal pole) versus the other pole (the animal pole). This causes cells within the animal pole to divide more, and thus to be smaller than those of the vegetal pole. Because of the distribution of the yolk, cleavage of the egg does not produce eggs that develop normally. If the egg is divided into an animal and vegetal pole, development does not proceed normally.

Which of the following processes produces embryonic germ layers?

A. gastrulation

B. cleavage

C. blastulation

D. organogenesis

Here's How to Crack It

The process that produces embryonic germ layers is gastrulation. Choice (B), cleavage, is the mitotic division of the zygote after fertilization. Choice (C), blastulation, is the hollow ball of cells produced by cleavage of a fertilized ovum. Choice (D), organogenesis, is the process by which organs develop. Therefore, (A) is the correct answer.

REPRODUCTION

Reproduction can be either **sexual** or **asexual.** You're probably most familiar with sexual reproduction, as it is how humans procreate. But asexual reproduction is an important piece in the puzzle, also.

Asexual Reproduction

Asexual reproduction is reproduction that does not involve meiosis or fertilization. Only one parent is involved in asexual reproduction, and the technical definition refers to reproduction without the fusion of gametes. This form of reproduction is the primary one used for single-celled organisms such as the archaea, bacteria, and protists, as well as many plants and fungi. A few types of asexual reproduction include **budding** (when cells split and result in a "mother" and "daughter" cell, with buds eventually breaking off from the parent, like hydra); **mitotic sporogenesis** (the spreading of spores by water or air, which is the way that some fungi and algae reproduce); and **binary fission** (used by all prokaryotes, resulting in the reproduction of a living prokaryotic cell by division into two parts each of which has the potential to grow to the size of the original cell).

Sexual Reproduction

Sexual reproduction in animals involves the production of eggs and sperm.

Since the ovaries release hormones, they are considered endocrine glands. The **ovaries** have two main responsibilities:

- They manufacture **ova.**
- They secrete **estrogen** and **progesterone,** sex hormones that are found in females.

The hormones secreted by the ovaries are involved in the menstrual cycle.

The Menstrual Cycle

The menstrual cycle on average is 28 days and affects two organs: the ovaries and the uterus. We can subdivide the menstrual cycle into what's going on in the ovaries and what's going on in the uterus.

So, lets start with the ovaries.

The Ovarian Cycle

The ovarian cycle is the 28 days of the menstrual cycle specifically looking at events in the ovary. We can subdivide the ovarian cycle into three phases.

1. Follicular Phase (Days 1–13)   The follicular phase takes place on days 1–13 of the menstrual cycle. Day 1 is always the first day of menstruation and so that is the first day of the cycle. During the follicular phase, the anterior pituitary secretes two hormones: **follicle-stimulating hormone (FSH)** and **luteinizing hormone (LH).** FSH stimulates several follicles in the ovaries to grow. A follicle is nothing more than an oocyte (egg or ovum) and all of its surrounding cells. Eventually, only one of these follicles gains the lead and dominates the others, which soon stop growing. The one growing follicle now takes command. The production of the follicle is regulated by follicle stimulating hormone. In response to FSH, the growing follicle produces estrogen. This increase in estrogen causes a sudden surge in LH. This release of LH is known as the LH surge. The LH surge triggers ovulation—the release of the oocyte from the follicle out of the ovary.

2. Ovulation (Day 14)   Ovulation takes place on day 14 of the cycle. The oocyte and some of the surrounding cells get kicked out of the follicle. This is triggered by the **LH surge.** The LH surge makes the follicle burst and release the oocyte. The oocyte then begins its journey into the **fallopian tube,** which is also known as the uterine tube or oviduct. Once the oocyte has been released, the oocyte is ready to move on to the next phase.

3. Luteal Phase (Days 15–28)   The luteal phase takes place on days 15–28 of the cycle. As a result of ovulation, the oocyte has moved into the fallopian tube and the follicle has been ruptured and left behind in the ovary. The ruptured follicle (now a fluid-filled sac) continues to function in the menstrual cycle. All of the stuff that stayed behind in the ovary now becomes a new structure called the **corpus luteum.** This is still somewhat under control of the LH surge. The LH surge triggers ovulation and causes the conversion of what's left into the corpus luteum. But a surge by definition is a short thing—so it gets this guy started, but in the absence of LH, the corpus luteum cannot maintain itself. So right away, the day after it formed, it starts degenerating. It has about a two-week life span, which is why we have a two week luteal period. The corpus luteum continues to secrete estrogen. In addition, it now starts producing the other major hormone involved in female reproduction, progesterone.

The Uterine Cycle

So during this same 28 day period, while things are happening in the ovaries, things are also happening in the uterus.

1. Menstruation (Days 1–5)   During these first five days, estrogen and progesterone levels are pretty low. In the absence of estrogen and progesterone, the **endometrium (uterine walls)** starts breaking down and is shed off. This "sloughing off," or bleeding, is known as **menstruation.**

2. Proliferative Phase (Days 6–14)   We see a rise in estrogen levels during this phase. As we discussed in the ovarian cycle, estrogen is being released from the growing follicle. An increase in estrogen levels promotes the proliferation of the endometrium. During this phase, the endometrium rebuilds itself since it was shed off during menstruation.

3. Secretory Phase (Days 15–28)   During the last half of the cycle, we are going to maintain and enhance the endometrium. Progesterone is responsible for readying the body for pregnancy. It does this by promoting the growth of glands and blood vessels in the endometrium. Without progesterone, a fertilized ovum cannot latch onto the uterus and develop into an embryo. After about 13–15 days, if fertilization and implantation have not occurred, the corpus luteum shuts down. Once it has stopped producing estrogen and progesterone, we go back to the beginning of the menstrual cycle yet again.

A great way to remember the order of the phases for both of the ovarian and uterine cycle is the nmemonic FOL(D) M(A)PS (disregard the D and A). The ovarian cycle: follicular, ovulation, and luteal. The uterine cycle: menstruation, proliferative, and secretory.

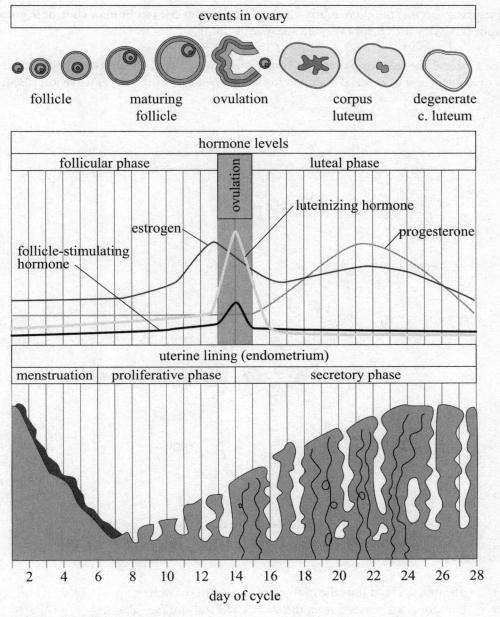

events in ovary

follicle | maturing follicle | ovulation | corpus luteum | degenerate c. luteum

hormone levels

follicular phase | ovulation | luteal phase

luteinizing hormone

estrogen

progesterone

follicle-stimulating hormone

uterine lining (endometrium)

menstruation | proliferative phase | secretory phase

2 4 6 8 10 12 14 16 18 20 22 24 26 28

day of cycle

Let's recap some of the major steps:

- In the follicular phase, the pituitary releases FSH, causing the follicle to grow.
- The follicle releases estrogen, which helps the endometrium to grow.
- Estrogen causes the pituitary to release LH, resulting in a luteal surge.
- This excess LH causes the follicle to burst, releasing the ovum during ovulation.
- The shed follicle becomes the corpus luteum, which produces progesterone.
- Progesterone enhances the endometrium, causing it to thicken with glands and blood vessels.
- If fertilization does not occur after about two weeks, the corpus luteum dies, leading to menstruation—the sloughing off of uterine tissue.

If pregnancy occurs, the extraembryonic tissue of the fetus releases **human chorionic gonado-tropin (HCG)**, which helps maintain the uterine lining.

Take a look at the following diagram. Familiarize yourself with the parts of the female reproductive system and pay special attention to the different sites of the stages we've just discussed.

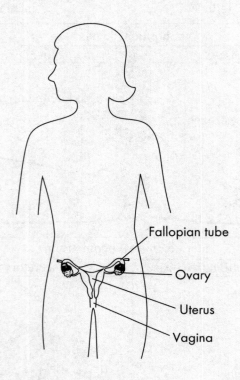

Female Reproductive System

Remember:

- The follicles (and thus the ova) are contained in the ovaries.
- Hormones are released from the ovaries and the pituitary gland.
- Fertilization occurs in the fallopian tube.
- The fertilized ovum implants itself in the uterus.

The Male Reproductive System

Now let's discuss the hormones in the male reproductive system. **Testosterone,** along with the cortical sex hormones, is responsible for the development of the sex organs and secondary sex characteristics. In addition to the deepening of the voice, these characteristics include body hair, muscle growth, and facial hair, all of which indicate the onset of **puberty.** Testosterone also has another function. It stimulates the testes, the male reproductive organs, to manufacture **sperm cells.** Testosterone does this by causing cells in the testes to start undergoing meiosis.

Take a look at the male reproductive system.

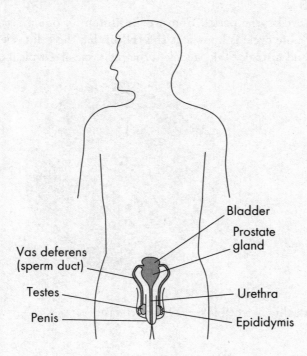

Male Reproductive System

Sperm and male hormones are produced in the testes. The main tissues of the testes, called the **seminiferous tubules,** are where spermatogonia undergo meiosis. The **interstitial cells,** which are supporting tissue, produce testosterone and other androgens. The spermatids then mature in the **epididymis.** Sperms then travel through the **vas deferens** and pick up fluids from the **seminal vesicles** (which provide them with fructose for energy) and the **prostate gland** (which provides an alkaline fluid that neutralizes the vagina's acidic fluids). Semen is transported to the vagina by the penis.

Unlike the female reproductive system, the male reproductive system continues to secrete hormones throughout the life of the male. FSH targets the seminiferous tubules of the testes, where it stimulates sperm production. LH stimulates interstitial cells to produce testosterone.

Cell Division

Every second, thousands of cells are dying throughout our bodies. Fortunately, the body replaces them at an amazing rate. In fact, epidermal, or skin, cells die off and are replaced so quickly that the average 18-year-old grows an entirely new skin every few weeks. The body keeps up this unbelievable rate thanks to the mechanisms of **cell division.**

Cell division is only a small part of the life cycle of a cell. Most of the time, cells are busy carrying out their regular activities. Let's now look at how cells pass their genetic material to their offspring.

The Cell Cycle

Every cell has a life cycle—the period from the beginning of one division to the beginning of the next. The cell's life cycle is known as the **cell cycle.** The cell cycle is divided into two periods: **interphase** and **mitosis.** Take a look at the cell cycle of a typical cell:

Want More?
For in-depth coverage of these topics, check out *ASAP Biology* or *Cracking the AP Biology Exam* from The Princeton Review.

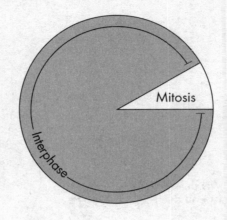

Notice that most of the life of a cell is spent in interphase.

Interphase: The Growing Phase

Interphase is the time span from one cell division to another. We call this stage interphase (*inter-* means between) because the cell has not yet started to divide. Although biologists sometimes refer to interphase as the "resting stage," the cell is definitely not inactive. During this phase, the cell carries out its regular activities. All the proteins and enzymes it needs to grow are produced during interphase.

Interphase can be divided into three stages: **G1, G2,** and **S phase.**

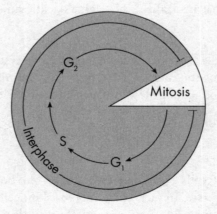

The most important phase is the S phase. That's when the cell replicates its genetic material. The first thing a cell has to do before undergoing mitosis is to duplicate all of its chromosomes, which contain the organism's DNA "blueprint." During interphase, every single chromosome in the nucleus is duplicated.

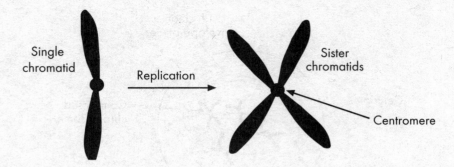

Single chromatid

Replication

Sister chromatids

Centromere

You'll notice that the original chromosome and its duplicate are still linked, like Siamese twins. These identical chromosomes are now called **sister chromatids** (each individual structure is called a chromatid). The chromatids are held together by a structure called the **centromere.** Although the chromosomes have been duplicated, they are still considered a single unit. Once duplication has been completed, we're ready for the big breakup: mitosis.

We've already said that replication occurs during the S phase of interphase, so what happens during G1 and G2? During these stages, the cell produces proteins and enzymes. For example, during G1, the cell produces all of the enzymes required for DNA replication. By the way, "G" stands for "gap," but we can also associate it with "growth."

Let's recap:

- The cell cycle consists of two periods: interphase and mitosis.
- During the S phase of interphase, the chromosomes replicate.
- Growth and preparation for mitosis occur during the G1 and G2 stages of interphase.

Mitosis: The Dance of the Chromosomes

Once the chromosomes have replicated, the cell is ready to begin mitosis. Mitosis is the period during which the cell divides. Mitosis consists of a sequence of four stages: **prophase, metaphase, anaphase,** and **telophase.**

Stage 1: Prophase.   One of the first signs of prophase is the disappearance of the nucleolus. In prophase, the chromosomes condense, forming coils upon coils, and become visible. (During interphase, the chromosomes are not visible. Rather, the genetic material is scattered throughout the nucleus and is called **chromatin.** It is only during prophase that we can properly speak about the chromosomes.)

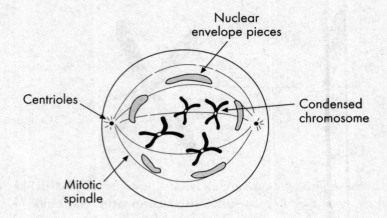

Nuclear envelope pieces

Centrioles

Condensed chromosome

Mitotic spindle

Now the cell has plenty of room to "sort out" the chromosomes. Remember centrioles? During prophase, these cylindrical bodies found within microtubule organizing centers (MTOCs) start to move away from each other, toward opposite ends of the cell. The centrioles will spin out a system of microtubules known as the **spindle fibers.** These spindle fibers will attach to a structure on each chromatid called a **kinetochore.** The kinetochores are part of the centromere.

Stage 2: Metaphase. The next stage is called metaphase. The chromosomes now begin to line up along the equatorial plane, or the **metaphase plate,** of the cell. That's because the spindle fibers are attached to the kinetochore of each chromatid.

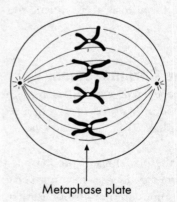

Metaphase plate

Stage 3: Anaphase. During anaphase, the sister chromatids of each chromosome separate at the centromere and migrate to opposite poles. The chromatids are pulled apart by the microtubules, which begin to shorten. Each half of a pair of sister chromatids now moves to opposite poles of the cell. **Cytokinesis,** or cell division, starts here in anaphase.

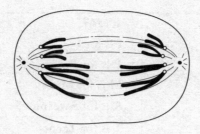

Stage 4: Telophase. The final phase of mitosis is telophase. A nuclear membrane forms around each set of chromosomes and the nucleoli reappear.

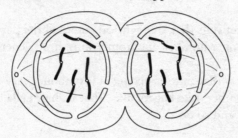

The nuclear membrane is ready to divide. This division of the cell, or cytokinesis, is finished here in telophase. Look at the figure below and you'll notice that the cell splits along a **cleavage furrow** (which is produced by actin microfilaments):

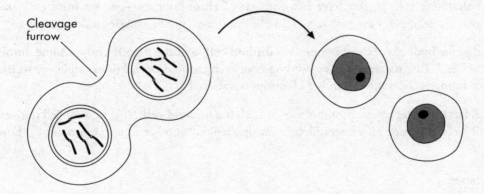

Cleavage furrow

A cell membrane forms about each cell and they split into two distinct daughter cells. This division of the cytoplasm yields two daughter cells.

Here's one thing to remember: cytokinesis occurs differently in plant cells. The cell doesn't form a cleavage furrow. Instead, a partition called a **cell plate** forms down the middle region.

Interphase. Once the daughter cells are produced, they reenter the initial phase—interphase—and the whole process starts over. The cell goes back to its original state. Once again, the chromosomes become invisible, and the genetic material is called chromatin.

But How Will I Remember All That? For mitosis, you may already have your own mnemonic. If not, here's a table with a mnemonic we created for you.

IPMAT	
Interphase	**I** is for **I**
Prophase	**P** is for **Propose**
Metaphase	**M** is for **More**
Anaphase	**A** is for **Awesome**
Telophase	**T** is for **Tacos**

Purpose of Mitosis.   Mitosis has two purposes:

- to produce daughter cells that are identical copies of the parent cell
- to maintain the proper number of chromosomes from generation to generation

For our purposes, we can say that mitosis occurs in just about every cell except sex cells. When you think of mitosis, remember: like begets like. That is, hair cells beget other hair cells; skin cells beget other skin cells; and so on.

Haploids versus Diploids

Every organism has a certain number of chromosomes. For example, fruit flies have 8 chromosomes, humans have 46 chromosomes, and dogs have 78 chromosomes. It turns out that most eukaryotic cells in fact have two full sets of chromosomes—one set from each parent. Humans, for example, have two sets of 23 chromosomes, giving us our grand total of 46.

A cell that has both sets of chromosomes is a **diploid cell,** and the zygotic chromosome number is given as "2n." That means we have two copies of each chromosome. For example, we would say that for humans the diploid number of chromosomes is 46.

If a cell has only one set of chromosomes, we call it a **haploid cell.** This kind of cell is given the symbol "n." For example, we would say that the haploid number of chromosomes for humans is 23.

Remember:

- *Diploid* refers to any cell that has two sets of chromosomes.
- *Haploid* refers to any cell that has one set of chromosomes.

Why do we need to know the terms *haploid* and *diploid*? Because they are extremely important when it comes to sexual reproduction. As we've seen, 46 is the normal diploid number for human beings. We can say, therefore, that human cells have 46 chromosomes. However, this isn't entirely correct.

Flashcards
You might want to make some flashcards to help with memorization of all this cellular vocabulary.

Human chromosomes come in pairs called **homologues.** So while there are 46 of them altogether, there are actually only 23 *distinct* chromosomes. The **homologous chromosomes** that make up each pair are similar in size and shape and express similar traits. This is the case in all sexually reproducing organisms. In fact, this is the essence of sexual reproduction: each parent donates half its chromosomes to its offspring.

Gametes

Although most cells in the human body are diploid (that is, filled with pairs of chromosomes), there are special cells that are haploid (unpaired). These haploid cells are called **sex cells,** or **gametes.** Why do we have haploid cells?

As we've said, an offspring has one set of chromosomes from each of its parents. A parent, therefore, contributes a gamete with one set that will be paired with the set from the other parent to produce a new diploid cell, or zygote.

Let's try a problem.

What occurs in sexual reproduction?

A.   Each parent donates half its chromosomes to its offspring.

B.   Each parent donates two full sets of chromosomes.

C.   Each parent donates 46 chromosomes.

D.   Each parent donates a diploid cell.

Here's How to Crack It

Don't be thrown by this question—it's a bit tricky. You know from your review that humans have 46 chromosomes—two full sets, one from each parent. Choices (B) and (C) must be wrong, because parents cannot donate all of their chromosomes to the child. Choice (D) is a bit confusing because it talks about a diploid, which is any cell that has two sets of chromosomes. This choice doesn't fit at all, so cross it off. So we're left with (A), the correct answer: in sexual reproduction, each parent donates half its chromosomes to its offspring.

EVOLUTION

All of the organisms we see today arose from earlier organisms. This process, known as **evolution,** can be described as a change in a population over time. Interestingly, however, the driving force of evolution, **natural selection,** operates on the level of the individual. In other words, evolution is defined in terms of populations but occurs in terms of individuals.

Natural Selection

What is the basis of our knowledge of evolution? Much of what we now know about evolution is based on the work of **Charles Darwin.** Darwin was a 19th-century British naturalist who sailed the world in a ship named the HMS *Beagle*.

Darwin developed his theory of evolution based on natural selection after studying animals in the Galapagos Islands.

Darwin concluded that it was impossible for the finches and turtles of the Galapagos simply to "grow" longer beaks or necks. Rather, the driving force of evolution must have been natural selection. Quite simply put, this means that nature would "choose" which organisms survive on the basis of their fitness. For example, on the first island Darwin studied, there must once have been short-necked turtles. Unable to reach the higher vegetation, these turtles eventually died off, leaving only those turtles with longer necks. Consequently, evolution has come to be thought of as "the survival of the fittest": only those organisms most fit to survive will survive.

Darwin elaborated his theory in a book entitled *On the Origin of Species*. In a nutshell, here's what Darwin observed:

- Each species produces more offspring than can survive.
- These offspring compete with one another for the limited resources available to them.
- Organisms in every population vary.
- The offspring with the most favorable traits or variations are the most likely to survive and therefore produce more offspring.

Artificial Selection

Artificial selection is similar to natural selection, except, as its name implies, it's artificial. It's a man-made phenomenon of deliberate breeding for certain traits or certain combinations of traits. Today, this phenomenon is quite prevalent, with mixed breed dogs such as the Labradoodle (Labrador Retriever and Standard Poodle). The Labradoodle is a product of artificial selection, as this is a man-made mixed breed dog that is bred for its combination of both Lab and Poodle qualities. Not only is this new breed highly intelligent and friendly, but it is also full of energy and a good watchdog.

Keep in mind that there is no real difference in the genetic processes underlying artificial and natural selection. Charles Darwin coined the term "artificial selection" as an illustration of natural selection. He noted that many domesticated animals and plants had special properties that were developed by intentional breeding to create and promote desirable characteristics. The bi-product of this type of breeding is a decrease in the proliferation of plants and animals with less desirable characteristics.

Evidence for Evolution

In essence, nature "selects" which living things survive and reproduce. Today, we find support for the theory of evolution in several areas:

- **Paleontology,** or the study of fossils. Paleontology has revealed to us both the great variety of organisms (most of which, including trilobites, dinosaurs, and the woolly mammoth, have died off) and the major lines of evolution.

- **Biogeography,** or the study of the distribution of flora (plants) and fauna (animals) in the environment. Scientists have found related species in widely separated regions of the world. For example, Darwin observed that animals in the Galapagos have traits similar to those of animals on the mainland of South America. One possible explanation for these similarities is a common ancestor. As we'll see below, there are other explanations for similar traits. However, when organisms share multiple traits, it's pretty safe to say that they also shared a common ancestor.

- **Embryology,** or the study of the development of an organism. If you look at the early stages in vertebrate development, all the embryos look alike! All vertebrates—including fish, amphibians, birds, and even humans—show fishlike features called gill slits.

- **Comparative anatomy,** or the study of the anatomy of various animals. Scientists have discovered that some animals have similar structures that serve different functions. For example, a human's arm, a dog's leg, a bird's wing, and a whale's fin are all the same appendages, though they have evolved to serve different purposes. These structures, called **homologous structures,** also point to a common ancestor.

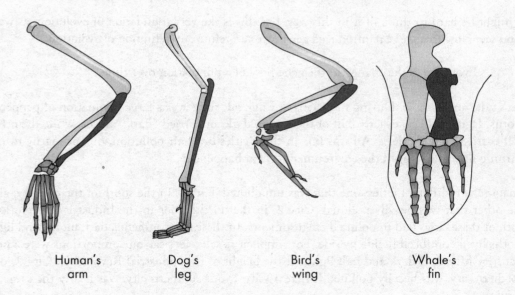

Human's arm   Dog's leg   Bird's wing   Whale's fin

In contrast, sometimes animals have features with the same function but that are structurally different. A bat's wing and an insect's wing, for example, are both used to fly. They therefore have the same function, but have evolved totally independently of one another. These are called **analogous structures.** Another classic example of an analogous structure is the eye. Though scallops, insects, and humans all have eyes, these three different types of eyes are thought to have evolved entirely independently of one another. They are therefore analogous structures.

- **Molecular biology.** Perhaps the most compelling proof of all is the similarity at the molecular level. Today, scientists can examine the nucleotide and amino acid sequences of different organisms. From these analyses, we've discovered that organisms that are closely related have a greater proportion of sequences in common than distantly related species. For example, most of us don't look much like chimpanzees. However, by some estimates, as much as 99% of our genetic code is identical to that of a chimp.

Genetic Variability

Different **alleles** are passed from parents to their progeny. An allele is an alternative form of a gene (one member of a pair) that is located at a specific position on a specific chromosome. For example, you might have an allele for brown eyes from your mother and an allele for blue eyes from your father. In this coupling, brown is considered **dominant**, as it masks blue eyes when both are present in the same organism. Blue eyes are said to be **recessive.** Since brown is dominant, you'll wind up with brown eyes. These alleles are in fact just different forms of the same gene. The two alleles are different (blue, brown), so this gene is **heterozygous.** If both parents had brown eyes, the gene would be **homozygous dominant.**

As you know, no two individuals are identical. The differences in each person are known as **genetic variability.** All this means is that no two individuals in a population have identical sets of alleles (except, of course, identical twins). How did all this wonderful variation come about? Through **random mutation.**

It might be hard to think of it in this way, but this is the very foundation of evolution, as we'll soon see. Now that we've reintroduced genes, we can refine our definition of evolution:

> Evolution is the change in the gene pool of a population over time.

Let's take an example. During the 1850s in England, there was a large population of peppered moths. In most areas, exactly half of them were dark, or carried "dark" alleles, while the other half carried "light" alleles. All was fine in these cities until air pollution, due primarily to the burning of coal, changed the environment. What happened?

Imagine two different cities: one that was unpolluted, City 1, in the south of the country, and the other that was heavily polluted, City 2, in the north. Prior to the Industrial Revolution, both of these cities had unpolluted environments. In these environments, dark moths and light moths lived comfortably side by side. For simplicity's sake, let's say our proportions were a perfect fifty-fifty, half dark and half light. At the height of the Industrial Revolution, City 2, our northern city, was heavily polluted, whereas City 1, our southern city, was nearly the same as before.

In the north, where all the trees and buildings were thick with soot, the light moths didn't stand a chance. They were impossible for a predator to miss! As a result, the predators gobbled up light-colored moths just as fast as they could reproduce, sometimes even before they reached an age where they *could* reproduce. However, the dark moths were just fine. With all the soot around, the predators couldn't even see them; they continued doing their thing—above all, *reproducing*. And when they reproduced, they had more and more offspring carrying the dark allele.

After a few generations, the peppered moth gene pool in City 2 changed. Although our original moth gene pool was 50 percent light and 50 percent dark, excessive predation changed that. By about 1950, the gene pool reached 90 percent dark and only 10 percent light. This occurred because the light moth didn't stand a chance in an environment where it was so easy to spot. The dark moths, on the other hand, multiplied just as fast as they could.

In the southern city, you'll remember, there was very little pollution. What happened there? Things remained pretty much the same. The gene pool was unchanged, and the population continued to have roughly equal proportions of light moths and dark moths.

Causes of Evolution

The allele frequency remains constant in a population unless something happens to alter the gene pool. In the case above, the pollution in City 2 altered the frequency of certain alleles in the peppered moth population.

Individuals in a population are always competing, whether it's for food, water, shelter, mates, or something else. When a population is subjected to environmental change, or "stress," those who are better equipped to compete are more likely to survive. As we saw above, this process is called natural selection. In other words, nature "chooses" those members of a population best suited to survive. These survivors then have offspring that will carry many of the alleles that their parents carried, making it more likely that they, too, will survive.

As time goes on, more and more members of the population resemble the better competitors, while fewer resemble the poorer competitors. Over time, this will change the gene pool. The result is evolution.

Wait a second—didn't we say earlier that *random mutation* was the foundation of evolution? In fact, we did. Yet our example seems to say that the **environment** caused evolution. The truth lies somewhere between these two.

For natural selection to operate, there must be variation in a population. In this case, the variation was due to a mutation. By the way, what other possible sources of variation exist in a population? Sexual reproduction is a major factor in genetic variability. Meiosis, through crossing-over, produces new genetic combinations, as does the union of different haploid gametes to produce a diploid zygote.

Now let's go back to our moths. Why did the dark moths in the north survive? Because they were dark-colored. But how did they become dark-colored? The answer is, through random mutation. One day, a moth was born with a dark-colored shell. As long as a mutation does not kill an organism before it reproduces (most mutations, in fact, do), it may be passed on to the next generation. Over time, this one moth had offspring. These, too, were dark. The dark- and the light-colored moths lived happily side by side until something from the outside—in our example, the environment—changed all that.

The initial variation came about by chance. This variation gave the dark moths an edge. However, the edge did not become apparent until something made it apparent. In our case, that something was the intensive pollution due to the burning of coal. The abundance of soot made it easier for predators to spot the light-colored moths, thus effectively removing them from the population.

Eventually, over long stretches of time, these two different populations might change so much that they could no longer reproduce together. At that point, we would have two different species, and we could say, definitively, that the moths had evolved. As a consequence of random mutation and the pressure put on the population by an environmental change, evolution occurred.

Types of Selection

The situation with the moths is an example of **directional selection.** One of the phenotypes was favored at one of the extremes of the normal distribution.

In other words, directional selection "weeds out" one of the phenotypes. In our case, dark moths were favored and light moths were practically eliminated. Here's one more thing to remember: directional selection can happen only if the appropriate allele—the one that is favored under the new circumstances—is already present in the population.

Two other types of selection are **stabilizing selection** and **disruptive selection.** Stabilizing selection means that organisms in a population with extreme traits are eliminated.

This type of selection favors organisms with common traits. It "weeds out" the phenotypes that are less adaptive to the environment. A good example is birth weight in human babies. If babies are abnormally small or abnormally large, they have a low rate of survival. The highest rate of survival is found among babies with an average weight. Disruptive selection, on the other hand, does the reverse. It favors both the extremes and selects against common traits. For example, females are "selected" to be small and males are "selected" to be large in elephant seals. You'll rarely find a female or male of intermediate size. Artificial selection, on the other hand, refers to the process by which a breeder *chooses* which traits to favor. A good example is how farmers breed seedless grapes.

Remember that there are three types of selection:

- directional selection
- stabilizing selection
- disruptive selection

Species

A dog and a bumblebee obviously cannot come together to produce offspring. They are therefore different **species.** However, a poodle and a Great Dane could reproduce (at least in theory). We would not say that they are different species; they are merely different breeds.

Let's get back to our moths. We said above that evolution occurred when they could no longer reproduce. In fact, this is simply the endpoint of that particular cycle of evolution: **speciation.** Speciation refers to the emergence of new species. The type of evolution that our peppered moths underwent is known as **divergent evolution.**

Divergent evolution results in closely related species with different behaviors and traits. As with our example, these species often originate from a common ancestor. More often than not, the "engine" of evolution is cataclysmic environmental change, such as pollution in the case of the moths. Geographical barriers, new stresses, disease, and dwindling resources are all factors in the process of evolution.

Convergent evolution is the process in which two unrelated and dissimilar species come to have similar (analogous) traits, often because they have been exposed to similar selective pressures. Examples of convergent evolution include aardvarks, anteaters, and pangolins. They all have strong, sharp claws and long snouts with sticky tongues to catch insects, yet they evolved from three completely different mammals.

There are two types of speciation: **allopatric speciation** and **sympatric speciation.** Allopatric speciation simply means that a population becomes separated from the rest of the species by a geographical barrier so that they can't interbreed. An example would be a mountain that separates two populations of ants. In time, the two populations might evolve into different species. If, however, new species form without any geographic barrier, it is called sympatric speciation. This type of speciation is common in plants. Two species of plants may evolve in the same area without any geographic barrier.

Although kangaroos, koalas, and opossums are very different mammals, they are all marsupials—that is, they have a maternal pouch. The process of similar traits arising in diverse species is an example of:

A.   divergent evolution.

B.   convergent evolution.

C.   disruptive selection.

D.   genetic variability.

Here's How to Crack It
These marsupials were exposed to the same environmental conditions and developed similar structures (pouches) because of it. This is an example of convergent evolution. Choice (A), divergent evolution, refers to two species that branched out from a common ancestor. Choice (D), genetic variability, is too broad a term for this question. Choice (C), discruptive selection, refers to a situation in which extreme phenotypes are favored in a population.

KEY TERMS

morphogenesis
corona radiata
zona pellucida
diploid cell
zygote
fertilization
cleavage
morula
blastula
blastocoel
gastrulation
ectoderm
mesoderm
endoderm
epidermis
neurula
notochord
neural tube
extraembryonic membranes
yolk sac
amnion
chorion
allantois
placenta
umbilical cord
induction
organizers
morphogen
homeotic genes
sexual reproduction
asexual reproduction
budding
mitotic sporogenesis
binary fission
ovaries
ova
estrogen
progesterone

follicular phase
follicle-stimulating hormone
  (FSH)
luteinizing hormone (LH)
ovulation
LH surge
fallopian tube (uterine tube
  or oviduct)
corpus luteum
uterine walls (endometrium)
menstruation
human chorionic
  gonadotropin (HCG)
testosterone
puberty
sperm cells
seminiferous tubules
interstitial cells
epididymis
vas deferens
seminal vesicles
prostate gland
cell division
cell cycle
interphase
mitosis
G1
G2
S phase
sister chromatids
centromere
prophase
metaphase
anaphase
telophase
chromatin
spindle fibers
kinetochore

metaphase plate
cytokinesis
cleavage furrow
cell plate
diploid cell
haploid cell
homologues
homologous chromosomes
sex cells (gametes)
evolution
natural selection
Charles Darwin
artificial selection
paleontology
biogeography
embryology
comparative anatomy
homologous structures
analogous structures
molecular biology
alleles
dominant
recessive
heterozygous
homozygous dominant
genetic variability
random mutation
environment
directional selection
stabilizing selection
disruptive selection
species
speciation
divergent evolution
convergent evolution
allopatric speciation
sympatric speciation

Chapter 12 Drill

Answers and explanations can be found in the final section of this book, beginning on page 617.

1. The phases of mitosis, in order of occurrence, are:

   A. telophase, anaphase, metaphase, prophase, interphase.

   B. telophase, metaphase, prophase, anaphase, interphase.

   C. interphase, prophase, metaphase, anaphase, telophase.

   D. interphase, prophase, metaphase, telophase, anaphase.

2. Which of the following is derived from embryonic endoderm?

   A. epidermis of skin

   B. muscular system

   C. stomach

   D. pancreas

3. The reduction in cell size from zygote to blastula in mammals is most likely due to:

   A. the loss of DNA in the embryo.

   B. decreases in the amount of cytoplasm per cell.

   C. feedback inhibition.

   D. the haploid nuclei of the embryo.

4. The greatest degree of genetic variability would be expected among organisms that reproduce via:

   A. budding.

   B. sporulation.

   C. sexual recombination.

   D. vegetative propagation.

5. Which of the following statements is true regarding mutations?

   A. Mutations are irreversible.

   B. Mutations are generally lethal to populations.

   C. Mutations serve as a source for genetic variation in a population.

   D. Mutations affect only certain gene loci in a population.

Summary

o   A single-celled egg develops into a complex, multicellular organism by dividing and going through many stages in a process called morphogenesis.

o   Organisms reproduce sexually or asexually, depending on their reproductive organs.

o   Sexual reproduction involves the meeting of eggs and sperm.

o   Asexual reproduction can occur in a few different ways, including budding, mitotic sporogenesis, and binary fission.

o   The cell cycle has two periods: interphase (growing) and mitosis (dividing).

o   Charles Darwin developed the evolutionary theories of natural selection and artificial selection.

Chapter 13
Earth and
Space Science

THE SOLAR SYSTEM AND UNIVERSE (ASTRONOMY)

Our **solar system** consists of the **Sun** and other celestial objects bound to it by **gravity**. It includes planets, moons, and other small bodies. The planet names in order from the Sun are **Mercury**, **Venus**, **Earth**, **Mars**, **Jupiter**, **Saturn**, **Uranus**, and **Neptune**. Until 2006, **Pluto** was considered a planet, but that year it was reclassified as merely a **dwarf planet.**

Asteroids, which are smaller bodies than the planets, also orbit the Sun. Asteroids are sometimes referred to as minor planets. Asteroids are comprised of carbonaceous or rocky-metallic materials.

Comets are distinctly different from asteroids in that they have significant amounts of ices and water. A comet is a small solar system body that orbits the Sun and exhibits a visible coma, or tail. Comets leave a trail of debris behind them.

Earth rotates on its own axis. It rotates once upon its axis every 24 hours with the actual time of day varying at points on its surface. Therefore, at one point on Earth it may be a particular time, say 9:00 A.M., and at another point on Earth it may be 9:00 P.M. relative to the hemispheric location of the point. For our daily purposes, Earth is viewed as a grid with latitude and longitude lines. **Longitudinal lines** are designated by linear forms from pole to pole, and there are 360 of these around Earth in one-degree increments. Each hour a given location on Earth's surface rotates through 15 degrees of longitude.

The Sun is in a fixed position in the sky. At dawn it appears before the eastern horizon and it sets below the western horizon at dusk. To an observer, the Sun appears to rise higher and higher in the sky each hour during the day.

The Sun is not unique in that it is really only one of billions of stars in what is known as the Milky Way galaxy. A **galaxy** is a large collection of stars which contains stars, hydrogen, dust particles, and various other gases. Galaxies are located light years away from Earth. Classification of galaxies is made according to appearance. An **irregular system** has no form. A **spiral system** tends to resemble a pinwheel. **Elliptical systems** appear round with spiral-like arms. The universe is composed of countless galaxies, many of which may yet remain unknown.

Stars are luminous balls made of plasma that is held together by its own gravity. They are made largely of hydrogen. The nearest star to planet Earth is the Sun.

Asteroids are comprised of:

A.   carbonaceous or rocky-metallic materials.

B.   ice, water, and a visible tail.

C.   stars, hydrogen, dust particles, and gases.

D.   hydrogen and helium.

Here's How to Crack It

You must simply memorize the information for this question, but you can cross off choices that seem familiar and go from there, if necessary. Choice (D) is describing the Sun—hydrogen and helium. Choice (B) should stick out immediately with the mention of a tail—that's a comet, like a sperm cell in the solar system. Cross off that one. Stars, hydrogen, dust particles, and gases are simply too much material to be an asteroid, so (C) must be wrong (and it's describing a galaxy). That leaves only (A), carbonaceous or rocky-metallic materials. Indeed, that's what asteroids are comprised of.

STRUCTURE AND COMPOSITION OF EARTH (GEOLOGY)

What Is Earth Made Of?

Planet Earth is made up of three concentric zones of rocks that are either solid or liquid (molten). The innermost zone is the **core**. The core has two parts: a solid inner core and a molten outer core. The inner core is composed mostly of nickel and iron, and is solid due to tremendous pressures. The outer core is composed mostly of iron and sulfur, and is semisolid due to lower pressures. Surrounding the outer core is the **mantle,** which is made mostly of solid rock. The mantle has an area, called the asthenosphere, which is slowly flowing rock. The **lithosphere,** a thin, rigid layer of rock, is the outermost layer of Earth. The lithosphere contains the rigid upper mantle and the **crust,** the solid surface of Earth.

Earth's Layers

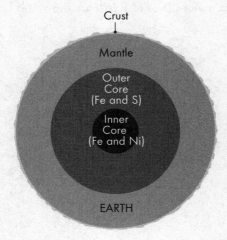

Lithosphere

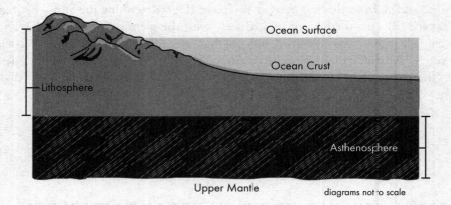

diagrams not to scale

Tectonic Plates

Because the lithosphere floats atop the asthenosphere like a cracker on a layer of pudding, it can move and break into large pieces, or **tectonic plates.** There are a dozen or so tectonic plates in the lithosphere that move independently of one another. The plates are made up of both mantle and crust. The majority of the land on Earth sits above six giant plates; the remainder of the plates lie under the ocean as well as the continents.

Some plates consist only of ocean floor, such as the Nazca plate, which lies off the west coast of South America, while others contain both continental and oceanic material. One example of the latter is the North American plate, where the United States is located; this plate extends out to the mid-Atlantic ridge. There is even a plate that is located exclusively within the Asian continent; its boundaries nearly coincide with those of Turkey. The largest plate is the **Pacific plate**—it primarily consists of ocean floor, but also includes Mexico's Baja Peninsula and southwestern California. The major plates of Earth are shown on the map below.

Earth's Plates

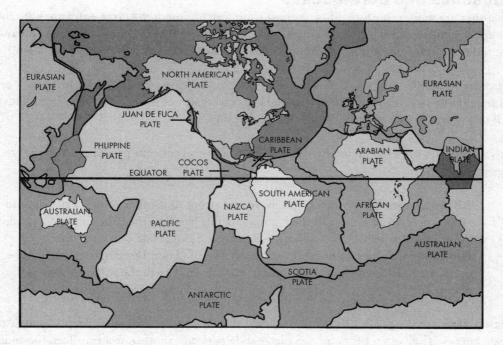

The edges of the plates are called **plate boundaries** and the places where two plates abut each other is where events like sea floor spreading and most volcanoes and earthquakes occur. There are three types of plate boundary interactions:

- **Convergent boundary.** Two plates are pushed toward each other. One of the plates will be pushed deep into the mantle.
- **Divergent boundary.** Two plates are moving away from each other. This causes a gap that can be filled with **magma** (molten rock), and when it cools new crust is formed.
- **Transform fault boundary.** Two plates slide from side to side relative to each other—like when you rub your hands back and forth. These are also called transform boundaries.

So, what happens when plates collide? It depends on what types of plates collide and where. Converging ocean-ocean and converging ocean-continent boundaries often result in **subduction,** in which a heavy ocean plate is pushed below the other plate and melts as it encounters the hot mantle. Converging continent-continent boundaries result in the uplifting of plates to form large mountain chains, like the Himalayas (which were created by a collision between the plate carrying India and the Asian plate), the Urals, the Alps, and the Appalachian Mountains.

One important result of plate movement is the creation of volcanoes and earthquakes. Let's examine those next.

Volcanoes and Earthquakes

Volcanoes are mountains formed by magma from Earth's interior. **Active volcanoes** are those that are currently erupting or have erupted within recorded history, while **dormant volcanoes** have not been known to erupt. It's thought that **extinct volcanoes** will never erupt again.

Volcanoes form where tectonic plates meet. At these junctures, breaks occur in Earth's crust and magma flows out. If no outlet is available as the plates push together, pressure builds up until it is relieved in an explosion—a volcanic eruption.

Active volcanoes are categorized by the kind of tectonic event that produces them. There are three types:

- **Rift volcanoes** occur when plates move away from each other. When a rift volcano erupts, new ocean floor is formed as magma fills in where the plates have separated.
- **Subduction volcanoes** occur where plates collide and slide over each other.
- **Hot spot volcanoes** do not form at the margin of plates. Instead, they are found over "hot spots," which are areas where magma can rise to the surface through the plates. The Hawaiian Islands are thought to have formed over a hot spot.

Earthquakes are the result of vibrations (often due to plate movements) deep in Earth that release energy. They often occur as two plates slide past one another at a transform boundary. The **focus** of the earthquake is the location at which it begins within Earth, and the initial surface location is the **epicenter.** The size, or magnitude, of earthquakes is measured by using an instrument known as a **seismograph,** which was devised by Charles Richter in 1935. The Richter scale measures the amplitude of the highest S-wave of an earthquake. Each increase in Richter number corresponds to an increase of approximately 33 times the energy of the previous number.

The 2004 Indian Ocean undersea earthquake, known by the scientific community as the Sumatra-Andaman earthquake, occurred on December 26, 2004, and was the second largest earthquake ever recorded. The earthquake generated a giant wave called a **tsunami** that was among the deadliest disasters in modern history, killing well over 240,000 people. During this earthquake, an estimated 1,200 km (750 miles) of faultline slipped about 15 m (50 ft.) along the subduction zone where the India Plate is subducted under the Burma Plate. The slip did not happen instantaneously, but took place in two phases that occurred over a period of several minutes.

The Rock Cycle

Rocks are all around us, in the soil, buildings, and the ore used in industry. So, where do all those rocks come from? The answer: other rocks. The oldest rocks on Earth are 3.8 billion years old, while others are only a few million years old. This means that rocks have to be recycled. The process that does this is the **rock cycle.** In the rock cycle, time, pressure, and Earth's heat interact to create three basic types of rocks.

- **Sedimentary rocks** are formed as sediment (eroded rocks and the remains of plants and animals) builds up and is compressed. One place this can occur is at a subduction zone where ocean sediments are pushed deep into Earth and compressed by the weight of rock above it. An example of a sedimentary rock is limestone.

- **Metamorphic rock** is formed as a great deal of pressure and heat is applied to rock. As sedimentary rocks sink deeper into Earth, they are heated by the high temperatures found in Earth's mantle. An example of a metamorphic rock is slate.
- **Igneous rock** results when rock is melted (by heat and pressure below the crust) into a liquid and then resolidifies. The molten rock (magma) comes to the surface of Earth. When it emerges, it is called **lava.** Solid lava is igneous rock. An example of an igneous rock is basalt.

The diagram below illustrates the rock cycle.

The Rock Cycle

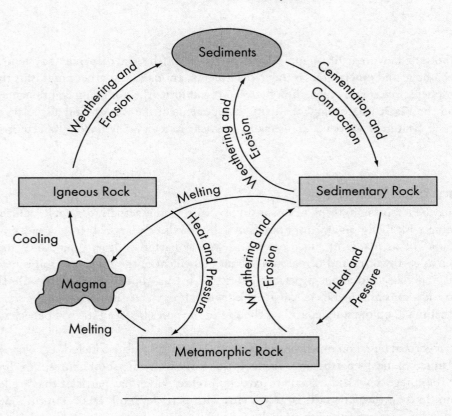

California is the site of more earthquakes than New York because of:

A. New York's location on the Pacific plate.

B. California's location on the Pacific plate.

C. California's location near the Scotia plate.

D. subduction.

Here's How to Crack It

Choice (A) should look wrong immediately, as New York is nowhere near the Pacific Ocean. Cross off that one and keep (B) until you know more. As we saw from the plates graphic earlier in this section, California is not located near the Scotia plate, so you can eliminate (C). Subduction is the phenomenon in which a heavy ocean plate is pushed below the other plate and melts as it encounters hot mantle—definitely not the answer to this question. That leaves just (B), which is correct. California experiences earthquakes because of its location on the Pacific plate.

Soil

One very important but often underappreciated player in Earth's interdependent systems is soil. Soil plays a huge and crucial role in the lives of plants, animals, and other organisms that live in the biosphere. It acts as a crucial link between the **abiotic** (the nonliving components of the world) and the **biotic** (that's right, the living components of the world). Soil also plays an active role in the cycling of nutrients. Let's take a moment to review the major characteristics of soil.

Soil Is More than Just Dirt

Although it may be tempting to think of soil as simply "dirt," soil is actually a complex, ancient material teeming with living organisms. Some soil is hundreds of years old! In just one gram of soil, there may be as many 50,000 protozoa, as well as bacteria, algae, fungi, and larger organisms such as earthworms and nematodes. About 50 percent of the volume of soil is made up of mineral materials, and about 5 percent is organic matter (both living and dead). The pores between the grains of minerals in soil are filled with air or water and, as a rule, the size of the particles that make up the soil determines the size of the pores between the soil particles.

Soils can be categorized based on numerous physical and chemical features including color and texture. The United States Department of Agriculture (USDA) divides soil textures into three large groups. The category with the smallest particles is **clay,** which has particles that are less than 0.002 mm in diameter. The next largest is **silt,** with particles 0.002–0.05 mm in diameter, and **sand** is the coarsest soil, with particles 0.05–2.0 mm in diameter. Sand particles are too large to easily stick together, and sandy soils have larger pores; which means that they can hold more water. Clays easily adhere to each other and there is little room between particles for water; clay soil is extremely compact.

Another very important characteristic of soil types is soil **acidity** or **alkalinity.** Recall that the pH of a substance ranges from 0–14, and is a measure of the concentration of hydrogen ions. Most soils fall into a pH range of about 4–8, meaning that most soils range in pH from being neutral to slightly acidic. Soil pH is important because it affects the solubility of nutrients, and this in turn determines the extent to which these nutrients are available for absorption by plant roots. If the soil in a region is too acidic or basic, certain soil nutrients will not be able to be used by the regional plants.

Where Does Soil Come From?

Basically, soil is a combination of organic material and rock that has been broken down by chemical and biological weathering. Therefore, it should not be surprising to learn that the types of minerals found in soil in a particular region depend on the identity of the base rock of that region.

Water, wind, and living organisms are all prominent agents of weathering, and all weathering processes are placed into the following three rather broad categories:

- **Physical weathering** (also known as **mechanical weathering**) is any process that breaks rock down into smaller pieces without changing the chemistry of the rock. The forces responsible for physical weathering are typically wind and water.
- **Chemical weathering** occurs as a result of chemical interactions between water and other atmospheric gases, and the bedrock of a region.
- **Biological weathering** takes place as the result of the activities of living organisms.

Soil is made up of distinct layers with very different characteristics. Let's discuss those next.

Soil Layers

Soil is comprised of distinctive layers known as **horizons,** which vary considerably in content.

- The **O horizon** is the uppermost horizon of soil. It is primarily made up of organic material, including waste from organisms, the bodies of decomposing organisms, and live organisms. The dark, crumbly material that results from the decomposition of organic material forms **humus.**
- The **A horizon** lives below the O layer. This layer is made up of weathered rock and some organic material that has traveled down from the O layer. The A layer, often referred to as **topsoil,** plays an important role in plant growth. This is the zone of **leaching.**
- The **B horizon** lies below the A horizon. The B layer receives all of the minerals that are leached out of the A horizon as well as organic materials that are washed down from the topsoil above. This is the zone of **illuviation.**
- The **C horizon** is the bottommost layer of soil. It is composed of larger pieces of rock that have not undergone much weathering.
- The **R horizon** is the bedrock, which lies below all of the other layers of soil.

We touched on soil in Chapter 11, but let's now discuss soil in the context of geology.

Soil Problems for (and Caused by) Humans

In order to be able to grow all of the foods that humans consume we must have enough **arable**—suitable for plant growth—soil to meet our agricultural needs. Soil fertility refers to soil's ability to provide essential nutrients, like nitrogen (N), potassium (K), and phosphorus (P), to plants. Humus (remember: it's in the O layer!) is also an extremely important component of soil because it is rich in organic matter.

Soils composed of roughly the same amount of all three textures (remember: clay, silt, and sand) are described as being **loamy,** and these types of soil are considered the best for plant growth. Another important characteristic of soil for agricultural purposes is the extent to which it **aggregates,** or clumps. The most fertile soils are aggregates (look: it's a noun, too!) of soils of different textures bound together with organic material.

Monoculture. Unfortunately, certain agricultural activities can change the texture of soil; for example, repeated plowing tends to break down soil aggregates, leaving "plow pan" or "hard pan," which is hard, unfertile soil.

While communities traditionally planted many different types of crops in a field, in modern agriculture the **monoculture,** or the planting of just one type of crop in a large area, predominates. Over the history of agriculture, a significant decrease in the genetic diversity of crop species has taken place. This creates numerous problems. First of all, a lack of genetic variation makes crops more susceptible to pests and diseases. Second, the consistent planting of one crop in an area eventually leaches the soil in that area of the specific nutrients that the plant needs in order to grow. One way of preventing this phenomenon is to practice **crop rotation,** in which different crops are planted in the area in each growing season.

Other problems with modern agriculture include its reliance on large machinery (which can damage soil), and the fact that as an industry, agriculture is a huge consumer of energy. Energy is consumed both in the production of pesticides and fertilizers, and in the use of fossil fuels to run farm machinery.

The past 50 years or so have seen a huge increase in worldwide agricultural productivity, and this is largely due to the mechanization of farming that resulted from the Industrial Revolution. The boom in agricultural productivity is known as the **Green Revolution,** and unfortunately it has since had many detrimental environmental effects. For example, the use of chemical pesticides resulted in the emergence of new species of insects that were pesticide-resistant. Recently, the introduction of genetically modified plants has enabled researchers to take steps in solving the problem of pesticide-resistant insect species.

Another drawback to the Green Revolution resulted from the dramatic increase in irrigation worldwide; over-irrigated soils undergo salinization. In **salinization,** the soil becomes waterlogged and when it dries out, salt forms a layer on its surface; this eventually leads to **land degradation.** In order to combat this problem, researchers have developed **drip irrigation,** which allots an area only as much water as is necessary, and it delivers the water directly to the roots.

Soil Erosion.   The small rock fragments that result from weathering may be moved to new locations in the process of **erosion,** and bare soil (soil upon which no plants are growing) is more susceptible to erosion than soil that's covered by organic materials.

Because of the constant movement of water and wind on Earth's surface, the erosion of soil is a continual and normal process. However, when erosion removes valuable topsoil or deposits soil in undesirable places, it can become a problem for humans. Eroded topsoil usually ends up in bodies of water, posing a problem for both farmers, who need healthy soil for planting, and people who rely on bodies of water to be uncontaminated with soil runoff (soil can contaminate the water with pesticides and other harmful chemicals).

The most significant portion of erosion caused by humans results from logging and slash-and-burn agriculture. The removal of plants in an area makes the soil much more susceptible to the agents of erosion.

EARTH'S ATMOSPHERE (METEOROLOGY)

In the broadest definition, the **atmosphere** is a layer of gases that's held close to Earth by the force of gravity. The layer of gases that lies closest to Earth is the **troposphere;** it extends from the surface of Earth to about 10–20 km (5–10 miles). The troposphere is where all of the weather that we experience takes place; this layer contains the majority of atmospheric water vapor and clouds. Generally the troposphere is vertically well mixed, and (with the exception of periods of temperature inversions) it gradually becomes colder with an increase in altitude (by about 6.5°C/km).

You've probably heard about the troposphere before in the news because of the **greenhouse effect.** The troposphere contains certain gases called **greenhouse gases,** the most important of which are H_2O and CO_2. As the Sun's rays strike Earth, some of the solar radiation is reflected back into space; however, greenhouse gases in the troposphere intercept and absorb a lot of this radiation.

The Greenhouse Effect

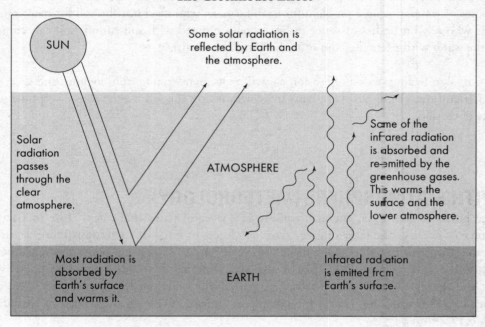

Crowning the troposphere is the **tropopause,** which is a layer that acts as a buffer between the troposphere and the next layer up, the stratosphere. In this buffer zone, the atmospheric temperature no longer decreases with altitude; instead the temperature begins to *increase* with altitude.

The **stratosphere** sits on top of the tropopause and extends about 20–50 km above Earth's surface. Unlike the troposphere, its gases are not very well mixed and, as in the tropopause, the temperature in the stratosphere increases as the distance from Earth increases. This warming effect is due to a thin band of **ozone** (O_3) that exists in this layer. The ozone traps the high-energy radiation of the Sun, holding some of the heat and protecting the troposphere and Earth's surface from this radiation.

Above the stratosphere are two layers called the mesosphere and the thermosphere (ionosphere). The **mesosphere** extends about 80 km above Earth's surface and is the area where meteors usually burn up.

The **thermosphere** is the thinnest gas layer; it is located about 110 km above Earth and is where auroras take place. It's also the layer of the atmosphere where space shuttles orbit! The thermosphere is also known as the **ionosphere** because of the ionization that takes place in this region; this region also absorbs most of the energetic photons (solar wind) from the Sun. Interestingly, the thermosphere also reflects radio waves, which is what makes long-distance radio communication possible.

What human activity/activities has/have increased the levels of erosion in the upper layers of Earth's soil?

A.   crop rotation

B.   land degradation

C.   urbanization and deforestation

D.   under-cultivation of agricultural fields

Here's How to Crack It
Choice (A), crop rotation, is actually a phenomenon that prevents soil problems caused by humans, so eliminate this choice. Choice (B), land degradation, is the same thing as erosion, so don't fall for that trick choice—cross it off. Choice (C) certainly seems correct, but let's take a gander at (D) before we decide for sure. Under-cultivation of agricultural fields is the opposite of what causes erosion, so cross that one off. Choice (C) is the correct answer.

Climate
Earth's atmosphere has physical features that change day to day as well as patterns that are consistent over a space of many years. The day-to-day properties such as wind speed and direction, temperature, amount of sunlight, pressure, and humidity are referred to as **weather.** The patterns that are constant over many years (30 years or more) are referred to as **climate.** The two most important factors in describing climate are average temperature and average precipitation amounts. **Meteorologists** are scientists who study weather and climate.

The weather and climate of any given area is the result of the Sun unequally warming Earth (and the gases above it) as well as the rotation of Earth.

Air Circulation in the Atmosphere
The motion of air around the globe is the result of solar heating, the rotation of Earth, and the physical properties of air, water, and land. There are three major reasons that Earth is unevenly heated:

- More of the Sun's rays strike Earth at the equator in each unit of surface area than strike the poles in the same unit area.

- Earth's axis points regions tilt toward or away from the Sun. When pointed toward the Sun, those areas receive more direct or intense light than when pointed away. This causes the seasons.
- Earth's surface at the equator is moving faster than the surface at the poles. This changes the motion of air into major prevailing winds, belts of air that distribute heat and moisture unevenly.

Solar energy warms Earth's surface. The heat is transferred to the atmosphere by radiation heating. The warmed gases expand, become less dense, and rise creating vertical currents called **convection currents.** The warm currents can also hold a lot of moisture compared to the surrounding air. As these large masses of warm moist air rise, cool air flows along Earth's surface into the area where the warm air was located. This flowing air, or **horizontal airflow,** is one way that surface winds are created.

As warm moist air rises into the cooler atmosphere, it cools to the **dew point,** the temperature at which water vapor condenses into liquid water. This condensation creates clouds. If condensation continues and the drops get bigger, they can no longer be held up by gravity and they fall as **precipitation** (which can be frozen or liquid). The cold dry air is now denser than the surrounding air. This air mass then sinks to Earth's surface where it is warmed and can gather more moisture, thus starting the **convection cell** rotation again.

Convection Cell

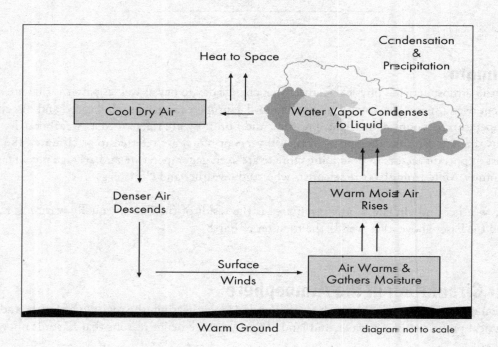

diagram not to scale

On a local level, this phenomena accounts for land and sea breezes. On a global scale, these cells are called **Hadley cells.** A large Hadley cell starts its cycle over the equator, where the warm moist air evaporates and rises into the atmosphere. The precipitation in that region is one cause of the abundant equatorial rain forests. The cool dry air then descends about 30 degrees north and south of the equator, forming the belts of deserts seen around Earth at those latitudes.

Hadley Cell

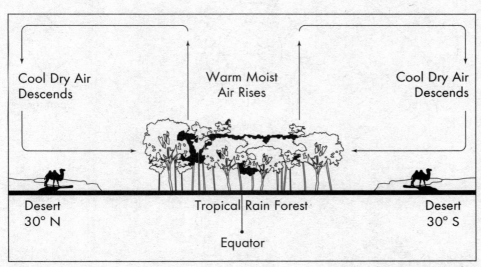

Cool Dry Air Descends

Warm Moist Air Rises

Cool Dry Air Descends

Desert 30° N

Tropical Rain Forest

Desert 30° S

Equator

diagram not to scale

Seasons

The motion of Earth around the Sun—and the fact that Earth is tilted on its axis by 23.5 degrees—together create the seasons that we experience on Earth. When Earth is in the part of its orbit in which the Northern Hemisphere is tilted toward the Sun, the northern half of the planet receives more direct sunlight for longer periods of time each day than does the Southern Hemisphere. This means that when the Northern Hemisphere is experiencing summer, the Southern Hemisphere is experiencing winter.

Interestingly, because of Earth's tilt, the Sun rises and sets just once a year at the North and South Poles. Approximately six months of the year at the poles is daytime, while the other six months is dark, and considered nighttime.

Seasons

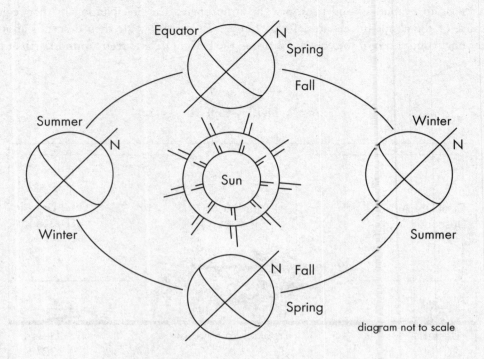

diagram not to scale

Weather Events

Monsoons, which occur primarily in coastal areas, are caused by the fact that land heats up and cools down more quickly than water does. In a monsoon, hot air rises from the heated land, and a low-pressure system is created. The rising air is quickly replaced by cooler moist air that blows in from over the ocean. As this air rises, it cools, and the moisture it carries is released in a steady seasonal rainfall. This process happens in reverse in the dry season, when masses of air that have cooled over the land blow out over the ocean. Check out the illustration on the next page.

How a Monsoon Forms

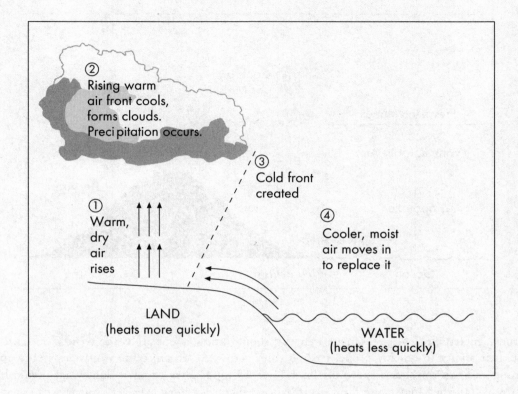

② Rising warm air front cools, forms clouds. Precipitation occurs.

③ Cold front created

① Warm, dry air rises

④ Cooler, moist air moves in to replace it

LAND (heats more quickly)

WATER (heats less quickly)

On a smaller scale, this effect can be seen on the shores of large lakes and bays. In these areas, again the land warms faster than does the water during the day, so the air mass over the land rises. Air from over the lake moves in to replace it, and this creates a breeze. At night, the reverse happens; the land cools more quickly than the water and the air over the lake rises. The air mass from the land moves out over the lake to replace the rising air, and this creates a breeze as well. If you live in San Francisco, you may have experienced this small-scale monsoon effect!

As we mentioned above, the air that moves in from over the ocean or a large body of water contains large amounts of water. An air mass may be forced to climb in altitude—if, for instance, it encounters an obstruction such as a mountain. When the air mass rises, it will cool and water will precipitate out on the ocean side of the mountain. By the time the air mass reaches the opposite side of the mountain, it will be virtually devoid of moisture. This phenomenon, known as the **rain shadow effect,** is responsible for the impressive growth of the Olympic rainforest on the Washington State coast. Interestingly, the Olympic rainforest receives up to 5 m of rain per year, while the opposite side (the leeward side) receives less than 50 cm of rain per year.

How the Rainshadow Effect Works

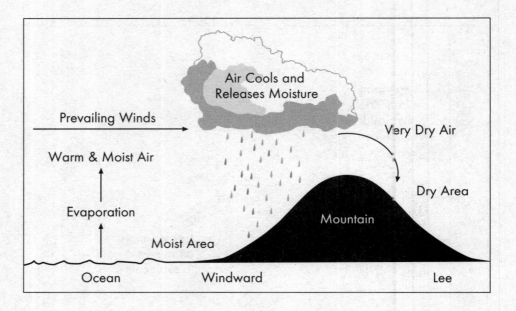

Crucial meteorological phenomena that you should know about are **trade winds.** So named for their ability to quickly propel trading ships across the ocean, trade winds are steady and strong and can travel at a speed of about 11 to 13 mph. They occur in somewhat predicable patterns, but they may cause local disturbances when they blow over very warm ocean water. When this occurs, the air warms and forms an intense, isolated, low-pressure system, while also picking up more water vapor from the ocean surface. The wind circles around this isolated low-pressure air area (counterclockwise in the Northern Hemisphere and opposite in the Southern Hemisphere). The low pressure system will continue to move over warm water, increasing in strength and wind speed; this will eventually result in a tropical storm.

Certain tropical storms are of sufficient intensity to be classified as **hurricanes.** Hurricanes can have winds with speeds in excess of 130 km/hr. The rotating winds of a hurricane remove water vapor from the ocean's surface, and heat energy is created by the condensing water vapor. This addition of heat energy continues to contribute to the increase in wind speed, and some hurricanes have winds traveling at speeds of nearly 400 km per hour! A major hurricane contains more energy than that released during a nuclear explosion, but since the force is released more slowly, the damage is generally less concentrated. Another important note about these types of storms is that they are referred to as hurricanes in the Atlantic Ocean, but they are called **typhoons** or cyclones when they occur in the Pacific Ocean. Go figure!

EARTH'S WATER (OCEANOGRAPHY)

Oceanography is the study of various bodies of water which include rivers, lakes, oceans, and estuaries. There are distinctions between these bodies of water. A **river** is a large, flowing water body that empties into the sea or ocean. A **lake** is a body of water surrounded by land on all sides. An **ocean** is a large body of saltwater that surrounds a continent land mass. Earth is covered by more than two-thirds with oceans. An **estuary** is a partly enclosed coastal body of water with one or more rivers or streams flowing into it, and with a connection to the ocean. It's basically the mouth of a river, where the current of the river comes up against the ocean's tide.

The term **tide** refers to the alternating rising and falling of the sea level with respect to the land and is produced by the gravitational attraction of the Moon and the Sun. Tides are also affected by other influences including the coastline, depth of a body of water, and the topography of the ocean. These factors and others can affect the frequency and timing of the tide arrival.

Water covers about 75 percent of planet Earth. Most of the water on Earth's surface is saltwater. On average, the saltwater in the world's oceans has a salinity of about 3.5 percent. This means that for every 1 liter (1,000 ml) of seawater, there are 35 grams of salts (mostly, but not entirely, sodium chloride) dissolved in it. In fact, one cubic foot of seawater would evaporate to leave about 1 kg of sea salt! However, **seawater** is not uniformly saline throughout the world. The planet's freshest seawater is in the Gulf of Finland, part of the Baltic Sea. The most saline open sea is the Red Sea, where high temperatures and confined circulation result in high rates of surface evaporation.

Freshwater is water that contains only minimal quantities of dissolved salts, especially sodium chloride. All freshwater ultimately comes from precipitation of atmospheric water vapor, which reaches inland lakes, rivers, and groundwater bodies directly, or after melting of snow or ice. Let's start with a discussion of freshwater before discussing the world's oceans.

Freshwater

Freshwater is deposited on the surface of Earth through precipitation. Water that falls on Earth and doesn't move through the soil to become groundwater moves along Earth's surface, via gravity, and forms small streams, and then eventually larger ones. The size of the stream continues to increase as water is added to it, until the stream becomes a river, and the river flows until it reaches the ocean. The land area that drains into a particular stream is known as a **watershed,** or drainage basin.

As water moves into streams, it carries with it sediment and other dissolved substances, including small amounts of oxygen. Turbulent waters are especially laden with dissolved oxygen and carbon dioxide, such as those found at the source, or head waters, of a stream. As a general rule, the more turbulent the water, the more dissolved gases it will contain.

As you probably know, freshwater that travels on land is largely responsible for shaping Earth's surface. Erosion occurs when the movement of water etches channels into rocks. The moving water then carries eroded material farther downstream.

Because of obstructions on land, moving water does not move in a straight line; instead it follows the lowest topographical path, and as it flows, it cuts farther into its banks to eventually form a curving channel. As the water travels around these bends, its velocity decreases and the stream drops some of its sedimentary load.

Rivers drop most of their sedimentary load as they meet the ocean because their velocity decreases significantly at this juncture. At these locations, landforms called **deltas** (which are made of deposited sediments) are created. Another important freshwater body that you should know about is the estuary. As we mentioned before, estuaries are sites where the "arm" of the sea extends inland to meet the mouth of a river. Estuaries are often rich with many different types of plant and animal species, because the freshwater in these areas usually has a high concentration of nutrients and sediments. The waters in estuaries are usually quite shallow, which means that the water is fairly warm and that plants and animals in these locations can receive significant amounts of sunlight.

Some of Earth's most important ecologically diverse ecosystems are the areas along the shores of fresh bodies of water known as **wetlands.** Types of wetlands include marshes, swamps, bogs, prairie potholes (which exist seasonally), and flood plains (which occur when excess water flows out of the banks of a river and into a flat valley).

A myriad assortment of plants and animal species are usually found in estuaries because:

A. landforms of deposited sediments are located there.

B. the freshwater in these areas has a high concentration of nutrients and sediments.

C. seawater isn't uniformly saline throughout the world.

D. the rain shadow effect encourages such assortments.

Here's How To Crack It

Remember that an estuary is where the "arm" of the sea extends inland and meets the mouth of a river. These areas are rich with different plants and species because the freshwater there has a high concentration of nutrients and sediments. Choice (B) is correct. Why are the others wrong? Choice (A) describes a delta, so cross off that one. Choice (C) presents a true statement—seawater isn't uniformly saline throughout the world—but that doesn't explain why many plants and animals are found in estuaries. The rain shadow effect is responsible for the growth of the Olympic rainforest on the Washington state coast, but this doesn't have anything to do with estuaries. You can cross off (D).

——————————⌒——————————

The World's Oceans

Before we get into our review of the world's oceans, let's consider another aquatic ecosystem (besides wetlands and estuaries) that's an important source of biodiversity—this one is a saltwater ecosystem. Certain landforms that lie off coastal shores are known as **barrier islands.** Because barrier islands are created by the buildup of deposited sediments, their boundaries are constantly shifting as water moves around them. These spits of land are generally the first hit by offshore storms, and they are important buffers for the shoreline behind them.

In tropical waters, a very particular type of barrier island, called a **coral reef,** is quite common. These barrier islands are formed not from the deposition of sediments, but from a community of living things. The organisms that are responsible for the creation of coral reefs are cnidarians that secrete a hard, calciferous shell; these shells provide homes and shelter for an incredible diversity of species, but they are also extremely delicate and thus very vulnerable to physical stresses, changes in light intensity, and changes in water temperature.

Like freshwater bodies, oceans are divided into zones based on changes in light and temperature. They're listed below:

- The **coastal zone** consists of the ocean water closest to land. Usually it is defined as being between the shore and the end of the continental shelf.
- The **euphotic zone** is the photic, upper layers of water. The euphotic zone is the warmest region of ocean water; this zone also has the highest levels of dissolved oxygen.
- The **bathyal zone** is the middle region; this zone receives insufficient light for photosynthesis and is colder than the euphotic zone.
- The **abyssal zone** is the deepest region of the ocean. This zone is marked by extremely cold temperatures and very low levels of dissolved oxygen, but very high levels of nutrients because of the decaying plant and animal matter that sinks down from the zones above.

Ocean Zones

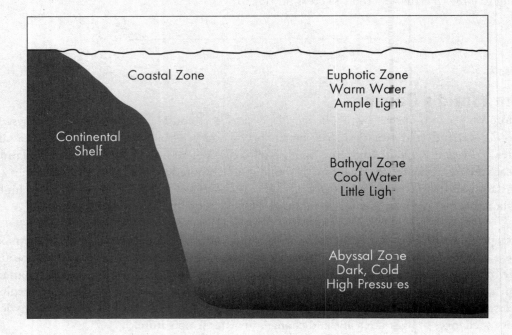

Both freshwater and saltwater bodies experience a seasonal movement of water from the cold and nutrient-rich bottom to the surface. These **upwellings** provide a new nutrient supply for the growth of living organisms in the photic regions. Therefore, they are followed by an almost immediate exponential growth in the population of organisms in these zones, especially the single-cell algae, which may form blooms of color called algal blooms. These algae can also produce toxins that may kill fish and poison the beds of filter feeders, such as oysters and mussels. One fairly notorious recurring toxic algal bloom is referred to as **red tide;** this is caused by a proliferation of dinoflagellates.

Ocean currents play a major role in modifying conditions around Earth that can affect where certain climates are located. As the Sun warms water in the equatorial regions of the globe, prevailing winds, differences in salinity (saltiness), and Earth's rotation set ocean water in motion. For example, in the Northern Hemisphere, the Gulf Stream carries Sun-warmed water along the east coast of the United States and as far as Great Britain. This warm water displaces the colder, denser water in the polar regions, which can move south to be rewarmed by the equatorial Sun. Northern Europe is kept 5 to 10°C warmer than if the current was not present.

Oceanographers also study a major current, the **ocean conveyor belt,** which moves cold water in the depths of the Pacific Ocean while creating major upwellings in other areas of the Pacific.

Ocean Circulation

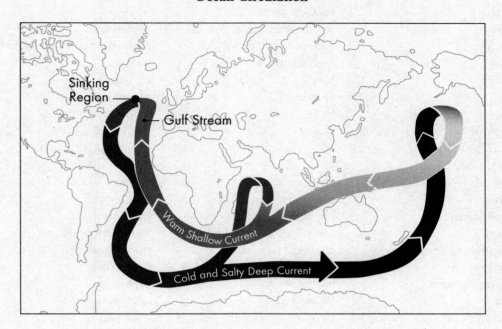

KEY TERMS

solar system
Sun
gravity
Mercury
Venus
Earth
Mars
Jupiter
Saturn
Uranus
Neptune
Pluto
dwarf planet
asteroids
comets
longitudinal lines
galaxy
irregular system
spiral system
elliptical system
stars
core
mantle
lithosphere
crust
tectonic plates
Pacific plate
plate boundaries
convergent boundary
divergent boundary
magma
transform fault boundary
subduction
volcanoes
active volcanoes
dormant volcanoes
extinct volcanoes
rift volcanoes
subduction volcanoes
hot spot volcanoes
earthquakes
focus

epicenter
seismograph
tsunami
rock cycle
sedimentary rocks
metamorphic rocks
igneous rocks
lava
abiotic
biotic
clay
silt
sand
acidity
alkalinity
physical weathering
  (mechanical weathering)
chemical weathering
biological weathering
horizons
O horizon
humus
A horizon
topsoil
leaching
B horizon
illuviation
C horizon
R horizon
arable
loamy
aggregates
monoculture
crop rotation
Green Revolution
salinization
land degradation
drip irrigation
erosion
atmosphere
troposphere
greenhouse effect

greenhouse gases
tropopause
stratosphere
ozone
mesosphere
thermosphere (ionosphere)
weather
climate
meteorologists
convection currents
horizontal airflow
dew point
precipitation
convection cell
Hadley cells
monsoons
rain shadow effect
trade winds
hurricanes
typhoons
oceanography
river
lake
ocean
estuary
tide
seawater
freshwater
watershed
deltas
wetlands
barrier islands
coral reef
coastal zone
euphotic zone
bathyal zone
abyssal zone
upwellings
red tide
ocean conveyor belt

Chapter 13 Drill

Answers and explanations can be found in the final section of this book, beginning on page 617.

1. Inner planets that orbit the Sun consist of:

    A. Mercury, Venus, Earth, and Mars.

    B. Mercury, Venus, and Pluto.

    C. Earth.

    D. Earth and Venus.

2. Asteroids are minor planets that are:

    A. rocky or metallic objects.

    B. collections of hydrogen gas.

    C. similar in structure to elements of Earth.

    D. non-orbital artifices.

3. Meteoroids are:

    A. non-orbital artifices.

    B. large bodies.

    C. small bodies.

    D. soft, liquid-like material.

4. Tides are most affected by:

    A. the location of the water body.

    B. the surrounding land temperature.

    C. the time of the day.

    D. the pull of gravity on Earth's force.

5. A researcher is preparing to study the effects of logging on the streams and lakes in the Amazon rainforest. Which of the following types of information would be a primary source of data to the researcher?

    A. blog posts about logging methods and potential environmental damage

    B. topographic maps of the Amazon rainforest, showing areas of clear-cutting and streams

    C. a *Newsweek* article about logging methods

    D. reports by an environmental-political group on the silting of a stream caused by logging in a forest in the Pacific Northwest

Summary

o   The solar system consists of the Sun and other celestial objects bound to it by gravity.

o   Since 2006, the planet names in order from the Sun are Mercury, Venus, Earth, Mars, Jupiter, Saturn, Uranus, and Neptune.

o   The nearest star to planet Earth is the Sun.

o   Planet Earth is in the Milky Way galaxy and is made up of three concentric zones of rocks that are either solid or liquid (molten).

o   The majority of the land on Earth sits above six tectonic plates. The movements of these plates sometimes cause earthquakes.

o   Volcanoes, which are mountains formed by magma from Earth's interior, form where tectonic plates meet.

o   Soil plays a crucial role in the lives of plants and animals, and soil erosion is an increasingly major problem as the mechanization of farming increases.

o   The atmosphere is the layer of gases that's held close to Earth by gravity.

o   Seawater is salty, but varies in levels of salinity; freshwater contains only minimal quantities of dissolved salts.

Chapter 14
Number Sense

NUMBERS

Integers include the counting numbers {1, 2, 3, ...}, zero {0}, and the negatives of the counting numbers {–1, –2, –3, ...}, so the whole set can be represented like this: {... –3, –2, –1, 0, 1, 2, 3, ...}.

Whole numbers are the counting numbers and zero {0, 1, 2, 3, ...}. **Positive numbers** are numbers greater than zero, such as 0.25, $\frac{2}{3}$, 1, 5, and 100, and **negative numbers** are numbers less than zero, such as –0.75, $-\frac{3}{4}$, –1, $-\frac{9}{2}$, –20, and –1,200. Notice that this means that zero is neither positive nor negative!

A **fraction** is a number represented as a quotient. The **numerator** of the fraction is the dividend, and it is written above the fraction bar. The **denominator** of the fractions is the divisor, and it is written below the fraction bar. So in the fraction $\frac{5}{8}$, 5 is the numerator and 8 is the denominator. Fractions include both **proper fractions** (in which the denominator is greater than the numerator) and **improper fractions** (in which the numerator is greater than the denominator). The latter can also be written as **mixed numbers** (for example, the improper fraction $\frac{12}{5}$ can also be written as the mixed number $2\frac{2}{5}$).

A **decimal** is another way to represent a non-integer number, using the decimal or base-ten system. The fraction $\frac{5}{8}$, written as a decimal, is 0.625. A **percentage** is a special fraction with a denominator of 100, and it can be represented by the symbol %.

A **rational number** is any number that can be expressed as the quotient of two integers (for example, $\frac{a}{b}$), with the denominator b not equal to zero. So fractions like $\frac{5}{8}$ and $\frac{12}{5}$ are rational numbers, and so are integers, such as 7 and –3, since they can also be represented as quotients of integers ($\frac{7}{1}$ and $-\frac{3}{1}$).

Real numbers are numbers that can be found on the number line, and they include both rational and **irrational numbers.** Any real number that can't be represented as the quotient of integers is irrational, and the decimal representations of these numbers are infinite and non-repeating: some examples of irrational numbers are π = 3.141592653589793... and $\sqrt{2}$ = 1.414213562373095....

Take a look at the number line below:

If you are comparing two numbers, the one farther to the right on the number line is the greater one. For example, 10 > 5, –2 > –5, and 7 > –3. The arrows on the number line represent its continuation: real numbers continue infinitely in both the positive and negative directions.

The CSET requires you to be able to order integers. If you ever aren't sure how to order them, visualize or draw a number line and place the numbers on it. The order they appear on the number line from left to right is their order from least to greatest.

Let's see how the CSET might ask a question about ordering integers.

Use the number line below to answer the question that follows.

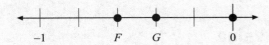

Which of the following numbers can be represented on the number line shown, between points *F* and *G*?

A. $-\dfrac{9}{13}$

B. $-\dfrac{6}{11}$

C. $-\dfrac{5}{14}$

D. $\dfrac{5}{9}$

Here's How to Crack It

Look at the number line given. The only points labeled with numbers are –1 and 0. That means the correct answer will be negative, so eliminate (D). Now determine the values of points *F* and *G*. Since there are 4 ticks between –1 and 0, they divide the interval into 5ths. So the values of the ticks are −0.8, −0.6, −0.4, and −0.2, from left to right. The two labeled F and G are −0.6 and −0.4, respectively. The correct answer has a value between those two. Find the values of the fractions in the remaining choices: $-\dfrac{9}{13} \approx -0.69230769$; $-\dfrac{6}{11} = -0.\overline{54}$; $-\dfrac{5}{14} \approx -0.35714286$. The value that is between −0.6 and −0.4 is (B), so that's the correct answer here.

The **absolute value** of a number is its distance from 0 on the number line. The key fact to remember is that distance is always positive (that comes in handy in geometry as well). So the absolute value of a negative number is positive. Absolute value is written like this:

$$|{-}10| = 10$$

The absolute value of a positive number is also positive: $|7| = 7$. And the absolute value of 0 is 0, because the distance from any number to itself is 0.

Digits and Place Value

Digits are the integers 0 through 9. **Place value** means the value of a digit in its **place,** or position, in a number. Each place to the left and right of the decimal point has a value that will determine the value of a digit placed there:

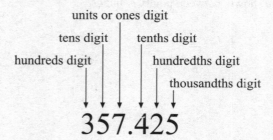

Look at each digit *and* its place to determine its value. For example, the digit 3 is in the hundreds place, so its value is $3 \times 100 = 300$. The digit 7 is in the ones, or units, place, so its value is $7 \times 1 = 7$. The digit 2 is in the hundredths place, so its value is $2 \times 0.01 = 0.02$, or 2 hundredths.

CALCULATIONS WITH INTEGERS

You need to be familiar with the basic operations of arithmetic: addition, subtraction, multiplication, and division, and the **standard algorithms** for those operations. An **algorithm** is just a process, or sequence of steps, to calculate.

Addition

Numbers that are being added together are called **addends,** and the result is a **sum.** The standard algorithm for addition is to stack the addends vertically according to place value, add columns from right to left, and carry amounts above 10 to the next place.

Remember the **Commutative Property of Addition:** $a + b = b + a$. In other words, two addends make the same sum no matter which order they are added in. Another way to say this is that *addition is commutative.*

The **Associative Property of Addition** means that addends can be grouped in different ways, and their sum will still be the same: $(a + b) + c = a + (b + c)$.

The **additive identity** is the number that, when added to another addend, doesn't change it: in other words, 0. You can see this for yourself: any number plus zero equals the original number.

An **additive inverse** of a number a is a number that can be added to a that gives the sum 0 (the additive identity). The additive inverse of 5 is –5: $5 + –5 = 0$. So the additive inverse of a number is usually its negative: $–(–5)$, or 5, is the inverse of –5, and –60 is the inverse of 60. The only exception is 0: its inverse is itself. This might help you remember that 0 is neither positive nor negative.

Subtraction

The number being subtracted from is the **minuend** and the number subtracted from it is the **subtrahend.** The result of a subtraction is the **difference.** The standard algorithm for subtraction is to stack the numbers vertically according to place value and subtract columns from right to left, borrowing from the next place value when needed to ensure that you are subtracting a lesser from a greater value.

Subtraction is the inverse operation of addition. **Inverse operations** reverse each others' effects: for example, $7 + 3 = 10$, and $10 – 3 = 7$.

Another thing to remember is that subtraction is NOT commutative: $9 – 5 = 4$, but $5 – 9 = –4$. Subtraction is also NOT associative: $(10 – 7) – 2 \neq 10 – (7 – 2)$, since $(10 – 7) – 2 = 3 – 2 = 1$ and $10 – (7 – 2) = 10 – 5 = 5$.

Multiplication

Multiplication can be thought of as repeated addition. In other words, if you want to add 3 groups of 5, or $5 + 5 + 5$, you can also represent that as 3×5. The two terms being multiplied are called **factors,** and the result of multiplication is called the **product.**

The standard algorithm for multiplication is to stack the numbers vertically and multiply each digit of the lower number by the upper number, carrying as needed and using place value, and then to add those products. Finally, decimal points are placed according to the number of places to the right of the decimal point in *both* factors.

$$
\begin{array}{r}
\overset{2\,1}{\overset{3\,2\,1}{175.2}} \\
\times \quad 3.5 \\
\hline
\overset{1}{8760} \\
+\; 52560 \\
\hline
613.20 \\
\end{array}
$$

Multiplication is both commutative and associative. Formally, the **Commutative Property of Multiplication** states that $a \times b = b \times a$. The **Associative Property of Multiplication** states that $(a \times b) \times c = a \times (b \times c)$. So it doesn't matter what order you multiply factors in, or how you group those factors: the product is the same.

The **multiplicative identity** is the number that, when multiplied by another number, doesn't change it: in other words, 1. You can see that any number times one equals the original number.

The **multiplicative inverse** of a number a is a number that can be multiplied by a so that it gives the product 1 (the multiplicative identity). The multiplicative inverse of 5 is $\frac{1}{5}$: $5 \times \frac{1}{5} = 1$.

You can think of the multiplicative inverse of a number as a fraction with 1 as the numerator and the number as the denominator: $\frac{1}{10}$ is the inverse of 10, and $\frac{1}{\frac{1}{5}}$, or 5, is the inverse of $\frac{1}{5}$. The inverse of 1 is $\frac{1}{1} = 1$. The only exception is 0: it has no multiplicative inverse, because division by 0 is undefined.

That makes sense if you think about multiplication by 0: any number multiplied by 0 is 0. So there is no number that you can multiply by 0 to get 1.

Rules to Remember about 0 and 1
- Zero is neither positive nor negative.
- Any number plus 0 is itself (0 is the additive identity): $a + 0 = a$.
- Any number times 0 is 0: $a \times 0 = 0$.
- Division by 0 is undefined.
- Any number times 1 is itself (1 is the multiplicative identity): $a \times 1 = a$.
- The multiplicative inverse of a is $\frac{1}{a}$.

Division

Division can be thought of as separating into equal groups. So 15 ÷ 3 can be thought of as 15 separated into groups of 3. There are 5 groups, so 15 ÷ 3 = 5.

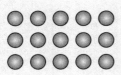 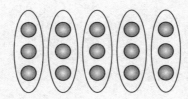

More Review
For more math review, check out *MathSmart* from The Princeton Review.

Division can be written with a division symbol: $a \div b$, a long division symbol: $b\overline{)a}$, or a fraction bar: $\frac{a}{b}$. All these symbolize the same operation.

The number being divided (the a above) is called the **dividend.** The number it's being divided by (the b above) is called the **divisor.** The result is called the **quotient.**

The standard algorithm for division uses the long division symbol. Each digit of the dividend is divided by the divisor, with the result written above that digit. The product is written underneath the digit. The result is subtracted and, if there is a remainder, that is added as a digit to the left of the next digit. Division proceeds until the decimal point is reached (for simple long division with a remainder if needed), or continues after it until the difference is 0 to get a decimal result.

Division is the inverse operation of multiplication. So, for example, 10 ÷ 2 = 5 and 5 × 2 = 10.

Just like subtraction, division is NOT commutative. In other words, 10 ÷ 5 ≠ 5 ÷ 10, because 10 ÷ 5 = 2, but 5 ÷ 10 = $\frac{1}{2}$. And similarly, division is NOT associative: (100 ÷ 10) ÷ 5 ≠ 100 ÷ (10 ÷ 5), because (100 ÷ 10) ÷ 5 = 10 ÷ 5 = 2 and 100 ÷ (10 ÷ 5) = 100 ÷ 2 = 50.

Remember that what variation of the division algorithm you choose should be dependent on the conditions of the problem. In other words, if you are dividing 31 yards into 5 equal lengths, you will find that each one is 31 ÷ 5 = 6.2 yards long.

$$
\begin{array}{r}
6.2 \\
5\overline{)\,31.0} \\
-30 \\
\hline
1\,0 \\
-1\,0 \\
\hline
0
\end{array}
$$

However, if instead you are asked to divide 31 shirts among 5 friends, you will need to notice that only a whole number of shirts will work as an answer. The problem should give you a hint with wording like "what is the greatest number of shirts you can give each friend to give them all the same number?"

Here, you want to divide to get a whole-number answer and discard the remainder. Each friend would get 6 shirts. A variation on that question might ask how many shirts are left over. That's a way of asking for the remainder, which is 1.

$$
\begin{array}{r}
6 \text{ R1} \\
5{\overline{\smash{\big)}\,31}} \\
\underline{-30} \\
1
\end{array}
$$

The Distributive Property

The **Distributive Property** (or Distributive Law) is a property involving multiplication and addition or subtraction. Here's what it looks like:

The Distributive Property

$$a(b + c) = ab + ac$$

$$a(b - c) = ab - ac$$

Basically what it means is that you can separate a factor into two pieces, and the product will still be the same. Let's say you were trying to find the cost of 54 toys that each cost $3. Rather than performing 54 × 3, you could split 54 into two pieces to make this calculation easier. For example, 54 = 50 + 4, so the Distributive Property says that 3(54) = 3(50 + 4) = 3(50) + 3(4). I bet you can do those two calculations in your head! 3(50) + 3(4) = 150 + 12 = 162. If you do it the hard way, you'll see that 3(54) does equal 162.

Using the property in reverse can also come in handy. If someone asks you, "Hey! What is 5 × 2 plus 5 × 3?" you could just say, "Please *try* to challenge me. That's obviously just a fancy way to say 5 × 5, which I know is 25."

Factoring

A **factor** of a number a is an integer that can be multiplied by another integer to yield a. Another name for a factor is **divisor.** If $b \times c = a$, then you can say that b and c are factors, or divisors, of a. You can also say that a is a **multiple** of b and of c. And you can say that a is **divisible** by b and by c.

To factor an integer is to find all of its factors. The easiest way to do that is to make a chart and list the factors, dividing them into pairs. Find the smallest factor of a, which will be 1, and then divide a by it to find its matching factor. Proceed by choosing the next-smallest factor and finding its pair. Continue until the next-smallest factor is already listed on the other side. The following charts illustrate how this is accomplished.

For example, let's find all the factors of 60:

60	
1	60
2	30
3	20
4	15
5	12
6	10

Notice that when you reach 6, and try the next few integers, 60 is not divisible by them: $60 \div 7$ is not an integer; $60 \div 8$ is not an integer; $60 \div 9$ is not an integer. The next choice is 10, but that is already in your chart on the other side. So that's how you can tell where to stop.

Here's another example:

45	
1	45
3	15
5	9

Notice that 45 is divisible by fewer numbers than 60, so it has fewer factors.

You can also use these lists to find the **greatest common factor** of a pair of numbers—just look for the greatest factor that shows up in both lists. For 60 and 45, the greatest common factor is 15.

Try this one:

13	
1	13

Notice that 13 has only one pair of factors: 1 and itself. This tells you that 13 is prime.

A **prime number** is a whole number that has only one pair of factors: 1 and itself. IMPORTANT: 1 is NOT prime. That's because 1 has only 1 factor—itself—rather than one *pair*.

Remember, 1 is NOT prime, because it has only ONE factor rather than one PAIR of factors.

Let's take a look at a list of the first several prime numbers:

2   3   5   7   11   13   17   19   23   29   31   37

Knowing the first handful of prime numbers will help you on the test, not just to be able to quickly spot prime numbers, but also for prime factorization.

Prime Factorization

Prime factorization is finding all the **prime factors** of a whole number, which of course are all the factors that are prime. For prime factorization, another algorithm works best, which is called a factor tree.

Start with the number you are factoring. Find any prime number that is a factor of it, and divide.

Let's try it with 60:

$$60$$
$$② \quad 30$$

Circle the prime factor. Then look at the other factor you have found. Find a prime number that is a factor of it, and then divide.

$$60$$
$$② \quad 30$$
$$③ \quad 10$$

Circle the prime factor. Keep doing this until the other factor is also prime. Then circle that as well, and you are done.

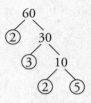

The numbers you have circled are the prime factors of 60: 2, 3, 2, and 5. You can write out a prime factorization like this: $2 \times 2 \times 3 \times 5 = 60$. Or like this: $2^2 \times 3 \times 5 = 60$.

Also notice that it doesn't matter what order you divide in: you will reach the same prime factorization. For example, make a factor tree for 60 in which the first prime factor you divide by is 5:

The numbers circled are the same: 5, 3, 2, and 2. Since multiplication is commutative, $5 \times 3 \times 2 \times 2 = 2 \times 2 \times 3 \times 5$. So the prime factorization is the same. Any whole number has a unique prime factorization.

Prime Number Facts

0 is NOT prime.
1 is NOT prime.
2 is the smallest prime number.
2 is the only EVEN prime number.

Prime numbers are whole numbers (positive integers): they are never negative or non-integers.

To find out whether a number is prime, try to divide it by smaller prime numbers. Try all the prime numbers up to the approximate square root of the number you are checking. This works because any prime factor you find that's *less* than the square root would have to have a matching factor that's *greater* than the square root, so you have to check only one side.

Example:

71        $\sqrt{71} \approx 8.43$

71 ÷ 2 = not divisible

71 ÷ 3 = not divisible

71 ÷ 5 = not divisible

71 ÷ 7 = not divisible

You can stop here, because the next prime number, 11, is greater than $\sqrt{71}$.

71 is prime.

Divisibility

One thing that can help with factorization and prime factorization is knowing the Rules of Divisibility. Try to memorize these so that you can use them whenever needed on the test.

- An integer is divisible by 2 if its units digit is divisible by 2. For example, we know just by glancing at it that 598,447,896 is divisible by 2, because the units digit, 6, is divisible by 2.
- An integer is divisible by 3 if the sum of its digits is divisible by 3. For example, we know that 2,145 is divisible by 3 because 2 + 1 + 4 + 5 = 12, and 12 is divisible by 3.
- An integer is divisible by 4 if its last two digits form a number that's divisible by 4. For example, 712 is divisible by 4 because 12 is divisible by 4.
- An integer is divisible by 5 if its units digit is either 0 or 5. For example, 23,645 is divisible by 5 because its units digit is 5.
- An integer is divisible by 6 if it's divisible by both 2 and 3. For example, 4,290 is divisible by 6 because it is divisible by 2 (it's even) and by 3 (4 + 2 + 9 = 15, which is divisible by 3).
- An integer is divisible by 8 if its last three digits form a number that's divisible by 8. For example, 11,640 is divisible by 8 because 640 is divisible by 8.
- An integer is divisible by 9 if the sum of its digits is divisible by 9. For example, 1,881 is divisible by 9 because 1 + 8 + 8 + 1 = 18, which is divisible by 9.
- An integer is divisible by 10 if its units digit is 0. For example, 1,590 is divisible by 10 because its units digit is 0.

Note that there is no good rule for divisibility by 7: you just have to try dividing.

Let's see how the CSET might test prime factorization.

If the number 480 is written as the product of its prime factors in the form f^5gh, what is the value of fgh?

A. 10

B. 30

C. 40

D. 60

Here's How to Crack It

Make a factor tree:

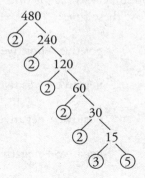

Write out the prime factorization: $2^5 \times 3 \times 5$. This matches with the form f^5gh from the question, so you can say that $f = 2$, $g = 3$, and $h = 5$. (Notice that which number is g and which is h doesn't matter, because you are going to multiply them back together in a minute. Which one is f is determined, because only 2 is repeated 5 times in the factorization.) Now find fgh: $2 \times 3 \times 5 = 30$. Choice (B) is the correct answer.

NEGATIVE NUMBERS

Negative numbers are real numbers that are less than 0. They lie to the left of 0 on the number line. Remember that when you compare negative numbers, the one with the greater absolute value is less. For example, $-12 < -3$. Calculations with negative numbers are like those with positive numbers, but there are a few more rules to remember.

Adding and Subtracting Negative Numbers

To add a negative number, remember that it's an opposite, so the result is the same as if you subtracted the absolute value:

$$5 + -6 = 5 - 6 = -1 \qquad\qquad -3 + -5 = -3 - 5 = -8$$

To subtract a negative number, use the rule that a negative of a negative is a positive:

$$5 - (-6) = 5 + -(-6) = 5 + 6 = 11 \qquad\qquad -3 - (-5) = -3 + -(-5) = -3 + 5 = 2$$

> **Non-negative and Non-positive**
>
> If you see the word *non-negative* (or *non-positive*) on your test, what are the test writers trying to say? The difference between *non-negative* and *positive* is that *positive* does not include 0, since 0 is neither positive nor negative. If the test writers tell you to use the set of *non-negative* numbers for something, they are purposefully including zero. You may want to try using 0 in your calculation, because they are probably including it for a reason. It's the same idea with *non-positive*: that means the negative numbers and 0.

Multiplying and Dividing Negative Numbers

Multiplying and dividing negative numbers works just like it does with positive numbers, but to determine the sign of the result, use these rules:

positive × positive = positive   positive ÷ positive = positive

negative × positive = negative   negative ÷ positive = negative

positive × negative = negative   positive ÷ negative = negative

negative × negative = positive   negative ÷ negative = positive

ORDER OF OPERATIONS

Now that you have reviewed addition, subtraction, division, and multiplication (for positive and negative numbers), what happens when you're asked to perform a few of these operations in a single question?

Let's try an example. Say you wanted to find the result of the following expression:

$$6 + 10 \div 5 - 3 \times 2 + (3 \times 5)$$

There are a number of different operations that you must perform in order to simplify this expression. In fact, you'll see many CSET questions that ask you to use many different operations to solve a problem. To simplify the expression correctly, you must perform these operations in the correct order. That correct order is called the **order of operations.** Just remember:

PEMDAS

Another Handy Mnemonic!
Remember IPMAT from Chapter 12 and PEMDAS from Chapter 14.

Most people remember this as "Please Excuse My Dear Aunt Sally" (though no one seems to remember the story behind that phrase). This acronym stands for the following math operations: **P**arentheses, **E**xponents, **M**ultiplication, **D**ivision, **A**ddition, and **S**ubtraction.

In a complex expression, the first thing you solve should be the operation inside parentheses—or, and this is important—other grouping symbols; next, simplify any term with exponents; then, perform all multiplication and division, going from left to right in the expression; finally, perform all addition and subtraction, again going from left to right in the expression.

Most CSET questions are designed to give you a clear understanding of the order in which you must perform operations. However, if you're ever unsure of exactly the order in which to solve a problem, be sure to use PEMDAS. Let's go back to the previous expression and solve it using PEMDAS:

$$6 + 10 \div 5 - 3 \times 2 + (3 \times 5)$$

Step 1: Solve all work inside the parentheses. $3 \times 5 = 15$, so our problem now looks like this:

$$6 + 10 \div 5 - 3 \times 2 + 15$$

Step 2: Since the problem has no exponents, move along to multiplication and division, moving from left to right in the expression:

$$6 + 2 - 6 + 15$$

Step 3: Finish the problem by performing the addition and subtraction, moving from left to right in the expression:

$$8 - 6 + 15$$
$$2 + 15$$
$$17$$

FRACTIONS

Recall that a **fraction** is a number represented as a quotient. The **numerator** of the fraction is the dividend, and it is written above the fraction bar. The **denominator** of the fraction is the divisor, and is written below the fraction bar.

Some fractions reduce to whole numbers: $\dfrac{6}{3} = 2$.

Others can be reduced to simplest terms: $\dfrac{5}{20} = \dfrac{1}{4}$; $\dfrac{12}{8} = \dfrac{3}{2}$.

Proper fractions (in which the denominator is greater than the numerator) have absolute values less than 1. For example, you can see that $\dfrac{2}{3}$ of an apple is represented here:

Grouping Symbols

The most common grouping symbols you'll see in a mathematical expression will be parentheses. But there are others you should know about.

Brackets—they look like this: [ ]—are grouping symbols that work the same way as parentheses. They are usually used if multiple sets are parentheses will look too confusing. So, for example, you might see an expression like $200 \div [(2 \times 5^2) \div 2]$. In that case, work the grouping symbols from innermost to outermost: find the value of (2×5^2) and substitute: $200 \div [(2 \times 25) \div 2] = 200 \div [50 \div 2]$; then simplify inside the brackets and substitute: $200 \div 25$; then solve the rest: $200 \div 25 = 8$.

Another important grouping symbol is the *fraction bar*!

It works by implying a set of parentheses surrounding the numerator and one surrounding the denominator:

$$\frac{4 + 5 \times 3^2}{10 - 3} = \frac{\left(4 + 5 \times 3^2\right)}{\left(10 - 3\right)} = \frac{\left(4 + 5 \times 9\right)}{7} = \frac{\left(4 + 45\right)}{7} = \frac{49}{7} = 7.$$

Make sure to keep this one in mind because it's less obvious than the other two.

You could describe the situation as cutting an apple into 3 pieces, and keeping only 2 of them.

Improper fractions (in which the numerator is greater than the denominator) have absolute values greater than 1. The latter can also be written as **mixed numbers** (for example, the improper fraction $\frac{12}{5}$ can also be written as the mixed number $2\frac{2}{5}$).

Here is a picture of $\frac{5}{2}$ apples:

You can see that each apple is divided into 2 pieces, and then 5 pieces are kept. You can also tell from this picture that $\frac{5}{2} = 2\frac{1}{2}$.

When the numerator and denominator of a fraction are equal, the fraction is equal to 1: $\frac{3}{3} = 1$.

This apple was divided into 3 pieces, and 3 pieces—the whole apple—were kept.

When the numerator is 1, such as in $\frac{1}{4}$, that's called a **unit fraction.** When the denominator is 1, the fraction will be equal to its numerator: for example, $\frac{4}{1} = 4$.

When the numerator of a fraction is 0, the fraction is always equal to 0, since 0 divided by anything equals 0. A fraction with a denominator of 0 is undefined, since division by 0 is undefined. The test will avoid giving you a fraction like that, along with any situation in which you would come up with one if you were working the problem correctly.

The CSET will ask you to interpret pictures as fractions. It will also ask you to perform operations with fractions. It's really important to understand and feel comfortable with fractions. Even though you'll have a calculator, a lot of operations with fractions get really messy when you convert them to decimals, and the calculator is not always as helpful as you would think.

Reducing Fractions

Remember the examples of reducing fractions given above: $\frac{6}{3} = 2$, $\frac{5}{20} = \frac{1}{4}$, and $\frac{12}{8} = \frac{3}{2}$? What is the operation you perform when you reduce a fraction?

To **reduce** a fraction, divide *both* the numerator and the denominator by the same number to get a simpler fraction. For example, use the fraction $\frac{20}{100}$. What number is a factor of both the numerator and the denominator? They are both even, so 2 will divide evenly into both of them.

$$\frac{20 \div 2}{100 \div 2} = \frac{10}{50}$$

Since both 10 and 50 still have a common factor, you can reduce again.

$$\frac{10 \div 10}{50 \div 10} = \frac{1}{5}$$

Since 1 has no other factors, 1 and 5 don't share any more factors, so this fraction is in **simplest terms.** Fractions that can be shown to be equal in this way are called **equivalent fractions.** For example, $\frac{20}{100}, \frac{1}{5}, \frac{4}{20}$, and $\frac{3}{15}$ are all equivalent: you can tell because they all reduce to $\frac{1}{5}$.

Multiplying and Dividing Fractions

To multiply fractions, simply multiply the numerators and multiply the denominators. Then you can reduce if needed. For example:

$$\frac{3}{5} \times \frac{1}{2} = \frac{3 \times 1}{5 \times 2} = \frac{3}{10}$$

To multiply a fraction by an integer, convert the integer to a fraction. That's easy: just use 1 as your denominator, since any fraction with a denominator of 1 is equal to its numerator.

$$\frac{3}{8} \times 2 = \frac{3}{8} \times \frac{2}{1} = \frac{3 \times 2}{8 \times 1} = \frac{6}{8} = \frac{6 \div 2}{8 \div 2} = \frac{3}{4}$$

Dividing fractions is almost the same as multiplying fractions, with one important difference: before you multiply you need to find the reciprocal of the second fraction. The **reciprocal** of a fraction is its multiplicative inverse. In practice, this means you invert the fraction. For example, the reciprocal of $\frac{2}{7}$ is $\frac{7}{2}$. You can tell by applying the rule from above about multiplicative inverse: the multiplicative inverse of a number a is a number that can be multiplied by a so that it gives the product 1. Since $\frac{2}{7} \times \frac{7}{2} = 1$, you know these two fractions are multiplicative inverses, or reciprocals.

So to divide fractions, just find the reciprocal of the second one, and multiply *that* by the first fraction. For example:

$$\frac{1}{8} \div \frac{2}{7} = \frac{1}{8} \times \frac{7}{2} = \frac{1 \times 7}{8 \times 2} = \frac{7}{16}$$

If you are dividing a fraction by a whole number, convert the number into a fraction and then find its reciprocal:

$$\frac{2}{5} \div 8 = \frac{2}{5} \div \frac{8}{1} = \frac{2}{5} \times \frac{1}{8} = \frac{2 \times 1}{5 \times 8} = \frac{2}{40} = \frac{2 \div 2}{40 \div 2} = \frac{1}{20}$$

Adding and Subtracting Fractions

To add or subtract fractions with like denominators, simply add or subtract the numerators, and keep the denominator the same. For example:

$$\frac{3}{20} + \frac{7}{20} = \frac{10}{20} = \frac{10 \div 10}{20 \div 10} = \frac{1}{2}$$

$$\frac{11}{12} - \frac{5}{12} = \frac{6}{12} = \frac{6 \div 6}{12 \div 6} = \frac{1}{2}$$

To add or subtract fractions with unlike denominators, you can find equivalent fractions with like denominators. That's called finding a **common denominator.** Then you can add or subtract the fractions with like denominators using the method above.

So how do you find a common denominator? One easy way is to just multiply the two denominators together. Let's try an example:

$$\frac{1}{2} + \frac{2}{5}$$

Try finding a common denominator by multiplying the denominators: $2 \times 5 = 10$. To convert the fractions to use this common denominator, find equivalent fractions for $\frac{1}{2}$ and $\frac{2}{5}$ with denominator 10 by multiplying each one by a fraction that's equivalent to 1. You can do that, because 1 is the multiplicative identity: multiplying any number by 1 yields the same number. Here, multiply $\frac{1}{2}$ by $\frac{5}{5}$ because $2 \times 5 = 10$. Multiply $\frac{2}{5}$ by $\frac{2}{2}$ because $5 \times 2 = 10$.

$$\left(\frac{1}{2} \times \frac{5}{5}\right) + \left(\frac{2}{5} \times \frac{2}{2}\right) =$$

$$\frac{1 \times 5}{2 \times 5} + \frac{2 \times 2}{5 \times 2} =$$

$$\frac{5}{10} + \frac{4}{10} =$$

$$\frac{9}{10}$$

Try it with subtraction:

$$\frac{2}{3} - \frac{1}{8} =$$

$$\left(\frac{2}{3} \times \frac{8}{8}\right) - \left(\frac{1}{8} \times \frac{3}{3}\right) =$$

$$\frac{2 \times 8}{3 \times 8} - \frac{1 \times 3}{8 \times 3} =$$

$$\frac{16}{24} - \frac{3}{24} =$$

$$\frac{13}{24}$$

Finding a common denominator by multiplying the denominators works well when the denominators are pretty small and don't share factors. When they share factors, it might be worth it to look for the **lowest common denominator:** the least common multiple of the denominators. The **least common multiple** of any set of numbers is the smallest number that is a multiple of all the numbers in the set.

For example, say you wanted to add $\dfrac{5}{12} + \dfrac{4}{9}$. To find the lowest common denominator, find the least common multiple of 12 and 9. To do that, list multiples of 12 and 9:

12: 12, 24, *36*, 48, 60, 72...

9: 9, 18, 27, *36*, 45, 54, 63, 72...

Then find the *first* set of factors that match between the two lists. In this case, the first factors that match are 36, so the least common multiple of 12 and 9 is 36. Make equivalent fractions and then add:

$$\frac{5}{12} + \frac{4}{9} =$$

$$\left(\frac{5}{12} \times \frac{3}{3}\right) + \left(\frac{4}{9} \times \frac{4}{4}\right) =$$

$$\frac{5 \times 3}{12 \times 3} + \frac{4 \times 4}{9 \times 4} =$$

$$\frac{15}{36} + \frac{16}{36} =$$

$$\frac{31}{36}$$

You could multiply $12 \times 9 = 108$ instead to get a common denominator, but then the fractions would have numbers that are quite large and more difficult to calculate.

Here's another example:

$$\frac{1}{3} + \frac{1}{6} + \frac{1}{9} + \frac{1}{18}$$

In this case, we could add the fractions pairwise, finding a common denominator each time, but that would take a long time. Faster would be to find a common denominator for all four fractions. That's not too difficult: 18 is a multiple of 3, 6, 9, and 18, so it can be a common denominator for all four fractions.

$$\left(\frac{1}{3} \times \frac{6}{6}\right) + \left(\frac{1}{6} \times \frac{3}{3}\right) + \left(\frac{1}{9} \times \frac{2}{2}\right) + \frac{1}{18} =$$

$$\frac{1 \times 6}{3 \times 6} + \frac{1 \times 3}{6 \times 3} + \frac{1 \times 2}{9 \times 2} + \frac{1}{18} =$$

$$\frac{6}{18} + \frac{3}{18} + \frac{2}{18} + \frac{1}{18} =$$

$$\frac{12}{18} = \frac{12 \div 6}{18 \div 6} = \frac{2}{3}$$

There is another technique for adding and subtracting fractions that you can memorize: it has the advantage that you can do it to any pair of fractions and it will work, and it's relatively quick. It's called the Bowtie.

Let's try it for adding these two fractions:

$$\frac{5}{7} + \frac{3}{4}$$

To perform the Bowtie, multiply diagonally up across the two fractions (the denominator of the first by the numerator of the second, and the denominator of the second by the numerator of the first). Write the products above your two fractions:

$$\overset{10}{\frac{2}{7}} \diagup\!\!\!\!\!\diagdown \overset{21}{\frac{3}{5}}$$

Then multiply across the bottom (multiply the two denominators). Use this as the denominator for your sum:

$$\overset{10}{\frac{2}{7}} \diagup\!\!\!\!\!\diagdown \overset{21}{\frac{3}{5}} = \frac{}{35}$$

Now add the two products from the first step to get your numerator:

$$\overset{10}{\underset{7}{2}} \overset{+}{\times} \overset{21}{\underset{5}{3}} = \frac{31}{35}$$

For subtracting fractions, the Bowtie works the same, except you subtract the products rather than adding them:

$$\frac{6}{7} - \frac{1}{4}$$

Once again, multiply diagonally up across the two fractions (the denominator of the first by the numerator of the second, and the denominator of the second by the numerator of the first). Write the products above your two fractions:

$$\overset{24}{\underset{7}{6}} \times \overset{7}{\underset{4}{1}}$$

Then multiply across the bottom (multiply the two denominators). Use this as the denominator for your difference:

$$\overset{24}{\underset{7}{6}} \times \overset{7}{\underset{4}{1}} = \frac{}{28}$$

Now subtract the two products from the first step to get your numerator:

$$\overset{24}{\underset{7}{6}} \overset{-}{\times} \overset{7}{\underset{4}{1}} = \frac{17}{28}$$

The Bowtie works by doing the addition/subtraction step and the common denominator step all at once, which can really save you some time! Practice it so you can use it on the test.

Comparing Fractions

Comparing fractions is actually very similar to adding and subtracting fractions—or at least to the first steps of that process. If the fractions being compared have like denominators, you just compare the numerators:

$$\frac{5}{6} > \frac{1}{6}$$

$$\frac{2}{5} < \frac{3}{5}$$

If the fractions you're comparing have unlike denominators, convert to a common denominator and then compare numerators:

$$\frac{3}{8} \; [?] \; \frac{3}{4}$$

$$\frac{3}{8} \; [?] \; \frac{3 \times 2}{4 \times 2}$$

$$\frac{3}{8} < \frac{6}{8}$$

You can also use the first step of the Bowtie to compare fractions! To use the Bowtie to compare, just multiply diagonally up across the two fractions (the denominator of the first by the numerator of the second, and the denominator of the second by the numerator of the first). Write the products above your two fractions, and then compare them. The fraction with the greater product is the greater fraction.

So you can say that $\frac{7}{8} > \frac{9}{11}$.

Mixed Numbers

A **mixed number** is a number that contains both an integer and a proper fraction, such as $4\frac{2}{3}$. You need to be able to represent, convert, and perform operations with mixed numbers.

Here's a representation of $4\frac{2}{3}$:

You can think of $4\frac{2}{3}$ as 4 whole cans of peas, plus $\frac{2}{3}$ of another can.

To convert a mixed number to an improper fraction, think of the mixed number as a sum of its two parts:

$$4\frac{2}{3} = 4 + \frac{2}{3} =$$

$$\frac{4}{1} + \frac{2}{3}$$

Now, use the Bowtie.

$$\overset{12}{\underset{1}{4}} \times \overset{2}{\underset{3}{2}} \;=\; \frac{14}{3}$$

So $4\frac{2}{3} = \frac{14}{3}$.

To convert an improper fraction into a mixed number, divide the numerator by the denominator; write down the whole number answer; and then write down any remainder above the denominator.

For example, to convert $\frac{16}{5}$ to a mixed number, divide 16 by 5:

$$
\begin{array}{r}
3 \ \text{R1} \\
5\overline{)\ 16} \\
-15 \\
\hline
1
\end{array}
$$

The whole number part is 3. Put the remainder over the original denominator: $\frac{1}{5}$. So $\frac{16}{5} = 3\frac{1}{5}$.

You can convert mixed numbers and use the rules for fraction operations to perform operations with them; or, you can separate their whole number parts from their fractions parts and calculate:

$$4\frac{1}{2} + 3\frac{1}{2} = \left(4 + 3\right) + \left(\frac{1}{2} + \frac{1}{2}\right) = 7 + \frac{2}{2} = 7 + 1 = 8$$

Let's look at a question that puts some of what we've reviewed about fractions together:

Use the diagram below to answer the question that follows.

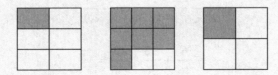

What is the sum of the shaded areas in the three rectangles above if each rectangle represents one unit?

A. $\dfrac{17}{18}$

B. $1\dfrac{1}{36}$

C. $1\dfrac{7}{36}$

D. $1\dfrac{43}{108}$

Here's How to Crack It

First, write down the fraction represented by each rectangle: $\dfrac{1}{6}$, $\dfrac{7}{9}$, and $\dfrac{1}{4}$. Next, determine what operation you need to perform. *Sum* means that you need to add:

$$\frac{1}{6} + \frac{7}{9} + \frac{1}{4}$$

Think about the easiest way to add these fractions. You could do the Bowtie twice, but it might be faster to find a common denominator for all three fractions so you can add them all at once.

Find the lowest common denominator by finding the least common multiple of the three denominators:

6: 6, 12, 18, 24, 30, *36*, 42, 48...

9: 9, 18, 27, *36*, 45, 54, 63, 72...

4: 4, 8, 12, 16, 20, 24, 28, 32, *36*...

The least common multiple is 36, so use that as your common denominator:

$$\left(\frac{1}{6} \times \frac{6}{6}\right) + \left(\frac{7}{9} \times \frac{4}{4}\right) + \left(\frac{1}{4} \times \frac{9}{9}\right) =$$

$$\frac{1 \times 6}{6 \times 6} + \frac{7 \times 4}{9 \times 4} + \frac{1 \times 9}{4 \times 9} =$$

$$\frac{6}{36} + \frac{28}{36} + \frac{9}{36} =$$

$$\frac{43}{36}$$

Choice (A) is a proper fraction, whereas the rest are mixed numbers, so you need to convert your answer to a mixed number. You can eliminate (A) right away, since the correct answer is greater than 1.

$$\begin{array}{r} 1 \text{ R7} \\ 36 \overline{)\ 43} \\ -36 \\ \hline 7 \end{array}$$

The whole number part is 1. Put the remainder over the original denominator: $\frac{7}{36}$. So $\frac{43}{36} = 1\frac{7}{36}$. The correct answer is (C).

RATIOS AND PROPORTIONS

A **ratio** is a relationship between two quantities showing their relative frequency: for example, if you have 2 apples and 3 oranges, then the ratio of apples to oranges is 2 to 3. You can also say that the ratio of oranges to apples is 3 to 2. There are several ways to write ratios: for example, 2 to 3 can also be written 2 : 3 or $\frac{2}{3}$. A ratio can be thought of as a part-to-part relationship, in contrast to a fraction, which is a part-to-whole relationship: the fraction of fruit you have that's apples is $\frac{2}{5}$.

When working with ratios, it's helpful to use a tool called the ratio box to keep track of all the parts. The ratio box looks like this:

			Total
Ratio			
Multiply by			
Actual Numbers			

The first two columns represent the parts of the ratio. Make as many columns as you need for the parts of the ratio, plus one more for the total. For example, if a question tells you that you have pears and kiwis in a ratio of 6 to 5, and that the number of kiwis is 15, you can fill in this much information, making sure to put ratios in the Ratio row and actual numbers in the Actual numbers row:

	Pears	Kiwis	Total
Ratio	6	5	
Multiply by			
Actual Numbers		15	

Guess what? That's enough information to find anything you need. You can fill in the whole box now, once you know how it works: look for any column in which you have a Ratio value and an Actual number value, and use that to find the multiplication factor: what value can you multiply by the ratio to find the actual number? Fill the Multiply by row up with that number. Here, it's 3:

	Pears	Kiwis	Total
Ratio	6	5	
Multiply by	3	3	3
Actual Numbers		15	

Next, multiply any other values on the Ratio row to get values for the Actual number row:

	Pears	Kiwis	Total
Ratio	6	5	
Multiply by	3	3	3
Actual Numbers	18	15	

Now add the first two columns of the Ratio row or the Actual Numbers row to find the values in the Total column.

	Pears	Kiwis	Total
Ratio	6	5	11
Multiply by	3	3	3
Actual Numbers	18	15	33

Notice that the values in the Total column work with the multiplication factor too.

If the question asked you the total number of Pears, you'd have it—18. Total pieces of fruit? 33. Fraction of the fruit that is Kiwis? You can find it using the Actual number row: $\frac{15}{33} = \frac{5}{11}$, but notice it's easier to look at the Ratio row—there, the fraction is already reduced.

Use the steps above in whichever order you can to fill in a ratio box and solve.

In a town with 1,400 adult residents, the ratio of men to women is 3 to 4. If 325 women are unmarried, how many women in the town are married?

A.   275

B.   475

C.   600

D.   800

Here's How to Crack It

Start by making a ratio box. Fill in the pieces of information you know:

	Men	Women	Total
Ratio	3	4	
Multiply by			
Actual Numbers			1,400

To get the multiplication factor, you need a ratio and an actual number in the same column. Add the parts of the ratio:

	Men	Women	Total
Ratio	3	4	7
Multiply by			
Actual Numbers			1,400

Now ask, what multiplication factor multiplies by 7 to yield 1,400? Yep, that's the same as 1,400 ÷ 7 = 200.

	Men	Women	Total
Ratio	3	4	7
Multiply by	200	200	200
Actual Numbers			1,400

So you can find the actual numbers of women and men:

	Men	Women	Total
Ratio	3	4	7
Multiply by	200	200	200
Actual Numbers	600	800	1,400

Since there are 800 women, and you know that 325 of them are unmarried, subtract to find the number who are married: 800 − 325 = 475. The correct answer is (B).

─────────────○─────────────

A **proportion** is a mathematical comparison between two equivalent fractions. For example, $\frac{3}{4} = \frac{75}{100}$ is a proportion. We know it's a true mathematical sentence because $\frac{3}{4}$ and $\frac{75}{100}$ are equivalent: you could multiply $\frac{3}{4}$ by $\frac{25}{25}$ (which is equal to 1) and get $\frac{75}{100}$.

When the CSET asks you about proportions, you usually need to solve for one of the parts. Here's an example.

─────────────○─────────────

Gayle is mixing soil to plant for the spring. For one plant she needs a special mix that's 3 parts compost to 2 parts sand. If she uses $3\frac{1}{4}$ lbs. of sand, how many pounds of compost does she need to include?

A. $1\frac{1}{12}$

B. $2\frac{1}{6}$

C. $2\frac{1}{4}$

D. $4\frac{7}{8}$

Here's How to Crack It

The question tells you three out of the four parts of the proportion. Label them so that you can set up the proportion properly.

$$\frac{3 \text{ compost}}{2 \text{ sand}} = \frac{}{3\frac{1}{4} \text{ sand}}$$

The question asks for the amount of compost she needs to go with the $3\frac{1}{4}$ pounds of sand she uses. That fits into your missing part. Label it with a variable.

$$\frac{3}{2} = \frac{x}{3\frac{1}{4}}$$

Now solve. One easy technique here is to cross multiply: multiply the numerator of one side of the proportion by the denominator of the other side, and vice versa. It's a shorthand for multiplying each side by the denominator of the other to get rid of the fractions—you are just doing it all in one step.

$$3 \times 3\frac{1}{4} = 2x$$

Convert the mixed number into an improper fraction so that you can multiply easier.

$$3\frac{1}{4} = \frac{3 \times 4}{4 \times 4} + \frac{1}{4} = \frac{12}{4} + \frac{1}{4} = \frac{13}{4}$$

Now back to the proportion:

$$3 \times \frac{13}{4} = 2x$$

Simplify the left side:

$$\frac{3}{1} \times \frac{13}{4} = 2x$$

$$\frac{3 \times 13}{1 \times 4} = 2x$$

$$\frac{39}{4} = 2x$$

Now, to isolate x, multiply both sides by $\frac{1}{2}$, the reciprocal of 2.

$$\frac{1}{2} \times \frac{39}{4} = \frac{2x}{1} \times \frac{1}{2}$$

$$\frac{1 \times 39}{2 \times 4} = \frac{2x}{2}$$

$$\frac{39}{8} = x$$

Now, just convert the improper fraction to a mixed number, since the answer choices are in that form.

$$\frac{39}{8} = 4\frac{7}{8}$$

The correct answer is (D).

───────────────○───────────────

Note that it might also be possible to solve the question above using a ratio box. Ratios and proportions are related: choose the tool that looks most helpful for a problem, but don't be afraid to try a different one if it's not working!

DECIMALS

Ah, decimals. Now you can relax and let your calculator do the work, right? Don't be so sure. The CSET doesn't just expect you to calculate—it also expects you to *interpret* calculations and *understand* the algorithms used. So knowing decimals inside and out is a must.

A decimal is a fraction whose denominator is a power of ten and whose numerator is expressed by figures placed to the right of a decimal point. In other words, fractions are decimals and decimals are fractions. So obviously, you need to know how to convert!

Decimals can be converted to fractions easily—just pay attention to place value. Each digit in a decimal represents a fraction with a denominator that is a power of 10. For example, in 0.005, since the 5 is in the thousandths place, it represents $\frac{5}{1,000}$. When there is more than one non-zero digit, just convert the digits after the decimal to a fraction with denominator equal to the *last* place represented: $0.32 = \dfrac{32}{100}$; $0.025 = \dfrac{25}{1,000}$. If there are non-zero digits *before* the decimal point, convert to a mixed number: $1.2 = 1\dfrac{2}{10}$; $60.006 = 60\dfrac{6}{1,000}$. Then you can reduce, simplify, and convert as needed.

Remember to use your mental math skills too: when you see 0.57, do you automatically think of 57 cents? That can help you. You know that that means $\dfrac{57}{100}$, since there are 100 cents in a dollar. If you were adding 0.024 and 0.341, you could estimate by thinking "that's around 2 cents plus 34 cents, which has a sum of 36 cents." If the answer choices weren't ridiculously close together, that would probably be enough to help you answer the question.

Estimating with decimals can be done in a more precise way, called rounding. **Rounding** is a process in which a number is approximated as the closest number that can be expressed using a given number of digits. So rounding to the nearest tenth means that the approximation will extend only to the tenths place, and so on. There is one rule for rounding: if the digit to the right of the place you are rounding to is greater than or equal to 5, you throw it out and all the digits to its right and make the digit to the left 1 greater—that's called rounding up. If the digit to the right of the place you are rounding to is less than 5, you throw out all the digits to its right and leave the digit to the left as it is—that's rounding down. Note: if you are rounding to a place to the left of the decimal point, fill in 0s in place of the digits you are throwing out between there and the decimal point. Here are some examples:

Rounding up:

> 0.035 rounded to the nearest *hundredth* becomes 0.04.

> 0.167 rounded to the nearest *hundredth* becomes 0.17.

> 125 rounded to the nearest *ten* becomes 130.

Rounding down:

> 0.032 rounded to the nearest *hundredth* becomes 0.03.

> 1.541 rounded to the nearest *hundredth* becomes 1.54.

> 323 rounded to the nearest *ten* becomes 320.

Adding and Subtracting Decimals

What's so great about decimals? One of the great things about decimals is that since they are fractions with denominators that are powers of ten, adding and subtracting them is very straightforward. All you have to do is make sure that you line them up according to their decimal places, so that you are adding tenths to tenths, hundredths to hundredths, and so on. If the addends don't have the same number of digits after the decimal point, add zeros until they do. Then you can use the standard algorithms for addition and subtraction of integers, with the small added step of keeping the decimal point in its place. For example:

$$
\begin{array}{r}
0.45 \\
+\ 0.1 \\
\hline
\end{array}
$$

$$
\begin{array}{r}
0.45 \\
+\ 0.10 \\
\hline
0.55 \\
\end{array}
$$

$$
\begin{array}{r}
0.01 \\
-\ 0.002 \\
\hline
\end{array}
$$

$$
\begin{array}{r}
0.010 \\
-\ 0.002 \\
\hline
0.008 \\
\end{array}
$$

Multiplying and Dividing Decimals

To multiply decimals, use the standard algorithm for multiplication of integers, ignoring the decimal point. Then count the *total* number of places after the decimal point in all of your factors, add them up, and place the decimal point that many places to the left in your product. Here are a couple of examples:

$$
\begin{array}{r}
\overset{2}{}0.5 \\
\times\ \ 4 \\
\hline
2.0 \\
\end{array}
\qquad
\begin{array}{r}
\overset{3}{}3.5 \\
\times\ 1.7 \\
\hline
245 \\
+\ 350 \\
\hline
5.95 \\
\end{array}
$$

A good way to check the placement of your decimal point is to approximate. For example, in the second product above, you could approximate 3.5 as 4 and 1.7 as 2. You can quickly calculate that $4 \times 2 = 8$; then you can check that your product, 5.95, is closer to 8 than to 80, 800, or 0.8.

Dividing decimals is pretty similar to multiplying them, in that you can use the standard algorithm for division of integers, with one extra rule. In the case of division, the extra rule is that the divisor must always be in the form of an integer. For example, to work the division problem $0.45 \div 0.3$, you need to convert 0.3 to an integer. The key is to think of it as a fraction: then you just find an equivalent fraction before you divide. You can always use a power of ten to find a denominator that's an integer:

$$\frac{0.45}{0.3} = \frac{0.45}{0.3} \times \frac{10}{10} = \frac{0.45 \times 10}{0.3 \times 10} = \frac{4.5}{3}$$

There's a shorthand version: just move the decimal point in the divisor to the right enough times to make it an integer, and move the decimal point in the dividend to the right the same number of times. That's the same as multiplying by the appropriate power of 10.

$$0.3\overline{)0.45}$$

$$3.\overline{)4.5}$$

In the quotient, write the decimal point directly above its position in the dividend. Then divide using the standard algorithm.

$$
\begin{array}{r}
1.5 \\
3\overline{)4.5} \\
-3 \\
\hline
1\,5 \\
-1\,5 \\
\hline
0
\end{array}
$$

You can use mental math to check your solution: how many groups of 30 cents are there in 45 cents? About $1\frac{1}{2}$, so our solution checks out.

Let's see how the CSET might test you on decimals.

Use the numbers below to answer the question that follows.

8.23
5.7
12.1
6.6
10.31
7.5

To estimate the sum of the numbers given above, Sloane first rounds each one to the nearest whole number, and then adds the rounded values. By how much will Sloane's estimate differ from the actual sum?

A. 0.04

B. 0.44

C. 0.56

D. 9.56

Here's How to Crack It

The question asks you to find a difference, so you need to find two quantities and then subtract to find the difference between them. What are the two quantities?

One is the answer Sloane obtains when she rounds the numbers. Find that. She rounds each value to the nearest whole number, so the list should look like this:

8
6
12
7
10
8

Add these to find Sloane's estimated sum: 8 + 6 + 12 + 7 + 10 + 8 = 51.

The question asks how much Sloane's estimate (which you just found) differs from the *actual sum*. So you need to find that too.

```
    3 2
    8.23
    5.70
   12.10
    6.60
   10.31
 +  7.50
   50.44
```

Now you can find the difference. Since all the answer choices are positive numbers, the question is asking for the positive difference. That means just subtract the lesser of your two numbers, 50.44, from the greater one, 51.

$$51 - 50.44 = 0.56$$

The correct answer is (C).

———————◯———————

PERCENTAGES

Here's the great news about percents: they're just fractions! I know, I know. You just did a bunch of work with fractions, and then when you looked at decimals, those were really fractions too. Now percents! When will you ever be done with fractions? Relax: this is the last kind of fractions—*for now*.

Converting Percentages to Fractions

Percents are pretty straightforward, because they all have the same denominator: 100. In fact, the word *percent* itself tells you that: *per cent* means per (or divided by) 100. Keep in mind that the symbol % stands for percent. So if you see any percentage, you can convert it to a fraction by using the number given as the numerator, and 100 as the denominator:

"Three percent" means $\dfrac{3}{100}$.

50% means $\dfrac{50}{100}$.

What about 100%? That just means $\dfrac{100}{100}$. Since anything divided by itself equals 1, 100% means 1, or the whole.

Don't be intimidated by strange percentages, like 0.05% (that just means $\dfrac{0.05}{100}$, or $\dfrac{5}{10,000}$) and 300% (that means $\dfrac{300}{100}$, or 3). Just put whatever number you see in the numerator, and 100 in the denominator.

If you see a percentage with a fraction in it, you can still convert it to a fraction in the same way. For example, $\dfrac{3}{4}\% = \dfrac{\frac{3}{4}}{100} = \dfrac{3}{4} \div 100 = \dfrac{3}{4} \times \dfrac{1}{100} = \dfrac{3}{400}$.

Do the same with mixed numbers: $66\dfrac{2}{3}\% = 66\% + \dfrac{2}{3}\% =$

$$\dfrac{66}{100} + \dfrac{\frac{2}{3}}{100} = \dfrac{66}{100} + \left(\dfrac{2}{3} \div 100\right) = \dfrac{66}{100} + \left(\dfrac{2}{3} \times \dfrac{1}{100}\right) = \dfrac{66}{100} + \dfrac{2}{300} = \left(\dfrac{66}{100} \times \dfrac{3}{3}\right) + \dfrac{2}{300}$$

$$= \dfrac{66 \times 3}{100 \times 3} + \dfrac{2}{300} = \dfrac{198}{300} + \dfrac{2}{300} = \dfrac{200}{300} = \dfrac{200 \div 100}{300 \div 100} = \dfrac{2}{3}$$

Converting Percentages to Decimals

To convert a percentage to a decimal, just remember that decimals are fractions too! The *hundredths* place is the one in which the denominator equals 100, just like in a percentage. So the number in your percent should *end* at the hundredths place in a decimal. In other words, move the decimal point two places to the left to convert (and remove the % symbol):

75% = 0.75   2% = 0.02   100% = 1   350% = 3.5   0.5% = 0.005

Converting Fractions and Decimals to Percentages

To convert a fraction or decimal to a percentage, just find an equivalent fraction with a denominator of 100. If it's not easy to find an equivalent fraction, you can convert to a decimal first.

$$\dfrac{3}{4} = \dfrac{3}{4} \times \dfrac{25}{25} = \dfrac{3 \times 25}{4 \times 25} = \dfrac{75}{100} = 75\%$$

$$0.05 = \dfrac{5}{100} = 5\%$$

$$1.753 = \dfrac{1{,}753}{1{,}000} = \dfrac{1{,}753 \div 10}{1{,}000 \div 10} = \dfrac{175.3}{100} = 175.3\%$$

$$\dfrac{12}{5} = \dfrac{12}{5} \times \dfrac{20}{20} = \dfrac{12 \times 20}{5 \times 20} = \dfrac{240}{100} = 240\%$$

$$\dfrac{3}{8} = 0.375 = \dfrac{375}{1{,}000} = \dfrac{375 \div 10}{1{,}000 \div 10} = \dfrac{37.5}{100} = 37.5\%$$

It is very helpful to have a handful of percentage-decimal-fraction equivalents memorized, since you can cut the time you spend on converting a *lot* if you don't have to actually convert! Here are some of the most common ones:

$$0.01 = \frac{1}{100} = 1\% \qquad 0.333... = \frac{1}{3} = 33\frac{1}{3}\% \qquad 0.666... = \frac{2}{3} = 66\frac{2}{3}\%$$

$$0.75 = \frac{3}{4} = 75\%$$

$$0.1 = \frac{1}{10} = 10\% \qquad 0.4 = \frac{2}{5} = 40\%$$

$$0.8 = \frac{4}{5} = 80\%$$

$$0.2 = \frac{1}{5} = 20\% \qquad 0.5 = \frac{1}{2} = 50\%$$

$$1.0 = \frac{1}{1} = 100\%$$

$$0.25 = \frac{1}{4} = 25\% \qquad 0.6 = \frac{3}{5} = 60\% \qquad 2.0 = \frac{2}{1} = 200\%$$

Translation

To find percentages of numbers (as you will in word problems), you need to translate them into math operations. Use this table to help:

These translations work in any word problem, not just percent problems.

Word	Equivalent Symbol
percent	$\overline{100}$
is	=
of, times, product	×
what (or any unknown value)	any variable *(x, k, b)*

Here's an example of how this might be tested on the CSET:

In a high school with 600 students, 12% of the student body is involved in student government. The students involved in student government are evenly distributed among grade levels 9–12. How many students in the 12th grade are involved in student government?

A.   18

B.   24

C.   72

D.   150

Here's How to Crack It

Translate the steps of the problem: first, it says that 12% of the student body is involved in student government.

12	%	of	the student body	is	in student government
12	÷ 100	×	600	=	?

Solve your translated problem to find the number of students involved in student government:

$$\frac{12}{100} \times 600 = 72$$

So 72 students *total* are involved in student government. Don't be fooled by (C), the partial answer trap! In fact, you can eliminate it now, as well as (D): since only some of these students are in the 12th grade, the correct answer will be less than 72.

Next, the problem states that the students involved in student government are evenly distributed among grades 9–12. That's four grades, so it means that the number of 12th-graders in student government will be $\frac{1}{4}$ of the 72 students involved:

$\frac{1}{4}$	of	the 72 students	are	12th-graders
$\frac{1}{4}$	×	72	=	?

Solve your translated problem:

$$\frac{1}{4} \times 72 = 18$$

The correct answer is (A).

Percent Change

You may also be asked questions dealing with a percentage increase or decrease. For those, you need the following formula:

Percent Change Formula

$$\text{Percent Change} = \frac{\text{Difference}}{\text{Original}} \times 100$$

When you are given a percent change problem, you'll be given two numbers. You need to find two pieces of information: the *difference* (which is the result when you subtract the lesser of the two numbers from the greater one) and the *original* (which is the one you "started with" in the problem). Sometimes the problem will say "from" and "to" (the "from" is the original), or use the word "original" or "originally." If not, keep in mind that in a **percent increase,** the original is the *lesser* number. In a **percent decrease,** the original is the *greater* number.

For example, find the percent increase from 3 to 4:

$$\text{Percent Change} = \frac{\text{Difference}}{\text{Original}} \times 100$$

Which number is the *original* here? The "from" number, 3, should be the original. You can check it by remembering that in a percent increase, the lesser number is the original.

The difference is 4 − 3 = 1.

$$\text{Percent Change} = \frac{\text{Difference}}{\text{Original}} \times 100 = \frac{1}{3} \times 100 = 33\frac{1}{3}\%$$

So the percent increase from 3 to 4 is $33\frac{1}{3}$%.

What about the percent decrease from 4 to 3?

Don't fall for the trap of assuming it's the same. In fact, it's not:

$$\text{Percent Change} = \frac{\text{Difference}}{\text{Original}} \times 100$$

Which number is the *original* here? The "from" number, 4, should be the original. You can check it by remembering that in a percent decrease, the greater number is the original.

The difference is still $4 - 3 = 1$.

$$\text{Percent Change} = \frac{\text{Difference}}{\text{Original}} \times 100 = \frac{1}{4} \times 100 = 25\%$$

So the percent decrease from 4 to 3 is 25%.

EXPONENTS

An **exponent** is just a mathematical shorthand for repeated multiplication. Rather than writing out $4 \times 4 \times 4$, you can use an exponent and write 4^3. The raised number, 3, is the **power** and the larger number, 4, is the **base.** The power tells you how many times to multiply the base by itself.

If the power (exponent) is 1, the base is repeated only one time. So any number to the power of 1 is itself: $a^1 = a$. If the base is 0, the result is always 0, since no matter how many times you multiply zero by itself you'll still get zero: $0^a = 0$.

When you raise a fraction to a power, both the numerator and the denominator are raised to the power. For example, $\left(\frac{3}{4}\right)^2 = \frac{3^2}{4^2} = \frac{3 \times 3}{4 \times 4} = \frac{9}{16}$.

Multiplying and Dividing Exponents

Here are some rules to remember when working with exponents.

Exponent Rules

When you are multiplying or dividing with exponents, or taking a power to a power, use the acronym **MADSPM,** which stands for:

Multiply
Add
Divide
Subtract
Power
Multiply

Multiply-Add

Let's look at what multiplying exponents really means. Let's say you need to multiply 4^3 by 4^2. Each of these powers tells you how many times to multiply the base, 4, by itself.

$$4^3 \times 4^2 = \left(4 \times 4 \times 4\right)\left(4 \times 4\right) = 4 \times 4 \times 4 \times 4 \times 4 = 4^5$$

Since 4^3 means three 4s multiplied together, and 4^2 means two 4s multiplied together, multiplying the two expressions is the same as just multiplying five 4s together. The powers sum to give a combined power. That's what we mean by Multiply-Add: when you multiply powers with the same base, just add the exponents.

$$4^3 \times 4^2 = 4^{3+2} = 4^5$$

Divide-Subtract

What about dividing exponents? Seems a little complex, but you can handle it. Let's say you want to divide 3^5 by 3^2. Again, the powers tell you how many times the base, 3, is multiplied by itself.

$$\frac{3^5}{3^2} = \frac{3 \times 3 \times 3 \times 3 \times 3}{3 \times 3} = \frac{3 \times 3 \times 3}{1} = \frac{3^3}{1} = 3^3$$

Notice that after you expand the powers to show the multiplication, you have five 3s in the numerator and two 3s in the denominator. Two sets of 3s cancelled: in other words, you reduced the fraction by dividing the numerator and denominator by 3×3. Since the denominator after reducing is 1, the result is just the three 3s that are left in the numerator: 3^3. That's what Divide-Subtract means: when you divide powers with the same base, just subtract the exponents.

$$\frac{3^5}{3^2} = 3^{5-2} = 3^3$$

Power-Multiply

When you take a power to a power, it starts to look pretty weird. Let's use the same process we've been using to discover how this rule works.

$$\left(6^2\right)^3 = \left(6^2\right)\left(6^2\right)\left(6^2\right) = \left(6 \times 6\right)\left(6 \times 6\right)\left(6 \times 6\right) = 6^6$$

Taking the expression 6^2 to the third power means multiplying it by itself 3 times. But each 6^2 means 6×6, so there end up being six 6s multiplied. The powers multiply to make the new exponent.

$$\left(6^2\right)^3 = 6^{2 \times 3} = 6^6$$

Keep in mind when you are using the MADSPM rules that the bases must be the same. You can't use these rules for an expression such as $\frac{3^3}{2^2}$, because the bases are different.

Negative Exponents

What happens in a situation like this: $\frac{8^3}{8^5}$?

Try expanding it out:

$$\frac{8^3}{8^5} = \frac{8 \times 8 \times 8}{8 \times 8 \times 8 \times 8 \times 8} = \frac{1}{8 \times 8} = \frac{1}{8^2}$$

It's very similar to the problem you worked above, but since there are more 8s in the denominator, the reduced fraction has 1 in the numerator.

Now try using the Divide-Subtract rule:

$$\frac{8^3}{8^5} = 8^{3-5} = 8^{-2}$$

From this, you can figure out what negative exponents mean. Confusingly, they do not make any of the values in the power negative. Instead, the negative sign indicates a multiplicative inverse. 8^{-2} is the multiplicative inverse, or reciprocal, of 8^2; in other words, $\frac{1}{8^2}$. Any term raised to a negative power is the reciprocal of that term raised to the positive power.

Zero Exponents

So, then, you might ask: what does a power of 0 mean? Any nonzero number raised to a power of 0 is equal to 1. For example:

$$4^3 \times 4^{-3} = 4^{3-3} = 4^0 = 1$$

0^0 is undefined. The CSET will not force you into that situation.

Adding and Subtracting Exponents

There is no MADSPM rule for adding or subtracting powers of the same base. However, you can sometimes use factoring in situations like this.

$$15^{15} - 15^{14}$$

What on Earth can you do here? Do they really expect you to find the values of 15^{15} and 15^{14}? Those are really large numbers! The calculator gives you scientific notation, which is not really helping.

Let's see what the answer choices would look like:

A.   15

B. $15^{14}(14)$

C. $15^{14}(16)$

D. 15^{29}

Okay, so you're not expected to calculate the values. But there has to be some way to simplify, right?

Try this: think of 15^{15} as a list of fifteen 15s, multiplied together. Think of 15^{14} as a list of fourteen 15s, multiplied together. What do those two products share? They each have fourteen 15s, multiplied together. 15^{15} just also has one extra one.

Remember the Distributive Property? Here's a refresher:

$$a(b + c) = ab + ac$$

$$a(b - c) = ab - ac$$

Let's look at the part that looks most like what we have: $ab - ac$. Write your expression in that form.

$$15^{15} - 15^{14} = 15^{14}(15) - 15^{14}(1)$$

What just happened? We wrote 15^{15} as $15^{14}(15)$: in other words, a list of fourteen 15s, multiplied together, times one extra 15. That's so we can see what it has in common with the other term. Then we wrote 15^{14} as $15^{14}(1)$, just to make it match. Now use the rule $a(b - c) = ab - ac$, in *reverse*. Here, a stands for 15^{14}, and b and c are 15 and 1, respectively:

$$15^{14}(15) - 15^{14}(1) = 15^{14}(15 - 1)$$

Now we're finally getting somewhere! You can subtract $15 - 1$ pretty easily.

$$15^{14}(14)$$

Great! The correct answer is (B).

Solving with Exponents

Let's look at one more example involving exponents:

$$64^3 = 8^x$$

Here you need to find the value of x, but the two powers have different bases. What gives?

The key is to rewrite terms using common bases.

Since 64 can be written as 8^2, the equation can be rewritten as $(8^2)^3 = 8^x$. Now that the bases are the same, you can use Power-Multiply: $8^6 = 8^x$. Since the bases are the same, the fact that both sides are equal tells you that the powers are the same as well: $x = 6$.

> If none of the bases in an exponent question seem to match up, see if you can find a way to rewrite the bases so that they match.

The Peculiar Behavior of Exponents

Here are a few more things to keep in mind about exponents:

- Raising a number greater than 1 to a power greater than 1 results in a greater number. For example, $2^2 = 4$.

- Raising a fraction that's between 0 and 1 to a power greater than 1 results in a lesser number. For example, $\left(\frac{1}{2}\right)^2 = \frac{1}{4}$.

- A negative number raised to an even power results in a positive number. For example, $(-2)^2 = 4$, because $(-2)(-2) = 4$.

- A negative number raised to an odd power results in a negative number. For example, $(-2)^3 = -8$, because $(-2)(-2)(-2) = -8$.

- A number raised to the first power ALWAYS results in the number itself. For example, $1{,}000^1 = 1{,}000$.

Scientific Notation

Scientific notation is a way of expressing numbers that are too big or too small to be conveniently written in decimal form. To write a number in scientific notation, first write it as a decimal. Move the decimal point so that the resulting number has a value between 1 and 10. Then use a power of 10 to represent the number of decimal spaces you moved the decimal point. Just remember that when you move the decimal point to the left, the power of 10 is positive. When you need to move it to the right, the power of 10 is negative. Here are a few examples.

$$1{,}256{,}000 = 1.256 \times 10^6$$

$$136 = 1.36 \times 10^2$$

$$0.00047 = 4.7 \times 10^{-4}$$

$$\frac{56}{1,000} = 0.056 = 5.6 \times 10^{-2}$$

As long as you remember how to interpret exponents, converting from scientific notation back to decimals should feel pretty straightforward.

$$7.502 \times 10^5 = 7.502 \times 100,000 = 750,200$$

$$6.25 \times 10^{-3} = 6.25 \times \frac{1}{1,000} = 0.00625$$

ROOTS

The inverse operation of a power is a **root.** In other words, while powers represent repeated multiplication, roots represent undoing repeated multiplication: a root tells you what number could be multiplied by itself a certain number of times to obtain a given number. The most common root you'll see is the square root.

Square Roots

The **square root** of a number is the quantity you would square to get that number. So for example, if you are asked for the square root of 9, you'd think: What number squared gives me 9?

It's a trick question, because there are two answers. You probably thought of 3 right away. And you are right! $3^2 = 9$. But there is also another number you can square to get 9: –3. That's right, $(-3)^2 = 9$ too! So the two square roots of 9 are 3 and –3.

The positive square root of a positive number is called the **principal square root.** So 3 is the principal square root of 9.

The sign for square root, called a **radical sign,** looks like this: $\sqrt{}$.

Remember, $\sqrt{}$ means the principal (positive) root only.

Here's where it gets a little weird: the radical sign *indicates only the principal root.* That means that although 3 and –3 are both square roots of 9, $\sqrt{9}$ is only equal to 3. If instead you see $x^2 = 9$, the solutions will be $x = 3$ AND $x = -3$.

So now you can see that $\sqrt{25} = 5$. How did you solve that? You probably asked yourself, "What times itself equals 25?" It wasn't too hard to get, because 25 is a **perfect square:** the square of an integer.

What happens if you are asked for the square root of a number that's not a perfect square? In this case, you can use your calculator. However, you may find that estimating is just as helpful. For example, you know that $\sqrt{13}$ is between 3 and 4, because $3^2 = 9$ and $4^2 = 16$, and $9 < 13 < 16$. Often, that's enough to answer the question.

Adding and Subtracting Square Roots

You can add or subtract square roots only if the values under the radical sign are equal. For example, the expression $2\sqrt{5} + 4\sqrt{5}$ can be simplified to $6\sqrt{5}$ because the values under the radical signs are equal, but $3\sqrt{3} + 4\sqrt{5}$ cannot be simplified because the values of the roots are not the same.

Multiplying and Dividing Square Roots

Multiplying and dividing square roots is different, though: *any* square roots can be multiplied or divided. Just put everything under the radical sign, and do your multiplying and dividing there. For example, $\sqrt{3} \times \sqrt{12} = \sqrt{3 \times 12} = \sqrt{36} = 6$. Similarly, $\dfrac{\sqrt{12}}{\sqrt{3}} = \sqrt{\dfrac{12}{3}} = \sqrt{4} = 2$.

Simplifying Square Roots

Sometimes when you are working with square roots, you'll find that the numbers under the radical sign don't work out to perfect squares. In that case, you can estimate, but you may also need to simplify. To simplify a square root, look for ways to factor the number under the radical sign so that at least one of the factors is a perfect square. For example, try working out the following expression:

$$\sqrt{2} \times \sqrt{10}$$

First, put these under the radical sign together and multiply:

$$\sqrt{2 \times 10} = \sqrt{20}$$

Now, look for ways to factor 20 that have at least one perfect square as a factor. The factors of 20 are:

20	
1	20
2	10
4	5

The only one of these factors that's a perfect square is 4. So factor 20 into 4 and 5:

$$\sqrt{20} = \sqrt{4 \times 5} = \sqrt{4} \times \sqrt{5} = 2\sqrt{5}$$

That's the form an answer choice would probably take, since it's as simplified as it can get.

Other Roots

Just as the square root of a number is the quantity you would square to get that number, other roots of a number represent the quantities you would take to other powers to get that number. You can take any root of a number, but you aren't likely to see too many of these on the CSET. Let's take a look at some.

The radical sign for a root other than a square root will show a little number on the left side indicating what root it is.

$$\sqrt[3]{8} = 2$$

The root above is called the **cube root** of 8. Since $2^3 = 8$, you know that the cube root of 8 is 2.

Notice that even if the problem were $x^3 = 8$, the solution would still be just 2, not 2 and –2. Why is that? Try cubing –2: $(-2)^3 = -8$. Remember the rule that a negative number raised to an odd power results in a negative number? That means that odd roots of positive numbers will be positive, and odd roots of negative numbers are negative.

$$\sqrt[4]{81} = 3$$

The root above is the fourth root of 81. Since $3^4 = 81$, you know that $\sqrt[4]{81} = 3$.

In this case, if the problem were $x^4 = 81$, the solutions would be 3 and –3. Why? Now you need the rule that a negative number raised to an even power results in a positive number. That means that even roots will always work like square roots (which are even roots!) in that there will be a principal (positive) root, and a second root that is negative. Pay attention to how the question is asked to determine whether you are being asked for both, or just the principal root.

Even and Odd Roots

Even roots have two solutions: a principal (positive) root, and a negative root.

Odd roots have only one solution. Odd roots of positive numbers are positive, and odd roots of negative numbers are negative.

$$\sqrt[5]{-32} = -2$$

In this example, you are finding the fifth root of –32. Since a negative number raised to an odd power is negative, you know the root is –2, and that there is no positive solution.

Another way to express roots is as fractional exponents.

For example, $\sqrt[3]{27}$ can also be written as $27^{\frac{1}{3}}$. This may help you combine roots and powers:

$$\sqrt[3]{4^6} = \left(4^6\right)^{\frac{1}{3}} = 4^{6 \times \frac{1}{3}} = 4^2 = 16$$

Notice that this also means $\sqrt[3]{4^6} = \left(\sqrt[3]{4}\right)^6$; it doesn't matter which order you do the root and the power in, because they can both be thought of as powers that will be multiplied together according to the Power-Multiply rule.

It will also help you to dissect something like $8^{\frac{2}{3}}$. You can separate this out to figure out what's going on: $8^{\frac{2}{3}} = \left(8^{\frac{1}{3}}\right)^2 = \left(\sqrt[3]{8}\right)^2 = 2^2 = 4$.

KEY TERMS

integer
whole number
positive number
negative number
fraction
numerator
denominator
proper fraction
improper fraction
mixed number
decimal
percentage
rational number
real number
irrational number
absolute value
digit
place value
place
standard algorithm
algorithm
addend
sum
Commutative Property of Addition
Associative Property of Addition
additive identity
additive inverse
minuend
subtrahend
difference
inverse operation
factor
product
Commutative Property of Multiplication
Associative Property of Multiplication
multiplicative identity

multiplicative inverse
dividend
divisor
quotient
Distributive Property (Distributive Law)
multiple
divisible
greatest common factor
prime number
prime factorization
prime factor
negative number
order of operations
unit fraction
reduce
simplest terms
equivalent fractions
reciprocal
common denominator
lowest common denominator
least common multiple
ratio
proportion
rounding
percent increase
percent decrease
exponent
power
base
scientific notation
root
square root
principal square root
radical sign
perfect square
cube root

Chapter 14 Drill

Answers and explanations can be found in the final section of this book, beginning on page 617.

1. **Use the problem below to answer the question that follows.**

   Angelina and her friends are having a book sale. Angelina has *v* books, Darcy has *w* books, and Cixin has *x* books. They want to stack the books in piles of equal number. How many books can they put in each stack?

   Which of the following methods could be used to find all the solutions to this problem?

   A. Find the divisors of $v + w + x$.

   B. Find the common factors of *v, w,* and *x*.

   C. Find the prime factors of *vwx*.

   D. Find the common multiples of *v, w,* and *x*.

2. Which of the following illustrates the operation $12\frac{3}{4} \times \frac{1}{3}$?

   A. It usually takes Suzanne $12\frac{3}{4}$ days to practice for her dance recital. This time, her practice took $\frac{1}{3}$ day longer. How many days did she practice this time?

   B. Suzanne is making a cake and the recipe calls for $12\frac{3}{4}$ cups of flour. She wants to make 3 times the recipe. How many cups of flour does she need?

   C. Suzanne has $12\frac{3}{4}$ hours to work on her presentation. She wants to split the presentation into 3 parts, and work the same amount of time on each part. How many hours will she work on each part?

   D. Suzanne has $12\frac{3}{4}$ feet of yarn. She wants to divide it into $\frac{1}{3}$-foot lengths for making tassels. How many pieces of yarn will Suzanne have?

3. The problem below shows a division problem setup, using the standard algorithm for division. The missing digits in the problem are represented by the symbol □.

$$\begin{array}{r} 5\square5\square \\ \square\overline{)17562} \end{array}$$

What is the ones digit of the quotient?

A.   3

B.   4

C.   5

D.   8

4. If the product of two integers is 91, which of the following values could represent the sum of the two integers?

A.   7

B.   13

C.   20

D.   91

5. The problem below shows steps to find the product of two decimals, using the standard algorithm for multiplication. The missing digits are represented by letters: all As represent the same missing digit, and all Bs represent the same digit.

$$\begin{array}{r} \overset{3}{17.A} \\ \times\ 3.2 \\ \hline 3AB \\ +\ A2AB \\ \hline A6.BB \end{array}$$

What is the value of the digit A?

A.   0

B.   3

C.   5

D.   6

6. Shelby needs to calculate the product 17×105. Which of the following is an equivalent expression that she can use to make the calculation easier?

A. $17 \times 100 \times 5$

B. $10 + 7 \times 100 + 5$

C. $(20 \times 105) - (7 \times 105)$

D. $(17 \times 100) + (17 \times 5)$

7. The town of Appleton had a population of 6,400 in 2005. By 2015, its population had grown to 9,600. If the town's population grew at a steady rate over the 10-year period, by what percent did its population increase each year?

   A. 5%

   B. $6\frac{2}{3}\%$

   C. 15%

   D. 50%

8. If $y \neq 0$, which of the following is equivalent to $\dfrac{y^9}{y(y^2)^3}$?

   A. y

   B. y^2

   C. y^3

   D. y^6

9. What value does the 7 represent in the number 5.073×10^{-2} ?

   A. $\dfrac{7}{100}$

   B. $\dfrac{7}{1,000}$

   C. $\dfrac{7}{10,000}$

   D. $\dfrac{7}{100,000}$

10. What is the value of $\dfrac{\sqrt{75}}{\sqrt{27}}$?

   A. $\dfrac{5}{9}$

   B. $\dfrac{5}{3}$

   C. $\sqrt{3}$

   D. $5\sqrt{3}$

Summary

- Integers include the counting numbers, zero, and the negatives of the counting numbers.

- A number line represents all the real numbers. Numbers farther to the left on the number line are less than numbers farther to the right, so you can use the number line to order integers, rational numbers, or real numbers.

- The absolute value of a number is its distance from 0 on the number line.

- Digits are the integers 0 through 9. Place value means the value of a digit in its place in a number. Each place to the left and right of the decimal point has a value that will determine the value of a digit placed there.

- You need to be familiar with the basic operations of arithmetic: addition, subtraction, multiplication, and division, and the standard algorithms for those operations.

- You should also be familiar with methods for finding all the factors of an integer, finding its prime factorization, and finding the greatest common factor of two integers.

- The order of operations is represented by the acronym PEMDAS: Parentheses, Exponents, Multiplication and Division, Addition and Subtraction.

- A fraction is a way to write a quotient and looks like this: $\dfrac{\text{numerator}}{\text{denominator}}$. The CSET will ask you to interpret pictures as fractions and perform operations with fractions. Reducing, finding a common denominator, and the Bowtie are essential tools.

- A ratio is a relationship of part to part. To work with ratios, remember the ratio box!

- A proportion is a mathematical comparison between equivalent fractions.

- A percentage is a fraction with a denominator of 100.

- Percent Change = $\dfrac{\text{Difference}}{\text{Original}} \times 100$

- An exponent is a mathematical shorthand for repeated multiplication.

- When you are multiplying or dividing with exponents, or taking a power to a power, use the acronym MADSPM: Multiply-Add; Divide-Subtract; Power-Multiply.

- A negative exponent means a reciprocal; any number to the power of 0 equals 1; a fractional exponent means a root.

- Scientific notation expresses numbers as decimals between 1 and 10 multiplied by powers of 10.

- A root is the inverse operation of a power. Even roots have two solutions: a principal (positive) root, and a negative root. Odd roots have only one solution: odd roots of positive numbers are positive, and odd roots of negative numbers are negative.

Chapter 15
Algebra and
Functions

EXPRESSIONS, EQUATIONS, AND FUNCTIONS

A **variable** is a symbol that represents a quantity in a mathematical expression. The variable's value is unspecified, and may vary (hence, the name). It may also be called an *unknown*. You'll usually see variables represented with letters in italics, such as a, b, c, x, y, or z. In a given expression or equation, all instances of the same variable represent the same quantity. For example, in the equation $-a = a^2$, you know that both a's represent the same value.

An **algebraic term** is a variable, a number, or a variable and a number combined by multiplication or division. For instance, $3x$ is a term, $\frac{a}{2}$ is a term, 5 is a term, and x is a term. But $3 + y$ is two terms, because the number and the variable aren't combined by multiplication or division, but by addition. In a term such as $3x$ (in which a variable is multiplied by a number), the number 3 is a **coefficient**—a number by which the variable is multiplied. When terms are combined by addition or subtraction, that combination is called an **algebraic expression.**

Expressions

Algebraic expressions are more or less the simplest sentences in the language of algebra. Some examples of algebraic expressions are:

$$3x - 4$$

$$x - y$$

$$\frac{4}{x} + \frac{x}{4}$$

Here's an algebraic expression showing a summary of the terms so far:

Manipulating Expressions

Like terms are terms with the same variables to the same exponents. In other words, $5x$ and $3x$ are like terms, because they both contain x (or x^1). So are $5x^2$ and $\frac{x^2}{2}$. The terms $3x$ and x^2 are NOT like terms, because the exponents are not the same. Neither are $3x$ and $5y$, because the variables are not the same.

In manipulating long, complicated algebraic expressions, combine all like terms before doing anything else. In other words, if one of the terms is $5x$ and another is $-3x$, simply combine them into $2x$. Then you won't have as many terms to work with. Here's an example:

$$(3x^2 + 3x + 4) + (2 - x) - (6 + 2x) =$$

$$3x^2 + 3x + 4 + 2 - x - 6 - 2x =$$

$$3x^2 + (3x - x - 2x) + (4 + 2 - 6) =$$

$$3x^2$$

Evaluating Expressions

Sometimes the CSET will give you the value of one of the variables or terms in an algebraic expression and ask you to find the value of the entire expression. In that case, substitute the given value for the specified variable or term, and then simplify. Here is an example:

$$\text{If } 2x = -1, \text{ then } (2x - 3)^2 = ?$$

Don't solve for x; just substitute the value you are given, -1, for the term it's equal to, $2x$:

$$(2x - 3)^2 = (-1 - 3)^2 = (-4)^2 = 16$$

Equations

An **equation** is a statement that the values of two expressions are equal. To show this, use the equals sign (=). Here are some examples of equations:

$$3g = 27$$

$$\frac{4}{x} = 12$$

$$3x - 4 = x + 5$$

$$x - y = 5y$$

Manipulating Equations

To **solve** an equation for the value of a variable, you must **isolate** the variable: in other words, get it by itself so that you can find its value. To do this, you can manipulate the equation—but you *can't change it.* What does that mean? The equal sign has to keep on being true: the two sides of the equation (on either side of the equal sign) have to keep being equal. That means that if you change one side of the equation, you must change the other side in *exactly the same way.*

Try it with the example $3g = 27$. To isolate g, you need to get rid of its coefficient, 3. There's an easy way to get rid of a number that's multiplied by a variable: perform the inverse operation. Since g is multiplied by 3, the inverse operation is to divide by 3. Here's where the balance of the equation comes in: you can't divide the left side by 3 *unless* you do the same to the right side:

$$\frac{3g}{3} = \frac{27}{3}$$

The equation is still in balance; the equal sign is still true. Now, simplify:

$$g = 9$$

The equation has been solved for g. To check that the solution is correct, you can substitute the value into the equation as it was originally written: does $3(9) = 27$? Yep. This solution is correct.

You can do the same process to equations with more than one term. Just make sure you remember inverse operations!

$$x + 5 = 12$$

$$x + 5 - 5 = 12 - 5$$

$$x = 7$$

You need to be aware of the order of operations when you solve in more than one step. You'll use the reverse order to solve.

$$2x - 6 = 26$$

$$2x - 6 + 6 = 26 + 6$$

$$2x = 32$$

$$\frac{2x}{2} = \frac{32}{2}$$

$$x = 16$$

Try another one:

$$5(4x + 3) = 25$$

$$\frac{5(4x + 3)}{5} = \frac{25}{5}$$

$$4x + 3 = 5$$

$$4x + 3 - 3 = 5 - 3$$

$$4x = 2$$

$$\frac{4x}{4} = \frac{2}{4}$$

$$x = \frac{1}{2}$$

You may also have to simplify at some steps.

$$12x - 23 = 4x + 5$$

$$12x - 23 + 23 = 4x + 5 + 23$$

$$12x = 4x + 28$$

$$12x - 4x = 4x - 4x + 28$$

$$8x = 28$$

$$\frac{8x}{8} = \frac{28}{8}$$

$$x = \frac{7}{2}, \text{ or } 3\frac{1}{2}$$

If you see fractions, remember that the fraction bar represents division, and the inverse operation to division is—that's right—multiplication!

$$\frac{x}{3} + 5 = 12$$

$$\frac{x}{3} + 5 - 5 = 12 - 5$$

$$\frac{x}{3} = 7$$

$$\frac{x}{3} \times 3 = 7 \times 3$$

$$x = 21$$

If you need to combine algebraic fractions (fractions with variables in them), or combine them with regular variable terms, remember what you know about manipulating fractions.

$$\frac{x}{3} + 2 = 4x$$

$$\frac{x}{3} - \frac{x}{3} + 2 = 4x - \frac{x}{3}$$

$$2 = 4x - \frac{x}{3}$$

$$2 = \frac{4x}{1} - \frac{x}{3}$$

What now? How about the Bowtie?

$$2 = \frac{4x}{1} \overset{12x}{\underset{}{\times}} \overset{-}{\underset{}{}} \overset{x}{\underset{3}{x}} = \frac{11x}{3}$$

Now deal with the fraction by using multiplication, and finish solving.

$$2 \times 3 = \frac{11x}{3} \times 3$$

$$6 = 11x$$

$$\frac{6}{11} = \frac{11x}{11}$$

$$\frac{6}{11} = x$$

Another way to deal with this equation would be to eliminate the fraction at the beginning. Here's the original equation:

$$\frac{x}{3} + 2 = 4x$$

To eliminate the fraction, just multiply *everything* on both sides of the equation by 3:

$$3\left(\frac{x}{3} + 2\right) = 3(4x)$$

Distribute the multiplication:

$$3\left(\frac{x}{3}\right) + 3(2) = 12x$$

$$x + 6 = 12x$$

Now solve the rest:

$$x - x + 6 = 12x - x$$

$$6 = 11x$$

$$\frac{6}{11} = \frac{11x}{11}$$

$$\frac{6}{11} = x$$

Finally, remember that the inverse operation to a power is a root:

$$x^3 = 27$$

$$\sqrt[3]{x^3} = \sqrt[3]{27}$$

$$x = 3$$

Patterns and Functions

Equations can be used to represent patterns. For example, if x increases by 3 every time y increases by 1, the equation $y = 3x$ can represent that pattern. Another kind of notation used to represent patterns is function notation.

A **function** is a special relationship between variables in which each input has a single output.

Function notation looks like this: $f(x) = 6x - 5$. Here the f is not a variable, but the name of the function. It's not being multiplied: it's just there to represent the *process* being applied to x. You might say "A function f of x is defined as $6x - 5$." Here's what this means: "To perform $f(x)$, multiply the value of x by 6 and then subtract 5." For each input (x-value), there will be one output ($f(x)$-value). To evaluate a function for a given value, substitute that value for the variable (in this case, x):

If $f(x) = 6x - 5$, what is the value of $f(7)$?

Substitute 7 for x:

$$f(7) = 6(7) - 5 = 42 - 5 = 37$$

What if a question asks you to find what input value yields a particular output?

If $f(x) = 6x - 5$, for what value of x does $f(x) = 13$?

Then substitute the value for $f(x)$, the output, and solve for x, the input:

$$13 = 6x - 5$$

$$13 + 5 = 6x - 5 + 5$$

$$18 = 6x$$

$$\frac{18}{6} = \frac{6x}{6}$$

$$3 = x$$

You may be asked to write a function that fits a given set of values. In that case, you must look for the pattern that describes the set of values given. Look for whether the terms increase by a fixed amount or whether there is a factor they are being multiplied by.

———————⌣———————

Use the table below to answer the question that follows.

x	$f(x)$
0	5
1	8
2	11
3	14
4	17

Which of the following is a function that can describe the values shown in the table?

A. $f(x) = x + 3$

B. $f(x) = x + 5$

C. $f(x) = 3x + 3$

D. $f(x) = 3x + 5$

Here's How to Crack It

Look at the values given in the table. While the x-values increase by 1, the $f(x)$-values increase by 3. That tells you the x-value will be multiplied by 3 as part of the function evaluation. Eliminate (A) and (B). Which function fits the values? Try the first pair in each function you have left to see whether it fits: $f(0) = 5$?

Try (C). Using this function would mean that $5 = 3(0) + 3 = 0 + 3 = 3$. That's not true, so that function doesn't fit.

Try (D). Using this function would mean that $5 = 3(0) + 5 = 0 + 5 = 5$. That's true.

You can make a good bet that (D) is correct, now that you've eliminated the other answer choices. If you have the time, it's good to check the other values to be sure you haven't made a mistake. Does $8 = 3(1) + 5$? Yes, $3(1) + 5 = 3 + 5 = 8$. Does $11 = 3(2) + 5$? Yes, $3(2) + 5 = 6 + 5 = 11$. Does $14 = 3(3) + 5$? Yes, $3(3) + 5 = 9 + 5 = 14$. Does $17 = 3(4) + 5$? Yes, $3(4) + 5 = 12 + 5 = 17$. Since all the values work, you know (D) is correct.

What function could describe the following data?

x	$f(x)$
1	1
2	4
3	9
4	16

Notice that the x-values increase by 1, but the $f(x)$-values don't increase by a constant difference. There must be a different kind of pattern here. Can you spot it?

If you noticed that $f(x) = x^2$, you're on your way!

Writing Expressions, Equations, and Functions

Since the CSET expects you not just to be able to *manipulate* algebraic expressions and equations, but also to *understand* them, it often gives you algebraic situations in words rather than algebra. Then it's up to you to translate. Use the skills you've just reviewed to put the following situations in algebraic terms.

———————○———————

Bowling at Fast Lanes costs $6 per game and $3 per pair of shoes. If Kelsey and 4 of her friends want to play *n* games, what will the total cost be?

A. $12 + $6*n*

B. $15 + $6*n*

C. $12*n* + $6

D. $15*n* + $6

Here's How to Crack It

This question is asking you to write an algebraic expression based on the situation. Think about what quantities contribute to the total cost. Kelsey and 4 of her friends will need 5 pairs of shoes, so you can calculate the cost of the shoes: $3 per pair of shoes × 5 pairs of shoes = $15.

Next, you need to find the cost of the *n* games. Each game costs $6, so multiply: *n* games × $6 per game = $6*n*.

Now just add the two costs to find the total: $15 + $6*n*. The correct answer is (B).

———————○———————

Here's one that sounds pretty vague:

———————○———————

If 15 more than twice a number is equal to 7 times that number, what is the value of the number?

A. −3

B. $1\frac{2}{3}$

C. $2\frac{1}{2}$

D. 3

Here's How to Crack It

This is actually a very specific math sentence that tells you exactly how to write an equation that you can solve for the variable. Just translate piece by piece:

15 more than	twice a number	is equal to	7 times that number
15 +	$2n$	=	$7n$

Now solve for n:

$$15 + 2n = 7n$$

$$15 + 2n - 2n = 7n - 2n$$

$$15 = 5n$$

$$\frac{15}{5} = \frac{5n}{5}$$

$$3 = n$$

The correct answer is (D).

REPRESENTING ALGEBRA

Dependent and Independent Variables

In real-world situations, relations can often be described in terms of dependent and independent variables. The value of a **dependent variable** depends on the value of the **independent variable.** In other words, the independent variable is the input, or cause. The dependent variable is the output; its value changes based on changes in the independent variable.

For example, imagine that Ximena is measuring her kitten's weight as it grows. Below is her record of the data she has collected.

Age (in days) of kitten	Weight in ounces
0	5
1	5.25
2	5.5
3	5.75
4	6
5	6.25
6	6.5
7	6.75
8	7

Ximena wants to write an equation to describe the kitten's growth. First, she needs to determine which is the independent variable and which is the dependent variable. Since the age of the kitten can't be affected by its weight, that's the independent variable. The kitten will grow over time as long as it eats and stays healthy, so its weight is the dependent variable.

What's the relationship between the numbers Ximena has recorded? As its age increases by 1 day, the kitten's weight keeps increasing by 0.25 ounces. Its original weight was 5 ounces (when its age was 0). You have enough information now to write an equation:

$$w = 0.25a + 5$$

Notice that this data could just as easily be represented by a function:

$$f(a) = 0.25a + 5$$

Tables and Graphs

In the example above, you used a table to generate an equation. The information contained in algebraic equations can be represented in different ways. **Tables** are useful for organizing data and looking for patterns, as well as for helping to plot points in graphs. In algebra, a **graph** is a line or curve drawn on a number line or coordinate plane by joining the points represented by certain ordered pairs.

You can graph equations in one variable on a number line. You use a closed dot to represent a single number on a number line. For example, let's graph $y = 5$:

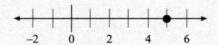

You can graph equations in two variables on a coordinate plane.

The **coordinate plane,** also known as the *x-y* coordinate plane or the Cartesian grid, looks like this:

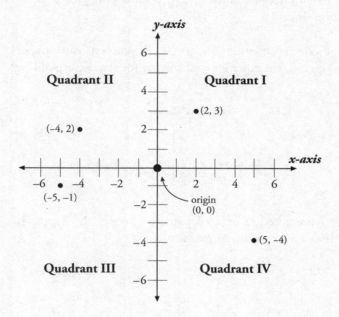

The horizontal axis in the coordinate plane is called the **x-axis.** It's just like a horizontal number line: values increase as you move to the right, with negative values to the left of 0 and positive values to the right.

The vertical axis in the coordinate plane is called the **y-axis.** It's just like a vertical number line: values increase as you move up, with negative values above 0 and positive values below.

The **origin** is the place where the two axes cross each other. It falls at the 0 point of both number lines. In an ordered pair, the origin's location is expressed as (0, 0).

An **ordered pair** is the way you express the locations of points in the coordinate plane. The **x-coordinate** (the point's horizontal location) is given first, and the **y-coordinate** (the point's vertical location) is given second. So to find the point (2, 3) in the coordinate plane above, start at the origin and move 2 units to the right (according to the *x*-coordinate) and 3 units up (according to the *y*-coordinate). The generalized form of an ordered pair is written (*x, y*), to remind us that the first coordinate is the *x*-coordinate and the second is the *y*-coordinate.

The coordinate plane is divided into four **quadrants,** or quarters, by the two axes. Quadrant I contains points with positive *x*- and *y*-values, like the point (2, 3) above. Quadrant II contains points with negative *x*-values and positive *y*-values, like the point (–4, 2) above. Quadrant III contains points with negative *x*- and *y*-values, like the point (–5, –1) above. And Quadrant IV contains points with positive *x*-values and negative *y*-values, like the point (5, –4) above.

Many kinds of equations can be represented by graphs in the coordinate plane. The most important kind are linear equations.

Linear Equations

A **linear equation** is an equation in two variables that gives a straight line when it's graphed; in linear equations, each term is either a constant or the product of a constant and a single variable (to the first power). (That's because equations with exponents greater than one, which will be discussed later, are non-linear.)

Here's an example of a linear equation: $y = 2x + 1$. To graph it, you can make a table of values by substituting x-values into the equation and solving for the corresponding y-values:

x	y
–2	–3
–1	–1
0	1
1	3
2	5

These values can be represented as ordered pairs: (–2, –3), (–1, –1), (0, 1), (1, 3), and (2, 5). Then you can plot those on a coordinate plane:

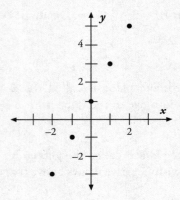

If you plot at least two points that satisfy a linear equation, you can connect them and form a **line.** A line is a basic geometric shape: it's a set of points that continue forever in two directions. Lines must be straight and have no thickness. Place a ruler so that the straight line it represents passes through both your points, draw the line, and add arrows at both ends to show that it continues in both directions:

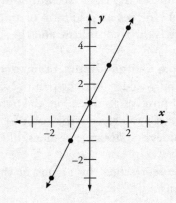

What's really cool is that any point on the line you drew will satisfy the linear equation $y = 2x + 1$. So you can think of it as a different way to represent that equation.

Slope and Intercepts

Linear equations are easiest to graph when they are in the **slope-intercept form.** The generalized version of that form is $y = mx + b$. You can tell that the equation you used above, $y = 2x + 1$, is already in this form.

When an equation you're given is not in slope-intercept form, you can solve it for y to get it into the form:

$$2x + 4y = 16$$

$$2x - 2x + 4y = -2x + 16$$

$$4y = -2x + 16$$

$$\frac{4y}{4} = \frac{-2x}{4} + \frac{16}{4}$$

$$y = -\frac{1}{2}x + 4$$

What's useful about slope-intercept form is that it can tell you useful pieces of information about the graph of the line. The two pieces of information it gives you are, unsurprisingly, the slope and the y-intercept. In terms of the generalized form, $y = mx + b$, the m tells you the slope and the b tells you the x-coordinate of the y-intercept. So let's review what those are!

Slope is a ratio that tells you the *steepness* of a line. The ratio compares the vertical change (or change in y-coordinates) to the horizontal change (or change in x-coordinates). Some people think of slope as $\frac{\text{rise}}{\text{run}}$:

$$\text{slope} = \frac{\text{rise}}{\text{run}} = \frac{\text{vertical change}}{\text{horizontal change}}$$

In other words, think of two points on your line. The **rise,** or vertical change, is how much the line goes *up* between the two points. If the line goes *down* instead, the rise is negative. The **run,** or horizontal change, is how much the line goes *to the right* between the two points. If the line goes *to the left* instead, the run is negative. Here's a formula that will give the slope if you know two ordered pairs representing two points:

$$\text{slope} = \frac{y_2 - y_1}{x_2 - x_1}$$

In the formula, x_1 represents the x-coordinate and y_1 represents the y-coordinate of the *first* ordered pair, and x_2 represents the x-coordinate and y_2 represents the y-coordinate of the *second* ordered pair. Which ordered pair you choose to be *first* and which you choose to be *second* doesn't really matter as long as you keep the 1s separate from the 2s. For example, take two points from the table above, say (0, 1) and (1, 3). If we call (0, 1) the first point and (1, 3) the second, then the formula gives:

$$\text{slope} = \frac{y_2 - y_1}{x_2 - x_1} = \frac{3 - 1}{1 - 0} = \frac{2}{1} = 2$$

That means that the line has a slope of 2: it goes up 2 units every time it goes to the right 1 unit.

Remember that the equation for this line, in slope-intercept form, is $y = 2x + 1$. The m part of $y = mx + b$ tells you the slope. Here, you can read that the slope is 2, because that's the number in the place of the m in the equation for this line.

The other piece of information the slope-intercept form tells you is the **y-intercept.** That's the point at which the line crosses the y-axis. Since all the points on the y-axis have x-coordinates of 0, the x-coordinate of the y-intercept is always 0, so the value of b in the equation tells you the y-coordinate. In other words, the y-intercept is the point $(0, b)$. Let's find the y-intercept of the line you graphed above, $y = 2x + 1$. Since the value of b here is 1, the y-intercept is $(0, 1)$. And you can see that that's a point on the graph of your line, and that it *is* the spot where the line crosses the y-axis.

A line with negative slope goes up and to the left (or down and to the right), rather than up and to the right (or down and to the left), as lines with positive slopes do. Steeper lines have slopes with greater absolute values. A line that has a slope of 1 or –1 makes a 45°-angle with the x-axis. And lines with slopes between 0 and 1, or between –1 and 0, have slopes that are less steep. Here are a few examples:

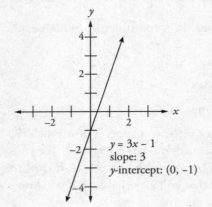

$y = 3x - 1$
slope: 3
y-intercept: (0, –1)

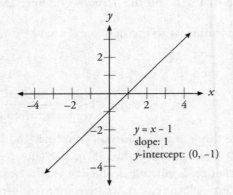

$y = x - 1$
slope: 1
y-intercept: (0, –1)

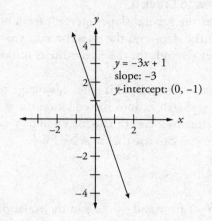

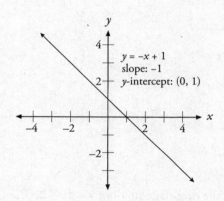

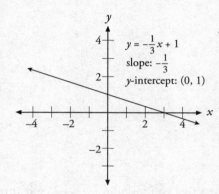

Also keep in mind that horizontal lines have slopes of 0, and vertical lines have slopes that are undefined. If a line *looks* horizontal or vertical, that doesn't guarantee that you know its slope: you need two points to verify that there is no vertical or horizontal change.

The CSET likes to ask questions about linear equations. Let's try an example:

What is the equation of the straight line that has slope 4 and passes through the point (–1, –6)?

A. $y = 4x - 2$

B. $y = 4x - 6$

C. $y = 2x - 4$

D. $y = 2x - 6$

Here's How to Crack It

Remember the general slope-intercept form of the equation for a line: $y = mx + b$. Since the m stands for the slope and the question tells you that the slope is 4, substitute 4 for m: $y = 4x + b$. Recall that b stands for the y-coordinate of the y-intercept, $(0, b)$. You need to find that value.

The easiest way to solve this takes advantage of a cool fact about linear equations: any point on the line (x, y) will fit into the equation. In other words, if you know a point on the line, you can substitute its x-coordinate for x and its y-coordinate for y in the equation, and it will still be true. Here you can use that to solve for b.

You know the point $(-1, -6)$.

Substitute -1 for x and -6 for y in the equation and solve for b:

$$y = 4x + b$$

$$-6 = 4(-1) + b$$

$$-6 = -4 + b$$

$$-6 + 4 = -4 + 4 + b$$

$$-2 = b$$

Since the value you found for b is -2, substitute that into the original equation: $y = 4x - 2$. The correct answer is (A).

Here's another way the CSET might test this:

Use the graph below to answer the question that follows.

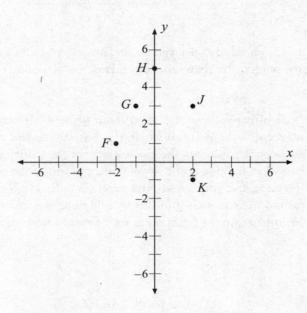

Point F is on a line with a slope of $\dfrac{1}{2}$ in the x-y plane.
Which of the following points is also on the line?

A. G

B. H

C. J

D. K

Here's How to Crack It

You can use the formula, $\text{slope} = \dfrac{y_2 - y_1}{x_2 - x_1}$, to check each point given in the answer choices with the given point, F, to find which gives the correct slope, $\dfrac{1}{2}$. But that's pretty time consuming. There is an easier way that works here. Try using your knowledge of what the given slope of $\dfrac{1}{2}$ means. You know that slope represents $\dfrac{\text{rise}}{\text{run}}$, or $\dfrac{\text{vertical change}}{\text{horizontal change}}$. That tells you that a slope of $\dfrac{1}{2}$ describes a line that goes up 1 unit every time it goes to the right 2 units. Try doing this, with the given point, F, as a starting point. From F, $(-2, 1)$, going up 1 unit and to the right 2 units gives you the point (0, 2). That's not one of the labeled points, but what happens if you try again? Go up 1 more unit and to the right 2 more units. You'll arrive at (2, 3). That point is labeled *J,* so the correct answer is (C). Don't forget that you could also have tried going *down* 1 unit and *to the left* 2 units if you hadn't found an answer in this direction.

Many test questions, like the one above, give you an advantage if you find the easiest way to get to the answer: you get the point faster than other test takers, and have more time left to answer other questions.

Another piece of information that you may be asked about is the *x*-intercept. This is just what it sounds like: the **x-intercept** is the point at which the line crosses the *x*-axis. Since all the points on the *x*-axis have *y*-coordinates of 0, the *y*-coordinate of the *x*-intercept is always 0. You can't find the *x*-intercept by just looking at the slope-intercept form of the equation of the line, as you can with the *y*-intercept. But you can use the equation to find it. Remember, any point on the line (*x*, *y*) will fit into the equation. In other words, since you know the *y*-value of the *x*-intercept, you can substitute it into the equation to solve for the matching *x*-value. Try it with the equation $y = 2x + 1$.

$$0 = 2x + 1$$

$$0 - 1 = 2x + 1 - 1$$

$$-1 = 2x$$

$$\frac{-1}{2} = \frac{2x}{2}$$

$$-\frac{1}{2} = x$$

So the *x*-intercept of the line $y = 2x + 1$ is $(-\frac{1}{2}, 0)$.

Equations of Parallel and Perpendicular Lines

One more thing you need to know about linear equations is how the equations of two lines relate when the lines are **parallel** (they are equidistant and never intersect) and when they are **perpendicular** (they form a 90° angle).

Parallel lines never meet. This happens because though they cross through different points, their slopes are the same, ensuring that they never get closer together at any point.

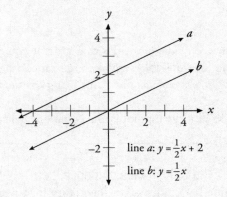

line *a*: $y = \frac{1}{2}x + 2$

line *b*: $y = \frac{1}{2}x$

The two lines above are parallel—they have the same slope. Their *y*-intercepts are different. What happens if two equations have the same slope and the same *y*-intercept? Then the two equations are the same—so they describe the same line.

Perpendicular lines do cross. At their **intersection** (the point at which they cross), they form a 90° angle. The equations of these lines also have a special relationship: their slopes are opposite reciprocals. That means that the slope of one line is the negative of the reciprocal of the other line's slope.

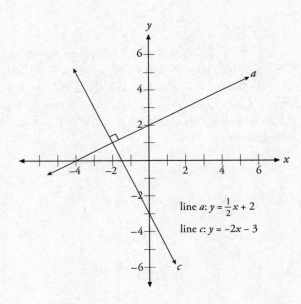

line *a*: $y = \frac{1}{2}x + 2$

line *c*: $y = -2x - 3$

INEQUALITIES

An **inequality** is a relation between two quantities that are not equal. It uses a symbol such as < to compare their values. The four possible symbols are >, meaning *greater than*, <, meaning *less than*, ≥, meaning *greater than or equal to,* and ≤, meaning *less than or equal to.*

Manipulating inequalities works just like manipulating equations, with one important difference.

> ### The Golden Rule of Inequalities
> When you multiply or divide both sides of an inequality by a negative number, flip the sign around.

Try a few examples:

$$-y < 25$$

$$-1(-y) > -1(25)$$

$$y > -25$$

That makes sense. If $-y < 25$, then the values of y have to be numbers that, once they are negated, are less than 25. So numbers like -5 will work: $-(-5) = 5$, which is less than 25; and any positive number will work: $-(6) = -6$, which is less than 25. But negative numbers with absolute values greater than 25 aren't going to work: $-(-26) = 26$, which is greater than 25. And the sign tells you that -25 won't work either: $-(-25) = 25$, which is not less than 25. So only values *greater than* -25 are solutions.

$$7 - 3x \leq -14$$

$$7 - 7 - 3x \leq -14 - 7$$

$$-3x \leq -21$$

$$\frac{-3x}{-3} \geq \frac{-21}{-3}$$

$$x \geq 7$$

When you divide by -3, don't forget to flip the sign around.

$$-5(4x + 3) < 25$$

$$\frac{-5(4x + 3)}{-5} > \frac{25}{-5}$$

$$4x + 3 > -5$$

$$4x + 3 - 3 > -5 - 3$$

$$4x > -8$$

$$\frac{4x}{4} > \frac{-8}{4}$$

$$x > -2$$

In that one, you flip the sign only in the first step, when you divide by –5. None of the later steps involve multiplication or division by a negative number.

$$-\frac{x}{3} + 5 \leq 12$$

$$-\frac{x}{3} + 5 - 5 \leq 12 - 5$$

$$-\frac{x}{3} \leq 7$$

$$-\frac{x}{3} \times (-3) \geq 7 \times (-3)$$

$$x \geq -21$$

In the inequality above, you flip the sign in the last step, when you multiply by –3.

Graphing Inequalities

When an inequality is in one variable, it can be graphed on a number line.

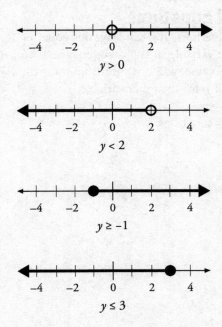

$y > 0$

$y < 2$

$y \geq -1$

$y \leq 3$

When an inequality is in two variables, it can be graphed on the coordinate plane. To graph, first graph the line that would be the solution if the inequality were an equation. A dotted line is used for < and >, and a solid line for ≤ and ≥. Then shade the portion of the graph that fulfills the inequality. If you are not sure which side that is, pick a point on one side of the line you drew and test it in the inequality. If it makes the inequality true, shade that side of the graph; if it makes the inequality false, shade the other side of the graph.

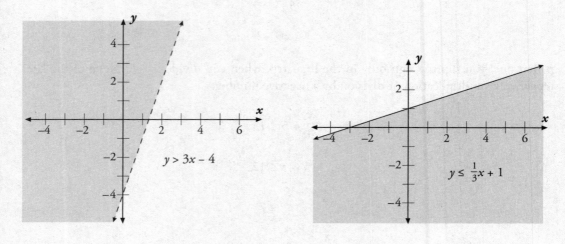

SYSTEMS OF EQUATIONS AND INEQUALITIES

If you have two linear equations in two variables, you can usually use them to find a solution that fits both: in other words, if you graph two lines, there will usually be one point that's on both lines: their intersection. It won't work if the two equations represent the same line (all the points are solutions) or if the lines are parallel (they do not intersect).

Solving Systems of Equations

To solve a system of linear equations, you can solve one equation for one variable, substitute the equivalent expression for the variable in the other equation, and then solve for the remaining variable. Once you have that value, you can substitute it for the variable it represents in one of the original equations and solve for the other variable.

Try it with the following two equations:

$$7x + 3y = 19$$

$$\frac{x}{2} - y = 5$$

Solve the second equation for *y*:

$$\frac{x}{2} - y = 5$$

$$\frac{x}{2} - \frac{x}{2} - y = 5 - \frac{x}{2}$$

$$-y = 5 - \frac{x}{2}$$

$$-1(-y) = -1(5 - \frac{x}{2})$$

$$y = -5 + \frac{x}{2}$$

Now substitute the equivalent expression for *y* in the other equation:

$$7x + 3y = 19$$

$$7x + 3(-5 + \frac{x}{2}) = 19$$

This is pretty ugly, but the good news is that it now has only one variable, *x*. So you can solve for *x*:

$$7x - 15 + \frac{3x}{2} = 19$$

Multiply the whole equation by 2 to get rid of the fraction:

$$2(7x - 15 + \frac{3x}{2}) = 2(19)$$

$$14x - 30 + 3x = 38$$

$$14x + 3x - 30 = 38$$

$$17x - 30 = 38$$

$$17x - 30 + 30 = 38 + 30$$

$$17x = 68$$

$$\frac{17x}{17} = \frac{68}{17}$$

$$x = 4$$

Now substitute 4 for x in one of the original equations:

$$7x + 3y = 19$$

$$7(4) + 3y = 19$$

$$28 + 3y = 19$$

$$28 - 28 + 3y = 19 - 28$$

$$3y = -9$$

$$\frac{3y}{3} = \frac{-9}{3}$$

$$y = -3$$

You can check your solution by trying both values ($x = 4$, $y = -3$) in the other of the original equations:

$$\frac{x}{2} - y = 5$$

$$\frac{4}{2} - (-3) = 5?$$

$$2 - (-3) = 5?$$

$$5 = 5 \checkmark$$

That process is pretty long and unwieldy. There is an easier way that often works with systems of linear equations. It works like this: stack the two equations and match up the coefficients of the two variables. If either pair is opposites, then add the equations. If either pair of coefficients are the same, then subtract the equations. That way you'll eliminate one of the variables, and be able to solve what's left for the other variable.

$$7x + 3y = 19$$

$$5x - 3y = 41$$

Since the coefficients of y are opposites, add the equations:

$$\begin{array}{r} 7x + 3y = 19 \\ +\ \ 5x - 3y = 41 \\ \hline 12x + 0 = 60 \end{array}$$

Since the *y*-terms added to 0, now the equation can be solved for *x:*

$$12x = 60$$

$$\frac{12x}{12} = \frac{60}{12}$$

$$x = 5$$

Substitute this value for *x* in either one of the original equations and solve for *y:*

$$7x + 3y = 19$$

$$7(5) + 3y = 19$$

$$35 + 3y = 19$$

$$35 - 35 + 3y = 19 - 35$$

$$3y = -16$$

$$\frac{3y}{3} = \frac{-16}{3}$$

$$y = -\frac{16}{3} = -5\frac{1}{3}$$

Now substitute both values in the other original equation to check:

$$5x - 3y = 41$$

$$5(5) - 3\left(-\frac{16}{3}\right) = 41?$$

$$25 - (-16) = 41?$$

$$25 + 16 = 41?$$

$$41 = 41 \checkmark$$

If the coefficients aren't the same or opposites, find a factor that you can multiply one equation by to make the coefficients the same or opposites.

$$2x + 3y = 12$$

$$5x + 6y = 16$$

Multiply the first equation by 2 (this will make the y-coefficients the same):

$$2(2x + 3y) = 2(12)$$

$$4x + 6y = 24$$

Now stack them again, and you can subtract:

$$4x + 6y = 24$$

$$5x + 6y = 16$$

$$\begin{array}{r} 4x + 6y = 24 \\ -\ \ 5x + 6y = 16 \\ \hline -x + 0 = 8 \end{array}$$

Since the y-terms added to 0, now the equation can be solved for x:

$$-x = 8$$

$$-1(-x) = -1(8)$$

$$x = -8$$

Substitute this value for x in either one of the original equations and solve for y:

$$2x + 3y = 12$$

$$2(-8) + 3y = 12$$

$$-16 + 3y = 12$$

$$-16 + 16 + 3y = 12 + 16$$

$$3y = 28$$

$$\frac{3y}{3} = \frac{28}{3}$$

$$y = \frac{28}{3} = 9\frac{1}{3}$$

Now substitute both values in the other original equation to check:

$$5x + 6y = 16$$

$$5(-8) + 6\left(\frac{28}{3}\right) = 16?$$

$$-40 + 56 = 16?$$

$$16 = 16 \checkmark$$

You might have to multiply *both* equations to get matching coefficients:

$$3x + 7y = 20$$

$$2x + 3y = 10$$

Multiply the first equation by 2 and the second equation by 3:

$$2(3x + 7y) = 2(20)$$

$$6x + 14y = 40$$

$$3(2x + 3y) = 3(10)$$

$$6x + 9y = 30$$

Now stack them again, and you can subtract:

$$6x + 14y = 40$$

$$6x + 9y = 30$$

$$\begin{array}{r} 6x + 14y = 40 \\ -\ 6x + \ \ 9y = 30 \\ \hline 0 + \ \ 5y = 10 \end{array}$$

Since the *x*-terms added to 0, now the equation can be solved for *y*:

$$5y = 10$$

$$\frac{5y}{5} = \frac{10}{5}$$

$$y = 2$$

Substitute this value for y in either one of the original equations and solve for x:

$$3x + 7y = 20$$

$$3x + 7(2) = 20$$

$$3x + 14 = 20$$

$$3x + 14 - 14 = 20 - 14$$

$$3x = 6$$

$$\frac{3x}{3} = \frac{6}{3}$$

$$x = 2$$

Now substitute both values in the other original equation to check:

$$2x + 3y = 10$$

$$2(2) + 3(2) = 10?$$

$$4 + 6 = 10?$$

$$10 = 10 \checkmark$$

Graphing Systems of Equations

When you graph a system of linear equations, the solution is the ordered pair that is a solution to both equations: their intersection. Let's graph the system of equations below to find their solution.

$$6x - 2y = 18$$

$$2x + 4y = -8$$

First, solve each equation for y to put it into slope-intercept form:

$$6x - 2y = 18 \qquad\qquad\qquad 2x + 4y = -8$$

$$6x - 6x - 2y = -6x + 18 \qquad\qquad 2x - 2x + 4y = -2x - 8$$

$$-2y = -6x + 18 \qquad\qquad\qquad 4y = -2x - 8$$

$$\frac{-2y}{-2} = \frac{-6x}{-2} + \frac{18}{-2} \qquad\qquad \frac{4y}{4} = \frac{-2x}{4} - \frac{8}{4}$$

$$y = 3x - 9 \qquad\qquad\qquad y = -\frac{1}{2}x - 2$$

Now use the slope and y-intercepts from those two equations to graph them on the x-y coordinate plane. The equation $y = 3x - 9$ has slope 3 (or $\frac{3}{1}$) and y-intercept $(0, -9)$. The equation $y = -\frac{1}{2}x - 2$ has slope $-\frac{1}{2}$ and y-intercept $(0, -2)$.

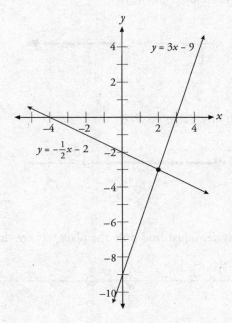

You can see from the graph that the two lines' point of intersection is $(2, -3)$. Check your solution by trying it in both equations:

$$y = 3x - 9 \qquad\qquad y = -\frac{1}{2}x - 2$$

$$-3 = 3(2) - 9? \qquad\qquad -3 = -\frac{1}{2}(2) - 2?$$

$$-3 = 6 - 9? \qquad\qquad -3 = -1 - 2?$$

$$-3 = -3 \checkmark \qquad\qquad -3 = -3 \checkmark$$

Since the ordered pair works in both equations, it is a solution to the system of equations.

Solving and Graphing Systems of Inequalities

If you have two inequalities in one variable, you can graph on a number line to solve.

Remember that the graph of $y > 0$ looks like this:

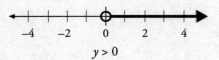

$$y > 0$$

And remember that the graph of $y < 2$ looks like this:

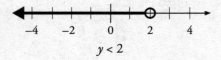

$$y < 2$$

To graph the solution to the system, just find only the places where the two graphs overlap.

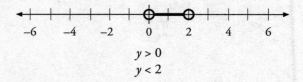

$$y > 0$$
$$y < 2$$

Notice that the solution may be bounded on two sides, as in the example above, or on only one side:

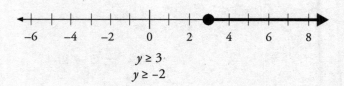

$$y \geq 3$$
$$y \geq -2$$

The solution is identical to the graph of $y \geq 3$, since all those solutions are in the overlap.

What about a system like $y > 5$, $y \leq -1$? Here are the graphs of these two equations:

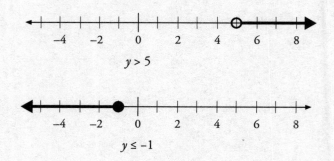

$$y > 5$$

$$y \leq -1$$

If you try to find their overlap, you'll find that they don't have any! There are no solutions to this system of equations. In other words, there are no numbers that are both greater than 5 and less than or equal to –1.

Here's one more example:

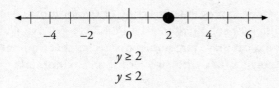

$$y \geq 2$$
$$y \leq 2$$

The only value that satisfies both of these inequalities is 2. Note that if these inequalities used > and <, rather than ≥ and ≤, there would be no solution.

If you have two linear inequalities in two variables, you can also usually use them to find solutions. Their solutions are all the ordered pairs that fit both inequalities: in other words, if you graph both inequalities, the region of the coordinate plane where their solutions overlap is the solution to the system. Just as with systems of one-variable inequalities, systems of two-variable linear inequalities sometimes have no solution.

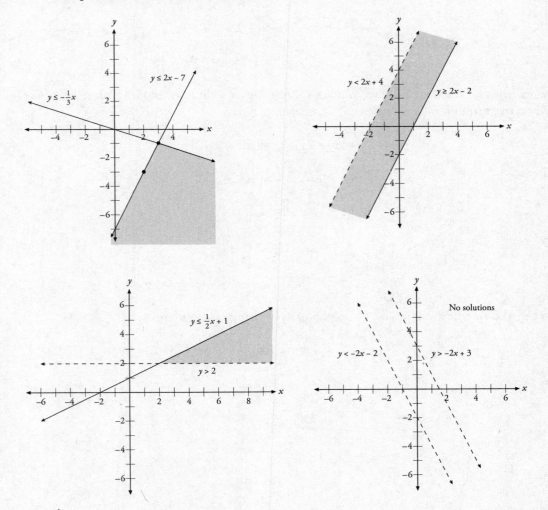

POLYNOMIALS

A **monomial** is an algebraic expression consisting of just one term (remember, a term is a variable, a number, or a variable and a number combined by multiplication or division). So y, $3x^2$, $14xy$, and $2x^2y3z$ are all monomials.

A **polynomial** is an algebraic expression consisting of two or more terms. Remember, separate terms are joined by addition or subtraction. So $3ab + 2b$, $4x^2 + 3xy + y^2$, and $x^2 + x - 6$ are all polynomials. A polynomial can have any number of terms that's more than one, so polynomials include **binomials** (polynomials with two terms) and **trinomials** (polynomials with three terms).

Operations with Polynomials

To add or subtract polynomials, just add or subtract the like terms. Here's an example:

$$(6x^2 + 3x - 2) + (3x^2 - 5x + 2) =$$

$$6x^2 + 3x - 2 + 3x^2 - 5x + 2 =$$

$$6x^2 + 3x^2 + 3x - 5x - 2 + 2 =$$

$$9x^2 - 2x + 0 = 9x^2 - 2x$$

Try one with subtraction. You can think of subtracting as adding the negative; then distribute the negative through the parentheses.

$$(5x^2 + 2x - 1) - (3x^2 + x - 2) =$$

$$(5x^2 + 2x - 1) + -(3x^2 + x - 2) =$$

$$5x^2 + 2x - 1 + -3x^2 + -x - (-2) =$$

$$5x^2 + 2x - 1 + -3x^2 + -x + 2 =$$

$$5x^2 + -3x^2 + 2x + -x - 1 + 2 = 2x^2 + x + 1$$

You can also multiply monomials by polynomials by using distribution:

$$(-4y)(y + 3) =$$

$$(-4y)(y) + (-4y)(3) =$$

$$-4y^2 - 12y$$

When you multiply polynomials by polynomials, you need to be more methodical. The CSET will expect you to be able to multiply two binomials together. To do this, carefully multiply each term of the first by each term of the second, following the acronym FOIL: *first, outer, inner, last.* For example, if you need to multiply $(x + 4)$ by $(x + 3)$, just multiply the first terms $(x \times x)$, the outer terms $(x \times 3)$, the inner terms $(4 \times x)$, and the last terms (4×3):

Another Mnemonic!
The tally so far:
IPMAT
PEMDAS
FOIL

$$(x + 4)(x + 3) =$$

$$(x \times x) + (x \times 3) + (4 \times x) + (4 \times 3) =$$

$$x^2 + 3x + 4x + 12 = x^2 + 7x + 12$$

Try one more. Notice that when one or both of the terms contain subtraction, you can change it to addition of a negative to keep the signs straight.

$$(y - 4)(y + 5) =$$

$$(y + {-4})(y + 5) =$$

$$(y \times y) + (y \times 5) + (-4 \times y) + (-4 \times 5) =$$

$$y^2 + 5y + {-4}y + {-20} = y^2 + y - 20$$

You can even divide polynomials by monomials by using distribution:

$$\frac{-16x^2 - 12x}{4x} =$$

$$\frac{4x(-4x - 3)}{4x} =$$

$$-4x - 3$$

And, of course, you can divide a polynomial by one of its factors:

$$\frac{(y - 7)(y + 5)}{y + 5} =$$

$$y - 7$$

As for how to factor a polynomial, first let's look at situations in which you might need to do that.

QUADRATICS

A **quadratic equation** is an equation that just has one variable, and its degree is 2: in other words, it contains a term in which the variable is squared. The standard form of a quadratic equation is $ax^2 + bx + c = 0$, where a, b, and c are constants, or numerical coefficients, and x is the variable.

You might notice that when you multiplied the binomials above, the results were quadratic expressions. This is a clue to one way to solve quadratic equations.

Solving Quadratics

Factoring to Solve Quadratics

If you are asked to solve a quadratic equation, the first thing you should try is factoring.

Let's start with quadratics in which $a = 1$ (the coefficient of the x^2-term is 1). To factor an equation like this, follow these rules:

- Put the equation in the form $x^2 + bx + c = 0$.
- Start by factoring the first term: $x^2 = x \times x$. Write down $(x\ \ \ )(x\ \ \ ) = 0$.
- Find two numbers that multiply to c and add to b. If necessary, write out the factors of c.

Here's an example:

If $x^2 + x - 20 = 0$, which of the following is a possible value of x?

A. −5

B. −4

C. 2

D. 5

Here's How to Crack It

Follow the steps above. Since the equation is already in the form $x^2 + bx + c = 0$, start by factoring the first term: $x^2 = x \times x$. Write down $(x\ \ \ )(x\ \ \ ) = 0$.

$$x^2 + x - 20 = 0$$

$$(x\ \ \ )(x\ \ \ ) = 0$$

Now find two numbers that multiply to c and add to b. Here, the value of b is 1, and the value of c is –20. Remember, you can write out the factors of c if you need to:

$$
\begin{array}{c|c}
\multicolumn{2}{c}{-20} \\
\hline
-1 & 20 \\
-2 & 10 \\
-4 & 5 \\
\hline
1 & -20 \\
2 & -10 \\
4 & -5 \\
\end{array}
$$

Which two factors of c, which is –20, add to b, which is 1? –4 and 5 add to 1, so those are the factors you need. Write them in to complete the factoring:

$$(x - 4)(x + 5) = 0$$

Now solve. Here's where making sure that the quadratic expression is set equal to 0 (which we did in the first step) comes in handy. When you have a product that equals 0, that tells you that at least one of the factors in the product equals zero. So at this step, you can split up the two factors and set each one equal to zero to solve:

$$x - 4 = 0 \qquad\qquad\qquad x + 5 = 0$$

$$x - 4 + 4 = 0 + 4 \qquad\qquad x + 5 - 5 = 0 - 5$$

$$x = 4 \qquad\qquad\qquad x = -5$$

Notice that the two solutions (these are also called roots) of the quadratic equation, 4 and –5, are the opposites of the number parts of the factors $x - 4$ and $x + 5$. Don't make the mistake of choosing (B) or (D) here when you are looking at the factors: the correct answer is (A). You'll get solutions quickly if you remember that they are always the opposites of the numbers contained in the factors.

———————————○———————————

Try another example:

———————————○———————————

If $49 = -x^2 - 14x + 1$, which of the following is a possible value of x?

A. –7

B. –6

C. 7

D. 8

Here's How to Crack It

Follow the steps above. To get the equation into the form $x^2 + bx + c = 0$, just move all the terms to the left side of the equation:

$$49 = -x^2 - 14x + 1$$

$$x^2 + 14x + 49 - 1 = -x^2 + x^2 - 14x + 14x + 1 - 1$$

$$x^2 + 14x + 48 = 0$$

Next, factor the first term: $x^2 = x \times x$. Write down $(x \qquad)(x \qquad) = 0$.

$$(x \qquad)(x \qquad) = 0$$

Now find two numbers that multiply to c and add to b. Here, the value of b is 14, and the value of c is 48. Remember, you can write out the factors of c if you need to:

48	
1	48
2	24
3	16
4	12
6	8

Which two factors of c, which is 48, add to b, which is 14? 6 and 8 add to 14, so those are the factors you need. Write them in to complete the factoring:

$$(x + 6)(x + 8) = 0$$

Now solve. Remember that the solutions are always the opposites of the numbers contained in the factors, so the solutions here must be -6 and -8. The correct answer is (B).

Here's one more example in which $a = 1$:

In the equation $x^2 + px - 18 = 0$, one of the roots is 6, and p is a constant. What is the value of p?

A. -6

B. -3

C.   3

D.   6

Here's How to Crack It

Here the question asks for a different piece of information. Remember, a constant is a number. So p stands for some specific number, and the question asks you to find out what that number is.

Follow the steps above and work with the information the question gives. Since the equation tells you that one of the roots is 6 (and remember—*roots* are *solutions* in quadratic-land), you know that one of the solutions is $x = 6$. That means that one of the factors has the opposite value: $(x - 6)$. When you write out the factors, write in the one you know, and fill in the first part of the other:

$$x^2 + px - 18 = 0$$

$$(x - 6)(x \quad\quad) = 0$$

Now, you know that the two numeric parts of the factors must multiply to c and add to b. Here, the value of b is the constant p, and you don't know what that is yet. So concentrate on the value of c, which is -18. Since you know one of the values is -6, you can just ask yourself "What times -6 is -18?" The other value is 3.

$$(x - 6)(x + 3) = 0$$

Now, use FOIL to multiply these binomials. Remember, the question asked for the value of the constant p, not the solutions.

$$(x \times x) + (x \times 3) + (-6 \times x) + (-6 \times 3) = 0$$

$$x^2 + 3x - 6x - 18 = 0$$

$$x^2 - 3x - 18 = 0$$

Since the value in the place of p is -3, $p = -3$. The correct answer is (B).

What happens when the value of a is not equal to 1? In that case, see whether you can factor any monomials out. Otherwise, you make have to think a bit about the factors of a.

$$x^2 + 12x = 0$$

Factor the monomial x out of the two terms:

$$x(x + 12) = 0$$

Since the two factors are x and $x + 12$, the solutions are $x = 0$ and $x = -12$.

How about this one?

$$4x^2 + 5x + 1 = 0$$

In this case, you can't factor out a monomial, so you are going to have to factor into two binomials. Think about how you can factor the *a* term, $4x^2$.

Here's one way that might work:

$$(2x \quad)(2x \quad) = 0$$

But when you look at *b* and *c*, you run into a problem: the factors of *c*, which is 1, are 1 and 1. But then your middle term comes out to $4x$, rather than $5x$:

$$(2x + 1)(2x + 1) = 0$$

$$(2x \times 2x) + (2x \times 1) + (1 \times 2x) + (1 \times 1) = 0$$

$$4x^2 + 2x + 2x + 1 = 0$$

$$4x^2 + 4x + 1 = 0$$

So that isn't the right factorization. How else can you factor $4x^2$? Try this:

$$(4x \quad)(x \quad) = 0$$

The factors of *c*, which is 1, are still 1 and 1. But now that yields the correct middle term:

$$(4x + 1)(x + 1) = 0$$

$$(4x \times x) + (4x \times 1) + (1 \times x) + (1 \times 1) = 0$$

$$4x^2 + 4x + x + 1 = 0$$

$$4x^2 + 5x + 1 = 0$$

Since this is the correct factorization, use the factors to find the solutions:

$$4x + 1 = 0 \qquad\qquad x + 1 = 0$$

$$4x + 1 - 1 = 0 - 1 \qquad\qquad x + 1 - 1 = 0 - 1$$

$$4x = -1 \qquad\qquad x = -1$$

$$\frac{4x}{4} = \frac{-1}{4}$$

$$x = -\frac{1}{4}$$

Common Quadratics

There are three **common quadratics** that can really help save you time on the test. Take a look at them:

Common Quadratics

$$(x + y)^2 = x^2 + 2xy + y^2$$

$$(x - y)^2 = x^2 - 2xy + y^2$$

$$(x + y)(x - y) = x^2 - y^2$$

You can get from any of the left sides of these equations to the corresponding right sides using FOIL. For example:

$$(x + y)^2 =$$

$$(x + y)(x + y) =$$

$$(x \times x) + (x \times y) + (y \times x) + (y \times y) =$$

$$x^2 + 2xy + y^2$$

And you could use factoring to reverse the process. However, either process takes time. If you have this step memorized, you can save some valuable time on your test. Additionally, if you memorize these patterns, you'll be able to use these shortcuts in questions with numbers as well as variables.

Here's an example:

_____ O _____

$$\left(4 + \sqrt{6}\right)\left(4 - \sqrt{6}\right) =$$

A.   −20

B.   6

C.   10

D.   16

Here's How to Crack It

You can use FOIL to work this question. However, if you can recognize that the calculation the question is asking you to perform falls into the pattern of one of the common quadratics, you'll get that point much faster.

$$\left(x + y\right)\left(x - y\right) = x^2 - y^2$$

Your x in this problem is 4. Your y is $\sqrt{6}$. Use the pattern of the common quadratic to find the solution:

$$\left(4 + \sqrt{6}\right)\left(4 - \sqrt{6}\right) = 4^2 - \left(\sqrt{6}\right)^2$$

$$= 16 - 6$$

$$= 10$$

The correct answer is (C).

_____ O _____

Completing the Square to Solve Quadratics

Some quadratics are difficult to solve with factoring because their solutions are not integers. Since the CSET may ask you to solve quadratics of this type, it's useful to have another process to use if factoring isn't helping.

This method takes its inspiration from a group of quadratics that happen to be easy to solve because they fit into the form "something squared equals some number." In that case, you can take the square root of both sides of the equation to solve.

Here's an example:

$$(x - 5)^2 = 7$$

$$x - 5 = \pm\sqrt{7}$$

$$x - 5 + 5 = 5 \pm\sqrt{7}$$

$$x = 5 \pm\sqrt{7}$$

Remember, when you take the square root of a value such as 7 (rather than evaluating a radical sign that's already there), you need to include both the values that square to 7: $\sqrt{7}$ and $-\sqrt{7}$. The symbol ± is a way to show both roots at once, and it means that there are really two solutions here: $x = 5 + \sqrt{7}$ and $x = 5 - \sqrt{7}$.

Those solutions are not integers, but do represent exact values. They would probably be written as $5 + \sqrt{7}$ and $5 - \sqrt{7}$ in answer choices, rather than converted into decimals.

Now what if the test gives you a quadratic equation that looks like this?

$$x^2 + 2x - 9 = 0$$

If you try to use your factoring process, you'll have trouble finding two integers that multiply to −9 and add to 2. Try something else instead.

This process is called **completing the square.** Basically, you want to use the simple process you used above to solve $(x - 5)^2 = 7$. How can you make that happen? First, you'll move the constant term to the other side of the equal sign:

$$x^2 + 2x - 9 + 9 = 0 + 9$$

$$x^2 + 2x = 9$$

That looks closer. But you need what's still there on the left side of the equation to be a square. Let's try to make it into a square! Remember the first common quadratic?

$$(x + y)^2 = x^2 + 2xy + y^2$$

We're trying to figure out what y would fit here. Look at the right side of the common quadratic form. You already have the term x^2. You also have the second term, which is your $2xy$: it's $2x$ here. So your y must be 1.

> To find the y, divide the coefficient of x by 2. Then square it to get the y^2 term.

The rule here to find the y is to divide the coefficient of x by 2. Since $\frac{2}{2} = 1$, our solution checks out. Now, since the final term in the common quadratic is y^2, you just need to *add* 1^2, which equals 1, to the left side of your equation. You can do that—as long as you keep your equation balanced by adding 1 to the right side as well:

$$x^2 + 2x = 9$$

$$x^2 + 2x + 1 = 9 + 1$$

Now use factoring or your common quadratic to write the left side as a square:

$$\left(x + 1\right)^2 = 10$$

This looks a lot like the problem we solved above! Now that you've completed the square (in other words, made the left side of your equation into a square), you can take square roots to solve:

$$x + 1 = \pm\sqrt{10}$$

$$x + 1 - 1 = -1 \pm \sqrt{10}$$

$$x = -1 \pm \sqrt{10}$$

Let's try another example.

Which of the following is a possible solution to $x^2 - 10x + 19 = 0$?

A. $1 - \sqrt{6}$

B. $5 - \sqrt{6}$

C. 5

D. 11

Here's How to Crack It

Since 19 does not factor into any two integers that add to −10, use completing the square to solve this problem.

$$x^2 - 10x + 19 = 0$$

$$x^2 - 10x = -19$$

Remember, to find the y, divide the coefficient of x by 2. Then square it to get the y^2 term.

$$\frac{-10}{2} = -5$$

$$(-5)^2 = 25$$

Since your y^2 term is 25, you need to add that value to both sides of the equation.

$$x^2 - 10x + 25 = -19 + 25$$

Use the second common quadratic, $(x - y)^2 = x^2 - 2xy + y^2$, to change the left side of the equation into a square.

$$(x - 5)^2 = 6$$

Now take the square roots and solve:

$$x - 5 = \pm \sqrt{6}$$

$$x = 5 \pm \sqrt{6}$$

Both $5 + \sqrt{6}$ and $5 - \sqrt{6}$ are solutions, but only $5 - \sqrt{6}$ is a given answer choice. Choice (B) is correct.

───────────────────

What happens if the first term (the x^2 term) has a coefficient that's not 1? You'll need to factor that coefficient out before solving.

Which of the following represents all possible solutions to $5x^2 - 30x + 10 = 0$?

A. $\pm\sqrt{7}$

B. $3 \pm \sqrt{7}$

C. $3 \pm \sqrt{35}$

D. $15 \pm \sqrt{215}$

Here's How to Crack It

Start by factoring out the coefficient of the x^2 term. You need to factor it out of all the terms on the left side:

$$5x^2 - 30x + 10 = 0$$

$$5\left(x^2 - 6x + 2\right) = 0$$

Now divide both sides of the equation by 5. This works out handily: $0 \div 5 = 0$, so the right side doesn't change.

$$x^2 - 6x + 2 = 0$$

Since there are no factors of 2 that add to −6, you need to use completing the square.

$$x^2 - 6x = -2$$

Remember, to find the y, divide the coefficient of x by 2. Then square it to get the y^2 term.

$$\frac{-6}{2} = -3$$

$$\left(-3\right)^2 = 9$$

Since your y^2 term is 9, you need to add that value to both sides of the equation.

$$x^2 - 6x + 9 = -2 + 9$$

Use the second common quadratic, $(x - y)^2 = x^2 - 2xy + y^2$, to change the left side of the equation into a square.

$$(x - 3)^2 = 7$$

Now take the square roots and solve:

$$x - 3 = \pm\sqrt{7}$$

$$x - 3 + 3 = 3 \pm \sqrt{7}$$

$$x = 3 \pm \sqrt{7}$$

The correct answer is (B).

————————————————————○————————————————————

Graphing Quadratics

You can graph quadratic equations on the coordinate plane, just as you can graph linear equations. The graphs of quadratic equations have a specific kind of shape, called a **parabola.** Let's look at the simplest quadratic equation and its graph:

$$y = x^2$$

Here's a table of values for this equation. Then we can plot them on the coordinate plane.

x	y
−3	9
−2	4
−1	1
0	0
1	1
2	4
3	9

When these values are plotted, they form a curve: the parabola.

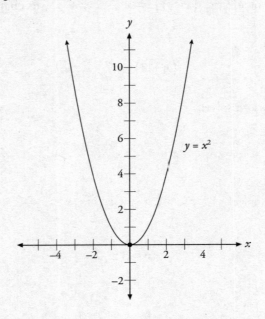

Now let's see what happens to the parabola's shape when we change the equation. For now, let's just change the coefficient of x (the a value):

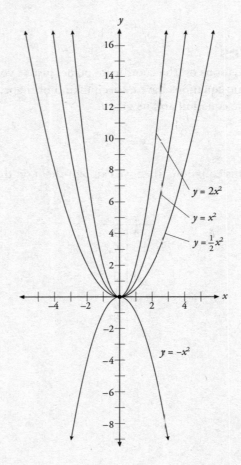

Notice that the shape of the graph of $y = 2x^2$ is thinner than that of $y = x^2$: its two "arms" are closer together. So increasing the value of a results in a thinner parabola. The shape of the graph of $y = \frac{1}{2}x^2$, conversely, is wider than that of $y = x^2$: its two "arms" are farther apart. So decreasing the value of a to a fraction between 0 and 1 results in a wider parabola. What about when a is negative? The graph of $y = -x^2$ is upside-down compared to that of $y = x^2$: its "arms" point downward instead of upward. So parabolas with negative a-values point downward.

What about graphs of quadratics in full general form $y = ax^2 + bx + c$?

Let's graph a specific example and see what we can tell about how its shape and placement on the coordinate plane is indicated by the values of a, b, and c.

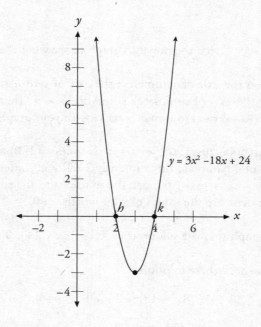

The values of a, b, and c for the equation $y = 3x^2 - 18x + 24$ are:

$a = 3$

$b = -18$

$c = 24$

Here are some tools to unpack the information the equation tells you. First of all, you can tell that the parabola will point upward, and be thinner than the graph of $y = x^2$, since the a-value is 3.

Next, you need to calculate (h, k), the vertex of the parabola. The **vertex** of a parabola is the point at which the parabola crosses its **axis of symmetry:** the line that divides the shape of the parabola into two congruent halves.

To find h, use the formula $h = \dfrac{-b}{2a}$.

$$h = \frac{-(-18)}{2(3)} = \frac{18}{6} = 3$$

Since (h, k) is an ordered pair that is a solution to the equation, substitute $h = 3$ into the equation for x, and solve for the y-value that matches it (k).

$$y = 3(3)^2 - 18(3) + 24$$

$$= 27 - 54 + 24$$

$$= -3$$

So the vertex, (h, k), is $(3, -3)$. Check the previous graph to see what the vertex looks like.

The value of h also tells you the axis of symmetry: the axis of symmetry of a parabola will be the line $x = h$. Thus, here the axis of symmetry is the line $x = 3$. That's the vertical line that passes through your parabola's vertex, so it makes sense with your graph.

Finally, notice that the parabola crosses the x-axis at the points $(2, 0)$ and $(4, 0)$: these are the x-intercepts. In the graph of a parabola, the x-intercepts tell you something important: the x-intercepts of the graph of $y = ax^2 + bx + c$ tell you the solutions to the equation $ax^2 + bx + c = 0$. This makes sense, because these are the values of x for which $y = 0$.

So you can tell from this graph that the solutions to $3x^2 - 18x + 24 = 0$ are $x = 2$ and $x = 4$.

You could use factoring to check these solutions:

$$3x^2 - 18x + 24 = 0$$

$$3(x^2 - 6x + 8) = 0$$

$$x^2 - 6x + 8 = 0$$

$$\left(x \quad\right)\left(x \quad\right) = 0$$

Find two numbers that multiply to 8 and add to -6:

$$\left(x - 2\right)\left(x - 4\right) = 0$$

$$x - 2 = 0 \qquad\qquad x - 4 = 0$$

$$x - 2 + 2 = 0 + 2 \qquad x - 4 + 4 = 0 + 4$$

$$x = 2 \qquad\qquad x = 4$$

The solutions check.

Try a problem involving the graph of a quadratic equation:

Use the graph below to answer the question that follows.

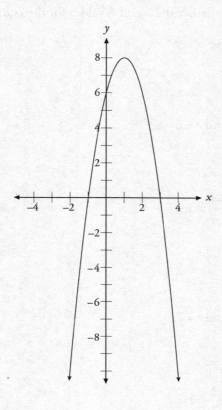

Which of the following equations is represented by the graph above?

A. $y = -2x^2 + 4x + 6$

B. $y = -x^2 + 2x + 7$

C. $y = x^2 - 2x + 9$

D. $y = 2x^2 - 4x + 10$

Here's How to Crack It
First, notice that the parabola opens downward. That tells you that the value of a is negative. Eliminate (C) and (D).

Next, match what you know about the graph to an equation. Remember that the vertex of a parabola can be represented as (h, k), where $h = \dfrac{-b}{2a}$. The vertex of the parabola shown on the graph is (1, 8). So you know that $h = 1$ and $k = 8$. You can also find the a, b, and c values in each of these equations. Find out whether the a and b values for the equations you have left in (A) and (B) give the correct h-value:

Try (A): $y = -2x^2 + 4x + 6$

Here, $a = -2$, $b = 4$, and $c = 6$.

Calculate h.

$$h = \frac{-b}{2a} = \frac{-4}{2(-2)} = \frac{-4}{-4} = 1$$

Try (B): $y = -x^2 + 2x + 7$

Here, $a = -1$, $b = 2$, and $c = 7$.

Calculate h.

$$h = \frac{-b}{2a} = \frac{-2}{2(-1)} = \frac{-2}{-2} = 1$$

Both these choices give the correct value of h, so try another point from the graph.

The graph contains the point (3, 0), which is an x-intercept. Try it in the two equations to see which one it fits in:

Try (A): $y = -2x^2 + 4x + 6$

$0 = -2(3)^2 + 4(3) + 6$?

$0 = -18 + 12 + 6$?

$0 = 0$ ✓

The point from the graph fits the equation in (A).

Try (B): $y = -x^2 + 2x + 7$

$$0 = -(3)^2 + 2(3) + 7?$$

$$0 = -9 + 6 + 7?$$

$$0 = 4 \ ✗$$

The point from the graph does not fit the equation in (B). The correct answer is (A).

—————————○—————————

Graphing Other Functions

Finally, the text may ask you to identify graphs of functions that you haven't seen yet: ones that are neither linear nor quadratic. Use a table of values or what you know about those functions to identify graphs.

—————————○—————————

Which of the following is a graph of the equation
$y = \dfrac{x^3}{2}$?

A.

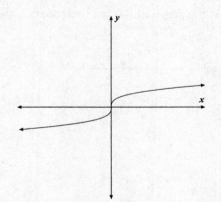

C.

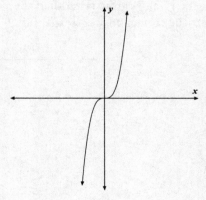

B.

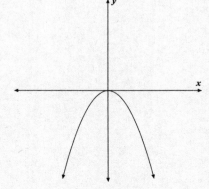

D.

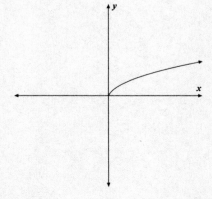

Here's How to Crack It

Think about the values that will satisfy the equation. When x is negative, what values will y have? Remember that when you cube negative numbers (or take them to any other odd power), the results are negative. When you cube positive numbers, the results are positive. So negative x-values should be paired with negative y-values, and positive x-values should be paired with positive y-values. Eliminate (B). Did you notice it is a parabola? That probably means its equation has x^2, not x^3. Choice (D) also looks like a parabola, but on its side. It also shows results for positive values only. This is what $y = \sqrt{x}$ and related equations look like when you graph them: no negative values can be evaluated for x, no negative values result for y, and the graph looks like half a sideways parabola. Eliminate (D).

To choose between the two options you have left, try some values in the equation you were given.

x	y
-2	-4
-1	$-\dfrac{1}{2}$
0	0
1	$\dfrac{1}{2}$
2	4

Since the y-values grow faster than the x-values, the graph in (C) is a better match than the one in (A). The correct answer is (C).

KEY TERMS

variable

algebraic term

coefficient

algebraic expression

like terms

equation

solve

isolate

function

dependent variable

independent variable

table

graph

coordinate plane (*x-y* coordinate plane or Cartesian grid)

x-axis

y-axis

origin

ordered pair

x-coordinate

y-coordinate

quadrant

linear equation

line

slope-intercept form

slope

rise

run

y-intercept

x-intercept

parallel

perpendicular

intersection

inequality

monomial

polynomial

binomial

trinomial

quadratic equation

common quadratics

completing the square

parabola

vertex

axis of symmetry

Chapter 15 Drill

Answers and explanations can be found in the final section of this book, beginning on page 617.

1. If $3z + 6 = 16$, what is the value of $9z$?

    A. $\dfrac{10}{3}$

    B. 10

    C. 30

    D. 66

2. $10y - 36 + 4y - 6 + y = 3$. What is the value of y?

    A. $-2\dfrac{3}{5}$

    B. $2\dfrac{4}{5}$

    C. 3

    D. 45

3. Lines c and d (not shown) are perpendicular lines. If the equation of line c is $y = -5x - 2$, which of the following is a possible equation for line d?

    A. $y = -5x + \dfrac{1}{2}$

    B. $y = -\dfrac{1}{5}x - 2$

    C. $y = \dfrac{1}{5}x + 2$

    D. $y = 5x - \dfrac{1}{2}$

4. **Use the graph below to answer the question that follows.**

    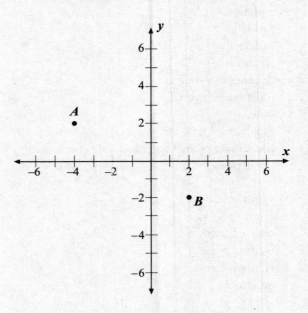

    Line m passes through points A and B in the coordinate plane above. Which of the following is an equation for line m?

    A. $y = -\dfrac{2}{3}x - \dfrac{2}{3}$

    B. $y = -\dfrac{2}{3}x - 1$

    C. $y = -\dfrac{3}{2}x - \dfrac{2}{3}$

    D. $y = -\dfrac{3}{2}x - 1$

5. **Use the table below to answer the question that follows.**

Hours	Cost
0.5	$60
1	$70
1.5	$80
2	$90
2.5	$100
3	$110

Ravi charges a service fee plus a fixed rate per hour to repair furniture, and the table shows his total charge for working the given amounts of time. Which of the following graphs best represents the data in the table?

A.

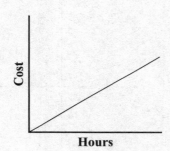

C.

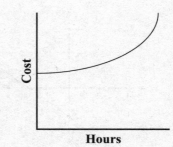

B.

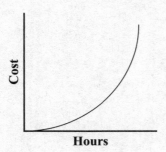

D.

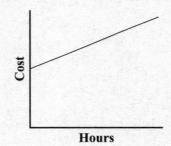

6. Which of the following is a correct graph of the inequality $y \leq \dfrac{3}{4}x - 2$?

A.

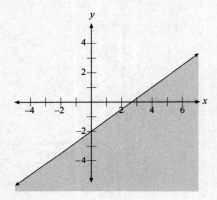

C.

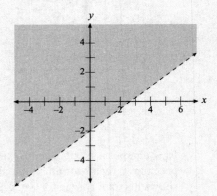

B.

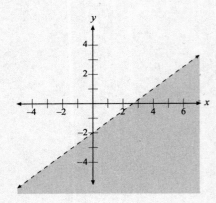

D.

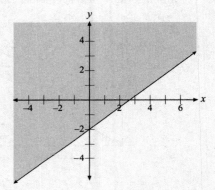

7. **Use the graph below to answer the question that follows.**

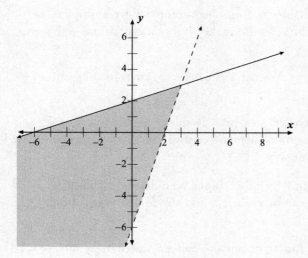

The graph above shows the solution of a system of inequalities. Which of the following points is in the solution set?

A. $(0, -6)$

B. $(2, 0)$

C. $(3, 3)$

D. $(-3, -3)$

8. The equation $x^2 + kx + 12 = 0$ has two solutions. If k is an integer and $k < 0$, which of the following is a possible value of k?

A. -13

B. -12

C. -6

D. 7

9. Which of the following represents all possible solutions to $3x^3 + 18x^2 + 12x = 0$?

A. $\sqrt{5}$ and $-\sqrt{5}$

B. $3 + \sqrt{5}$ and $3 - \sqrt{5}$

C. $0, \sqrt{5}$, and $-\sqrt{5}$

D. $0, 3 + \sqrt{5}$, and $3 - \sqrt{5}$

10. Which of the following represents the vertex of the graph of the equation $y = -\dfrac{1}{2}x^2 + 2x + 1$?

A. $(3, 2)$

B. $(2, 3)$

C. $(-2, -1)$

D. $(-1, -2)$

Summary

- Algebraic terms, which are variables, numbers, or variables and numbers combined by multiplication and division, can be combined by addition or subtraction to make algebraic expressions—the sentences of algebra.

- You can manipulate expressions by combining like terms. You can evaluate expressions by substituting values for variables and simplifying.

- An equation is a statement that the values of two expressions are equal. To solve equations for a variable, isolate the variable by performing inverse operations. When you change one side of an equation, you must change the other side in exactly the same way.

- A function is a special relationship between variables in which each input, or independent variable, has a single output, or dependent variable. Functions can be evaluated and solved just as equations can.

- The information contained in algebraic equations and functions can also be represented using tables and graphs.

- The coordinate plane is the graphing space for algebraic equations in two variables. It consists of an x-axis and a y-axis joined at the origin. You can plot ordered pairs on the coordinate plane in the form (x, y).

- A linear equation is one that gives a straight line when graphed on the coordinate plane. The slope-intercept form of the equation of a line, $y = mx + b$, gives information that is helpful for graphing: m is the slope, or steepness, of the line, and b is the y-intercept (the place where the line crosses the y-axis).

- Parallel lines have equal slopes. Perpendicular lines have opposite reciprocal slopes.

- An inequality is a relation between two quantities that aren't equal. Manipulating inequalities works just like manipulating equations, with one exception: when you multiply or divide both sides of an inequality by a negative number, you must flip the sign around.

o   Inequalities can also be graphed on number lines and the coordinate plane.

o   Systems of equations and inequalities are pairs of equations (or inequalities) that use the same variables. You can use them to find solutions that work in both equations (or inequalities), as long as solutions are possible.

o   Systems of linear equations and inequalities can also be graphed. The solution to a system of linear equations is the point at which the two lines intersect. The solution to a system of linear inequalities is the portion of the coordinate plane where both inequalities are true.

o   Polynomials are algebraic expressions consisting of two or more terms. You can use like terms to simplify them using addition, subtraction, and distribution. To multiply binomials, use FOIL.

o   A quadratic equation has one variable with degree 2. Its general form is $ax^2 + bx + c = 0$.

o   Two good methods for solving quadratic equations are factoring and completing the square.

o   The common quadratics are $(x + y)^2 = x^2 + 2xy + y^2$, $(x - y)^2 = x^2 - 2xy + y^2$, and $(x + y)(x - y) = x^2 - y^2$.

o   The graphs of quadratic equations form parabolas. The vertex of a parabola is the point at which it crosses the axis of symmetry. You can use the information in a parabola's equation to calculate its vertex.

Chapter 16
Measurement and Geometry

PLANE GEOMETRY

In geometry, a **point** is defined as a location with no size. A **line** is made up of points—it's a series of points that extends infinitely in either direction and has no width (it's one-dimensional). ∠A **plane** is two-dimensional: it extends infinitely in two dimensions.

A line is drawn with arrows at each end, to represent the fact that it continues on forever in both directions. The line below is called line *AB,* or $\overleftrightarrow{AB}$.

Plane geometry is the study of figures in two dimensions, including points, lines, and figures made up of them.

Lines and Angles

The most important figures made up of points and lines are line segments and rays, because they are used to make up the rest of the figures. A **line segment** is just what it sounds like—a segment of a line. Like a line, it's straight and has no width. But unlike a line it doesn't extend indefinitely: it ends at definite **endpoints.** The endpoints can be used to name the line segment. For example, you can call this one line segment *AB,* or $\overline{AB}$:

A line segment has two endpoints, but a ray has only one: a **ray** is a portion of a line that extends indefinitely in one direction from an endpoint in the other. When you name a ray, the endpoint is the first letter and any other point on the ray is the second: ray *AB,* or $\overrightarrow{AB}$.

When two rays share an endpoint but aren't part of the same line, they form an **angle.** Their common endpoint is called the **vertex** of the angle. Point *B* is the vertex of the angle below.

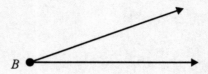

One way to name an angle is for its vertex—so this angle can be called angle *B*. The symbol $\angle$ means *angle,* so it can also be called $\angle B$. Angles can be measured in terms of their width—in other words, how much of the plane they sweep out between their two rays—and they are usually measured in **degrees.** The symbol for degrees is °. There are 360° in a circle; in other words, 360° sweeps out the full plane. To state the measure of an angle, you can say "the measure of angle *A* is 30 degrees." In writing, this is often expressed as $m\angle A = 30°$.

One of the most important ideas in geometry is congruence: **congruent** figures have the same size and shape. That means that lengths are equal, and angle measures are equal. The symbol for congruence is $\cong$. Two angles with the same measure are congruent, since that is the only size they have. All angles have the same shape.

A line can be thought of as an angle: place a point anywhere on the line and call that the vertex. This is called a **straight angle.** The measure of a straight angle is 180°—in other words, the two rays of a straight angle sweep out *half* of the plane $\left(360° \times \dfrac{1}{2} = 180°\right)$. Of course, the other side of the straight angle sweeps out 180° as well—the other half of the plane!

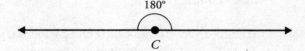

Almost any pair of lines in the same plane will eventually cross somewhere. When they do, they form four angles:

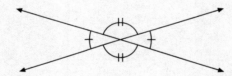

The angles that are formed by lines that cross come in two pairs of **vertical angles:** the angles opposite one another. A useful fact about vertical angles is that each pair of vertical angles has the same measure. The tick marks in the figure above indicate congruence: the angles with one tick have equal measure, and the angles with two ticks have equal measure. However, the one-tick angles do not have the same measure as the two-tick angles.

If an angle cuts a line in half, its measure is 90° (remember that a straight angle measures 180°, and $180° \times \dfrac{1}{2} = 90°$). This angle is called a **right angle,** and lines that cross at right angles are called **perpendicular lines.**

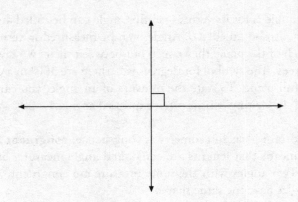

The symbol shown on the perpendicular lines above is called the **right angle symbol.** Any time a figure includes this symbol, you know for sure that the angle is a right angle—the lines are perpendicular. Without the symbol, you can't necessarily guess that an angle that looks like it measures 90° really does—it may just be close.

Angles other than right and straight angles can also be classified according to their measures: an angle with a measure between 90° and 180° is referred to as **obtuse.** An angle with a measure between 0° and 90° is called **acute.**

Two angles with measures that add up to 90° are called **complementary angles.** Two angles with measures that add up to 180° are called **supplementary angles.** In the figures below, angles a and b are complementary, and angles c and d are supplementary.

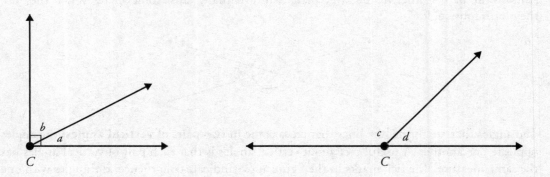

What happens if two lines in the plane never cross? These lines are called **parallel lines.** Since they don't cross, they stay the same distance apart—they are **equidistant.**

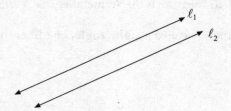

The symbol for parallel is ‖: in the drawing above, $\ell_1 \parallel \ell_2$. You'd read this as "line 1 is parallel to line 2."

Specifically, this means that if you choose any point on one of the parallel lines and cross it with a perpendicular line, that line will also be perpendicular to the other parallel line, and the distance between the two along the perpendicular will be the same as the distance at any other point on the original line. In the figure below, $\ell_1 \parallel \ell_2$, so $\overline{AD} \cong \overline{BC}$. In other words, AD (the length of $\overline{AD}$) = BC (the length of $\overline{BC}$).

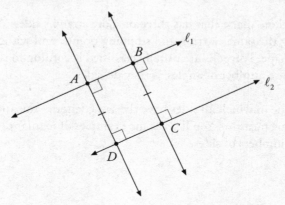

There's one more useful rule to keep in mind about lines and angles. It concerns a situation in which two parallel lines are crossed by a third line. That line is called a **transversal.**

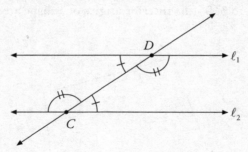

In the figure above, $\ell_1 \parallel \ell_2$. The transversal is $\overleftrightarrow{CD}$. Whenever two parallel lines are crossed by a transversal, the **alternate interior angles,** angles inside the parallel lines on opposite sides of the transversal, are congruent. There are two pairs of alternate interior angles. They are marked in the figure above.

In addition, the angles outside the parallel lines form pairs of vertical angles with the alternate interior angles. You can see which angles have same measures in this figure:

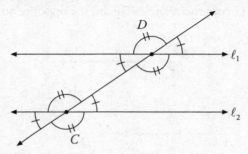

So when two parallel lines are crossed by a transversal, two kinds of angles are formed: obtuse ones and acute ones. All the obtuse angles have equal measure, and all the acute angles have equal measure. In addition, any pair of angles made up of one obtuse angle and one acute angle is supplementary: their measures add up to 180°.

Polygons

A **polygon** is a closed plane shape that has three or more straight sides. A **closed shape** is one that can be traced using the same starting and stopping points, and without crossing or retracing any section of the shape. Polygons are usually classified according to their numbers of sides, and usually have the same number of angles as they do sides.

A **regular polygon** is one in which all sides have the same length. The angles in a regular polygon also all have the same measure. You'll see some examples of regular polygons as you explore polygons with specific numbers of sides.

Quadrilaterals

A **quadrilateral** is a closed, two-dimensional shape that has four sides. A quadrilateral always has four angles as well as four sides. One useful property of quadrilaterals is that the measures of their interior angles sum to 360° (the **interior angles** of a shape are the angles formed *inside* its boundary).

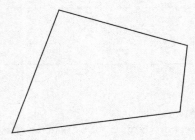

Quadrilaterals come in different shapes. Certain quadrilaterals have special properties.

Parallelograms

A **parallelogram** is a quadrilateral with two pairs of parallel and congruent sides (its opposite sides). It also has two pairs of congruent angles (again, the opposite ones).

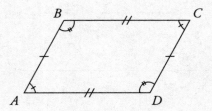

In parallelogram $ABCD$ above, $\overline{AB} \parallel \overline{CD}$, $\overline{BC} \parallel \overline{AD}$, $\overline{AB} \cong \overline{CD}$, $\overline{BC} \cong \overline{AD}$, $\angle A \cong \angle C$, and $\angle B \cong \angle D$.

An important measure in plane geometry is area. The **area** of a closed shape is the amount of space inside its boundary. To measure the area of a parallelogram, use the formula $A = bh$. It stands for "area equals base times height."

So what are the base and the height? The **base** of a figure is just the length of one of its sides. You can think of the base as the bottom side—as long as you remember that it's okay to turn any shape around until the side that is useful to you is on the bottom, and call that the base!

The **height** of a shape is a length from its base to its "top." In the case of a parallelogram, the "top" is the side opposite the base. The main thing to remember about height is that it must be the length of a line segment that's *perpendicular* to the base.

For a parallelogram, draw a line segment, connecting the base to the opposite side, that's perpendicular to the base. Any such line segment will have the same height, since the base and "top" are parallel and therefore equidistant. So you can draw the height anywhere between them:

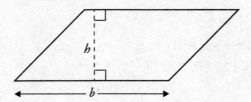

Then multiply those values together to find the area. Try it:

Use the diagram below to answer the question that follows.

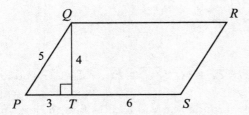

What is the area of parallelogram *PQRS* in square units?

A. 12

B. 24

C. 36

D. 45

Here's How to Crack It

Use the formula $A = bh$ to find the area of a parallelogram. What are the values of the base and the height? Since the height is any line segment perpendicular to the base and touching the opposite side, $\overline{QT}$ is a height of parallelogram $PQRS$. Its value is 4, so $h = 4$.

The base it's perpendicular to is $\overline{PS}$, so find its length. It's made up of two segments, $\overline{PT}$ and $\overline{TS}$, and their lengths are 3 and 6. Since they are segments on the same line, you can add their lengths to find the length of $\overline{PS}$: $3 + 6 = 9$. So $b = 9$.

Substitute these values into your area formula: $A = bh = (4)(9) = 36$. The correct answer is (C).

───────────────○───────────────

Another important measure for two-dimensional shapes is perimeter. The **perimeter** of a shape is the distance around its boundary. For a quadrilateral, this is the sum of the lengths of its four sides.

The perimeter of a parallelogram is the sum of the lengths of its four sides, which come in pairs. If the sides have lengths a and b, then $P = 2a + 2b$.

Rhombuses

A **rhombus** is a special parallelogram with all sides congruent. So in a rhombus, all sides are congruent, opposite sides are parallel, and opposite angles are congruent. One thing to note: the plural of *rhombus* can be either *rhombuses* or *rhombi*.

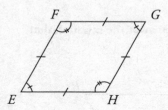

In rhombus $EFGH$ above, $\overline{EF} \parallel \overline{GH}$, $\overline{FG} \parallel \overline{EH}$, $\overline{EF} \cong \overline{FG} \cong \overline{GH} \cong \overline{EH}$, $\angle E \cong \angle G$, and $\angle F \cong \angle H$.

To find the area of a rhombus, use the same formula that you used to find the area of a parallelogram: $A = bh$. To find the perimeter of a rhombus, add the lengths of the four sides. Since they all have the same length, $P = 4s$.

Rectangles

A **rectangle** is also a special parallelogram. In a rectangle, opposite sides are congruent and parallel, and all angles are right angles.

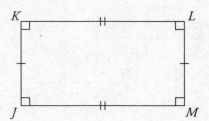

To find the area of a rectangle, use the formula $A = lw$, where l means length and w means width. Length and width are the two dimensions of the rectangle: in other words, the lengths of two *different* sides. It doesn't matter which one you call length and which one width.

Why is there a different formula for the area of a rectangle? Isn't it just a special parallelogram? If you look at it, you can see that this formula is really just your old friend $A = bh$. But in a rectangle, the sides are perpendicular, since all the angles are right angles. So whichever side you decide is the base already has a built-in height to go with it: either of the sides that meets it in a right angle!

Try an example:

Use the diagram below to answer the question that follows.

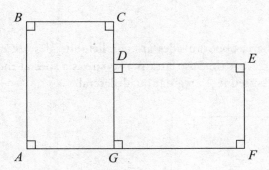

The figure above represents Ale's two garden beds. If $AB = DE = 6$ ft and $BC = EF = 4$ ft, what is the area of the two beds combined?

A.   24 ft²

B.   32 ft²

C.   48 ft²

D.   96 ft²

Here's How to Crack It

When the question tells you measurements that are not shown on the picture, redraw the picture and add all the extra information:

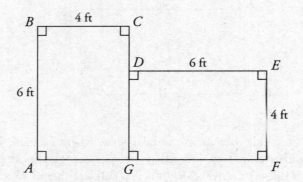

There are two rectangles here. Rectangle *ABCG* has length 4 ft and width 6 ft, so its area is $A = lw = 4 \text{ ft} \times 6 \text{ ft} = 24 \text{ ft}^2$. Rectangle *DEFG* has length 6 ft and width 4 ft (but remember, it doesn't matter which is the length and which is the width), so its area is $A = lw = 6 \text{ ft} \times 4 \text{ ft} = 24 \text{ ft}^2$ as well.

Add the two areas to find the area of the two beds combined: $24 \text{ ft}^2 + 24 \text{ ft}^2 = 48 \text{ ft}^2$, so (C) is correct.

The perimeter of a rectangle is the sum of the lengths of its four sides, the two lengths and the two widths. So $P = 2l + 2w$.

Squares

A **square** is a special rectangle. In a square, opposite sides are parallel, all sides are congruent, and all angles are right angles. Notice that this also means a square is a special rhombus! What's another name for a square? You guessed it—a regular quadrilateral!

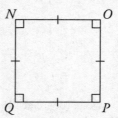

To find the area of a square, use the formula $A = s^2$, where *s* means the length of any side.

To find the perimeter of a square, use the formula $P = 4s$.

Fatima is building a rectangular sandbox for her daughter. She has 8 m of wood board to build the sides. If she can make the sides any length, what dimensions will result in the greatest area?

A. 0.5 m by 3.5 m

B. 1 m by 3 m

C. 1.5 m by 2.5 m

D. 2 m by 2 m

Here's How to Crack It

One way to work this problem is just to find the area for each answer choice, and see which is the greatest:

Choice (A) gives measurements 0.5 m by 3.5 m. To find the area, multiply the length by the width: $A = lw = 0.5 \text{ m} \times 3.5 \text{ m} = 1.75 \text{ m}^2$.

Choice (B) gives measurements 1 m by 3 m. To find the area, multiply the length by the width: $A = lw = 1 \text{ m} \times 3 \text{ m} = 3 \text{ m}^2$.

Choice (C) gives measurements 1.5 m by 2.5 m. To find the area, multiply the length by the width: $A = lw = 1.5 \text{ m} \times 2.5 \text{ m} = 3.75 \text{ m}^2$.

Choice (D) gives measurements 2 m by 2 m. To find the area, multiply the length by the width: $A = lw = 2 \text{ m} \times 2 \text{ m} = 4 \text{ m}^2$.

The greatest area is given by the measurements in (D). Notice that since these measurements are equal, the rectangle in (D) is a square. That's okay! Squares are just special rectangles.

This question points out a rule that might help you get points faster: for a given perimeter, the rectangle with the greatest area will always be the square. If you knew that rule, this question would be a snap! Remember it and it may come in handy.

Trapezoids

A **trapezoid** is the last special type of quadrilateral you are likely to see. It's different from the other types in that it has exactly one pair of parallel sides—the other two sides are not parallel.

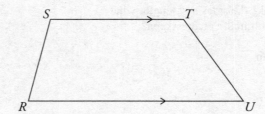

To find the area of a trapezoid, use the formula $A = \dfrac{a+b}{2}h$, where a and b are the lengths of the two parallel sides, and h is the height—the distance between those two sides along a perpendicular.

Since there is no special relationship between the lengths of the sides in a trapezoid, to find the perimeter of a trapezoid, you'll need to add the lengths of the four sides.

Use the diagram below to answer the question that follows.

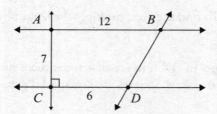

Lines *AB* and *CD* are parallel. What is the area of figure *ABDC* formed by the four lines shown, in square units?

A. 32

B. 42

C. 63

D. 84

Here's How to Crack It

The figure formed has to be a trapezoid, since the lines *AB* and *CD* are parallel, but opposite sides are not congruent. Use the formula $A = \dfrac{a+b}{2}h$. Here *a* and *b* are the lengths of the parallel sides, so they are 12 and 6; and *h* is the height.

Look carefully at the trapezoid: since line *AC* is perpendicular to line *CD*, *AC* = 7 can be your height!

$$A = \frac{a+b}{2}h = \frac{12+6}{2}(7) = \frac{18}{2}(7) = 9(7) = 63$$

The correct answer is (C).

There is one special kind of trapezoid—an isosceles trapezoid. In an **isosceles trapezoid,** both angles coming from a parallel side are equal, and the sides that aren't parallel are equal in length.

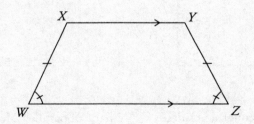

Types of Quadrilaterals

Parallelogram

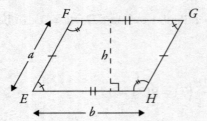

2 pairs of parallel and congruent sides, 2 pairs of congruent angles
$$A = bh, P = 2a + 2b$$

Trapezoid

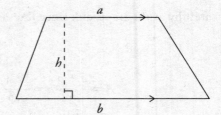

exactly 1 pair of parallel sides

$$A = \frac{a + b}{2}h$$

Rectangle

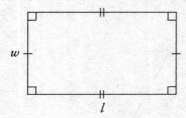

2 pairs of parallel and congruent sides, 4 right angles
$$A = lw, P = 2l + 2w$$

Rhombus

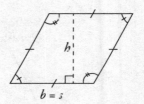

2 pairs of parallel sides, 4 congruent sides, 2 pairs of congruent angles
$$A = bh, P = 4s$$

Square

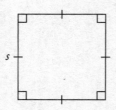

2 pairs of parallel sides, 4 congruent sides, 4 right angles
$$A = s^2, P = 4s$$

Try this quadrilateral question:

──────────────────◯──────────────────

Use the diagram below to answer the question that follows.

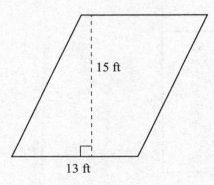

15 ft

13 ft

Carlo has a large piece of carpet in the shape of a parallelogram. He needs to carpet a rectangular room that measures 11 feet by 13 feet, and he thinks he can use this piece to cover it by cutting and rearranging the parallelogram into a rectangle. What is the area of the piece(s) of carpet that will be left over?

A.   4 ft²

B.   26 ft²

C.   52 ft²

D.   97.5 ft²

Here's How to Crack It

This problem centers around rearranging a parallelogram into a rectangle. How can you do that? Easy: Draw any height and chop the parallelogram into two pieces. Slide one of them around to the *other side* of the other piece and stick them back together, and hey presto! A rectangle. Try it with Carlo's carpet parallelogram:

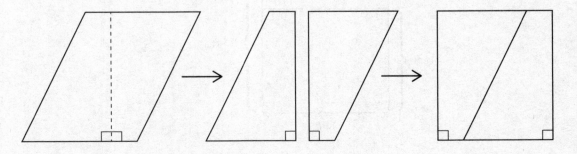

What is the width of this new rectangle? Since the parallelogram was cut along its height, and the two pieces were rearranged so that the height is now two sides of the rectangle, the width of the rectangle is equal to the height of the parallelogram: 15 ft.

What is the length of this new rectangle? Since the base of the parallelogram was cut into two pieces and then those two pieces were put back together, the length of the rectangle is equal to the base of the parallelogram: 13 ft. This is true no matter what the sizes of the pieces were. Neato.

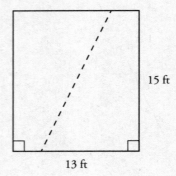

Now, the rectangular room Carlo needs to cover measures 11 feet by 13 feet. Find the area of the carpet and the area of the room and then subtract:

$$A_{carpet} = lw = 13 \text{ ft} \times 15 \text{ ft} = 195 \text{ ft}^2$$

$$A_{room} = lw = 11 \text{ ft} \times 13 \text{ ft} = 143 \text{ ft}^2$$

$$A_{left over} = 195 \text{ ft}^2 - 143 \text{ ft}^2 = 52 \text{ ft}^2$$

The correct answer is (C). Notice that now that you know that rearranging the parallelogram gives a rectangle *of the same area,* you wouldn't have to actually *do* it: you could just subtract the area of the rectangular room from the area of the carpet parallelogram! Carlo's still going to have to do it, though.

If you do better with visualizations, you might solve this problem a different way: draw the two rectangles overlapping to find the area of the extra piece:

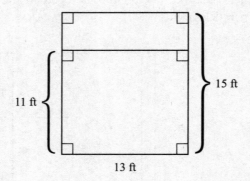

Subtract 15 ft − 11 ft = 4 ft to find the width of the extra piece:

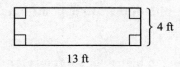

$A_{\text{extra piece}} = lw = 13 \text{ ft} \times 4 \text{ ft} = 52 \text{ ft}^2$

Triangles

Split a quadrilateral diagonally, and what do you get? Triangles!

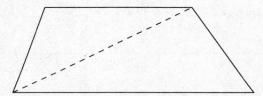

A **triangle** is a closed, two-dimensional shape that has three sides. A triangle always has three angles as well as three sides (hence, the name).

The measures of the interior angles of a triangle sum to 180°—that's known as the **rule of 180°.** This makes sense: since a quadrilateral (which, remember, has interior angles that sum to 360°) can be split into two triangles, the sum of the measures of the interior angles of a triangle is half that of a quadrilateral.

Another cool rule is that any exterior angle of a triangle is equal to the sum of the two opposite interior angles. What's an **exterior angle?** If you extend any of the sides of a triangle, you get an angle *outside* the boundary of the triangle that is supplementary to the adjacent interior angle:

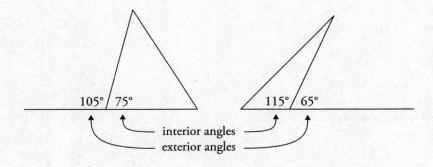

Those are the exterior angles. If you think about the rule of 180°, you can figure out the rule above: since the exterior angle is supplementary to the interior angle, its measure is 180°– the measure of the interior angle. The sum of the two opposite interior angles is the same: 180°– the measure of that interior angle.

In fact, you can use similar thinking to figure out a formula for the area of a triangle. Any triangle can be looked at as half of a parallelogram:

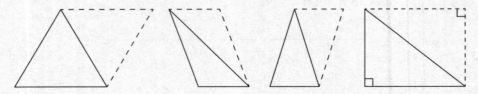

The parallelograms above were made by making an identical triangle to each given triangle, and then sticking the two together. Since the area of a parallelogram is $A = bh$, it follows that the area of any triangle will be $A = \frac{1}{2}bh$.

Use the diagram below to answer the question that follows.

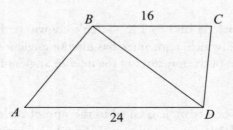

The area of trapezoid *ABCD* is 100 square units.
What is the area of triangle *ABD*?

A.   40 square units

B.   50 square units

C.   60 square units

D.   100 square units

Here's How to Crack It

The question tells you the area of the trapezoid and gives you the lengths of its base and the side opposite its base. Can you use the formula for the area of a trapezoid to get more information?

$$A = \frac{a + b}{2} h$$

Substitute the given values:

$$100 = \frac{16 + 24}{2} h$$

Now you can solve for h:

$$100 = \frac{40}{2} h$$

$$100 = 20h$$

$$\frac{100}{20} = \frac{20h}{20}$$

$$5 = h$$

Now you know the height of the trapezoid. Is this helpful? The question asks for the area of triangle ABD, and you know that the area of a triangle is given by $A = \frac{1}{2}bh$. Draw the height of the triangle:

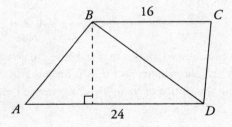

So it turns out knowing the height of the trapezoid *is* helpful, because the height of triangle ABD is also a height of the trapezoid!

Now you can substitute the values of *b* and *h* into the formula for the area of a triangle:

$$A = \frac{1}{2}bh$$

$$A = \frac{1}{2}(24)(5)$$

$$A = 60$$

The correct answer is (C).

Note that the area of the triangle is *not* half of the area of the trapezoid: that only works with parallelograms. Choice (B) is a trap!

To find the perimeter of a triangle, add the lengths of its three sides.

Isosceles Triangles

Another useful triangle rule: the angles of a triangle are directly proportional to the sides opposite them; in other words, the largest angle is always opposite the longest side, and the smallest angle is always opposite the shortest side. This also means that congruent angles are opposite congruent sides!

A triangle with at least two congruent sides is an **isosceles triangle.**

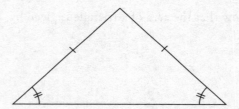

This means that if you are told that two angles in a triangle are congruent, you also know that the two sides opposite them are congruent; and if you are told that two sides are congruent, you also know that the two angles opposite them are congruent. That information can come in handy!

Triangle *TUV* is isosceles. Angle *V* measures 100 .
What is the measure of angle *U*?

A.   40

B.   60

C.   80

D.   100

Here's How to Crack It

The question doesn't show a picture, so draw one. You need a triangle with one angle that measures 100°, and that is isosceles. Since an isosceles triangle has two angles (and two sides) that are congruent, the first question you need to ask yourself is, which two angles are congruent? Is angle *V* one of the two congruent ones, or is it the other two angles that are congruent?

If you try to draw a triangle with two 100° angles, you'll find a problem:

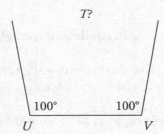

Why can't you draw a triangle with two 100° angles? It goes back to the rule of 180°: the sum of the interior angles of a triangle is 180°. Since 100° + 100° = 200°, you would have already used up more than the allotted 180°, just on two of the angles!

The general rule here is that a triangle can't have two obtuse or right angles, since any angle of 90° or greater will cause this problem.

> A triangle can't have two obtuse or right angles!

So that helps you figure out that *V* is not one of the two congruent angles in this problem. Eliminate (D).

Now draw the triangle that *does* work:

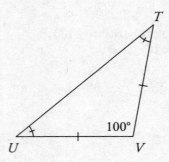

You know that $m\angle U = m\angle T$, and you know that $m\angle T + m\angle U + m\angle V = 180°$. Substitute the value of $m\angle V$ and simplify: $m\angle T + m\angle U + 100° = 180°$, so $m\angle T + m\angle U = 180° - 100° = 80°$.

Now you can substitute $m\angle U$ for $m\angle T$ because you know they are equal: $m\angle U + m\angle U = 80°$, so $2m\angle U = 80°$, and $m\angle U = 40°$. The correct answer is (A).

Equilateral Triangles

A triangle with three congruent sides is an **equilateral triangle.**

Since all three sides are congruent, you also know that the three angles opposite them are congruent. What happens when all the angles in a triangle are congruent?

Well, you know the sum of the three angles is 180°. Since the three angles have the same measure, each one must be one-third of 180°:

$$3a = 180°$$

$$\frac{3a}{3} = \frac{180°}{3}$$

$$a = 60°$$

So, all three angles in an equilateral triangle *always* measure 60°! That information is useful: you should label equilateral triangles with three 60° angles whenever you draw them.

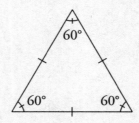

And in the same vein, if you find out that there are three 60° angles in a triangle (or even two—then the third one will have to be 60° as well!), then you know the triangle is equilateral!

Use the figure below to answer the question that follows.

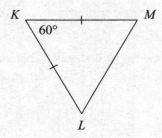

In isosceles triangle *KLM*, $m\angle K = 60°$. What is $m\angle M$?

A.   30°

B.   60°

C.   90°

D.   120°

Here's How to Crack It

The question tells you that the triangle is isosceles, and the figure shows you which two sides are the same: *KM* and *KL*. That tells you that angles *M* and *L* are congruent. Since the three angles must add to 180°, subtract the angle measure you know to find what's left:

$$m\angle K + m\angle L + m\angle M = 180°$$

$$60° + m\angle L + m\angle M = 180°$$

$$m\angle L + m\angle M = 180° - 60° = 120°$$

Since the two angles left are congruent, their measure is half of what's left:

$$m\angle L = m\angle M = \frac{120°}{2} = 60°$$

Wait a sec, they're both 60° too? Is that okay?

Yes! An equilateral triangle is a special type of isosceles triangle. So even though the question told you it's isosceles, it can really be equilateral.

In fact, if you ever run into the situation again in which a 60° angle is between two congruent sides of an isosceles triangle, you know now what's going to happen. The two other angles are going to have to be 60°: the triangle is really equilateral. Good to keep in mind.

The correct answer is (B).

So what is a triangle called if it has no congruent sides (and therefore no congruent angles)? That kind of triangle is called a **scalene triangle.**

Right Triangles

A **right triangle** is a triangle that contains a right angle. (Remember, a triangle can't have more than *one* right angle.)

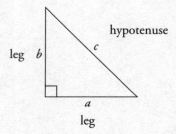

The side opposite the right angle is called the **hypotenuse,** and the other sides of the triangle are called **legs.**

There is a special relationship between the lengths of the legs and the length of the hypotenuse of a right triangle:

> The Pythagorean Theorem
> $$a^2 + b^2 = c^2$$
>
> Where a and b are the lengths of the legs, and c is the length of the hypotenuse, of a right triangle.

So you can find a missing length of a side of a right triangle any time you know the lengths of the other two sides:

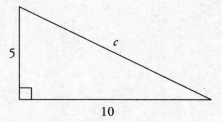

Find the missing length using the Pythagorean Theorem. Here the missing length is the length of the hypotenuse, so make sure to substitute the lengths you know for *a* and *b* (it doesn't matter which is which).

$$a^2 + b^2 = c^2$$

$$5^2 + 10^2 = c^2$$

$$25 + 100 = c^2$$

$$125 = c^2$$

Take the square root of both sides to solve. Since you are solving for a length, or distance, you don't need to worry about the negative root, because distance is always positive.

$$\sqrt{125} = c$$

Simplify the root:

$$\sqrt{25} \times \sqrt{5} = c$$

$$5\sqrt{5} = c$$

In the triangle below, use the Pythagorean Theorem to find the missing length *a*.

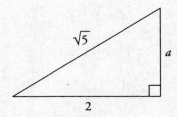

In the triangle on the previous page, the missing length is the length of a leg. Make sure to substitute the length of the hypotenuse for c, and the length of the known leg for either a or b.

$$a^2 + b^2 = c^2$$

$$a^2 + 2^2 = \left(\sqrt{5}\right)^2$$

$$a^2 + 4 = 5$$

$$a^2 + 4 - 4 = 5 - 4$$

$$a^2 = 1$$

Take the square root of both sides to solve. Since you are solving for a length, or distance, you don't need to worry about the negative root, because distance is always positive.

$$a = \sqrt{1} = 1$$

The converse of the Pythagorean Theorem also holds. In other words, if the lengths of the sides of a triangle fit into the relationship $a^2 + b^2 = c^2$, then the triangle is a right triangle.

Find the value of z in the triangle below.

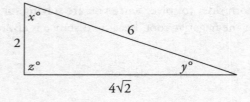

The angles aren't given, so you don't know what kind of triangle it is. But you *are* given lengths of sides, so you can try them in the Pythagorean Theorem to see whether the triangle is a right triangle or not. Remember that if it is, the hypotenuse must be the longest side. So make sure to substitute the greatest value, 6, for c.

$$a^2 + b^2 = c^2$$

$$2^2 + \left(4\sqrt{2}\right)^2 = 6^2 ?$$

$$4 + 16(2) = 36?$$

$$4 + 32 = 36?$$

$$36 = 36 \checkmark$$

These values *do* fit the Pythagorean Theorem. So the angle opposite the hypotenuse, c, measures 90°. Thus, $z = 90$.

There are some right triangles that test makers really love to use, because they happen to have side lengths that are all integers. You should memorize the most common three, to save yourself time on the test. What's faster: solving using the Pythagorean Theorem, or already knowing the answer?

Here are the **common right triangles:**

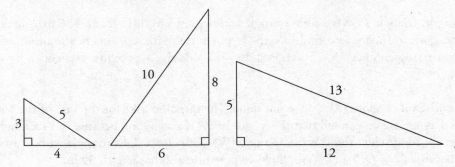

Become familiar enough with these that you can spot when a question is asking about one of them. Did you notice that the second one has the same ratio as the first one? You should also keep an eye out for other multiples, such as 30-40-50 or 10-24-26.

Use the figure below to answer the question that follows.

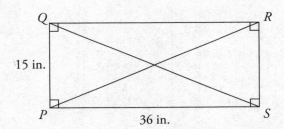

Shay is building a rectangular shelf to display toys. He needs to support the back with diagonal struts. If the length of the shelf is 36 in. and the width is 15 in., what is the sum of the lengths of the diagonals QS and PR?

A.   39 in.

B.   78 in.

C.   270 in.

D.   540 in.

Here's How to Crack It

The question looks like it's asking about rectangles. However, notice that each diagonal of the rectangle forms two right triangles with the rectangle's length and width as legs.

The diagonals of rectangles always form right triangles with their legs, so right triangles come in handy quite often on rectangle problems!

For example, triangle *PQS* is a right triangle with legs of length 15 in. and 36 in. You could use the Pythagorean Theorem to find *QS*, the hypotenuse, but...yep, this is a multiple of a common right triangle. Since 15 = 5 × 3, and 36 = 12 × 3, the hypotenuse has got to have length 13 × 3 = 39.

Watch out! Don't choose (A): you're not done! The question asks for the *sum* of the lengths of the two diagonals. You can tell that the length of *PR* is also 39 in., because in a rectangle opposite sides are congruent. You can use triangle *PRS*—it's also a right triangle with legs of length 15 in. (because *RS* = *QP*) and 36 in. So its hypotenuse also has length 39 in.

Since 39 in. + 39 in. = 78 in., the correct answer is (B).

Another couple of right triangles you should know like the back of your hand are the **special right triangles.** These are two triangles with fixed ratios of sides: the 45-45-90 triangle and the 30-60-90 triangle. They come up often enough that knowing the ratios is worth your time.

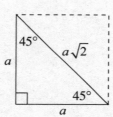 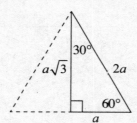

So if you see a right triangle problem that gives you the length of only *one* side, it may be testing special right triangles: if you determine the triangle is one of these, you need only one length—then you can use the ratio to find the other two.

The 45-45-90 triangle is also known as the isosceles right triangle. That's because it's the only way a triangle can be both isosceles and right.

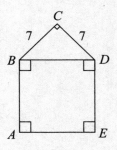

In the figure above, what is the area of square
ABDE ?

A. 49

B. $49\sqrt{2}$

C. 98

D. $98\sqrt{2}$

Here's How to Crack It

In order to figure out the area of square *ABDE*, we need to know the length of one of its sides.

We can get the length of *BD* by using the isosceles right triangle attached to it. *BD* is the

hypotenuse, which means its length is $7\sqrt{2}$. To get the area of the square we have to square the

length of the side we know, or $\left(7\sqrt{2}\right)\left(7\sqrt{2}\right) = (49)(2) = 98$. That's (C).

One place the 30-60-90 triangle comes up often is in finding the heights of equilateral triangles.

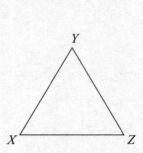

Triangle *XYZ* in the figure above is an equilateral triangle. If the perimeter of the triangle is 12, what is its area?

A. $2\sqrt{3}$

B. $4\sqrt{3}$

C. 8

D. $8\sqrt{3}$

Here's How to Crack It

Here we have an equilateral triangle with a perimeter of 12, which means that each side has a length of 4 and each angle is 60 degrees. Remember that in order to find the area of a triangle, we use the triangle area formula: $A = \frac{1}{2}bh$, but first we need to know the base and the height of the triangle. The base is 4, which now gives us $A = \frac{1}{2}4h$, and now the only thing we need is the height. Remember that the height always has to be perpendicular to the base. Draw a vertical line that splits the equilateral triangle in half. The top angle is also split in half, so now we have this:

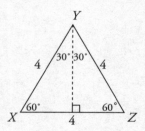

What we've done is create two 30-60-90 right triangles, and we're going to use one of these right triangles to find the height. Let's use the one on the right. We know that the hypotenuse in a 30-60-90 right triangle is always twice the length of the short side. Here we have a hypotenuse (*YZ*) of 4, so our short side has to be 2. The long side of a 30-60-90 right triangle is always equal to the short side multiplied by the square root of 3. So if our short side is 2, then our long side must be $2\sqrt{3}$. That's the height.

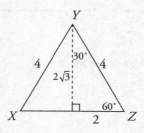

Finally, we return to our area formula. Now we have $A = \dfrac{1}{2} \times 4 \times 2\sqrt{3}$. Multiply it out and you get $A = 4\sqrt{3}$. The answer is (B).

Circles

A **circle** is a round plane figure whose boundary (the **circumference**) consists of points equidistant from a fixed point (the **center**). A line segment with one endpoint at the center of the circle and the other anywhere on its boundary is called a **radius.** Since all points on the circle are equidistant from the center, the length of every radius of the same circle is equal. A line segment with both its endpoints on a circle is called a **chord.** A chord that passes through the center of the circle is called a **diameter:** a diameter is the longest chord in a circle.

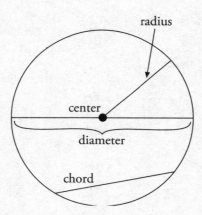

There are some important relationships between the measurements of a circle. **Circumference** is the name for the circle's boundary, but it's also the word for the length of that boundary. Given a circle's radius r, you can find its diameter d, circumference C, and area A. You can tell that $d = 2r$, since a diameter is made up of two radii. The other two relationships are very important to memorize:

$$C = 2\pi r$$

$$A = \pi r^2$$

For circles, remember:
r
$d = 2r$
$C = 2\pi r$
$A = \pi r^2$

What is the area of a circle with a diameter of 16 units?

A. 16π square units

B. 32π square units

C. 64π square units

D. 256π square units

Here's How to Crack It

Think about the four pieces of information that tell you about a circle (think *r, d, C, A*). Which do you know? Which does the question ask for?

You are given the diameter and asked for the area. Use the diameter to find the radius:

$$d = 2r$$

$$16 = 2r$$

$$8 = r$$

Now use the radius to find the area:

$$A = \pi r^2$$

$$A = \pi(8)^2$$

$$A = 64\pi$$

The correct answer is (C).

Parts of Circles

Some questions will ask you for the length of a *piece* of the circumference of a circle, or the area of a *piece* of the area of a circle. In this case, you need to know about arcs and sectors.

An **arc** is a piece of the circumference of a circle. It always has a corresponding **central angle:** the angle made by the radii with the same endpoints as the arc.

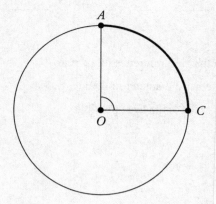

Arcs are named for their endpoints on the circle. The arc above is minor arc *AC*. A **minor arc** is an arc with a central angle that measures less than 180°. The other arc connects the same two endpoints going in the opposite direction around the circle: it's called a **major arc** because its central angle measures greater than 180°. Major arc *AC* is the arc that's not marked above.

Another way to name arcs is with three points: the endpoints and one point in between them. With this method, only one arc is described, so you don't have to call the arc *minor* or *major*.

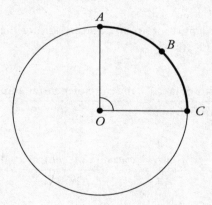

The arc above is called arc *ABC*, and its central angle is ∠*AOC*.

The central angle that corresponds to an arc is important, because you need it to find the arc's measure. The length of an arc is a fraction of the circumference proportional to the central angle's measure divided by 360°, the central angle of the whole circle:

$$\frac{\text{length of arc}}{\text{circumference}} = \frac{\text{measure of central angle}}{360°}$$

Points *C, D,* and *E* lie on the circumference of a circle with center *O*. If the circle has a diameter of 4 and arc *CDE* has a length of $\frac{2\pi}{15}$, what is the least possible measure of angle *COE*?

A.   6°

B.   12°

C.   48°

D.   180°

Here's How to Crack It

Think *r, d, C, A* first. The question tells you that the diameter is 4. You need the circumference in order to use the information about the arc's length. If *d* = 4, then *r* = 2, and *C* = 4π.

Now use your formula for the length of an arc, and substitute the values you have—the circumference and the length of the arc:

$$\frac{\text{length of arc}}{\text{Circumference}} = \frac{\text{measure of central angle}}{360°}$$

$$\frac{\frac{2\pi}{15}}{4\pi} = \frac{\text{measure of central angle}}{360°}$$

Don't forget: to divide by a fraction, multiply by the reciprocal: $\frac{\frac{2\pi}{15}}{4\pi} = \frac{2\pi}{15} \times \frac{1}{4\pi} = \frac{2\pi}{60\pi} = \frac{1}{30}$.

Use this information to solve for the measure of the central angle:

$$\frac{1}{30} = \frac{\text{measure of central angle}}{360°}$$

$$\frac{1}{30} \times 360° = \text{measure of central angle}$$

$$12° = \text{measure of central angle}$$

The correct answer is (B).

A **sector** is a piece of the area of a circle. It looks like a piece of pizza or pie: the shape bounded by an arc and the two radii of its central angle.

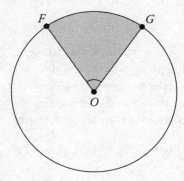

Again, you need to know the measure of the central angle in order to determine the area of a sector. The area of a sector is a fraction of the circle's whole area proportional to the central angle's measure divided by 360°, the central angle of the whole circle:

$$\frac{\text{area of sector}}{\text{area of circle}} = \frac{\text{measure of central angle}}{360°}$$

Use the figure below to answer the question that follows.

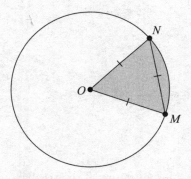

The circle above has center *O,* and points *N* and *M* are on its circumference. If triangle *NOM* is equilateral and *NM* = 12, what is the area of the shaded portion of the circle?

A.   6π

B.   24π

C.   36π

D.   144π

Here's How to Crack It

Again, think *r, d, C, A* first. The question doesn't explicitly tell you the radius, diameter, circumference, or area of the circle. That means you probably can find at least one of them from the information it *does* give you.

The question does tell you that *NM* = 12, and that triangle *NOM* is equilateral. That's what you need: since the triangle is equilateral, all its sides have the same length, so *ON* = *OM* = 12 too. Those are both radii of the circle, so now you can get your *r, d, C, A*. Which value do you need? Since the question asks for the area of a portion of a circle, and the portion is a sector, you need the area of the circle to put into your sector formula.

You also need the central angle. What is it? That's right! All angles in an equilateral triangle measure 60°.

$$A = \pi r^2 = \pi (12)^2 = 144\pi$$

$$\frac{\text{area of sector}}{\text{area of circle}} = \frac{\text{measure of central angle}}{360°}$$

$$\frac{\text{area of sector}}{144\pi} = \frac{60°}{360°}$$

Reduce, and then multiply both sides by 144π:

$$\frac{\text{area of sector}}{144\pi} = \frac{1}{6}$$

$$\text{area of sector} = \frac{1}{6} \times 144\pi = 24\pi$$

The correct answer is (B).

Inscribing

An **inscribed figure** is one that's drawn within another figure so that their boundaries touch but do not intersect. For some reason, test writers love to inscribe shapes and angles inside circles and semicircles. Occasionally, a circle will be inscribed inside another shape.

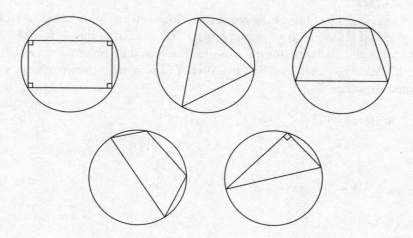

Sometimes problems involving inscribed figures really have to do with what the figures have in common:

———————————○———————————

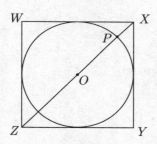

In the figure above, a circle with the center O is inscribed in square $WXYZ$. If the circle has radius 3, then $PZ =$

A. $3\sqrt{2}$

B.   6

C. $3 + 3\sqrt{2}$

D. $6 + \sqrt{2}$

Here's How to Crack It

The question tells you the radius of the circle is 3. Since you are being asked to find PZ, think about what pieces of information you need. Since PO is a radius of the circle, $PO = 3$. If Z were at the other end of the diameter from P, this problem would be easy and the answer would be 6, right? But OZ is longer than PO. So the answer will be greater than 6 You can estimate to eliminate some answers:

A. $3\sqrt{2} \approx 3(1.4) = 4.2$

B. 6

C. $3 + 3\sqrt{2} \approx 3 + 3(1.4) = 3 + 4.2 = 7.2$

D. $6 + \sqrt{2} \approx 6 + 1.4 = 7.4$

Eliminate (A) and (B).

OZ is part of the diagonal of square $WXYZ$. In fact, it's exactly half. What else do you know about the square? The diameter of the circle is the same as the side of the square, since you can draw a horizontal or vertical diameter that's parallel to the sides of the square and will have the same length.

Find the diameter: $d = 2r = 2(3) = 6$.

How can you find the length of the diagonal of a square?

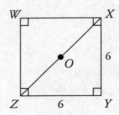

Remember that when you draw a diagonal of a square, it splits the square into two 45-45-90 triangles. The length of the hypotenuse of a 45-45-90 triangle is $\sqrt{2}$ times the lengths of its legs, so the diagonal ZX has length $6\sqrt{2}$.

You wanted to find OZ, which is half the diagonal, so it's $\dfrac{6\sqrt{2}}{2} = 3\sqrt{2}$.

To find PZ, all you have left to do is to add $PO + OZ = 3 + 3\sqrt{2}$. The correct answer is (C).

And sometimes problems involving inscribed figures have to do with corresponding angles.

Corresponding Angles

When you inscribe an angle in a circle, there are three points on the circumference of the circle involved: the angle's vertex and the other endpoint of each chord. If you connect these same endpoints to the center of the circle, you get a central angle that's related to the inscribed angle in a specific way: it's called the **corresponding angle** of the inscribed angle. For example, in the first circle below, the inscribed angle is 60° and the corresponding angle is 120°.

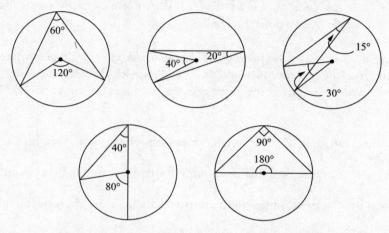

An angle inscribed in a circle with endpoints *a* and *b* measures half of its corresponding angle (the angle with the same two endpoints, and the center as its vertex).

One upshot of this rule is that any angle inscribed in a semicircle (such that the endpoints are the endpoints of the semicircle's arc) is a right angle, since its corresponding angle is a straight angle: the diameter of the semicircle.

Use the figure below to answer the question that follows.

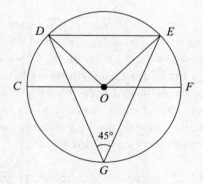

The circle above has center *O*, and diameter *CF* measures 12 units. What is the area of triangle *DOE*?

A.   12 square units

B.   18 square units

C.   36 square units

D.   144 square units

Here's How to Crack It

To find the area of the triangle you must know its base and its height, so you need to determine which dimensions of the triangle you already know.

Since the diameter of the circle is 12 units, the radius is 6 units.

Happily, two of your triangle's sides are radii. This does not necessarily mean that you know the height of the triangle in question, though.

To find the height, you need a perpendicular. Look at the triangle to see what information it contains, and what the measure of angle *EOD* is. Since it's the corresponding angle of the inscribed angle, it must be twice the inscribed angle's measure, or twice 45, which is 90 degrees. Aha!

The corresponding angle is a right angle, meaning you've got a right isosceles triangle on your hands. You can use the two sides formed by the radii as your height and base—since they have a right angle, they are perpendicular. So the area of the triangle is

$$A = \frac{1}{2}bh = \frac{1}{2}(6)(6) = \frac{1}{2}(36) = 18 \text{ square units: the correct answer is (B).}$$

ANALYTIC GEOMETRY

Analytic geometry is just a fancy term for using algebra and geometry together, in the place they most like to meet: the coordinate plane.

First, remember the basics of the coordinate plane from Chapter 15: it's made of two perpendicular axes, the *x*-axis (horizontal) and the *y*-axis (vertical). The place where they meet is called the origin and its location expressed as an ordered pair is (0, 0). Other points in the form (*x*, *y*) can be plotted by moving away from the origin *x* units horizontally (right for positive values and left for negative values) and *y* units vertically (up for positive values and down for negative values). Linear, quadratic, and other types of equations have representations in the coordinate plane: lines, parabolas, and other shapes. You can also find solutions to inequalities, systems of equations, and systems of inequalities using the coordinate plane.

Now that you've reviewed the basics of Geometry, let's look at some important geometric concepts that can be represented and solved using the coordinate plane: distance, midpoint, and plotting shapes.

Distance

Let's say you have two points on your grid, (1, 3) and (6, 3).

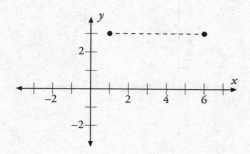

To calculate the distance between them is a fairly easy matter: just count along the x-axis, or subtract the x-coordinates (see how those are the same operation?) and you've found the distance between the points.

When you need to find a length or distance that's not just in the vertical or horizontal direction in the coordinate plane, you can take advantage of its cool properties: since the x-axis and the y-axis are perpendicular, it's really easy to make right triangles in the x-y coordinate plane.

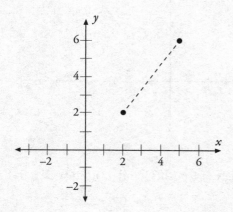

Suppose you need to find the distance between the two points in the figure above. Connect your points and make the distance you are finding the hypotenuse of a right triangle. Then just draw connecting vertical and horizontal segments to make the legs of the triangle. Since any horizontal segment is parallel to the x-axis and any vertical segment is parallel to the y-axis, you know the segments you drew are perpendicular to each other: so you've made a right triangle.

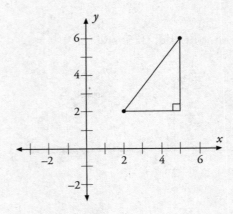

Now, find the lengths of the legs of your triangle by counting along the *x*- and *y*-axes. Then use the properties of right triangles to find the length of the hypotenuse: see whether your triangle is a common or special right triangle, and if not, use the Pythagorean Theorem.

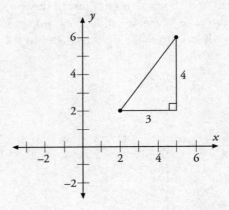

Since the right triangle has legs of lengths 3 and 4, it must be a 3-4-5 triangle, and its hypotenuse has length 5.

To do this without graphing, you can use the **distance formula.**

The Distance Formula

$$d = \sqrt{\left(x_2 - x_1\right)^2 + \left(y_2 - y_1\right)^2}$$

Where (x_1, y_1) and (x_2, y_2) are the points in the coordinate plane, and *d* is the distance between them.

If you square both sides of the distance formula, you can see that it's really just the Pythagorean Theorem, with the horizontal distance (horizontal leg of the right triangle) as a and the vertical distance (vertical leg of the right triangle) as b:

$$d^2 = (x_2 - x_1)^2 + (y_2 - y_1)^2$$

Midpoint

There's one more formula that relates to line segments in the coordinate plane, and you might want to have it on hand in case anyone ever asks you, "Hey, would you happen to know the midpoint of the line segment between the two points (x_1, y_1) and (x_2, y_2)?" And how often do you hear that one? On the CSET—you very well may!

The **midpoint** of a line segment is its exact middle: the point that splits it exactly in half. The midpoint of a line segment with endpoints (x_1, y_1) and (x_2, y_2) has the following coordinates:

$$x = \frac{x_1 + x_2}{2} \text{ and } y = \frac{y_1 + y_2}{2}$$

In other words, the x-coordinate is the average of the two x-coordinates and the y-coordinate is the average of the two y-coordinates. Seems pretty obvious, doesn't it? Well it is. Go ahead and enjoy it, you deserve an easy and obvious formula by now.

Using Coordinate Geometry to Represent Geometric Objects

As you saw above, it's easy to make right triangles in the coordinate plane. You can also graph just about any of the plane geometry figures you've reviewed so far in the coordinate plane, and you should be prepared to see some questions dealing with this topic on the CSET. You need to be able combine what you know about graphing with what you know about plane geometry.

Use the diagram below to answer the question that follows.

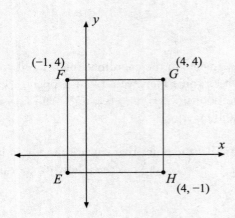

If figure *EFGH* is a square, what are the coordinates of point *E*?

A.   (1, 1)

B.   (–1, –1)

C.   (–4, 1)

D.   (–4, –4)

Here's How to Crack It

Since you know the figure is a square, think about what you know about squares. In a square, all angles are right angles, and both pairs of opposite sides are parallel and congruent. That means *EH* is parallel to *FG*, and has the same length. *FG* is horizontal, since there is no vertical change between its coordinates ($y_2 - y_1 = 4 - 4 = 0$). So *EH* has to be horizontal too, and you can figure that the *y*-coordinate of *E* will be the same as that of *H:* –1. The same reasoning can be applied to sides *EF* and *GH:* so *E* will have the same *x*-coordinate as *F:* –1. Its coordinates are (–1, –1), so the correct answer is (B).

SYMMETRY, CONGRUENCE, AND SIMILARITY

Symmetry and Transformations

What is symmetry? **Symmetry** describes how certain things *don't* change: it's the property that something does not change under a set of rigid transformations. So the next question is: what are transformations?

A **transformation** is a function that maps points of a figure (sometimes called the **preimage**) onto another figure (sometimes called the **image**). A **rigid transformation** is one that preserves all distances in the figure: in other words, the figure keeps the same shape and size. Where have you seen that before? That's right: the image resulting from a rigid transformation is *congruent* to its preimage!

There are three types of rigid transformations: translations, reflections, and rotations.

Translations

A **translation** is a transformation that doesn't change the original shape's size, shape, or orientation. All points are moved in the same direction over the same distance.

To perform a translation, move the points the appropriate distances by adding or subtracting values to or from the coordinates. To move *to the right,* add the number of units to the x-coordinate; to move *to the left,* subtract the number of units from the x-coordinate. To move *up,* add the number of units to the y-coordinate; to move *down,* subtract the number of units from the y-coordinate.

Use the diagram below to answer the question that follows.

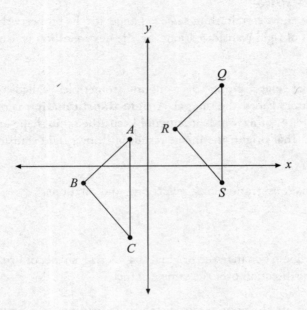

Triangle *ABC* above has vertices *A* (–2, 3), *B* (–7, –2), and *C* (–2, –8). Triangle *ABC* was translated 6 units up and 10 units to the right. If triangle *QRS* is its image under this translation, what are the coordinates of its vertices?

A.   (4, 13), (–1, 8), and (4, –2)

B.   (8, –3), (3, –8), and (8, –14)

C.   (8, 9), (3, 4), and (8, –2)

D.   (9, 8), (4, 3), and (–2, 8)

Here's How to Crack It

The translation is described in the question: the triangle was moved 6 units *up* and 10 units *to the right*. Since you know that the lengths of the sides will be preserved under the transformation, just concentrate on how the vertices moved.

For each vertex, to move it 10 units to the right is the same as *adding* 10 to its *x*-coordinate. To move it 6 units up is the same as *adding* 6 to its *y*-coordinate. Do that to the coordinates of each vertex of the triangle:

$A\,(-2, 3)$	add 10 to *x*-coordinate, add 6 to *y*-coordinate	(8, 9)
$B\,(-7, -2)$	add 10 to *x*-coordinate, add 6 to *y*-coordinate	(3, 4)
$C\,(-2, -8)$	add 10 to *x*-coordinate, add 6 to *y*-coordinate	(8, -2)

The correct answer is (C).

You can see for yourself that the translation above results in a shape (triangle *QRS*) with the same size, shape, and orientation as its preimage (triangle *ABC*).

The rest of the rigid transformations don't necessarily preserve the shape's orientation.

Reflections

A **reflection** is a transformation in which the preimage is reflected (or flipped) across a **line of reflection** to create the image. Each point of the image is on the opposite side of the line of reflection from its corresponding point in the preimage, but is the same distance from the line.

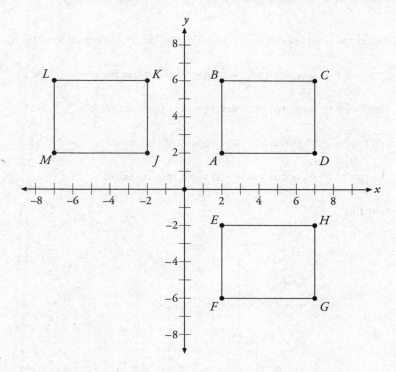

In the coordinate plane above, think of rectangle *ABCD* as the preimage. There are two images shown: rectangle *EFGH* and rectangle *JKLM*. Rectangle *EFGH* is the image after a reflection over the *x*-axis, while rectangle *JKLM* is the image after a reflection over the *y*-axis.

Notice that these reflections are relatively easy in terms of the coordinates of the points. To reflect a figure over the *x*-axis, just keep its *x*-coordinates the same, and take the opposites of its *y*-coordinates. So the point (2, 2) in the preimage becomes (2, -2) in the image.

To reflect a figure over the y-axis, just keep its y-coordinates the same, and take the opposites of its x-coordinates. So the point $(2, 2)$ in the preimage becomes $(-2, 2)$ in the image.

This works even when the preimage has parts on both sides of the line of reflection. Try reflecting trapezoid $NOPQ$ over the y-axis.

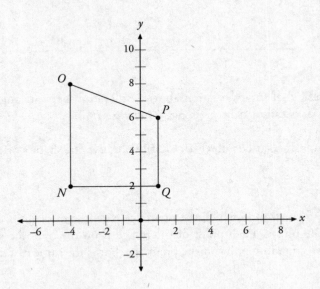

To flip it, write down the coordinates of the vertices and apply the transformation:

$N\ (-4, 2)$ opposite of x-coordinate, keep y-coordinate same $(4, 2)$

$O\ (-4, 8)$ opposite of x-coordinate, keep y-coordinate same $(4, 8)$

$P\ (1, 6)$ opposite of x-coordinate, keep y-coordinate same $(-1, 6)$

$Q\ (1, 2)$ opposite of x-coordinate, keep y-coordinate same $(-1, 2)$

Here's what it looks like:

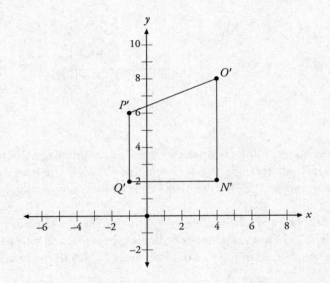

Another line you may be asked to reflect over is the line $y = x$.

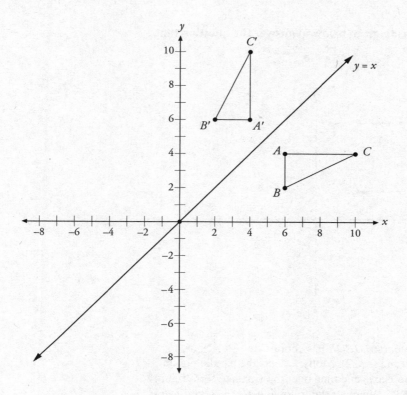

Can you tell what happened to the coordinates? They've been reversed! When you reflect a given point over the line $x = y$, the x-coordinate and y-coordinate are switched in the image.

Another thing you may be asked about is compositions of transformations. A **composition of transformations** is just doing multiple transformations in a given order. Make sure you do them one at a time!

Reflections	
Line of Reflection	Effect on x- and y-coordinates
x-axis	$(x, y) \longrightarrow (x, -y)$
y-axis	$(x, y) \longrightarrow (-x, y)$
$y = x$	$(x, y) \longrightarrow (y, x)$

Use the diagram below to answer the question that follows.

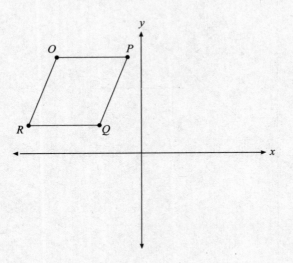

Parallelogram *OPQR* has coordinates (–6, 7), (–1, 7), (–3, 2), and (–8, 2). Molly reflects the parallelogram over the *x*-axis and then over the *y*-axis to form figure *O″P″Q″R″*. Which of the following are the coordinates of the resulting figure?

A. (7, –6), (7, –1), (2, –3), and (2, –8)

B. (6, 7), (1, 7), (3, 2), and (8, 2)

C. (–6, –7), (–1, –7), (–3, –2), and (–8, –2)

D. (6, –7), (1, –7), (3, –2), and (8, –2)

Here's How to Crack It
Follow the steps one at a time. First, Molly reflects the figure over the *x*-axis. You know that to do that, you keep the *x*-coordinates the same, and take the opposites of the *y*-coordinates. Call the image *O′P′Q′R′*:

O (–6, 7)	keep *x*-coordinate same, opposite of *y*-coordinate	*O′* (–6, –7)
P (–1, 7)	keep *x*-coordinate same, opposite of *y*-coordinate	*P′* (–1, –7)
Q (–3, 2)	keep *x*-coordinate same, opposite of *y*-coordinate	*Q′* (–3, –2)
R (–8, 2)	keep *x*-coordinate same, opposite of *y*-coordinate	*R′* (–8, –2)

Now do the second transformation to the points of the image. Since Molly next reflects over the *y*-axis, now you'll keep the *y*-coordinates the same, and take the opposites of the *x*-coordinates.

O' (–6, –7)	opposite of *x*-coordinate, keep *y*-coordinate same	*O"* (6, –7)
P' (–1, –7)	opposite of *x*-coordinate, keep *y*-coordinate same	*P"* (1, –7)
Q' (–3, –2)	opposite of *x*-coordinate, keep *y*-coordinate same	*Q"* (3, –2)
R' (–8, –2)	opposite of *x*-coordinate, keep *y*-coordinate same	*R"* (8, –2)

The correct answer is (D).

Rotations

A **rotation** is a transformation in which a plane figure is turned around a fixed center point. In other words, one point on the plane, the **center of rotation,** is fixed, and the preimage rotates around that point by a given angle to form the image.

When rotations are described, you are given a center of rotation and an angle. If you're not told otherwise, assume the angle is counterclockwise.

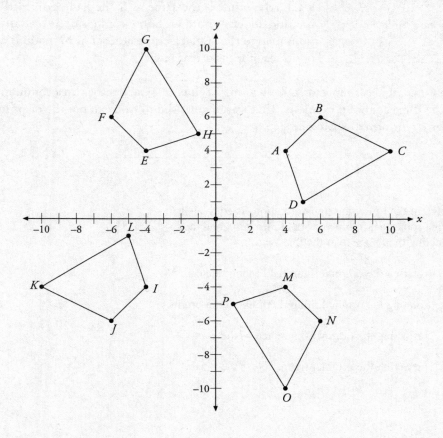

In the figure above, quadrilateral *ABCD* is rotated about the origin. Quadrilateral *EFGH* is its image after a rotation of 90° (counterclockwise). Quadrilateral *IJKL* is its image after a rotation of 180°. Quadrilateral *MNOP* is its image after a rotation of 270° counterclockwise, which is the same as a rotation of 90° clockwise.

What happens to the *x*- and *y*-coordinates of points when they are rotated around the origin? You can memorize these three cases, since they are the most common.

To make a 90° (counterclockwise) rotation about the origin (or, equivalently, a 270° clockwise rotation), a point (x, y) maps to the point $(-y, x)$.

To make a 180° (counterclockwise or clockwise) rotation about the origin, a point (x, y) maps to the point $(-x, -y)$.

To make a 270° (counterclockwise) rotation about the origin (or, equivalently, a 90° clockwise rotation), a point (x, y) maps to the point $(y, -x)$.

A 360° rotation maps an image directly onto its preimage: it does not change the figure at all. In other words, a point (x, y) maps to itself.

You might notice that in the question above, when Molly reflected her quadrilateral across first the *x*- and then the *y*-axis, the result is the same as if she had performed a 180° rotation about the origin. Some compositions of transformations map to the same places as other transformations or compositions of transformations.

Rotations Around the Origin

Rotation (about the origin)	Effect on *x*- and *y*-coordinates
90°	$(x, y) \rightarrow (-y, x)$
180°	$(x, y) \rightarrow (-x, -y)$
270°	$(x, y) \rightarrow (y, -x)$
360°	$(x, y) \rightarrow (x, y)$

Remember: Rotations are *counterclockwise* unless otherwise described.

It's probably a good idea to memorize how to map points (x, y) across the three common reflections and the three common rotations. That way, if you need to, you can put the maps together and compose transformations in one step.

Which of the following transformations is equivalent to first rotating a figure 90° about the origin and then reflecting the image over the line $y = x$?

A.   rotating the original figure 180° about the origin

B.   rotating the original figure 270° about the origin

C.   reflecting the original figure across the *x*-axis

D.   reflecting the original figure across the *y*-axis

Here's How to Crack It

The question doesn't give you a specific figure, or any specific points. Write down what you know about the two transformations:

To rotate a figure 90° about the origin, map (x, y) to $(-y, x)$.

To reflect a figure over the line $y = x$, map (x, y) to (y, x).

To put these together, you can try them on a test point: say you wanted to do these transformations to the point $(5, 7)$. First do the 90° rotation: $(-7, 5)$. Now do the reflection over $y = x$: $(5, -7)$.

What happened to the x- and y-coordinates of your test point? Since $(5, 7)$ became $(5, -7)$, you can say that (x, y) mapped to $(x, -y)$. Which of the choices has the same map?

Reflection across the x-axis maps (x, y) to $(x, -y)$. The correct answer is (C).

Forms of Symmetry

Remember symmetry, which describes how certain things *don't* change under rigid transformations? What does it mean when somebody says that a shape *has* symmetry?

A shape has symmetry, or is **symmetric,** if it can be divided into identical pieces, and there is some transformation that moves individual pieces of the object but doesn't actually change its overall shape. There are different ways an object can be symmetric:

- A figure has **translational symmetry** when it can be translated without changing its overall shape. An example is a line: a line can be translated along itself without changing the shape of the line.
- A figure has **reflectional symmetry** when there is some line through it (a **line of symmetry,** of course) that divides it into two pieces that are mirror images.
- A figure has **rotational symmetry** when it can be rotated about some fixed point without changing its overall shape.

Reflectional symmetry is also called line symmetry or mirror symmetry. Some shapes have no lines of symmetry, and some may have several. For example, triangles can have three, one, or no lines of symmetry:

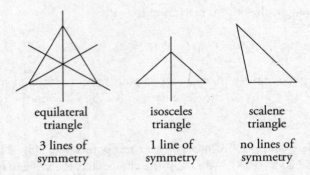

equilateral triangle	isosceles triangle	scalene triangle
3 lines of symmetry	1 line of symmetry	no lines of symmetry

Quadrilaterals can have four, two, one, or no lines of symmetry:

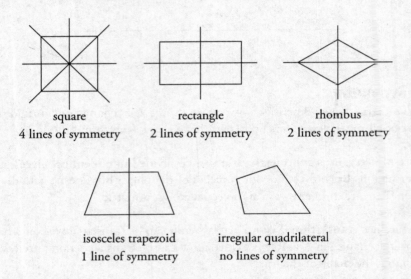

square	rectangle	rhombus
4 lines of symmetry	2 lines of symmetry	2 lines of symmetry

isosceles trapezoid
1 line of symmetry

irregular quadrilateral
no lines of symmetry

One pattern to notice with polygons is that regular polygons have the same number of lines of symmetry as they have sides and angles:

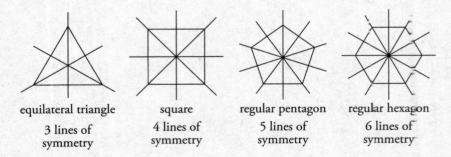

equilateral triangle	square	regular pentagon	regular hexagon
3 lines of symmetry	4 lines of symmetry	5 lines of symmetry	6 lines of symmetry

Since any line containing a diameter of a circle is a line of symmetry for the circle, a circle is said to have infinite lines of symmetry.

Rotational symmetry is also called **radial symmetry.** The **order** of a figure's rotational symmetry is the number of distinct orientations in which the figure looks the same.

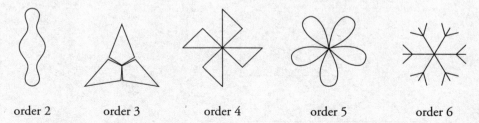

order 2   order 3   order 4   order 5   order 6

One more thing to notice is that shapes may have both rotational and reflectional symmetry, or just one of those. For example, the flower and snowflake above have reflectional symmetry as well as rotational symmetry, but the pinwheel does not.

Congruence and Similarity

Congruence

Remember that **congruent** figures have the same size and shape. That means that lengths are equal and angle measures are equal. Two angles with the same measure are congruent, since an angle's rays are infinite and so all of them are the same length.

Circles are congruent if they have the same radius. This makes sense, because given the radius of a circle, you already know that you can find its other important characteristics: diameter, circumference, and area.

Polygons are congruent if they have the same number of sides, congruent angles, and equal side lengths. Once you know that two figures are congruent, you can use that knowledge to transfer information from one figure to the other, or in both directions.

Use the diagram below to answer the question that follows.

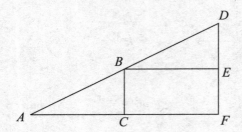

In the figure above, triangle *ABC* is congruent to triangle *BDE*. If *CF* = 10 cm and rectangle *BEFC* has area 50 cm², what is the area of triangle *ADF*?

A. 25 cm²

B. 50 cm²

C. 100 cm²

D. 200 cm²

Here's How to Crack It

The question tells you a lot of information about the figure. Redraw it and add all the information you know about congruence. Since triangles *ABC* and *BDE* are congruent, figure out which sides and angles are the same.

You know that *BCEF* is a rectangle, so angles *ACB* and *BED* are right angles. You can also match sides of triangles with sides of the rectangle. Since *BC* is a side of triangle *ABC* and of the rectangle, and *BE* is a side of triangle *BDE* and of the rectangle, these must be different sides in matching the triangles, since they are different sides of the rectangle.

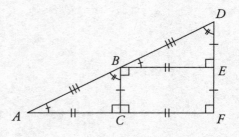

(Can you see the exception here? If the rectangle is really a square, then each triangle is an isosceles right triangle, and the four legs can have the same length. That doesn't end up working for the lengths given, but don't discount the possibility until you know for sure.)

You know that angles *ACB* and *BED* are right angles, since they are supplementary to right angles. So you can match up angle *CAB* with angle *EBD*, and angle *ABC* with angle *BDE*.

Since you know the length and the area of rectangle *BEFC*, you can find its width:

$$A = lw$$

$$50 = 10w$$

$$\frac{50}{10} = \frac{10w}{10}$$

$$5 = w$$

Add the lengths of sides to your diagram:

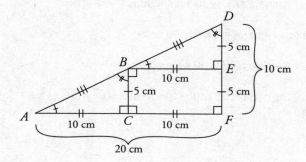

Since triangle *ADF* is a right triangle, you can use its legs as its base and height:

$$A = \frac{1}{2}bh$$

$$A = \frac{1}{2}(20)(10)$$

$$A = 100$$

The area of triangle *ADF* is 100 cm². The correct answer is (C).

───────────── ○ ─────────────

Make sure that you do not assume congruence when it may not be present!

Use the diagram below to answer the question that follows.

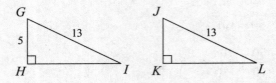

Which of the following statements about the figures must be true?

A.   The area of triangle *JKL* is 30 square units.

B.   The perimeter of triangle *JKL* is 30 units.

C.   The area of triangle *GHI* is 30 square units.

D.   The sum of the perimeters of the two triangles is 60 units.

Here's How to Crack It

Here, you know some information about each triangle. They are both right triangles, and you can see that triangle *GHI* is a 5-12-13 triangle: since two of its sides fit that relationship, you know that *HI* = 12.

The two triangles *look* congruent. However, you don't know the lengths of either of triangle *JKL*'s other two sides, nor do you know either of its other two angles. Ask yourself: could this triangle look completely different from triangle *GHI* while keeping the information I know true?

Here's an example:

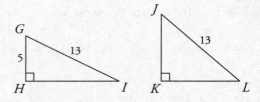

Now that you can tell the two triangles *don't* have to be congruent, what can you prove about them? You don't know much about triangle *JKL*—it's a right triangle and you know its hypotenuse length. Stick to triangle *GHI*. Since you know it's a 5-12-13 triangle, you could add those to find its perimeter. But both choices that mention perimeter require knowing the perimeter of triangle *JKL*. What about area? Since *GHI* is a right triangle, you can use its legs as its base and height, so its area is

$$A = \frac{1}{2}bh$$

$$A = \frac{1}{2}(5)(12)$$

$$A = 30$$

You can prove that the area of triangle *GHI* = 30 square units, so (C) is correct.

Similarity

Similar figures have angle measures that are equal and side lengths that are proportional. With equal angles, the *shape* of a figure is the same, so it's just the *size* that differs. That means you can use proportions to figure out missing lengths.

Some classes of figures are automatically similar. For example, all circles are similar, since they all sweep the same angle measure (360°), and it's only their defining length (radius) that differs between them.

All regular polygons of a given number of sides are similar too. This has to do with a rule about their interior angle measure: the sum of the measures of the interior angles of a polygon is $(n - 2)180°$, where *n* is the number of sides in the polygon. In other words, a triangle's interior angle measures sum to 180°: for each additional side the polygon has, add another 180°.

You can use this rule to find the measure of each angle inside a regular polygon, since regular polygons have angles that are all congruent. The angle measure of any angle in an *n*-sided regular polygon is $\dfrac{(n - 2)180°}{n}$: the total interior angle measure divided by the number of angles, which is the same as the number of sides.

So since all regular pentagons, for example, have five interior angles that each measure $\dfrac{(5 - 2)180°}{5} = \dfrac{(3)180°}{5} = \dfrac{540°}{5} = 108°$, they are all similar to each other, while all regular hexagons are similar to each other, etc.

When polygons are not regular, you need to know the angles to determ ne whether they are similar: then match them up according to their angles. The symbol for s milarity is ~. When you say that figure *ABC* ~ figure *DEF*, that means you have matched up the angles: $m\angle A = m\angle D$, $m\angle B = m\angle E$, and $m\angle C = m\angle F$. It tells you that the proportional s des match up in the same way: $\dfrac{AB}{DE} = \dfrac{BC}{EF} = \dfrac{AC}{DF}$.

Use the diagram below to answer the question that follows.

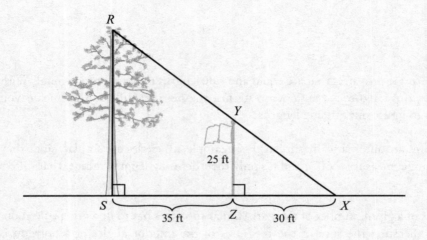

Solvei wants to find the height of the tree in front of her school. She knows the flagpole is 25 feet high, and she measures the distances to it and the tree along the same line from a common point, *X*. If $XZ = 30$ feet and $ZS = 35$ feet, what is the height of the tree, to the nearest foot?

A.   29 ft

B.   39 ft

C.   54 ft

D.   85 ft

Here's How to Crack It

First, determine whether triangles *RSX* and *YZS* are similar. You know that whatever the angle is at point *X*, it's shared by both triangles. Angles *XZY* and *XSR* are both right angles. And knowing that two angles are congruent, you know that the third is, since the measures of both angles *SRX* and *ZYX* are complementary to angle *X* because of the rule of 180°. The triangles are similar: $\triangle RSX \sim \triangle YZX$.

Next, use proportions to find the height of the tree, *RS*. The bases of the two triangles are in proportion, and their heights must be too. Find the base of triangle *RSX*. It's just the sum of the two lengths given: 30 ft + 35 ft = 65 ft. Now use the proportion to make an equation for *h*, the height of the tree:

$$\frac{ZX}{SX} = \frac{YZ}{RS}$$

$$\frac{30}{65} = \frac{25}{h}$$

Cross multiply and solve:

$$30h = 65 \times 25$$

$$30h = 1{,}625$$

$$\frac{30h}{30} = \frac{1{,}625}{30}$$

$$h = 54.1\overline{6}$$

Since the question asks for the height of the tree *to the nearest foot,* round your answer: $h \approx 54$ ft. The correct answer is (C).

———————————————○———————————————

Note that though the sides are proportional, the areas are not in the same proportion. What are the areas of the triangles formed above?

The area of triangle *XYZ* is:

$$A = \frac{1}{2}bh = \frac{1}{2}\left(30 \text{ ft}\right)\left(25 \text{ ft}\right) = 375 \text{ ft}^2$$

The area of triangle *XRS* is:

$$A = \frac{1}{2}bh = \frac{1}{2}(65 \text{ ft})(54.1\overline{6} \text{ ft}) = 1,760.41\overline{6} \text{ ft}^2$$

The areas don't fit the same proportion because they are two-dimensional, rather than one-dimensional, measures. They are in proportion with the *squares* of the side lengths.

SOLID GEOMETRY

So far, you've reviewed a ton of geometry in two dimensions. The CSET also tests some three-dimensional geometry, so don't neglect it. You need to know the basic three-dimensional shapes, and how to find their volumes and surface areas.

Volume is a measure of the amount of space inside a three-dimensional figure. It's measured in cubic units. **Surface area** is the total (two-dimensional) area of all the surfaces, or **faces,** of a three-dimensional figure. It's measured in square units, just like any other area.

The common three-dimensional shapes you need to know about are prisms, pyramids, cylinders, cones, and spheres.

Prisms

A **prism** is a three-dimensional figure with two parallel congruent bases that are both polygons. The lateral, or side, faces of a prism must all be parallelograms or rectangles. Prisms are named for the shapes of their bases.

Rectangular Prisms

A **rectangular prism** is a three-dimensional shape with 6 faces that are all rectangles: the two bases are rectangles and all the lateral faces are rectangles too. You can just think of the faces of a rectangular prism as three pairs of congruent faces: the front and the back, the left side and the right side, and the top and the bottom. Any pair could be thought of as the bases in this kind of prism.

A rectangular prism thus has three measurements: its length, its width, and its height. You can use these to find its volume *(V)* and its surface area *(SA).*

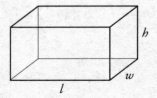

You can see why these statements are true: to find the volume of the shape, since its faces are all perpendicular, you just multiply the three dimensions together; to find its surface area, you just add up the areas of its faces. Since a rectangular prism's six faces come in pairs, two of them have area *lw*, two of them have area *lh*, and two of them have area *wh*.

A special case of the rectangular prism is the cube. A **cube** is a rectangular prism in which all side lengths are equal—all its faces are squares.

Since all the side lengths are equal, you need to know only one length to calculate volume and surface area for cubes.

You don't *have* to memorize these; they are the same as the formulas for rectangular prisms, but using the same length for all sides, *s*. However, knowing them might save you a little time if you are dealing with a cube.

Triangular Prisms

A **triangular prism** is a prism with triangles as its bases.

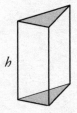

The general formula for the volume of a prism is Volume = Area of Base × Height of Prism. The height of the prism is the perpendicular distance between the two parallel bases. Though this formula works for oblique prisms (those whose bases are not perpendicular to their other faces), you'll likely only ever be asked about right prisms on the CSET.

Similarly, the surface area of any prism can be found by adding the areas of the two bases to the areas of all the rectangular (or parallelogram-shaped) lateral faces. The number of lateral faces is the same as the number of sides on each base.

Triangular Prisms

$$V = \text{Area of triangular base} \times h$$

where the area of the triangular base can be found from *its* base and height $\left(A = \dfrac{1}{2}bh \right)$.

$SA = 2(\text{Area of triangular base}) + \text{Area of lateral face}_1 + \text{Area of lateral face}_2 + \text{Area of lateral face}_3$

where the area of the triangular base can be found from *its* base and height $\left(A = \dfrac{1}{2}bh \right)$,

and the area of each lateral face can be found from *its* length and width ($A = lw$).

Notice that if the triangular base in a right triangular prism is an isosceles or equilateral triangle, then some or all of the lateral faces will be congruent.

Use the diagram below to answer the question that follows.

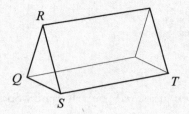

In the right triangular prism above, $QR = RS = 5$, $QS = 6$, and $ST = 10$. What is the surface area of the solid?

A.   120 square units

B.   134 square units

C.   172 square units

D.   184 square units

Here's How to Crack It

Remember, the surface area of a three-dimensional shape is the sum of the areas of its faces, and a right triangular prism has 2 triangular bases and 3 rectangular lateral faces.

First, find the area of a triangular base. The formula for the area of a triangle is $A = \frac{1}{2}bh$. Redraw just the base, label it with the information you know, and draw in a height:

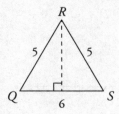

This triangle's base has length 6. What is the height?

Since the triangle is isosceles, the height splits the base into two equal parts. Draw one of the two resulting right triangles:

Did you notice it? Yep, this is a 3-4-5 triangle! You just saved yourself some work.

Since the height is 4, find the area of triangular base *QRS:*

$$A = \frac{1}{2}bh = \frac{1}{2}(6)(4) = 12$$

The opposite base has the same area, 12.

Now find the areas of the three lateral faces, which are all rectangles. All of them have length 10. Two have width 5, and one has width 6.

$A = lw = (10)(5) = 50$

$A = lw = (10)(5) = 50$

$A = lw = (10)(6) = 60$

Add the areas of the five faces together:

SA = 2(Area of triangular base) + Area of lateral face$_1$ + Area of lateral face$_2$ + Area of lateral face$_3$

$$SA = 2(12) + 50 + 50 + 60 = 184$$

The correct answer is (D).

Other Prisms

A prism can have any polygon for a base, so you could see a pentagonal prism, a hexagonal prism, a heptagonal prism, and so on. Triangular and rectangular ones are far more likely to be on the test, however. If you do see a weird prism, remember the general formulas: the volume of a prism is its height times the area of its base. The surface area of a prism is the sum of the areas of all its faces: 2 polygonal bases and *n* rectangular (or parallelogram-shaped) lateral faces, where *n* is the number of sides in the base.

Pyramids

A **pyramid** is a three-dimensional figure that has a base, which can be any polygon, and three or more triangular faces that meet at a point called the **apex.** Pyramids are also named for the shapes of their bases.

In a right pyramid, the apex lies directly above the center of the base. You won't see oblique pyramids (ones that aren't right) on the test.

Pyramids

$$V = \frac{1}{3}\left(\text{Area of base}\right)h$$

where h, the height of the pyramid, is the vertical distance from the apex of the pyramid to its base.

$$SA = \text{Area of base} + \text{sum of the areas of all (triangular) lateral faces}$$

For example, let's find the volume and surface area of a square pyramid.

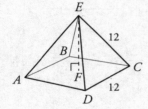

First, find the volume:

Since $V = \frac{1}{3}\left(\text{Area of base}\right)h$, you need to find h, the height of the pyramid, and the area of its base. Since the base is a square, its area is $A = s^2$. You know the length of a side is 12, so $A = 12^2 = 144$. What about the height?

To find the height of the pyramid, draw triangle *EFC*.

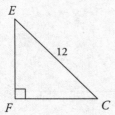

You know the length of its hypotenuse is 12. If you can find another side length, you'll be able to find the third.

The key is to look back at the square base. Leg *FC* in this triangle is half the diagonal of the square base *ABCD*.

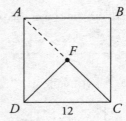

Since the diagonal of a square is the hypotenuse of an isosceles right triangle, you can find that $AC = 12\sqrt{2}$ (using the ratio of sides in a 45-45-90 triangle), and so $FC = \dfrac{12\sqrt{2}}{2} = 6\sqrt{2}$.

Go back and apply this to triangle *EFC*:

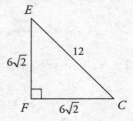

Since $FC = 6\sqrt{2}$, you know that $EF = 6\sqrt{2}$ as well (this is another 45-45-90 triangle). That's the height of the pyramid!

Substitute the values for area of base and height into the formula for the volume of a pyramid:

$$V = \frac{1}{3}\left(\text{Area of base}\right)h = \frac{1}{3}(144)\left(6\sqrt{2}\right) = 288\sqrt{2}$$

Good job! Next let's find the surface area:

For a pyramid, *SA* = Area of base + sum of the areas of all (triangular) lateral faces. You already found the area of the base, so concentrate on the areas of the triangular lateral faces. Let's draw one:

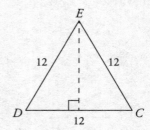

It's an equilateral triangle! You need to find its area, and you know that for a triangle, $A = \frac{1}{2}bh$.

How do you find the height of an equilateral triangle? That's right: use your knowledge of 30-60-90 triangles! Split the lateral face in half, and look at the resulting 30-60-90 triangle:

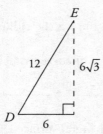

The fixed ratio of sides of a 30-60-90 triangle tells you that if the hypotenuse has length 12, then the short leg has length 6 (which is half of the length of DC), and the long leg—the height—has length $6\sqrt{3}$.

So the area of a lateral face is $A = \frac{1}{2}bh = \frac{1}{2}(12)(6\sqrt{3}) = 36\sqrt{3}$. Now put together the areas of the different faces:

$$SA = \text{Area of base} + \text{sum of the areas of all (triangular) lateral faces}$$

$$SA = 144 + 4(36\sqrt{3}) = 144 + 144\sqrt{3}$$

Whew!

You can see that finding the volumes and surface areas of even pretty simple pyramids requires pretty complicated calculations. Don't look to see too many problems asking about this on your test—although this kind of thing might make for a good Constructed Response Assignment!

Cylinders

A circular **cylinder** is a three-dimensional shape with two circular bases and a third face that curves around to enclose the shape. It looks like a tin can. You can think of it as similar to a prism, but with circles for its bases. (There is such a thing as a non-circular, or elliptic, cylinder, but again: you won't see the CSET test that, or oblique cylinders either.)

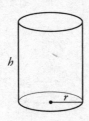

Fortunately volumes and surface areas of (right circular) cylinders are a lot easier to calculate:

Right Circular Cylinders

$$V = (\text{Area of base})h = \pi r^2 h$$

where h is the height of the cylinder and r is the radius of the base.

$$SA = 2(\text{Area of base}) + \text{area of curved lateral surface} = 2\pi r^2 + 2\pi rh$$

Can you see why the area of the curved lateral surface is $2\pi rh$? Try opening up all the surfaces and laying them out flat. This is called a **net:** an arrangement of the faces of a three-dimensional figure, joined at the edges, all flattened into a plane.

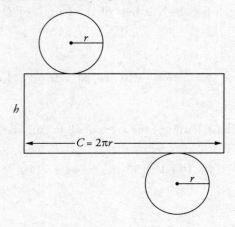

You can see that the length of the rectangle that makes up the curved lateral surface of the cylinder is actually the *circumference* of the circular bases: so the area of the lateral surface is $A = lw = 2\pi rh$.

Cones

A circular **cone** is a three-dimensional shape with a circular base and a curved face that tapers smoothly to a point called the apex, or vertex. It looks like an ice cream cone, of course!

You can think of it as similar to a pyramid, but with a circle for its base. (There is such a thing as a non-circular, or elliptic, cone, but you guessed it: you won't see the CSET test that or oblique cones.)

Right Circular Cones

$$V = \frac{1}{3}\left(\text{Area of base}\right)h = \frac{1}{3}\pi r^2 h$$

where h is the height of the cylinder and r is the radius of the base.

$$SA = (\text{Area of base}) + \text{area of curved lateral surface} = \pi r^2 + \pi r l$$

where r is the radius of the base and l is the lateral height of the cone.

Lateral height, or slant height, is the distance from any point on the circle to the apex of the cone. You can find it, if you need to, by making a right triangle with the radius and height as legs and the lateral height as hypotenuse.

Spheres

A **sphere** is a three-dimensional shape that's defined as the set of points equidistant from a given point, its center, in three-dimensional space. In other words, it's like a circle, but in three dimensions. It looks like a ball. As with a circle, one value will tell you everything you need to know about a sphere: the radius.

Spheres

$$V = \frac{4}{3}\pi r^3$$

$$SA = 4\pi r^2$$

These formulas are a little too complicated to derive here, but you should memorize them.

A sphere with center A has a radius of 9 cm. Which of the following statements about the figure must be true?

A. The surface area of the figure is 81π cm².

B. The surface area of the figure is 108π cm².

C. The volume of the figure is 324π cm³.

D. The volume of the figure is 972π cm³.

Here's How to Crack It

You know the formulas for the volume and surface area of a sphere. The first two choices give values for the surface area, so find that:

$$SA = 4\pi r^2 = 4\pi(9)^2 = 4\pi(81) = 324\pi$$

The surface area of the sphere is 324π cm². This is not one of the choices. (Don't fall for (C)—it's giving this value as the sphere's *volume*!)

The next two choices give values for the volume, so find that:

$$V = \frac{4}{3}\pi r^3 = \frac{4}{3}\pi(9)^3 = \frac{4}{3}\pi(729) = 972\pi$$

The volume of the sphere is 972π cm³. The correct answer is (D).

MEASUREMENT

It's not just angles, lengths and distances, and areas and volumes (which you've seen plenty of already in this chapter) that can be measured: all sorts of other measurements are part of the daily life and use of mathematics. Some important ones are measurements of time, rate, temperature, and weight/mass.

You need to know what units are used for each type of measurement, how to convert between those units, and what steps to take to solve problems involving measurement. First, let's look at the units.

Units of Measurement

Customary or English System		Metric or International System	
Length			
		millimeter (mm)	= 0.001 meter
inch (in.)		centimeter (cm)	= 0.01 meter
foot (ft)	= 12 inches	decimeter (dm)	= 0.1 meter
yard (yd)	= 3 feet, or 36 inches	meter (m)	
mile (mi)	= 5,280 feet, or 1,760 yards	decameter (dam)	= 10 meters
		hectometer (hm)	= 100 meters
		kilometer (km)	= 1,000 meters

Here are some approximations for converting between systems:

- A meter is a little longer than a yard.
- An inch is 2.54 centimeters.
- A mile is a little more than 1.6 kilometers.

Customary or English System		Metric or International System	
Weight/Mass			
		milligram (mg)	= 0.001 gram
		centigram (cg)	= 0.01 gram
ounce (oz)		decigram (dg)	= 0.1 gram
pound (lb)	= 16 ounces	gram (g)	
ton (T)	= 2,000 pounds	decagram (dag)	= 10 grams
		hectogram (hg)	= 100 grams
		kilogram (kg)	= 1,000 grams

Here are some approximations for converting:

- An ounce is about 28 grams.
- A kilogram is about 2.2 pounds.
- A *metric ton* is 1,000 kilograms.

Customary or English System		Metric or International System	
Capacity/Volume			
		milliliter (mL)	= 0.001 liter
cup (c)		centiliter (cL)	= 0.01 liter
pint (pt)	= 2 cups	deciliter (dL)	= 0.1 liter
quart (qt)	= 2 pints = 4 cups	liter (L)	
gallon (gal)	= 4 quarts	decaliter (daL)	= 10 liters
		hectoliter (hL)	= 100 liters
		kiloliter (kL)	= 1,000 liters

Here are some approximations for converting between systems:

- A liter is a little more than a quart.
- A gallon is about 3.8 liters.

Time	
second (sec)	
minute (min)	= 60 seconds
hour (hr)	= 60 minutes
day (d)	= 24 hours
week (w)	= 7 days
year (yr)	= 52 weeks = 365 days
decade	= 10 years
century	= 100 years

Temperature	
The standard unit to measure temperature is the degree (°). This is used in both systems, so an extra letter is used to indicate which system is being used.	
Fahrenheit	**Celsius**
degrees Fahrenheit (°F)	degrees Celsius (°C)

To convert from Celsius to Fahrenheit, multiply by 1.8 and then add 32 to the product.

$$°F = 1.8(°C) + 32$$

To convert from Fahrenheit to Celsius, subtract 32 and then divide the difference by 1.8.

$$°C = \frac{°F - 32}{1.8}$$

Here are a few examples of how you might see measurement tested on the CSET:

──────────────────○──────────────────

Jae has a thermometer outside her window. If her thermometer showed 77°F on Tuesday, and 59°F on Thursday, how much did the temperature drop in degrees Celsius?

A.   10°C

B.   18°C

C.   34°C

D.   62°C

Here's How to Crack It

You know the formula for converting temperatures in degrees Fahrenheit to degrees Celsius:

$$°C = \frac{°F - 32}{1.8}$$

Convert both temperatures from Fahrenheit to Celsius:

$$\frac{77°F - 32}{1.8} = 25°C$$

$$\frac{59°F - 32}{1.8} = 15°C$$

The question asks for the amount the temperature *dropped,* so find the difference:

$$25°C - 15°C = 10°C$$

The difference is 10°C, so the correct answer is (A).

──────────────────○──────────────────

Roman is training to compete in a physical fitness tournament, and he records the amount of time he spends at each task. Yesterday he spent 30 minutes stretching, 2 hours weight training, and 3 hours and 20 minutes running. Today he spends twice as long at each task. What is the total time he spends in the two days on all his training?

A.   5 hrs 50 min

B.   11 hrs 40 min

C.   16 hrs 30 min

D.   17 hrs 30 min

Here's How to Crack It

Find the amount of time Roman spent training yesterday:

$$30 \text{ min} + 2 \text{ hrs} + 3 \text{ hrs } 20 \text{ min} = 5 \text{ hrs } 50 \text{ min}$$

Then multiply the time he spent yesterday by 2 to find the amount of time he spent today:

$$5 \text{ hrs } 50 \text{ min} \times 2 = 10 \text{ hrs } 100 \text{ min}$$

You need to convert the minutes, since the number of minutes is greater than 60.

$$100 \text{ min} = 60 \text{ min} + 40 \text{ min} = 1 \text{ hr } 40 \text{ min}$$

So 10 hrs 100 min = 11 hrs 40 min. Now, add the totals for yesterday and today to find the total time:

$$5 \text{ hrs } 50 \text{ min} + 11 \text{ hrs } 40 \text{ min} = 16 \text{ hrs } 90 \text{ min}$$

Again, since you have a number of minutes greater than 60, convert:

$$90 \text{ min} = 60 \text{ min} + 30 \text{ min} = 1 \text{ hr } 30 \text{ min}$$

So 16 hrs 90 min = 17 hrs 30 min, and the correct answer is (D).

Brook needs to move a large pile of cinder blocks with his truck. He can haul only 1 ton (customary) per load. If each cinder block weighs 30 lbs, how many cinder blocks can Brook fit in a single load?

A.   33 cinder blocks

B.   66 cinder blocks

C.   67 cinder blocks

D.   2,000 cinder blocks

Here's How to Crack It
This question involves converting units in the customary system. The conversion you need is 1 ton = 2,000 pounds.

Since Brook can haul 1 ton per load, that's 2,000 pounds per load. Divide the total he can haul per load by the weight of each cinder block:

$$\frac{2{,}000 \text{ lbs}}{30 \text{ lbs}} = 66.\overline{6}$$

Brook could haul $66\frac{2}{3}$ cinder blocks in a load, but you have to take the real-world considerations of the problem into account: he can't break a cinder block into pieces, so he can fit only 66 blocks. When real-world problems involve whole-number amounts, that affects how you round.

The correct answer is (B).

Rate and Scale
Another type of question in which units and conversion come up is rate and scale problems. The test may ask you to use rates to find values of distance, work, or time, or to use scale drawings and models to find values of length, distance, area, or volume.

SCALE

To solve problems involving scale drawings, scale models, or maps, use proportions. The scale tells you one side of the proportion: fill in the other side with the information you know and a variable representing the value you need to solve for.

On a map, the scale is 1 inch = $\frac{1}{2}$ mile. If the parade route drawn on the map makes a rectangle with length 2 inches and width 1 inch, and the parade will start at one corner of the rectangle and follow the route until returning to the starting place, what is the total parade route distance?

A.   0.5 miles

B.   1.5 miles

C.   3 miles

D.   6 miles

Here's How to Crack It

First, recognize that the question is asking for the *perimeter* of the rectangle: the total distance from one corner, around the sides, and back to the same point. The perimeter of a rectangle is $P = 2l + 2w$. The rectangle is 1 inch by 2 inches on the map. You can convert first, and then find the perimeter, or find the perimeter first and then convert:

$$P = 2l + 2w = 2(2 \text{ in.}) + 2(1 \text{ in.}) = 4 \text{ in.} + 2 \text{ in.} = 6 \text{ in.}$$

The perimeter on the map is 6 inches.

To convert, make a proportion:

$$\frac{1 \text{ inch}}{\frac{1}{2} \text{ mile}} = \frac{6 \text{ inches}}{x \text{ miles}}$$

Cross multiply to solve:

$$1x = 6 \times \frac{1}{2}$$

$$x = 3$$

The perimeter is 3 miles. The correct answer is (C).

RATE

To solve rate problems, use a tool to keep track of all the parts. The rate pie looks like this:

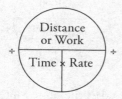

Here's how the rate pie works: if you divide the *distance* or *amount of work* by the *time,* you get the *rate.* If you divide the *distance* or *amount of work* by the *rate,* you get the *time.* If you multiply the *rate* by the *time,* you get the *distance* or *amount of work.* There's just one important rule to remember when using rate pies: always write in and check your units. That way, you'll notice if you need to convert first!

Try it on the next problem.

It takes Zahra 3 hours to drive to her brother's house at an average speed of 50 miles per hour. If she takes the same route home, but her average speed is 60 miles per hour, how much time does it take her to drive home?

A.   2 hours

B.   2 hours 30 minutes

C.   3 hours

D.   3 hours 30 minutes

Here's How to Crack It

First, notice that the question is asking about rate. Since *speed* means *rate,* you can tell this is a rate problem. Go ahead and draw a rate pie and fill in the information you know, including units:

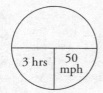

Since the units (hours and miles per hour) are compatible, you can multiply to find the distance:

So Zahra travels 150 miles. Since she takes the same route home, you can assume the distance will be the same. You also know her rate on the return trip. Draw another rate pie and fill in the information you know:

The units are compatible, so divide to find the time:

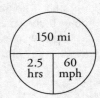

Zahra drives for 2.5 hours on the return trip. Convert the 0.5 hours to 30 minutes to match the answer choices: her time is 2 hours 30 minutes, so the correct answer is (B).

———————————○———————————

KEY TERMS

point
line
plane
plane geometry
line segment
endpoint
ray
angle
vertex
degree
congruent
straight angle
vertical angles
right angle
perpendicular lines
right angle symbol
obtuse
acute
complementary angles
supplementary angles
parallel lines
equidistant
transversal
alternate interior angles
polygon
closed shape
regular polygon
quadrilateral
interior angle
parallelogram
area
base
height
perimeter

rhombus
rectangle
square
trapezoid
isosceles trapezoid
triangle
rule of 180°
exterior angle
isosceles triangle
equilateral triangle
scalene triangle
right triangle
hypotenuse
leg
Pythagorean Theorem
common right triangles
special right triangles
circle
circumference
center
radius
chord
diameter
arc
central angle
minor arc
major arc
sector
inscribed figure
corresponding angle
distance formula
midpoint
symmetry
transformation

preimage
image
rigid transformation
translation
reflection
line of reflection
composition of
  transformations
rotation
center of rotation
symmetric
translational symmetry
reflectional symmetry
line of symmetry
rotational symmetry
  (radial symmetry)
order
similar
volume
surface area
face
prism
rectangular prism
cube
triangular prism
pyramid
apex
cylinder
net
cone
lateral height
sphere

Chapter 16 Drill

Answers and explanations can be found in the final section of this book, beginning on page 617.

1. **Use the diagram below to answer the question that follows.**

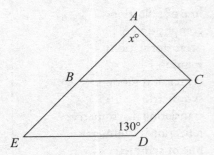

   If *BCDE* is a parallelogram and *AB = AC*, which of the following is the value of *x* ?

   A. 50

   B. 60

   C. 80

   D. 130

2. **Use the diagram below to answer the question that follows.**

   Clementine has made a regular hexagon by tiling 6 equilateral triangles as part of an art project. If the hexagon has perimeter 24 in., what is the area of one of the triangles?

   A. 4 in.²

   B. $4\sqrt{3}$ in.²

   C. 12 in.²

   D. $24\sqrt{3}$ in.²

3. **Use the diagram below to answer the question that follows.**

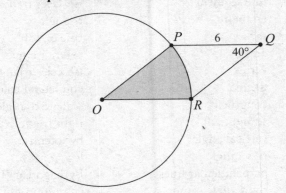

   In the figure, parallelogram *OPQR* overlaps the circle with center *O*. If *P* and *R* are points on the circle, what is the area of the shaded sector of the circle?

   A. $\dfrac{4}{3}\pi$

   B. 3π

   C. 4π

   D. 9π

4. Alex plots a line segment in the coordinate plane: its endpoints are *J* (−3, 5) and *K* (4, −2). Which of the following describes its length and midpoint?

   A. Its length is $7\sqrt{2}$ and its midpoint is $\left(\dfrac{1}{2}, 1\dfrac{1}{2}\right)$.

   B. Its length is $7\sqrt{2}$ and its midpoint is $\left(3\dfrac{1}{2}, -3\dfrac{1}{2}\right)$.

   C. Its length is 14 and its midpoint is $\left(\dfrac{1}{2}, 1\dfrac{1}{2}\right)$.

   D. Its length is 14 and its midpoint is $\left(3\dfrac{1}{2}, -3\dfrac{1}{2}\right)$.

5. Square *FGHI* has vertices (0, 0), (4, 0), (4, 4), and (0, 4) in the coordinate plane. Dani translates the square 3 units to the right and 2 units up. Then he rotates the image 270° about the origin. What are the coordinates of the resulting figure?

   A.   (3, 2), (7, 2), (7, 6), and (3, 6)

   B.   (–2, 3), (–2, 7), (–6, 7), and (–6, 3)

   C.   (–3, –2), (–7, –2), (–7, –6), and (–3, –6)

   D.   (2, –3), (2, –7), (6, –7), and (6, –3)

6. **Use the diagram below to answer the question that follows.**

   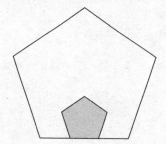

   Amir is building a birdhouse for his yard: the front face of it is shown. It's in the shape of a regular pentagon. He makes a door that's also a regular pentagon. If the sides of the door are $\frac{1}{3}$ the length of the sides of the birdhouse, what is the ratio of the area of the door to the area of the rest of the front of the birdhouse (not including the door's area)?

   A.   1 to 2

   B.   1 to 3

   C.   1 to 8

   D.   1 to 9

7. **Use the diagram below to answer the question that follows.**

   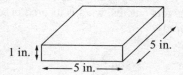

   Marcus is building a miniature of a stepped pyramid. He uses rectangular prisms made of wood, starting with the block shown above and stacking smaller blocks on top of it. All the blocks have heights of 1 in., and the top and bottom faces are squares. However, each block's square faces have side lengths 1 in. less than those of the block below. If Marcus uses 5 layers, what is his structure's total volume?

   A.   25 in.³

   B.   35 in.³

   C.   55 in.³

   D.   125 in.³

8. Anya made a prop for her son's play: a very simple "tree" in the shape of a cone. The diameter of the base is 1 yard, and the height of the cone is 1.2 yards. She makes the "tree" out of cardboard and covers the whole cone (including the circular bottom) with green felt. What is the surface area of the cone in square yards?

   A.   0.1π yd²

   B.   0.25π yd²

   C.   0.65π yd²

   D.   0.9π yd²

9. An acre is a unit of measurement for area. It's defined as the area of 1 chain (22 yards) by 1 furlong (220 yards). If a new property covers 6 acres, what is its area in square yards?

   A. $806\dfrac{2}{3}$ yd²

   B.   4,840 yd²

   C.   29,040 yd²

   D.   261,360 yd²

10. On Bessie's map, the scale is 1 centimeter = 25 kilometers. Her map shows the distance from Santiago to San Juan as 7 centimeters. About how long will it take Bessie to drive at an average speed of 90 kilometers per hour from Santiago to San Juan?

    A.   1 hr 45 min

    B.   1 hr 57 min

    C.   2 hr 34 min

    D.   5 hr 21 min

Summary

- Plane geometry is the study of figures in two dimensions, including points, lines, and figures made up of them.

- A line segment is a piece of a line with two endpoints, and a ray is a piece of a line with one endpoint. An angle is formed when two rays join at a vertex. Angles are measured in degrees.

- A straight angle measures 180°. A right angle measures 90°.

- When two lines cross, the vertical angles that form are congruent.

- Parallel lines are equidistant, and they never cross each other. Perpendicular lines form right angles. When parallel lines are crossed by a transversal, pairs of congruent angles are formed.

- Polygons are closed plane shapes with straight sides; they are regular when all their sides have the same length and all their angles have the same measure.

- The two most important measures of a polygon are its area (the amount of space it contains) and its perimeter (the distance around its boundary).

- Quadrilaterals are four-sided polygons. The sum of the interior angles of any quadrilateral is 360°. Some types of quadrilaterals with special properties are: parallelograms, rhombuses, rectangles, squares, and trapezoids.

- Parallelograms have 2 pairs of parallel and congruent sides and 2 pairs of congruent angles; their areas are $A = bh$ (base times height) and their perimeters are $P = 2a + 2b$, where a and b are the lengths of the sides.

- Rhombuses have 2 pairs of parallel sides and all 4 sides congruent, with 2 pairs of congruent angles; their areas are $A = bh$ (base times height) and their perimeters are $P = 4s$, where s is the length of a side.

- Rectangles have 2 pairs of parallel and congruent sides and 4 right angles; their areas are $A = lw$ and their perimeters are $P = 2l + 2w$, where l is length and w is width.

- Squares have 4 congruent sides and 4 right angles; their areas are $A = s^2$, and their perimeters are $A = 4s$, where s is the length of a side.

o Trapezoids have exactly 1 pair of parallel sides. Their areas are $A = \dfrac{a+b}{2}h$, where a and b are the lengths of the parallel bases and h is the height. To find the perimeter of a trapezoid, add all its side lengths.

o Triangles are three-sided polygons. The sum of the interior angles of any triangle is 180°. Some types of triangles with special properties are scalene, isosceles, equilateral, and right triangles.

o A scalene triangle has 3 sides of different lengths; its angles have different measures.

o An isosceles triangle has at least 2 congruent sides, and 2 congruent angles opposite them.

o An equilateral triangle has 3 congruent sides and 3 congruent angles, which all measure 60°.

o A right triangle is a triangle that has one right angle. (Triangles can't have more than one right or obtuse angle.)

o The relationship between the lengths of the legs and hypotenuse of a right triangle is represented by the Pythagorean Theorem: $a^2 + b^2 = c^2$, where a and b are the legs and c is the hypotenuse. In addition, if the three sides of a triangle fit into this relationship, the triangle must be a right triangle.

o Some common right triangles have side lengths in the ratios 3-4-5, 6-8-10, and 5-12-13.

o The special right triangles have fixed ratios of sides: in the 45-45-90 triangle (isosceles right triangle) if the two legs have length a, then the hypotenuse has length $a\sqrt{2}$; and in the 30-60-90 triangle (which is half of an equilateral triangle) if the short leg has length a, then the long leg has length $a\sqrt{3}$ and the hypotenuse has length $2a$.

o A circle is a round plane figure whose boundary (circumference) consists of points equidistant from a fixed point (its center). The important measures of a circle are radius, diameter, circumference, and area. Remember: $d = 2r$, $C = 2\pi r$, and $A = \pi r^2$.

o An arc is a piece of the circumference of a circle, while a sector is a piece of the area. To find the length of an arc or the area of a sector, use proportions: $\dfrac{\text{length of arc}}{\text{circumference}} = \dfrac{\text{area of sector}}{\text{area}} = \dfrac{\text{measure of central angle}}{360°}$.

o An inscribed figure is one that's drawn within another figure so that their boundaries touch but do not intersect.

○ An angle inscribed in a circle with endpoints a and b measures half of the measure of its corresponding angle (the angle with the same two endpoints, and the center as its vertex).

○ To find the distance between two points (x_1, y_1) and (x_2, y_2) in the coordinate plane, draw a right triangle and use the Pythagorean Theorem. (Or use common or special right triangle ratios!) Or, you can use the distance formula: $d = \sqrt{(x_2 - x_1)^2 + (y_2 - y_1)^2}$.

○ The midpoint of a line segment with endpoints (x_1, y_1) and (x_2, y_2) has coordinates $x = \dfrac{x_1 + x_2}{2}$ and $y = \dfrac{y_1 + y_2}{2}$.

○ A rigid transformation is a function that maps points of a figure onto another figure while preserving the figure's shape and size. There are three kinds: translations, reflections, and rotations.

○ To perform a translation, add (or subtract) the number of units to the x-coordinate that the preimage moves right (or left), and add (or subtract) the number of units to the y-coordinate that the preimage moves up (or down).

○ To perform a reflection, flip the preimage over the line of reflection. Some common reflections are:

Line of Reflection	Effect on x- and y-coordinates
x-axis	$(x, y) \rightarrow (x, -y)$
y-axis	$(x, y) \rightarrow (-x, y)$
$y = x$	$(x, y) \rightarrow (y, x)$

○ To perform a rotation, turn all the points of the figure around the center of rotation. Rotations are *counterclockwise* unless otherwise described. Some common rotations are:

Rotation (about the origin)	Effect on x- and y-coordinates
90°	$(x, y) \rightarrow (-y, x)$
180°	$(x, y) \rightarrow (-x, -y)$
270°	$(x, y) \rightarrow (y, -x)$
360°	$(x, y) \rightarrow (x, y)$

○ A composition of transformations is just doing multiple transformations in a given order.

- A shape is symmetric if it can be divided into identical pieces, and there is some transformation that moves individual pieces of the object but doesn't actually change its overall shape. Shapes can have translational, reflectional, and/or rotational symmetry.

- Congruent figures have the same size and shape: lengths are all equal, angles have equal measure, and the number of sides is the same.

- Similar figures have the same shape but different sizes: angles have equal measure and side lengths fit into proportions.

- The sum of the measures of the interior angles of a polyon is $(n-2)180°$, where n is the number of sides of the polygon.

- The angle measure of any angle in an n-sided regular polygon is $\dfrac{(n-2)180°}{n}$: the total interior angle measure divided by the number of angles, which is the same as the number of sides.

- Solid geometry is the study of figures in three dimensions.

- Volume is the amount of space inside a three-dimensional figure. Surface area is the total (two-dimensional) area of all its faces.

- Some common three-dimensional shapes are prisms, pyramids, cylinders, cones, and spheres.

- A prism is a three-dimensional figure with two parallel congruent bases that are both polygons, and lateral faces that are all parallelograms or rectangles. Prisms are named for the shapes of their bases. The volume of a prism is the area of its base times its height. The surface area is the sum of the areas of the two bases and the areas of all the lateral faces.

- A rectangular prism is a three-dimensional shape with 6 faces that are all rectangles. Its volume is $V = lwh$ and its surface area is $SA = 2lw + 2lh + 2wh$.

- A cube is a special rectangular prism in which all faces are squares. Its volume is $V = s^3$ and its surface area is $SA = 6s^2$.

- A triangular prism is a prism with triangular bases. Its volume is the area of its triangular base times its height, and its surface area is the sum of the areas of its two triangular bases and the areas of its three lateral faces.

- A pyramid is a three-dimensional shape that has a base, which can be any polygon, and three or more triangular faces that meet at its apex. Pyramids are also named for the shapes of their bases. The volume of a right pyramid is $V = \frac{1}{3}\left(\text{Area of base}\right)h$, and the surface area is the area of the base plus the sum of the areas of all the triangular lateral faces.

- A right circular cylinder is a three-dimensional shape with two circular bases and a third face that curves around to enclose the shape. Its volume is $V = \pi r^2 h$, and its surface area is $SA = 2\pi r^2 + 2\pi rh$.

- A circular cone is a three-dimensional shape with a circular base and a curved face that tapers smoothly to its apex. Its volume is $V = \frac{1}{3}\pi r^2 h$, and its surface area is $SA = \pi r^2 + \pi rl$, where l is the lateral height of the cone.

- A sphere is a three-dimensional shape that looks like a ball: it's the set of points equidistant from a given point, the center. Its volume is $V = \frac{4}{3}\pi r^3$, and its surface area is $SA = 4\pi r^2$.

- Measurement involves finding a numerical value for some quality of an object, such as length or distance, angle measure, area, volume, time, temperature, and weight/mass.

- The customary system and the metric system are the two most commonly used systems of units for measurement.

- A scale uses proportions to represent measurements. Make proportions to find values using a map or scale model.

- Use the rate pie to solve for rate, time, or distance/work in rate problems. Don't forget to include the units!

Chapter 17
Statistics, Data Analysis, and Probability

COLLECTION, ORGANIZATION, AND REPRESENTATION OF DATA

Statistics is the science of data. We all use data to estimate unknown quantities, to check our experiences against a larger context, to see patterns, to make decisions, and to develop and implement policies. To draw any sensible conclusions from collected data, we need to summarize the data or examine the patterns that it forms.

Collecting Data

Data is raw information, facts, and qualitative and quantitative values. People collect data in order to draw conclusions from it. To do that, the data must be organized so that it can be interpreted.

Data collection is the process of gathering and measuring information on targeted variables in an established systematic fashion. Data collection is part of research in pretty much all fields of study, including the physical and social sciences, engineering, humanities, and business.

Different researchers may have different goals and methods in collecting data, but they all share a very important concern: an emphasis on ensuring accurate and honest collection.

Usually, the variables for which data is being collected are defined beforehand. Variables fall into two types: categorical (or qualitative) and numerical (or quantitative). A **categorical variable** is one that can take on values that are names or labels, with a fixed or limited number of names to choose from. For example, the color of a flower (red, blue, yellow, etc.) and the gender of a person are categorical variables. The researcher must decide on the number of categories and their names before assigning data points to them.

A **numerical variable** is one that can be assigned a quantity, or number. These may be discrete or continuous. For example, age of a person, temperature, mass, and number of rooms in a house are all numerical variables.

Univariate data is made up of information about a single characteristic or attribute, while **bivariate data** is made up of information about two variables, where each data point about one variable is paired with a data point relating to the other variable. Bivariate data is useful when one is investigating possible relationships between variables.

Data can be collected in a variety of ways. The least complicated tend to be surveys and polls. A **sample study** is a collection of data from a given population according to a sampling method, while an **observational study** is a collection of data arranged around variables that the researcher can't control. When the researcher can control the study to a greater extent, by assigning groups, controlling for unexpected influences, and managing the changes in the independent variable, it becomes an **experiment.**

Surveys, studies, and experiments are all ways to estimate patterns and information that are true for a larger population. In statistics, the **population** is the group that the information gathered is meant to describe. Using a sample, or smaller subset of the population, makes data collection more manageable. However, it can introduce bias.

Bias is any way in which the data collected about a sample differs systematically from the data that would be collected if the whole population were studied. Bias can occur at any stage in data collection, including selection of subjects or samples, detection of data, and reporting. Bias can also be introduced later, during interpretation of the data collected. The job of good research is to avoid bias as much as possible.

Surveys, Studies, and Experiments

The first step in any study, survey, or experiment is making a plan. Studies aren't likely to be accurate and informative if they aren't well planned! This plan must include the question or questions to be answered, as well as an appropriate method of data collection and analysis.

More Review
For more statistics review, check out *Cracking the AP Statistics Exam* from The Princeton Review.

First, let's talk about one special kind of survey or study: a **census** collects information from ALL the units in a population. The sample in this case is the whole population.

It is feasible to do a census if the population is small and the process of getting information does not destroy or modify units of the population. For example, if a school principal wants to know the educational background of the parents of all the children in his school, he can gather this information from every one of the school children. It is possible to do a census of a large population—the United States Census takes place every 10 years—but it requires a *huge* amount of work, time, and money.

In order to plan a census, the person (or usually, organization) collecting the data needs to establish and check a complete list of the population units, survey all the units, and check for missing or wrong data. This also means you need some way of making sure the whole population can and will take part in the survey: for example, if you are surveying people or animals, they may not want to comply.

Most surveys are sample surveys. A **sample survey** uses a **sample,** a representative group from the target population, to gather data about the whole population.

The most important aspect of planning a sample survey is that the sample is **representative.** This means that it matches the general population in all the important characteristics, rather than being biased. That way, the data collected from the sample can be generalized to draw conclusions about the entire population.

There are many ways that researchers go about trying to ensure that their samples are representative. The most common are simple random sampling, systematic sampling, and stratified sampling.

In **simple random sampling,** statistical methods are used to generate a list of random units of the population, and check that it's a truly random list. On average, most characteristics of the general population should be well-represented by a random sample. However, when sampling is random, **sampling error** can introduce bias: any given random sample may not accurately represent the population in some characteristics. If the survey is repeated, a different sample will give different results: the aim is to minimize those differences.

In **systematic sampling,** the study population is arranged according to some order, and units are selected at regular intervals (such as every 5th unit) from a random starting point. This helps make sure the sample is not a cluster of the population, but you still have to be careful: if the units are listed in a way that has periodicity to it, bias can come in because certain characteristics show up too often or too little in the sample.

In **stratified sampling,** the study population is divided into layers (or strata) according to categories. This can be helpful if the person doing the study wants to make sure these categories are all included in the study, and especially if data is already available about how those categories are represented in the whole population (such as data from a census). For example, if you know the census data on different races in the general population in a country, you can stratify your sample based on race to ensure that your sample contains the right percentages of each race. Within each stratum, a random sample is taken.

The aim of random sampling, systematic, and stratified sampling is to avoid possible sources of bias. For example, if you collect a sample for your study on food preferences by talking only to your friends, handing out surveys at a local restaurant, or conducting a poll on your website, those samples are probably not representative of the general population: your friends may have similar food preferences to each other (and to you!), the customers at a restaurant are more likely to like the kind of food served there, and the people who go to your website may also be similar to each other in ways that could include food preference.

Another kind of bias can be introduced if the wording and context of the survey or study are not carefully thought out. For example, asking questions that are worded strongly or hint at one response being "better" can also result in biased results. For example, "Would you prefer a delicious steak or green, healthy vegetables?" can create bias because it implies that the vegetables are not delicious (and also because it implies the steak is not healthy). Asking questions that can be considered private, such as about diet, smoking, or sexual activity, in front of others can result in inaccurate results because people may not always be truthful in front of their peers. Even the presence of an interviewer can create bias if the person responding to the question perceives any social pressure to answer in a specific way.

Use the information below to answer the question that follows.

At Angelina's school, students arrive on average 30 minutes before classes begin. Angelina is conducting a survey to determine whether students in her school prefer to spend this extra time indoors or outdoors.

Which of the following is a question Angelina can use in her survey that is least likely to introduce bias?

A. "Do you feel like more outdoors time would be good for student's wellbeing?"

B. "Do you feel that keeping all students inside would be safer?"

C. "Would you prefer to be bored indoors, or to be free to be outside?"

D. "Would you prefer to spend any extra time indoors or outdoors?"

Here's How to Crack It

The question asks for the choice that is least likely to introduce bias based on its wording. Look for ways that the wording of the questions may influence the responders. In (A), only the outdoor option is mentioned, and it is painted in a positive light. That may make students more likely to choose the outdoor option. In (B), only the indoor option is mentioned, and it implies that being outside is less safe. That may make students more likely to choose the indoor option. In (C), both choices are mentioned, but the negative "bored" and the positive "be free" make it biased. The correct answer is (D): it simply asks which choice students prefer, without loading either choice with any qualifiers.

Once you have determined your sampling method, you need a study design. This includes what type of observation or questions you will perform, and how you will administer questions (questionnaire, poll, or verbal survey) if you ask them. You also need to record results.

In an experiment, the design is more complex. Since the researcher can control what happens to the **experimental group,** it makes sense to also have a **control group:** a group in which subjects are left alone—the "treatment" is not performed on them. This allows the person doing the experiment to compare the two groups, and to determine whether the things they might think are effects really resulted from the treatment, or are present in the control group as well. Some of the best experimental designs are **single-blind:** either just the subject or just the researcher does not know which group is the control and which is the experimental; or **double-blind:** neither party knows. That helps avoid bias introduced when people know which group is which and change their actions because of that knowledge.

Use the information below to answer the question that follows.

Suppose a doctor is interested in comparing an anxiety-controlling drug out on the market now (the current medicine) with two new drugs (new medicine X and new medicine Y). A group of patients from a local clinic, all of whom are already taking the current medicine, is available for the experiment.

Which of the following describes an experimental design most likely to yield useful information about the effectiveness of each of the two new drugs compared with that of the current one?

A.   The researcher divides the patients into 3 groups of equal size based on their experience with the current medicine: Group 1 contains patients for whom the medicine works well and Groups 2 and 3 contain patients that want to try something different. Group 1 is administered the current medicine, Group 2 new medicine X, and Group 3 new medicine Y. The anxiety level of each patient is measured after a designated time period, and then the results for the 3 groups are compared.

B.   The researcher divides the patients into 2 groups of equal size based on their experience with the current medicine: Group 1 contains patients for whom the medicine works well and Groups 2 and 3 contain patients that want to try something different. Group 1 is administered the current medicine, and each person in Group 2 receives either new medicine X or new medicine Y. The anxiety level of each patient is measured after a designated time period, and then the results for the 2 groups are compared.

C. The researcher uses random methods to divide the patients into 3 groups of equal size. Group 1 is administered the current medicine, Group 2 new medicine X, and Group 3 new medicine Y. The anxiety level of each patient is measured after a designated time period, and then the results for the 3 groups are compared.

D. The researcher uses random methods to divide the patients into 2 groups of equal size. Group 1 is administered the current medicine, and each person in Group 2 receives either new medicine X or new medicine Y. The anxiety level of each patient is measured after a designated time period, and then the results for the 2 groups are compared.

Here's How to Crack It

The question asks for the best experimental design. Look for ways that the design could be flawed to eliminate answers. In (A) and (B), the patients are divided according to whether they are satisfied with the effects of the current medicine. This introduces bias: the groups are fundamentally different, and the results will be suspect. Eliminate (A) and (B). In (C) and (D), the patients are divided into groups randomly, which will ensure less bias. The difference between (C) and (D) is that the patients are split up differently: should they be divided into 2 groups, or 3? The experiment will be more useful if it yields information about the two new drugs *separately:* then the researchers can evaluate the effects of each new drug, rather than having them lumped together. The correct answer is (C).

Organizing and Representing Data

Organizing data involves putting numerical values in order, and putting categorical data in categories. There are some basic measures that it's useful to think about when organizing numerical data.

Mean, Median, Mode, and Range

The **mean** of a set of data is a measure you probably know well—the average. To find the average, divide the total (the sum of all the data points) by the number of data points.

$$2, 3, 5, 8, 10, 13, 13, 17$$

In the data set above, the sum of the values is $2 + 3 + 5 + 8 + 10 + 13 + 13 + 17 = 71$. Therefore, the mean is $\frac{71}{5} = 8.875$.

The **median** of a data set is the number in the middle when the set is ordered. In the case of a set with an odd number of values, there will be one value in the middle, which is the median. In the case of an even number of values, the median is the *average* of the two middle values.

The data set above is ordered from least to greatest. Since it has 8 values, there are two middle values: 8 and 10. Take their average to find the median of the set: $\frac{8+10}{2} = \frac{18}{2} = 9$.

The **mode** of a data set is the value that occurs the greatest number of times. In this set, 13 is the only number that appears more than once, so it's the mode.

Mean, median, and mode are **measures of central tendency.** In other words, they are all ways to think about where the middle of a set of data is.

The **range** of a data set is the difference between its greatest and least values. In the set above, the range is $17 - 2 = 15$. The range of a set lets you know how "wide" it is: how much the values vary. That's why it's called a **measure of variation** (or spread).

Another common measure of variation is the standard deviation. Simply put, **standard deviation** is a measure of the dispersion of a data set from its mean. Sets with low standard deviation have values that are clustered close together; sets with high standard deviation have values that are spread farther apart.

The calculation for standard deviation of a data set is pretty complex, and it takes a long time. Fortunately, the test writers won't make you do that on the CSET. It's a good idea to have a sense of what standard deviation shows about data—but that's it!

Use the table below to answer the question that follows.

Gerbil	A	B	C	D	E	F	G	H	I	J	K	L
Weight (g)	75	69	75	76	78	73	74	81	72	75	72	80

Hayao measured the weights of the gerbils in his lab for an experiment, and he recorded the data in the table above. Then he discovered that his scale was incorrect—the gerbils each weighed 2 grams more than what was recorded in his table. Which of the following values will not be affected by the change?

A. range

B. mode

C. median

D. mean

Here's How to Crack It

The question asks for the measure that does NOT change its value. Check the measures to see which stays the same.

The mean of the data set as it is recorded is

$$\frac{75 + 69 + 75 + 76 + 78 + 73 + 74 + 81 + 72 + 75 + 72 + 80}{12} = \frac{900}{12} = 75.$$

What will happen to this value when the new data points are used? Each value in the sum will be greater by 2. So the total will be greater by 2(12) = 24. Since $\frac{924}{12} = 77$, the value of the mean increases by 2 as well.

Put the data set in order to find the median and mode:

$$69 \quad 72 \quad 72 \quad 73 \quad 74 \quad 75 \quad 75 \quad 75 \quad 76 \quad 78 \quad 80 \quad 81$$

The mode is 75. The median is $\frac{75 + 75}{2} = 75$.

When the data points are increased by 2, the data set becomes:

$$71 \quad 74 \quad 74 \quad 75 \quad 76 \quad 77 \quad 77 \quad 77 \quad 78 \quad 80 \quad 82 \quad 83$$

The new mode is 77. The new median is $\frac{77 + 77}{2} = 77$.

Since the mean, median, and mode all increased by 2, check the range.

The range of the original set is 81 − 69 = 12. The new range is 83 − 71 = 12. The range doesn't change. The correct answer is (A).

You can also work this problem using reasoning rather than calculation:

> Since the mean is the total divided by the number of values, and the total will definitely change when 2 is added to each value, you can tell that the mean will change.

> Since median is the average of the middle two values, and those two values will change, you can tell that the median will change.

> Since mode is the number that occurs the most frequently, that number will also change, since the original mode plus 2 will be the new mode.

Range, however, is the difference between the maximum and the minimum values. Since each value will be increased by two, the difference will remain the same:

$$\text{(maximum + 2)} - \text{(minimum + 2)} = \text{maximum} - \text{minimum}$$

The correct answer is (A).

Tables and Graphs

To organize data, you can represent it in a table or graph. There are many kinds of tables and graphs that can help you look at data and see its patterns and characteristics; different types work best for different kinds of data. It's good to keep in mind that in general, you cannot look at data from all possible angles using only one method. So it's best to use more than one method when summarizing a data set, even if the different methods produce some overlap of information.

A **table** is an arrangement of data in rows and columns. The data must be arranged so that it's easy to read: if the information is categorical, it's arranged into its categories. If it's numerical, it should be arranged in order of its values. Data can also be grouped: in a frequency distribution table, for instance, the values can be grouped into ranges.

Degree of Agreement	Number of Responses
Agree strongly	10
Agree somewhat	15
Neither agree or disagree	25
Disagree somewhat	20
Disagree strongly	18

Score Range	Number of Students
90–100	7
80–89	12
70–79	11
60–69	5
0–59	4

	For	Undecided	Against	Total
Men	26	6	14	46
Women	11	7	36	54
Total	37	13	50	100

The examples above show different types of tables. In the first two, the data is univariate, and the table shows how may data points correspond to each category or range of categories. In the last table, the data is bivariate, and the columns and rows separate it according to different category sets.

A chart or graph is a way to represent information visually. Here are some of the most common types of charts and graphs and the kind of data they fit best with.

Pie Charts

A **pie chart** is a type of chart or graph in which a circle is divided into sectors that each represent a proportion of the whole. They show each data point as a simple share of a total, so they can only be used to show the composition of a data set, not to show comparisons or relationships. It's also good to note that pie charts are not considered a very good method for representation of data: they have been shown to be misleading and hard to read. That doesn't stop them from being tested though! Unsurprisingly, questions about pie charts usually ask about fractions or percentages of a total.

Use the chart below to answer the question that follows.

World Population by Continent, 2016

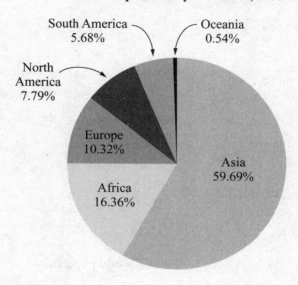

The chart shows the distribution of the world population by continent in 2016. If South America had a population of approximately 423 million in 2016, what was the approximate population that year, in millions, of Africa?

A.   147

B.   888

C.   1,218

D.   4,445

Here's How to Crack It

The pie chart shows percentages of the world population for each continent. The question tells you the actual population of South America in 2016, so use that to find the total. Since the information given and asked for is all in millions, it's safe to keep that as a label rather than writing out all the zeros.

423 million	is	5.68	%	of	the total world population
423 million	=	5.68	÷ 100	×	W

$$423 \text{ million} = \frac{5.68}{100} \times W$$

$$423 \text{ million} \times \frac{100}{5.68} = W$$

$$7{,}447.183 \text{ million} \approx W$$

Now find the amount represented by Africa:

Africa's population	is	16.36	%	of	the total world population
A	=	16.36	÷ 100	×	7,447.183 million

$$A = \frac{16.36}{100} \times 7{,}447.183 \text{ million} \approx 1{,}218.359 \text{ million}$$

Since the question asks for the *approximate* population, the correct answer is (C).

Line Graphs

Everybody knows line graphs. A **line graph** is a chart that displays information as a series of data points connected by line segments or curves. It's used to show trends in data points, usually over time. A typical line graph has time intervals as its x-axis values, and some data that changes over time as its y-axis values. The data needs to be numerical. Some line graphs show multiple lines, showing trends for separate data sets over time.

Use the chart below to answer the question that follows.

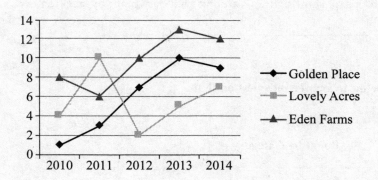

The line graph shows the number of new residents in three different living communities over the course of 5 consecutive years. What was the ratio of the total number of new residents over the 5 years at Lovely Acres to the total number of new residents at Eden Farms during the same time?

A. 4 to 7

B. 7 to 12

C. 14 to 15

D. 7 to 4

Here's How to Crack It

The question asks for a ratio, so look for the two parts of the ratio: 1) the total number of new residents over the 5 years at Lovely Acres and 2) the total number of new residents at Eden Farms during the same time. Make sure you put the elements in that order:

new residents over all 5 years
at Lovely Acres   to   new residents over all 5 years
at Eden Farms

Now find the values for each part. The line for Lovely Acres is the one marked with squares, and the line for Eden Farms is marked with triangles.

4 + 10 + 2 + 5 + 7 = 28   to   8 + 6 + 10 + 13 + 12 = 49

Reduce the ratio just as you would a fraction: 28 to 49 = 4 to 7. The correct answer is (A).

Bar Charts

A **bar chart,** or bar graph, is a chart that shows categorical data with rectangular bars whose heights (or lengths) correspond to the values being represented. The data on one axis must be in discrete categories, while the other axis shows numerical values. Sometimes bar charts have multiple data sets in groups, or show divisions among each data point by stacking.

Use the chart below to answer the question that follows.

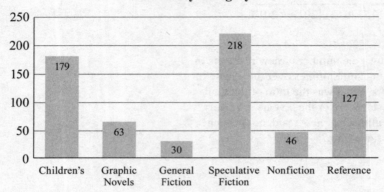

Ali recorded the numbers of books in various categories on her shelves, and represented the data with the bar graph above. If she then adds 6 new Children's books, 4 new Speculative Fiction books, and 5 new Reference books, what will be the approximate percent increase in her total number of books?

A.   2.21%

B.   2.26%

C.   3.94%

D.   9.12%

Here's How to Crack It

The question asks for the percent increase in her total number of books. You need the percent change formula:

$$\text{percent change} = \frac{\text{difference}}{\text{original}} \times 100$$

First, find her current total, the original:

$$179 + 63 + 30 + 218 + 46 + 127 = 663$$

Then find the total of the new books:

$$6 + 4 + 5 = 15$$

You could add this and then subtract the original from the resulting number to get the difference, but notice that you don't need to: 15 is the amount she's adding, so it's the difference. Substitute the values into the percent change formula:

$$\text{percent change} = \frac{15}{663} \times 100 \approx 2.2624434...\%$$

Since the question asks for the *approximate* percent increase, round to the number of digits you see in the choices. The correct answer is (B), 2.26%.

Histograms

A **histogram** is like a bar chart, but for continuous numerical data. One axis shows numerical data, while the other shows numerical data in ranges. Histograms are useful for examining distributions of data in a single variable.

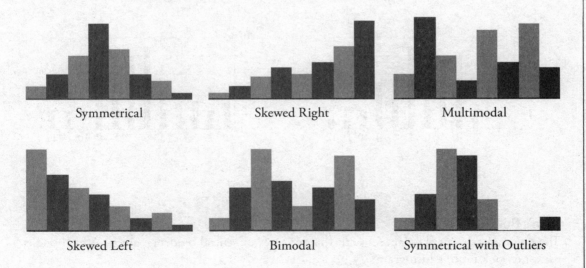

Symmetrical   Skewed Right   Multimodal

Skewed Left   Bimodal   Symmetrical with Outliers

As you can see in the examples above, the shape of a histogram shows clearly some information about distribution: the mode is obvious as the tallest bar, and when there is more than one mode or several local maxima—modes of parts of the data set—the shape of the graph shows that too. Note that it's common to call a set **bimodal** (2 modes) or **multimodal** (more than 2 modes) even when referring to local maxima. Range is easy to find, since you can see what the greatest and least values are.

Histograms also help you see some other characteristics of data sets. **Skew** is how much a data set clusters in lower or higher parts of its range: in other words, how asymmetrical it is. Sets can be skewed in any direction. **Outliers** are data points that are significantly farther from the mean than the main group of data points. Sometimes measures of central tendency are taken after first excluding the outliers, to give a better measure of the main set.

Which of the following data sets has a mean of 6.5, a median of 6, and a mode of 6?

A.

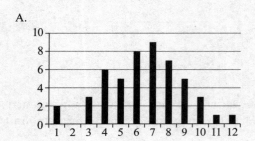

B.

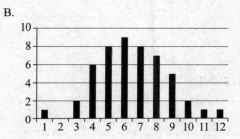

C.

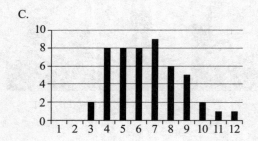

D.

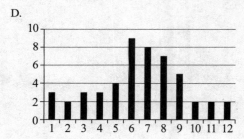

Here's How to Crack It

The question asks for the data set with the measures of central tendency given. Which one is easiest to look for in a histogram?

That's right, mode. Which of these sets have modes of 6? Look for the highest bar.

Choices (A) and (C) have modes of 7: eliminate them. Choices (B) and (D) both have modes of 6.

So what's the next-easiest to check for? Median is easier than mean. Think of the data as a list. It's a long list, so don't write the whole thing out. Instead, think of taking chunks off the ends to work toward the middle.

Look at (B): How many data points are in the columns 1–5? Add up the numbers of data points each bar represents: 1 + 0 + 2 + 6 + 8 = 17. How many data points are in the columns 8–12? Add them up too: 7 + 5 + 2 + 1 + 1 = 16.

They are almost balanced. Take one more data point from the "top end" to match: look at the 7 bar. Take it down by 1, so now you have 8 − 1 = 7 sevens left. Since you are left with 7 sevens and 9 sixes, you can tell that the middle of the list will be two 6s, and their average will be 6. That's the correct median!

What about (D)? How many data points are in the columns 1–5? Add up the numbers of data points each bar represents: 3 + 2 + 3 + 3 + 4 = 15. How many data points are in the columns 8–12? Add them up: 7 + 5 + 2 + 2 + 2 = 18.

Those are pretty close to balanced. Take three data points from the "bottom end" to match: look at the 6 bar. Take it down by 3: now you have 9 − 3 = 6 sixes left, and you have 8 sevens. That means the middle of the list will be two 7s, so the median will be their average: 7. Eliminate (D).

You can bet that (B) is correct, since you already eliminated all the other choices. Check the mean, if you have time, in case you made any errors. Find the total of the values of all the data points, and divide it by the total number of data points:

$$\frac{1(1) + 0(2) + 2(3) + 6(4) + 8(5) + 9(6) + 8(7) + 7(8) + 5(9) + 2(10) + 1(11) + 1(12)}{1 + 0 + 2 + 6 + 8 + 9 + 8 + 7 + 5 + 2 + 1 + 1} =$$

$$\frac{1 + 0 + 6 + 24 + 40 + 54 + 56 + 56 + 45 + 20 + 11 + 12}{50} =$$

$$\frac{325}{50} = 6.5$$

Since that's the correct mean, (B) is the correct answer.

Another type of graph used to show data in the same way as a histogram is a **density plot.** This kind of graph might be familiar to you: it's what people usually use to show normal distributions of data, though of course the distribution does not *have* to be normal to use this type of graph! Basically, statistical methods are used to smooth the data represented into curves. That's good if what you are looking at is the *shape* of the data. Density plots are great for showing characteristics of distribution, like skew, how concentrated your data is, and how close to the shape of a normal distribution it is.

Scatter Plots

A **scatter plot** is a graph that's used to display bivariate data, and it's useful for showing whether there is a **correlation** between the two variables—a statistical relationship indicating how close they are to having a linear relationship. A scatter plot shows data points plotted on two axes, and the shape of the "scatter" of points shows the correlation, or lack of it. If there is a relationship between the variables, you can look for key things in a scatter plot:

- The *form* of the relationship—is it linear or nonlinear?
- The *direction* of the association—is it positive (one set of values increases as the other increases) or negative (one set of values increases as the other decreases)?
- The *strength* of the correlation—a strong correlation is much closer to a linear relationship than a weak one
- *Outliers*—you can see data points that are unusually far away from the main pattern

Here are some examples:

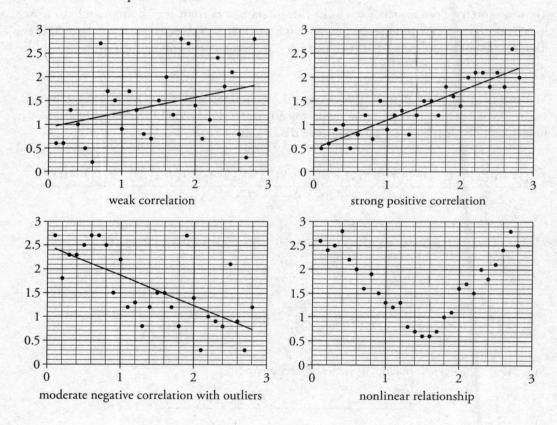

weak correlation

strong positive correlation

moderate negative correlation with outliers

nonlinear relationship

The lines shown on the scatter plots above are **lines of best fit,** straight lines that form the best approximations of the linear relationships the data shows. (The last one has no line of best fit, because you can tell that its relationship is nonlinear.) There are statistical methods for calculating lines of best fit, but you won't need to do that on the CSET. The test may ask you to choose the best line though: look for a line positioned so that about half the data points are above it and half below it. It's okay if the line goes through some of the points too!

INTERPRETING DATA

You can use all the methods you know for representing data to draw conclusions from it and use it to make inferences, arguments, and decisions. Some of the most straightforward conclusions involve estimating the values of variables on the basis of a relationship determined from data collected. **Interpolation,** or estimating within the range of the data that was observed, is more reliable than **extrapolation**, estimating beyond the original observation range.

Keep in mind that good studies come with statistical values not just for the observations, but also for how certain the methods used allow you to be about generalizing those observations. Confidence intervals, effect sizes, probability values, and significance levels are ways to estimate how well the collected data can be used to describe the population and draw conclusions.

When you draw conclusions about a population from data taken from a random sample, remember the biases inherent in that process. A sample of a population, if it's taken according to good methods, should give a relatively good guess about the characteristics of the population as a whole, on average. It's not likely to represent characteristics that are true of only tiny portions of the whole population, and it isn't a perfect guess: it may be off by a small amount. You can't use it to conclude things about populations other than (or larger than) the population the sample was drawn from. And remember not to conclude things that weren't actually studied!

Here's a question about drawing conclusions from collected data.

Use the graph below to answer the question that follows.

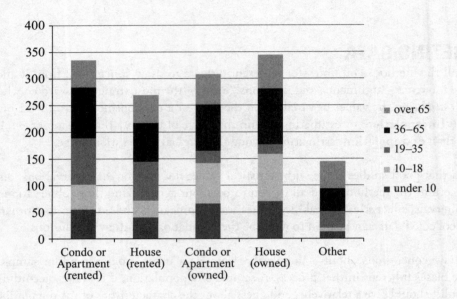

Lakshmi obtained the data above by surveying a random sample of the residents of her city. Her survey included questions asking the age of residents and the type of homes in which they currently live. Which of the following conclusions is reasonable to draw from Lakshmi's data?

A.   More people own houses than rent houses in the United States.

B.   People over 65 are more likely to live in assisted living facilities than in houses or apartments in Lakshmi's city.

C.   Residents of her city say they would prefer to have more rental housing options available.

D.   The number of children in Lakshmi's city who live in owned properties is greater than the number who live in rented properties.

Here's How to Crack It

The question asks which conclusion is reasonable. Look for reasons that a conclusion might not be supported by the data.

For example, (A) is incorrect because it draws a conclusion about the wrong population: Lakshmi's sample is of the residents of her city, not the whole United States.

Choice (B) looks incorrect from the graph: it doesn't offer information specifically about assisted living facilities, but the Other category for the Over 65 range is not bigger than the four specified categories combined.

Watch out for conclusions outside the scope of the data: her data does not offer any information about what residents would prefer, so (C) is incorrect.

Choice (D) draws a reasonable conclusion: the categories Under 10 and 10–18 combined show more residents in the Owned categories than in the Rented ones, so (D) is the correct answer.

Remember, graphical representations of data can also be misleading, which introduces bias into interpretation.

For example, try this question:

Use the table below to answer the question that follows.

Year	Number of surgeries	Year	Number of surgeries	Year	Number of surgeries	Year	Number of surgeries
1991	20	1998	17	2005	35	2012	41
1992	22	1999	30	2006	25	2013	33
1993	18	2000	23	2007	32	2014	38
1994	21	2001	24	2008	37	2015	45
1995	16	2002	28	2009	29	2016	49
1996	19	2003	22	2010	38	2017	42
1997	25	2004	29	2011	45	2018	51

Emilio is using data in the table, showing the numbers of a certain type of surgery performed at his local hospital over the years 1991–2018, to make a graph. Which of the following graphs is the best representation of the data, with the least bias?

A.

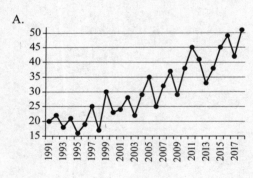

B.

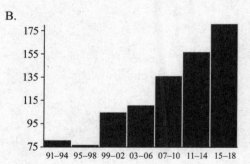

C.

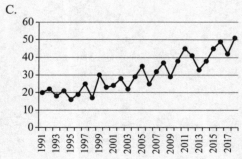

D.

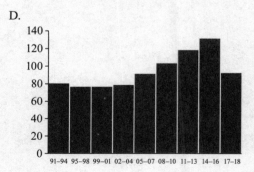

Here's How to Crack It

The question asks for the best representation with the least bias, so you can bet that some of these graphs present the data in a biased way. Which ones? It's not preferable to bin continuous data like years unless there's a good reason, so start by looking at (B) and (D). Is there anything off about how the data is presented?

In (B), notice that the vertical axis doesn't start at zero. That can be misleading when people are reading your chart: in fact, it looks like almost no surgeries were performed in 1995–1998, even though the actual number was close to 75. Making an axis that doesn't start at zero tends to exaggerate the ups and downs of a set and make the lower values look too small. Eliminate (B).

In (D), the axis starts at zero, so that's good. However, there is a trickier bias in how this data is represented. You might notice it by looking at the last column: in all the other representations (and in the table!), the last year has the greatest number, showing an overall upward trend. Here the last column is much shorter—what gives? When you look closely at the labels on the horizontal axis you'll find the culprit: these bins are not equal in number of years! In fact, the first two are groups of 4 years, the middle 6 are groups of 3 years, and the last one shows only 2 years. That really distorts the data, since the columns are shown with equal widths and *look like* they each represent the same number of years. You can see that the overall "trend shape" of the graph is different. Eliminate (D).

Choices (A) and (C) both use line graphs, which is a better choice for data with time as an axis. Look for anything biased or misleading in either of these graphs. You'll notice that (A) makes the same mistake (B) did: its axis starts at 15 rather than 0. This makes the ups and downs of the data look more extreme. Eliminate (A).

Choice (C) is correct: its vertical axis starts at zero, its axes both use even scales, and it's a good type of chart to choose to show this kind of data.

Effects of Bias

Now you've reviewed many of the possible causes of bias in data, from the way it's collected, organized, and represented, to the way it's interpreted and the conclusions that are drawn from it. The reason it's so important to be aware of all this, of course, is the *effects* those kinds of biases can have on the conclusions, arguments, decisions, and policy that people make using data.

For example, imagine that conclusions about patient safety and risks of unnecessary surgery were being made from the graphs in the example above. If the graphs for which the vertical axes did not start at zero were used, and if you don't read carefully, you might jump to the conclusion that rates in that hospital have skyrocketed. This could lead to the wrong kind of initiatives for policy change, addressing a problem that doesn't exist. Worse yet is bias that enters in during data collection: even reading the chart or graph correctly, one can still draw the wrong conclusions if the data is inaccurate or incomplete. With biased or incomplete data, needed policy for problems that *do* exist might never happen.

That's why it's a number-one priority for people doing research of any kind to ensure that all steps of data collection, organization, representation, and use are as accurate, complete, clear, and unbiased as possible.

PROBABILITY

Probability is a measure of how likely it is that a given event will occur. Most of the time when probability comes up, what's meant is **theoretical probability.** That's the probability you calculate based on what is expected to happen. However, theoretical probability is rooted in **experimental probability**—the probability you calculate based on conducting trials and recording the results.

For either type of probability, to find it you make a fraction. You can think of it as $\frac{\text{want}}{\text{total}}$:

$$P\left(\text{outcome meets a condition}\right) = \frac{\text{number of outcomes that meet the condition}}{\text{total number of possible outcomes}} = \frac{\text{want}}{\text{total}}$$

Experimental Probability
To calculate experimental probability, find the number of outcomes of your experiment that meet the condition, and divide by the number of total outcomes observed.

A probability experiment is called a **simulation.** You conduct a simulation by repeating a trial over and over, and recording the results. Greater numbers of trials result in experimental probabilities that more closely approximate theoretical probabilities for the same event.

For example, consider a fair coin toss ("fair" means the chance of getting either outcome is equal). When you toss a coin just a few times, you may see experimental probabilities that vary widely, but as you toss it more and more times, you'll see your result approaching $\frac{1}{2}$.

Here are the results of one such experiment:

Number of Tosses	Number of Heads	Experimental Probability: *P*(heads)	Number of Tosses	Number of Heads	Experimental Probability: *P*(heads)
2	0	0	30	17	$0.5\overline{6}$
3	2	$0.\overline{6}$	35	17	0.48571
4	3	0.75	40	18	0.45
5	5	1	45	18	0.4
6	3	0.5	50	23	0.46
7	5	0.71429	60	32	$0.5\overline{3}$
8	5	0.625	70	29	0.41429
9	7	$0.\overline{7}$	80	34	0.425
10	4	0.4	90	48	$0.5\overline{3}$
15	10	$0.\overline{6}$	100	49	0.49
20	9	0.45	150	74	$0.49\overline{3}$
25	12	0.48	200	106	0.53

The graph below plots this data:

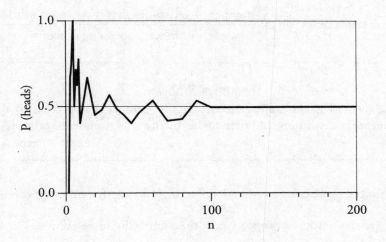

Notice that as the number of tosses increases, the experimental probability—the fraction of the time that the coin lands on heads—gets closer and closer to 50 percent. In other words, in the long run, the relative frequency of getting heads approaches $\frac{1}{2}$, which is what you expected, right?

That's the basic idea of theoretical probability—when you already know what the experimental probability approaches (like you knew that fair coins should come up heads $\frac{1}{2}$ of the time), you can use that knowledge to predict the chances of a given event.

To calculate theoretical probability, you need a **sample space**—a set of possible, equally likely, outcomes. You can represent the sample space as a list. For example, the following is a sample space of possible choices for three-digit numbers composed of the digits 0, 1, and 2:

000, 001, 002, 010, 011, 012, 020, 021, 022, 100, 101, 102, 110, 111, 112, 120, 121, 122, 200, 201, 202, 210, 211, 212, 220, 221, 222

Or you can use tables to keep track of your sample spaces. Here's a table showing the same data:

000	001	002	010	011	012	020	021	022
100	101	102	110	111	112	120	121	122
200	201	202	210	211	212	220	221	222

The outcomes in a sample space are **mutually exclusive:** the occurrence of one outcome means the other outcomes did not occur. Then theoretical probability can be expressed as the same kind of ratio you used for experimental probability: the ratio of the number of successful outcomes (the ones that meet your condition) to the total number of possible outcomes (the whole sample space).

$$P\left(\text{outcome meets a condition}\right) = \frac{\text{number of outcomes that meet the condition}}{\text{total number of possible outcomes}} = \frac{\text{want}}{\text{total}}$$

> ### Theoretical Probability
> To calculate theoretical probability, determine the number of outcomes in the sample space that meet the condition, and then divide by the total number of possible outcomes.

It's easiest to think of probability as a fraction, but just like any fraction, you can also represent it as a decimal, percent, ratio, or proportion. If the probability of an event is $\frac{1}{2}$, that probability can also be expressed as a 1 to 2 chance, a 50% chance, or a probability of 0.5.

For the sample space above, since there are 27 numbers in it, the probability of picking any one number, say 012, randomly from the set is $\frac{1}{27}$.

What's the probability of an event that's impossible? If you know the event definitely won't happen, then the number of outcomes that meet the condition is 0. Since the numerator of the $\frac{\text{want}}{\text{total}}$ fraction is 0, the probability equals 0. That's the least probability an event can have.

What about an event that is guaranteed to happen? If all possible outcomes satisfy the condition, then the number of outcomes that meet it is equal to the total number of outcomes. Since the numerator and denominator of the $\frac{\text{want}}{\text{total}}$ fraction are equal, the probability is equal to 1. That's the greatest probability an event can have.

$$0 \le P\left(\begin{array}{c}\text{any}\\ \text{given}\\ \text{event}\end{array}\right) \le 1$$

Most probabilities fall somewhere in between. In other words, for an event A, $0 \le P(A) \le 1$.

Another useful measure related to probability is **odds:** the ratio of the number of outcomes that meet the condition to the number of outcomes that don't meet the condition. You can think of it as $\frac{\text{want}}{\text{don't want}}$:

$$\text{odds that an outcome meets a condition} =$$

$$\frac{\text{number of outcomes that meet the condition}}{\text{number of outcomes that don't meet the condition}} = \frac{\text{want}}{\text{don't want}}$$

Odds, like probability, is a non-negative value, but since the number of outcomes that meet the condition may be greater than the number that don't, the value of the odds can be greater than 1.

Simple Events

A **simple event** is one outcome in a sample space of equally likely outcomes. To calculate the probability of a simple event, just use the $\frac{\text{want}}{\text{total}}$ fraction.

Of the 364 students at Arrow Bowl Cooperative School, 52 are in kindergarten. The rest of the students are divided evenly into grades 1–4. If one student is chosen at random for a prize, what is the probability that the student chosen is in the 3rd grade?

A. $\dfrac{1}{7}$

B. $\dfrac{3}{14}$

C. $\dfrac{9}{14}$

D. $\dfrac{6}{7}$

Here's How to Crack It

The question asks for the probability of a simple event: one choice of student. The outcomes that meet the condition are those in which the student chosen is a 3rd-grader. The total number of possibilities is given: there are 364 students, any of whom could be chosen.

Find the number of 3rd-grade students. First, the question tells you that 52 students are kindergarteners, so subtract them from the total: $364 - 52 = 312$. Then the question tells you that the rest are *evenly* divided into 4 grades. That means the same number are in each grade, so you can divide 312 by the 4 grades: $\frac{312}{4} = 78$. Now make your fraction and reduce it:

$$\frac{\text{want}}{\text{total}} = \frac{78}{364} = \frac{3}{14}$$

The correct answer is (B).

What if the question had asked for odds rather than probability? You can subtract to find the number of outcomes that don't meet the condition: $364 - 78 = 286$. Now make the ratio and reduce it:

$$\frac{\text{want}}{\text{don't want}} = \frac{78}{286} = \frac{3}{11}$$

The odds are 3 to 11 that a 3rd-grader will be chosen.

Sometimes even though a question is asking for a simple probability, multiple events are mentioned. You need to ask yourself whether these other events matter to the probability you are calculating. Mainly you need to know whether the events are independent or dependent.

Independent events do not affect one another: in other words, the outcome of one event does not change the outcome of the next event. This happens when your events aren't related, use separate objects (as with rolling separate dice), or when **replacement** is occurring. If objects (like marbles, coins, cards, or fruit) are being chosen from a collection, it matters whether they are replaced after each draw, or kept out. You can see why—if they aren't replaced, that changes what's left in the pile to draw from! "With replacement" is a clue that you are dealing with independent events.

Dependent events affect each others' outcomes. In other words, the outcome of one event changes what happens next. "Without replacement," as you've already guessed, is a big clue that you're dealing with dependent events.

What's the probability that a pregnant couple who already have had 6 daughters will have a son? In general, these are independent events: each child has a $\frac{1}{2}$ chance of being either sex. (Unless you know some very specific details about conception I guess!) The chance the current baby is male is approximately $\frac{1}{2}$.

Devon has 12 blue and 6 green marbles in a jar. He chooses 3 marbles from the jar without replacing them. If the first two marbles he chooses are both blue, what's the probability that the third marble will also be blue?

A. $\frac{1}{3}$

B. $\frac{5}{8}$

C. $\frac{5}{9}$

D. $\frac{3}{4}$

Here's How to Crack It

Again, the question is asking for the probability of a simple event: the third marble is blue. However, it's a dependent event: since the marbles from the previous choosings were not replaced, the number of marbles in the jar has changed. There were 12 blue, and 12 + 6 = 18 total marbles in the jar originally. Since he took out two blue marbles already, there are 12 − 2 = 10 blue marbles left. The total also changed: there are 18 − 2 = 16 marbles left. Make the fraction and reduce it:

$$\frac{\text{want}}{\text{total}} = \frac{10}{16} = \frac{5}{8}$$

The correct answer is (B).

Compound Events

A **compound event** is an event that includes more than one possible outcome, like choosing a blue marble first and a green marble second, flipping a coin 3 times and getting 3 heads, or having 6 children who are all girls.

To make the question about the seventh child into a question about a compound event, you have to change what it's asking: What's the probability that a couple bears 7 daughters (or 6 daughters and then a son)? This probability is *not* $\frac{1}{2}$. It's very small!

When you are representing sample spaces involving compound events, you can still use lists and tables, but sometimes it's helpful to use a **tree diagram,** which is what it sounds like—a diagram that branches out like a tree to show possible choices in a sample space.

For example, you can keep track of the outcomes in the sample space for rolling a 6-sided die and flipping a coin like this:

```
die        coin
              H
1  <
              T
              H
2  <
              T
              H
3  <
              T
              H
4  <
              T
              H
5  <
              T
              H
6  <
              T
```

Then you can write the results in a list or table: 1H, 1T, 2H, 2T, 3H, 3T, 4H, 4T, 5H, 5T, 6H, 6T.

To calculate probabilities of compound events, you need to know whether you are looking for the union or intersection of the events. You also need to keep track of dependence/independence.

The **intersection** of two events (let's call them *A* and *B*) is all the outcomes that satisfy both *A* and *B:* in other words, only the ones that fit both sets of conditions.

For example, if you are rolling a die and flipping a coin (independent events), what's the probability that the number you roll is even and the coin lands on tails?

One way to think about this is to make a list of all outcomes. Use the list or the tree diagram you made above:

1H, 2H, 3H, 4H, 5H, 6H, 1T, 2T, 3T, 4T, 5T, 6T

There are 12 outcomes in the combined sample space. Which ones meet your condition? The ones for which the number on the die is even and the coin shows tails are: 2T, 4T, and 6T.

The probability is $\frac{3}{12} = \frac{1}{4}$.

How can you do this without having to write out all the ways? When you are calculating probability for an intersection, you multiply. The only caveat is that your events have to be independent.

Probability for Intersection
$$P(\text{event}_1 \text{ AND event}_2) = P(\text{event}_1) \times P(\text{event}_2)$$

When the two events are independent.

$$P(\text{even AND tails}) = P(\text{even}) \times P(\text{tails})$$

The probability the result is even is $\frac{3}{6} = \frac{1}{2}$, since 3 of the 6 numbers are even: 2, 4, and 6. The probability the coin lands on tails is the same: $\frac{1}{2}$, since 1 of the 2 outcomes meet that condition. So the probability that you roll an even number and get tails is $\frac{1}{2} \times \frac{1}{2} = \frac{1}{4}$.

When the events are not independent, you may have to count which outcomes meet the conditions.

If you are rolling a die, what's the probability that the result is both even and greater than 3?

sample space for rolling a die: 1, 2, 3, 4, 5, 6

There are 6 outcomes in the sample space. Which ones meet your conditions? The ones that are even are 2, 4, and 6; the ones that are greater than 3 are 4, 5, and 6. Two outcomes occur in both sets: 4 and 6. So the probability the result is even and greater than 3 is $\frac{2}{6} = \frac{1}{3}$.

One way to skirt this problem when dealing with some dependent events is to think of them one at a time. Assume the previous event was successful (met the condition) when you are calculating the next event.

Shawn has 3 gold marbles and 2 black marbles in a jar. He chooses 3 marbles from the jar without replacing them. What's the probability that all three marbles will be gold?

A. $\dfrac{6}{125}$

B. $\dfrac{27}{125}$

C. $\dfrac{1}{10}$

D. $\dfrac{3}{10}$

Here's How to Crack It

Here you need to notice that the question asks for the probability of a compound event: choosing 3 marbles that are all gold. You also need to notice that the events affect one another: "without replacing" means the numbers of gold marbles and total marbles will change. Assume each event is successful (the marble was gold) when you calculate the probability of the next event:

$$P(\text{gold}_1 \text{ AND gold}_2 \text{ AND gold}_3) = P(\text{gold}_1) \times P(\text{gold}_2) \times P(\text{gold}_3)$$

For the first choice, the total number of marbles is $3 + 2 = 5$, and the number of gold marbles is 3: $P(\text{gold}_1) = \dfrac{3}{5}$.

For the second choice, assume the first marble chosen was gold. The total number of marbles is $5 - 1 = 4$, and the number of gold marbles is $3 - 1 = 2$: $P(\text{gold}_2) = \dfrac{2}{4}$.

For the third choice, assume Shawn already chose 2 gold marbles. The total number of marbles is $5 - 2 = 3$, and the number of gold marbles is $3 - 2 = 1$: $P(\text{gold}_3) = \dfrac{1}{3}$.

Now you can multiply.

$$P\left(gold_1\right) \times P\left(gold_2\right) \times P\left(gold_3\right) = \frac{3}{5} \times \frac{2}{4} \times \frac{1}{3} = \frac{6}{60} = \frac{1}{10}$$

The correct answer is (C).

─────────────○─────────────

The **union** of two events (let's call them A and B again) is all the outcomes that satisfy A or B: in other words, anything in either event. When you are calculating probability for a union, you add. It's really simple if the two events are mutually exclusive.

> **Probability for Union of Mutually Exclusive Events**
> $P(event_1 \text{ OR } event_2) = P(event_1) + P(event_2)$

For example, if you are rolling a die, what's the probability that you get either a 4 or a 5?

$$P(\text{rolling a 4 OR rolling a 5}) = P(\text{rolling a 4}) + P(\text{rolling a 5})$$

Since the probability for each one is $\frac{1}{6}$, the probability of getting either a 4 or a 5 is $\frac{1}{6} + \frac{1}{6} = \frac{2}{6} = \frac{1}{3}$. Easy! That's because there is no way to get both outcomes (you can't roll a 4 and a 5 at the same time).

What happens when the events aren't mutually exclusive? The complication is that there is some overlap between them, and when you add their probabilities together, that overlap gets counted twice. You need the following formula.

> **Probability for Union**
> $P(event_1 \text{ OR } event_2) = P(event_1) + P(event_2) - P(event_1 \text{ AND } event_2)$

Let's crack out the Venn Diagrams to show why.

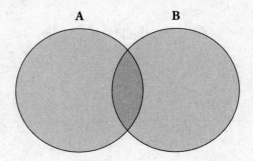

The Venn Diagram above represents your sample space: the circle labeled A stands for one event, and the one labeled B stands for another event. You can see that the total shaded area is their union, and the area that's shaded darker is their intersection. If you want to think about the number of items in the sample space, you need to add the ones in A to the ones in B. But then everything in the intersection has been counted twice. Subtract it once, and you'll get the true total. You use the same process when you are thinking about probabilities: in terms of the outcomes that meet the condition (the numerator of $\frac{\text{want}}{\text{total}}$), you must add the ones in A to the ones in B and then subtract the intersection.

In the pool of candidates applying for a position at Company X, there are 12 men and 13 women. Of all the candidates, 10 have the necessary qualifications for the job, while the other 15 are not qualified. Two of the qualified candidates are men. What are the chances that a randomly chosen candidate is either qualified or a man?

A.   2 to 25

B.   1 to 5

C.   4 to 5

D.   22 to 25

Here's How to Crack It

First of all, don't let how the choices are represented throw you. Remember, a 1 to 5 chance is the same as a probability of $\frac{1}{5}$. Work the problem with fractions, and then write your answer in the correct form when you are done.

The question asks for probability of a union: either the candidate is qualified, or a man. However, the information you are given tells you these two sets overlap: there are two candidates who are both qualified and men. Use the formula for union:

$$P(\text{qualified OR man}) = P(\text{qualified}) + P(\text{man}) - P(\text{qualified AND man})$$

The probabilities of each of these parts is easy to find. There are 12 + 13 = 25 total candidates, so:

$$P(\text{qualified}) = \frac{\text{want}}{\text{total}} = \frac{10}{25}$$

$$P(\text{man}) = \frac{\text{want}}{\text{total}} = \frac{12}{25}$$

$$P(\text{qualified AND man}) = \frac{\text{want}}{\text{total}} = \frac{2}{25}$$

Now apply the formula: $\frac{10}{25} + \frac{12}{25} - \frac{2}{25} = \frac{20}{25} = \frac{4}{5}$.

Rewrite this in the correct form to match the choices: a probability of $\frac{4}{5}$ is the same as a 4 to 5 chance. The correct answer is (C).

———————————◯———————————

Complements

Another important feature of a sample space is the complement. The **complement** of an event A is the event "NOT A": that is, the event that A does not occur. Notice that an event and its complement are mutually exclusive: they can never *both* happen.

The neat thing about the fact that events have complements is that events and their complements are also **exhaustive.** That means that together they cover all the possible outcomes in the sample space.

Think about the probability of rolling a 2 on a 6-sided die. What's its complement? Rolling "NOT 2" is the same as rolling any side but 2: a 1, 3, 4, 5, or 6. What's the probability of rolling a 2? That's 1 event out of 6 possibilities, so the probability is $\frac{1}{6}$. What's the probability of rolling "NOT 2," the complement? Well, that covers the other 5 out of 6 possibilities, so it's $\frac{5}{6}$.

Notice anything about these two fractions? That's right, they sum to 1. It makes sense: if together an event and its complement cover the whole sample space, then the sum of their probabilities (the chance that one or the other happens) must be 1.

Complements

Given an event A,

$$P(A) + P(\text{NOT } A) = 1$$

In other words,

$$P(\text{NOT } A) = 1 - P(A)$$

Jalys has a bag full of color counters in which 30% of the counters are white and 25% are yellow. The rest are green and blue, and she knows the numbers of green and blue counters are equal. If Jalys draws a counter at random, what is the probability that it is not blue?

A. 22.5%

B. 27.5%

C. 72.5%

D. 77.5%

Here's How to Crack It

The question asks for the probability that the counter drawn is NOT blue. You can find the probability that it *is* blue, and then subtract that from 1:

$$P(\text{NOT blue}) = 1 - P(\text{blue})$$

These probabilities are given in percentages, so you can either work with them that way or, if it's easier for you, convert them to fractions. Remember, percentages are just fractions with the denominator 100.

Write down what you know:

30% white

25% yellow

the rest green and blue, numbers are equal

You can add up the percentages for white and yellow counters: 30% + 25% = 55%. You know that the rest are green and blue: find that total percentage by subtracting from 100% (remember, that's the same as 1):

100% − 55% = 45% green and blue

Since the numbers of green and blue counters are equal, divide this percentage by 2 to find what percent of each there are:

$$\frac{45\%}{2} = 22.5\%$$

22.5% green

22.5% blue

Remember what the question asked for! Choice (A) is a trap: eliminate it.

$P(\text{NOT blue}) = 1 - P(\text{blue}) = 100\% - 22.5\% = 77.5\%$

The correct answer is (D).

The fact that the probabilities of an event and its complement sum to 1 also provides an alternate way to think about *any* probability question, especially those that look monstrous to calculate. What if you can find the probability that the event *doesn't* happen, and then just subtract that from 1? It may be an easier way to calculate!

Complements of Complements

Given an event A,

$$P(A) + P(\text{NOT } A) = 1$$

Which also means that

$$P(A) = 1 - P(\text{NOT } A)$$

Some words to look for to indicate that this might be the best way to work a probability question are "at least" and "at most."

For the next 5 days, the weather forecast says the chance of rain on each day is 33%. What is the approximate probability that it rains on at least one of the next 5 days?

A.   0.39%

B.   13.50%

C.   86.50%

D.   99.61%

Here's How to Crack It

The question tells you the probability of rain on each of 5 days: 33%. Then it asks for the probability that it rains on *at least* one of the next 5 days.

You might think you need to calculate all the probabilities of rain on different possible numbers of days, since "at least one" includes the possibilities that it rains on 1, 2, 3, 4, or all 5 of the days, and then add those probabilities together. That's a way to do this! But it's the *long* way. It could take quite a while.

Instead, since the clue "at least" is there, you can think to yourself, "Maybe for this question I should look to find the complement of the complement."

What's the complement of "it rains on at least one of the next 5 days"? If it does NOT rain on at least one of the days, then it rains on none of them.

$$P(\text{rains at least once}) = 1 - P(\text{never rains})$$

How would you find the probability that it doesn't rain on any of the days? Just find the probability that it doesn't rain on day 1 AND it doesn't rain on day 2 AND it doesn't rain on day 3 AND it doesn't rain on day 4 AND it doesn't rain on day 5.

Start by finding the probability that it doesn't rain on a given day by using—you guessed it—the complement!

$$P(\text{NOT rain}) = 1 - P(\text{rain}) = 100\% - 33\% = 67\%$$

Then find the probability that it never rains:

$$P(\text{never rains}) = P(\text{NOT rain}) \times P(\text{NOT rain}) \times P(\text{NOT rain}) \times P(\text{NOT rain}) \times P(\text{NOT rain})$$

$$P(\text{never rains}) = 67\% \times 67\% \times 67\% \times 67\% \times 67\% \approx 13.50\%$$

Now use the complement of the complement:

$$P(\text{rains at least once}) = 1 - P(\text{never rains}) \approx 100\% - 13.50\% = 86.50\%$$

The correct answer is (C).

KEY TERMS

statistics
data
data collection
categorical variable
numerical variable
univariate data
bivariate data
sample study
observational study
experiment
population
bias
census
sample survey
sample
representative
simple random sampling
sampling error
systematic sampling
stratified sampling
experimental group
control group
single-blind
double-blind
mean (average)
median
mode
measure of central tendency
range
measure of variation
standard deviation
table

pie chart
line graph
bar chart
histogram
bimodal
multimodal
skew
outlier
density plot
scatter plot
correlation
line of best fit
interpolation
extrapolation
probability
theoretical probability
experimental probability
simulation
sample space
mutually exclusive
odds
simple event
independent events
replacement
dependent events
compound event
tree diagram
intersection
union
complement
exhaustive

Chapter 17 Drill

Answers and explanations can be found in the final section of this book, beginning on page 617.

1. **Use the information below to answer the question that follows.**

   Teddy is designing a survey with the aim of collecting data from his neighborhood about use of shared spaces, such as the neighborhood park, walkways, and the nearby nature preserve.

   Which of the following is a way Teddy can collect data for his study that will yield the most accurate data with the least bias?

   A.   approaching people using the outdoor spaces mentioned on random days of the week and asking them to complete the survey

   B.   mailing the survey with a return envelope included to all the residents on Teddy's block

   C.   going door-to-door at 3 p.m. each Friday and asking those who answer to complete the survey

   D.   mailing the survey with a return envelope included to a random sample of all neighborhood residents

2. **Use the chart below to answer the question that follows.**

   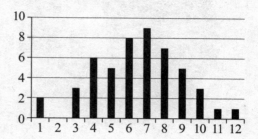

   Which of the following is true of the data represented above?

   A.   The mean of the data is 7.

   B.   The standard deviation of the data is 0.

   C.   The range of the data is 12.

   D.   The median and mode of the data are equal.

3. **Use the graph below to answer the question that follows.**

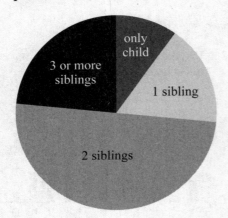

Hong took a survey of his classmates and recorded their answers about number of siblings. In his class, there are 30 students: 7 of them are only children, 5 of them have 1 sibling, 15 of them have 2 siblings, and 3 of them have 3 or more siblings. Hong made the pie chart above with the data, but his teacher told him his graph is incorrect. What must Hong do to fix it?

A. Increase the wedge for "1 sibling" and decrease the one for "3 or more siblings."

B. Increase the wedge for "1 sibling" and decrease the one for "2 siblings."

C. Increase the wedge for "3 or more siblings" and decrease the one for "2 siblings."

D. Increase the wedge for "only child" and decrease the one for "3 or more siblings."

4. **Use the table below to answer the question that follows.**

	Response	Number of respondents
1	disagree strongly	12
2	disagree somewhat	25
3	disagree a little	32
4	neither agree nor disagree	53
5	agree a little	29
6	agree somewhat	21
7	agree strongly	13

Calliope made the table above to show responses to one question from her survey. Now she plans to make a histogram of the data. Which of the following best describes the shape of the histogram?

A. It has one mode and is tightly clustered.

B. It is bimodal with a gap.

C. It is strongly left-skewed.

D. It is right-skewed with outliers.

5. The following scatter plots show the same data. Which line of best fit has been drawn correctly?

A.
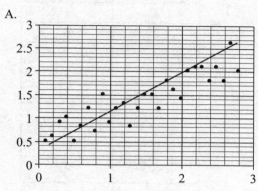

B.
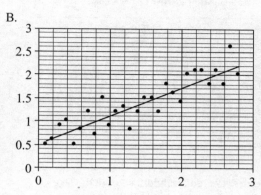

C.
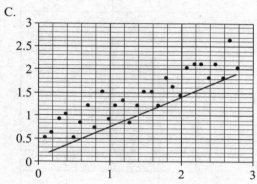

D.
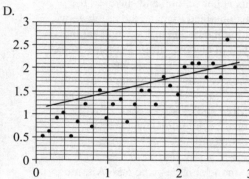

6. **Use the graph below to answer the question that follows.**

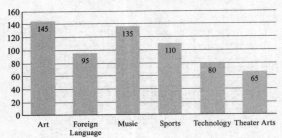

Students by Elective Course Choice

Maggie surveyed a random sample of students at her school, and she used the data she obtained to make the graph above estimating the number of students taking each type of elective offered at her school. Which of the following conclusions is reasonable to draw from Maggie's results?

A. More students take Sports than take Technology and Theater arts combined.

B. Among students who take Art, more take Drawing and Painting than take Sculpture.

C. At least 25 students would take Home Economics if it were offered.

D. The total number of students taking Art and Foreign Language is about the same as the total number taking Music and Sports.

7. **Use the table below to answer the question that follows.**

Trial	Result
1	1
2	6
3	5
4	4
5	3
6	1
7	2
8	5
9	3
10	1
11	2
12	3
13	2
14	6
15	4
16	3
17	2
18	3
19	1
20	6

Cornell is running a simulation to test the experimental probability for tossing a fair 6-sided die. The table shows his results. Which of the following is the experimental probability of rolling a 6 in his simulation?

A. $\dfrac{1}{20}$

B. $\dfrac{3}{20}$

C. $\dfrac{1}{6}$

D. $\dfrac{1}{5}$

8. What is the probability that a randomly generated number between 1 and 100, inclusive, is a multiple of 3?

   A. 0.32

   B. $0.\overline{32}$

   C. 0.33

   D. $0.\overline{3}$

9. In a deck of cards, there are 52 cards divided evenly into 4 suits, two black and two red. The cards are numbered 1–10, followed by 3 face cards, in each suit. What is the probability that a randomly chosen card is either red or a face card?

   A. $\dfrac{3}{26}$

   B. $\dfrac{5}{13}$

   C. $\dfrac{8}{13}$

   D. $\dfrac{19}{26}$

10. Sarah flips a coin 4 times. What is the probability that the coin lands on heads at most 3 times?

   A. $\dfrac{1}{16}$

   B. $\dfrac{1}{8}$

   C. $\dfrac{7}{8}$

   D. $\dfrac{15}{16}$

Summary

- Statistics is the science of data: collecting, organizing, representing, and using data to draw conclusions and make decisions.

- Data collection involves defining variables: categorical (or qualitative) and numerical (or quantitative) variables describe different types of data.

- Researchers use censuses, surveys, studies, and experiments to collect data. With the exception of censuses, studies use samples to represent the populations they describe, and those samples must be representative of their populations in order for studies to avoid bias.

- Random, systematic, and stratified sampling are different methods of sampling that help to ensure representativeness.

- Researchers also need to be careful to avoid bias that comes from the wording or context of their studies, by using neutral questions and situations that maximize the chance of truthful and accurate reporting.

- Experiments are controlled studies in which researchers are able to compare experimental and control groups to observe the effects of treatments or other changes introduced by the experiments.

- When organizing data, measures of central tendency—such as mean, median, and mode—and of variation—such as range and standard deviation—can be useful for describing features of the data.

- The mean is the average of the data—the total of all values divided by the number of values.

- The median is the middle value when the data is arranged in numerical order (the average of the two middle values in a set with an even number of numbers).

- The mode is the value that occurs the greatest number of times.

- The range is the difference between the greatest and least values in a data set.

- The standard deviation is a measure of how closely clustered the values are to the mean.

○ Once it's collected and organized, data can be represented in tables and graphs. Different types of tables and graphs are best for representing different types of data, and they help show different features of data sets.

○ A table is an arrangement of data in rows and columns organized to show ordering or categories.

○ Pie charts are circular charts with sectors that each represent a fraction of the whole and are used to show composition of data sets.

○ Line graphs are charts that display information as a series of data points connected by line segments or curves, with numerical data (usually time) on the x-axis. They are used to show trends (usually over time).

○ Bar charts are charts that show categorical data with rectangular bars whose heights or lengths correspond to values. One axis is categorical and the other is numerical.

○ Histograms are charts much like bar charts except that the bars represent ranges of numerical data; they are useful for examining characteristics of distribution, such as clustering, skew, and outliers.

○ Scatter plots are graphs used to display bivariate data as points plotted on two axes. They are useful for examining correlation or lack of correlation between two variables, and characteristics such as the form, direction, and strength of the correlation, as well as outliers. You can find a line of best fit to represent the trend of the relationship between variables when the data has a linear correlation.

○ When interpreting data and making conclusions, inferences, arguments, and decisions based on it, make sure to remember the limitations of the data and not make unsupported conclusions. Remember as well that charts and graphs can be misleading. Bias from anywhere in the processes of data collection, organization, representation, and interpretation can cause the conclusions drawn to be incorrect or dangerous.

○ Probability is a measure of how likely it is that a given event will occur. Theoretical probability is the ratio of the number of outcomes from a sample space that meet a condition to the total number of possible outcomes; experimental probability is the ratio of the number of outcomes from a simulation, or experiment, that meet the condition to the total number of trials. As more trials are conducted, experimental probability tends to approach theoretical probability.

o   Probability can be expressed as a fraction, decimal, percentage, or ratio between 0 and 1, inclusive.

o   The odds of an event is another ratio: the number of outcomes that meet the condition to the number of outcomes that don't.

o   To calculate the probability of a simple event, use $\frac{\text{want}}{\text{total}}$.

o   Independent events do not affect each other, but dependent events are events in which each one affects the next. You must take into account changes to the sample space when calculating probabilities of dependent events.

o   A compound event is one that includes multiple outcomes. When calculating probabilities for compound events, look for whether the situation involves union or intersection.

o   To calculate probability for intersection of independent events, multiply the probabilities for the simple events together.

o   To calculate probability for intersection of dependent events, you may have to write out the sample space using a list or tree diagram and count the outcomes; but when you are dealing with separate events in an order, you can usually assume the previous event was successful when calculating the next probability for each simple event, and then multiply the results.

o   To calculate probability for union of mutually exclusive events, add the probabilities for the simple events together.

o   To calculate probability for union of non-mutually exclusive events, add the probabilities for the simple events and then subtract the probability of the intersection.

o   The complement of an event A is the event NOT A. Events and their complements are mutually exclusive and exhaustive, so their probabilities sum to 1.

o   To find the probability of the complement of an event A, find $1 - P(A)$.

o   Sometimes you can use the complement of the complement to find the probability of an event; in other words, to find the probability of an event A, you can find $1 - P(\text{NOT } A)$. This is likely to be helpful when the calculation using the normal method looks monstrous, or when you see the phrase "at least" or "at most."

Subtest III: Physical Education, Human Development, Visual and Performing Arts

Chapter 18
Physical Education

IT'S NOT JUST DODGEBALL ANYMORE

Elementary school Physical Education classes may incorporate which of the following activities?

A. swimming, water ballet, kayaking, and fishing
B. juggling, stilt walking, unicycle riding, and tightrope walking
C. tennis, golf, fencing, and croquet
D. all of the above

The correct answer is (D), all of the above.

You mean they actually plan that stuff?

You may recall "gym," "P.E.," or "Phys. Ed." as nothing more than a teacher in shorts and a T-shirt blowing a whistle while you ran or climbed or jumped until you were gasping for air—or until the bell rang, whichever came first. But just like any other class, Physical Education requires careful planning, extensive subject matter knowledge, and no small amount of creativity.

I LIKE TO MOVE IT, MOVE IT

Basic Movement Skills

Basic movement skills are the foundation to more complex skill sets needed to exercise and play games and sports. The three main categories of movement skills are **traveling, stabilizing,** and **control** (of objects).

Movement Concepts

In Physical Education, students learn to become aware of their bodies and movements. Movement concepts are often referred to as the *how*, the *where*, and the *what* of body movement.

- **Body awareness** teaches children about body shapes, body parts, and relationships.
- **Space awareness** refers to personal and shared space, and the body in relation to dimensions in space.
- **Movement exploration** allows students to experiment with time, space, force, and flow as the elements of movement.

Locomotor and Nonlocomotor Skills

The term **locomotor** indicates the movement of the body from one place to another—in other words, you use your feet to get you someplace.

Locomotor skills are used to walk, run, leap, jump, hop, skip, gallop, and slide.

The term **nonlocomotor** indicates body control and balance, with limited emphasis on movement. Nonlocomotor skills are used to balance, bend, stretch, and pull.

Activities

Physical Education (PE) teachers build their lessons around the fundamentals of basic skills. Even the simplest of activities requires multiple skills. For example, two students tossing a ball back and forth have to throw, catch, balance, adjust force and speed, and gauge distance. It's the teacher's job to help them to become aware of all of those components, and to assess their progress.

HEALTH AND PHYSICAL FITNESS

In Physical Education, students learn how physical fitness affects their overall health, including both the benefits and risks of physical activity.

Health Benefits and Risks

The benefits of regular exercise include:

- weight management
- better sleep patterns
- heart and lung (cardiovascular) efficiency
- higher energy levels
- stress relief

The risks of regular exercise include:

- injury
- illness, such as heatstroke
- dehydration
- aggravation of existing conditions, such as asthma

Exercise Principles

Part of your job as a PE teacher is to help students learn exercise principles that promote physical fitness. Think FITT: Frequency, Intensity, Type, and Time. **Frequency** refers to how often we exercise; kids should get activity daily. **Intensity** refers to how hard a person is working, which is most easily gauged by heart rate. Both moderate intensity (e.g., brisk walking) and vigorous intensity (e.g. running) exercise should be incorporated in a comprehensive fitness plan. Different **types** of activities, such as aerobic and muscle strengthening exercises, should also be part of a comprehensive plan. Time can be measured in minutes, which is typical for aerobic activity, or repetitions, which is typical for muscle strengthening exercises. The Department of Health and Human Services recommends kids get 60 minutes of activity per day.

FITT: Frequency, Intensity, Type, Time

Other principles of exercise vary slightly in terminology but can include the following:

- **Balance:** To be effective, exercise should require the use of different muscles and parts of the body.
- **Variety:** Varying activities reduces boredom and aids or increases motivation.
- **Recovery:** During recovery, muscles are given a chance to rest.
- **Overload:** To achieve a training effect, the workload must exceed the normal demands placed on a body.

Physical Fitness Components

There are two types of physical fitness components: **health-related components** and **skill-related components**.

The following are health-related components:

- body composition
- cardiovascular fitness
- muscular endurance
- muscle strength
- flexibility

The following are skill-related components:

- agility
- balance
- coordination
- power
- speed
- reaction time

CURRICULUM

You're expected to be able to take your knowledge of movement and physical fitness and apply it to teaching Physical Education through a strong curriculum.

Activities

We weren't kidding at the beginning of the chapter—it's standard now for Physical Education teachers to incorporate a wide variety of activities into the curriculum. It's important for a number of reasons, including employing all of the components of physical fitness, and keeping the students interested and motivated. Additionally, it will help you make sure you include all students. You must be able to recognize and accommodate individual differences such as gender, culture, ability, or disability.

Rules and Etiquette

You should familiarize yourself with as many sports and games as you can, both traditional and nontraditional. You may also want to learn about other types of movement, such as dance, yoga, or martial arts, so you can incorporate different movement concepts into your curriculum. Regardless of the activity, make sure can explain the **rules** and **social etiquette** associated with it.

Content Areas

Anytime a Physical Education teacher can integrate activities with other content areas, it's beneficial to everyone. It helps students build on prior knowledge, and reinforces concepts learned in other disciplines.

- Math: hurrying to form groups in the number called out by the teacher
- Science: using weights to balance bottles and then attempting to knock them down
- Social Science/History: jousting, Native American hand wrestling, capoeira, lacrosse
- Language Arts: creating words or sentences while throwing and catching a ball

---

Which of the following is an example of body awareness?

A. timing a run

B. checking your heart rate

C. serving a volleyball

D. walking on a balance beam

Body awareness is the understanding of the parts that make up one's body, including what they can do and how they feel (hence, the term). Which of the above activities shows some type of bodily awareness? Running, (A), hitting a volleyball, (C), and walking on a balance beam, (D), take some type of effort: speed, force, and coordination. Determining your heart rate, (B), though, is a form of body awareness.

WATCH THEM GROW

Physical Growth and Development

Picture a group of kindergarteners walking in a line. All of the students are about the same height and weight, give or take a few inches and pounds. Now picture a group of sixth graders walking in a line: they could conceivably vary by up to two feet and 100 pounds. And those are just the superficial differences.

Gross Motor Skills

Gross motor skills are the basic skills acquired by children in the early stages of development, using the large muscle groups. They include major bodily skills like walking, climbing, and throwing. Skills are acquired in a natural progression. Children learn to stand before they can jump, walk before they can run. In typically developing children, gross motor skills are fully present by age five or six.

Fine Motor Skills

Fine motor skills are sometimes referred to as hand skills, because that's what they are: skills you can perform with your hands. As with gross motor skills, they are acquired in a natural progression. Babies first reach for things, then learn to grasp, and later learn to hold and carry.

Fine motor skills are much more complex and continue to develop well into the school years. Fine motor skill development varies more by age than does gross motor skill development, which progresses at generally the same rate—think about things like writing, drawing, and cutting. By first grade, some children are adept at all of those skills, while others are still in the early stages of development.

Growth Spurts and Puberty

The most rapid growth occurs in infancy. By one year old, average babies triple their birth weight and grow up to a foot in length. After that, children grow slowly and steadily until adolescence. And then…welcome to puberty.

The onset of **puberty** in healthy girls can occur anywhere from age 8 to age 13. The actual growth spurts usually start around age 11 or 12 and last until age 15 or 16.

Boys' **growth spurts** start a little later, usually around age 12 or 13, and can last until age 19. Some boys don't reach their full height until they're in college.

Puberty includes many body changes: the appearance of pubic and underarm hair, weight gain, voice changes, development of sex organs, and, in girls, menstruation.

All of these factors affect students' physical abilities. Growth spurts can lead to awkwardness and discomfort, which in turn may hinder movement. Adolescents have to learn to adjust to different heights, weights, and hand and foot sizes. This adjustment makes it difficult for them to do some physical activities they previously performed with confidence and skill, like running, jumping, and playing certain sports.

SELF-IMAGE

Exercise and fitness play a major part in children's **self-image.** Staying active relieves stress, burns off excess energy, both physical and emotional, and builds confidence.

There are a number of skills children learn and use in Physical Education that build self-esteem and promote overall health, including the following:

- helping others
- thinking positively
- joining groups or clubs
- having healthy family relationships
- taking on responsibilities
- goal setting
- working hard to succeed academically

Building self-esteem and psychological skills through Physical Education will promote students' lifelong participation in physical fitness activities.

Which activity would most challenge a person's fine motor skills?

A.   bowling

B.   basketball

C.   origami

D.   swimming

Here's How to Crack It

When you see the term *fine motor skills*, focus on the word *fine*. What does the word make you think of? Small? Precise? Refined? Those are all good descriptions of fine motor skills. If you don't have a confident grasp on the word, take a different route and remember the other type of motor skills, *gross motor skills*. Those refer to large muscle groups and movements. While all of the activities above require some measure of fine motor skills, all primarily utilize gross motor skills. The delicate art of origami, (C), would be the biggest challenge for fine motor skills.

SOCIAL DEVELOPMENT

Physical Education class can be considered the most important class of the day when it comes to students' social development. Students interact far more in Physical Education than they do in traditional academic classes. It's important for teachers to factor in social dynamics when planning curriculum and structuring class sessions.

Class Setting

Teachers can create a healthy classroom environment by selecting activities that are developmentally appropriate, inclusive, and promote students' responsible social behavior. Some strategies to do so include:

- creating heterogeneous teams with a mix of genders and cultures regardless of the sport or activity
- choosing activities, games, and sports from different cultures
- planning a wide range of activities in which all students have the opportunity to showcase their skills
- frequently changing and mixing groups so that students interact with as many other peers as possible
- monitoring students' verbal and nonverbal attitudes toward themselves and their peers
- balancing cooperation and competition
- giving each student a turn at being in a leadership/team captain role

KEY TERMS

traveling
stabilizing
control
body awareness
space awareness
movement exploration
locomotor skills
nonlocomotor skills
FITT
balance
variety
recovery
overload
health-related components
skill-related components
rules
social etiquette
gross motor skills
fine motor skills
puberty
growth spurt
self-image
sportsmanship
movement exploration
nonlocomotor skills
biomechanics
flexibility
strength
endurance

Chapter 18 Drill

Answers and explanations can be found in the final section of this book, beginning on page 617.

1. Which of the following would most likely be considered poor sportsmanship?

   A. a baseball player loudly cheering a home run by a member of his team

   B. a football team captain designating player positions based on her team members' strengths

   C. a skilled soccer player scoring as many goals as she can in order to ensure her team's win

   D. a basketball player consistently blocking an opponent's attempt to shoot baskets

2. A child whose fine motor skills are slower to develop might be the last one in his peer group to be able to:

   A. use scissors.

   B. hop on one foot.

   C. kick a ball.

   D. make a noise like a train.

3. In order to effect positive changes to the body through exercise, it is best to:

   A. stop before you are out of breath.

   B. exercise for at least one hour.

   C. work to the point of exhaustion.

   D. push yourself slightly farther than you've gone before.

4. In general Physical Education classes, students should usually be grouped:

   A. by gender, because there will be less discomfort and embarrassment.

   B. according to skill level, to keep activities moving at a steady pace and to prevent boredom.

   C. in a variety of ways, to promote equality and interaction.

   D. randomly, because it is the most fair.

5. Which of the following effects of growth spurts is LEAST likely to impact a student's physical activity?

   A. having larger feet than before the growth spurt

   B. weight gain

   C. joint discomfort

   D. reduced self esteem

Summary

- Basic movement skills are the foundation from which more advanced physical skills develop.

- When developing curriculum, Physical Education teachers should draw from a wide variety of sports, games, and activities.

- Children grow and develop at very different rates and in very different ways.

- Exercise and fitness are good for children both physically and emotionally.

- Physical Education is greatly beneficial to students' social development.

Chapter 19
Human
Development

NO TAXONOMY WITHOUT REPRESENTATION

Read the example; then answer the two questions that follow.

At the end of a Social Studies unit on the Colonial Era, Mr. Yeh asked his students, "A family of Quakers who had left England because of religious persecution would probably have chosen to settle in which of the Middle Colonies?"

1. The correct answer is:

   A.   New York.

   B.   New Jersey.

   C.   Pennsylvania.

   D.   Delaware.

Because you'll have studied your history, you'll remember that Pennsylvania was founded by William Penn, a Quaker, so the first question will be a breeze. But then…

2. Which level of Bloom's taxonomy does Mr. Yeh's question represent?

   A.   knowledge

   B.   application

   C.   analysis

   D.   synthesis

Unfortunately, *Huh?* is not one of the answer choices. The answer is (B), *application*, but that won't do you any good if you have no idea why.

TEACHING TO THE TEST

Above all, the CSET is an exam for teachers, and as a teacher, you'll be tested not only in subject matter, but also on your understanding of how to apply that knowledge in the learning environment.

The Human Development section of the test can be divided into three main areas: cognitive, social, and physical development. Cognitive development focuses on how children learn, and you will need to identify the different stages of cognitive development and how they build on each previous stage. Social development encompasses the theories that help with moral development, the importance of play, and the impact of society and culture on student expectations. Physical development reviews the different physical attributes at different ages and the important role it plays even with disabled students. A strong understanding of all three areas and how they correlate are necessary in order to answer situational questions about how to promote correct behaviors and growth in the classroom.

Let's start our review with cognitive development theories.

COGNITIVE DEVELOPMENT

You'll need to know the basic developmental theories and theorists in cognitive, social, and moral development. Cognitive development is the acquisition of learning and knowledge. These theories allow teachers to understand their student's learning patterns and make teaching more effective. While understanding the full age range of human development theories will help with your complete knowledge, the CSET: Multiple Subjects test will focus mainly on the theories from birth to adolescence. Here's an overview of the big ones.

Piaget's Theory

Jean Piaget was a Swiss psychologist whose theory of **cognitive development** may be alluded to in CSET questions. Piaget theorized that cognitive development precedes learning. In other words, Piaget believed that the brain needs to develop first before learning can actually take place. You should be familiar with the basics of this theory and some common examples used to illustrate its principles.

Piaget believed that learning happens as people adapt to their physical environments. He suggested that cognitive development proceeds as follows: when faced with a situation, you first try to use or apply what you already know, and if that doesn't work, you figure out something else based on what's new or different about that situation. The first idea, using your existing **framework** or **schema,** he called **assimilation.** Schema can be thought of as mental frameworks that help us to interpret information, ideas, thoughts, and concepts. A lot of schemas are rooted in experiences or previous ideas. The assimilation process achieves cognitive equilibrium in terms of the current existing schema and doesn't promote further learning. The second, developing new frameworks, he called **adaptation.** During adaptation, schemas are changed in order to re-establish cognitive equilibrium, and this change is seen as learning. He believed that we are constantly refining our frameworks.

Based on his observations, Piaget theorized that this ongoing process of assimilation and adaptation leads all children to pass through identical stages of cognitive development, but not necessarily at identical times. He identified four stages; let's review them in order.

Sensorimotor Stage (approximate age 0 to 2 years)

Because most children pass through the **sensorimotor stage** by the time they reach the age of formal instruction, it's unlikely that you'll see questions dealing with it. You should know, however, that things that babies do and the types of games that parents typically play with babies are all relevant to this stage. For instance, one of the characteristics of the sensorimotor stage is understanding **object permanence**—the concept that things continue to exist even though you can't see them. Some educational psychologists and social anthropologists agree that the game of peek-a-boo is practically universal in human cultures specifically because it reinforces the concept of object permanence. Another hallmark of the sensorimotor stage is the early development of **goal-oriented behavior.** For example, a very young child who is able to roll over at will, but not yet able to crawl, may consciously roll over multiple times to reach a bottle or favorite toy.

Preoperational Stage (approximate age 2 to 7 years)

At the **preoperational stage,** children are developing language skills quickly. They also begin to use symbols to represent objects, a process known as animism in which objects take on greater qualities, such as feelings or opinions. Children in this stage will be able to think through simple problems, but only in one direction—that is, they won't be able to reverse the steps mentally, which is known as reverse logic. They also will have difficulty seeing things from another person's point of view. This idea is called **egocentrism.** Although this sounds like a negative quality, it's best understood as the child's assumption that everyone else sees things the same way that he does. For example, a child may assume that everyone likes orange juice simply because he likes orange juice. Children at this stage also lack the concept of conservation and objects do not retain their original qualities. For example, if you poured the child's favorite orange juice from a tall glass into a shorter but wider glass, the child might think there was less juice. The concept of juice is still there, but the volume is dependent on its appearance.

Concrete Operational Stage (approximate age 7 to 11 years)

Children in the **concrete operational stage** develop the ability to perform a mental operation and then reverse their thinking back to the starting point, a concept called **reversibility,** or **reverse logic.** They demonstrate the concepts of **transitivity** (they can classify objects according to a specific characteristic, even if the object has many different characteristics) and **seriation** (they can put objects in order according to a given criterion such as height or volume). One important concept is that of **conservation**—the idea that the amount of a substance doesn't change just because it's arranged differently. For example, conservation of mass might be demonstrated by taking a large ball of clay and creating several smaller balls of clay out of it. A child in the concrete operational stage will understand that the total amount of clay hasn't changed, while a child in the preoperational stage might think that there is more clay (because there are more balls). Children in the concrete operational stage also understand the concept of **class inclusion**—they can think about a whole group of objects while also thinking about the subgroups of those objects. For example, while thinking about the whole class, a child could also think about how many girls or boys are in the class. At this stage, children can solve concrete, hands-on problems logically. In fact, all of the cognitive developments at this stage lead to the acquisition or learning of logical application.

Formal Operational Stage
(approximate age 11 years to adulthood)

Not all students reach the **formal operational stage.** In fact, some theorists estimate that only about 35 percent of the adult population ever achieves this stage. It's characterized by the ability to solve abstract problems involving many independent elements. The thought process necessary to frame and solve such problems is called **hypothetical-deductive reasoning.**

Vygotsky's Theories

Lev Vygotsky was a Russian educational psychologist in the early 20th century whose theories you should be familiar with. You might see questions about his four major ideas.

Unlike Piaget, Vygotsky based his theories on the idea that learning precedes cognitive development and actually leads to the development of the brain. Vygotsky also emphasized the influences of language, society, and culture on the learning and development process. You could even say that Vygotsky was more a promoter of the nurture philosophy versus the nature aspects presented by other theorists. According to Vygotsky, parents, teachers, and communities are key actors in a child's cognitive development, making a teacher's role vital to the healthy development of children.

Culture

Vygotsky believed that environmental and cultural factors have an enormous influence on what children learn. Piaget argued that children are constantly developing methods of adapting to the world around them; Vygotsky argued that **environment** and **culture** dictate what methods the children will find useful, and what their priorities will be.

Private Speech

To Vygotsky, language use is a critical factor in cognitive development. Young children frequently talk to themselves as they play or solve problems. This is called **private speech.** While Piaget would cite private speech as evidence of egocentrism in the preoperational stage, Vygotsky believed that private speech allows children to use language to help break down a problem and solve it—in effect, the children talk themselves through it. He believed that a fundamental stage in development comes when children begin to carry on this speech internally, without speaking the words aloud. Children who routinely use private speech learn complex tasks more effectively.

Zone of Proximal Development

At any given stage, there are problems that a child can solve by herself, and there are other problems that a child couldn't solve even with prodding at each successive step. In between, however, are problems that a child could solve with the guidance of someone who already knows how. That range of problems is what Vygotsky referred to as the **zone of proximal development.** He believed that real learning takes place by solving problems in that zone.

Scaffolding

Scaffolding is another idea fundamental to Vygotsky's notion of social learning. It's about providing children with help from more competent peers and adults. Children are given a lot of support in the early stages of learning and problem solving. Then, as the child is able, he takes on more responsibility, and the supporter diminishes the support. Supportive techniques include clues, reminders, encouragement, breaking the problem into steps, providing examples, and anything that helps a student develop learning independence.

Piaget vs. Vygotsky

Piaget and Vygotsky are two of the most influential cognitive development theorists. They show up on the Human Development test quite a bit, and there might be some answer choices that are meant to test your knowledge of them. To make sure you understand the major differences between the two, think through the following questions:

- What is the major difference in approach between the two theories? Does learning come before development or vice versa?
- How do Piaget and Vygotsky use the idea of cognitive equilibrium? What factors allow children to progress through each of their stages?
- How does the physical environment affect development in both theories? How about cultural influences?

CONSTRUCTIVISM

Piaget's and Vygotsky's theories (among others') led to an educational philosophy called **constructivism,** which essentially says that learning is a constant assimilation of new knowledge and experiences into each student's unique worldview. Because each student's point of view will be different from everyone else's, a strict constructivist would be in favor of guided hands-on learning rather than traditional lecture-based teaching, because hands-on learning would more likely be related to a student's own experience. In fact, the new Common Core curriculum tested on the CSET: Multiple Subjects test emphasizes this "show, don't tell" teaching idea. The curriculum focuses on guiding teachers to create more interactive lessons that allow students to scaffold their own learning and development.

Bloom's Taxonomy

Bloom's taxonomy is broadly encouraged and utilized in teacher preparation and instruction—in other words, if you don't know it already, you should! It's broken down into the six levels in which students develop thinking skills: in order, they are knowledge, comprehension, application, analysis, synthesis, and evaluation. In the early grades, students are limited to facts and other rote knowledge. As they develop, they're capable of processing information at levels of greater and greater complexity. In general, teachers should try to develop higher-order thinking skills (those at the end of the list). Let's take a look at the types of questions that would stimulate these types of thinking. Remember Mr. Yeh, and his unit on the colonization of the United States?

Bloom Taxonomy Level	Description	Question Example
Knowledge	Recalling factual information	What were the names of the New England colonies?
Comprehension	Using factual information to answer a specific question	What crops were common to the New England Colonies and the Southern colonies? What were the major religious differences between the New England colonies and the Middle Colonies?
Application	Taking an abstract concept together with specific facts to answer a question	In which area of the colonies would a Freethinker have been most likely to find like-minded people?
Analysis	Breaking down a question into concepts and ideas in order to answer a question	What characteristics of the New England colonists made them the most likely to rebel against British rule?
Synthesis	Connecting concepts and ideas to create a new product or idea	What steps could the king have taken to appease the New England colonists that might have prevented the American Revolution?
Evaluation	Making considered judgments by breaking down and reconnecting ideas, concepts, and facts and comparing the judgments to standards	In which area of the colonies did the colonists have the best natural resources from an economic standpoint?

In planning the unit, Mr. Yeh built a base of facts and concepts and then developed lessons that would encourage students to ask and answer increasingly complicated types of questions based on those facts and concepts.

Cognitive, Affective, and Psychomotor Domains

Bloom's taxonomy deals with skills in the cognitive area, or domain. The other two widely recognized areas are the affective and psychomotor domains.

The **affective domain** includes class participation, including listening as well as speaking, defending positions, and recognizing the opinions of others.

The **psychomotor domain** includes abilities related to physical prowess ranging from reflexes through basic motions such as catching and throwing a ball, to skilled motions such as playing tennis and playing the piano. It also includes the ability to communicate through motion, as in dancing or miming.

Which of the following examples best demonstrates Vygotsky's theory of the zone of proximal development for a sixth-grade student?

A. She reads a chapter in her geometry textbook, and is asked to define the key terms.

B. She is given a book to read in French, even though she has never studied the subject.

C. She can already solve one-variable algebra equations, and is asked to solve multi-variable algebra equations.

D. She is asked to complete a spelling assignment, which reviews words that she learned last year.

Here's How to Crack It

Remember that the *zone of proximal development* refers to a situation in which the student is asked to build upon prior learning, and has a reasonable chance to solve the problem, with some assistance. To crack this question, look to see which answer fits each part of that theory and use POE to eliminate the rest. The first answer you can rule out is (B), which is obviously wrong because the student has no prior knowledge to build on. Choice (D) is incorrect for the opposite reason: the student is using prior knowledge, but she is not building anything new out of it. Technically, both (A) and (C) can be considered within the student's zone of proximal development, but remember, the CSET asks for the "best" example. Choice (A) is too vague. Choice (C) is specific and shows very clearly the student's current knowledge base as well as the logical next learning stage, and that is how you know it is the correct answer.

SOCIAL DEVELOPMENT

While cognitive development looks at the ways children learn, social development focuses on the ways children develop and society's influence on who they become. Similar to other development sections, the CSET: Multiple Subjects test will focus only on the ages from birth to adolescence.

Erikson's Eight Stages of Psychosocial Development

You should be familiar with **Erik Erikson's stages of psychosocial development.** Erikson, a German-born American psychologist, identified eight stages of personal and social development, each of which takes the form of a resolution of an identity crisis.

In other words, children need to achieve the first stage before moving on to the second stage, and the completion of each stage is marked by the resolution to a specific identity crisis. An identity crisis can simply be characterized by a life task or conflict that requires a re-balance to achieve equilibrium. Each stage also widens the child's interactions with others and society. Here they are in chronological order.

More Review
For more in-depth coverage of this content, check out *Cracking the AP Psychology Exam* from The Princeton Review.

1. Trust vs. Mistrust (birth to 18 months)

If children are well cared for during this time, they will become naturally trusting and optimistic. The goal is for infants to develop basic trust in their families and the world, and learning and interaction happens most frequently with the primary caregiver. Again, due to the age range involved, you will probably not see questions dealing with this stage.

2. Autonomy vs. Doubt (18 months to 3 years)

Children learn the mechanical basics of controlling their world, including walking, grasping, and toilet training. The "terrible twos" fall into this stage, with common traits including stubbornness and willful behavior as the child pushes the limits of control and develops autonomy. Children want to become independent and still rely on their support system. In fact, unlike the first stage, learning is expanded to multiple caregivers. Ideally, parents need to be supportive of the children's needs so that they come out of this stage proud of their abilities rather than ashamed.

3. Initiative vs. Guilt (3 to 6 years)

After becoming autonomous, children start wanting to do things. They have ideas and plans and carry out activities. Some activities aren't allowed, and it's important for children to feel that their activities are important and valued by adults. If this feeling isn't there, children believe that what they do is wrong, and guilt develops, which restricts growth.

4. Industry vs. Inferiority (6 to 12 years)

In these elementary-school years, children are expected to learn and produce. Parental influence decreases. Teachers and peers become more important, and children begin to develop an awareness that everyone and each person is different in sometimes even small ways. Success creates high self-esteem, while failures lower self-image. Just the perception of failure can cause children to feel inferior, even if the failure is not real. If children can meet the expectations of themselves, parents, and teachers, they learn to be industrious. If they do not, they risk feeling inferior. In this stage, learning expands to include the whole family and not just the parents.

5. Identity vs. Role Confusion (12 to 18 years)

During this stage, adolescents answer the question "Who am I?" It's quite common for teenagers to rebel, some very strongly. Erikson believed that the social structure of the United States was a healthy one for teenagers. They are offered the opportunity and leeway to try out different personalities and roles, and decide which ones suit them best. Acceptance by peer groups is of extreme importance.

Because the last three stages, described below, are stages that adults go through, it is unlikely that you will see any questions about them on the exam. They're listed here only for the purpose of completing the list.

6. Intimacy vs. Isolation (Young adulthood)

Being able to form mutually beneficial intimate relationships is the defining characteristic of this stage.

7. Generativity vs. Self-Absorption (Middle adulthood—around 40 years)

Adults need to be productive in helping and guiding future generations, both procreatively and professionally. If adults don't, they risk being self-absorbed.

8. Integrity vs. Despair (Late adulthood)

Finally, adults need to feel complete and comfortable with themselves and the choices they've made in their lives. The ego has a great effect during this stage. If the person feels like they have accomplished their expectations, they will feel satisfied. If not, then they can be left with the feeling of frustration. They need to accept their eventual deaths.

Mildred Parten's Stages of Play Development

Play is an important way in which children learn to socialize, but unlike other development theories, the age ranges for play development vary more widely. Mildred Parten, a child psychologist in the 1930s, was one of the first people to study children at play. Play not only helps development in all other areas, but can also be an indicator of development progress. The CSET: Multiple Subjects test will usually test play concepts as situational indicators for social development. Here are **Mildred Parten's six stages of play development**, which are linked to different levels of social interaction.

1. Unoccupied Play

This stage of play is likely not tested on the CSET: Multiple Subjects test. However, it can still be helpful to be familiar with this stage. This stage is characterized by observing and not active participation in play.

2. Solitary Play

During this stage, children play by themselves. While children may continue to do this throughout their childhoods, in the context of social interaction, this is usually observed in children less than two years of age.

3. Onlooker Play

At around two years, children watch others play without doing anything themselves or making any effort to join in. This is closely followed in the same time frame by parallel play.

4. Parallel Play

In parallel play, children do the same thing that other children are doing. There is no interaction between the children.

5. Associative Play

Normally, by age four or five, children engage in associative play. Associative play is similar to parallel play, but there is increased interaction. Children share, take turns, and are interested in what others are doing.

6. Cooperative Play

Finally, usually by age five to seven, children play together in one activity.

APPROPRIATE ATTACHMENTS

Play can also help children build appropriate attachments, but in the earlier stages, key attachments are formed mostly with primary caregivers. However, even the initial attachments can help to define how children move from one stage of psychosocial development to the next.

Harlow's Discoveries in Attachment

In the 1950s, the Harlow couple used experiments with baby monkeys to study the need for attachment. They discovered that attachment is more than just for food or necessity; it is also for contact and comfort. Physical attachment and touch with caregivers can lead to emotional, moral, and psychological developments. How did they know? The monkeys that were given inappropriate environments for attachment or caregivers to attach to were unable to form proper social bonds, even with other monkeys, throughout the remainder of their lives.

Mary Ainsworth's Strange Situation

In the mid-1960s, American-Canadian social psychologist Mary Ainsworth noted separation reactions and attachments in infants. Observing a mother and child, she would record the child's reactions when the mother was replaced with a stranger and then returned. Using her "Strange Situation" experiment, she concluded that there were three different attachment styles with corresponding responses.

1. Secure Attachment

Children who develop secure attachments will play freely and interact with their primary caregiver normally. Children show signs of being upset when the caregiver leaves, and are immediately happy when the caregiver returns.

2. Insecure Ambivalent Attachment

Children who form insecure ambivalent attachments are uncomfortable or even distressed in the presence of strangers despite the primary caregiver's position. These children are also difficult to console in the absence of the caregiver or upon their return. For example, this could be a child who is unable to play in the caregiver's absence or the child who is upset with the caregiver after their return.

3. Insecure Avoidant Attachment

Insecure avoidant attachments are characterized by relative non-reactivity. For example, insecure avoidant children show little emotion when the caregiver leaves and returns. In some cases, the child even ignored their primary caregiver.

Ainsworth theorized that the two forms of insecure attachment were a result of the caregiver being over responsive or less responsive.

The Development of Self-Concept

Attachment also helps to develop our ideas of self-concept by the age of 12. This idea of self-concept will later help children to build confidence and is usually a result of three different control styles. Authoritarian control is more dictatorial and less instructional. Permissive control is more a lack of control around boundaries and limits. Finally, authoritative control is structured with reasons explained. The Common Core curriculum, for example, favors the authoritative methodology because it incorporates the "why" behind lesson plans and helps to build student motivation for learning.

MORAL DEVELOPMENT

Lawrence Kohlberg was a developmental psychologist at Harvard University in the late 20th century. He conducted extensive research in the field of moral education. You should be familiar with **Kohlberg's stage theory of moral reasoning.** He split moral development into three levels, each of which contains two stages.

Level 1: Preconventional Moral Reasoning (Elementary School)

Rules are created by others. This level of moral reasoning is seen mostly in children under the age of 9 and is primarily concerned with self-interest.

Stage 1: Punishment and Obedience Orientation

Young children obey rules simply because there are rules, and they understand that they risk punishment by breaking them. Whether an action is good or bad is understood in terms of its immediate consequences.

Stage 2: Instrumental Relativist Orientation

Children internalize the system from Stage 1 and realize that following the rules is generally in their best interests. An action is right or good if it gets you what you want. A simple view of "fair's fair" develops, so that, for example, favors are done with the expectation of something in return. This stage is need-based driven, and actions are ego-driven for self need.

Level 2: Conventional Moral Reasoning (Junior High–High School)

Kohlberg called this level conventional because most of society remains at this level. Judgment is based on tradition and others' expectations and less on consequences. Individuals adopt rules and sometimes put others' needs before their own in an effort to conform. This level often correlates with Erikson's Identity vs. Role Confusion stage of social development.

Stage 3: Good Boy–Good Girl Orientation

An action is right or good if it helps, pleases, or is approved by others.

Stage 4: "Law and Order" Orientation

An action is right or good if it's expected out of a sense of duty or because it supports the morals or laws of the community or country. This reflects the common sentiment "It's right because it's the law."

Level three is unlikely to be tested because Kohlberg believed that it's not fully attained until adulthood, if it's ever attained at all. It's included here for completeness.

Level 3: Post-Conventional Moral Reasoning

People determine their own values and ethics. Even though this level might not be tested on the CSET: Multiple Subjects test because it develops after adolescence, if at all, it is still important to be able to identify this stage.

Stage 5: Social Contract Orientation

An action is right or good if it meets an agreed-upon system of rules and rights (such as the United States Constitution). Unlike stage four, this phase recognizes that rules can be changed for the betterment of society.

Stage 6: Universal Ethical Principle Orientation

Good and right are relative, not absolute, and require abstract thinking in terms of justice, equality, and human dignity. One's conscience determines right from wrong. (In his later years, Kohlberg decided that stages 5 and 6 were actually the same.)

Heinz Dilemma Thought Exercise

To memorize the different levels and stages of Kohlberg's moral development, it can be helpful to think about the Heinz Dilemma.

Situation: A woman is close to death from a rare form of cancer. There is a medicine that could save her, but it is very expensive. The woman's husband, Heinz, didn't have enough money to pay for the medicine even after borrowing all that he could. He begged the druggist to sell it to him cheaper, but was denied. After trying all other options, Heinz stole the medicine for his wife.

Now think about how people in each level would answer the question: Should Heinz have stolen the medicine? Why or why not? Remember to focus on the reason behind the answer to identify the stage.

- Level 1: Heinz was right for stealing because he was fulfilling a need.
- Level 2: Heinz was wrong because it doesn't conform to the laws of society.
- Level 3: Heinz was not right or wrong because he tried other methods and the morality in the dilemma is debatable.

STUDENTS AS DIVERSE LEARNERS

Not all students learn the same way, and students have strengths and weaknesses in a variety of areas. The major ideas you should be familiar with are multiple intelligences, different learning styles, gender-based and culture-based differences, and exceptional students.

Multiple Intelligences

What is intelligence? This question may never be fully answered. Nonetheless, you should be familiar with Howard Gardner's work because it might show up on the CSET. **Howard Gardner** is a developmental psychologist at Harvard University who categorized the following nine **types of intelligence**:

1. **Logical-mathematical intelligence** relates to the ability to detect patterns, think logically, and make deductions. Scientists and mathematicians tend to be logical-mathematical thinkers.

2. People who have **linguistic intelligence** are particularly sensitive not only to words themselves, but also to the relationship between the meanings and sounds of words and the ideas and concepts that words represent. Poets and journalists tend to possess linguistic intelligence.

3. **Musical intelligence** is the ability to recognize and reproduce rhythm, pitch, and timbre—the three fundamental elements of music. Obviously, composers and musicians possess musical intelligence.

4. People with **spatial intelligence** have the ability to create and manipulate mental images. They also perceive spatial relationships in the world accurately and can use both the mental and actual perceptions to solve problems. Both artists and navigators use well-developed spatial intelligence.

5. **Naturalist intelligence** relates to being sensitive to natural objects like plants and animals and making fine sensory discriminations. Naturalists, hunters, and botanists excel in this intelligence.

6. **Bodily-kinesthetic intelligence** is the ability to consciously and skillfully control and coordinate your body's movements and manipulate objects. Athletes and dancers need a strong bodily-kinesthetic intelligence.

7. **Interpersonal intelligence** is the ability to understand and respond to the emotions and intentions of others. Psychologists and salespeople make good use of interpersonal intelligence.

8. **Intrapersonal intelligence** is the ability to understand and respond to your own emotions, intentions, strengths, weaknesses, and intelligences.

9. **Existential intelligence** is the sensitivity and capacity to tackle deep questions about human existence, such as the meaning of life, why we die, and how we got here.

> **Intelligence**
> The different types of intelligence usually appear as identification questions on the CSET: Multiple Subjects test. Most of these questions will present a situation, and sometimes they will include identifying learning difficulties or differences necessary for the Common Core curriculum.

Gardner believes that we all possess some degree of these intelligences, and that each of these must be relatively well developed in order for us to function well in society.

Although the intelligences are categorized separately, we rarely use them strictly independently. It is difficult to think of a profession or activity that wouldn't combine some of these intelligences. For instance, a pianist needs not only musical intelligence, but also interpersonal (to be able to relate to an audience) as well as bodily-kinesthetic (to control the actions of her hands on the keyboard).

Different Learning Styles

Not all people learn the same way. Different students process information differently depending on how it's presented. Many theorists split learning styles into the following three categories:

You will need to be able to identify student learning styles and differences on the CSET: Multiple Subjects test. Again, this will likely be tested through situational and Common Core curriculum will focus on various learning style teachings to bolster traditional classroom environments.

1. **Visual learners** learn by seeing. They prefer graphs and charts to summarize information, rather than text or a spoken summary. They prefer maps and diagrams to step-by-step directions. They're more likely to remember faces than names when they meet someone. Traditional lecture-based lessons can be good for visual learners as long as the teacher makes good use of visual aids.

2. **Auditory learners** learn by hearing. They're more likely to remember what was said about a painting they've studied than to be able to describe its appearance. Traditional lecture-based lessons are effective with aural learners.

3. **Kinesthetic learners** learn by doing. They remember things best if they try them out and see for themselves. They're more likely to remember what they were doing when they met someone than what they talked about. Traditional lecture-based lessons are not good for kinesthetic learners. Lessons that involve laboratory work or hands-on experimentation tend to be effective.

Theorist Lawrence Kohlberg would most likely agree with which of the following statements about first-grade students?

A.   Children have no clear morality.

B.   Children show concern for others and try to live up to expectations.

C.   Children are able to differentiate between legality and morality.

D.   Children have a generalized sense of respect for rules and expectations.

Here's How to Crack It

You know that Kohlberg split moral development into three levels, and as soon as you read the words "first grade," you know the question refers to Level 1: preconventional moral reasoning. Choices (B) and (C) are farthest from that level—much too advanced. When you look at the two choices that are left, though both seem plausible, remember that Kohlberg designated Level 1 for elementary school students. First graders are pretty low on the elementary school totem pole, so he most likely would agree with the statement that refers to the most basic stage of moral reasoning, which is (A).

PHYSICAL DEVELOPMENT FROM CHILDHOOD TO ADOLESCENCE

Since 2010, the CSET: Multiple Subjects test has also started to test physical developments from childhood to adolescence. Some of these questions might overlap or resemble physical education topics, but they will be characterized more as identifying stages and proper physical development. You will be required to identify the proper expected physical developments in children with consideration to genetic and environmental differences.

Genetic and Environmental Influences on Physical Development

Many of the questions on the CSET: Multiple Subjects test will address the factors that can affect a child's physical development. These differences can be grouped into two main categories: genetic and environmental. It is important to distinguish the appropriate cause for a specific physical development in order to address deficiencies or promote proper growth.

Genetic Influences

Genetic influences can be thought of as a given. For example, a child with short parents is likely to be shorter themselves. Genetic factors can also lead to physical limitations, such as a child who is born with a physical handicap and needs the assistance of a wheelchair. Below is a sample list of genetic factors to consider.

- race or ethnicity
- gender
- physical disabilities
- other genetics that lead to differences in hair color, eyesight, etc.

Environmental Influences

Environmental factors can sometimes be harder to identify, but these factors can lead to a wide range of physical capabilities in the classroom. Environmental influences come from everything inside and outside of the classroom. For example, a child who comes from poverty can show slower physical development compared to children from a more affluent family environment. Some things to consider:

- culture
- socio-economic background
- family structure
- lifestyle, such as active or non-active

> Physically disabled students still undergo physical developments but it might present differently. The CSET: Multiple Subjects test will expect you to identify physical limitations and assign appropriate modifications for students who are physically disabled. The test might also present 1–2 questions regarding how the disability can also affect cognitive, social, or moral development areas.

The Five Stages of Physical Development

The CSET: Multiple Subjects test physical development section focuses mostly on identifying the difference between the five various stages of physical development. However, since the test only tests up to the adolescence stage, you should focus most of your review on the first three stages. It can also be helpful to identify the differences between gross motor developments and fine motor developments at each stage. Gross motor movements include larger body movements that involve a limb or whole part of the body. Fine motor movements are smaller and use fingers or hand movements. Here are the five main stages:

- **Infancy: 0–3 years.** This stage is marked by rapid physical growth. Infants and toddlers will see a dramatic change in height and weight ratios. Most of the physical development revolves around involuntary reflexes and reactions. For example, most children during this stage will exhibit the Palmar hand grasp where they naturally begin to grasp fingers or things just to practice the holding action. By the end of this stage, children should be able to crawl, walk, sit independently, and grab smaller objects.

- **Childhood: 3–12 years.** This is also often referred to as the school age stage, because this is usually the age that children are in school and play becomes more physically interactive. Children during this stage will continue to improve their gross motor control by running, jumping, and catching balls. By the age of 6, most children will be able to perform dual actions. For example, riding a bike requires steering the bike with your arms and peddling up and down with your legs. Furthermore, children during this stage start to develop their fine motor skills. For example, they begin to use scissors, write letters, and draw.

- **Adolescence: 12–18 years.** Adolescence can be identified as the second stage of rapid growth with the onset of puberty. Children shed their "baby fat" or weight and stretch out in height. Hair growth is also an indicator of puberty for both girls and boys. Girls tend to start this stage earlier than boys, so there might be a time when girls appear to be more physically developed compared to boys. Both gross and fine motor skills should be mastered during this stage, and children toward the end of this age are usually very aware of their physical capabilities and limitations. Adolescents are also able to maintain physical activity for a longer period of time since their lungs and heart also grow quickly during this period.

- **Adulthood: 18–65 years.** Adults do not experience growth but rather the beginnings of the decline in growth. Physical development is at its peak from ages 20–40, and begins to decline steadily until the senior stage. The decline can manifest as a slow loss of vision, muscle strength, agility, etc.

- **Senior: 65+ years.** This stage is marked with the further decline of physical attributes. Muscles slow down, hair whitens or is lost, fine motor control becomes less specific, and gross motor control is slower.

STUDENT MOTIVATION AND THE LEARNING ENVIRONMENT

Despite the typical nature-versus-nurture argument among social psychologists, most would agree that there are several factors that can influence a child's learning. For example, the family structure and traditions, culture, race, and religion can teach children to behave in a specific, more appropriate way. Additionally, as teachers and on the CSET: Multiple Subjects test, we need to understand the socioeconomic factors that can also affect children's development. For example, a child in a well-off family will likely be able to learn and practice art skills sooner and show confidence at an earlier age. External socio-economic factors are also important to consider in the classroom and on this test, because you may be asked to identify signs of abuse or neglect that are interfering with learning and development.

Now that we've looked at how children develop and how they learn, let's take a look at how motivation and the classroom environment can have an impact. There are several major theorists you should be familiar with: Edward Lee Thorndike, Ivan Pavlov, Abraham Maslow, B. F. Skinner, and Albert Bandura.

Thorndike's Laws

Edward Lee Thorndike was an early behavioral psychologist whose work led him to three major conclusions:

- **Law of effect.** An action that produces a positive result is likely to be repeated. This law mostly explains trained behavior using an emotional response. A child who is recognized for achievement continues to show interest in that subject or area.
- **Law of readiness.** Many actions can be performed in sequence to produce a desired effect. This focuses on the effect of a student who is more ready to learn and the influence of having an intrinsic motivation to learn.
- **Law of exercise.** Actions that are repeated frequently become stronger. This law builds confidence, but it does not necessarily lead to further learning. Repeating a task does not establish a new equilibrium.

Maslow's Hierarchy of Needs

Abraham Maslow was an educational theorist who believed that children must have certain needs met before they're ready to learn and grow. He organized these needs into a hierarchy, and taught that you couldn't progress to the next level until you'd achieved the previous one. Here's the hierarchy from low to high:

Deficiency Needs

Physiological needs—food, sleep, clothing, and so on
Safety needs—freedom from harm or danger
Belongingness and love needs—acceptance and love from others
Esteem needs—approval and accomplishment

Growth Needs

Cognitive needs—knowledge and understanding
Aesthetic needs—appreciation of beauty and order
Self-actualization needs—fulfillment of one's potential

Maslow called the first four **deficiency needs.** They are the basic requirements for physical and psychosocial well-being. Desire for these declines once you have them, and you don't think about them unless you lack them. He called the other three **growth needs.** They include the need for knowing, appreciating, and understanding. People try to meet these needs only after their basic needs have been met. He believed that meeting these needs created more desire for them. For example, having adequate shelter and food doesn't make you crave more shelter and food. By contrast, learning and understanding sparks the desire to learn and understand more.

Pavlov's Conditioned Responses

Ivan Pavlov, a Russian psychologist, proved through experimentation that behavior could be learned according to a system of stimulus and response. His most famous experiment conditioned dogs to salivate at the sound of a bell. He did so by noting that dogs normally salivate at the smell of food, an unconditioned (that is, innate or reflexive) response to an unconditioned stimulus. The ringing of a bell has no natural meaning for dogs. Such a signal is called a neutral stimulus. He introduced the sound of the bell at feeding time, thereby linking the sound of the bell and the smell of the food in the dogs' minds. Eventually, the dogs salivated at the sound of the bell alone, which was now a conditioned (that is, learned) response to a conditioned stimulus.

Skinner's Operant Conditioning

B. F. Skinner was a psychologist who believed that you could use a system of positive and negative reinforcements to affect voluntary behavior. He called a positive reinforcement a **reinforcing stimulus,** or **reinforcer,** and the behavior that leads to the positive reinforcement an **operant.** The classic lab scenario is that of a rat pressing a bar in a cage in order to receive food. The pressing of the bar is the operant and the food is the reinforcer. If, after a time, the operant no longer leads to positive reinforcement, the behavior will decrease, and eventually stop. That process is called **extinction.**

A **negative reinforcement** is the removal of an unpleasant stimulus after a certain desired behavior occurs. For instance, a parent wishing to reward a teenager for consistently following a 10:00 P.M. curfew might extend the curfew until 10:30 P.M.

Presentation punishment is what we normally think of as being punished for bad behavior. For instance, a teenager that violated curfew rules might be grounded.

Pavlov vs. Skinner

Pavlov and Skinner both experimented with learning behaviors. Here are some of the distinctions between them:

- Both sociopsychologists controlled natural voluntary behaviors to teach or trigger learned behaviors.
- Learning was associated with past experiences for both Pavlov and Skinner.
- Skinner focused on a cause-and-effect relationship with behavior. For example, you would give a dog a treat after a specific trained behavior like sitting. On the other hand, Pavlov linked two behaviors together, such as salivating at the sound of a dinner bell before the smell of food. In this way, Pavlov's trained behavior had a longer-lasting effect compared to Skinner's.

Bandura's Concept of Reinforcement

Albert Bandura, a psychologist, theorized that people learn behavior by watching others, trying the behavior themselves, and deciding whether the behavior is beneficial or detrimental. A positive result means that the behavior is **reinforced,** and therefore likely to be repeated. Bandura believed that peer group modeling and images from the media provided very strong suggestions for new behavior patterns. Peer group modeling is typically seen during the adolescence stage of development, and will be tested as a situation question on CSET: Multiple Subjects test.

EXTRINSIC AND INTRINSIC MOTIVATION

One important idea with respect to classroom management is **extrinsic, or external, motivation** (motivation that comes from outside factors) versus **intrinsic, or internal, motivation** (motivation that comes from within). In general, while external motivation can be used, the long-term goal is that students' motivation for learning be intrinsic. This also means that on the CSET: Multiple Subjects test, the answer choice that leads to intrinsic motivation will likely be the best answer choice.

Putting all this together means that children learn best in an environment in which they are encouraged to reach their potential, are inwardly motivated to learn, and are exposed to positive behaviors that allow learning to happen. Sounds easy, right?

Extrinsic or Intrinsic Motivations

It is important to realize how motivations can integrate with other social and motivated learned behaviors to fully understand the powers of certain motivations. Think about this: how did extrinsic or intrinsic motivations each play a role in Pavlov and Skinner's theories and experiments?

Here are important things to keep in mind.

Consistency

Whatever approach you take to classroom management, you must be consistent. Rules that aren't followed consistently cease to have any weight. There should be consistent, regular procedures for daily activities (such as putting chairs on the top of desks at the end of the day).

Structure

Students need structure and direction. Lessons or tasks should have clear, well-articulated goals. Students should always know what they're supposed to be doing at any given point during the day.

Discipline

Discipline techniques that are too harsh and autocratic run the risk of suppressing students' internal motivation. Discipline techniques that are too laissez-faire run the risk of not providing enough structure. Striking that balance is challenging, but can be made easier by establishing guidelines immediately. Guidelines should be age-appropriate. First graders can simply be told that they need to raise their hands and wait for a teacher to call on them before they can start speaking. A sixth-grade teacher might use part of the first day of school having the class as a whole decide what types of behavior should be prohibited, and what consequences should arise from prohibited behavior.

Inappropriate behavior should be dealt with immediately, consistently, and in a manner that does not unwittingly provide positive reinforcement. For instance, a verbal reprimand should occur out of earshot from the rest of the class. A troublemaker who craves attention will continue to act out if the teacher gives him/her attention for each inappropriate behavior. For the student, the teacher's attention is positive reinforcement.

Time on Task

It's easy to lose the forest for the trees, but remember that students are there to learn. Structure and discipline serve to make sure there's as much time as possible available for actual learning.

Transitions

Procedures should be in place for getting students from one task to another in an efficient manner. Suggestions include agreed-upon signals such as flipping the lights on and off or clapping your hands.

CREATIVE THINKING VS. CRITICAL THINKING

Good teachers promote both **critical** and **creative thinking** in their students. The difference between the two might best be described by thinking about the following questions:

- How many different ways can you think of to get from New York to San Francisco?
- What's the best way to get from New York to San Francisco?

Answering the first question involves creative thinking. Answering the second involves critical thinking. Let's compare the two.

Creative Thinking

The first question involves **divergent thinking**—there are many possible answers, and no particular answer is necessarily right or wrong. One technique that a good teacher can use to help with questions such as these is **brainstorming,** in which students are encouraged to come up with as many solutions as possible without stopping to evaluate their merits. Imagine posing the question to a group of active sixth graders. At first, you'd probably get some relatively predictable responses that you'd write down as the students came up with them:

- You could fly; you could drive; you could take a train.

Then, you could start to expect some more "outside the box" ideas:

- You could bike; you could run; you could walk; you could take a boat around the tip of South America and come back up the other side.

And some with less critical thought behind them:

- You could hitchhike. How about a hot air balloon? You could drive to Florida and take the space shuttle. You could wrap yourself up and have yourself FedExed. Could you dig a tunnel?

And after a while the responses would taper off, and you'd be left with a large list of possibilities on the board.

You should be familiar with two other important ideas regarding creative thinking:

- **Restructuring** is a term that describes the process of thinking about an old problem in a new way. Many educational psychologists believe that time away from the problem is an important element that encourages restructuring—some believe that dreaming is also an important component.
- Also, **play** encourages creative thinking, and good teachers use well-designed in-class games for this purpose.

Critical Thinking

Let's go back to the results of the brainstorming exercise. There's a large list of possibilities on the board, and you're now ready to ask the second question:

What's the best way of getting from New York to San Francisco?

This question requires **convergent thinking**—from many possible answers the student is expected to choose and defend the best one. A good teacher will use this opportunity to show how the answer to this question depends on the criteria used. Does "best" mean "cheapest"? If so, then hitchhiking might be a good choice, but you'd have to factor in the cost of food and shelter, because the trip would take longer than it would if you flew. Does "best" mean "quickest"? If so, then flying is probably the best way to go. A good teacher would also seize the opportunity to allow for **transfer,** the application of previously learned skills or facts to new situations. For example, if the class had recently completed a unit on the environment, the teacher could ask, "What if 'best' means 'most environmentally friendly,' but you have to get there within three days?"

Two important aspects of critical thinking are inductive and deductive reasoning.

Inductive Reasoning

Inductive reasoning occurs when, after viewing several examples, students perceive underlying rules or patterns. For example, students could be given many different parallelograms, and asked what they all have in common. Through measurement and comparison, students might induce that opposite sides of parallelograms are parallel, and that the sum of any two adjacent angles in a parallelogram is 180 degrees.

Deductive Reasoning

Deductive reasoning works in the opposite direction. For example, students might be told that if the sum of any two adjacent angles in a given quadrilateral is 180 degrees, then that quadrilateral is a parallelogram. Then, they'd be given many quadrilaterals, and asked to determine which ones are parallelograms. Both inductive and deductive reasoning are important cognitive skills.

INSTRUCTIONAL STRATEGIES

Different teaching approaches should be taken to stimulate different types of thinking. You should know what options are available to you and which strategies are most likely to accomplish a given educational goal.

Direct Instruction

Direct instruction is the most common form of teaching, the traditional model in which the teacher stands in front of the room, presents new material, and guides the class toward understanding. You should be familiar with the following concepts.

Hunter's Effective Teaching Model and Mastery Learning

Madeline Hunter, an educational psychologist, expanded on the basic idea of direct instruction and broke the process down into discrete steps:

1. Prepare students to learn:
   - Review the previous day's material with a question or two.
   - Get the students' attention with an **anticipatory set,** a question or problem designed to spark students' curiosity and imagination.
   - Outline the lesson's objectives.
2. Use input and modeling:
   - Teach well.
   - Organize your presentation.
   - Present the information clearly.
   - Connect new ideas to old ideas.
   - Use examples and analogies. (The Common Core curriculum tested will focus mostly on actual or historical examples rather than hypothetical.)
   - Demonstrate and model new techniques.
3. Make sure students understand. Ask both individual and group questions.
   - Have students apply new techniques immediately.
   - Work several short examples—**guided practice.**
   - Monitor student ability—**independent practice.**

> Hunter's teaching model incorporates many of the learning and conditioning theories previously presented in this chapter. Can you identify which ones are used in each of the three steps of Hunter's teaching model?
>
> Step 1: Thorndike's Law of Readiness
> Step 2: Bandura's Concept of Reinforcement
> Step 3: Thorndike's Law of Exercise

Ausubel's Advance Organizers

David Ausubel's theory expands on some aspects of Hunter's model. **Advance organizers** are the structure (also known as **scaffolding** or **support**) and information that students will need to learn new material effectively. They fall into two categories:

1. A **comparative organizer** relates previously mastered material to the material that's about to be presented. For example, a middle-school lesson about sonnet form might begin with a comparative advance organizer that reminds students of a previous lesson on iambic pentameter or simple ABAB rhyme schemes.
2. An **expository organizer** is a new idea or concept that needs to be understood before a specific lesson can be understood. For example, a high-school literature class already familiar with rhyme schemes might need an expository advance organizer that discussed the purpose of analyzing poetry and showing that rhyme scheme analysis is just one method of doing so.

Demonstrations

Visual learners in particular respond well to **demonstrations.** Showing is more effective than simply telling. New computer technology allows for imaginative and compelling demonstrations. Good teachers take advantage of all tools at their disposal.

Mnemonics

Provide students with memory devices to help them retain factual information. For instance, "Please excuse my dear Aunt Sally" is a common **mnemonic** for the order of mathematical operations: parentheses, exponents, multiplication, division, addition, and subtraction. We have seen quite a few mnemonics throughout this book.

Note-Taking

Students need to be taught how to take notes effectively. One important technique involves giving students a general outline of the major points to be discussed and having them fill in the blanks as the lesson progresses.

Outlining

A clear order of presentation with a well-defined hierarchy of ideas is crucial so that students have an understanding of what the most important parts of a lesson are.

Use of Visual Aids

As with demonstrations, visual aids can make new information stick in students' minds better than it would if it were presented through lecture alone.

Student-Centered Models

In contrast to direct instruction, **student-centered models** make students, not teachers, the center of attention while new material is being learned. These methods do not lessen the demands on the teacher; in fact, use of student-centered models requires more planning and as much active participation by the teacher as does use of direct instruction. Here are some important student-centered models.

Emergent Curriculum

In **emergent curriculum,** students are given a strong voice in deciding what form the curriculum will take. For instance, students could decide that they were interested in studying leaves. It would then be incumbent upon the teacher to find useful leaf-related activities and experiments that would meet established educational goals. Alternatively, the teacher could present a variety of possible topics, and the students could choose which they wanted to study.

Cooperative Learning

In **cooperative learning,** students are split into mixed-ability groups, assigned well-defined tasks to accomplish or problems to analyze, and are given individual roles within the group (such as note-taker or illustrator). Students learn from each other and interact in a way that is not possible with direct instruction. One well-known method of organizing cooperative learning in the classroom is called **STAD (student teams achievement divisions)** in which cooperative learning cycles through the following stages:

1. teaching, in which the teacher presents basic material and gives teams a task;
2. team study, in which students work on the project;
3. test, in which students take individual quizzes; and
4. team recognition, in which the best-performing teams are rewarded.

In another model, called the **think-pair-share method,** students research a topic on their own, discuss their theories and ideas with one other student, and then participate in a classroom discussion.

Discovery Learning

Discovery learning is closely aligned with inductive reasoning. Students are given examples and are expected to find patterns and connections with minimal guidance from a teacher during class. Students are encouraged to use **intuitive thinking,** and then make an effort to prove or disprove their intuition given the available information.

Concept Models

Concept models are part of an organizational strategy that helps students to relate new ideas to old ideas. There are three aspects that you should be familiar with:

- **Concept development.** The concept is promoted by the identification of a prototype, or stereotypical example of the concept. For example, if the concept is polygons, a prototype might be a square or a triangle. From the prototype, students generate the definition, in this case, a closed plane figure with a finite number of straight-line sides.
- **Concept attainment.** Students learn to identify examples (pentagons, right triangles) and non-examples (circles, open figures) and sub-define the category according to given criteria (a rectangle is a special polygon having four sides and four equal angles).
- **Concept mapping or webbing.** Students draw a pictorial representation of the concepts or ideas about some topic and the links between them. Teachers can look over these maps and discern areas of misunderstanding. There are several different types of methods that currently go by names like **concept mapping, mental mapping,** and **concept webbing.**

Inquiry Method

The **inquiry method** is related to discovery learning. A teacher poses a question, and the students have to gather information and then formulate and test hypotheses in order to answer it. Although this method could conceivably be used in teaching almost any discipline, it's particularly well-suited to teaching science and math. For instance, a teacher could pose the question "Do all triangles have 180 degrees?" Students could then try to find different ways of proving or disproving the statement (drawing triangles, measuring the angles, and adding them up; comparing the degree measures to a straight line; and so on), and eventually conclude that yes, all triangles have 180 degrees.

Metacognition

Teachers can also encourage students to think about their own learning processes. This is called **metacognition.** For example, a teacher might assign a journal assignment in which students would answer the questions "What did I learn today?" and "How did it relate to things I've learned earlier?"

QUESTIONING

Good teachers ask good questions that encourage different kinds of thinking in students. Use Bloom's Taxonomy as a sorting mechanism for different types of questions.

In addition to asking good questions, teachers should also be aware that how questions are asked can have a large impact on student learning. You should be familiar with the following concepts.

Frequency

Frequency simply refers to the number of questions you ask. Socrates notwithstanding, if everything you say is a question, it's difficult for students to learn. On the other hand, nothing is duller than a lecture with no questions. Strike a balance and use questions well to enhance learning.

Equitable Distribution

Call on individual students to ensure that all students are participating. Gear specific questions to specific students, ensuring that a question will be challenging for a given student, but will be something the student has a good chance of answering correctly.

Cueing

Cueing is further prompting by the teacher after the initial question is met with silence or an incorrect or partially correct response. For a rote-memory sort of question such as "What's the capital of Kansas?" a teacher might cue with a reference to a previously learned mnemonic such as "Remember: 'Everyone in Kansas wears sandals, so...,'" thereby eliciting the student response of "Topeka!" More complicated questions could require more extensive cueing.

Wait-Time

Wait-time is the amount of time a teacher waits for a response after asking a question. Students need time to process the question, think of the answer, and formulate a response. A wait-time of three to five seconds is shown to have a strong positive impact on student learning.

Further, a good teacher can use questioning as a mechanism to support classroom management techniques. One common technique is called **group alerting**, in which the teacher asks the whole class the question, waits, and then selects one student to answer. Naming the student before the question is asked increases the likelihood that the other students will stop paying attention.

Ms. Barabian finds that her fourth-grade class loses focus when she switches from subject to subject. Which of the following techniques would help Ms. Barabian manage her class more effectively?

A.   modeling

B.   guided practice

C.   transitions

D.   assertive discipline

Here's How to Crack It

This is really a common sense question. You know that (A) and (B) are teaching techniques, but the question is looking for a classroom management technique. You're left with two choices, and in this case, the easiest way to determine the right answer is to look for key words within the question. The phrase *switches from subject to subject* tells you that the problem Ms. Barabian is having relates to (C), transitions.

PLANNING INSTRUCTION

How does a teacher decide what to teach? Ideally, teachers have long-term and short-term objectives for their students. It's important that these objectives are well-defined, because planning instruction and assessment is easier and more meaningful if goals are clearly specified.

There are two fundamental approaches to defining objectives. Good teachers apply both.

Teaching Objectives

Teaching objectives are defined in general terms. A cognitive objective might be, "Students will understand the hierarchical relationships among the different types of quadrilaterals." The advantage to a teaching objective is that it's general enough to encompass a wide variety of teaching approaches and techniques. The disadvantage is that it's difficult to measure student understanding of any given concept in all its various forms. Could you write a test that would measure whether students understood all "the hierarchical relationships among the different types of quadrilaterals"?

Learning Objectives

Learning objectives are defined in concrete terms, and can be directly observed. Students are expected to exhibit the desired behavior at the end of the lesson(s). For example, "Students will be able to construct a perfect square of a given length using a compass and straightedge." These goals are easy to assess—you can simply watch a student perform the construction—but their specificity makes it difficult to include large-scale concepts. For instance, imagine how long the list of learning objectives would be to describe the body of knowledge and skills covered in the first semester of a geometry class.

The type of objective a teacher will use depends on the plan he/she is creating. A daily lesson plan will require learning objectives; a unit or monthly plan will include teaching objectives. Here's an example:

Type of Lesson	Type of Objective	Example of Objective
Unit lesson plan	Teaching objective	Students will understand the hierarchical relationships among the different types of quadrilaterals.
Daily lesson plan	Learning objectives	Students will recite the definition of a quadrilateral. Students will be able to demonstrate the hierarchical distinction between squares and rectangles. Students will be able to prove that every rhombus is a parallelogram.

ASSESSMENT STRATEGIES

Just as you'd use different teaching strategies to teach different ideas, you should use different assessment strategies to measure student achievement. Here are some terms you should be familiar with.

Norm-Referenced Tests

If you've ever been graded on a curve, then you've experienced a **norm-referenced test.** That means that your grade depended on how well you did compared to everyone else who took the test.

Criterion-Referenced Tests

Your driver's license test was probably a **criterion-referenced test.** Perhaps there were 25 questions, and you needed to answer 20 of them correctly in order to pass. It didn't matter how many people had aced the test and how many people had answered only 10 questions correctly. You needed to prove a certain proficiency in order to pass.

Standardized Tests

If you're reading this book, then we probably have a pretty good idea about what you think of **standardized tests.** The term *standardized* means that test content, conditions, grading, and reporting are equivalent for everyone who takes the test. We tend to think of them as purely multiple-choice, but that's not true.

- Most standardized tests given are **achievement tests,** administered to measure specific knowledge in a specific area.
- **Aptitude tests** purport to measure how well a student is likely to do in the future.

Remember, of course, that you don't have to give standardized tests to your students. You have a much wider range of options, including the following.

Assessments of Prior Knowledge/Pretesting

It's important to take into account the level of knowledge a student had before beginning a given lesson or semester. Would it be fair to hold a recent immigrant to the same standards as a native English speaker on an oral grammar test? Probably not. Some curricula are designed so that a specific set of knowledge and skills is necessary before instruction in a new area can occur. Such a set of knowledge and skills is called a **prerequisite competency.**

Structured Observations

These are particularly well-suited to situations in which cooperative learning is taking place. The teacher can observe the interactions within a group and evaluate student performance accordingly. This is an example of an **informal assessment,** meaning that there is no grading rubric or checklist that a teacher follows. An informal assessment is more subjective and situation-specific than it is during a **formal assessment** such as a standardized test.

Student Responses During a Lesson

This shouldn't necessarily be considered the same as grading on class participation, but a teacher can get a strong sense of student understanding (or lack thereof) based on responses during classroom discussions. This is another example of an informal assessment.

Portfolios

Portfolios aren't just used in art classes. They're are often used to give students a place to collect their best work over a longer period of time, such as a unit or even a semester. Teachers can get a sense of the level of student work holistically, without placing undue influence on a specific test. Portfolios allow teachers to assess learning growth over a period of time.

Essays Written to Prompts

While these take longer to grade, and depend upon students possessing sufficient writing skills, essays give insight into student thought in a way that multiple-choice tests cannot.

Journals

Many good teachers use **journals** not only as tools to promote individual self-expression, but also to gauge understanding.

Self-Evaluation

Sometimes, a good teacher will give students an opportunity to grade their own work. While it's not usually binding, the grade a student chooses to give himself (along with the explanation of why it's deserved) can provide the teacher valuable insight.

KEY TERMS

Jean Piaget
cognitive development
framework (schema)
assimilation
adaptation
sensorimotor stage
object permanence
goal-oriented behavior
preoperational stage
egocentrism
concrete operational stage
reversibility (reverse logic)
transitivity
seriation
conservation
class inclusion
formal operational stage
hypothetical-deductive
  reasoning
Lev Vygotsky
environment
culture
private speech
zone of proximal
  development
scaffolding
constructivism
Bloom's taxonomy
affective domain
psychomotor domain
Erik Erikson's stages of
  psychosocial development
Mildred Parten's stages
  of play development
Lawrence Kohlberg's
  stage theory of moral
  reasoning
Heinz Dilemma
Howard Gardner's
  multiple intelligences
secure attachment
insecure ambivalent
  attachment
insecure avoidant attachment
logical-mathematical
  intelligence
linguistic intelligence

musical intelligence
spatial intelligence
naturalist intelligence
bodily-kinesthetic
  intelligence
interpersonal intelligence
intrapersonal intelligence
existential intelligence
visual learners
auditory learners
kinesthetic learners
genetic factors
environmental factors
5 stages of physical
  development
fine motor skills
gross motor skills
Edward Lee Thorndike's
  laws
Abraham Maslow's
  hierarchy of needs
deficiency needs
growth needs
Ivan Pavlov's conditioned
  responses
B. F. Skinner's operant
  conditioning
reinforcing stimulus
  (reinforcer)
operant
extinction
negative reinforcement
presentation punishment
Albert Bandura's concept
  of reinforcement
extrinsic (external)
  motivation
intrinsic (internal)
  motivation
critical thinking
creative thinking
divergent thinking
brainstorming
restructuring
play
convergent thinking
transfer

inductive reasoning
deductive reasoning
direct instruction
Madeline Hunter's
  effective teaching model
  and mastery learning
anticipatory set
guided practice
independent practice
David Ausubel's advance
  organizers
scaffolding (support)
comparative organizer
expository organizer
demonstrations
mnemonics
student-centered models
emergent curriculum
cooperative learning
STAD (student teams
  achievement divisions)
think-pair-share method
discovery learning
intuitive thinking
concept models
concept mapping
  (concept webbing,
  mental mapping)
inquiry method
metacognition
frequency of questions
cueing
wait-time
group alerting
teaching objectives
learning objectives
norm-referenced tests
criterion-referenced tests
standardized tests
achievement tests
aptitude tests
prerequisite competency
informal assessment
formal assessment
portfolios
journals

Chapter 19 Drill

Answers and explanations can be found in the final section of this book, beginning on page 617.

1. Jean Piaget stated a theory of four stages of cognitive development in young children. Which stage is most associated with a fourth-grade student whose thinking becomes organized and logical?

   A. sensorimotor

   B. preoperational

   C. concrete operational

   D. formal operational

2. Students in third grade are given a spelling test. The skills measured in this test are aligned with what stage in Bloom's taxonomy of learning?

   A. knowledge

   B. comprehension

   C. synthesis

   D. evaluation

3. Mr. Meyer's 10th grade students are speaking out of turn in class, and it is disruptive. Mr. Meyer separates the students with assigned seating, and the class becomes more focused.

   Mr. Meyer appropriately identified Erikson's psychosocial development stage and addressed the issue. What stage are these students exhibiting?

   A. industry vs. inferiority

   B. identity vs. role confusion

   C. intimacy vs. isolation

   D. initiative vs. guilt

4. After presenting a lecture on the human circulatory system, Ms. Burns demonstrated how blood travels toward and away from the heart. Ms. Burns is in what stage of Madeline Hunter's effective teaching model?

   A. anticipatory set

   B. input

   C. modeling

   D. guided practice

5. A first-grade class plays at recess and one of their favorite games is tag. This is an example of:

   A. just-for-fun play that doesn't impact development.

   B. a distraction from learning.

   C. practicing gross motor developments through play.

   D. following rules in games.

6. Ms. Wylan catches a student helping a classmate on a test. When she asks the student why he was helping the other student, the student responds that the other student would bring him cookies.

   This student is in which stage of moral development?

   A. punishment and obedience

   B. instrumental relativist

   C. good boy-good girl

   D. law and order

7. A student has trouble reading out loud and always struggles with spelling tests. However, the same student doesn't seem to have the same issue with math problems.

   Why could the student be struggling?

   A. The student doesn't practice enough reading at home with their family.

   B. The student doesn't speak English.

   C. The student is just trying to be disruptive in class.

   D. The student is dyslexic and has trouble reading because he/she sees letters backwards.

Summary

- For the CSET, you should know a few theories of cognitive development: Jean Piaget, Lev Vygotsky, and Bloom's taxonomy.

- Social development is extremely important. You should be familiar with theories from Erik Erickson, Mildred Parten, and Lawrence Kohlberg.

- There are many types of intelligence, according to Howard Gardner's list of eight types of intelligence.

- As a teacher, you should also be aware that your students will have different learning styles.

- You should be familiar with major theorists of student motivation and the learning environment: Edward Lee Thorndike, Ivan Pavlov, Abraham Maslow, B.F. Skinner, and Albert Bandura.

- Teachers should promote both critical and creative thinking in their students.

- There are many different instructional strategies that can be used to stimulate different types of thinking in students.

- When planning instruction and assessment, teachers should think about both teaching objectives and learning objectives.

- Many different types of assessment strategies can be used, including norm-referenced tests, criterion-referenced tests, standardized tests, pretesting, journals, self-evaluation, and more.

Chapter 20
Visual and
Performing Arts

IS THAT PAINT-BY-NUMBER?

The painting reproduced above depicts:

A. an ancient game of tag.

B. an unfortunate Superglue incident.

C. the earliest known experiment with static electricity.

D. the creation of Adam.

ART IMITATES LIFE

A comprehensive arts program in schools includes four disciplines: dance, music, theater, and the visual arts. For each grade level, the standards are grouped under five strands.

Artistic Perception

Artistic perception, the first of the five strands, refers to the way students learn to respond to, process, and analyze sensory information. They learn and use the vocabulary and skills unique to each of the disciplines.

Creative Expression

In **creative expression,** students are expected to participate and perform. They learn to create their own works, using a variety of means to communicate intent and meaning, and apply processes and skills in composing, arranging, and performing their works.

Historical and Cultural Context

Students analyze the function and development of an artistic medium in past and present cultures throughout the world.

Aesthetic Valuing

Through the process of **aesthetic valuing,** students analyze, interpret, derive meaning from, and critique works in each discipline, including works of their own creation.

Connections, Relationships, and Applications

The final strand is called **connections, relationships,** and **applications.** Students connect and apply what they learn in each discipline to other arts disciplines and to other subject areas. They learn about careers in and related to arts disciplines.

DANCE

Elements of Dance

While ballet and breakdancing may not appear to be similar, they have more in common than you might think. All dance is based on the same basic elements.

Space

Space in dance refers to the area covered by movements.

- level: the distance from the floor
- directions: up, down, forward, backward, and so on
- shape: the "design" of the body
- pathways: patterns made by the body as it moves
- relationship: with whom or what the body is moving

Time

Time has several designations.

- duration: the length of time the movement takes
- tempo: the speed of the dance
- beat: even or uneven

Force

Force, or **dynamics,** implies there is a spectrum or gradation in the action performed. A heavy action requires more force than a light action, and a sharp action requires differing force than a smooth action. All motions can be placed on a spectrum between opposite types of movement by varying degree's of force.

Form

The structural organization of the work is called **form.** All elements of Force, Time, and Space are organized by the form of the work.

Dance Techniques

Each style or genre of dance has its own specific techniques, or physical skills required to perform the movements and steps. Of course, many skills overlap between genres. Basic techniques include the following:

- balance
- weight shift
- alignment
- patterns
- mirroring
- positioning
- extension

While teachers should try to incorporate as many different styles of dance as possible, some genres are taught most frequently to children, in part because of the basic movement skills utilized. Those genres include ballet, line dancing, jazz, tap, folk dancing, modern dance, and ballroom dancing.

Cultural and Historical Context

You should be familiar with types of dances developed in different historical eras and geographical settings, and purposes of dance in various cultures.

Purpose

These are some examples of how dance is used:

- ceremonies and celebrations: Native American, Japanese, Greek
- artistry: Japanese, Russian, Mexican
- communication: African, Chinese, Indian
- recreation: American, Spanish

Origins

Here are some of the historical and geographical origins of the more well-known forms of dance:

- ballet: Renaissance Italy and France
- jazz: early- to mid-20th-century African Americans
- tap: based on Irish step dancing, African drum rhythms, and English clog dance; popularized during the Vaudeville Era
- flamenco: Spanish gypsies, strongly influenced by Indian and colonial African dance
- tango: Argentina, developed centuries ago but modernized and popularized in the early- to mid-20th century
- waltz: 17th-century Austria
- modern dance: early 20th-century North America and Germany

Important Terms and People

People

Twyla Tharp (b. 1941)—American dancer and choreographer who started her own dance company that blends the use of classical, jazz, and contemporary pop music.

Bob Fosse (1927–1987)—American dancer, musical theater choreographer, director, screenwriter, and actor known in choreography for the "Fosse Amoeba" (sideways shuffling, rolled shoulders, and jazz hands).

Martha Graham (1894–1991)—American modern dancer and choreographer. Her style, the Graham Method, reshaped American dance and is still taught worldwide.

George Balanchine (1904–1983)—American choreographer who was known for his expressiveness and musicality, creating his signature "neoclassical" style.

Vaslav Nijinsky (1889–1950)—Russian dancer and choreographer celebrated for his virtuosity and for the depth and intensity of his characters.

Terms and Technique

Pas de deux—a dance for two people, typically a man and a woman.

Plié—a movement in which a dancer bends the knees and straightens them again.

Promenade—a movement in which couples follow one another in given directions, each couple with both hands joined.

Relevé—a movement—a ballet technique and training system by Russian dancer Agrippina Vaganova. This technique was used throughout the late 19th century.

Fox-Trot—a ballroom dance in 4/4 time with alternation of two slow and to two quick steps.

Waltz—a dance in triple time performed by a couple who as a pair turn rhythmically around as they progress around the dance floor.

Cha-Cha—a ballroom dance with small steps and swaying hip movements, performed to a Latin American rhythm.

Swing—a style of dance with an easy flowing but vigorous rhythm.

Horton Technique—a technique used in the 1920s–1940s based on Native American dances by choreographer Lester Horton.

Limon Technique—a technique developed by Doris Humphrey and Charles Weidman, which is based upon the movement style and philosophy of theater.

Which of the following dances allows a dancer the widest range of levels?

A. tap

B. ballet

C. cha-cha

D. line dancing

Here's How to Crack It

Level in dancing refers to how high or low a dancer is in relation to the floor. To help you determine the answer, pull up a mental video of each of the types of dances. Tap dancing, (A), cha-cha, (C), and line dancing, (D), are all generally performed in an upright position, with some bending at the knees and waist. On the other hand, it is entirely common to see a ballet dancer lying on the floor or leaping high in the air, which is how you know that ballet, (B), is the best answer choice.

Here's an example of a constructed-response question on this topic.

—————————————○—————————————

Complete the exercise that follows:

> Choose a style of dance;
>
> Name and define two specific criteria that could be used to assess the quality of a dance performance in that style;
>
> Discuss how a teacher would prepare a lesson using these criteria to have students create, develop, and memorize patterns and sequences.

Here's How to Crack It

Pick the style of dance you know best! We will use ballet for this example. Two elements that could be identified to use as judging criteria are extension and posture. For both, quality could be defined by the fullest extension, straight line, or clean angles of the body. To use these elements in a lesson plan, one solution is to have students work in pairs and improvise body movements requiring involvement of posture and extension. One student makes a motion extending one part of the body, and the other copies and adds. With each turn, the motions are repeated and added upon until the pattern is forgotten.

—————————————○—————————————

MUSIC

Elements of Music

There are seven basic elements of music.

Rhythm

Rhythm is the duration of sound, or how long or short the notes are. There are three parts to rhythm:

- **beat**: the pulse; a rhythmic unit of time
- **tempo**: the speed of the beat
- **meter**: the organization of strong and weak beats; indicated by measures and time signatures

Melody

Melody refers to a tune created by playing a series of notes.

Harmony

Harmony is the combination of two or more pitches. There are two types of harmony:

- **Consonance**: a combination of two or more pitches that are harmonious (they sound pleasing)
- **Dissonance**: a combination of two or more pitches that are not harmonious (they don't sound pleasing)

Timbre

Timbre is the quality of sound that distinguishes one instrument or voice from another. It is also referred to as *tone color*.

Form

Form is the structure of music. There are four basic forms:

- **Binary form**, or AB form: two melodies—Melody A followed by Melody B
- **Ternary form**, or ABA form: two melodies—Melody A, then Melody B, back to Melody A
- **Theme and variation**: presentation of a melody, and repeats of melody with variations
- **Popular song**, or AABA form: verse-chorus, verse-chorus, bridge-chorus, verse-chorus

Texture

Texture is the overall quality of sound of a piece, most often indicated by the number of layers of voices. There are three types of texture:

- **Monophonic**: one melody on the same pitch and same rhythm
- **Homophonic**: one melody in harmony on the same rhythm
- **Polyphonic**: two or more melodies in different pitch or rhythm at the same time

Density is also an aspect of texture and refers to the number of instruments playing.

Dynamics

Dynamics are symbols or abbreviations used to indicate the volume of, or change of volume within, a piece of music. Examples of dynamic signs include the following:

- *p* : *piano* (soft)

- *f* : *forte* (loud)

- > : *decrescendo* (gradually softer)

Musical Notation

The CSET will ask you some questions that require you to read and interpret short excerpts of sheet music, so you should be able to recognize some of the more common signs and symbols of **musical notation.**

Staff

The **staff** is the five-line foundation on which notes are written.

The **treble staff** opens on the left with a **treble clef,** which looks a little like the "and" symbol on your keyboard. From the bottom line up, the notes on the lines are named E, G, B, D, F. You can remember them with the mnemonic device "Every Good Boy Does Fine." From the bottom up, the notes in the spaces between the lines are named F, A, C, E—which lends itself to an easy mnemonic device, "FACE."

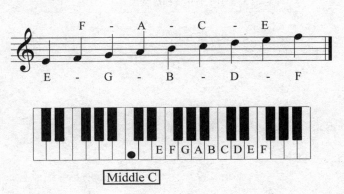

The piano keyboard below the staff shows the keys relating to the notes on the staff. "Middle C" represents the middle of the keyboard, which is the point where the treble staff and the bass staff overlap.

The **bass staff** opens with a **bass clef.** The bottom line represents G, and the lines follow the same upward order. A mnemonic device to remember the notes on the lines in the bass staff is "Good Boys Don't Fight Anyone." To remember the notes in the spaces, which start with the note A, you can use "All Cows Eat Grass."

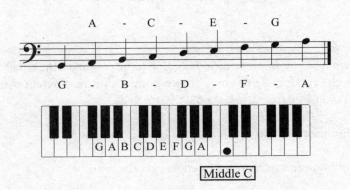

The **grand staff** is what you'd normally see in piano music, because of the range of pitches on that instrument. It is a combination of the treble staff (top) and the bass staff (bottom). The note "C" above the bass staff and the "C" below the treble sound the same and the point where the bass clef and treble clef transfer.

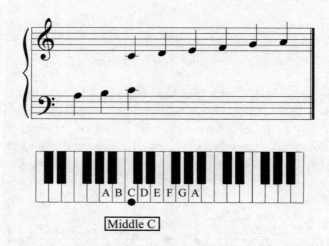

Notes
Musical notes represent the length of beats.

- ○ Whole note

- ♩ Half note

- ♩ Quarter note

- ♪ Eighth note

- ♪ Sixteenth note

These different durations are divisions of one another. For instance, one whole note equals two half notes, two half notes equal four quarter notes, etc. The name half note or sixteenth could be thought of as a fraction of a whole note, the half note being half the length of a whole note, and likewise the sixteenth being one-sixteenth of a whole note.

Time Signatures
The **time signature** tells you how the music is going to be counted. The time signature appears to the right of the clef and key signature. The two numbers mean different things to the length of a measure, a straight line that divides the staff into cells.

The top number refers to the number of beats per measure.

The bottom number refers to which note gets the beat.

The same notes from above will be represented as a number and represent the lower number in the time signature. For instance, 1 for whole note, 2 for half note, 4 for quarter note, 8 for eighth note, 16 for sixteenth note. Any note can be divided into multiple notes: one whole note equals two half notes, two half notes equal four quarter notes, etc.

- 𝅝 = 1

- 𝅗𝅥 = 2

- 𝅘𝅥 = 4

- 𝅘𝅥𝅮 = 8

- 𝅘𝅥𝅯 = 16

Examples:

Four beats in a measure.
The quarter note gets the beat.

Six beats in a measure.
The eighth note gets the beat.

Key Signature

The **key signature** is a set of either sharp symbols, which look like tilted number signs (#), or flat symbols, which look like pointed b's (♭), located just after the clef on a musical staff. It tells you which notes will be sharp or flat throughout the piece. The number of sharps or flats gives you the **key** of the melody or work.

A note that is **sharp** is raised from its note name, while a note that is **flat** is lowered from its note name. When looking at the keyboard graphic previously, a sharp or flat would move one key in the direction needed, even if that means a black key between two white keys.

The Circle of Fifths

The **circle of fifths** is a theoretical tool for understanding key signatures relationships; a key signature always represents both a major and minor key. Below, the chart has capital letters on the outside of the circle representing the major key, and lowercase on the inner circle representing minor keys.

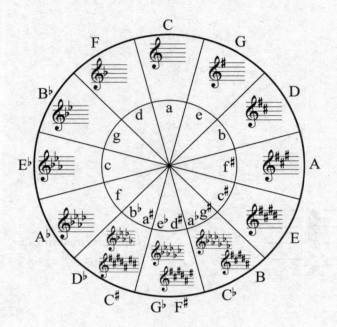

There is a little trick to figuring out a key signature's name. When confronted with a major key signature that consists of flats, look at the flat second from the far right. This flat is on the line or space the key signature is named after. One flat is F, since you can't go to the next-to-last flat. To find the name of a major key signature with sharps, look at the sharp farthest to the right. The key signature is the note a half step above, or one piano key up from, that last sharp. No flats and no sharps indicates the key of C major or a minor. To determine the name of a minor key, find the name of the key in major and then count backwards three half steps, or three piano keys. Remember that sharps and flats affect names.

Musical Instruments

In its broadest definition, a musical instrument is considered to be any device used to produce sound. Instruments can be broken into four categories: woodwind, brass, string, and percussion.

Woodwind Instruments

Woodwind instruments produce sound when air is blown against an edge or opening in the instrument, usually past a thin piece of wood called a reed, causing the air to vibrate. Woodwinds include:

- flute
- clarinet
- saxophone
- oboe
- bassoon

Brass Instruments

With **brass instruments**, tone is produced by the vibration of the lips, and valves or a slide are used to change the pitch. Brass instruments include:

- french horn
- trumpet
- trombone
- tuba

String Instruments

String instruments produce tone by vibrating taut strings. While percussive and plucked techniques may be used, string instruments primarily use bows as their main mode of sounding. String instruments include:

- violin
- viola
- cello
- double bass

Percussion Instruments

Percussion instruments are sounded by striking, plucking, shaking, or scraping with hands or another apparatus. Percussion instruments fall into one of three categories: unpitched, pitched, or keyboard.

An **unpitched percussion** instrument is played by striking the instrument with your hands, stick, or mallet as to produce sounds of indeterminate pitch. Examples of unpitched percussion are the snare drum, bass drum, cymbal, tam-tam, and maracas.

A **pitched percussion** instrument is played by striking the instrument with your hands, stick, or mallet to produce pitched sounds. To do achieve this, the percussion instrument will have multiple surfaces of different sizes, or multiple instruments that look similar but are various sizes. While often characterized as a string instrument, a guitar is characterized as a pitched percussion instrument because the initiation of sound occurs from the fingers. Other examples of pitched percussion include timpani, gongs, and temple blocks.

Keyboard instruments are played by hands or mallets typically in order to produce pitched sounds. It is possible keyboard instruments will be lumped into the pitched percussion category at times, as they both require a similar method to produce pitch. However, keyboard instruments pitched "keys" will typically be laid out like a piano, or very similarly. Examples of keyboard instruments are piano, marimba, crotales, xylophone, and tubular bells.

Origins

Beyond the classifications, you should be familiar with the historical and cultural origins of musical instruments, such as the ones listed below.

- Drums: dating back to 5,000–6,000 BCE in many parts of the world
- Piano: developed from the clavichord and harpsichord, and perfected in Italy, Germany, and Austria during the early 1700s
- Guitar: based on early Egyptian and Mesopotamian stringed instruments; the modern version first appeared in 16th-century Italy and Spain
- Flute: earliest known version traced to China, approximately 900 BCE; popularized in Western Europe in the early 15th century
- Violin: originated in Italy in the early 1500s
- Harmonica: 19th-century Germany
- Trumpet: originally used as a signaling device in ancient Greece, Egypt, and parts of Asia; first used as a musical instrument in 16th-century Germany
- Tambourine: can be traced back to its use in festivals and processions by civilizations in many parts of the world, including Ancient Egypt, Greece, and Rome; China; Eastern Europe; and Native Americans in Canada; popularized in Western Europe in the mid-18th century
- Saxophone: mid-18th-century Belgium

Important Terms and People

People

Giovanni Pierluigi da Palestrina (c. 1525–1594): Italian Renaissance composer of sacred music, and known for establishing the guidelines for modern counterpoint. Works: *Stabat Mater, Missa Papae Marcelli.*

Antonio Vivaldi (1678–1741): Italian Baroque composer and virtuoso violinist. Works: *The Four Seasons.*

Johann Sebastion Bach (1685–1750): German Baroque composer who established a tonal system (chordal system) and the guidelines for four-part harmony used today. Works: *Brandenburg Concerto, Mass in B minor.*

Wolfgang Amadeus Mozart (1756–1791): Austrian Classical composer and child prodigy who expanded the forms and harmonic language from the Baroque period. Works: *The Marriage of Figaro, Don Giovanni, The Magic Flute.*

Ludwig Van Beethoven (1770–1827): German Classical and Romantic composer who expanded the harmonic language and championed the symphony. Works: *Symphony No. 5, Moonlight Sonata.*

Pyotr Ilych Tchaikovsky (1840–1893): Russian Romantic composer who pushed harmony further including modulations to new keys and playing with different time signatures. Works: *The Nutcracker Suite, 1812 Overture, Swan Lake.*

Terms and Techniques

Allegro: moderately fast

Andante: walking pace

Ballet: a music form progressed from simply a complement to dance, to a concrete compositional form that often had as much value as the dance that went along with it

Concerto: a musical composition for a solo instrument or instruments accompanied by an orchestra

Counterpoint: the art or technique of setting, writing, or playing a melody or melodies in conjunction with another

Fugue: a composition in which a short melody or phrase is introduced by one part and successively taken up by others and developed

Homophony: music in which the voices or instruments sing or play chords

Lento: slowly

Mass: a form of sacred musical composition; a choral composition that sets the invariable portions of the Eucharistic liturgy to music

Moderato: moderate

Monophony: music with a single "part" or a single vocal melody

Opera: a form of theater in which music has a leading role and the parts are taken by singers. The music and performance is staged as a full theatrical performance.

Ostinato: a continually repeated musical phrase or rhythm

Pedal: a sustained, unchanging tone that remains when chords change

Plainsong: unaccompanied church music sung in unison in medieval modes and in free rhythm

Polyphony: music that combines a number of parts, each forming an individual melody and harmonizing with each other

Sonata: a composition for an instrumental soloist, often with a piano accompaniment, typically in several movements with one or more in sonata form

Symphony: an elaborate musical composition for full orchestra, typically in four movements, at least one of which is traditionally in sonata form

---

Which of the following is a woodwind instrument?

A. bassoon

B. timpani

C. cello

D. tuba

Here's How to Crack It

Narrow down the answer choices based on what you know. A woodwind instrument produces sound when the player blows air through a thin opening in the instrument, causing the air to vibrate. Based on that, you can eliminate (B), the timpani, which is a type of kettle drum, and (C), the cello, which is a large string instrument. You're left with two wind instruments, and you know one of them has to be a brass instrument. One of the defining characteristics of a brass instrument is the use of buzzing lips to produce sound; the tuba, (D), uses buzzing lips, so you can rule it out. The correct answer is (A), the bassoon, which we also know because it uses a reed.

Here is an example of a potential constructed-response assignment.

―――――――――――――――――――

Using your knowledge of vocal music, prepare a response in which you:

Describe the melody, rhythm, and form of this song;

and

Discuss one reason why this song would be appropriate for elementary school students to sing.

Twinkle Twinkle Little Star

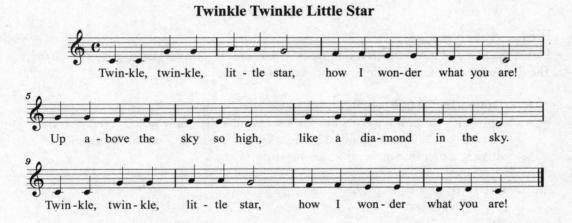

Here's How to Crack It

It is important to identify all aspects of a melody at hand, including clef, key signature, meter, rhythm, range of notes, and form (repetition and difference). The clef is identified as a treble clef. Looking at the key signature, we see that there are no flats or sharps, which indicates that the key is C. The meter tells us that there are four quarter notes per measure, as the "C" on the clef is equivalent to 4/4. The range can be determined loosely by looking at the lowest note and the highest note and counting the lines and spaces between them. Here, there is an interval of a sixth between the lowest and highest note. Finally, form can be identified in small or large portions by identifying repetition and difference. While the notes are often the first thing we look at, patterns in rhythm can also be telling. Here, notice the first two measures (up to the half note) and the second two measure (up to the second half note), and notice the exact repetition in rhythm. These can be considered two **phrases**, essentially like clauses of a sentence. Additionally, each line changes, and lines 1 and 3 are exactly the same. This would be ABA form (ternary Form), where line 1 is A, line 2 is different so we call it B, and line 3 returns to the original and is A again. Due to the small range and easily recognizable melody, this song is ideal for a kindergartener who is expected to sing simple melodies by memory, not by sight, and be able to recognize the beat and direction on the melody.

$\frown$

THEATER

In schools, theater is often referred to as drama (not to be confused with what ensues during recess when someone decides to change best friends without warning).

Elements of Theater

Plot

Plot is the first and most important dramatic element, as it provides structure to the narrative. There are two major kinds of plots for theater: dramatic and episodic.

- **Dramatic**: The plot contains rising action and an eventual climax.
- **Episodic**: The plot is a series of scenes or episodes that show various events. At the end, the routine is still changed by these events, but there is no single suspenseful driving action that moves the plot forward.

All plots, however, have three parts.

- **The beginning**: The beginning of a plot includes the background, setting, and introduces the characters. It is usually called the exposition. The beginning lets the audience know the routines of the world of the play.
- **The end**: Events of plays change routines in plays, so the end of a play usually establishes new routines of characters.
- **The middle**: The middle is the meat of the story—the point in the story when the normal routines of characters' change. The middle creates a sense of rising action and eventual climax.

Character

Characters that seem to have deep personalities and complex personalities are known as three-dimensional characters. These characters often must make tough decisions in which right and wrong are difficult to decipher. Some characters are two-dimensional. They are not as complex, and they are usually not as engaging for longer periods of time in a play or movie. Two-dimensional characters are often called stock characters.

Thought

Thought is often more equivalent to the more used term, **theme.** The theme embodies the central questions at the heart of the narrative. For example, in "The Tortoise and the Hare," we know the tortoise races the hare—the hare being fast and arrogant, and the tortoise being slow and steady. There is not one theme, but several: "Slow and steady wins the race," and "Don't be arrogant." More themes can make the narrative more interesting.

Diction

Diction is the words and language used, even more so exactly how those words are used to make a statement. Take Shakespeare's *Hamlet,* for example:

"To be or not to be: that is the question."

"Do I kill myself, or not?"

The same statement is made twice, the first by Shakespeare and the latter another possible modern translation. The poetic nature in which Shakespeare made the same statement provides a better diction.

Music

Music encompasses all sound in the play or film. While a soundtrack would be most noticeable as music, the sound design down to the creation of an individual sound falls into this category. For instance, a sound designer may recreate the sound of a gunshot for a play so that no one has to actually fire a real gun onstage.

Spectacle

Simply put, **spectacle** comprises the visual elements. Spectacle includes the set design, costumes, properties (the things the actors hold like swords, etc.), lighting, and special effects.

Roles of the Theater

Acting

Actors bring characters to life by conveying emotions through words that elicit responses from an audience. Acting comes in many forms, including the following:

- improvisation
- monologue/soliloquy
- pair or group scenes
- singing
- mime

When reading **dialogue,** actors have to take into account not only the words, but the emotions, relationships, and situations involved. Take the following sample lines of dialogue. Read them with the assumption that Lance is Tori's fiancé and has come home early from a business trip to surprise her. She wasn't home, so he checked with her roommate, Fiona, and tracked her down at work with a giant bouquet of flowers.

> TORI: Lance! What are you doing here?
> LANCE: I just had to see you.
> TORI: How did you find me?
> LANCE: Fiona told me where you were.

Now, read the lines over again, but this time, imagine that Lance is Tori's psychotic ex-boyfriend. He has escaped from prison and managed to find her, even though she has changed her name and moved hundreds of miles away. Fiona is Tori's sister, and the only person who knows where Tori lives. Tori knows Fiona would never betray her unless her life had been threatened.

After these two very different readings, you should see how much the context, relationships, and **backstory** (background story) affect the delivery of dialogue.

Directing

The **director** of a play or film takes his or her vision of the script and guides the cast and crew into making it a reality.

A director has a lot to do with how actions are expressed and how the actors play their characters. For example, in William Shakespeare's scripts, there is virtually no stage direction: no movement, no expressions of emotion. Every now and then, there will be a "He falls" or "Exeunt" (all exit). The director of a Shakespeare play has the enormous task of creating the setting, the action, and the character development based almost solely on the dialogue.

Scriptwriting

Scripts should have all of the elements of any type of story: theme, setting, character development, and a solid plot. The challenge in scriptwriting is to move the action along by primarily using dialogue.

Design

Design is the setting of the play or film. It includes elements such as shapes, colors, props, costumes, pictures, and background.

Styles of Theater

Theatrical styles, or **genres,** can be categorized by a number of aspects, including theme and dialogue style. Some plays and playwrights overlap more than one genre.

Realism

Realism is grounded in fact. Plays of this genre depict real people in real situations, without any idealism or appeal to the imagination. Henrik Ibsen's *A Doll's House* (1879) is one example.

Classicism

Classicism, classicalism, or **neoclassicism** in theater exemplifies the aesthetic principals rooted in ancient ("classic") Greek and Roman art: an emphasis on simplicity, formality, and restraint. *The Discovery* (1763) by Frances Sheridan is considered a play of this genre.

Romanticism

Romanticism developed as a rebellion against classicism. Romantic plays emphasized emotion and feeling rather than form and restraint. Shakespeare (1564–1616) was a Romantic playwright.

Modernism

Modernism is a genre that breaks from the past; it focuses on the contemporary, drawing a distinction between itself and previous genres. T.S. Eliot's play *The Cocktail Party* (1949) is an example.

Expressionism

Expressionism in theater is a style of presentation, both in content and in design, focusing on symbolic and abstract representations of reality. Emphasis is placed on the emotions and reactions of the characters. Eugene O'Neill's *The Hairy Ape* (1922) is an expressionist play.

Existentialism

Existentialism is the belief that each person is wholly responsible for his or her own feelings, thoughts, and actions, and that it is up to the individual to make sense of the universe. An example of an existentialist play is Samuel Beckett's *Waiting for Godot* (1952).

Absurdism

Absurdism is similar to existentialism in that it is a philosophy based on the idea that there is no meaning in the universe in relation to humanity, and any attempt by humans to find any sense or logic out of this chaos is absurd. One of the most well-known plays of this genre is Tom Stoppard's *Rosencrantz and Guildenstern Are Dead* (1966).

Epic Theater

Epic theater is probably the most difficult theatrical style to explain. It follows a familiar story, such as a historical event or a fable, but is presented in loosely connected episodes. Epic theater employs what is called the **alienation effect,** which refers to a technique intended to detach the audience's emotions from the drama. Bertolt Brecht was possibly the most famous playwright of this genre; one of his more well-known plays is *Mother Courage and her Children* (1938).

Historical and Cultural Context

Forms of theater date back to ancient times, when primitive peoples performed rituals and ceremonies by creating actions, or early **scenes,** through dance.

Egypt

There is evidence of dramatic productions in Egypt dating back to about 2000 BCE. Most likely, these were passion plays, which depicted the suffering and sacrifices of gods.

China

Though historians have pieced together evidence of ceremonial dances and theatrical performances well before the Common Era, the commonly recognized "first period" of Chinese drama occurred in the 8th century, when dramatic productions focusing on extraordinary themes and heroic characters were performed before the Imperial Court.

India

Indian and Hindu theater developed from an ancient custom whereby the national poetry was recited at social and religious gatherings. Dramatic gestures and music were gradually added to the recitations; eventually, religious legends and stories, usually featuring Krishna or Shiva, were transformed into performances.

Greece

Greek drama originated in the worship of Dionysus, the god of wine and agriculture, now recognized as the patron god of the Greek stage. Dramatic performances developed through choral songs and dances.

Native American

Native American theater began with ceremonies and rituals regarding gods and nature. It utilized symbolism, engaged all of the senses, and incorporated active audience participation.

Important Terms and People

People

William Shakespeare (1564–1616): an English poet and playwright regarded as the greatest writer in the English language. Works: *Hamlet, Romeo and Juliet, Macbeth.*

Sophocles (497 BCE–406 BCE): One of three ancient Greek tragedians, that is, a master of the Greek Tragedy style. Works: *Oedipus Rex, Electra.*

Aphra Behn (1640–1689): British playwright and poet from the restoration era. Behn was the first woman author to make her living solely by writing. Works: *The Rover, Love Letters Between a Nobleman and his Sister.*

Konstantin Stanislavsky (1863–1938): a Russian character actor and director who garnered a reputation for his "system" of actor training, preparation, and rehearsal technique.

Terms and Technique

Ensemble: Sometimes called "the chorus," members of the ensemble are called upon to sing, dance, and play smaller roles in a musical.

In the round: A circular playing space in which the audience completely surrounds the playing space and the performers.

Proscenium: The most traditional stage set-up. The stage is removed from the audience and framed by an arch that separates it from the audience.

The fourth wall: An invisible dividing "wall" between the stage and audience.

Understudy: Usually a member of the ensemble, this actor will be responsible for learning the part of a leading or supporting actor and act as a backup or alternate.

Which would be the best choice for a third-grade teacher to use as a culminating project in a theater unit?

A.   Pairs or small groups of students write and perform short plays.

B.   Students watch scenes from various plays and identify the genres.

C.   Pairs or small groups of students memorize and perform famous one-act plays.

D.   Students memorize and perform monologues.

Here's How to Crack It

First, consider the age group you're given: third-grade students. That should help you eliminate some answers; for example, identifying genres, (B), is too advanced. Choice (C), memorizing and performing one-act plays, is also too difficult; you should know that *one-act* is not necessarily synonymous with *short*. Now that you're down to your last two choices, switch to teacher mode. For many reasons, including teamwork and writing across the curriculum, (A), is the best choice.

Here is an example of a potential constructed-response assignment.

---○---

Using your knowledge of theater, prepare a response in which you:

Identify a theatrical production available for viewing in the classroom; then using theatrical terminology, discuss the character personalities or relationships; and create a scenario in which students act out their understanding of the characters.

Here's How to Crack It

First, identify a drama that could be viewed in the classroom; *The King and I* is a classic. Identify some main characters and ask students to identify their personality or interactions with each other. Numerous qualities come to mind about the character Anna: courageous, kind, nurturing, etc. One possible scenario would be to ask some students to act out one such characteristic silently, and ask others to identify the characteristic.

---○---

VISUAL ARTS

The area of **visual arts** is comprised of many sub-disciplines, such as drawing, painting, sculpture, and photography. We'll focus here on the general principles and elements, most of which apply to more than one category.

Elements of Art

Line

A **line** is a continuous mark going from one point to another. Lines can be used to express a variety of things such as feelings, moods, and movement.

Color

Color has three characteristics: **hue,** which is the shade of color; **value,** which represents the lightness or darkness; and **intensity,** which refers to the dullness or brightness of a color.

Space

Space gives depth by creating visual perspective. Space can be positive, negative, or three-dimensional.

Shape

Artists use a variety of **shapes,** such as circles, rectangles, and triangles, to enclose areas of specific lengths and widths.

Form

A **form** has three dimensions and encloses volume. A sphere and a cube are examples of forms.

Texture

Texture is usually created by shading and lines to represent the quality of a surface. Texture can be actual, simulated, or invented.

Principles of Art

Balance

Balance refers to the way the elements of art are arranged within a piece. Balance can be symmetrical, asymmetrical, and radial.

Emphasis

Artists often use the principle of **emphasis** to make one or more features of the piece stand out, or catch the viewer's eye. In a predominantly black-and-white drawing, for instance, an artist may use a splash of a bright color in one spot.

Contrast

Contrast refers to a method of stressing the difference between particular artistic elements. For example, an artist may combine bright and dark colors, or different shapes.

Unity

Unity, or **harmony,** gives a sense of belonging to a piece. Artists use similar elements to create a cohesive look or feel.

Rhythm

Rhythm is also referred to as **pattern** or **repetition.** Artists use repeated elements, such as lines and shapes, to give the piece a visual rhythm.

Movement

Artists can use the elements of art to create a sense of **visual movement,** causing the viewer's eye to move from one place to another.

Proportion

Proportion usually refers to the size of images in relation to each other. For example, an artist may draw a large flower in the center of a piece, then a very small building to one side, which gives the sense that the flower is much closer than the building.

Variety

Artists create **variety** by combining different artistic elements to create complex and intricate relationships.

Styles of Visual Arts

Historical Context

Art history dates back to ancient times. The following list contains some early forms of art from the various regions of the world:

- Prehistoric times: cave and rock painting, simple sculptures
- Egypt: colorful drawings
- Mesopotamia: pottery, jewelry, sculpture, architecture
- China: bronzeware, terracotta, silk drawings
- Japan: pottery
- India: rock paintings, petroglyphs
- Persia: jewelry, animal art
- Mexico: ceramics, jade carvings
- Rome: busts, architecture
- Greece: ceramics, frescoes, jewelry, architecture

Art Movements

The following list contains a few of the major art movements and the artists and cultures commonly associated with each:

- Gothic: 13th- and 14th-century France; linear, graceful style
- Renaissance: 15th- through 17th-century Europe; associated with Leonardo and Michelangelo; balance, harmony, scientific perspective, secular subjects
- Baroque: 17th- and early 18th-century Europe; strong emotion, dramatic lighting, violent movement
- Neoclassicism: late 18th- and early 19th-century Europe; revived order and harmony of ancient Roman, Greek art
- Romanticism: late 18th- and early 19th-century Europe; spontaneous expression, energy, brilliant colors
- Impressionism: late 19th-century France; associated with Renoir and Monet; often painted from nature with an emphasis on changing effects of light and color
- Cubism: early 20th-century Europe; associated with Picasso; fragmentation, multiple viewpoints
- Surrealism: early 20th-century France; associated with Dali and Magritte; dreams, spontaneity, juxtaposition
- Expressionism: early 20th-century Europe; communication of emotion with emphasis and distortion
- Pop art: mid-20th-century Britain and United States; associated with Lichtenstein and Warhol; images and techniques of mass media and irony

Important Terms and People

People

Leonardo Da Vinci (1452–1519: Italian mathematician, engineer, artist, and more. His works explore humanity, religion, and science. Works: *Mona Lisa*, *The Last Supper*, *The Vitruvian Man*.

Michelangelo Buonarroti (1475–1564): well known for his sculptures, though his most famous work is his *Sistine Chapel* painting.

Pablo Picasso (1881–1973): a Spanish visual artist known for co-founding the Cubist movement and the Collage. Works: *Les Demoiselles d'Avignon*, *Guernica*.

Frida Kahlo (1907–1954): a Mexican painter and powerful figure in Latin American art. Kahlo is known for her surreal self-portraits which explore beauty and power with bold colors. Works: *The Two Fridas*, *Self-Portrait with Thorn Necklace and Hummingbird*.

Andy Warhol (1928–1987): an American artist and a leading figure in pop art. His works explore the relationship between artistic expression, celebrity culture, and advertising. Works: *Campbell's Soup Cans*, *Marilyn Diptych*.

Terms and Techniques

Abstract: the modification of a (usually) natural form by simplification or distortion

Collage: French word for cut and pasted scraps of materials, such as paper, cardboard, chair caning, playing cards, etc., to a painting or drawing surface

Engraving: a general term used to describe traditional printing processes, such as etching, aquatint, dry point, etc., in which an image is made by the use of metal plates and engraving tools, and printed, usually through a printing press

Figurative: a term used to describe art that is based on the figure, usually in realistic or semi-realistic terms

Focal point: in two-dimensional images, the center of interest visually and/or subject-wise

Found object: any object that an artist comes upon, and uses in an artwork, or as the artwork itself

Hue: the actual color of a form or object

Installation: a type of art, usually sculptural, which is often large enough to fill an entire space, such as a gallery, and consists of a number and variety of components

Medium: material or technique an artist works in

Motif: a French term that refers to the subject matter or content of a work of art

Negative space: in a painting or sculpture, the areas where there are no forms (the "empty" areas)

Perspective: a semi-mathematical technique for representing spatial relationships and three-dimensional objects on a flat surface

Interpretation

The CSET may present an image of a work of art and ask you to derive meaning, or make an interpretation. This is a tough one, because interpretation is very subjective. Your best bet is to use what you know to gather as many details as you can. Ask yourself questions such as these:

- What type of art is it?
- Which artistic elements seem to be most predominant?
- How well does the artist present the principles of art?
- How old does the piece seem to be?
- What culture might the piece be from?
- What art movement might the piece be indicative of?
- What does the purpose of the piece seem to be?

The traditional Japanese art of using gold-dusted lacquer to repair broken pottery is called:

A. kabuki.

B. terracotta.

C. glassblowing.

D. kintsugi.

Here's How to Crack It

Knowing that the answer is a "Japanese art," eliminate terracotta, (B), and glassblowing, (C), which are not Japanese terms. The term kabuki, (A), refers to a type of theater, leaving kintsugi, (D), the correct answer.

KEY TERMS

General Terms
artistic perception
creative expression
aesthetic valuing
connections
relationships
applications

Dance Terms
force (dynamics)
form
pas de deux
plié
promenade
relevé
fox-trot
waltz
cha-cha
swing
Horton technique
Limon technique
level

Music Terms
rhythm
beat
tempo
meter
melody
harmony
consonance
dissonance
timbre (tone color)
form (binary, ternary)
theme and variation
popular song
texture
monophony
homophony
polyphony
density

dynamics
musical notation
staff
treble staff
treble clef
bass staff
bass clef
grand staff
time signature
key signature
key
sharp
flat
circle of fifths
woodwinds
brass
string
percussion
unpitched percussion
pitched percussion
keyboard

Theater Terms
plot (dramatic, episodic)
characters
thought (theme)
diction
spectacle
actors
dialogue
backstory
director
script
design
genres
realism
classicism (classicalism,
   neoclassicism)
romanticism
modernism
expressionism

existentialism
absurdism
epic theater
alienation effect
scenes
ensemble
in the round
proscenium
the fourth wall
understudy

Visual Arts Terms
line
color
hue
value
intensity
space
shape
form
texture
balance
emphasis
contrast
unity harmony)
rhythm (pattern, repetition)
visual movement
proportion
variety
abstract
collage
engraving
figurative
focal point
found object
installation
medium
motif
negative space
perspective

Chapter 20 Drill

Answers and explanations can be found in the final section of this book, beginning on page 617.

1. Which of the following is NOT an example of recreational dancing?

   A. ballet

   B. square dancing

   C. tango

   D. twist

2. The numbers in the music staff above are used to indicate:

   A. key.

   B. harmonics.

   C. instrumentation.

   D. meter signature.

3. Which term refers to the intended volume of a piece of music?

   A. timbre

   B. harmony

   C. dynamics

   D. tempo

4. In theater, a soliloquy is a type of:

   A. pantomime.

   B. monologue.

   C. plot.

   D. costume.

5. Which principle of art is most apparent in the work represented above?

   A. movement

   B. rhythm

   C. proportion

   D. variety

6. Which of the following would a third-grade student be expected to identify by ear?

   A.   the key signature

   B.   differences in monophony, homophony, and polyphony

   C.   an ostinato

   D.   the families of the orchestra

7. Which of the following is typically NOT an aspect to Japanese Kabuki theater?

   A.   acting

   B.   singing

   C.   dancing

   D.   masks

8. Which of the following was a Russian choreographer known for intensity in portraying characters?

   A.   Vaslav Nijinsky

   B.   George Balanchine

   C.   Bob Fosse

   D.   Evgeni Plushenko

9. Which of the following is an art movement NOT from the 19th century?

   A.   realism

   B.   dadaism

   C.   romanticism

   D.   impressionism

10. A student dancing spontaneously in a free-form hip style is practicing:

   A.   structure.

   B.   improvisation.

   C.   counterbalancing.

   D.   dynamics.

Summary

o   The four art disciplines are dance, music, theater, and the visual arts.

o   The five strands of standards for each discipline are artistic perception; creative expression; historical and cultural context; aesthetic valuing; and connections, relationships, and applications.

o   Elements of dance include space, time, and force.

o   Elements of music include instruments, timbre, dynamics, melody, harmony, rhythm, form, and texture.

o   Four basic classifications of musical instruments are woodwind, brass, percussion, and string.

o   Elements of theater include plot, character, thought, diction, music, and spectacle.

o   There are many theatrical styles, including realism, existentialism, classicism, and romanticism.

o   Elements of art include line, color, space, shape, form, texture, and value.

o   Principles of art include balance, emphasis, contrast, unity, rhythm, movement, proportion, and variety.

Answers and Explanations to Chapter Drills

CHAPTER 3 DRILL

1. **C** Critics argue that the alphabetic principle is flawed because it is based on the concept that each letter has a corresponding sound, but in English, so many letters and letter combinations have more than one possible sound that children can't count on any kind of consistency.

2. **D** load + ed. Were you fooled by "speakers"? It actually has two suffixes: speak + er + s.

3. **B** /f/ /l/. The consonant sounds don't change when you put the letters together.

4. **C** *Alter* and *altar* are reversed, and *cite* means *quote* or *mention*.

5. **B** The first part of the sentence is an independent clause, and *as long as* is a subordinating conjunction that attaches the dependent clause.

CHAPTER 4 DRILL

1. **C** A Venn diagram is used to compare and contrast two or more things: In this case, it would be reasonable to use it for the two main characters in the novel.

2. **A** Again, this is one of those questions that seems subjective, but there are clear wrong answers. Choices (B) and (C) sound like informational reports, not persuasive pieces, and (D) just wouldn't be interesting to a second-grade student or her classmates. Choice (A) is the only option that is both accessible and relevant to the age group.

3. **D** Choice (D) is the only pair in which both sources are primary.

4. **A** In an "either...or" construction, when both parts of the subject are singular (Uncle Henrik/Peter), the verb should be singular. You are assuming that only one or the other is performing the action. Either "Uncle Henrik *has* to help" or "Peter *has* to help."

5. **C** If you happen to see a question like this on the test, *don't* throw your hands up and guess at random. You don't have to memorize every possible citation type. If you can remember a few basics, you can at least narrow the field. Remember that the title of a book is always italicized or underlined, which in this case immediately cuts your choices down to two. If you also remember that the date comes last in MLA format, you've nailed it.

CHAPTER 5 DRILL

1. **B** The Sun did with gentleness what the Wind could not do with brute force.

2. **C** One of the main characteristics of fables is the use of non-human characters. None of the other answers is specifically indicative of a fable.

3. **A** Look for what there *isn't* in the sentence rather than what there *is*. There is no alliteration, which rules out (B); there is no metaphor, which rules out (C) and (D). There is a very clear simile, though, and the word slice is onomatopoeia.

4. **C** Yes, you may run into a question or two that does specifically test your content knowledge. If you are familiar with all of the pieces, or at least the one that you know fits the bill, then you'll have no problem. If not, use POE to narrow down your choices based on what you do know. A narrative poem is long and tells a story: you can eliminate any of the other three poems if you recognize that they don't meet the criteria.

5. **D** Choice (A) is improbable, but not impossible. Choices (B) and (C) are simple similes. Choice (D) is an extreme exaggeration. And...pretty gross.

CHAPTER 7 DRILL

1. **B** Islam originated in the Arabian peninsula, but it spread farther west and south across Africa and east into Central and Southeast Asia within the first century of its founding. Buddhism (A) originated in India and is prevalent mainly in Asia. Zoroastrianism, (C), is prevalent in Central Asia in the area of Iran. Christianity, (D), spread around the area of the Mediterranean Sea in all four directions.

2. **A** Plant and animal domestication, (A), was crucial to allowing human populations to settle. More efficient means of warfare, (B), help deplete populations, not increase them! Humans compete primarily with one another for food, so eliminate (C). Spoken language, (D), developed well before 3000 BCE. In fact, the first evidence of written language dates to about 3200 BCE.

3. **D** This map shows a large portion of modern-day Mexico. The Incas (A) occupied the Andes, not Central America. The Spanish Empire, (B), did not include this territory until later. The Olmecs, (C), were long gone by 1510. The Aztec Empire, (D), ruled over this region until it was finally defeated by the Spanish in 1521.

4. **C** The Senate persisted throughout Roman history and beyond. Choices (A), (B), and (D) are all serious issues that the Romans encountered in the imperial period and all are arguably far worse than the existence of the Senate. Therefore, you can eliminate those three choices and choose (C).

5. **A** Remember that Gutenberg's revolutionary invention was the printing press, which made books easier to produce and more affordable, (A). This had no impact on painting (B). While it might seem logical that this invention impacted industrialization and craftspeople, its primary impact was the availability of books, so you can eliminate (C) and (D).

6. **D** All of Europe knew of the New World, (A), which Columbus had "discovered" in 1492. The Spanish made no efforts to assimilate to New World Cultures, (B), and they had not negotiated for rights to the New World, (C). The Spanish Armada, Spain's Navy, controlled the Atlantic and kept other European powers from establishing much of a foothold in the New World. The correct answer is (D).

7. **A** The concept of federalism is central to the Constitution, and describe a system of government under which the national government and local governments share powers. Choice (B), nationalism, is not a governmental system. Autocracy, (C), refers to a government that answers only to itself. Socialism, (D), refers to a system in which the means of production is owned by the community as a whole.

8. **A** Remember that most slaves had no job skills and could neither read nor write. They had no money and nowhere to go when slavery was abolished. Some slaves took off in search of their scattered families, but most stayed exactly where they were and worked as tenant farmers or sharecroppers. Choice (C) is incorrect for reasons stated above. The Great Migration of Southern blacks into Northern cities did not take place until World War I, long after Reconstruction. Choice (D) is incorrect because Chinese immigrants were used to construct our nation's railroad system, much of which had been completed by the end of the Civil War.

9. **B** Ask yourself: was this a 19th-century development or not? Choices (A), (C), and (D) seem reasonably set in the 19th century, but (C), assembly-line technique, should jump out as a later innovation (Henry Ford's company was one of the first to use it to build Model T's in 1910).

10. **B** The Louisiana Purchase grew out of the government's efforts to purchase New Orleans from the French; President Jefferson wanted control of the city because it sits at the mouth of the Mississippi River, an essential trade route. Jefferson sent James Monroe to France to negotiate the sale. The French, desperate for cash and nearly as desperate to divest themselves of New World holdings, offered to sell the entire massive Louisiana Territory, giving the United States control of both banks of the Mississippi River (as well as a tremendous amount of western land). As a result, American traders could travel the length of the river unimpeded, and trade subsequently boomed. Many of the incorrect answers to this question are anachronistic; the date of the purchase was too early for there to be "numerous French factories" in the territory, as in (C), or to allow for "the immediate completion of the transcontinental railroad," as in (D).

11. **B** Discrimination against the Chinese began well before their work on the railroad; in fact, that is considered one of the reasons they were desirable for the work. As for the farmland, the amount of land used for the railroad versus the sheer size of California is just not proportional. Choice (D) is simply wrong.

12. **C** This question is testing your knowledge of three Progressive Era Reforms in the California Constitution—initiative, referendum, and recall. Choices (B) and (D) are not examples of these reforms, so you can eliminate them. An initiative is an effort to change the law, not an elected official, so eliminate (A). Recall allows voters to remove officials from office, which is what happened in 2003. Choice (C) is the correct answer.

13. **D** The mission system was established by Father Junipero Serra during the time Spain ruled California. The missions were self-contained and self-sufficient communities, and were not intended to generate income; eliminate (A). While travelers may have stayed at the missions while traveling and agriculture was one of the ways the missions sustained themselves, neither of these was a primary purpose of the mission system, so eliminate (B) and (C). Father Serra attracted many Native Americans to the missions with the specific goal of Christianizing the population; (D) is the correct answer.

14. **A** If you haven't read *The Grapes of Wrath*, pick it up sometime. And in this case, you can still rule out a couple of the answers: no family would have been traveling from Oklahoma to California during the Mission Period, and during the gold rush, men left their families and traveled alone.

15. **B** The Central Valley of California has a mild climate and fertile soil, which should make you think of agriculture. Think logically on this one. While the population may be a bit more spread out, it isn't sparse, so eliminate (A). Agriculture seems pretty logical given the climate, so leave (B). The capital did move from San Jose to Sacramento, but this wasn't a result of climate, so eliminate (C). The Central Valley is rich in resources, so it doesn't logically follow that regional conflict would be created; eliminate (D). The correct answer is (B).

CHAPTER 8 DRILL

1. **D** There are only two major storage forms of carbohydrates, starch and glycogen. Starch is the storage form of sugars in plants. Cellulose, (A), is a structural component of the cell wall. Choices (B) and (C), maltose and fructose, are monosaccharides.

2. **D** A change of pH equals a tenfold change in hydrogen ion concentration. Therefore, if the pH changes from 8 to 10 (a pH change of 2), the resulting solution is 10×10, or 100, times more basic.

3. **D** For lactose to be hydrolyzed to glucose and galactose, a water molecule must be added. The other species—O_2, H_2, and ATP—will not hydrolyze lactose.

4. **A** WC22 must be a liquid, as the liquid phase of matter is characterized by the ability of the material to conform to the shape of the container that holds it, but an inability of the material to expand to fit the available volume.

5. **B** Glucose is the most abundant monosaccharide, the most popular sugar around, and plants produce it by capturing sunlight for energy, while cells break it down to release stored energy. Don't be thrown off by photosynthesis, (D), which is described in the question. Glucose is what plants produce during photosynthesis, so (B) is correct.

CHAPTER 9 DRILL

1. **C** Statement I is false since a projectile experiencing only the constant acceleration due to gravity can travel in a parabolic trajectory. Statement II is true: zero acceleration means no change in speed (or direction). Statement III is false: an object whose speed remains constant but whose velocity vector is changing direction is acceleration.

2. **C** The baseball is still under the influence of Earth's gravity. Its acceleration throughout the entire flight is constant, equal to g downward.

3. **B** Because the person is not accelerating, the net force he feels must be zero. Therefore, the magnitude of the upward normal force from the floor must balance that of the downward gravitational force. Although these two forces have equal magnitudes, they do not form an action/reaction pair because they both act on the same object (namely, the person). The forces in an action/reaction pair always act on different objects.

4. **D** The color of an object is determined by the colors of light reflected. Choice (D) is correct because a red shirt must reflect red light.

5. **C** We know that opposite poles attract and like poles repel. In the diagram, we see that B is attracted to the south pole (above it), so B must be north and A must be south. We can see that C is repelled by a north pole (thus the gap), so C must be north and D is south. Thus, the north poles are B and C, and (C) is the correct answer.

CHAPTER 10 DRILL

1. **C** Bacterial cells have a cell wall made up of peptidoglycan, while animal cells don't. Both bacterial cells and animal cells have ribosomes and plasma membranes made of phospholipids, so eliminate (A) and (B). Choice (D) is wrong because bacterial cells do not have nuclear membranes and vacuoles.

2. **A** Choice (A) is correct. The nucleolus is the site where rRNA is formed. Choice (B) is a description of smooth ER, (C) is a description of microtubules, and (D) is a description of the cell wall.

3. **D** The anther is the male part of the flower. The pistil is the female part of flowering plants. It consists of the ovule, style, ovary (which contains the female gametes), and the stigma (sticky protein that traps pollen trains).

4. **B** Enzymes that digest fats are called lipase, (B). Choice (A), bile, isn't an enzyme; rather, it emulsifies fats. Choice (C), amylase, digests carbohydrates. After eliminating (A) and (C), you're down to two answer choices. You may not know what proteases are, but you should know that lipase digests fats.

5. **C** There are four blood types: A, B, AB, and O. Blood type O is the universal donor, and AB is the universal recipient. Individuals with blood type AB can receive blood from all of the other blood groups without any blood clotting.

CHAPTER 11 DRILL

1. **C** A producer is an organism that is capable of converting radiant or chemical energy into carbohydrates. The only example of this is (C), grass.

2. **D** Plants are autotrophs, mice are heterotrophs, and fungi are decomposers.

3. **D** Different species can use slightly different parts of the habitat to avoid direct competition with other species. For example, there are five species of warblers that can live in the same pine tree. They can coexist because each species feeds in a different part of the tree: the trunk, at the ends of the branches, and at other sites.

4. **C** Humans don't undergo photosynthesis; therefore, we can eliminate (B) and (D). Humans obtain their energy from consuming plant and/or animal matter and therefore are classified as heterotrophs, so eliminate (A).

5. **C** Choice (A), cost-benefit analysis, is the comparison of the benefit of an action relative to the costs of that action. Choice (B), external costs, refers to the costs that occur after someone purchases something. For example, after you buy a car, the cost of gasoline is an external cost. Choice (D), marginal benefits, refers to the tradeoff between how much we gain by buying forest land (for example) or using the money to do some other beneficial activity. Choice (C), marginal costs, refers to the costs of each step in a process. Thus, (C) is the correct answer.

CHAPTER 12 DRILL

1. **C** Use the handy IPMAT mnemonic and tricks of thinking I, Propose, More, Awesome, Tacos to remember that the phases of mitosis (in order) are interphase, prophase, metaphase, anaphase, and telophase.

2. **D** The pancreas is derived from the endoderm. Choice (A), the epidermis of the skin, is derived from the ectoderm. Choice (B), the muscular system, and (C), the stomach, are derived from the mesoderm.

3. **B** The reduction of the cell size is most likely due to decreases in the amount of cytoplasm in each cell since the embryo does not enlarge during this stage. The embryo does not suffer a loss of DNA, so eliminate (A). Choice (C), feedback inhibition, is not responsible for the reduction in cell size. The cells within the zygote are diploid not haploid (D).

4. **C** Genetic variability is usually due to a mutation during meiosis (sexual reproduction). Choices (A), (B), and (D) are all examples of asexual reproduction. They create identical offspring.

5. **C** One way to get genetic variability is by mutations. Mutations are reversible, so we can eliminate (A). They are able to revert. Mutations are not always detrimental or lethal; as we mentioned earlier they can contribute to genetic variability—so eliminate (B). Mutations can influence any gene locus in a population, so eliminate (D).

CHAPTER 13 DRILL

1. **A** Mercury, Venus, Earth, and Mars are known as inner planets in our solar system.

2. **A** Asteroids are known as minor planets that orbit the Sun in the asteroid belt between Mars and Jupiter. They are made of rocky and metallic objects. Hydrogen is found in planets. Asteroids are not substantially similar to Earth's surface and they are orbital.

3. **C** Meteoroids are small bodies, smaller than asteroids, and are very tiny. They travel through space. The other answers are incorrect because they do not meet the definition of a meteoroid.

4. **D** Tides are affected by gravity and its pull in the Earth-Moon-Sun system and the movement of those bodies within the system.

5. **B** Remember that primary sources are also known as direct sources, and they are generally sources that experienced the phenomenon, were around during the time of study, or have first-hand knowledge of the situation. Secondary sources are generally commenting on, citing, or referencing primary sources. The blog post, *Newsweek* article, and report written by an environmental-political group are all considered secondary sources.

CHAPTER 14 DRILL

1. **A**   Angelina and her two friends will combine their books and then divide them into equal stacks. So first you need to find $v + w + x$. Then you need to divide the total number of books into equal numbers to make the stacks. The problem doesn't give you a number to divide by: any factor of $v + w + x$ will yield a solution, and the question asks how to find *all* the solutions, so you need to find *all* the factors. You don't need to find common factors of the separate amounts, you need to find factors of the total, so eliminate (B). Similarly, prime factors aren't necessary, and you need to find the sum of v, w, and x, not their product, so eliminate (C). Multiples wouldn't help either, so eliminate (D). Recall that *divisor* is another word for *factor:* (A) is correct.

2. **C**   The question asks you to choose which situation illustrates the operation $12\frac{3}{4} \times \frac{1}{3}$. Translate the answer choices into mathematical operations to find the correct answer. Choice (A) involves addition: since she practiced $\frac{1}{3}$ day longer than she usually does, add the values: $12\frac{3}{4} + \frac{1}{3}$. Eliminate (A), since it's the wrong operation. Choice (B) involves multiplication, but making 3 times the recipe means that Suzanne will need $12\frac{3}{4} \times 3$ cups of flour, so the values don't match. Eliminate (B). In (D), Suzanne is dividing $12\frac{3}{4}$ feet of yarn into $\frac{1}{3}$-foot lengths. This indicates division: $12\frac{3}{4} \div \frac{1}{3}$. Again, it's the wrong operation, so eliminate (D). In (C), Suzanne is splitting $12\frac{3}{4}$ hours of work into 3 parts; this can be represented by $12\frac{3}{4} \div 3$, or $12\frac{3}{4} \times \frac{1}{3}$. Choice (C) is correct.

3. **B**   You don't know what the divisor is, and knowing it would help solve the problem, so try to find it first. It is a single digit. Look at the beginning of the division problem: the first step will be $17 \div \square = 5$, with some remainder. You know that $17 \div 1 = 17$, which is not close to 5: in fact, there would be a digit above the 1 if 1 were the divisor. Try 2: $17 \div 2 = 8$ R 1, and this answer doesn't match the 5 in that place. It's close though, so try 3: $17 \div 3 = 5$ R 2. Try working the whole problem with 3 as the divisor to see if the solution matches the given digits:

$$
\begin{array}{r}
5854 \\
3{\overline{\smash{\big)}\,17562}} \\
\underline{-15} \\
25 \\
\underline{-24} \\
16 \\
\underline{-15} \\
12 \\
\end{array}
$$

Since all the digits you were given match, this must be the correct divisor, so find the ones digit of the quotient: it's 4. Choice (B) is correct.

4. **C**   Find all the factors of 91.

$$
\begin{array}{c|c}
& 91 \\
\hline
1 & 91 \\
7 & 13 \\
\end{array}
$$

Try adding each pair to find a possible sum: 1 + 91 = 92, which is not one of the solutions given; 7 + 13 = 20, which is one of the answers. Choice (C) is correct.

5. **C**   You can use some clues to simplify this problem. Look at the two partial products that are added together to get the final product at the bottom. In the second one, the last digit is B. Remember that that digit has to be 0: it's a placeholder showing that you are multiplying the tens digit of your second factor by your first factor. Now you know that B = 0. So what's A? Substitute 0 for B throughout the problem:

$$
\begin{array}{r}
17.A \\
\times\ \ 3.2 \\
\hline
3\,A\,0 \\
+\ A\,2\,A\,0 \\
\hline
A6.00 \\
\end{array}
$$

Now use your knowledge of multiplication facts: since the first partial product also ends in 0, you know that A × 2 ends in 0. That means that A is either 0 or 5. Try substituting 0 for A:

$$
\begin{array}{r}
17.0 \\
\times\ \ 3.2 \\
\hline
3\,40 \\
+\ 51\,00 \\
\hline
54.40 \\
\end{array}
$$

This doesn't match the problem given, so A must not be 0. Try substituting 5 for A instead:

$$
\begin{array}{r}
17.5 \\
\times\ \ 3.2 \\
\hline
3\,50 \\
+\ 52\,50 \\
\hline
56.00 \\
\end{array}
$$

That matches: all the As are 5s, and all the rest of the digits are the ones given. A = 5, so (C) is correct.

6. **D** The question asks for an equivalent expression to 17×105. Eliminate (A), since that product would be considerably greater. You can calculate to check: $17 \times 105 = 1,785$, while $17 \times 100 \times 5 = 8,500$. Choice (B) is wrong because you need to follow the correct Order of Operations: $10 + 7 \times 100 + 5 = 10 + 700 + 5 = 715$. Choice (C) isn't quite right either: $(20 \times 105) - (7 \times 105) = 2,100 - 735 = 1,365$. Choice (D) is correct: $(17 \times 100) + (17 \times 5) = 1,700 + 85 = 1,785$. This is an example of using the Distributive Property to make a calculation easier.

7. **A** This is a percent change question with an extra twist. First, remember the formula for percent change: Percent change $= \dfrac{\text{difference}}{\text{original}} \times 100$. Find the difference: $9,600 - 6,400 = 3,200$. Which number is the original? It's the lesser number, $6,400$. Substitute those values into the formula for percent change: $\dfrac{3,200}{6,400} \times 100 = 50$. The total percent increase is 50%. However, the question asks for the percent increase *each year*. Since the increase was at a steady rate, you can divide the total percent increase by the number of years to find the percent increase per year: $\dfrac{50\%}{10} = 5\%$. The correct answer is (A).

8. **B** Begin by simplifying the denominator of the fraction. Use the Power-Multiply rule to combine $(y^2)^3$ into y^6. Since a number, or in this case a variable, by itself is the same thing as having that number or variable raised to a power of 1, use the Add-Multiply rule to combine $y(y^6)$ into y^7. Now use the Divide-Subtract rule to solve the problem: $\dfrac{y^9}{y^7} = y^2$, so the correct answer is (B).

9. **C** This is a question about scientific notation and place value. First, rewrite the number as a decimal. Since the exponent of the 10 is -2, move the decimal point 2 places to the left: 0.05073. The digit 7 is in the ten-thousandths place, so it represents $\dfrac{7}{10,000}$. The correct answer is (C).

10. **B** First, simplify each of these roots. In the numerator, 75 has a factor that is a perfect square: 25. So $\sqrt{75}$ can be rewritten as $\sqrt{25 \times 3} = \sqrt{25} \times \sqrt{3} = 5\sqrt{3}$. Similarly, in the denominator, 27 has the perfect square 9 as a factor, so $\sqrt{27}$ can be rewritten as $\sqrt{9 \times 3} = \sqrt{9} \times \sqrt{3} = 3\sqrt{3}$. This means that $\dfrac{\sqrt{75}}{\sqrt{27}} = \dfrac{5\sqrt{3}}{3\sqrt{3}}$. The $\sqrt{3}$ s in the numerator and denominator cancel, leaving $\dfrac{5}{3}$. The correct answer is (B).

CHAPTER 15 DRILL

1. **C** Simplify the equation, but keep in mind what the question asks for.

   $$3z + 6 = 16$$

   $$3z + 6 - 6 = 16 - 6$$

   $$3z = 10$$

   Since you are solving for $9z$, you don't need to solve for z. Just multiply both sides of the equation by 3:

   $$3(3z) = 3(10)$$

   $$9z = 30$$

   The correct answer is (C).

2. **C** First, combine like terms:

   $$10y + 4y + y - 36 - 6 = 3$$

   $$15y - 42 = 3$$

   Now solve for y:

   $$15y - 42 + 42 = 3 + 42$$

   $$15y = 45$$

   $$\frac{15y}{15} = \frac{45}{15}$$

   $$y = 3$$

   The correct answer is (C).

3. **C** The key point to remember here is that perpendicular lines have *opposite reciprocal* slopes. Since the slope in the equation $y = -5x - 2$ is -5, find the opposite reciprocal of that: $\frac{1}{5}$. The y-intercept is not important: any line with slope $\frac{1}{5}$ is perpendicular to the original line. The correct answer is (C).

4. **A** Since the question asks for the equation of a line, use the form $y = mx + b$. Use the two points given to find the slope:

$$\frac{y_2 - y_1}{x_2 - x_1} = \frac{-2 - 2}{2 - (-4)} = \frac{-4}{6} = -\frac{2}{3}$$

The slope is $-\frac{2}{3}$, so eliminate (C) and (D). Now write the equation so far:

$$y = -\frac{2}{3}x + b$$

You need to find b, the y-intercept. Substitute the x- and y-values from one of your points into the equation to solve for b.

Use $(2, -2)$:

$$-2 = -\frac{2}{3}(2) + b$$

$$-2 = -\frac{4}{3} + b$$

$$-2 + \frac{4}{3} = b$$

$$-\frac{6}{3} + \frac{4}{3} = b$$

$$-\frac{2}{3} = b$$

So the equation is $y = -\frac{2}{3}x - \frac{2}{3}$: the correct answer is (A).

5. **D** The question asks you to choose the graph that represents the data in the table. There are no units labeled on the graphs, so you need to use the shape and characteristics of the graphs to choose, rather than matching up points. Should the graph be a line or a curve? Ravi charges a fee (a constant) plus a rate per hour (a variable multiplied by a coefficient), so an equation for this data would be of the form $y = ax + b$. It's a linear equation, so the graph should be a line. Eliminate (B) and (C). What's the difference between the two graphs left? The graph in (A) passes through the origin, while the one in (D) has a y-intercept that's greater than 0. Think about Ravi's cost for 0 hours of work: the cost would be just the amount of the service fee, which is greater than 0, plus his hourly rate times 0. Since the cost is not 0, (D) is the correct answer.

6. **B** First, notice that all four graphs show inequalities based around the same line, which has equation $y = \frac{3}{4}x - 2$. So you can't use the slope or intercepts to eliminate answers here. The differences between the answer choices are in whether the line is dotted or solid, and which part of the graph is shaded. Should the line for the given equation be dotted or solid? Recall that $\leq$ means *less than or equal to*, so the line should be included in the solution: it should be solid in the graph. Eliminate (A) and (C). To figure out which portion of the graph should be shaded, choose a point to try. For example, try (0, 0) in the equation. If it makes the equation true, then the portion of the graph containing (0, 0) should be shaded; if it makes the equation false, then the other portion should be shaded.

$0 \leq \frac{3}{4}(0) - 2?$

$0 \leq 0 - 2?$

$0 \leq -2 \ X$

The point (0, 0) is NOT in the solution set, so the correct answer is (B).

7. **D** The question asks which point is in the solution set of the system of inequalities shown in the graph. Find each point on the graph and determine whether it's a solution. Choice (A), (0, −6), is the *y*-intercept of the dotted line. Keep in mind that a dotted line is not part of the solution set! So a point on this line is not a solution: eliminate (A). Choice (B), (2, 0), is the *x*-intercept of the dotted line, so eliminate (B) for the same reason. Choice (C) is a trap! It's the solution to the set of equations representing the lines shown in the graph. But since it's also part of the dotted line, it's not in the solution set for the inequalities. Choice (D) is inside the shaded portion of the graph, so it's the correct answer.

8. **A** First, notice that the question tells you that $k < 0$. Eliminate (D) right away. To solve, factor the quadratic. This question is a twist on the regular factoring question type, but don't worry that you don't know the value of k. Since k is an integer, you can probably safely factor since the solutions are likely to be integers as well. What are the factors of 12? Notice that since k is negative, you'll need two negative factors to multiply to positive 12 and add to a negative sum, k.

	12
−1	−12
−2	−6
−3	−4

So here are the possible factorizations of the equation:

$$x^2 + kx + 12 = (x - 1)(x - 12)$$

$$x^2 + kx + 12 = (x - 2)(x - 6)$$

$$x^2 + kx + 12 = (x - 3)(x - 4)$$

FOIL to find the equations represented by each of the factorizations:

$$(x - 1)(x - 12) = x^2 - 13x + 12$$

$$(x - 2)(x - 6) = x^2 - 8x + 12$$

$$(x - 3)(x - 4) = x^2 - 7x + 12$$

The three possible values of k are –13, –8, and –7. Since only –13 is given, (A) is correct.

9.   **D**   When you notice that this equation includes x^3, don't panic. It's probably just testing the same things you've been studying. Can you simplify so that it looks more like a question you've done before? You sure can. Start by factoring out the monomial $3x$:

$$3x^3 + 18x^2 + 12x = 0$$

$$3x(x^2 + 6x + 4) = 0$$

Now the portion inside the parentheses looks like a quadratic, and you know what to do with those. First, split the two factors you already have and solve the simple one:

$$3x = 0 \qquad x^2 + 6x + 4 = 0$$

$$x = 0 \qquad x^2 + 6x + 4 = 0$$

So one of the solutions is $x = 0$. Eliminate (A) and (B). Now look at the quadratic. Since there aren't any integer factors of 4 that add to 6, you need to complete the square.

$$x^2 + 6x + 4 = 0$$

$$x^2 + 6x = -4$$

Remember, to find the y, divide the coefficient of x by 2. Then square it to get the y^2 term.

$$\frac{6}{2} = 3$$

$$3^2 = 9$$

Since your y^2 term is 9, add that value to both sides of the equation.

$$x^2 + 6x + 9 = -4 + 9$$

$$(x + 3)^2 = 5$$

$$x + 3 = \pm \sqrt{5}$$

$$x + 3 - 3 = -3 \pm \sqrt{5}$$

$$x = -3 \pm \sqrt{5}$$

This means that $-3 + \sqrt{5}$ and $-3 - \sqrt{5}$ are the other two solutions. The correct answer is (D).

10. **B** The question asks you to find the vertex of a parabola. Remember that the vertex of a parabola

can be represented as (h, k), where $h = \dfrac{-b}{2a}$. Use the equation given to find the a and b values:

$a = -\dfrac{1}{2}$ and $b = 2$. So $h = \dfrac{-2}{2\left(-\dfrac{1}{2}\right)} = \dfrac{-2}{-1} = 2$. Use this value for h to find the corresponding

y-value, k: $h = -\dfrac{1}{2}(2)^2 + 2(2) + 1 = -2 + 4 + 1 = 3$. The vertex of the parabola is $(h, k) = (2, 3)$,

so the correct answer is (B).

CHAPTER 16 DRILL

1. **C** Redraw the figure and label everything you know:

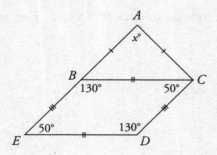

You can fill in the values of the angles in the parallelogram if you remember your parallelogram rules: opposite angles are congruent, and the total interior angle measure is 360°. (Or you can use the rules for parallel lines cut by a transversal to find the measures of these angles!)

Now, notice that angle *ABC* is supplementary to angle *EBC*. That means you can find its measure: 180° − 130° = 50°. Remember that in an isosceles triangle, congruent sides are opposite congruent angles. So angle *ACB* measures 50° as well:

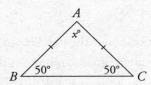

Now use the Rule of 180° to find the value of *x*:

$$50° + 50° + x° = 180°$$

$$100° + x° = 180°$$

$$x° = 80°$$

The correct answer is (C).

2. **B** First, remember what a regular polygon is: all its sides are congruent, and all its angles are congruent. So even though a hexagon is an unfamiliar shape, you know a lot about Clementine's hexagon.

For starters, since the perimeter of the hexagon is 24 in. and all its sides are congruent, you can find the length of each side: 24 in. ÷ 6 = 4 in.

Now concentrate on the triangles. The question asks you for the area of *one* of them. You know the formula for the area of a triangle is $A = \frac{1}{2}bh$, so try to find the base and height of one triangle.

These are equilateral triangles, so you know all their sides have length 4 in., the length of the sides of the hexagon. To find the height of an equilateral triangle, use 30-60-90 triangle rules!

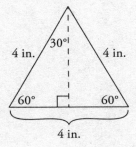 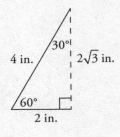

The height is $2\sqrt{3}$ in. Substitute the values of the base and height into the formula for the area of a triangle:

$$A = \frac{1}{2}bh$$

$$A = \frac{1}{2}(4)(2\sqrt{3})$$

$$A = 4\sqrt{3}$$

The area is $4\sqrt{3}$ in.², so (B) is correct.

3. **C** The question gives you information about the parallelogram and asks you about the circle. Think about what the two figures have in common, and what information you have. In a parallelogram, opposite sides are congruent, so you know that $OR = 6$. That's a radius of the circle! Now you can start thinking r, d, C, A:

$r = 6$ $d = 12$

$C = 12\pi$ $A = 36\pi$

What are you being asked to solve for? The question asks you to find the area of the shaded sector of the circle. The area of a sector is a piece of the area of the circle that's in proportion to its central angle:

$$\frac{A_{sector}}{A_{circle}} = \frac{\text{measure of central angle}}{360°}$$

So what is the measure of the central angle, $m\angle POR$? Remember that $OPQR$ is a parallelogram. (In fact, it's a rhombus, which you know because OP is a radius too, so it's length is also 6... but that doesn't really matter here.) In a parallelogram, opposite angles are congruent, so $m\angle POR$ is also 40°. Substitute that and the area of the circle into the proportion:

$$\frac{A_{sector}}{36\pi} = \frac{40°}{360°}$$

Solve for the area of the sector:

$$\frac{A_{sector}}{36\pi} = \frac{1}{9}$$

$$9(A_{sector}) = 36\pi$$

$$A_{sector} = \frac{36\pi}{9} = 4\pi$$

So (C) is correct.

4. **A** Ah, coordinate geometry. You need to find the length and midpoint of a line segment, and you have its endpoints. The midpoint is pretty straightforward:

$$\text{midpoint } (x, y) = \left(\frac{x_1 + x_2}{2}, \frac{y_1 + y_2}{2} \right) = \left(\frac{-3 + 4}{2}, \frac{5 + -2}{2} \right) = \left(\frac{1}{2}, \frac{3}{2} \right), \text{ or } \left(\frac{1}{2}, 1\frac{1}{2} \right)$$

You can eliminate (B) and (D) now that you know the midpoint.

To find the length, you could use the distance formula, but it might be easier to draw a right triangle. One of the two possible right triangles looks like this:

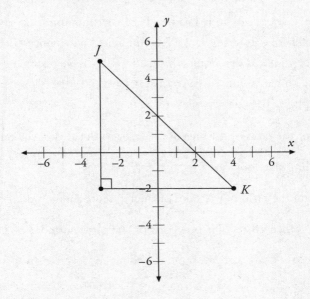

To find the lengths of the legs, you can count the horizontal distance from –3 to 4, which is 7, and the vertical distance from –2 to 5, which is also 7. This is an isosceles right triangle! So that means it's a 45-45-90 triangle. The hypotenuse of a 45-45-90 triangle is $\sqrt{2}$ times the length of its legs, so $JK = 7\sqrt{2}$. The correct answer is (A).

5. **D** Remember, when you are composing transformations, work one step at a time. First, Dani does a translation.

Moving each vertex 3 units to the right is the same as adding 3 to its x-coordinate. Moving each vertex 2 units up is the same as adding 2 to its y-coordinate. Do that to the coordinates of each vertex of the square:

(0, 0)	add 3 to x-coordinate, add 2 to y-coordinate	(3, 2)
(4, 0)	add 3 to x-coordinate, add 2 to y-coordinate	(7, 2)
(4, 4)	add 3 to x-coordinate, add 2 to y-coordinate	(7, 6)
(0, 4)	add 3 to x-coordinate, add 2 to y-coordinate	(3, 6)

Next, Dani does a rotation of 270° about the origin. Remember that if direction is unspecified, that means the rotation is counterclockwise. To rotate a figure 270° counterclockwise, map its coordinates (x, y) to $(y, -x)$.

(3, 2)	(x, y) to $(y, -x)$	(2, -3)
(7, 2)	(x, y) to $(y, -x)$	(2, -7)
(7, 6)	(x, y) to $(y, -x)$	(6, -7)
(3, 6)	(x, y) to $(y, -x)$	(6, -3)

If you can picture the square in your head and see that moving it up and to the right keeps it in Quadrant 1, and then that rotating it 270° counterclockwise moves it to Quadrant IV, you can check the ballpark of your answer. Points in Quadrant IV have positive x-coordinates and negative y-coordinates. Since all the points in your answer have those characteristics, you've landed Dani's square in the right place. The correct answer is (D).

6. **B** The question asks for the ratio of the area of the door to the area of the rest of the front of the birdhouse, NOT including the door's area: $\dfrac{A_{door}}{A_{front} - A_{door}}$.

The question tells you the ratio of the sides of the regular pentagon door to the sides of the regular pentagon front: $\dfrac{1}{3}$. Since all regular polygons of the same number of sides are similar, the ratio should be all you need—don't worry too much about the fact that this problem didn't give you any actual values!

However, you do need to be careful. The ratio of the areas will NOT be the same as the ratio of the lengths, because area is a two-dimensional measure. Instead, the ratio of the areas will match the ratio of the *squares* of the side lengths: $\dfrac{1^2}{3^2} = \dfrac{1}{9}$.

But don't pick (D)! You need $\dfrac{A_{door}}{A_{front} - A_{door}}$, so think of the front pentagon as 9 equal pieces, one of which is the missing door: $\dfrac{1}{9 - 1} = \dfrac{1}{8}$. The correct answer is (C).

7. **C** This question looks pretty complicated, so just take it a step at a time. Can you find the volume of the block Marcus starts with (the one in the picture)?

It's just a rectangular prism, and those have a pretty straightforward volume formula: $V = lwh$. It's height is 1 in. and its length and width are each 5 in.: $V = (1)(5)(5) = 25$ in.^{3}

You can get rid of (A) now: you know the total volume will be greater than the volume of just this piece!

The next block up also has height 1 in., but its length and width are each 1 in. less: 5 − 1 = 4, and $V = (1)(4)(4) = 16$ in.^{3}

There are 5 layers total in Marcus's structure, so you need 3 more:

4 − 1 = 3, and $V = (1)(3)(3) = 9$ in.^{3}
3 − 1 = 2, and $V = (1)(2)(2) = 4$ in.^{3}
2 − 1 = 1, and $V = (1)(1)(1) = 1$ in.^{3}

This is kind of a patterns question as well as a geometry question: each layer's area is the next perfect square less than the area of the layer below it.

Now you can just add up all the volumes to get the total volume of the stepped pyramid: 25 in.^{3} + 16 in.^{3} + 9 in.^{3} + 4 in.^{3} + 1 in.^{3} = 55 in.^{3}

Choice (C) is the correct answer.

8. **D** This one is a snap! As long as you remember the formula for the surface area of a cone, that is. Here it is: $SA = \pi r^2 + \pi r l$, where r is the radius of the circular base and l is the lateral height. Draw a picture of Anya's "tree." If the diameter of the base is 1 yard, then its radius is 0.5 yard:

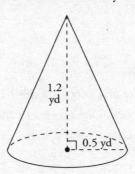

To find the lateral height, you'll need to notice that it forms the hypotenuse of a right triangle. The legs of the triangle are the radius of the base, and the height. Since you have both of those values, you've got enough information to use the Pythagorean Theorem...but wait! Aren't 0.5 and 1.2 an awful lot like 5 and 12? Yep. This is a 5-12-13 triangle, *divided* by 10! So the hypotenuse (your lateral height) is 1.3 yards.

Substitute all the values into the surface area formula:

$$SA = \pi r^2 + \pi r l = \pi(0.5)^2 + \pi(0.5)(1.3) = 0.25\pi + 0.65\pi = 0.9\pi$$

So the total surface area of Anya's "tree" that she needs to cover with felt is 0.9π square yards, and (D) is correct. She should probably estimate the value for the cloth-seller, though.

9. **C** While this question is a fascinating treatise on the definitions of several weird units of measure, the information you really need is that an acre is 22 yards by 220 yards. So 1 acre = 22 yards × 220 yards = 4,840 square yards. Now it's not that hard of a question:

$$\frac{1 \text{ acre}}{4840 \text{ yd}^2} = \frac{6 \text{ acres}}{x \text{ yd}^2}$$

Solve for the missing piece:

$$x = 6 \times 4,840 = 29,040$$

Since 6 acres is equal to 29,040 square yards, the correct answer is (C).

10. **B** This question has a few parts, so take them one at a time. First, the scale on the map is 1 cm = 25 km, so find out how far Bessie needs to drive. The distance is 7 cm on the map. Use a proportion to find the actual distance:

$$\frac{1 \text{ cm}}{25 \text{ km}} = \frac{7 \text{ cm}}{x \text{ km}}$$

Solve for the missing piece:

$$x = 25 \times 7 = 175 \text{ km}$$

Next, the problem gives you a rate and asks for a time. Draw a rate pie and put in the distance you found and the rate from the problem. Don't forget to check the units! Since 175 km and 90 km per hour are compatible, you don't need to convert first.

Divide the distance by the rate to find the time:

You can tell it's one hour and some number of minutes. You can get rid of (C) and (D), but you need to convert to hours and minutes to match the answer choices. Multiply $0.9\overline{4}$ by 60 to find how many minutes $0.9\overline{4}$ of an hour is: $0.9\overline{4} \times 60 = 56.\overline{6}$. Since the question asks *about* how long it will take, round up to 57 minutes: the correct answer is (B).

CHAPTER 17 DRILL

1. **D** The question asks for the data collection method that will give the least biased results. Look for a random sample that is likely to be representative of the entire population being studied—Teddy's neighborhood. Choice (A) is random in terms of what day the questions are asked on, but it has a clear bias in that the only people being asked are those using the outdoor spaces. Since Teddy wants data on how people use the space, he's likely to find different answers from these respondents than from those not covered—the ones not using the space. Choice (B) is not random—the respondents are chosen only from Teddy's block, and may not be representative of other parts of his neighborhood. Choice (C) involves asking residents at their homes at a specific time. The problem here is that many of the residents may not be home, either because they are working, or because they are outdoors using the spaces he's studying. Choice (D) is more random and likely to be more representative than the other choices—it is a random sample, and allows residents to answer at whatever time they are home, so (D) is the best answer.

2. **D** The question asks what conclusion is true based on the data given. Use the histogram to check whether the measures of spread and central tendency match the values given in the choices.

    To find the mean of the data, find the total of the values of all the data points, and divide it by the total number of data points:

    $$\frac{2(1) + 0(2) + 3(3) + 6(4) + 5(5) + 8(6) + 9(7) + 7(8) + 5(9) + 3(10) + 1(11) + 1(12)}{2 + 0 + 3 + 6 + 5 + 8 + 9 + 7 + 5 + 3 + 1 + 1}$$

    $$= \frac{2 + 0 + 9 + 24 + 25 + 48 + 63 + 56 + 45 + 30 + 11 + 12}{50}$$

    $$= \frac{325}{50}$$

    $$= 6.5$$

    Eliminate (A).

    Don't let (B) make you panic! The test is *not* asking you to calculate standard deviation. What is (B) really saying? A set with a standard deviation of 0 would have *no* variation from the mean. In other words, it would be a set composed of all the same number. That's clearly not true here: the data does have some variation, so eliminate (B).

    Find the range of the data by subtracting the minimum value from the maximum value: $12 - 1 = 11$. Eliminate (C).

    Find the mode of the data by finding the value that appears the most: in other words, the tallest bar. The mode is 7.

Now find the median of the data by thinking of the set as a list. It's too long a list to write it all out, so think of taking chunks off the ends to work toward the middle. How many data points are in columns 1–5? Add up the numbers of data points each bar represents: 2 + 0 + 3 + 6 + 5 = 16. How many data points are in the columns 8–12? Add them up too: 7 + 5 + 3 + 1 + 1 = 17. That's not quite balanced: there is 1 more on the "top end" than on the "bottom end." To add 1 to the "bottom end," take it from the next bar: column 6. That leaves 8 − 1 = 7 sixes and 9 sevens left in your list. Great! Take off all 7 sixes and 7 sevens to match. You are left with 2 sevens, and their average will be 7. Since both the mode and the median are 7, (D) is correct.

3. **D** To fix Hong's chart, first figure out what's wrong with it. Look at the numbers given and think what proportions should be represented on the chart. Since there are 30 total students, what fractions are represented by each group? Since there are 15 who have 2 siblings, $\frac{15}{30} = \frac{1}{2}$ of the pie chart should show that group. Since about half the pie is labeled "2 siblings," that looks right. The number of students who have 3 or more siblings is 3, which is $\frac{3}{30} = \frac{1}{10}$ of the pie. That part looks wrong: it's a much bigger slice than $\frac{1}{10}$. The number who have 1 sibling is 5, which is $\frac{5}{30} = \frac{1}{6}$ of the pie—that looks right. Lastly, the number who are only children is 7, which is a little less than $\frac{1}{4}$ of 30. This one looks too small. Looking at the two pieces that are wrong, you can tell they've been switched. Look for an answer that tells you Hong needs to switch the proportions of "only child" and "3 or more siblings" in his chart. Choice (D) is correct—"only child" is too small, while "3 or more siblings" is too big.

4. **A** The question asks for a description of the histogram to be made from the data in the chart. Look for the kinds of information that a histogram will show; you can use the answer choices to give you some ideas. Is the data clustered? It seems reasonably close together. How many modes or local maxima does it have? The data has one clear mode and seems to drop off on either side of it: eliminate (B). Since it's not skewed to the left or right, eliminate (C) and (D) as well. The correct answer is (A).

5. **B** Remember, to choose a good line of best fit, make sure there are about the same number of data points above the line as there are below it, and that the direction of the line follows the general trend of the data. Compare the choices: in (A), 6 points are above the line, 5 are on the line, and 17 are below, while the slope of the line is too steep to match the data: not a good fit. In (B), 12 data points are above, 5 are on the line, and 11 are below, which is pretty even, and the slope fits the data as well. In (C), most of the data points are above the line, with only one below: not a good fit either, even though the slope matches well. In (D), the opposite problem happens: most of the points are below, with about 4 clearly above. In addition, this line's slope doesn't really follow the direction of the data. The best answer is (B).

6. **D**   The question asks which conclusion is reasonable to draw. Look for reasons that a conclusion might not be supported by the data. For example, (A) is incorrect because the total for Sports, 110, is not greater than the sum of the totals for Technology and Theater: 80 + 65 = 145. Choice (B) is incorrect for a different reason: this information is not presented! Though Art is represented, there are no subcategories of it shown. Choice (C) is also beyond the scope of the chart—what students would prefer to take *if* it were offered cannot be concluded from what they do take. Choice (D) is reasonable: the sum of the totals for Art and Foreign Language, 145 + 95 = 240, is very close to the sum of the totals for Music and Sports, 135 + 110 = 245.

7. **B**   The question asks for an experimental probability. What's the difference between that and theoretical probability? Theoretical probability is calculated using a sample space, by finding the fraction of possible outcomes that meet a condition. In experimental probability, you calculate using a simulation (experiment), by finding the fraction of the actual results that meet the condition. In Cornell's simulation, the result 6 is obtained 3 times (on rolls 2, 14, and 20) out of his 20 total trials, so the experimental probability of rolling a 6 in his simulation is $\frac{3}{20}$. Choice (B) is correct.

8. **C**   Since the question asks for probability of a simple event, think $\frac{\text{want}}{\text{total}}$. What is the total number of possible outcomes? It's the number of numbers between 1 and 100, inclusive. There are 100 of them! Now, what's the number of outcomes that meet the condition "multiple of 3"? In other words, how many multiples of 3 are there between 1 and 100? You could count them, but that would take a long time. Think about it this way: what's the least multiple of 3 in the range? That's right, 3. What's the greatest? Count down from 100 until you hit a multiple of 3. If you aren't sure, use your divisibility rule: in multiples of 3, the sum of the digits is also divisible by 3. You know 100 is not divisible by 3 since 1 + 0 + 0 = 1, which is not divisible by 3. What about 99? Yup, it's divisible: 9 + 9 = 18, which is divisible by 3 (18 ÷ 3 = 6).

Now that you know you need to count all the multiples of 3 between 3 and 99, how many are there? Well, every third number in there is a multiple of 3. In other words, the multiples of 3 between 3 and 99 can be thought of as 1 × 3, 2 × 3, 3 × 3, ... , 33 × 3. How many terms are in the sequence? Since the numbers that are multiplied by 3 increase by 1 each term, and they count up from 1 to 33, there are 33 of them!

So the probability of choosing a multiple of 3 out of the numbers 1–100 is $\frac{33}{100}$, or 0.33. Choice (C) is correct.

9. **C** This question asks for the probability of a compound event. Is it asking about union or intersection? The word "or" is a big clue: it's asking about union. To find probability for union, you need to know whether the events are mutually exclusive or not. Can the two events overlap? Sure, a card can be both red and a face card, so use the formula for non-mutually exclusive events:

$$P(\text{event}_1 \text{ OR event}_2) = P(\text{event}_1) + P(\text{event}_2) - P(\text{event}_1 \text{ AND event}_2)$$

$$P(\text{red OR face}) = P(\text{red}) + P(\text{face}) - P(\text{red AND face})$$

Find each of these probabilities:

How many red cards are in the deck? There are 13 cards in each suit, and 2 of the suits are red, so there are $13 \times 2 = 26$ red cards out of the 52 total:

$$P(\text{red}) = \frac{\text{want}}{\text{total}} = \frac{26}{52}$$

It's a good idea *not* to reduce here, so that the addition and subtraction you're going to do can use fractions with a common denominator.

How many face cards are in the deck? There are 4 suits, with 3 face cards in each, so there are $4 \times 3 = 12$ face cards.

$$P(\text{face}) = \frac{\text{want}}{\text{total}} = \frac{12}{52}$$

How many cards meet *both* conditions? There are 3 face cards in each suit, and 2 of the suits are red, so there are $3 \times 2 = 6$ red face cards.

$$P(\text{red AND face}) = \frac{\text{want}}{\text{total}} = \frac{6}{52}$$

Now substitute the values into the formula:

$$P(\text{red OR face}) = P(\text{red}) + P(\text{face}) - P(\text{red AND face})$$

$$= \frac{26}{52} + \frac{12}{52} - \frac{6}{52}$$

$$= \frac{32}{52} = \frac{8}{13}$$

The correct answer is (C).

10. **D** This question has a big clue in its wording: "at most." Remember that "at least" and "at most" usually signal that finding the complement of the complement is a faster way to solve. What's the complement of "the coin lands on heads at most 3 times" out of 4 tosses? Since the coin can land on heads 0, 1, 2, 3, or 4 times, and "at most 3" covers 0, 1, 2, and 3 times, the complement is 4 heads.

$$P(\text{heads at most 3 times}) = 1 - P(\text{4 heads})$$

What's the probability that all 4 tosses land heads? That's just the probability that the first toss lands heads AND the second toss lands heads AND the third toss lands heads AND the fourth toss lands heads. These are independent events, so you can multiply to find the probability of their intersection:

$$P(4 \text{ heads}) = P(\text{heads}) \times P(\text{heads}) \times P(\text{heads}) \times P(\text{heads}) = \frac{1}{2} \times \frac{1}{2} \times \frac{1}{2} \times \frac{1}{2} = \frac{1}{16}$$

Choice (A) is a trap! Eliminate it.

Find the complement of the complement:

$$P(\text{heads at most 3 times}) = 1 - P(4 \text{ heads}) = 1 - \frac{1}{16} = \frac{15}{16}$$

The correct answer is (D).

CHAPTER 18 DRILL

1. **C** Let's break it down. The only reason cheering loudly for his own teammate, (A), might be considered poor sportsmanship by a baseball player would be if he countered it by jeering or booing the other team, but there's no indication of that here. The football team captain, (B), has the prerogative to designate positions, and playing on her teammates' strengths will allow all of them to showcase their skills; there's not much wrong with that. One of the basic rules of basketball is to block opponents' attempts to score, (D), so there's nothing unsportsmanlike about simply following the rules. But a soccer player taking it upon herself to score all or most of the goals indicates that she's not giving her teammates the same opportunity, which makes (C) the correct answer.

2. **A** Fine motor skills, sometimes referred to as hand skills, are involved in small and/or complex movements. Choices (B) and (C) involve gross motor skills and can be eliminated. Making a noise like a train (D) might be considered, well, a loco*motive* skill. Eliminate it. Choice (A) is the only one that involves a fine motor skill.

3. **D** The reference here is to the term *overload* that you read about earlier. To achieve maximum training results, you should exert yourself more than you can comfortably withstand (D). Stopping before you're out of breath (A) indicates that you're not putting forth enough effort. Exercising for at least an hour (B) doesn't mean much: the health benefits would depend on the type and intensity of exercise, and the person's body composition and size. And it's never healthy to work to the point of exhaustion (C).

4. **C** The question asks for the best grouping in general Physical Education classes. You can usually interchange the words *general, average, usual, normal, most common,* and similar terms, and they all mean the same thing. Don't think about the exceptions. Go with the majority. Most of the time, teachers would avoid grouping students by gender, (A), or skill level, (B), because both promote inequality and separatism. And beware of (D): choosing groups at random—by methods such as

"counting off" or drawing names—is just as dangerous, because it's possible that the groups will end up with a majority of one gender, or one culture, or a higher skill level, leaving one or a few "different" others feeling singled out. It's best for teachers to regroup frequently, and to try to make the groups as heterogeneous as possible. Therefore, the correct answer is (C).

5. **D**   This question asks what is least likely to impact a student. An increase in foot size, (A), and weight gain, (B), may make a student awkward as they adjust and therefore hinder physical activity. Joint discomfort, (C), can occur with rapid growth, and may make physical activity uncomfortable or even impossible. While reduced self-esteem may follow a growth spurt, it is the least likely among the answer choices to impact physical activity. The answer is (D).

CHAPTER 19 DRILL

1. **C**   During the concrete operational stage, students' thinking becomes operational, which means that concepts become organized and logical, as long as they are working with or around concrete materials or images.

2. **A**   In the knowledge stage, students are asked to remember specifics, recalling terms, formulas, and theories.

3. **B**   Mr. Meyer's students were rebelling, which is a key characteristic of the identity vs. role confusion stage, because that is when adolescents seek acceptance from peer groups.

4. **C**   In the modeling stage, the skills or procedures are being taught or demonstrated. Notice the clue in the question, which indicates that a lecture had already been given. A lecture would qualify as *input*, or the presentation of new information.

5. **C**   Running at this stage is helping children to become more confident with their gross motor skills.

6. **B**   The student is helping the other student to get something else he wants.

7. **D**   The student seems to struggle only with letters and this can be a sign of a learning difference.

CHAPTER 20 DRILL

1. **A**   Recreational dancing is dancing for fun, exercise, and social interaction. Square dancing, (B), tango, (C), and the twist, (D), all fall into one or more of those categories. Ballet, (A), however, is a classical and artistic form of dance.

2. **D**   The two vertical numbers at the beginning of a music staff represent the meter signature, or time signature. The top number indicates the number of beats in each measure, and the bottom number

indicates the duration of each beat. In this staff, there are four beats in each measure, and each beat is one-quarter note in length.

3. **C** Timbre, (A), is the quality of sound that distinguishes one voice or instrument from another. Harmony, (B), refers to combinations and relationships. Tempo, (D), refers to the speed at which a piece is played. The correct answer is (C), dynamics.

4. **B** The word *soliloquy* should make you think "solo." A soliloquy is a speech given when an actor is alone on the stage. Pantomime, (A), is performed without words, so you can eliminate that answer choice. Plot is the overall action of the play, which rules out (C) as well. And costume, (D), has nothing to do with spoken lines. A soliloquy is a type of monologue, (B); the main difference is that monologues can be performed within the context of a conversation with other characters on stage.

5. **A** Use your basic knowledge of the principles, and one of the answers should stand out to you. Choice (B), rhythm, indicates repetition or pattern, and there is nothing particularly indicative of that here. The same holds true for proportion, (C), which does not appear to have been altered or skewed in any way, and variety, (D), of which there is nothing striking. The position of the figure, bent and twisted, with the arm back, draws the eye up and out, giving the piece a great sense of movement, (A): one almost expects to see him uncoil and spring forward to throw the disc.

6. **D** Developmentally, a third grader listening to music would not have the ability to recognize theoretical or structural elements by ear, so eliminate the key signature, (A), and an ostinato, (C). While a student may be able to start understanding the differences between a melody in unison and in harmony, the differences of monophony, homophony, and polyphony are a more complicated, so eliminate (B). The families of the orchestra, (D), is the most feasible answer.

7. **D** Kabuki is a type of theater, and thus acting, (A), will be involved. The term *kabuki* is often translated to "the art of singing and dancing." This eliminates both singing, (B), and dancing, (C). Traditionally, Kabuki theater does not use masks, but instead elaborate makeup. Thus, masks, (D), is the correct answer.

8. **A** Look for a Russian name. Eliminate Bob Fosse, (C), because this is not a Russian name. Of the remaining figures, Vaslav Nijinsky, (A), fits the criteria because of his work portraying characters such as the faun in Claude Debussy's tone poem, and he choreographed multiple Igor Stravinsky works portraying Russian themes. While George Balanchine, (B), was a Russian choreographer, he worked with more abstract, plotless concepts. Evgeni Plushenko, while a Russian name, is not a choreographer.

9. **B** The 19th century had many art movements, so identifying what each movement was about is key. Realism, (A), is the attempt to represent subject matter truthfully and fits in the 19th century. Dadaism, (B), is a movement that rejects logic and reason, typically not consistent with 19th century. Romanticism, (C), in all arts is the dominant movement through the 19th century, and

Impressionism, (D), can be linked to Vincent Van Gogh whom we know lived during the late 1800s. Dadaism, (B), is the correct answer.

10. **B** *Free-form* and *spontaneous* are the key words to unlocking this question. Structure is the opposite of free-form, eliminating (A). Improvisation, (B), means to do something without preparation and fits with the word *spontaneous*. Counterbalancing, (C), means dealing with weight and does not apply to this question. Dynamics, (D), deals with the energy expended into a dance movement, but not a technique. Choice (B) is correct.